Daniel Defoe

"The God that gave me brains will give me bread."

—DANIEL DEFOE, *An Elegy on the*
Author of the True-Born-Englishman

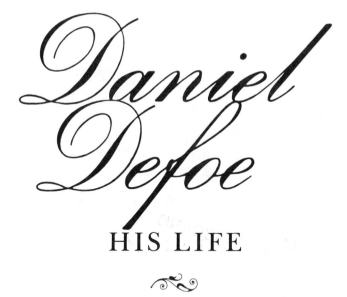

HIS LIFE

Paula R. Backscheider

The Johns Hopkins University Press
Baltimore and London

The Johns Hopkins University Press, 701 West 40th Street,
Baltimore, Maryland 21211
The Johns Hopkins Press Ltd., London

The paper used in this publication meets the minimum requirements of
American National Standard for Information Sciences—Permanence
of Paper for Printed Library Materials, ANSI Z39.48-1984.

LIBRARY OF CONGRESS CATALOGING-IN-PUBLICATION DATA
Backscheider, Paula R.
Daniel Defoe : his life / Paula R. Backscheider.
p.   cm.
Bibliography: p.
Includes index.
ISBN 0-8018-3785-5 (alk. paper)
1. Defoe, Daniel, 1661?–1731—Biography. 2. Authors, English—
18th century—Biography.   I. Title.
PR3406.B24   1989
823'.5—dc19

[B]   88-26752
                                                           CIP

For Andrea Gayle
Nick III
and VSR

CONTENTS

ILLUSTRATIONS

PREFACE

Few men seem to be better subjects for a biography than Daniel Defoe. Author of one of the best-known books in all the world, he came from obscure parents and a persecuted religious minority to lead a life of adventure, difficulty, accommodation, error, and perseverance. He offers us the puzzle of genius without advantage and achievement without aid. His experiences might have embittered or warped him, but instead he became endlessly versatile, courageous, and resilient. His struggle to support himself and his large family could have drained his creativity and energy, yet in his fifty-ninth year he wrote *Robinson Crusoe*.

Even the times in which he lived make him a great subject. Born in the year of the Restoration, he lived through the plague and the Great Fire of 1666, joined Monmouth's Rebellion, and dreamed of better times because of the Glorious Revolution of 1688. He saw some of the greatest political achievements in English history: his country's rise to military preeminence, the Protestant Settlement, the Union between England and Scotland, and the establishment of a modern economic system. His own life offers a number of traditionally attractive kinds of biographical material: he was an ordinary man whom historical forces influenced in dramatic ways; he was a literary genius whose achievements have no simple explanations; he led an exciting life—he was imprisoned as a bankrupt, convicted for sedition, acted as a double agent, created a spy network, infiltrated newspapers, and knew some of the most famous and notorious people of his time; he participated in almost every British religious and political controversy for thirty years; he is seldom included in standard anthologies of English literature, and yet the idea that he is the father of the novel, of modern journalism, and of political propaganda cannot be dismissed lightly.

In other ways, however, Defoe is a dreadful subject for a biography. He came from a family and social class incapable of imagining future interest in a child of the Cornhill Ward. For much of his life, Daniel Defoe was obscure, disgraced, or employed in jobs requiring secrecy and even subterfuge. Time after time he described his work as "being all things to all men." He was not the kind of man whom others bragged of knowing, nor did they return home to write descriptions of meetings, dinners, and conversations with him. Even those who admired him seem not to have saved his letters. Moreover, he was one of the most prolific writers who ever lived, but he was the kind of man about whom journalistic and political rivals lied. His works are sprinkled with appar-

ently autobiographical anecdotes, but he was an inveterate teller of tales
and believed firmly in the effectiveness of illustrative stories, true or
fabricated, thus sorting between them is next to impossible.

The existing biographies of Defoe teach the lessons of bones found
in crossing a desert. They mark the ways to lose the path: in the sheer
number of his works and in the complexities and drama of the historical events, or in imposing consistency and seizing upon a psychological
key. His biographers have variously called him the greatest liar who
ever lived, accused him of not speaking to his wife for twenty-eight
years, found him "strangely isolated as a man and as a writer," and rated
him "next to Chaucer and Milton." This is not to say that some of their
books are not fine biographies, but that the man and his mind have not
yet come to life for us is clear when we remember that as recently as
1977 Peter Earle devoted twelve pages of his book *The World of Defoe* to a
discussion of why there would never be an adequate biography of
Defoe. Since the publication of the last full biography of Defoe in 1958,
we have learned a great deal about his life, work, and time. In addition,
during the years I have worked on this biography, I have found unpublished manuscript material from almost every period of his life,
material that changes the interpretation of some of the most significant
periods of his life.

My interest in Defoe's life comes from three sources: his uncommon
aspirations, both moral and material; his absorption in the great issues
of his time; and his engagement with pen and paper. Seldom have the
life of writing and the life of action come together as completely as they
do with Defoe, and the challenge is to understand the times, the issues,
and Defoe's opinions and actions without losing the sense of the private
man and the dynamic creative energy that made Defoe a great writer.
Even if the literary life is the mind and emotions poured onto paper, is
the mysterious process that transforms experience, memory, and
thought into a complex work of art that somehow seems beyond the
power of a man at a desk, yet there is always a man at the desk who is
more like us than not.

I have tried to recreate the way the world felt to Defoe, to capture
him in the act of living and writing, and to let him—and his contemporaries—speak for themselves whenever possible. I freely admit that
there are periods of his life still obscure because of a lack of information
or, ironically, because of the copiousness of complex, contradictory
material, and that there are aspects of his personality that I do not
completely understand. So it is with our closest friends and perhaps
even with ourselves. Far more of Defoe survives than the great novels
and the more than five hundred works he is reputed to have written;
there is a sturdy personality with lifelong values and aspirations that

animates the man at his desk, on his horse, and in his beloved coffee-houses.

⤳

Biographers incur debts without number, and mine are nearly as voluminous as Defoe's writings. My end notes acknowledge scores of gifts—information, references, translations. This biography could not be what it is without the generosity of these first-rate scholars from England, Scotland, Canada, and the United States. The community of Defoe scholars especially has encouraged my work and answered numerous queries; at one time or another, almost every one of them has given me an expert opinion. J. A. Downie, Paul Hunter, Spiro Peterson, and John Richetti read portions of the manuscript. I owe the librarians and archivists in the United Kingdom and in this country a major debt. They have located items lost for decades, helped identify holdings never considered to have Defoe material, and brought to my attention items I would not have found. I am particularly grateful to the staffs of the London Public Record Office and the Scottish Record Office, and to the University of Rochester librarians, especially Phyllis Andrews and Shirley Ricker, I shall always be indebted. My graduate assistants, David Ames, Maryellen Potts, and Laurie A. Sterling worked tirelessly, carefully, and with great intelligence and ingenuity, and I thank them—perhaps most of all for their alacrity. With what Defoe would call providential good fortune, I was assigned to teach an undergraduate seminar on Defoe in the fall of 1987—the semester during which I reworked most of the chapters on the novels; these students' spontaneous, candid, and highly intelligent responses to Defoe contributed richly day after day.

The Duke of Buccleuch, the Duke of Hamilton, the Earl of Bute, Sir John Clerk of Pennicuik, Mrs. Violet De Foe Vasey, the Worshipful Company of Butchers, the British Library, Cambridge University Library, Oxford University Library, Harvard's Houghton Library, Yale's Beinecke Library, the Robert Taylor Collection at Princeton, Miami University of Ohio, the University of Illinois, the Harry Ransom Humanities Research Center at the University of Texas, the House of Lords Record Office, the City of London Record Office, the Essex Record Office, the Public Record Office in London, the Guildhall Library, the Scottish Record Office, the National Library of Scotland, the Manuscript Room of the University of Edinburgh, the Edinburgh Town Council, the Dr. Williams Library (London), the Victoria and Albert Museum, the Massachusetts Historical Society, the American Antiquarian Society, the Society in Scotland for Propagating Christian Knowledge, the Church of Scotland, and the Society for the Propagation of Christian Knowledge have allowed me to publish manuscript material and, in many cases, helpfully supplied microfilm or photographs.

I am grateful to the National Endowment for the Humanities, the American Philosophical Society, and the Institute for Advanced Studies, University of Edinburgh, all of which supported my research with several fellowships and grants. The Provost of the University of Rochester, Brian Thompson, provided a research fund at a crucial time. These grants made the long periods of archival research possible and reminded me that people can believe in projects stretching over a decade.

I acknowledge with appreciation the following journals for allowing me to rework and republish material: *PMLA* for parts of chapters 5 and 6; *ELH* for part of 8; *Modern Philology, Philological Quarterly*, and *Modern Language Review* for parts of 9, 10, and 11.

It is with pleasure that I thank the three people to whom I owe most. Lewis White Beck, Tom Gavin, and my husband, Nick Backscheider, read the biography chapter by chapter, sometimes more than once, and commented meticulously. Surely few people have been fortunate enough to have a philosopher, a novelist, and a Renaissance man as first critics. Had I been able to achieve the full potential of their suggestions, this biography would be unmatched. As it is, I offer my gratitude and take full responsibility for my obstinacies and deficiencies.

A note on the works ascribed to Defoe is in order. The most recent students of the Defoe canon have said that "it could never be definitive," and every responsible Defoe scholar and critic would probably agree. My own use of the received canon is conservative. Except for a few works in one category, I have reexamined and reevaluated every work attributed to Defoe, used for significant arguments only those about which I am certain, scrupulously noted my reservations about others, and avoided the use of those I consider not Defoe's, or probably not Defoe's. The exceptions are the post-1713 periodicals attributed to Defoe, including those ascribed by William Lee; I have discussed some of them with the awareness that they may have been edited rather than written by Defoe. In order to preserve the narrative flow of the biography, I have relegated discussion of the canon to notes and, for the reader's convenience, indexed them under "attribution."

Notes give author, short title, and page references, and readers should consult the bibliographies for full citations. The bibliographies are divided into three sections: works attributed to Defoe (and by this, I mean those listed in *NCBEL* and J. R. Moore's *Checklist of the Writings of Defoe*; I am not claiming them all for Defoe); primary sources; and secondary sources. George Healey's *The Letters of Daniel Defoe* are cited in the text as, for instance, "H 23" for "Healey, p. 23." Some material in my footnotes can also be found in the notes of Defoe's earlier biographers, especially James Sutherland and J. R. Moore. I have no desire to diminish their contribution, and my decision is based partly upon the redundancy that citing them in every case would necessarily produce. So much material has been discovered by myself and others, and enough corrections have been made in the more than twenty years since the publication of these biographies, that I found it easier to work from manuscripts and articles than their books. In the interest of narrative flow, I have usually corrected earlier biographers silently. At first I tried to check every archival reference in the published scholarship. Life is not so long nor grants so numerous; wherever possible, however, I have checked and cited the published and archival sources for the convenience of future scholars. Full citations to the hundreds of manuscripts, many never before published in relation to Defoe, are given in the notes alone.

Dates pose special problems. Until 1752 England retained the Julian, or Old Style, calendar, but Scotland had converted to the Gregorian, or New Style, in 1660. Dates in Scotland, then, and most of Europe differed from those in England in two ways: Old Style was eleven days behind New Style, and the New Year began on 25 March. I have retained the Old Style dates for England but taken the year to begin on 1 January.

I have spelled names as the people themselves did. When quoting from manuscripts, I have written out abbreviations such as y^t for *that* and regularized spelling of words in which the eighteenth-century writers used macrons to double letters and ς for *t*. As is standard modern practice, the Johns Hopkins University Press seldom uses ellipsis points at the beginning or end of quoted passages and alters initial letters of quotations according to the syntax of the sentences in which they appear.

PART I
1660–1703

CHAPTER 1

FIRE AND PLAGUE

*And now I began to think my Fortunes were settled for this World,
and I had nothing before me, but to finish a Life of infinite
Variety. . . . But an unseen Mine blew up all this apparent Tranquility at once.*

    —DEFOE, *Colonel Jack* (1722)

*But in the Middle of all this Felicity, one Blow from unforeseen
Providence unhing'd me at once.*

    —DEFOE, *The Farther Adventures
of Robinson Crusoe* (1719)

*Admirable therefore is the Man who has chearfully past thro' Life,
without the least desire of distinguishing himself.*

    —annotation on Defoe's copy of Francis Bacon's
Advancement of Human Learning [1720s]

Defoe wrote all of these lines, and they are the lessons of experience. His was a life of struggle and survival and of hard-won economic security and literary achievement. Indeed, the nature of his life was marked by his birth in the busiest, most crowded part of London and by the upheaval in his early years. Daniel was the third child of James and Alice Foe; while his mother carried him, General Monk entered London at the head of an army to restore order. Two months later a new House of Commons met, and Charles II was invited to assume the English throne. The "Restoration" raised hopes of better times but led to turmoil and dramatic change. Daniel was to survive the plague, the Great Fire, and several moves before he was ten years old.

Daniel was in the first generation of the Foe family to be born in London. The births of his older sisters, Mary, on 13 November 1657, and Elizabeth, on 19 June 1659, are neatly inscribed in the St. Giles, Cripplegate, parish records, but his is not. From two of his own offhand statements, it has been surmised that he was born in the fall of 1660. The evidence to support this opinion is entirely circumstantial, but there is no evidence to refute it. In the first few years after Oliver Cromwell's death, many citizens' lives and some record keeping were disrupted, and Daniel's birth may be recorded as this child's was in a parish where he might well have been born, Chadwell, Essex, in 1662:

Daniel son of a stranger baptized July 27.

We can trace Defoe's ancestry back only as far as his grandfather Daniel Foe and his wife, Rose, of Etton, Northamptonshire.[1] Although he died young, Daniel Foe was prosperous enough as a yeoman to own his own farm; to leave ten shillings each to his pastor Samuel Temple, his church, and the poor fund; set aside £80 for his eldest son and £50 for each of his three younger children; and leave a decent estate for his widow. Rose Foe, the writer's grandmother, married Soloman Fall of Maxie, Northants, on 4 August 1633, but was widowed again in February 1641. At this time the eldest of her children, Daniel, was at least eighteen, and he seems to have worked the family farm until his death in 1647.

James, the youngest child of Daniel and Rose Foe, was baptized on 13 May 1630 in the tiny village of Etton in the gently rolling hills sixty miles northwest of London. His father was buried there ten months later on 8 March 16$\frac{30}{31}$. James's older brother, Henry, served as an apprentice to a London saddler and, when he was old enough, James followed his brother to the City. By the time his son Daniel, the writer, was born, James had served an apprenticeship under John Levitt of the parish of St. Botolph, Aldgate, where Henry would live out his life. James was a respected tallow chandler with a talent for accounting that his son would claim.

Cripplegate, where James practiced his trade in the heart of the Old City, was characterized by narrow, crooked streets and small, crowded shops and houses. Six years after Daniel's birth, however, only three houses were left standing in all of the Broad Street Ward where the Foes lived, and three years after that James Foe was still pledging money to his livery company and paying special taxes and tithes to help rebuild London.[2] In the Great Fire, 229 houses in Cornhill alone burned to the ground, and the official survey report gave 13,200 as the number of houses destroyed in London. Ninety percent of the city's living accommodations burned. Begun on a Sunday evening in a bakery near London Bridge, the fire spread inexorably through the city until the land between the Tower and the Temple was a wasteland. During the four-day fire, eighty-nine churches burned, including St. Paul's, which was gutted. Property loss totaling about ten million pounds, or between half and three-quarters of a billion pounds in today's money, threatened the entire economy. Witnesses never forgot the frantic, confused people hurrying through the city carrying hastily gathered, untidy bundles of their possessions. "The streets and the highways are crowded with people, running and riding and getting of

"A Plan of the City of London after the Dreadful Conflagration,"
with the ruins represented by white.

carts at any rate," Samuel Pepys wrote on 3 September, the second day
of the fire. Richard Baxter recalled the horror: "To see the Flames
mount up towards Heaven. . . . To see the streets filled with people
astonished, that had scarce sense left them to lament their own calamity. . . . To see the Air, as far as could be beheld, so filled with smoak,
that the Sun shined through it, with a colour like Blood."[3] Others
described the clutter of household goods flung into the center of streets
as fire spread through the houses on both sides.

Even more memorable to witnesses were the unfamiliar sounds and
the appalling, unnatural glow in the night sky. John Evelyn describes
"the noise & crackling & thunder of the impetuous flames, the shreek-
ing of Women & children, the hurry of people, the fall of [buildings]. . .
like an hideous storme"; citizens heard the fire howl, glass shatter,
stones fall, and described the sound of houses "cracking." "How hor-
ridly the sky looks, all on a fire in the night," they wrote. The fire made
the night "as light as day for 10 miles round about after a dreadfull
manner" and was visible for forty miles. Thomas Vincent described the
burning of Guildhall as a "fearful spectacle, for the whole body of it
stood whole, for several hours together, after the fire had taken it,
without flames (I suppose because the timber was such solid oak) in a
bright shining coal, as if it had been a palace of gold, or a great building

of burnished brass." Strong men recorded emotional reactions. "God grant mine eyes may never behold the like," wrote Evelyn, who compared the devastation, as many of his countrymen did, to that of Sodom and of Troy. "It made me weep to see it" and "was enough to put us out of our wits," Pepys said.[4] The pavement itself glowed like hearthstones, and people described how their feet were burned through their shoes by walking past destroyed buildings. Apparently the Foes' house did not burn,[5] but four days of panic and devastation must have made a strong impression on Daniel. His family probably took what they could to his uncle's in St. Botolph's. They, like their neighbors, probably returned on 7 September and found, in the words of a survivor, "ruines, for it was no longer a Citty." If the days of the fire produced fragmented impressions, the aftermath must have seemed a prolonged nightmare. Entire streets were blocked by debris; twisted iron and buckled glass were objects of wonder in fields of rubble where not one building remained on an entire block; blowing ashes turned people white until they appeared to be "dismal ghosts" walking a "barren desert." The official survey reported 373 acres "within the wall of the City of London, and 63 acres, three roods without the walls" to be "consumed"; only "75 acres three roods yet standing within the walls unburnt."[6] Here and there a steeple, a chimney, or a building survived, startling in its isolation. Fires still broke out in collapsed warehouses and, as late as January of that winter, in smoldering cellars.[7] The Post House, the Custom House, the Royal Exchange, Guildhall, the civil courts, the prisons, and all of the markets but Leadenhall had been destroyed; inhabitants found they could buy nothing, and their prisoners were loose among them, with looters, arsonists, and vandals attracted from distant parishes. Forty-seven years later, Defoe wrote: "I remember very well what I saw with a sad Heart, *tho' I was but Young.* . . . the whole City was laid in Ashes" (*Review* 9:115).

King Charles, the lord mayor of London, and the City's aldermen and Common Council worked with remarkable efficiency to establish a new General Letter Office (in Bishopsgate), Custom House (Mark Lane), and government offices (Gresham College) and to find places for the courts and three thousand merchants, who needed the equivalent of the Royal Exchange and Guildhall as they rebuilt their businesses. In spite of this achievement, signs of the fire's destruction remained for more than thirty years, and the citizens were taxed and taxed again to pay for the rebuilding. Living and working in Cripplegate in 1666 would have meant approaching winter in a makeshift hut or crowded together in an undamaged house with families like the Foes, with shops inconveniently distant. The landscape of ash-coated rubble resembled modern pictures of bombed cities or of Colombia after the earthquake of 1983. As late as 1668 one of the typical inner city parish registers took a whole page to record in ornate script: "The First (After the sad Devastation by Fier of this whole Parish & most Part of this Citty) that was Borne . . . was Elizabeth . . . Ravenscraft . . . on All Saints Day being the First of November 1668."[8]

Even before the Great Fire, Daniel's childhood was not placid. Only one year earlier the last great plague in London had killed more than 97,000 people. Perhaps Daniel, like so many others, had been evacuated then as well as during the Great Fire. Even a child of five might remember a time when shops were shut, few people on the street, and open coffins and even bodies occasionally in plain view. It was, as Sir John Reresby reported, "usual for people to drop down in the streets." Both Daniel's own parish of St. Giles, Cripplegate, and his uncle's were particularly hard hit. The St. Botolph Aldgate's clerk begins the September 1665 registry with the words, "in the sad tyme of visitation." Of this parish, Defoe's *Journal of the Plague Year* says that there was "no parish in or about London where it raged with such violence." The Cripplegate vestry minute book notes the disruption caused by the deaths of the parish clerk and the sexton with the solemn words, "Whereas it hath pleased Almighty God to visit the Citty . . . especially this our parish . . . with a great mortality." In January the new clerk wrote: "Such multitudes have dyed that our Churchyard and burying places are now almost so filled with dead corpes [sic] that not any more can scarcely be buried there."[9]

More significant even than two successive years of public disaster, however, was the fact that the Foes became Nonconformists, Protestant "Dissenters" who refused the sacraments and membership in the Church of England. Daniel, therefore, grew up as part of a persecuted minority.

Samuel Annesley, the Foe's family pastor, chose to join the "Dissenters" on 24 August 1662, when 1,800 clergymen were ejected from their churches by the Act of Uniformity, and the Foes left St. Giles, Cripplegate, Church with him. By doing so they lost their right to worship openly and gave up their son's chance for a university education and a civil or military career. The Act of Uniformity, the second act in the "Clarendon Code," required clergymen, "heads, fellows, chaplains, and tutors" of "any college, halls, houses of learning or hospitals," and "every person instructing or teaching any youth in any house or private family" to take the oaths required of magistrates, officers, and employees of corporations by the first act of the Clarendon Code, the Corporation Act. Almost every provision of the oaths either contradicted an earlier oath or violated the consciences of non-Anglicans. They were to promise "non-resistance," which forbad taking arms against the king under any circumstances, to disclaim the Solemn Oath and Covenant that had been required of all men over eighteen in 1645, subscribe to all

Thirty-Nine Articles of the Church of England's creed, be ordained by a bishop, use the Book of Common Prayer in all services, and assent "to all and every thing contained and prescribed" in it. Chief among the objections were those to the words used in the baptism ceremony and to the "absolution" of the dying, to including the Apocrypha in the canonical books, and to using liturgical, rather than original, prayers "from the heart." Many men did not even have a chance to see the Book of Common Prayer before the August date.[10]

Some men gained stature from persecution, and Annesley, a man already remarkable for his character, diligence, and preaching style, was among them.[11] In childhood Annesley had begun his lifelong practice of reading twenty chapters of Scripture a day. During Defoe's childhood, when Dissenters were most actively persecuted, he preached almost daily. During his last illness he had to be restrained from preaching a second sermon on Sundays. He was particularly known for his care for other Nonconforming ministers and was acknowledged to have "won many souls." Despite harassment and persecution he managed to make the meeting house at Little St. Helen's the largest in London. The first public ordination of Dissenters in the city was held there in 1694.

He was a courageous and steady man. When he was twenty-two, his first parishioners opposed his appointment and met him with pitchforks, spits, and stones, but he told them that he was "resolved to continue with them, till God had fitted them by his Ministry to entertain a better." How many times he was arrested cannot be certainly determined, but the City records cite dozens of informers' reports on his preaching and numerous court appearances. In 1670, for example, he appeared before Sir John Robinson and was convicted and fined but refused to pay. Robinson issued warrants against him, but Annesley's meetings (and those of two other Presbyterian preachers) "were defended by 3000 or 4000 people who refused to move but by violent force." In 1682 the Entering Book records: "Dr. Ansley's house was broke into by the Informers &c. on Saturday & his Goods distrained upon for severall latent Convictions." His funeral sermon was preached by Dr. Daniel Williams, the most influential Dissenter in London.

Annesley, like so many of the Nonconformists of Defoe's childhood, was an unlikely object of institutional discrimination. He had been educated at Oxford, served as the earl of Warwick's chaplain, received an honorary doctor of civil laws degree at Oxford through the influence of the earl of Pembroke, had preached before the House of Commons, had his position at St. Giles confirmed by two post-Restoration committees and King Charles II, and was the nephew of the earl of Anglesey, but he resisted powerful men's urging and refused to "conform." One of the sticking points for Annesley was the demand that he

Sam! Annesley, D.D.
1619. — 1696.

The Reverend Samuel Annesley, the Foe family's pastor.

be reordained by a bishop. His own ceremony had been a dramatic one on 18 December 1644 abroad the *Globe*, a ship in the fleet commanded by the earl of Warwick, Lord High Admiral of Parliament's navy. Presided over by the seven Presbyterian ministers then required by parliamentary ordinance, it included the traditional "laying on of hands." Many ministers believed that to accept reordination would be to render all the marriages, baptisms, and commissions they had performed invalid, even as this first ordination would be.

He moved to Spital Yard in the liberty of Norton Folgate, Stepney, where he lived until his death thirty-five years later. Within a year of his ejectment, he recorded an incident in which he was slapped in the face for his decision. However, he began preaching illegally in his own home at least as early as January, only five months after his ejectment from St. Giles. By 1664 he preached openly at several places, including his home and the Seven Stars on Ludgate Hill. During the plague he was one of the most visible men to take the place of the parish ministers. By 1669, the Episcopal Returns tell us that he was preaching to eight hundred Presbyterians, including the Foes, in "a New House built for that purpose, with Pulpit & Seates." Immediately after Charles's Act of Indulgence in 1672, Annesley built the Little St. Helen's meeting house, complete with "three good galleries," for his congregation. Defoe was, according to a friend, a "great *Admirer* and *constant Hearer*" of Annesley's.[12]

As little as we know about Defoe's early life, the strength of the influence of his membership in the Dissenting community is unmistakable. Annesley, among others, represented the cost of the choice and the possibilities. During the first twenty years of his life, Defoe would have taken for granted scheming informers, interrupted Dissenting meetings, and the fining and imprisonment of Dissenters. Fines, which began at five shillings for the first offense of attending a conventicle, doubled with the second offense. Minister and owner of the building each forfeited £20 for the first offense and £40 for the second. Constables who failed to report conventicles to justices of the peace could also be fined.

Some 15,000 families were ruined, 5,000 died in prison (notably, Defoe says 8,000), and as many as 60,000 may have suffered for dissent. A contemporary of Defoe's wrote that "the vilest of Men" were encouraged to break up meetings and "some of the best Blood that ever run in *English* Veins was then spilt as Water upon the Ground; Juries were pack'd [and] false Witnesses suborned." Oliver Heywood, a man Defoe's family knew, was forcibly removed from church every Sunday by the churchwarden but fined four shillings for not attending when he did not go. Defoe remembered trapdoors in pulpits, secret passages from one house to another, and hidden rooms with doors disguised as cupboards. Persecution was most intense in 1662–1664, in 1670, and again from 1681 to 1685; Defoe was ten years old when Quaker children were put in the pillory, boys publicly scourged, children as young as twelve sent to Bridewell Prison at hard labor, and doors broken down in order to search houses. So threatened were Dissenters in Defoe's youth that he and others like him copied out large sections of the Bible, fearful that the king would prohibit privately owned Bibles.[13] One of his schoolmates, Samuel Wesley, father of Charles and John, believed that his father died as a direct result of his arrest for preaching at a meeting in 1670: "By lying on the cold Earth, whence he was not permitted to remove as our people then told the story, he contracted a sickness, which in tenn days cost him his life."[14] Above all, young Daniel learned that the government as surely as fire and plague could be the "unseen Mine" that destroyed a family's tranquillity.

The Dissenting community and Annesley gave Defoe the ideal of conduct he would praise throughout his life and articulate in his defense of *Robinson Crusoe* nearly fifty years after Annesley's house was raided: "Here is invincible patience recommended under the worst of misery, indefatigable application and undaunted resolution under the greatest and most discouraging circumstances."[15] He saw men remain "of a sweet natural temper, and a generous public spirit" in the face of injustice and persecution; he saw his religious group resist reactionary tendencies and become the bulwark of progressive education, and he saw a people barred from civil life become the backbone of mercantile England. Defoe learned piety, hard work, economy, long-suffering, self-discipline, and service, but he also learned resistance, distrust for authority, and independence of thought that tended to self-righteousness.

Defoe, then, grew up in a time of rebuilding. His people adjusted to their devastating change in social status. Many of them had been respected, substantial citizens influential in politics, education, religion, the military, and commerce. Most of their ministers were between thirty and fifty; Richard Baxter ranked the ejection of these devout, pastoral, scholarly men with the plague and fire as tragedies. Powerful, educated *Protestants*, they found themselves suddenly excluded from municipal corporations, barred from civil and military service, from teaching, from the universities as students or teachers, and subject to discriminatory fines and laws, for they were now identified in nearly everyone's mind with faction and rebellion. In tract after tract they were described as "turbulent and factious spirits" and "ever discontent with the present government." As late as 1725 a popular novelist, Mary Davys, wrote, "I once heard an impudent Papist say, *Guy Faux* was a Presbyterian, and that it was by them the Gunpowder-Plot* was set on foot. I dare say, it wou'd be no hard matter, to persuade half the *Tories* in the Nation to be of that Opinion."[16]

As these men reconstructed their lives and found new ways to educate their children, practice their religion, and exert influence, they

---

*Guy Faux, or more commonly "Fawkes," was one of the five men who joined in an oath to blow up Westminster Palace in 1605 while King James I, the royal family, and both Houses were present for the opening of Parliament. They were all Catholic and protesting the renewed enforcement of the Elizabethan Catholic acts. The men were betrayed, and Fawkes was caught in the gunpowder-filled cellar. "Guy Fawkes Day" is still celebrated in England with bonfires, fireworks, and a parade of effigies, or "guys."

and their Church of England brothers rebuilt the city of London. Men like Thomas Sprat, historian of the Royal Society, recorded the triumph. He wrote that men "beheld the Ashes of their *Houses*, and *Gates*, and *Temples*, without the least expression of Pusillanimity" and praised the "greatness of heart" found among "the obscure *multitude*"; John Reresby said, "the dreadful destruction [of London] was not more extraordinary than the speed, regularity, and cost wherewith . . . a new London, far exceeding the old, [was] erected." Dryden dedicated *Annus Mirabilis* to the City of London in these words: "You who are to stand a wonder to all Years and Ages, and who have built your selves an immortal Monument on your own ruines."[17] In truth, London struggled with mountains of debris and inadequate funding, supplies, and labor for many years. The Coal Dues, chosen by Parliament to support the rebuilding, were hopelessly inadequate for financing such a massive effort. In 1670 not more than a dozen of the fifty-three livery company halls had been rebuilt and none of the churches. In ten years, however, London had begun to flourish again. Nine thousand brick houses, whose size and architecture were regulated by the Rebuilding Act, replaced the ramshackle wooden ones destroyed by the fire. More spacious and beautiful, the city benefited from better water supplies, sewage systems, and public administration. Vincent had written in 1667 that "the glory of London . . . Queen city of the land . . . is now fled away like a bird, the trade of London . . . shattered." Soon, however, London was again "the beauty, riches, strength, and glory of the whole Kingdom."[18]

During this time, the English government shaped itself upon the remains of the Interregnum. Most significantly, the House of Commons maintained the power attained in the 1640s and continued to define its prerogatives, thereby gradually circumscribing the powers of the monarch. Resolutions in 1661, 1671, and 1678 gave the Commons the power to initiate money bills and to appropriate supplies for England's wars. Committees of Parliament continued to control the administration of the navy and the army and of trade policies; in 1667 a Committee of Public Accounts was established. In one encounter after another, control shifted from the crown to the Commons. For example, in 1673, in response to Charles II's Act of Indulgence, the Commons voted "that penal statutes, in matters ecclesiastical, cannot be suspended but by act of Parliament." By 1679 the Commons felt free to refuse to accept the royal nominee as their Speaker. This struggle for ascendancy gave birth to the country/court division that fostered the rise of the powerful political parties that would engage so much of Defoe's adult attention.[19]

Some time between 1668 and 1671 Defoe's mother, Alice, died,[20] and the young Defoe had yet another adjustment to make. Certainly the Dissenting community continued to be the primary influence on his life. Samuel Annesley may have been responsible for Defoe's youthful plans to enter the ministry. Defoe's elegy "The Character of the late Dr. Samuel Annesley" (1697) praised Annesley for his piety, humility, and zeal, as well as for qualities more likely to be known by personal acquaintance (congeniality, humor). Above all, Defoe saw Annesley as the personification of God's love. His devotion to his calling, generosity toward all in need, preaching style, and creative means of service led even his most distinguished contemporaries to praise him extravagantly. "He had a large soul and a flaming zeal, and his usefulness was very extensive"; "A most sincere, godly and humble man. An Israelite indeed," Edmund Calamy wrote.[21]

Annesley's sermons were distinguished by homely illustrations and an affecting delivery "very peculiarly" expressing "his heartiness in the things he spoke."[22] In the introduction to the first edition of *The Morning-Exercise* at Cripple-gate: Or, Several Cases of Conscience Practically Resolved*, he begins, "To my most unfeignedly *Beloved* Parishioners of Saint GILES *Cripplegate*" and continues, "These *Sermons*, both *preached*, and *printed*, are the meer product of love to your *Souls*. I never yet (that I remember) went thorow the *Parish* without *some* (though not *sutably compassionate*) heart-akeing *yearnings* towards my *charge*. . . . hate sin with a perfect hatred, yet . . . love sinners with an infinite Love." Deservedly known as "a considerable textuary," his familiarity with Scripture allowed him to begin sermons with a strikingly firm grasp of an entire book of the Bible and its significance for his congregations: "Solomon, upon the Review of his Life . . . at last demonstrates the utter Insufficiency of all Things *merely* worldly to make us happy. In the first six Chapters of [Ecclesiastes], he shews wherein Happiness doth *not* consist . . . and in the six last Chapters, he shews wherein it *doth* consist." Anecdotes, mundane metaphors, and clear prose bring his precepts to life. For example, in one sermon he calls conscience God's inextinguishable candle, compares it to gravel in the shoe, and concludes with simple admonitions: "There's nothing in the world for us to do, but to mind our duty"; "What you can't say, the Blessing of the Lord be upon it, do not meddle with it."[23]

Annesley may also have had a part in James Foe's decision to send Daniel to Charles Morton's academy in Newington Green. Morton was

---

*Established during the Civil War when parishioners turned in more requests for prayers for friends and relatives serving in the army than could be read on Sundays, the Morning Exercises met at 7:00 A.M. on alternate Sundays and were conducted by the most eminent ministers of the time. One half of the service was devoted to prayers for the welfare of the public and individuals and the other half to a sermon. After the war ended, the Morning Exercises also answered questions posed by the parishioners. After the death of their founder, Thomas Case, Samuel Annesley became the "main support" of the Morning Exercises.

another Oxonian and had lived quietly, preaching "privately to a few people in a neighbouring village," after his ejection from the Blisland, Cornwall, church. The Great Fire destroyed his income-producing St. Ives property, however, and forced him to earn a living. He had his own house in Kennington, Lambeth, licensed as a meeting house in 1672, and shortly afterwards opened his famous Newington Green Academy. Defoe probably entered Morton's academy in 1674. Since the academies were virtually one-man ventures, the personality of the master influenced his students deeply.

Charles Morton was as memorable a man as Samuel Annesley.[24] Like Annesley, he was universally respected for his benevolence, selflessness, public spirit, and good nature, but Morton was also known as a first-rate mind. He had been a fellow of Wadham College during the residency of the "Oxonian Sparkles," men like Robert Boyle, Christopher Wren, Thomas Sprat, and William Petty. His quickly became one of the most respected Dissenting academies in England and added to the academies' reputation for leading educational reform. One of the great ministers of Defoe's generation described Defoe's classmates as having "very agreeable Society and great advantages" at Morton's. Even Samuel Wesley, whose harsh criticism of the academies sparked a painful controversy, called Morton "an ingenious and universally learned Man" who taught moderation and tolerance and might have been "the most considerable [teacher] in *England*." Again Defoe saw a respected, good man continually harassed. By teaching, Morton was violating the "Stamford Oath"* that forbad graduates of Oxford and Cambridge to teach "as in a University without the approval of their alma mater."[25] Before he emigrated to America to accept Increase Mather's invitation to assume the presidency of Harvard College, he had been excommunicated, apprehended on a *capias*,† repeatedly arrested, and, in his own words, "infested with Processes from the Bishops Court." He and Annesley had both been rounded up and imprisoned as "disaffected and dangerous" men during the fear of a rebellion in October 1684.

Lay students at the Newington Green Academy were expected to spend three years there, while theological students spent five.[26] Since

---

*Administered at commencement at the universities, the oath was so named because a group of masters and scholars withdrew from Oxford in 1334 and, encouraged by "the patronage of some great persons," began to build colleges and lay the foundation for a new degree-granting university at Stamford. Oxford and Cambridge used their influence with "prelates and princes," and Stamford was suppressed. The oath was required after 1335 and interpreted in Defoe's time to mean that "no man, who had taken the degree of Master in Arts in either of our universities, might lawfully instruct so much as privately in any other place, any persons in any art or science professed publicly in the universities." The result was to set up an exclusive claim to the privilege of giving a university education and to label those Dissenters who set up academies "perjurors." The oath was required until 1827.

†A writ beginning, "you are to arrest," from the Latin *capias*.

Defoe entered in 1674 and did not leave until late 1679 or early 1680, he must have begun the theological curriculum. In his own words, he was "first . . . set a-part for, and then . . . set a-part from the Honour of that Sacred Employ."[27] To the end of his life he spoke of his education there with pride, and many of his interests, abilities, and opinions show the influence of Morton's school. The curriculum, like most designed by the ejected ministers, continued the university tradition of the Medieval Trivium (rhetoric, logic, and Latin grammar) and Quadrivium (arithmetic, geometry, astronomy, and music). After a year of philosophy and logic, students studied Aristotle's three branches of philosophy in the order the universities followed: moral (political, economic, ethical), metaphysical, and natural (physics, biology, botany, zoology).

These university-educated Nonconformist teachers were the intellectual equals of their contemporaries at Oxford and Cambridge, often exceeded them in devotion to their work, and had inquiring, skeptical minds. The academies were conspicuous for freedom of inquiry. For example, Dissenting schoolboys, including Morton's, read Locke's *Essay concerning Human Understanding*, which was forbidden at Oxford, and surviving textbook lists include such nonstandard readings as the tract *Lucius Junius Brutus*, which opposed a Roman Catholic succession to the English throne; a book of metaphysics by a Jesuit; and works by Pierre Gassendi, who was infamous in Morton's time for his defense of Epicureanism. The theologians on Morton's reading list were remarkably diverse; a Morton student reports that they were assigned "the best books both of the *Episcopal, Presbyterian,* and *Independent Divines.*" These included, for example, Baxter, Tillotson, and Charnock for practical divinity; *Altare Damascenum*, Bishop Hall, and Baxter on episcopacy; and Rutherford, Strangius, and Amyraldus on grace and free will. Morton clearly made an effort to represent theological variety and conflicting stances on disputed issues.

More significantly, Morton broke with educational tradition by emphasizing self-discipline, by teaching in English, and by insisting upon the importance of such additional subjects as history, geography, modern languages, and physics. Morton lists the specific benefits of various subjects in his *Spirit of Man* (1693); in part, it reads, "Intellectual & Moral Habits . . . are formed much according to the Information men meet with, especially in their younger dayes. . . . *Mathematicks* Solidness and Sagacity; *Physicks* good conjecture at the Reasons of things; *Moral Philosophy* and *History,* Prudence; *Rhetorick,* Fairness and Confidence of Address; *Poetry,* quickness of fancy, and Imagination."[28]

Most revolutionary of all was Morton's and the academies' science instruction. Unlike the universities, they used the experimental approach, equipped laboratories, and included current theories and discoveries as soon as they were published. A student of Morton's tells us that his laboratory held "air-pumps, thermometers, and all sorts of mathematical instruments."[29] Furthermore, they legitimized the study of science by explaining that it revealed "God as manifested in the world." Morton wrote a textbook for his students, *Compendium Physicae,* in which he presented the discoveries of Harvey, Newton, and Hooke and attempted to synthesize ideas, as he did in the section that posits a theory of the universe based on molecules from the work of Boyle, Gilbert, Gassendi, and Descartes. So good was Morton's work that this text was used at Harvard College for over thirty-five years.[30] Defoe retained his lively interest in science, and Morton's theories can be found in works from the early *Storm* to the very late *General History of Discoveries and Improvements.*

None of the events of Defoe's childhood, the harassments, arrests, and indignities, could diminish Annesley or Morton. They taught him the revolutionary Protestant idea that God's love gave his people status that no person, no law, could take away. When faced with hardship, he himself found direction and strength in their examples. In 1704, when he was imprisoned in Newgate, he referred to himself as "dead in Law" and "silenced," the words applied to those ejected on St. Bartholomew's Day, 1662. In 1712, in the wake of new discrimination against Dissenters and unmistakable evidence of government upheaval sure to threaten his employment, he wrote, "I have always been . . . Chearful, Easy and Quiet; enjoying a perfect calm of Mind . . . By a constant serious Application to the great, solemn and weighty Work of Resignation to the Will of Heaven." He concludes this preface to volume 8 of the *Review* with a hymn much like many of the hymns of Isaac Watts:

> I by his Rule, direct my Steps,
> And on him stay my Mind.
>
> Upon his various Providence
> *With Satisfaction* rest,
> I unexalted can enjoy,
> And *suffer* Undepress'd.

This hymn repeats nearly every idea he used to describe Annesley in his eulogy. Typically, the themes of acceptance, resignation, and endurance so common in the writings of Annesley and Morton dominate Defoe's writings in times of personal trouble.

In this same preface Defoe affirms his willingness to die for truth. His conception of his work, duty, and method show yet another major legacy from his Dissenting training. Both Morton and Annesley had a passion for practical teaching. Zealous, modest men, they followed Morton's injunction that duty lay in teaching men what they should do, not what the teacher could do. Both used mundane illustrations and concerned themselves with conduct rather than with theory. "Direct your Speech," Morton wrote, "not as if you intended to beat the Air over Mens Heads, but as designing to teach and touch . . . their Hearts." Morton's words from his "Advice to Candidates for the Ministry" might serve for both men: "Let your Discourses be mostly Practical, both as to the Subjects, and Manner of Handling," and Annesley described his intention in his calling to be "to promote *Practical Godliness*."[31] Supporting their every injunction was an honest recognition of human concerns. "If difficult Circumstances do really pinch you, be not discourag'd, God will provide for you. But when? and what? and where? and how?" Morton once asked. On his deathbed he observed, "That which can't be cur'd must be endur'd," but admitted that he "desired" rather than did "patiently . . . submit to the hand of God" at that time.

Above all, they communicated personal challenge animated by a tone of urgent demand for personal commitment. Daniel Williams' funeral sermon for Annesley bore the title, "The Excellency of A Publick Spirit." He called Annesley "the whole Text exemplified: *he served his Generation*, and he is *fallen asleep*." Those who aspire to Annesley's success "must spend, do, adventure, and suffer most, and yet must resolve to allow, intreat, connive, yield, thank, forbear, forgive, deny themselves, and endure most."[32] Defoe's rhetoric echoed these aspirations. He frequently said that he refused to take offense and would never answer in kind those who slandered him. His very last works consistently alluded to his desire to publish his beneficial ideas "and leave, at least, a Testimony of my good Will to my Fellow Creatures." Williams had called public spirit the "Spring that sets all the Wheels in Motion," and more than a quarter of a century later Defoe wrote, "A Commonwealth is a Machine actuated by many Wheels. . . . Every Man ought therefore as much as in him lies, to contribute in his Station, to the publick Welfare."[33]

Both Annesley and Morton wanted to make their teachings accessible. In his defense of teaching in English and particularly of teaching women, Morton writes, "What pitty is it that reasonable souls should not be improved to the uttermost, that Ingenuous minds should Languish for want of mater [*sic*] to work upon."[34] Neither he nor Annesley was self-conscious about his use of story. Morton explains,

Romances, & parables, or fables, that have no truth In the Matter, but Morall honesty In the Designe; As also Enlargment of stories by variety of phrases, & manner of expression, (Provided they are no part of a testimony) are noe Lyes, but Ingenuous Poesie (—In the propper Notion, distinct from the art of versifying, or poetry) or handsome Oratory, The better to Inculcate the virtue, or expose the vice they Designe to represent: and are of singular Use in all Discourses.[35]

Defoe learned this lesson well, for he almost never wrote anything without interspersing entertaining, illustrative stories. "All I could have

said would have yielded no diversion, and perhaps scarce have obtained a reading, or at best no attention. . . . Facts that are formed to
touch the mind must be done a great way off. . . . The fable is always
made for the moral, not the moral for the fable," he explains in the
preface of *Serious Reflections during the Life . . . of Robinson Crusoe*. He
compares *Moll Flanders* to plays that are "useful" and "fail not to recommend Virtue, and generous Principles, and to discourage and expose
all sorts of Vice and Corruption of Manners."[36] In his pamphlets he
would move from hypothesis to discussion with examples to summary;
even within parts of an argument he often relied upon the techniques
of triple statement, summarizing couplets, or the question-and-answer
arrangement found in Annesley's, Morton's, and other polemical writers' work. Even his fondness for medical analogies follows Annesley's
and Morton's.[37] In one of his last works Defoe explains his method of
inquiry in words reminiscent of theirs; in *An Effectual Scheme for the
Immediate Preventing of Street Robberies* (1731) he calls street violence a
"raging Pestilence" and says that he intends to search out the "Nature
and Original of the Disorder," for that is always the first step toward a
"Cure" (15).

Perhaps the most striking thing about the Newington Green Academy's educational week was the amount of time devoted to declamation
and dispute. Saturdays were dedicated to "useful subjects" and two
other mornings to philosophical controversies; other times were set
aside for similar debates on divinity, history, and science. Morton emphasized writing and speaking, and his students weighed, considered,
and argued endlessly. In addition to wide reading and rhetorical skills
came habits of thought that marked Defoe's personality as strongly as
his personal faith.

He was trained to consider many points of view, take a stand, and
develop a consequential argument; significantly, this training had a
casuistical bent. Casuistry, a branch of ethics that applied general rules
of religion and morality to individual "cases of conscience," held particular fascination for Defoe's generation, for it attempted to illuminate
apparent conflicts of duty. Casuistry paid closer attention to concrete
situations than abstract theory does. In ordinary times circumstances
might bring divine, positive, and natural law into apparent conflict. In
Defoe's time the literal interpretation of biblical code ethics came into
conflict with the legal absolutism of some of the Restoration laws, especially within the concept of a national church. A great many people
began to feel that their consciences dictated deviation from an established legal directive, and even more believed themselves faced with the
demand that they swear oaths contradicting earlier oaths. Many men of
James Foe's generation had been bound by oath to support Charles I,
Parliament, the Solemn Oath and Covenant, Cromwell, and then

Charles II and the Non-Resistance Act. Such demands made a generation that believed all oaths were binding under God reconsider the idea
that church and state, religious and legal codes were inseparable. They
were generations away from the kind of distinction Immanuel Kant
was to make between a government that restricts itself to its legitimate
powers, and can thus demand absolute disclosure of its subjects, and a
government that may be treated evasively because it violates the natural
rights of its subjects. As Protestants, however, they *felt* they were unique
souls whose highest allegiance was to God as represented by their "consciences." Such an emphasis upon the *individual* soul made code ethics
or a general norm unsatisfactory in the extreme. Casuistry offered
Annesley's generation a way to mediate between the individual and the
abstract; it seemed to offer ways to examine conscience and learn to
choose correct moral action. Both Annesley and Morton were habitually described by their contemporaries as "considerable Casuists." Almost all of the theologians on Morton's reading list for students were
casuists of note, and William Ames's *De conscientia et eius iure, vel casibus*,
a nearly complete guide to casuistry, was standard reading. Wesley
charged that Morton's way of argument was "*Words* and fine *Turns*,
mine is stubborn *Matter of Fact and Reason*."[38] Annesley's "normal
preaching" was described as dealing with "'cases of conscience,' or practical matters of Christian conduct and belief," and much of the universal praise for Morton's teaching ability is directed at his ability to make
knowledge immediately useful and moral. In order to be clear, Annesley divided his sermons into propositions, inferences, reproof, exhortation, directions, considerations, answers to objections, and questions. "How may we be universally and exactly Conscientious?" is a fine
illustration of his typical subject matter and method. It states his own
case ("arraign'd as a Malefactor, charged with Sedition, Schism, and
Heresie") and goes on to explain how conscience acts and how man may
test the correctness of his decisions. "How may we attain to love God
with all our Hearts, Souls, and Minds?" defines loving God with the
whole heart, offers suggestions for developing this love, and concludes
by urging the congregation to try. Annesley's sermons are full of illustrative, familiar anecdotes.

Morton also organized his work by the rules of classical rhetoric and
logic and incorporated a sturdy strain of reasoning on practical cases.
His *Spirit of Man*, for example, is divided into clearly marked sections,
such as "Text Opened," "Expositors Differ," "The most proper Interpretation . . . ," "Constitution of our Spirit," "types of spirits," and "Inference." In a postscript to a 1692 copy of his *System of Logick*, Morton
explains that he tries to present his material three times: "(1) that you
may have a more General notion (2) that you may distinctly Judge of it
(3) that you may reclaim it," and in three different ways.[39] The atten-

tion to the ways the mind works and decisions are made shows clearly in sections such as "Inference" and in the number of homely examples and analogies. John Dunton, the nephew of one of Morton's students and an acquaintance of Defoe's, explained the effectiveness of Morton's teaching style by praising it as "always new and occasional, for whatever subject was at any time started, he had still some pleasant and pat story for it."[40]

Morton's and Annesley's "cases" were presented as stories embedded in ordinary life and experience. Earnest dedication to enlightening men and women and intense interest in contemporary events, discoveries, and ideas, combined with the unshakable conviction that God was revealed in subjects such as history and science, invigorate Morton's writings. The interweaving of eternal context, concern for history, and passionate involvement with the immediate gives his and Annesley's works a modernity, an immediacy, and a heightened, even urgent, tone.

Defoe's pamphlets and periodical essays depend upon these habits of mind and rhetorical strategies, but it is in the novels that their artistic value is most clear. Character after character in Defoe's novels faces casuistical choices, and Defoe dramatizes the conflict between the "natural" instinct to survive and the "codes" of the Ten Commandments or of English law by emphasizing the character's thoughts, decisions, reactions, reconsiderations, and judgments. This emphasis does much to separate his novels from the fiction of plot so common in his own time.[41] Casuistry focuses on motives and thought processes leading to action, on conflicts and dilemmas, and develops empathy. Throughout his life Defoe thought like a Protestant casuist and used the clear, plain style he had learned from Morton to present concrete, instructive cases.

Even in this tumultuous, serious world, Defoe must have done the things children always do. He must have played in the vacant lots and built with the stones and boards in the wreckage from the fire. He undoubtedly knew the markets, shops, warehouses, and wharves of the city well. He surely saw pickpockets pumped,* thieves hanged, and the carriages of the wealthy crowd the narrow streets. He appears to have spent some part of his boyhood in the country, and he writes easily about boxing, wrestling, foxhunting, cardplaying, cockfighting, football, racing, and a number of children's games. Here and there he recounts a youthful prank or adventure, as he does in *An Essay on the History and Reality of Apparitions* (1727) when he describes making a

---

*Petty criminals caught on the streets were often held in the trough in the center of a public square, ducked repeatedly, and held while others pumped water on them.

vacant house seem haunted (374–76). His books are full of realistic domestic scenes and innocent recreations.

Thus Defoe grew up in a pious tradesman's home, reared primarily by a father who sought out exemplary men with unusual minds and talents to teach his son. The plague, the Great Fire, and the persecution of Dissenters dramatized the lessons of fortitude, patience, and diligence he heard preached. In the midst of the most severe period of persecution, Annesley had reminded his congregation: "Blessed Paul wrote more Epistles in his Bonds, than any one of the Apostles in their Liberty." Defoe saw the insecurity of life and the rewards of perseverance; he learned to fear "the unseen Mine," but he learned to play and absorbed the lesson of one of Annesley's sermons: "To give way to Sorrow, disspirits us for any considerable service either to God or Man; it unfits us for every thing . . . a Life of Sorrow is a degree of Hell upon Earth, and such Persons torment themselves before their time." Defoe himself wrote, "A Man that will lie still, should never hope to rise; he that will lie in a Ditch and pray, may depend upon it he shall lie in the Ditch and die."[42]

CHAPTER 2

MERCHANT-REBEL

*While such publick, scandalous Practices are found among us,
which Men can neither Justifie [nor] . . . defend by their Constitution, or by their Consciences—Which Reproach them as Men,
as Citizens, as* English Men, *and as Christians; it shall never be
said, that my Father's Son liv'd to see it, and fear'd to speak it.*
—DEFOE, *Review,* 21 July 1711

*As a livery man of this ancient city, Daniel Defoe had often to bear
himself bravely in defence of popular rights.*
—from memorial speech at the dedication of
the Defoe monument, Bunhill Fields, 1870

When the choice of occupation came to be made, Defoe chose his
father's path. James Foe was as admirable a man as Annesley and Morton, and his life brought Defoe into a tradition of independence and
brotherhood even older than that of the Dissenters. James was a freeman of the City of London and a member of an ancient livery company.
As such, he could practice his trade and vote "in the City," the one
square mile that had grown behind its Roman wall to become the center
of power, wealth, and commerce for the entire nation. Although the
ordinary householder and ratepayer could vote in some ward elections,
and freemen (those granted "the freedom" to carry on a trade within
the City) could vote for Common Councilmen, only the liverymen
could vote for the higher officers of the Corporation—the lord mayor,
the sheriffs, the auditors—and members of Parliament.[1] In addition to
the voice the M.P.'s had in national government, the sheriffs had the
right to make formal statements at the Bar of the House of Commons,
and the Court of Aldermen had the right of access to the throne itself.

The freemen of the City of London knew that they were different
from other Englishmen. Because of their success and importance to
the nation's economy, they were unusually free to express opinions and
could respect ability more than noble birth. Defoe sounded like a typical City man when he publicly condemned the 1711 elections for attempting to violate the orderly advancement of Sir Gilbert Heathcote

to the lord mayorship and for deliberately electing Nonconformist sheriffs who could not serve (Lambe was assessed a fine of £400 and Staverton £1,000 for declining office; some said Mansion House was built with the fines from Dissenters who could not serve). Defoe wrote that he had been threatened for speaking his mind and said, "I have a Right to make this Complaint, being born a Freeman, and for having been near 30 Years a *Livery-Man* of this City, and therefore Claim of Right to be concern'd in the Preservation of the Priviledges of the said City." Because he was a freeman, he always saw himself possessing special rights and responsibilities, including personal involvement in guarding the "privileges" of the City. His phrases ring with the special history of London, and "born a Freeman" invokes James Foe's special legacy to his son: "It shall never be said, that my Father's Son liv'd to see it, and fear'd to speak it." Moreover, Defoe appreciated his father's concern for him; as a man, he reacted to a satiric attack with the words, "I owe this Justice to my Ancient Father . . . that if I am a Blockhead, it was no Bodies Fault but my own; he having spar'd nothing in my Education."[2]

Defoe had grown up with the ancient ritual of City elections, livery company meetings and dinners, processions on Lord Mayor's Day, and trained band drills in Finsbury Field. Few men could have passed the spirit of the City on to their sons better than James. In 1644, almost exactly on his fourteenth birthday, James Foe had been apprenticed to John Levitt, a tallow chandler, Master of the Butcher's Company, and a lieutenant colonel in the City of London's trained bands.[3] James, fatherless now for thirteen years, followed in Levitt's footsteps, and Daniel was truly his father's son.

To be John Levitt's apprentice in 1644 was enviable. Levitt had already been a leader in the Butchers' Company for more than fifteen years. He had served a term as Warden in 1631,[4] the year James's father died, had been elected Assistant every year from 1632 through 1638, been a Warden again in 1639, an Assistant in 1640, the Master in 1641, an Assistant again for 1642 and 1643, and was then serving an unusual second term as Master.

The Master of a Livery Company held an administrative and ceremonial post. He sat at the head of the Company court, was responsible for enforcing the Company, City, and court rules governing the butcher's trade, and responded to the crown's requests for funds and provisions for England's wars. His varied duties included riding in the barge hired to accompany the lord mayor to Westminster for his oaths of office, presiding at the many company dinners, such as the Audit Dinner, and awarding prizes at wrestling matches at Bartholomew Fair. As one of the oldest companies—the Butchers had been fined by Henry II in 1180—Levitt's Company was highly respected.

The Presentiments of Apprentices, James Foe apprenticed to John Levitt.

In 1644 the companies* were extremely powerful. Besides their voting privileges, their Court of Common Council managed the City's property, contracts, and income; levied taxes and assessments; heard petitions; and enacted the legislation for the governing of the City. London owned the shrievalty of Middlesex and the bailiwick of Southwark, held a legal monopoly of the markets within a seven-mile radius, levied coal duties within twelve miles of the City, regulated and taxed the entire port of London, and governed eighty miles of the Thames.[5] Aldermen were justices of the peace; sheriffs appointed juries; and the lord mayor, aldermen and other wealthy Common Council members

*A company included apprentices; the Yeomanry, who were journeymen or small tradesmen; and the substantial businessmen admitted to the livery. Fifteen Assistants were chosen from the liverymen to help the Wardens and Master govern the company and protect its interests. The Master and five Wardens were elected from former Assistants by the liverymen and, after a time, had quite specific duties; for instance, the Renter Warden was treasurer.

held the "Commission of Lieutenancy"* from the monarch. Thus, the companies and the City controlled the executive, judicial, and legislative branches of the government and had such important rights as levying taxes and appealing directly by personal appearance to the king and Parliament. Men of Levitt's and James Foe's generations took pride in the City's economic importance, power, and independence.

The company when James Foe became an apprentice was a paternal, even familial organization.[6] Apprentices were bound to their masters for at least seven years and, ordinarily, until they were twenty-four. The company expected reliability, punctuality, piety, and respect. It fined apprentices for failing to meet its standards of appropriate dress and provided activities for them such as the Christmas Breakfast. The company kept its own charitable funds; many owned and administered almshouses and pensions, and members attended liverymen's funerals en masse. Both Levitt and Foe attended meetings faithfully.

The orderly rise through the company's ranks marked a respected way of life and provided lifelong friends. For example, Walter Tuffley, perhaps a relative of the man whose daughter would marry James Foe's son, was a yeoman in the Butchers' Company. He, like Levitt and James's second brother, Henry, lived in the parish of St. Botolph's, Aldgate. Henry would serve as executor of Levitt's will. The names Stancliffe, Newins, Marsh, Dunton, Shower, and Lodwick appear again and again in connection with the lives of James and his son. Marriage licenses, wills, petitions for appointed offices, company records, deeds, and lawsuits weave the lives of these City families together. Charles Lodwick, for example, who had grown up in Cornhill, signed Defoe's marriage license, and his half-brother, Thomas Lodwick of St. Botolph's, Aldgate, signed a petition with Defoe and others in favor of the appointment of another friend and Morton classmate, Matthew Clarkson, as secretary to the Council of New York. William Marsh, for whose mother's will James had been executor in 1671, moved from Dorking to London, and in 1692 was still in touch with Defoe. Samuel Stancliffe, whose father was a stocking seller at the corner of Bread Street and Cheapside, became Defoe's business partner.[7]

When James Foe became Levitt's apprentice, London was an armed camp enjoying a brief lull. As a member of the Court of Assistants in the Butchers' Company and a lieutenant colonel in the trained bands, Levitt had many stories to tell. The struggle for power between king and Parliament had entered its final phase. Beginning in 1640 both the king and Parliament repeatedly asked the Common Council to lend them money for their armies. Aldermen were jailed for refusing to give

---

*The commission designated them lord-lieutenants of the militia and volunteers and entitled them to choose the officers of the trained bands. In times of crisis, they had great power.

the king lists of wealthy citizens whom he might pressure or imprison. The City tried to remain neutral and granted a grudging £50,000 instead of requested sums as high as £200,000, regardless of which side asked.

By 1642 London felt threatened. Although Londoners were deeply divided into Royalists and Roundheads, they were united in their loyalty to London. Inspired by stories of the sacking of Brentford, they provided against an occupation of the City by Charles's army. When Charles besieged Gloucester, they believed London would be his next target. They denied the king's demand for £100,000 but granted that sum to a deputation from the Houses of Parliament. The Grocers' Company alone raised £9,000; the Butchers' share, £300, was given "by consent of the whole Board." When Parliament set aside a place to receive money, plate, arms, and horses for the defense of the City, so much was brought in that the earl of Clarendon describes it as "hardly credible," "there being hardly men enough to receive it, or room to lay it in." Women donated rings, bodkins, thimbles, and even their caudle cups.[8]

Just as London had twice raised *and* equipped 1,000 men within twelve hours in 1596, so it could tap apparently bottomless resources in the present crisis. The trained bands grew from thirty companies in January 1642 to forty by May and fifty-two by October, with Cripplegate ward alone contributing nearly 1,000 men; 1,000 light horse, 3,000 dragoons, and cannons and arms were added to existing forces within a week. The fortifications around London seemed to "spring up nearly overnight." Men, women, and children "of all ranks" worked side by side; 8,000 tailors with forty-six colors, the entire Common Council, and even 1,000 oyster wives from Billingsgate joined the estimated 100,000 people who worked in the trenches and ramparts that would enclose the entire City.[9]

This response was consistent with the City's history, in harmony with its tradition of self-defense. Many of their citizens knew that "the men of London whose forefathers had beaten back Swegen and Cnut, whose brothers died round the standard of Harold, were not men to surrender their mighty city [to William the Conqueror] . . . without at least meeting the invader in the field."[10] And that is what London and the trained bands thought in 1643. Two regiments chosen by lot were sent to relieve Gloucester and to withstand Prince Rupert's attacks at Newbury. Clarendon wrote, "The London trained bands, and auxiliary regiments, (of whose inexperience of danger, or any kind of service . . . men had till then too cheap an estimation), behaved themselves to wonder; and were, in truth, the preservation of that army that day. For they stood as a bulwark and rampire . . . though prince Rupert himself led up the choice horse to charge them . . . he could make no impression upon their stand of pikes" (1:458). They met the king's forces on the field and forced Charles to retreat and negotiate as William the Conqueror had. John Levitt's regiment fought under the banner JEHOVA PROVIDEBIT and saw service at Newbury. Levitt, like all officers of the trained bands, was also a member of the Honourable Artillery Company, and he paid the quarterage, his company dues, faithfully.

It was in his work as a public servant and administrator, however, that Levitt distinguished himself. He was a leader of the St. Botolph's, Aldgate, vestry for more than twenty years in addition to the Butchers' Company. The vestry, composed of the vicar, churchwardens, and all who had been churchwardens, elected such parish administrators as the surveyors of the highways and the overseers of the poor fund, administered leases, and conducted other business "concerning the good of the parish." Levitt was very regular in his attendance and was chosen repeatedly to audit the accounts and to mediate disputes. Several times he belonged to committees of twelve that had been carefully chosen to represent the interests of the parish.[11]

James Foe completed his apprenticeship in 1654 and followed in Levitt's footsteps to become a solid, prosperous tallow chandler, a responsible citizen, and a leader of the Butchers' Company. The work of tallow chandlers required the skill of craftsmen as well as strength and stamina. From antiquity, they had been closely associated with butchers, for they themselves melted, skimmed, and strained the rough fat they used for candles. The carefully purified tallow went into prism-shaped vessels, into which the chandler dipped rods with wicks. The chandler dipped the wicks to the same depth three times, then had to hold them almost motionless over the vessel while they dripped. He then hung them on racks to harden before two more dippings. On the final dip, he "necked" them—dipped them deeper to form an attractive top. Finally, he finished the bottoms by passing them over a heated brass plate. The quality and color of the wax as well as the uniformity and beauty of the final product depended on his skill.[12]

Within a few years, James came to be styled "merchant" and even "gentleman" rather than "tradesman." In addition to whatever skill he had as a tallow chandler and whatever acumen as an entrepreneur, he had respected accounting ability. During his term as Renter Warden, he made major changes in the bookkeeping procedures, and between 1698 and 1705 the vestry of St. Stephens parish continuously elected him an auditor of the accounts and an overseer for the collection and distribution of the poor rates. He also served his parish in such responsible, elected positions as Questman, churchwarden, and upper churchwarden.[13] His years on the Butchers' Company Court of Assistants were especially difficult, however, and at the family fireside young

Daniel would have heard the talk of special taxes, tense negotiations with the crown, and loss of civil rights.

During the most trying years for the City, James served in increasingly sensitive positions. In 1678, the first year he was an Assistant, the City angered King Charles II by electing strongly Whig M.P.'s and an equally partisan lord mayor, and in 1680 London overwhelmingly defeated the court's candidates for sheriff. Simultaneously the Dissenters began a concerted campaign against informers, and many were convicted of perjury and stood in the pillory. Next the City supported the Exclusion Bill with a delegation composed of the lord mayor and aldermen, who accompanied Lord William Russell when he presented the bill from the Commons to the Lords. So annoyed was the king with this new alliance between the City and the Commons that he convened Parliament in the conservative, Tory city of Oxford. The City petitioned Charles repeatedly to hold Parliament and continued to elect whomever it pleased to office; in 1682 this struggle between the crown and the City led Charles to begin *Quo Warranto* proceedings against the City.* The court decided against the City, and it and the livery companies lost their charters. That year James was Fourth Warden, the man responsible for enforcing the lord mayor's and aldermen's orders.[14] From then until October 1688, the City was governed by a royal commission with "all officers appointed by the King to act during his pleasure."[15]

The City never accepted the verdict. In 1684 the Butchers' Company assessed each Assistant forty shillings "to defray the charges of obtaining regrant of the Charter," and James was one of the collectors. On 24 May 1685, however, the warrant for removing the charter of the Master Wardens and Commonality of the company displaced all of those who had not taken the oaths and Anglican communion within six months. Now only those who took communion in the Church of England could be admitted to the livery, and no one could be elected who did "frequent or be present at any Conventicle . . . upon pretext of religious Worship."[16] Thus, James Foe like Levitt before him, sat on the court that listened to appeals for money from the king and Parliament, deliberated over raising the sums, and participated in the attempts to preserve the City's privileges and independence.

⁂

In 1681, his twenty-first year, Defoe was in London writing *Meditations* on John Collins's sermons and in the last throes of deciding a

---

*The City's representatives were summoned to appear at King's Bench to prove their right to the privileges they claimed from their charter. These rights were (1) to be of themselves a body corporate and politic, (2) to have sheriffs of the city and county of London and of Middlesex, and to name, elect, and constitute them, and (3) to have the mayor and aldermen be justices of the peace and hold Sessions of the Peace.

course for his life. He had completed four of the five years expected of ministerial candidates at Morton's Newington Green Academy. Now he saw that the lines were drawn between the City and the court, and that the Dissenters faced a new wave of persecution. London, "virtually a republic" and "the stronghold of militant protestantism," was defying the king on every front. Refusing to enforce the Clarendon Code, supporting the Exclusion Act, and petitioning for a convening of Parliament, the City seemed to bait its king.[17]

Defoe weighed the necessarily retired life of a Dissenting clergyman-teacher against the tense excitement of his father's official and private meetings. James Foe was serving his third year as one of the twenty-one members of the Court of Assistants of the Butchers' Company and had just completed his term as Renter Warden; his prosperity and influence had never been greater. Even before that year Defoe must have had reservations about the ministry. Years later he was to lament the "want of Conversation," that is, stimulating company, in the academies.[18] His *Meditations* are full of charged comparisons, prayers for "A Heart / To Vallue Thee," and emotional exclamations. As he listened to John Collins, perhaps the best preacher in London, whom his contemporaries knew as "mighty in the scriptures," Defoe could contemplate what might be the zenith of his own future success: Collins had a large, prosperous Lime Street congregation and was one of the original Pinners' Hall lecturers.[19] Collins preached almost every Sunday, but Defoe kept a notebook devoted to but six sermons preached between 20 February and early October on the highly pertinent text: "And he said unto them, Go ye into all the world, and preach the gospel to every creature. He that believeth and is baptized shall be saved; but he that believeth not shall be damned" (Mark 16:15–16).

The *Meditations* of 1681 have a restless, frenetic quality quite strongly in contrast with the witty, philosophic tone of the 1682 *Historical Collections*. "A Thousand, Thousand Wants I have," "Empty wishes Set the Mind on Fire," "I ask a Heart / To Vallue Thee . . . / A Will Resign'd to Thee, Desyres Confin'd / To What's Thy will," Defoe writes. There is a Donnian quality of fretting, of complexity, and of awareness of paradox: "Say Lord I can Not Come yet Here am I." "How is it Then That I / So Much Aversion To My Duty Find." In "shall the Clay Say unto the Potter?" Defoe draws upon one of the books of the Bible that meant the most to him throughout his life, Jeremiah. Here (18:1–10) he takes the familiar biblical theme of discontent and tells a fable of a clay pot that asks why it is a "Rude ill-fashion'd Nasty Pott / Destin'd To Every Slavish use" rather than a flower pot or painted dish. The potter then curses the complaining pot by making it "For Ever Shapeless Useless Unemploy'd." Here the longing for achievement and greatness stands starkly beside the fear of finding no useful, satisfying work. "Did But my [Meditations] More Enclyne To View What Tis I am," "Lord I should Never Then Repyne / I am Not This Or That / Or Have Not This or That Thats great," he exclaims.

The obscure service of a Dissenting divine or the opportunities of trade and London's battle of wits with her monarchs; the probability of persecution or the hope of prosperity; the Court of Aldermen or Pinners' Hall? By the end of 1681 Defoe had made his choice: he would become a wholesale hosier. The stocking knitting trade had become a large industrial occupation. Its rapid growth as a fashion industry meant that dealers needed to use more than thirty code numbers to identify their merchandise, and consumers demanded the latest colors, patterns, and designs. Some stockings came with decorations, and jersey workers produced ever more delicate, sheerer hose. Even as demand for the coarse, heavy stockings worn by laborers and soldiers and the thick, warm wools continued high, the poorest people began to buy fashion hosiery.[20] The merchant who had a variety of sizes, lengths, textures, and patterns made with different kinds of raw wool, yarns, dyes, and decorations could expect to prosper. Since stocking knitting had been a handicraft, districts still tended to produce different kinds of hosiery. As a wholesaler, then, Defoe would need suppliers from all over England, and he could expect to sell in these towns as well as London.

Defoe hoped his future included a young woman whom he called "Excellent," "Incomparable," and "Divine" in the dedication of a book he made for her in 1682. He described himself as "The meanest & Truest of all your Adorers & Servants" and hoped she would enjoy the book that is a definite compliment to her intelligence.

Mary Tuffley was the seventeen-year-old daughter of John and Joan Rawlins Tuffley of St. Botolph's, Aldgate. Her father, the son of a Wapping carpenter, had not had an easy life but had made a good trade pay off.[21] Bound an apprentice to the cooper John Rolph in January 1652, he was turned over to Thomas Stayins. Stayins died, but John was admitted a freeman in October 1659 upon testimony of Alexander Fowler, the new husband of the widow Stayins. Coopering, the trade described as "sweating, muscle-aching, back-breaking labour," took a long time to learn but was much in demand. Almost everything shipped traveled in casks and barrels made by coopers: beer, ale, wine, spirits, cider, oil, tar, pitch, sauces, jam, butter, soap, sugar, tobacco, fruit, oysters, crockery, nails, gunpowder, paint, meat, seeds, and even things like shoes. Every cask bore a master cooper's "mark" testifying to standard quality. Coopers also made buckets, tubs, churns, and chairs. As England's trade increased, the demand for casks multiplied, and coopers began to specialize. John, like almost all coopers, ended his apprenticeship only to become an improver and then a journeyman.

Before he could receive his own mark, he had to present work to the company. His casks could not leak, had to bear the strain of rough transportation, resist internal pressure sometimes as great as forty pounds per square inch, and hold exact amounts. A full nine years after he became a freeman, John received his mark: ⓣ. Fifteen years later Tuffley was a rich man. His will shows that he owned houses, lands, tenements, cellars, and vaults in St. Botolph's, property in Nutfield and Bletchingly, Surrey, in addition to the annuity for his sister, the estate he left his wife, and the £500 he left to his son.

Defoe's 1682 gift must have distinguished him from Mary's many other "Adorers." The *Historical Collections* was a kind of commonplace book made up of stories collected and retold from a wide variety of sources. Defoe complimented Mary's knowledge and sense in the dedication, and the anecdotes were of the sort often found in discourses or registers for the education of princes. Defoe's wide reading and serious interest in history, his artful presentation of the stories and his witty dialogue contrast jarringly with the stylized address to Mary as "Clarinda" from her worshipful "Bellmour" and to the arch statement that he lays the book at her feet. Such addresses were in vogue. In 1705 his friend John Dunton would publish his letters to his "Dear Iris" (Elizabeth Annesley Dunton) that he had signed "Philaret."

Mary could certainly learn a great deal about her suitor's mind and aspirations from the book. As might be expected in the work of a man contemplating the ministry, examples of piety and salvation figure prominently in the anecdotes that make up the *Historical Collections*; so, too, do fame, justice for seekers of place, virtuous women, and the devotion of servants and even pets. At the beginning, awareness of mortality and a concern with salvation appear in the majority of the stories; although these topics never disappear, anecdotes about virtuous women and lighter, more amusing tales increase in the last third of the book. This change may mark the time when Defoe made the decision to abandon the ministry and give Mary the book. In sequential paragraphs, for example, he tells of Mary of Arminia, who noticed her husband alone at the wedding of a king; of Hiero's wife, who gave no clue that his breath stank; and of a painted woman about whom "St. Hierome" said, "How can she weep for her sins when fearing her tears should make furrowes in her face?" Above all, the 132-page manuscript collects stories of wise, witty rejoinders:

Thales . . . being Asked what was the Easyest thing in the world replyed[,] to Spye other mens faults, and to see none of our owne. (22).

A young man . . . Addicted to his pleasures . . . Turned About to . . . the Companions of his jollity, and said, "Oh! that I Could live with you [and] Dye with [St. Ambrose]." (37)

Castilles the harlott . . . would prove that she Excelled Socrates, And her Argument was that she Could when she list Drawe from him All his Auditours, yea
(Quoth Socrates) And no Marvaile is it . . . for thou Allurest to wickedness, to
which the way is . . . Easye, But I Exhort unto vertue whose way is hard. (66–67)

The subjects that would intrigue Defoe to the end of his life appear.
For example, he is already fascinated with the ways people gain hearings and impress audiences. He tells the story of Marcus Servilius, who,
when he saw that the Romans were "not much moved with his words,"
tore open his shirt and let his "many honorable" battle scars reinforce
his description of valor. And the future crime reporter for *Applebee's
Journal* repeats stories of murders with the familiar moral of the *Newgate Calendar*, "murder will out," and writes,

> Tho' murtherers their guilt would faine protract,
> Concealing both the actor and the act,
> The Beasts, the Brutes, the stones will it Detect.
> (114)

He includes a large number of stories about monarchs performing the
various duties of kings as military leaders, judges, and patrons, and he
praises especially those strong enough to appreciate instructive
criticism.

The *Historical Collections* has a strong moral flavor, but Mary must
have been somewhat amazed at a book that included both a harrowing
account of a soldier rolled to death in a hogshead penetrated by many
nails for betraying the *other* side and the lovely tale of the sparrow that
nestled in Xenocrates' bosom to escape the hawk. Surely she had to
admire the wit and succinct wisdom found on every page; a typical
paragraph reads,

> Saladine the great Turkish king, Sensible of the mortallity of the greatest
> men, gave Order that At his funerall A shirt should be Carried on A Speare
> [with] these words . . . Saladine . . . carried nothing with him to his grave but
> this Shirt onely. (19–20)

The mingling of moral and fable, the love of stories, and the desire to
communicate useful knowledge are already present in Defoe's writing.
Like so many men who conclude they are not temperamentally suited
for the ministry, Defoe continued to seek ways to witness and serve. His
later pamphlets written in the interest of Dissenting causes, his elegy
for Annesley, his conduct books, and even his novels are more than
pragmatic uses of his religious education; they include attempts to
exhort, warn, and even save his readers. The freeman of the City
overwhelms the preacher-manqué in the writing as in life, however.
Even when Defoe would write in support of Dissenting causes, he
would be drawn to conflicts over natural and legal rights, to expression

of the "rights" of citizens, to protests against the exclusion of Dissenters from such civic involvement as military and public office, and to defenses of them against charges of rebellion and lack of patriotism.

On 1 January 1684 he married Mary. In books like *The Complete English Tradesman* Defoe always recommended that a man establish himself before he married. His father had served a full apprenticeship, spent a few years beyond its 1654 completion setting up his trade as a tallow chandler, then married. And though James had married Alice by 1657, it was nine years before they had their first child. In the two years between his decision to go into trade and his marriage, Defoe had done well for himself, and he and Mary would also wait to have children. He and his childhood friend Samuel Stancliffe went into partnership. Stancliffe had inherited his father's haberdashery in 1680 and had been joined by his cousin James, who had served an apprenticeship; they and Defoe would continue to be associated in business until Samuel Stancliffe's death in 1695.[22]

Mary's father provided a dowry of £3,700, and Defoe brought her to his home and warehouse in Freeman's Yard, Cornhill. At that time the major streets in Cornhill were occupied "by the most substantial dealers in plate, woollen manufacture," millinery, linen, and hardware in "houses of the first class"; the courts and smaller streets were the home of merchants and "reputable tradesmen." Nearby Drapers' Hall had a large, pleasant garden, where "those living near take their pleasure . . . at all seasons and especially on Sundays." Defoe's home was in a center of Dissent; a Presbyterian meeting house led by a man named Cruyo stood on Freeman's Yard itself.[23]

Defoe's *Collections* suggest that he married a woman he loved and respected. The dedication and selections seem consistent with everything else he says about the wife he occasionally mentions in his letters. He describes her as "virtuous" and "excellent" and habitually commends her good sense. During the time he was imprisoned for writing *The Shortest Way*, he not only sent her to Nottingham to discuss terms but described her as encouraging him to stand firm. Throughout his life, whenever he was away, she was the "faithfull Steward" who would not misuse his stock "One Penny," the resourceful woman who could manage ten days without money, and the loving wife and mother. He kept in close touch with her; at one point he mentioned writing three letters to her in a short time. The anecdotes he selected for her suggest an intelligent, discerning mind, and the descriptions of happy marriages in his works argue a temperate, virtuous woman whose conversation was a pleasure and whose home orderly. With Mary and her dowry behind him, Defoe could explore and test the options before him and begin to assume a confident, adult role.

He had come from a stable, comfortable home, and he expected to establish the same. By the time he was six, his parents had been settled in the St. Benet Fink parish of the St. Stephen, Coleman Street Ward. James's name appears on the tax rolls for St. Benet Fink from March 1666 to 1668, and again from 1672 through 1683.[24] An entry in the St. Benet Fink records for 1673 suggests that he had left the ward for a while ("James ffoe . . . being but lately come into the Ward"). In 1679 James Foe was one of two collectors for the Poor Tax and chosen an Assistant of the Butchers' Company. It appears that the Foes moved to French Court in the Broad Street Ward when they returned to the ward in the fall of 1671, about the time James proved Elizabeth Marsh's will in London. James prospered steadily and continued to hold his respected position and to serve his ward; except for three years, the Foes lived in a single neighborhood. Daniel grew up in a solid, middle-class circle. His uncle Henry, a successful saddler, lived less than a mile away on Well Alley in a house with six hearths, one of the ten largest houses in Portsoken Ward. Henry shared his brother's skill at accounting and belief in civic responsibility; like James he was occasionally tax collector for his precinct.

Defoe, like his father and uncle, began to serve his ward. In the year of his marriage he was chosen to the ward's petty jury, the jury appointed by the sheriff to try both civil and criminal cases. He knew what the life of a successful merchant should be like, and to have such an establishment in the heart of the busiest part of the City at twenty-four was unusual and showed ambition, promise, and credit with family and friends. Like many men in his twenties, Defoe was deeply concerned with his family and establishing his business.

Even a petty juryman and neophyte tradesman could not ignore the growing tension between City and crown and the rising threats to Dissenters. James II became king on 6 February 1685 and immediately alarmed the already pessimistic Londoners. Almost immediately after the accession of the Catholic James, the City and especially the Dissenters could see that their reservations about James were well-founded and that the harsh policies of Charles II were to continue. The Privy Council bypassed Parliament to extort the customs and excises granted Charles. The king managed parliamentary elections so that only 9 of 195 M.P.'s from boroughs were Whigs. Narcissus Luttrell describes the "great tricks and practices" used to keep out "whiggs or trimmers" and elect the king's supporters:

At some places . . . they chose at night, giveing no notice of it; in other buroughs . . . they have new regulated the electors by new charters . . . a selected number [instead of] inhabitants at large: in counties they adjourned the poll from one place to another, to weary the freeholders, refuseing also to take the votes of excommunicate persons and other dissenters . . . [the] king commanding some to stand, and forbidding others, polling many of his servants at Westminster to carry an election.[25]

As pressure on the City increased, the persecution of the Dissenters also intensified. In Southwark alone £9,680 in fines was assessed against Dissenting ministers in December, and Samuel Annesley was one of the men fined. Several Dissenters died in prison, including Thomas Delaune, his wife and two children.[26] Delaune had been convicted of seditious libel for *A Plea for the Nonconformists*, an explanation of the Dissenters' reasons for separating from the Church of England. In January 1684 he was fined 100 marks, which he could not pay. Delaune's treatment, Defoe wrote, "Will stand as a Monument of the Cruelty of those Times"; he lists him among the "near 8000 Protestant Dissenters that perish't in Prison," and calls him "a Monument of *English Tyranny* . . . and *Selfish Principles*."[27]

In another place Defoe compares the courts of that time to beargardens,[28] and the trial of the Reverend Richard Baxter approximates such a vulgar show. The popular, moderate Baxter was tried for sedition on flimsy evidence gleaned from his commentary, *Paraphrase on the New Testament*, fined 500 marks, and sentenced to prison until he could pay. At his trial Lord Chief Justice George Jeffreys ridiculed Baxter and his counselors, acted as prosecutor and judge, and gave an improper charge to the packed Tory jury. Baxter asked if "any jury will convict a man on such a trial as this?" And when they did, wrote, "to be ragingly reviled . . . and called Rogue and Knave, and not suffered to speak . . . and my Council reviled that offered to speak for me, was far harder than my Imprisonment."[29] This trial served further notice that a time of intensified persecution of Dissenters was at hand, and rumors that Jeffreys was to be lord keeper of the Privy Seal made James's approval clear.[30]

⟆⟆

In June 1685 Daniel Defoe left his family and his business to join the duke of Monmouth's doomed rebellion. Facing new religious persecution and the prospect of a lifetime barred from public office, living in a charterless City no longer able to protect Dissenters from the rigors of the Clarendon Code, Defoe joined the rebellion. Monmouth, the illegitimate son of King Charles II, was a favorite of his father's and a hero of the Dutch war. After 1662 he had grown in popularity as the choice to succeed Charles, for he would be a Protestant heir to the throne. Most of Monmouth's army were men like Defoe who had left established occupations and young families in the hope of making life "tolerable and safe." Later Defoe would say that most of the men who joined Monmouth were Dissenters who feared James's tyranny and considered themselves fighting for their religion: "Everyone knows, that those who join'd . . . did not do it till after King *James II* declar'd himself a Papist, and contrary to Law encourag'd those of his own Perswasion to set up their Worship publickly; and he had likewise in an

The painting of the Duke of Monmouth as John the Baptist suggests that
Monmouth represented the coming triumph of the Protestant Settlement
effected by the accession of William of Orange.

arbitrary and tyrannical Manner invaded our Civil Liberties."[31] They fought under the banner "Fear Nothing but God," cheered a proclamation that declared war against James II "as a murderer . . . traitor to the nation, and tyrant over the people," and described themselves as "in arms for the defense and vindication of the Protestant Religion."[32] As they opened battle, they shouted, "God with us," the battle cry of the Parliament forces in Cromwell's time. Testimony that they were unusual rebels filled the histories and journals of their contemporaries.

Even after Monmouth deserted them, the Mendip miners and local farmers fought on, and the conduct of the rebels captured and executed impressed the nation. Gilbert Burnet described them as maintaining their "calm firmness" through their executions and as having "such a zeal for their religion, which they believed was then in danger, that it made great impressions on the spectators."[33]

Although London was seen by Monmouth's *and* the king's supporters as largely in sympathy with Monmouth, Defoe was among only a few hundred men to join the rebellion. Captain Edward Matthews; John Jones, a London cabinetmaker; Crispe Grange, a brewer; and others had been working within London to raise support for the rebellion since early April.[34] On 11 June 1685 Monmouth landed at Lyme Regis and took stock of his forces. When the news of his landing reached London, the City was sealed. Later Defoe would say, "I remember, how boldly abundance of Men talk'd for the Duke of *Monmouth*, when he first landed; but if half of them had as boldly joyn'd him Sword in Hand, he had never been routed" (*Review* 9:154). In fact, it was not easy to join "Sword in Hand." Since late May warrants to search for "Traytors and Conspirators" and orders to seize arms, horses, and wagons had been issued. Now, however, the lieutenancy of London received specific, emergency instructions. The night Monmouth landed, "in as Little space of tyme as possible," they were to "make diligent search in the houses, warehouses, stables & Coach houses & other places of the persons herein named" for weapons. The list of fifty-eight people included most of the leading Nonconformist citizens, including several future lord mayors, Humphrey Edwin among them. Furthermore, the lieutenancy followed orders to man four boats on the Thames "with as many files of men as they can well bear to watch and apprehend all persons that goe on the Thames in the night & Seize all Arms that they find Conveying away." In order to prevent fatigue and assure vigilance, these men were to be relieved every two hours and the guards at all of the gates and "other Avenues of the Citty" every hour.

King James kept a substantial number of his troops in London and sent part of his army to Bow, Stratford, Highgate, Islington, and Holloway to seal the north and east sides of the City. Two hundred prominent Dissenters were immediately arrested, and others closely watched. Five livery halls and two Quaker meeting houses were commandeered to augment the Woodstreet and Poultry Compters.* Orders to search more and more houses followed. New justices of the peace who were "willing to prosecute" were sworn, and Robert Spencer, second earl of Sunderland, then secretary of state, gave orders to apprehend and hold "all disaffected and suspitious persones and particularly all Non Conformist Ministers."[35] Monmouth had landed with only 82 men; he could expect nothing from London, yet the next day over 1,200 men, including the London reinforcements that had slipped out or left before the City was closed, arrived; within ten days, Monmonth had an army of 3,000 men.[36]

After days of circuitous marching, these troops, whom Defoe called "unfortunate," tried a surprise night attack on the king's forces at Sedgemoor on 6 July. This battle and the aftermath were unforgettable. The troops deployed at ten P.M. and marched five miles, silently, in a heavy mist. A single shot, as Defoe said, "by accident, or treachery," alerted the king's troops; the pace had to be accelerated, and Monmouth's regiments were never well organized after that. The first three regiments withstood the fire of two battalions and six cannons for two hours but never advanced, mistakenly believing that a stream in front of them was too deep. Later Defoe would brood over their guide's "treachery, or mistake."[37] When they broke, they exposed the two unprepared, advancing regiments to the brutal charge of the pursuing royalists. The king's cavalry charged the running infantry, rode them down, and, with the force of their speed, height, and weight, slashed them with swords from behind with full arm blows. Men ran until they came to a boggy fen, sloshed through that, and then ran through waist-high corn, under attack all the way. Dragoons and infantrymen followed to shoot those struggling through the bog or corn beyond. About 2,000 men escaped from the battle of Sedgemoor, but within two weeks between 1,400 and 1,500 had been caught. Men hid in ditches, trees, fields, barns, and disguised meeting houses, but high rewards, willing informers, and forcible searches discouraged sympathizers from hiding the survivors. Carefully documented estimates are that a few score escaped abroad and that only a few hundred remained unapprehended in England.

Defoe, probably among the cavalry that failed to withstand the first round of fire or a member of Edward Matthews' Yellow Regiment, the second on the attack, had more than a hundred miles to go to reach London. Most of the men who escaped the slaughter around Sedge-

---

*The "compters," prisons under the responsibility of the sheriffs, were so called because prisoners were required to "account for the cause of their commitment" before discharge. The other prisons were filled with persons charged with crimes, including high treason.

moor scattered. "Within an hour [they] so disperst that you could not see anywhere ten of their men living," says one report.[38] Some headed for the Channel ports, but most were taken in Stourton, Lymington, and other towns. Others went to hide in wilder, friendlier country and hoped to reach the less guarded port cities such as tiny Ilfracombe or Lynmouth; rebels were taken in Devon, Exeter, and dozens of villages. British ships drove back those in boats. A few went south to ports such as Weymouth, but these routes were heavily patrolled. Matthews escaped to Holland and went on to fight for William, prince of Orange, in the Low Countries; other refugees became mercenaries in European armies or settled in Holland in the cloth industry. The majority of the rebels, however, tried to get home by traveling on foot at night and hiding during the day in cornfields, woods, sheds, barns, and the homes of sympathizers. With luck and horses Defoe could have reached London in two or three days, but the hunt was vigorous, lasted nearly nine months, and turned provincial and city gaols into overcrowded, stinking deathtraps for the wounded and the well alike.[39] Diligence, informers, and coincidences trapped rebels in every disguise, posture, and hiding place.

Defoe was luckier than most. He probably had a horse, and he may have carried the kind of pass merchants got from the lord mayor or the secretary of state. Certainly he had traveled enough on his business to be a more credible traveler than most.[40] Although a London wholesale hosier might well have been in the west country on business at that unlucky time, Defoe would have needed to get to a port at least as far west as Brighton to be credible as a merchant on his way to the continent on business. When necessary, of course, he could have pretended to be going *toward* some of the clothmaking towns rather than coming from them. Concentrations of Dissenters lived in Taunton, Exeter, Wilton, and a dozen villages like Gillingham, and the manufacture of cloth was their major occupation. Defoe tells us that at one time 1,100 looms were employed in Taunton alone.[41]

Each parish was ordered to "go to every house" and produce lists of men absent, in arms, giving supplies, or offering aid, and some of Defoe's friends, including John Dunton, appear on the list ordered by the lord mayor on 9 July 1685.[42] Although careful selection, supervision, and coercion kept the list-makers honest, Defoe's habitual travels, his mother-in-law's house in nearby Kingsland, where he was known to visit for extended periods, the reputation of the Foe family, and the anti-James City temper helped keep Defoe's name off the list.[43]

Once back in London, he would not be spared the results of a hunt that included such abuses as rewards of five shillings or the rebel's property, whichever was greater, for militia able to capture a rebel. As late as November warrants for house searches and seizure of "dis-

affected persons" continued to be issued. More than 850 men were
ordered transported, and courtiers squabbled over the grants that
would allow them to sell the rebels in Barbados, Jamaica, and other
non-Puritan colonies. The "Bloody Assizes" and the ghastly, botched
beheading of Monmouth at Bulwark Gate, London, followed. Defoe
wrote,"The young . . . Prince was taken and put to Death openly, &
Great Cruelties were exercis'd in cold Blood upon the poor unhappy
People that were taken in the Defeat!" Years later, when the aftermath
of the Jacobite rebellion of 1715 drew comparisons to 1685–86, Defoe's
own recollections surfaced. He wrote of the people executed, transported, burned, and whipped; the proceedings, he said, "did not only
exceed the Law, but were carry'd on with such Barbarity as is shocking
to Human Nature."[44]

King James waited until March of 1686 to issue his General Pardon,
but even then it excepted many rebels. Of the thirty-two men pardoned
with Defoe in May 1687, at least one had already been executed and
two transported. At least four of Defoe's classmates from Morton's
academy were executed; another, John Shower, was pardoned.[45] That
Defoe had remained uncaptured was simply amazing, at best a one-in-
fifteen chance.

CHAPTER 3

BANKRUPT

It is said of England *by way of distinction . . . that it is a trading
country. . . . the greatest trading country in the world.*
——DEFOE, *The Complete English Tradesman* (1726)

*What Agonies of Mind, does the Distress'd tradesmen go thro'. . .
and at last like a Deer, hunted down, are driven to stand at bay
with the World!*
——DEFOE, *Review,* 19 February 1706

The years immediately after Monmouth's rebellion were a kaleido-
scope of expanding, joining, experimenting, contracting, and litigating
for Defoe. A defeated rebel, he tried to put Sedgemoor and the fear of
arrest aside. He committed himself to his family and his business with
new energy and turned to his friends, the sons of Dissenting City
merchants and to a group of young men, many his schoolmates, with
literary aspirations.

His brief absence had not affected his wholesale hosiery business,[1]
and he returned to the Cornhill petty jury and other mundane activities. His first child was born. In January 1687 his father presented
him for membership in the Butchers' Company. Prosperous enough to
meet the economic and social standards required to become a livery-
man and to pay a £10.15 fee to be exempt from election to offices,[2] he
became a freeman of the City, thus increased his power in his ward, and
allied himself with a group of respected citizens. Until 1691 he paid his
company dues faithfully but seldom attended elections.

A potential leader in the Dissenting community, he already shared
many of their burdens. Legend makes him the organizing force behind
the Presbyterian church begun in Tooting, Surrey, around 1686. A
merchant, Joshua Gearing, contributed to this church, and the first
minister was Joshua Oldfield, a man Defoe may have known. Only four
years older than Defoe, Oldfield, the son of an ejected minister, had
assisted Samuel Doolittle at Turner's meeting house on Fetter Lane in
the heart of the City. In 1683 Oldfield had been fined £20 a day for each
of eight days of preaching.[3]

Especially severe measures against the Dissenters since Monmouth's

The Butchers' Company stained glass window of
Defoe, destroyed in World War II.

rebellion meant that informers, magistrates, and trained bands broke up all the meetings they could find. The lord mayor and the chief aldermen, most hand-picked by the king, willingly imposed fines and often called the accused "hard names" such as "jade and pimp." On 24 January 16$\frac{85}{86}$ a number of people were "taken at an unlawfull meeting or Conventicle" at a Mrs. Somers' house on Tenter Alley, Little Moorefields. Tenter Alley, a tiny street off Little Moorefields and Moorelane, was home for a nest of Dissenters. The wife of the Monmouth rebel Edward Matthews still lived there, as did Daniel Burgess, a soon-to-be famous preacher. Some of these people escaped, but fourteen, including the two men held responsible for the escape, were indicted and released on bail. Defoe stood for £20 recognizance each for Mary Deering and Jane Foe, both widows who lived at Mrs. Somers'. Mary Deering came from a Croyden family, the Surrey community where Mary Defoe's brother lived. Jane Foe, or Du Foe, was a recent widow; she and her husband had lived a few blocks from Defoe on St. Bartholomew Lane, near the Exchange. Tax and tithe assessments show that her prosperity hardly diminished after the death of her husband sometime after 1675. She continued his business, for an apprentice was listed as an inhabitant in her house in 1678 and 1681. Deering was convicted and fined at the Session of the Peace on 22 February 1686; Jane Foe was cleared. The Lord Mayor's Waiting Book for 1685–86 has many records of such arrests.[4] Macaulay wrote, "Never had spies been so actively employed in detecting congregations," and Defoe saw a number of Dissenters, including his teacher Charles Morton and his friend John Dunton, go to America.

The court accompanied the harassment of the Nonconformists with continued pressure on the City. The reign of Charles had proved that the king could dispense with Parliament; now the City was governed by a royal commission. Charles and James had taught the City the truth of Charles's words, "you are not Common Council of the Nation."[5] Perhaps even more difficult than steady persecution was James's inconsistent, unpredictable behavior. James's policies in the two years after Monmouth's rebellion were a curious combination of bribes and threats. Defoe repeatedly experienced the inherent contradictions in James's actions. For example, the Butchers' Company charter had been restored in 1686, but the court of the Company had to take the oath, and the king insisted upon the right to remove officers. The company was allowed only forty-two members, all of whom had to be "of approved loyalty." Yet Defoe, veteran of Monmouth's rebellion and of a court appearance for a conventicle arrest, could become a member. He saw his father's longtime friend Edward Newins, three wardens, and six other assistants ordered displaced in February 1688, only to be reinstated in October.[6] Similarly, although Defoe must have shared his people's relief at seeing the thousands of Dissenters released from prisons as the result of James's April 1687 Declaration of Liberty of Conscience, he recognized that James's action ignored the Constitution and repealed a law without parliamentary consent. With his declaration James had proclaimed his "sovereign authority, prerogative royal, and *absolute* power, which all his subjects were to obey *without reserve*,"[7] and he had opened the way for the appointment of Catholics to powerful positions.

After Monmouth, Defoe and others gave up on armed rebellion but not on mass resistance. They had grown up during a time when political events were often the subject of numerous hastily written, cheap pamphlets. In some cases, fifty or even a hundred would be published, and Defoe could not have avoided seeing some of the tracts written on ephemeral controversies as well as about such sensational events as the Popish and Rye House plots. Such pamphlets were brazen propaganda with the intentions of all propaganda: to "warn" the unwary, make a few converts, and strengthen the opinions of those already in agreement. They were published at the expense of the writer or his party, on commission, or by booksellers who sometimes hired hacks to keep a profitable paper war alive. By 1690 some pamphlets would be published to coincide with the opening of Parliament and before major votes.[8] As extensions of headline news, the political treatise attracted avid readers.[9] Defoe's generation saw its potential as shapers of opinion, and Defoe would write more of such pamphlets than anyone else.

His education admirably prepared him to write polemical essays. His years of training in "declamation and dispute," in rhetoric, and in the evaluation of opposing opinions at Morton's school could hardly be matched. His knowledge of the Bible and of history gave him a wealth of illustrative and admonitory examples. So good was his memory that he could repeat a minor anecdote from the 1682 *Historical Collections* in the 1726 *Complete English Tradesman*. The times, his experiences, and his strong opinions about government policies made his decision to use print to carry on his resistance to James inevitable.

His first two publications sprang from his experiences as a Dissenter and have a hint of the impetuousness and extremism that made him Monmouth's soldier. In neither case could he gain personally, and in both he took risks. According to his *An Appeal to Honour and Justice* (1715), he wrote a short essay arguing that England should want the Turks defeated at the siege of Vienna in 1683.[10] Defoe saw the Turks as vigorous propagators of the Muslim religion, and thus a greater threat to Christianity than a potential alliance between France and the Empire that would strengthen Catholicism. The Turks' history, Defoe said, was one of "Cruelty and perfidious Dealings" and demonstrated that they had "rooted out the Name of the Christian Religion in above Three-score and Ten Kingdoms."[11] To take such a position, Defoe must have felt the lessons of history to which he alludes to be more important than the dramatic action Louis XIV had taken when he "suddenly announced that, because of the Turkish danger to Christendom, he would raise the siege of Luxemburg."[12] There is some likelihood that by the time Defoe wrote the pamphlet, he could see that the Turks were too weak to take Vienna or that Louis would be unable to send troops because he was so engaged on other fronts. Certainly, Defoe was giving a precocious example of his mature ability to analyze politico-military decisions. Here he saw the relation of France to the Empire as the key to the position the English Dissenters ought to take on the Turks.

The second essay Defoe wrote is probably *A Letter to a Dissenter from His Friend at the Hague, concerning the Penal Laws and the Test.* Identified as Defoe's in part by his summary of it in *An Appeal to Honour and Justice*, the four-page publication warns the Dissenters about the motives Defoe sees behind King James's second Declaration of Indulgence in April 1688. "We know there was no talk of *Liberty of Conscience*, till the Nobility and Gentry of the *Church of England* refused to take off the Test," Defoe reminds the nation (2). The pamphlet expresses the opinions Defoe gives in *An Appeal* and elsewhere. For example, it catches Defoe's (and Presbyterian) distrust of the Catholic James well; in an *Appeal* he would say,

I told the *Dissenters* I had rather the Church of *England* should pull our Cloaths off by Fines and Forfeitures, than the Papists should fall both upon the *Church*, and the *Dissenters*, and pull our Skins off by Fire and Fagot. (233)

He, like the majority of Presbyterians, chose to join with the Anglicans rather than form the Roman Catholic/Dissenter alliance that James hoped would balance the Church of England's power.[13] Just as a Catholic was better than an "infidel" Turk, an Anglican (even with fines and forfeitures) was better than a Catholic. The "Fire and Fagot" of *An Appeal* are "the lash of a *Popish Supremacy*" and "the most despicable *Slavery*" in the pamphlet (4).

The modes of persuasion are already those that would become distinctively Defoe's. Here he argues, as he will later when he discusses Queen Anne's intentions regarding the Protestant succession and regarding the Church of Scotland at the time of the Union, that, once monarchs have given their word, to demand more is both insulting and pointless. Those who will break their word will easily find "some occasion to pretend a *forfeiture* of this *Liberty*," he says (2). He questions and badgers, jeers and rallies, and, above all, demands "common sense."

He has a firm grasp of James's inconsistencies in *A Letter to a Dissenter*. The letter is ostensibly written from the Hague, and it was the Dutch whom James was holding up for imitation by insisting that their economic success was based on religious toleration. To have an inhabitant of a "tolerant" country warn a Dissenter about James's offer is clever. The pamphlet uses the same verb to describe James's efforts that *An Appeal* uses twenty-seven years later: *wheedle*. The pamphlet is rash and immoderate in its attack on James: his "Zeal" for "Liberty of *Conscience*" is carried out by denying "Liberty of *Judgment*" and with "high displeasure" toward those who disagree with him; "for the sake of *Liberty of Conscience*, the whole Clergy must be *forced* to Publish the Declaration, though they declare it to be *against* their *Consciences*" (3).

The fear and rage that had motivated Defoe to risk his security with Monmouth flare up in this pamphlet. The awareness of human psychology and of history invigorates his descriptions of the operation of tyranny in general and of the implications of James's actions in particular. For example, he who would "[seize] into Popish hands" Magdalen, the wealthiest of the Oxford colleges, would not demand moderation from Catholics granted "*Liberty of Conscience*."[14] Despite its anonymity and the subterfuge on the title page, "Tot de Hague, gedruckt door Hans Verdraeght, 1688," *A Letter to a Dissenter* is Defoe's and seditious by any standard. Soon afterwards, a London mob attacked Henry Hill's printing shop and destroyed the presses of James's favorite printer.[15] This extraordinary action testifies to the skepticism, resentment, and hatred James had bred in his City subjects and explains the climate in which men could publish such straightforward attacks on the monarch.

⁓

William of Orange landed in Torbay on 5 November 1688,* and on 13 February the convention Parliament offered William and Mary the English crown jointly. The City rejoiced and honored William with its special privileges. For instance, he was made a member of the Grocers' Company (*London Gazette*, 31 October 1689), and a special volunteer regiment was formed. Defoe felt a new expansiveness and sense of involvement. His future suddenly seemed bright and his own position enviable. On the first Lord Mayor's Day after the "Glorious Revolution," 29 October, he participated conspicuously in a special event in honor of William and Mary; John Oldmixon, soon to be a journalistic rival, described the event as he remembered it in his *History*:

The City of *London*, in gratitude for the Care his Majesty took of their *Liberties* . . . prepar'd [a Balcony] for them at the *Angel* in *Cheapside* to see the *Show*, which, for the great number of Livery men, the full Appearance of the *Militia* and *Artillery* Company, the rich Adornments of the *Pageants*, and the splendid and good Order of the whole Proceeding, out-did all that had been seen before

---

*James's 1687–1688 attempts to pack Parliament and to increase Catholic influence backfired. After William landed he feared for his life and on 10 December attempted to flee to France. Caught by a Kentish fisherman, he returned to London and debated his course of action, but on 22 December he finally left England.

upon [Lord Mayor's Day]; and *what deserv'd to be particularly* mention'd . . . was a *Royal* Regiment of *Volunteer* Horse, made up of the chief Citizens, who being gallantly mounted and richly accoutred, were led by the Earl of . . . *Peterborough.* . . . Among these Troopers, who were for the most part Dissenters, was *Daniel Foe*, at that time a Hosier in *Freeman's* Yard, *Cornhill.* (2:37).

This procession attended the king and queen from Whitehall to Guildhall, where they joined the lord mayor and the Corporation for the city feast. The regiment, chosen to be "Guards for their Majesties persons," was commanded by Charles Mordaunt,* one of the Council of Nine to advise Queen Mary whenever William was abroad. A contemporary wrote proudly of the occasion:

> The nobler Citizens themselves present,
> To Guard his Person, and his Government
> No Hireling Soldiers for their Countries good,
> But freely spend their Treasure as their Blood. . . .[16]

Plans to form the regiment of "about 400 wherein such may serve as cannot take that part of the Test as related to the Sacrament" had been the subject of "great discourse and a great many meetings." Originally the king himself was to be the colonel, as the lord mayor served the senior regiment of the trained bands. Mordaunt was the lieutenant colonel and the captains included Humphrey Edwin, John Fleet, Thomas Lane, and William Ashurst.

From the beginning, the regiment attracted some envy and ridicule. In "The City Regiment," Joseph Haynes described their motley appearance:

> Some smoking, some whistling, all meaning no harm,
> Like Yorkshire attorneys coming up to a term.
> On bobtails, on longtails, on trotters, on pacers!
> On pads, hawkers, hunters, on higglers and racers![17]

The next year when King William considered sending them to fight the Jacobites in Ireland, the fact that the men considered their group strictly ceremonial provoked hilarity. "Some feigned themselves lame, some feigned themselves clapped," Haynes wrote. Charles Gildon was still laughing in 1719 when he included a reference to the incident in his satire of *Robinson Crusoe*. He has Defoe say: "I was most damnably frighted with the Dream; nay, more than ever I was in my Life; even more, than when we had News that King *William* design'd to take into *Flanders* the *Royal Regiment*."

That same year, Defoe was chosen Butler of the Cornhill Inquest. This office gave him a seat on the ward's eleven-member governing

---

*Mordaunt, former Viscount Aveland, had become the earl of Peterborough. In April 1689 William made him earl of Monmouth.

body, but it also obligated him to "find all manner of" linen, plate, cups, candlesticks, and other "necessaries."[18] Thirty years later he was still occasionally putting his knowledge of such things to use, as he does in his novel *Roxana*, in which his heroine often lays out elaborate meals. He was elected to the Cornhill Grand Jury in 1690. In November he signed a certificate of character for Matthew Clarkson, who was petitioning for the office of secretary of New York. Thomas Lodwick, a friend and respected resident of Henry Foe's St. Botolph, Aldgate, neighborhood signed, as did Robert Knight, another lifelong friend and substantial property holder.

About this time Defoe joined seventy-seven other merchants with trading interests in New England in signing a petition asking that the king restore the charter rights and privileges of the New England colonies, and that frigates be sent "for the Security of these Coasts and subduing the French at Canada by Sea, whilst you [sic] Subjects in New England are acting by Land and Sea." This group of men were the leading citizens of London. Among those who signed were Justice Richard Meriwether, who would be Defoe's host in Brentford in July 1705,[19] and Sir Humphrey Edwin, who was chosen alderman in 1687 and would become lord mayor in 1697; it was Edwin who was the official Defoe would chide for attending both church and meeting house in his 1698 *An Enquiry into the Occasional Conformity of Dissenters*. King William himself, impatient with the Admiralty, ordered a frigate to North America in January 1692.

Always a clubbable man who enjoyed the conversation around a fire, Defoe frequented several of the coffeehouses around Guildhall and the Exchange. He was probably part of the unusually long-lived literary group composed of Dissenting ministers and laymen that met at Chew's Coffeehouse on Bow Lane. Satires of Defoe occasionally mentioned his presence at "Sue's," another name for this coffeehouse. The chairman of the club proposed two questions "to be freely and candidly" debated, and the members took turns giving "learned or amusing" essays.[20] After Morton's educational emphasis on debate, Defoe must have loved this recreation. At Smith's Coffeehouse in the Poultry he met with Dunton and others to work on the *Athenian Mercury*.

He joined, too, in what turned out to be one of the most sustained pamphlet wars in history, one that labeled Englishmen "Jacobites" or "revolution" men for the rest of their lives: the "Allegiance Controversy." Some two and a half million words were spent justifying, condemning, or explaining the "right" of William and Mary to King James's throne.[21] Defoe, who believed entirely in a Protestant monarchy and held as many hopes for William's reign as anyone, joined a number of Dissenters, including his classmate Timothy Cruso, in publishing his opinions about the legality of William's accession. Cruso expressed the joy he and other Dissenters felt. He "preached and published a discourse, in which, after gratefully acknowledging the interposition of Providence, he expressed his admiration for the hero."[22] Like Defoe, Cruso was a man of "lively invention," had shared Morton's course on political ethics, and must have heard Morton's views on oaths several times.

Morton, Cruso, and Defoe all adhered to the theory of contract government, and Defoe consistently defended it throughout his life. Defoe relied primarily on biblical precedent and what we now consider Lockean arguments for the moral right of revolution.[23] In a typical statement Defoe says, "A *Compact* and Agreement between the Prince and People, is the very Corner-stone of Monarchy it self" and "Kings do derive their Authority from the Laws [and] their power to . . . that Original Contract which is made between the People and the Person [chosen to be King]." He tended to see the "rights" of Englishmen as built into their Constitution and inherited. In a burst of rather callow enthusiasm, he wrote, "we ought to commemorate the Courage of those Noble Patriots, who . . . have opposed the Encroachments that some of our Kings would have made upon our Laws and Liberties, which, blessed be God, were derived intire to us." Defoe agreed with those who argued that James had "forfeited" his right to be king by abusing his power, by doing what all of "the greatest Asserters of the Monarchical Right hold to be Forfeitures."[24]

Defoe is in no way extraordinary in his stand on the allegiance controversy; almost every "Whig" tract published used the "contractual resistance"[25] argument, and explications of the books of Samuel and Kings and the story of Saul are ubiquitous and usually conclude, as Defoe does, "Therefore 'tis from the Statute-Book, not the Bible, that we must judge of the Power our Kings are invested withal."(35).

What is somewhat unusual is Defoe's special interest in the City. The 1691 *An Account of the Late Horrid Conspiracy to Depose Their Present Majesties* includes in its title "*and ruine the City of London*." Even in the first allegiance pamphlet, *Reflections upon the Late Great Revolution*, he uses the City government as an analogy of the king's rule, reminds his readers that William the Conqueror confirmed the "Ancient Rights and Priviledges of the People," and even concludes that the power of the first king of the Saxons was not so "great" or "extensive" as that of the lord mayor (41). He sees James's "invading the Rights of Corporations" and "despoiling them of all their Ancient Privileges" striking at the "Foundation of Government" and the "Fountain of our Laws."[26] Without much evidence, Defoe sees personal animosity toward the City in the "plot" in which Lord Preston, secretary of state under James, was arrested on his way to France carrying plans for James's restoration. "*London* still sticks in their Stomachs," he writes.[27]

As he became more involved in politics, he continued to expand his business interests. He began to trade with other English towns, to invest in ships, and to deal in other commodities. He had been trading in wine, spirits, beer, and cloth goods for some time. Now he signed a bill of charter-party with Humphrey Ayles, who was to sail to Boston, then New York, and then Maryland. Ayles would deliver Defoe's cargo to his factors, return with tobacco and logwood, and try to pick up as many passengers as possible going both ways. By this time several of Defoe's Cornhill neighbors, including Josiah Abbott, John Sharp, and Joseph Beaton in Boston and Charles Lodwick and Matthew Clarkson in New York, were merchants and officials in the colonies. Lodwick, for example, reported on New York to the Commissioners of Trade and Plantations when in England. Wealthy enough to be able to advance the British troops in New York £500 sterling in 1701, he often appeared on lists of "principal merchants."

In spite of outward appearances, Defoe suffered private misfortunes. His daughter Mary died in early September 1688 and was buried in the lower vault, south aisle, of St. Michaels. His father-in-law had died in 1686 and left him without the adviser who had introduced him to the wine and spirit trade.[28] Moreover, he was in financial trouble. In 1687 his mother-in-law had had to pay off the £300 mortgage on his land in Tilbury.[29] By July 1688 he owed a Joseph Braban of Lynn Regis £396 7s. in unpaid bills for goods he was to have sold on commission. Braban allowed Defoe nine more months to pay on condition that he sign a penal bill for £600. When the time expired Defoe insisted that he had paid Braban more than he had been able to collect from "a great many several persons," those to whom he had sold the goods, and Braban accepted several notes from Defoe. When Defoe did not pay off the full sum, Braban went to court to demand payment of the notes and the penal sum, which was a standard part of a contract providing security against one partner's failing to keep his part of an agreement. In November 1689 Defoe agreed to pay Braban what he owed immediately but without the penal sum.[30] In August 1688, perhaps to raise money, Defoe decided to sell his share of a ship (or three-quarters thereof) to a man named Robert Harrison, who traded with France. He was ambivalent about becoming Harrison's partner, and his indecision lasted so long that Harrison was misled (or chose to appear so) and sailed for France before the agreement was final.

In 1689 Defoe's affairs fell apart. King William's accession to the throne had engaged England in the war to "reduce the exorbitant power" of France, and French privateers and men-of-war attacked British ships wherever they sailed. When an embargo was imposed against France, Harrison had taken his cargo to Portugal, but, on the way back to England, his ship was captured by a French man-of-war, and he was imprisoned. Harrison's representatives sued Defoe in Chancery for £62 allegedly owed for his share of the loss. Both Harrison's witness and Defoe agreed that Harrison had left London without discussing his cargo and destination with Defoe. Another witness for Harrison gave testimony that suggests Defoe may have changed his mind about the partnership and told Harrison so. Some legal papers, including a bill of sale and a bill of charter-party that Harrison was to have given Defoe, were missing, and Defoe consistently refused to "pay for this man's foolishness in losing" the ship.[31]

Depositions and affidavits reveal that rather than lose money Harrison still owed him for the ship, Defoe may have agreed to keep a quarter share. Several witnesses described the ship as "weake and Leakey," and one believed the £62 Defoe owed was for repairs, not the loss. Harrison's witnesses testified that the ship was not worth more than £150. Roger Cooper, a Rothehithe, Surrey, mariner, who said he had known Defoe since childhood testified that Defoe admitted that he "was not well versed in such Accounts." What Defoe could have done to protect himself from this loss is hard to say, but his willingness to give people credit and his lack of scrupulous attention to collecting is a factor here, as it was in the Braban case. Defoe spread himself too thin, trusted rather too much, and suffered the consequences. He also showed a litigious spirit and a carelessness about records. As early as 1684 he had lost a trivial case in the Lord Mayor's Court, where the lord mayor, acting as a justice of the peace, sat daily to "determine any differences that may happen among the citizens." On 15 October the lord mayor adjudicated between Defoe and a man named William Whetton. Defoe was ordered to pay seventeen shillings "in full of all clayms and demands whatsoever and so all differences between them to cease."[32]

Ayles's voyage had also been unfortunate. He had been delayed in getting to Maryland, and the tobacco load he was to pick up for Defoe had been sent by another ship. Because there remained only seven hogsheads of tobacco to be loaded, Ayles sued Defoe for £1,500, the amount of the penal bond. He noted that Defoe owed him only £424 and that he would settle for that. In a countersuit, Defoe demanded an exact account from Ayles and an explanation of his delay; he refused to pay Ayles's charge for "demurrage" days, days on which the ship was delayed while Ayles tried to find another cargo in Maryland. Ayles listed Defoe's outbound cargo as a trunk, a few passengers, and five servants.[33] He said he took in no passengers, servants, or goods in Boston, but accepted five and a half tuns of logwood and £71.6.6 from Charles Lodwick in New York. At Maryland he met Defoe's agent, Samuel Sandford, who sold the servants, one for £8.5.0, and took in the seven hogsheads of tobacco. His accounts, he insisted, were complete.

In November 1691 the judge was asked to rule on the sufficiency of his answer, and in December Ayles turned in yet another answer. With these two suits Defoe was fortunate. Harrison died in prison in France; his wife quickly remarried and eventually lost interest in wrongs done her former husband. Ayles and Defoe exchanged long depositions, and the case never came to judgment.

Defoe's losses continued. A cargo sent to Belfast arrived late, unfortunately six days after a new import duty had come into effect. On board Defoe had "six pipes of beer, 6 pipes of Porto wine, 4 hogsheads and 2 barrels of tobacco, one barrel of pipes, 2 trunks of hoses and stuffs, 120 gallons of English spirits, 100 lb. of Spanish snuff."[34] A typical cargo for him, it illustrates the way he bought and sold goods from Spain, Portugal, and the New World, added English goods, and sent mixed loads to a number of ports. The authorities held the cargo for payment. Defoe and other merchants whose cargo was on the ship petitioned the Treasury for its return on 19 March, but they seem to have been granted no relief.

In the face of the increasing dangers to shipping because of the Nine Years War with France,* Defoe continued to invest in foreign trade. He began to borrow heavily; in 1689, for example, he used some land in which he had an interest as collateral for a £300 loan with which he may have paid Braban. A number of people were willing to advance him money. His father may have paid his taxes in 1688, for an entry for Cornhill reads that James, not Daniel, paid 3s. 4d.[35] In addition to his partner Samuel Stancliffe, there were Robert Stamper, Peter Maresco, and John Ghiselyn. He had borrowed £400 from Peter Maresco and £200 from John Ghiselyn; both loans, as well as the £300 borrowed earlier from Robert Stamper and Ghiselyn, were due 18 May 1691.[36] As the due dates for these loans and others approached, the situation became desperate. In his old age Defoe would describe the life of a man in his situation in unforgettable terms:

1706: If I were to run through the Infinite Mazes of a Bankrupt, before he comes to the *Crisis*; what Shifts, what Turnings, and Windings in Trade, to support his Dying Credit; what Buying of one, to raise Money to Pay another; What Discounting of Bills, Pledgings and Pawnings; what Selling to Loss for present Supply; What Strange and Unaccountable Methods, to buoy up sinking Credit! (*Review* 3:85)

1727: I might instance here the miserable, anxious, perplexed life, which the poor Tradesman lives under before he Breaks . . . how harass'd and tormented for money . . . how many, little, mean, and even wicked things will even the

---

*Variously called King William's War, the War of the League of Augsberg, and the War of the Grand Alliance, this conflict began because of French territorial aggression. The British, Dutch, Austrian Hapsburgs, and others fought France; the Treaty of Ryswick ended the war temporarily in October 1697.

most religious tradesman stoop to in his distress, to deliver himself? even such things, as his very soul would abhor at another time; and for which he goes, perhaps with a wounded conscience all his life after? (*Complete English Trades-man* 1:79)

༄

In 1691, however, he had not given up. In fact, *A New Discovery of an Old Intreague*, his first published poem, appeared and signaled a new direction for his political action and his ambitions. The subject of this first poem by Defoe is, appropriately, the petition presented Parliament by 117 members of the London Common Council asking that election abuses be corrected. The protested election, held five months earlier, was the first after the restoration of the City's charter. Some 12,000 householders, mostly liverymen, were "Common Hall" and voted in their wards to elect the two hundred common councilors; these councilors tended to be ordinary merchants rather than the wealthy and powerful.[37]

Their complaint was about the election of Thomas Pilkington as lord mayor. In this petition perceptive Englishmen could see deep divisions. Throughout William's and Anne's reigns, the Council tended to be Tory, while the lord mayor and Court of Aldermen were dominated by Whigs. Pilkington had been knighted by William, and the Council resented the harmony between the king and the Court of Aldermen. The most dangerous issue was the succession to the throne, and Defoe and others were quick to point out the work of the "High-Flyers" in the petition.[38] Among other complaints, the common councilors who signed the petition argued that some of the aldermen should not have voted, because they had been appointed by the commissions that governed the City for King James during the time he tried to woo the Dissenters and were, therefore, exercising illegal authority.[39]

Defoe was already enamoured of William and a firm supporter of the Protestant succession, and, as a liveryman and freeman of the City, he felt personally concerned about the election and the issues raised. Even before the expiration of the Licensing Act in 1695, there was a lively tradition of circulating hurriedly written poems that explained or commented upon City politics.[40] These poems reviewed the situation in a biased manner, characterized the major participants, and insisted that fools and knaves alone would hold the opinion opposed by the author. These manuscript or clandestinely printed poems were often circulated in Parliament itself. That they had some impact is clear from the fact that quotations from them occasionally appear in the minutes of Parliament.[41] The poems are idiomatic, loosely constructed, and inartistic. At best they contain a devastating epithet or a memorable couplet.

Defoe's *A New Discovery* is no exception to the subgenre. A loose narrative framework allows Defoe to satirize the petitioners and praise their opponents. The petitioners are allied with madmen, criminals, and James II's "enforcers"; King William with God. This device gained popularity steadily after *Paradise Lost* and *Absalom and Achitophel*; numerous poets found devils and contemptible biblical characters populating English political disputes. Defoe's metaphors and allusions would have been clichés to his contemporaries. For example, the unthinking extremists are "Jehu-driven," and Englishmen are compared unfavorably to the grumbling, discontented Hebrews of Saul's time.[42] Defoe traces recent English history and ridicules the years of James's rule as "A *Protestant* Body with a *Popish* Head." Rough-and-ready satiric portraits of men like the earl of Feversham and Sir Peter Rich seldom rise above the level of turn-of-the-century abuse: "As much a Souldier, and as much an Ass." Some of Defoe's lines are unabashedly "low" and the stuff of *Hudibras* and lampoon: "Now if you'd hear some Loyal City Farce, / Hear *Bed[ingfiel]d*, hee'l bid you kiss his Ar——" (ll. 553–54).

Like all English schoolboys, Defoe had been educated since boyhood to write poetry as well as prose. Men of his generation often thought of themselves as the kind of nonprofessional but skilled poets who wrote to advance themselves and their causes.[43] These men did not devaluate poetry as art but enlarged its value by arguing its usefulness as a mode of discourse and argument. All of the great poets of the generation before Defoe had written public, political poetry, and Dryden's models reigned. For example, Defoe often quoted the poetry of Waller, Denham, Cowley, Marvell, Rochester, and Butler, all of whom wrote political poetry, as well as the works of Davenant, Milton, and Halifax, who excelled in both poetry and prose. He admired the best of this poetry, remarking at one point on "*Dryden's* inspired *Absalom*" (*Review* 4:396). His own generation continued to write public poetry in the hope of recognition and political patronage. Charles Montagu, William Congreve, Matthew Prior, and Joseph Addison all advanced their careers by writing successful poems.[44] In fact, Defoe's career as a poet was longer and more prolific than his career as a novelist.

Defoe and dozens of minor poets of his time incorporated common elements of political verse into their poems. His poem lacks the strong fable and smooth verse of Dryden's work, but the use of history as setting and precedent, the satiric portraits, the allusions selected to establish types, and the final verses show the strong influence of the tradition. The "Conclusion" of *A New Discovery* deliberately echoes the ending of *Absalom and Achitophel*. Dryden begins, "Thus from his royal throne, by Heav'n inspir'd, / The godlike David spoke." Defoe writes, "Great *Nassau* from his envied Throne look't down." Defoe describes William's contempt and impatience with his subjects' behavior and explains how "His Conquering Mercy did his Justice stay." Dryden has Charles speak, "Thus long have I, by native mercy sway'd . . . So much the father did the king assuage," "Must I at length the sword of justice draw?" and, finally, "Th' Almighty, nodding, gave consent; / And peals of thunder shook the firmament." Defoe has William, like Jove, drive his opponents to hell with thunderbolts. Three times in the last eleven lines he anchors lines with images of thunder and lightning that drive William's opponents farther and farther out of his empire.

No evidence that Defoe's poem had impact survives. Certainly others recognized "the old intreague," the Jacobite efforts in James's behalf, in the Common Council petition. After a few days' hearings, the House of Commons simply let the matter drop.[45] In any event, Defoe's friends probably praised him for the poem and laughed at the lines that speared their mutual enemies.

This poem and his friendship with John Dunton led to his next published poem, "To the Athenian Society" [1692]. Dunton says that he asked Defoe for the poem, which was prefixed to Charles Gildon's *History of the Athenian Society* and later reprinted in editions of *The Athenian Oracle* and Defoe's *True Collection*. Here Defoe attempts another common late seventeenth-century form, the historical survey ending with a tribute. Defoe locates the beginning of the reign of "King Ignorance" with the Tower of Babel. The story in this middle verse has intriguing parallels with recent English history. King Ignorance, like James, had influence behind the apparently reigning monarch, and Ignorance's child, Sloth, was heir to the throne because none of the Old Monarch's "numerous Progeny" could inherit the throne. Among those who joined Defoe in contributing poems to the *History of the Athenian Society* were Nahum Tate, the poet laureate, and Peter Motteux, a successful dramatist. Gentlemen of his time were expected to be able to write occasional verse, and perhaps Defoe was beginning to think of himself as that kind of amateur poet.

As harried as Defoe might have felt when he was alone with his account books, he still appeared to be one of the rising young City businessmen. He and his partner paid their Cornhill taxes, and he paid his Butchers' Company quarterage promptly. He kept a man and a maidservant,[46] and began to take new initiatives to raise enough capital to prevent bankruptcy. As he said, it is "hard to restrain youth in trade" and human nature not to think, "I have undertaken such a project . . . if it succeeds I may recover again . . . I'll never drown while I can swim . . . who knows but I may get over it at Last?"[47]

In April 1692 he bought seventy civet cats from John Barksdale for about £850. At this time the Dutch manufactured perfume with the cats' musk as base and exported the perfume or the musk itself. The potential existed for a steady income from this investment, but Defoe lost money on the cats. He may have failed partly because he detested them; in *Captain Singleton* he called them "furious wild Cats" and described their "flesh" as "the worst of Carrion." Indeed, harvesting the musk was not pleasant. Periodically, an attendant put the cats in special wooden cages so narrow that they could not turn around and used a small spatula to scrape out the butterlike secretion that had collected in the pouches between the tail and the anus.[48]

Defoe lost the cats, however, because he never paid for them. He got £400 of the £850 from his friend Samuel Stancliffe to whom he already owed £1,100, but he paid the cats' owner only £200 and some promissory notes.[49] Barksdale gave him "use" of the cats without ownership. In June, Barksdale discovered Defoe's notes to be worthless and signed the cats over to Sir Thomas Estcourt to pay his own debts. Estcourt's deed included a clause stating that Defoe would take care of the cats until 17 February 1693.

In October 1692 Stancliffe had the cats seized for a debt now approaching £1,500. Defoe bought them back at the public auction for the sheriffs' appraised price of £439.7s. This time he used his mother-in-law's money. Joan Tuffley's servants thereafter fed and "looked after" the cats until they were collected by Sir Thomas Estcourt's servants in March. At the time he allowed Joan Tuffley to buy the cats, Defoe knew they were already the property of Estcourt. Joan Tuffley went to Chancery claiming her losses at £600, including the meat and other things necessary for maintaining the cats.

Thus, Defoe had involved two friends in his desperate maneuvers and had cheated his mother-in-law. Had he been an experienced con-man, he could hardly have done better than he did with the civet cats: he purchased something he knew to be profitable with the knowledge he could not pay for it; he borrowed money for this purchase and used the money elsewhere; he participated in the sheriffs' sale of the cats when he knew they could not legally be sold; and he knew the money from this invalid sale would go toward his own debts. He may even have tried to make his wife's family think he paid more for the cats than he did.

About the time he bought the civet cats, he invested £200 in a diving bell scheme to recover sunken treasure. In June 1692 Defoe became secretary-treasurer of the company that had been formed to finance the expeditions. As impractical as the plan sounds, others had succeeded in similar ventures; for example, Sir William Phipps had salvaged a valuable cargo from a Spanish ship in 1688. Phipps, a Massachusetts merchant, had recovered thirty-two tons of silver from the *Concepción* where it lay on a submerged coral reef eighty miles off the coast of what is today the Dominican Republic. Sir Edmund Halley had improved the diving bell from an open-bottomed cone into a bell weighted with lead from which air could be expelled and replaced. In Halley's model the diver could stay below nine fathoms for about an hour and a half. Unfortunately too few shareholders joined Defoe's company and fewer still paid the extra assessments for explorations. A dispute over £120 pounds issued in a charge of fraud brought against Defoe by the diving bell's inventor. Joseph Williams turned in a list of sums he had paid or collected from others and complained that Defoe refused to reimburse him for repairs made to the diving engine. Defoe answered that he had no knowledge of Williams' repairs, but some of the notes given him were worthless anyway.[50]

Later Defoe was to reflect on the diving bell investment in *An Essay upon Projects* (1697). He points out the difference between inventions and projects that improve the manufacture or land, "which tend to the immediate Benefit of the Publick," and "Projects fram'd by subtle Heads . . . to bring People to run needless and unusual hazards." He says that Phipps's expedition was "a Lottery of a Hundred thousand to One odds" and, had it failed, Phipps would have been "as much ridicul'd as *Don Quixot's Adventure upon the Windmill*" and a subject for ballads. In a sober, mature moment, he concludes that this sort of project is not at all dishonest, "save that there is a kind of Honesty a Man owes to himself and to his Family, that prohibits him throwing away his Estate in impracticable, improbable Adventures; but still . . . Phips . . . brought home a Cargo of Silver of near 200000 l. sterling" (15-18).

And things got worse and worse. On 30 May 1692 Defoe paid his friend William Marsh £60 on account for a £100 bill of exchange that belonged to John Hoyle.[51] Hoyle had died several days before Marsh took the bill to Defoe, and when the executor, Thomas Nisbett, came to London he found the bill missing. Marsh may have initially taken advantage of Defoe, but Defoe's conduct when he had to confront the fact of Hoyle's death conformed to a pattern of prevaricating, procrastinating, and hiding that became increasingly common. On 20 June he passed the bill to the goldsmith to whom he owed money and received credit for the full £100. When Nisbett demanded the money, Defoe insisted Marsh had the £60 and, when pressed sternly, agreed to pay £40 if the court so ordered. Defoe called William Marsh, probably the fourth son of a respected Dorking justice of the peace, "an Ancient Acquaintance" and "a person of unquestionable creditt." Yet Marsh denied that he had received any of the money, and Nisbett pursued the case relentlessly. Defoe failed to appear in court several times. After much stalling Defoe filed a countersuit in Common Pleas. He lost this as well and on 30 January 16$\frac{92}{93}$, was ordered to pay Nisbett a total of damages of £41.10s and costs of £15.10s. He immediately filed a writ of error in the Exchequer Chamber asking that the verdict be revoked and quashed.

Defoe describes the experience of failing in several places in the writings of his next forty years. The metaphors of twisting, turning, tacking, trimming, compromising, and regretting convey both action and thought. The theme of regret runs through all of his descriptions: "Little, mean, and even wicked things . . . as his very soul would abhor . . . with a wounded conscience all his life after." The man who would have every major character in his novels suffer and explore guilt had the wife whom he had addressed so romantically only ten years earlier and her trusting, generous mother as reproachful reminders to his conscience. His characters would examine the motives for actions over and over; they would question intention, and they would test "necessity." They would feel ambition and fall to the temptation of putting on a prosperous, genteel front. They would have fertile minds and speculative schemes. They would try to reform, and they would have nightmares. They would be solitaries.

The end was ignominious. Defoe broke for the enormous sum of £17,000,[52] and it might have been more had he not been committed to the Fleet Prison in October 1692 on the complaint of several of his creditors. The Commitment Book entry tells us Defoe was bankrupt because of his problems with men like Joseph Braban rather than because of captured ships and civet cats. The plaintiffs were very ordinary London citizens:

Daniel Foe was committed to the prison of Fleet on the twenty ninth of October in the fourth year of the reign of the King and Queen William and Mary . . . by John Powell, knight, one of the Justices of the Bench . . . in discharge of the recognizances . . . of Walter Ridley of Cheapside, London, haberdasher, and Cornelius Lovett of Shadwell in the County of Middlesex, Distiller, at the suit of John Selby and £100 upon contract.

And also in discharge of their recognizances, that is, of Jerome Whitchcote of Love Lane, London, merchant, and Nicholas Barrett of Whitechapel in the County of Middlesex, Sailmaker, at the suit of Edward Lambert for £60 upon pledge.[53]

Quite simply, Defoe's creditors had run out of patience. When Defoe agreed in July 1692 to pay John Selby £90 for "various goods and merchandise sold and delivered," Defoe already owed him £160. He did not pay, and Selby went to court. Defoe was ordered to "satisfy all damages which shall be adjudged" against him or to "render his body in execution of this judgment to the prison of the Fleet."[54] On 29 October Defoe surrendered at the Fleet Prison and was transferred 'to the King's Bench Prison on the same day. By swearing to answer the charges and finding recognizances, Defoe was discharged.

On 4 November, he went through the entire process again:

And the aforesaid Daniel was committed to the prison of the Fleet . . . by John Powell, knight . . . in discharge of recognizances . . . of Walter Ridley . . . and of

Charles Noakes of Lothbury, London, gentleman, at the suit of Thomas Martin for £200 debt.

And also in discharge of recognizances at the suit of Henry Fairfax, Esquire. Attached in a plea of debt.

Defoe owed Martin £700. In this case, Defoe acknowledged his liability, and the Common Pleas plea roll carries the annotation "Execution."[55] On 5 November yet another debt case went to trial. William Stanlacke complained that Defoe owed him £200, and the Court of Common Pleas agreed, awarding Stanlacke an additional 46s. in damages.[56]

In Hilary term Selby's case was heard. Defoe did not appear nor did he enter "anything in bar or preclusion of the . . . action," and the court decided that "John should recover his damages occasioned by the promises and undertakings of . . . Daniel." In addition to the £270 debt, Selby received £4.6.8 costs and £95.13.4 damages.[57] At the same session of the court, Defoe lost the Nisbett case, and was ordered to pay the disputed £100 plus £5.13.4 costs and £48.10.0 damages. He immediately appealed on a writ of error to the Court of Exchequer.[58]

And Defoe's affairs continued to unravel. In May, Timothy Bird, a London "trader," appeared before Lord Chief Justice Holt to claim an unpaid debt and damages. He alleged that in April 1692 Defoe had promised to pay him £33 within three months. Although Defoe already owed him money, Defoe paid nothing. In the conventional language Bird's accusation states that

The aforesaid Daniel little caring about his separate promises and undertakings . . . but plotting with fraudulent intent wickedly and cunningly to deceive . . . Timothy . . . and to defraud him of the separate sums of money . . . did not pay the same Timothy, nor up to this moment has he paid or even satisfied him at all for them.[59]

Bird was awarded the sum he claimed Defoe owed, £5.3.4 costs, and £31.10.0 damages on 27 May 1693. A few days later Williams complained in Chancery that Defoe had been subpoenaed but refused to appear to settle the diving bell dispute. Defoe had begun a countersuit in the Court of Common Pleas, but in October was forced to answer Williams in Chancery. The judge issued an "Attachment," sometimes called a "Commission of Rebellion," empowering the sheriffs to apprehend him as an outlaw and commit him to the Fleet if he failed to appear in court.[60] In June and again in August, Peter Maresco, Robert Stamper, and John Ghiselyn obtained subpoenas to force Defoe to appear in Chancery for nonpayment of the money he owed them.[61] In this case and many of the others, Defoe tried to buy time by filing a countersuit in another court.

In November the Court of Exchequer affirmed the judgment against Defoe in the Nisbett case, and Nisbett received an additional £8.10.0

for costs. On 12 February Defoe was committed to the King's Bench prison at Nisbett's petition.[62] In April, Maresco, Stamper, and Ghiselyn filed for possession of the Tilbury land. Defoe finally appeared in court on 15 November, and the case was continued yet again.

Surely the war and Defoe's ambitious speculations contributed, but his bankruptcy was, at the core, boringly mundane. The greatest causes were his inattention to detail and his speculations, and his initial mistakes probably as basic as inexperience, investing in too much stock, and having too many of his debts due before he could collect money owed him.[63] In the 1690s his conduct was reprehensible. He cheated his friends and relatives, took advantage of men like Selby and Bird who kept extending his credit in order to give him time to recover, and borrowed money he could not repay in order to delay court actions or to invest in yet another enterprise.

He was now, however, unable to delay the reckoning and in a desperate situation. Bankrupts could be imprisoned until they paid all of their debts plus the prison fines and charges that quickly added up. While he was in prison, everything he owned could be divided among his creditors. Although debtors were usually separated from other prisoners, they shared the miserable conditions of London prisons. Overcrowded, underfed, and poorly protected from cold, the prisoners lived in stench and squalor. Visitors to the prisons uniformly record the raucous babble and nauseating odor experienced as the gates opened. Reports on the prisons such as the 1702 "Report of the Justice's [sic] concerning the abuses of the poor Debtors in Newgate" found that keepers demanded garnish money (between nine and seventeen shillings) and "stript, beat and abused" those who did not or could not pay; that beef allowances did not always reach the prisoners; that bedding was sold, not divided; that "leud women, strumpets, and shoplifters lay with the men all night," and that those who complained were often threatened and beaten.[64]

Defoe's horror was probably greater than some new prisoners because his fall was greater. The apparently successful, highly visible, somewhat pretentious man about town found himself in squalor with desperate felons and lice-infested beggars. His dreams died; he would never be an alderman. Moreover, he remembered some entire families who had died in prison for debt, including Thomas Delaune's.[65] Defoe used an anecdote from one of Delaune's books in his own *Historical Collections* and later would write an introduction to a reissue of one of Delaune's books. Delaune had described Newgate as "that horrid place which you describe when you mention hell"; these very phrases Defoe would use in *Moll Flanders*.

Defoe's wife, his daughter Maria, and the new baby moved in with Joan Tuffley in Kingsland; what happened to Defoe's five servants,

Richard, Ralph, Mary, Anne, and "Nourse," is not known.[66] The Corn-hill "Estreats into the Exchequer" for 1694 rather poignantly reads,

Dan: ffoe Hozier   freemans yard   gone   19s.

Except for the aftermath, nothing is remarkable about Defoe's failure. The story is the familiar one of overexpansion, unwise speculation, divided attention, and unsuccessful efforts to recover, with a touch of vanity, deceit, and overconfidence. The enormous contradiction of five servants and a debt of £17,000, the attack on Defoe's self-image, the years of financial struggle, and the final financial collapse changed Defoe forever from a prominent joiner of respected groups to a solitary with secrets, and from a tradesman to a writer.

CHAPTER 4

RECOVERY

*The Losses and Casualties which attend all Trading Nations in
the World . . . have reach'd us all . . . ; if this has put me, as well as
others, on Inventions and Projects, . . . 'tis no more than a proof
of the Reason I give for the general Projecting Humour of the
Nation.*

—DEFOE, *An Essay upon Projects* (1697)

His credit gone and his life in shambles, Defoe negotiated terms with
his creditors and emerged as full of schemes as ever. His greatest need
was for a large, steady income, and he set about securing it in a variety
of ways. According to a witness in one of his lawsuits, he was living in
Kingsland,[1] probably with his mother-in-law, Joan Tuffley, and had
thereby reduced his expenses considerably. In addition, he joined a
group of petitioners asking for relief under the "Merchant Insurers"
Bill presented by Edmund Waller, first to a committee of the House of
Commons and, after its passage in the Commons, to the House of
Lords. Defoe's application states that he had "sustained divers losses by
insurances* since the war with France, and having met and proposed to
his creditors a means for their satisfaction, some few of them would not
come into those proposals." Had the bill passed, Defoe's creditors
would have been legally bound to negotiate new terms for repayment.
Defoe would then either have had more time to pay, been allowed to
pay a percentage of each pound owed, or both. The Lords rejected the
bill.[2]

Defoe received help almost at once from Thomas Neale, King
William's Groom Porter.[3] He and Defoe had many interests in common. Neale had investments in the American colonies, a scheme for
employing the poor, and licenses to dive for wrecks in several places,
including off the Cornish coast, where Defoe's brother-in-law salvaged

---

*As Defoe explained "insurances" in *An Essay upon Projects,* he and his contemporaries
meant "a Compact among *Merchants*" made when one has a larger cargo in one ship than
he can afford to lose. The second merchant agrees to "bear part of the Hazard for part of
the Profit; Convenience made this a Custom, and Custom brought it into Method" (112–
13).

silver bars. He employed Defoe as a "manager-trustee" for some of his private lotteries. A handbill for the November 1693 lottery promised 250 prizes to be awarded upon 50,000 tickets sold at 10s apiece. The drawing would be held "round a Table in a great Room in Freeman's Yard, Cornhill"; this room, part of a Mrs. Hugh's house, was only a few doors away from Defoe's former home and warehouse. Men like Dalby Thomas and William Lowndes, secretary to the Treasury, served as overseers and trustees. Later lotteries promised a chance for the top prize of £50,000 on a 20s. ticket. A lottery on 20 November 1695 went particularly well, and Neale advertised another on 28 December. Neale, Defoe, and the other "managers" were again to be paid from ticket sales, but this lottery failed. Although lotteries had to be licensed, Neale had many competitors. In the fall and winter, the *Post-Boy* carried lottery ads for half a dozen others, including "The Fair Adventure," "The 20,000 l. Adventure," and the "Million Lottery" for the Land Bank. On 25 February Neale's lottery had to be readvertised, and, on 17 March, ticket holders were warned that the prize would depend on ticket sales and were offered their money back. In *An Essay upon Projects,* published less than a year later, Defoe described private lotteries as fraudulent, badly managed, and patronized by fools. He offers a plan for a lottery and grumbles, "[My] Specimen will inform any body what might be done by Lotteries, were they not hackney'd about in Private Hands, who . . . put them out of Repute" (184, 187).

Perhaps through Neale, Defoe gained dependable additional income from a government appointment. In the fall of 1695 Defoe became an accountant to Dalby Thomas, one of the commissioners of the glass duty. The commission administered the taxes on such things as bottles, dishes, and other glassware. Defoe received £100 per year, had two clerks working for him, and held the position until 1699, when the duty ended. Thomas and the "other officers," however, continued to be paid for their services through 1 November 1700.[4] Again Defoe had benefited from connections. Thomas was a friend of Neale's and co-author of Thomas's projecting pamphlet, *A Further Account of the Proposals . . . for Exchanging the Blank Tickets* (1695). In 1697 Neale became commissioner of the transfer office for duties on salt, beer, ale, and other liquor at £1,200 a year, with another £600 for an office and clerks. He already held the position of master of the mint for Norwich, York, Chester, Bristol, and Exeter. Dalby Thomas went on to become governor of the African Company's settlement in Guinea.[5]

Somewhat ironically, because it was mortgaged to Ghiselyn, Maresco, and Stamper and under litigation, the one property that Defoe could not lose after his bankruptcy was his land in Essex. From their suit it is clear that Defoe received "rents and profits" from this property in Chadwell and Tilbury parishes. For some reason this land held a special place in Defoe's heart. Intriguingly located partly in the parish where "Daniel son of a stranger" had been born in 1662, it carried the magic for him that Tilbury had for all English people who glorified Queen Elizabeth and remembered how she had gathered her forces there in 1588 before defeating the Spanish Armada, but it also seemed to have or to gain some special personal appeal. A 1687 lawsuit initiated by Robert and Sarah Knight against Defoe and their own son Robert reveals that Defoe had bought a very long-term lease to five pieces of land "diverse years" before.[6] Defoe had immediately leased it to a man named Peter Sainthill, but his continued possession of the property is clear from the £300 mortgage payment made by his mother-in-law, Joan Tuffley, in August of that same year. This receipt shows that Robert Knight held a mortgage for £300 signed by "Daniel ffoe of London factor of the one part and the said Joane Tuffley and Peter Sainthill of London Chiurgeon of the other part, to be paid . . . by . . . Joane Tuffley."[7]

In 1689 Defoe mortgaged the land again, this time to Peter Marescoe for £300. A contract drawn up in that year shows Tuffley and Sainthill as partners, Maresco and his partner Stamper as the second party, John Ghiselyn the third party, and Defoe and Robert Knight the fourth.[8] Defoe had possession of about thirty acres, and in November 1690 he leased an additional thirty-eight acres from Knight. Defoe mentions corn and cattle on the land, but he may have hoped to resell part of the land to the Admiralty for an arsenal, naval dockyard, or fortification.[9] At some point he and these partners, or he and some other group, began the manufacture of bricks and pantiles; he himself was proprietor of the brick works. Good bricks were in demand for the ongoing rebuilding and expansion of London, and pantiles, S-shaped tiles developed in Holland, were economical and could be highly ornamental. Because of their shape, pantiles required no mortar and could be easily laid by roofers. Defoe's were varnished, then glazed, and had a fine red color with good texture. The Dissenters, who, in the more tolerant reign of William, were now building public meeting houses, were probably his chief market. So common was the use of pantiles in their buildings that the high-pitched hip-roofs with the distinctive curved tiles became almost as symbolic as steeples and led some countrypeople to call the Dissenters "Pantilers."[10] Defoe's knowledge of pantiles and of civet cats suggests that he may have gone to Holland for a short business trip at least, but the numbers of Dissenters educated there and of English merchants who regularly visited the continent confuse the issue. Even had he been in Holland, Defoe probably would have had to hire a Dutch foreman or overseer.

This Essex factory appears to have been Defoe's major business effort, and he came to clear about £600 a year from it.[11] Among the contracts he secured was one for bricks for the new hospital and home for mariners and sailors in Greenwich. In both 1696 and 1697 Defoe sold place bricks to the clerk of the works there. In spite of continued problems with supply and quality, the hospital continued to buy most of its bricks from a man named Nicholas Goodwin. In 1696 Defoe sold 162,500 bricks to them and 20,000 in 1697. Dalby Thomas was on both the Grand and Fabric committees and probably helped Defoe secure the contract. In 1696, however, the Greenwich Hospital committee recorded that it had spent £5,000, although its treasurer had received only £800; by March of 1698, it was £4,000 in debt to the workmen. Defoe had to accept payment for bricks sold in July 1696 in two installments (March and August 1697) and was not paid for bricks delivered in August and October 1696 until October 1697. Moreover, he had to pay the treasurer, John Evelyn, £20 a year for his contract. He therefore cleared only £85.12s. after waiting a year for payment. He appears not to have bothered to collect the £13 owed him for the 1697 bricks and did not bid for the contract in 1698. Occasionally the committee heard complaints about bricks. The fact that Defoe's escaped criticism suggests that he did not do what most London brickmakers did to save money: mix soil called "Spanish" in the bricks or use ashes and cinders, "breeze," instead of pure coal in the kiln. The level ground and quality of the Tilbury clay allowed him to make place bricks rather than the more fragile stock bricks that required wooden supports for drying. He tried innovative ways of mixing the water in the clay, and his trade in pantiles made him a pioneer in manufacturing still called "a late Invention in *England*" in 1726.[12]

The enterprise, which Defoe undoubtedly believed to be a firmer foundation for his family's future economic security than his other projects, was never free from the effects of his dishonorable business practices. In April 1694 Peter Maresco, Robert Stamper, and John Ghiselyn went back to Chancery to demand that the contractual provision of "peaceable default" be honored. They accused Defoe of keeping the "rents and profits" of the property in Chadwell and Tilbury parishes long after he should have surrendered possession of the land. In November an "Officer of the Shore of London" apprehended Defoe, and he appeared in court to file an answer to the charges. The case was continued.[13] Less than a year later Henry Lickbarrow, one of the tenants on the Chadwell land, sued Defoe for losses he had sustained because of a neglected seawall. Lickbarrow had had to repair it himself and had even had to pay the taxes on the land. Already angry because he had lost a court decision and had had to pay one of Robert Knight's loans for which he had stood surety and because Defoe had brought suit against him for unpaid rent amounting to £300, Lickbarrow demanded that Defoe pay him £60 for repairs and crop losses and drop his own suit. Unlike some other adversaries, Lickbarrow actively pursued the case; in November he got an order to have Defoe subpoenaed and then apprehended by the sheriff. When Defoe still failed to appear, Lickbarrow obtained an injunction that halted Defoe's suit in the Court of Common Pleas.[14]

The Lickbarrow case seems to have been settled out of court, but Maresco, Stamper, and Ghiselyn could not be pacified for £60 or £70. Counsel for the three creditors filed suits again in 1698 and 1699 in attempts to get Defoe to comply. Finally in May 1699 he answered their charges, claimed he had paid most of the money owed from his rents and profits, and asked for four more years to pay the principal and interest. The judgment was fairly generous to Defoe. The plaintiffs were to continue to receive Defoe's profits in lieu of additional interest charges, and Defoe had until 29 September 1703 to pay Maresco £466.13s.4d., Stamper £408.6s.8d., and Ghiselyn £175. Considering that Defoe had borrowed £150 from Ghiselyn, £400 from Maresco, and £350 from Stamper at 6 percent and had signed penal bonds as early as 1689, he was lucky to keep his land and have some time to recover.[15] The ways that Defoe borrowed repeatedly, pieced loans together, promised profits from expansion, renegotiated agreements, delayed, and used the courts to delay yet more suggest a slippery, clever, reprehensible, and perhaps desperate man.

In yet another ingenious effort, Defoe began negotiating with Christ's Hospital in May 1696 for permission to build "Twelve New Brick Tenements" where its "Woolstaple" houses were leased.[16] In his proposal Defoe says he has already bought the leases to the two houses he wants to replace. The fairly ambitious plan included a new passage from the Thames to Westminster Market and claimed purchase of the two leases as well as Lord Weymouth's coachhouse and stable. Defoe and his partner, [William?] Gillingham, a bricklayer, estimated their costs for the tenements would be £1,200. A few days after receiving the proposal, however, the governors of Christ's Hospital found the lots too small for the plan and proposed that Defoe and Gillingham include the land on which a house leased to George Styles stood. Defoe could start building the houses on the south side of his proposed new passage while Christ's Hospital concluded arrangements with Styles, whose lease expired in 1698. Negotiations broke down in July over the amount of a fine* to be paid by Defoe and Gillingham; Defoe renewed his proposal in April 1698 and in March 1700 became the sole owner of the Sherman house lease. He appears to have lived there at least part of

---

*Rent was often very low, but "fines," short for the common law term, "final concord," were usually several hundred pounds. The fine was a nonreturnable lump sum paid by the prospective tenant to the landlord at the time of the lease signing. It was incontestable proof of the transaction.

the time until he fell four years in arrears on his rent. He lost the lease in 1705.

Like so many of Defoe's money-making schemes, this one was based on an intelligent analysis of market potential. London was growing rapidly, particularly toward the west, and the proposed passage would increase access to the market and raise the desirability of Christ's Hospital's Woolstaple houses. Defoe, however, seemed to lack the perseverance required for success and the ability to conceive process and detail. His proposal was correctly criticized by the Christ's Hospital committee for planning too many buildings in too little space—he was proposing twelve houses on a 33′ x 130′ lot, out of which he intended to carve a 10′ wide passage. Furthermore, he surely did not have his share of the £1,200. The collapse of negotiations at what can only be described from a business standpoint as a ridiculous impasse—Gillingham proposing a twenty-guinea fine when an offer of a fine of £50 was made on *one* of the leases in 1704—suggests either naiveté or lack of real seriousness. The pattern of intense negotiation followed by long lapses is also far too characteristic of Defoe's business style.

Defoe's active life in the City, his friendships, and his new association with Dalby Thomas and Thomas Neale helped him find his way into the booksellers' world. Although literary and political patronage continued, booksellers recognized that there were reader demands unmet by the books and pamphlets published by authors who received such support. The growth of London with the accompanying rise in literacy and desire for information, the rapid changes in a less monarchical government, and a growing national middle class for whom reading was an important leisure and self-improvement activity encouraged the booksellers. Their trade became increasingly diverse and competitive, and we can see the effects in a number of ways. For example, the kinds of books sold in increasingly large numbers were neither the classics nor those usually supported by patrons. The demand for travel books, collections of sermons, and novellas encouraged booksellers to hire translators and hacks to add more titles to those offered by independent writers.[17] Furthermore, booksellers encouraged writers who offered pamphlets on news events such as crimes or controversial political issues and regularly paid some to feed the debate with additional tracts. Clients demanded more choice, and booksellers swapped titles and held auctions. Andrew Baldwin's advertisement announcing "all the pamphlets against a standing army" available at his shop was rather typical.[18] Also booksellers could identify groups of readers now numerous enough to make publishing for them feasible. For instance, the death of Samuel Annesley was promising material because of the size and prosperity of his congregation and his prominence as a preacher and benefactor. The Dissenting community could be counted on to buy his funeral sermon and his elegy, both printed by John Dunton, Annesley's son-in-law. Defoe was almost certainly paid for the elegy for Samuel Annesley, *The Character of the Late Dr. Samuel Annesley*, and, by the time the standing army controversy flared anew, Elizabeth Whitlock, the publisher of the elegy, would have been willing to pay for Defoe's *Some Reflections on a Pamphlet Lately Publish'd, Entituled, An Argument Shewing that a Standing Army Is Inconsistent with a Free Government* (1697). This pamphlet went into a second edition almost immediately, the first of many Defoe pamphlets to do so.

An Essay upon Projects, published in the same year as Defoe's elegy for Annesley, might have been expected to make money. Pamphlets and books that presented "projects" (that is, plans or schemes) were designed to attract not just readers but also investors or patrons. England was in the midst of an economic crisis.[19] King James left William with a revenue of barely two million pounds per year, and William's war expenses alone averaged £5,500,000 a year. At first William had increased all taxes, including the poll and land taxes, and relied upon such stop-gap remedies as the lottery. By 1693, however, the inadequacy of these measures was clear. Creditors had stopped honoring the "tallies," receipts for payments due on short-term government loans, because the Exchequer could no longer pay on the due dates. By 1696 holders of tallies accepted a 33 percent discount from those willing to take them. Rising war costs and the depreciation of coinage—a result of the gold and silver imported from the New World—left no doubt that England was in a crisis. Because England had no machinery for public finance, the government relied heavily on arrangements with joint stock companies such as the East India Company and the Bank of England.*

When Defoe began writing his *Essay upon Projects* (by his account in 1692), Englishmen invested with individuals (as Defoe had in Joseph Williams' diving bell scheme) or formed companies (as William Paterson had, first with the Bank of England and then with the Scottish Darien Company). Many of these investment schemes began with published explanatory tracts. At least one projecting club existed, and "The Wednesday Club" published *Conferences on the Public Debts* (1695), written by Paterson. That Defoe read them cannot be doubted; in his *Essay upon Projects*, he mentions the existence of other proposals for improving the English language, praises John Asgill's pamphlet on

---

*Subscribers to the "Company of the Bank of England" raised £1,500,000 to carry on the war with France; £1,200,000 would be loaned the government at 8 percent interest (about 2 percent above the current rate) to go for the war effort and the rest to pay annuities guaranteed to subscribers by the government. The subscription list filled in ten days. The Bank could issue notes and carry on the other functions of a bank but was not guaranteed a monopoly.

land as an alternative to gold and silver as backing for bank bills, and uses William Petty's *Political Arithmetick* to support two of his own ideas. Moreover, Defoe addressed his preface to Dalby Thomas, himself the author of several projecting pamphlets, including *A Proposal for a General Fishery* (1694) and *Propositions for General Land-Banks* (1695). Thomas Neale received a series of letters of patent for a wide variety of things, including "mathematical," cheat-proof dice and a new method for making tapestry hangings.[20] Charles Montagu had made his fortune in Parliament with such "projects" as the duty on beer and the tonnage bill that led somewhat indirectly to approval of the Bank of England. The House of Commons Ways and Means committee encouraged proposals, and Defoe's projects were of the kind brought to this committee.

Several of Defoe's proposals were aimed at providing for those who became indigent and were therefore a drain on the economy. Seven of the eleven had the potential for increasing the wealth of England and thereby generating revenue for the government. For example, Defoe sees an improvement in roads as the heart of inland trade and, by extension, England's greatness, an argument he was to continue to make eloquently for the rest of his life. He believed communities should exchange goods rather than strive for self-sufficiency:

The more Hands . . . Manufacture . . . passes through . . . so much the greater Benefit is that Manufacture to the publick Stock of the Nation.

If the Pulse of the Trade beats true and strong, the Body is sound.[21]

Defoe even saw an improvement in the recruitment and maintenance of the navy in terms of the benefit to trade rather than to national security (314, 322, 333). Proposals included in the banks, bankrupts, and "Court Merchants" chapters of the *Essay upon Projects* were aimed at keeping credit, cash, and goods flowing. Impounded imports and imprisoned merchants generated no wealth.

At this point, Defoe's thinking is representative of his rapidly changing world. Many of his ideas depend upon the kind of administration that characterized parishes. For example, his scheme for road building, which assessed days of labor and use of horses, resembled the road surveyor's work in Newington Green, now called Stoke Newington.[22] At other places, he demonstrates the weaknesses of the Bank of England with a sophisticated analysis of the new credit economy or draws upon the infant science of the actuary for his friendly society* calculations (119–20, 139–40, 151). At times Defoe is very much the secular

---

*Groups of people who formed an association to help each other in times of "Disaster or Distress." Defoe describes several, including one formed by a troop of horse to "Remount any of the Troop who by Accident shou'd lose his Horse."

capitalist, as he is when he discusses merchant courts (specialized courts for merchants along the lines of the Admiralty courts). At others he is so conversant with contemporary warfare that he can propose a military academy to teach mining, entrenching, surveying, and other practices taught on the continent by men like Vauban. But Defoe could still be very much the Puritan. He tells us that the mentally retarded "are a particular Rent-Charge on the *Great Family of Mankind*" and describes them with real compassion. His plan for supporting a home for them comes from an idea of a built-in sense in the world that is more than social justice or even charity: Defoe would tax books, thereby taxing those with "a Portion of Understanding extraordinary" (179–81) to pay for those with little intelligence. Not only does this extraordinary suggestion give us insight into Defoe's conception of a divine plan built into the details of creation, but it reminds us how much Defoe valued writing books.

An Essay upon Projects did not make Defoe much money. The book was published in January 1697 and reissued with a new title page in 1700. In 1702 the original sheets were reissued with four different title pages, two with Thomas Ballard's imprint and two from "the Booksellers of *London* and *Westminster*," a sign that they belonged to Defoe. In January 1703 Ballard advertised *An Essay* among the "Books Publish'd this Month."[23] All of Defoe's projects required a substantial outlay of capital, and most would have taken years to become profitable. Defoe's own business ventures were often like this, and, along with the occasional handicaps of fuzzy details and naiveté, flowed from some of the same admirable impulses. Later Defoe would write proudly that his brick and tile factory once employed "a hundred *Poor* Familys" (emphasis added) (H 17).

A close look at the publishers of Defoe's early works indicates the usefulness of his City and Dissenting friends. A key figure was Samuel Annesley's son-in-law, the eccentric writer and publisher John Dunton,[24] whose home had been on Seven Stars Alley, the street on which Annesley had held meetings for a while. Dunton had opened a bookshop in 1688 at the sign of the Black Raven, opposite Poultry Compter, and in the 1690s was at the height of his career. At that time a "bookseller" purchased manuscripts from authors, employed his own or someone else's printers to print them, published them, sold them, and exchanged copies with other booksellers in order to offer more stock.[25] Dunton had asked Defoe to write "To the Athenian Society," and when Annesley died in 1697, he asked for the elegy.[26] Another Dunton acquaintance, Richard Chiswell, had printed two of Defoe's allegiance pamphlets. Thomas Cockerill, the publisher of *An Essay upon Projects*, was, like Defoe, a member of Annesley's congregation.[27] In Defoe's youth, Cockerill's shop was in Cornhill, and his second, occupied in

1678, was near Dunton's in the Poultry. Both Chiswell, who had had a huge success with Tillotson's sermons, and Cockerill, who had printed the *Morning Exercises,* were among the most respected men in the business and part of a large, active group of Nonconformist publishers.

The quality of Defoe's publications and his contacts put him in a position to earn a small but reasonably dependable sum from writing. The standing army controversy that followed the Treaty of Ryswick in 1697 engaged a number of respectable writers and generated thousands of words. Understanding continental politics and French ambitions better than his adopted countrymen, William wanted to maintain a peacetime army under the control of Parliament. This proposal awakened memories of Cromwell and fears of an absolutist government, and it threatened the seductive image of every man a potential member of the English army for liberty, an image that lay behind the arguments for relying upon a militia alone to defend the country. A former Williamite, Sir John Trenchard, began the paper war with his attack on William's request entitled *An Argument, Shewing That a Standing Army Is Inconsistent with a Free Government* (October 1697). William was supported by his outraged cabinet and particularly by John Somers, his lord chancellor, who quickly published the widely read *Letter, Ballancing the Necessity of Keeping a Land-force in Times of Peace, with the Dangers* (November 1697). In Parliament Paul Foley and Robert Harley united a group of Whigs and Tories into the "New Country Party" to oppose William. Parliament voted successively to reduce the army to 10,000 men in 1697 and to 7,000—all English-born—in 1698, and to deny William his Dutch Guards in 1699.[28]

Defoe's first standing army tract was another specific "reply" to Trenchard and went through two editions before the 3 December opening of Parliament; his other two standing army pamphlets, *An Argument Shewing, That a Standing Army . . . Is Not Inconsistent with a Free Government* and *A Brief Reply to the History of Standing Armies* (both 1698) almost certainly earned him the usual payment of two to four guineas from the booksellers. Both went into second editions shortly after publication; again, Defoe would have earned a few guineas. In fact, Defoe may have been paid an additional sum by the government, for Somers was probably correctly described as "organizing" the government's propaganda in favor of a standing army.[29] The other major writers in favor of the standing army were Matthew Prior, who had been secretary to the embassy at the Congress of Ryswick, and Richard Kingston, who had been employed to write political pamphlets for the government since 1689.[30] Although there is no direct evidence to prove a collaboration between Defoe and either Somers or King William, his pamphlets contain information about treaties, correspondence between monarchs, and troop sizes that would not have been readily available to everyone. For example, he repeats an exchange between William and the treaters at Nijmegen in *An Argument* (11) and lists the reductions in the army that William had made voluntarily in *A Brief Reply* (21). The timing of his publications and his forceful presentation of the point of view associated with William's strongest supporters also mark Defoe as one of William's pamphleteers. Whether Defoe acted independently or not, the fact that "parties" were known to have produced almost all of the standing army pamphlets and the nature of Defoe's work associated him firmly with the court Whigs and labeled him a "party writer."

Clearly Defoe was beginning to have a more mixed group of friends, to know some of the people at the fringes of the court, such as Dalby Thomas, and to identify with the causes of others, such as Halifax and Somers. Since his path to alderman had probably been blocked by his bankruptcy, he may have transferred his ambitions to national civil service. Certainly his writings in those ten years conform to those of other ambitious young men, and his appointment as accountant of the glass duty could have allowed him to dream of others, such as William Congreve's as one of the commissioners for licensing hackney coaches.

Soon after his first imprisonment for debt, Defoe began writing pamphlets in support of William's policies. Such pamphlets as *An Answer to the Late K. James's Last Declaration* (1693) and *The Englishman's Choice* (1694) defended William's accession to the throne and the war with France.* Three pamphlets in favor of William's standing army, five on the Protestant interest and William's "balance of power" politics on the continent, and three on parliamentary elections were published before March 1701. Even when Defoe wrote about speculation and abuse in the new credit economy (*The Villainy of Stock-Jobbers Detected*) or about a City election (*The Livery Man's Reasons, Why He Did Not Give His Vote for a Certain Gentleman to Be Lord Mayor*), he considered William and national interests. For example, in *Villainy*, he says, "Whoever wounds the publick Credit, wounds the whole Nation and the Government" (14). The publication of *An Essay upon Projects* may have been inspired partly by the spirit notable in William's 3 December 1697 speech to Parliament, in which he would say, "I esteem it one of the great Advantages of the Peace, that I shall now have Leisure . . . to discourage . . . Immorality: And I shall employ my Thoughts in promoting Trade, and advancing the Happiness and flourishing Estate of the Kingdom."

Defoe seems to have realized early that poetry could lead to political favor beyond the ambitions of a writer like Kingston. Charles Montagu,

---

*It is with sound reason that the North American colonists called this war "William's War." When he became king of England, William was already Louis XIV's most formidable opponent, and the English knew from the start that he would make the country part of the Grand Alliance to fight France.

the earl of Dorset, and Dryden had all profited from their poetry, and Cleveland, Waller, Cowley, Denham, Davenant, Milton, Marvell, Butler, and many more had written political poetry and used their art to champion the causes that pamphlet writers argued in prose. *An Encomium upon a Parliament* (1699) was an ironic address to the M.P.'s who opposed William's requests for funding for the war against France. Even *The Pacificator*, a poem apparently about the ancient/modern controversy as exemplified by Richard Blackmore's *Prince Arthur* and Samuel Garth's *Dispensary*,[31] comments on the state of the English nation in 1700. Defoe, like so many poets including Dryden, labels Englishmen contentious and stubborn, discontented and short-sighted, and complains that they will endanger the nation with their internal disputes. He and many other Englishmen fear domestic unrest even more than the rapidly increasing strength of France. The poem begins, "What *English* Man, without Concern, can see / The Approach of Bleeding *Britain*'s Destiny?" "In vain Victorious NASSAU did Advance / His Conquering Arms against the Power of France, / . . . But here's a Civil War broke out at Home." Lines 41–46 give a warning and summarize the common subordination of art to politics:

> The Pen's the certain Herald of a War,
> And Points it out like any Blazing Star:
> Men Quarrel first, and Skirmish with ill Words,
> And when they're heated then they draw their Swords;
> As little Bawling Curs begin to Bark,
> And bring the Mastive on you in the Dark.

Defoe understands how writers worsen political situations and make money for themselves without holding any real commitment to the issues. He compares such writers to "Bawling Curs" and contrasts them to Cowley, Milton, Rochester, Waller, Roscommon, Bhen [*sic*], and others who were "*Giants*" of "Wit and Sense" together.

Perhaps because most Dissenters did not attend the theatre, Defoe was unengaged with the literary issues raised by Jeremy Collier and Blackmore that roused the anger of men like Congreve and Dryden. Collier, author of *A Short View of the Immorality and Profaneness of the English Stage*, insisted that Restoration theatre encouraged debauchery by offering examples of fashionable, unpunished sinners. His opponents emphasized the classical theory that dramatic satire assumes an objective viewer rather than one who identifies with the characters. In contrast to those engaged in the critical debate, Defoe sees some of the practical problems caused by a paper war and the political differences behind the literary issues. By the time *The Pacificator* appeared, the controversy was five years old, and Defoe could see the Jacobite cast to the Garth forces.[32] He perceived the split to reflect party attitudes toward people's abilities to think and judge for themselves. Those who were insisting upon hereditary monarchy and nonresistance (High Church) wanted Collier's unambiguous, didactic theatre. Defoe gives the victory to Blackmore, who had, by the way, written a pro–standing army tract in December 1698, but warns that he sees no end to the conflict: "For which way ere the Conquest shall encline, / The loss *Britannia* will at last be thine" (ll. 418–19). Defoe calls for an appropriate union of Wit and Sense that will join England's poets in the common improvement of their country.

The Pacificator and *An Encomium upon a Parliament* mingle the literary and political partly because every major writer of Defoe's generation and the one before had been deeply involved in political writing and partly because Defoe was becoming increasingly concerned about national elections and the differences between William and his Parliaments. He had now seen the paper war over the Exclusion Crisis, participated in the allegiance controversy, and shared the nation's wonder at the ways pamphleteers sought to influence M.P.'s during the standing army debates. Undoubtedly that controversy taught Defoe a great deal. For the first time he saw the power of the press. Trenchard's *An Argument, Shewing that a Standing Army is Inconsistent* made the issue common knowledge and "the talk of the town." William wrote Anthony Heinsius, grand pensionary of Holland, that his request for troops was being discredited in pamphlets.[33] Once before William had used political writers to good effect, and the appearance of Somers's, Defoe's, and an anonymous tract's refutations of Trenchard before Parliament opened on 3 December, combined with William's statement to Heinsius that "nothing is neglected to oppose" the anti–standing army faction, suggests that he did so again in 1697.[34] In November 1698 Trenchard published *A Short History of Standing Armies in England*, and Somers, Defoe, and others once again raced to counter its effect before the opening of Parliament. Copies of the tracts were given to M.P.'s and distributed in the country, public attention stayed on the controversy, pressure was applied to M.P.'s, and opinions and votes were influenced.

Unlike those on the allegiance controversy and other earlier groups of pamphlets, the standing army tracts abandoned religious arguments in favor of practical history. For example, speeches from the 1670s and 1680s in favor of James II's request for an army were frequently quoted, as were passages from Machiavelli and Robert Molesworth's *An Account of Denmark*. Books that made the combatants' points, such as Algernon Sidney's *Discourses concerning Government*, which included the standing army = tyranny equation that the opposition sought to establish, were reprinted. These pamphlets articulated and appeared to defend such perceived supports of "English liberty" as the militia and Polybius's mixed government, both seen as threatened by a standing army. The weapons of the anti–standing army writers—historical precedents, a set of much-repeated, emotional phrases, and recourse to common values—always defeat explanations of complex, specific circumstances, individual intentions, and change—the methods of the pro-writers. The opponents to a standing army assumed naiveté about the methods of modern warfare, and that strengthened the anti–standing army arguments because it favored a picture of a brave militia defending its country without the need of the services of a mercenary group of specially trained career soldiers. Defoe must have seen the advantages of distortion, oversimplification, and nostalgia. He also saw the king's tormentors go unpunished.

The great literary triumph of Defoe's lifetime followed. *The True-Born Englishman* saw fifty editions by midcentury and became Defoe's signature. It came at a time when Englishmen were tired of internal disputes, when they wanted to believe that more united them than divided them, and when political poetry had an eager audience more ready to appreciate a good line than to take offense. A count of the standing army pamphlets contradicts the modern conception that William and his policies lacked widespread support,[35] and Defoe's poem is additional evidence that the majority of Englishmen appreciated many things about William.

In *The True-Born Englishman* Defoe uses inversions of conventional techniques, idiomatic language and metaphors, startling fictions, and incorporations of fairly sophisticated philosophical arguments to create a highly original apologia for William's kingship. This poem, like many of Defoe's early works, is a "reply," this time to John Tutchin's *The Foreigners*. Defoe addresses Satyr as the most appropriate character to explain English behavior, and she accepts the charge. For her, the world is the devil's kingdom and England is a fallen woman; part 1 explains English history and part 2 English character. Satan's regents have divided the world and rule without challenge because the temper of each nation now matches its ruler (for example, Avarice characterizes the Dutch, England's trading rival). The influence of Milton is not hard to see in Defoe's poem; he adapts the story of Satan, Sin, and Death into an allegory of the mythical time when Satan assigns Ingratitude to England. Satan ruins England, "possesses" her, and subjects her to "Crowds of Wandring Thieves," so that she is "oft subdu'd" and her children "oft undone." Like Milton's incestuous triumvirate, England, Ingratitude, and the first children mingle. Wave after wave of immigrants—some conquerors, some opportunists, some refugees—come in a variant on the seventeenth-century satiric poem's review of actual historical events until Defoe concludes, "[England's] Rank Daughters, to the Parents just, / Receiv'd all Nations with Promiscuous Lust," and "still the Ladies lov'd the Conquerors." Defoe includes details designed to remind the reader of the facts of reproduction; for example, the red hair of the descendants of invading Norsemen and Charles's "Bastard Dukes," who are named and described explicitly. Words like "medley," "common," "mixture," and "jumbled" are repeated and multiplied until the idea that "A *True-Born Englishman*'s a Contradiction, / In Speech an Irony, in Fact a Fiction" becomes an indisputable conclusion. Defoe makes lines like Tutchin's "Why should the *Gibeonites* our Land engross, / And aggrandize their Fortunes with our loss?" ludicrous. In addition to this fable, Defoe praises William by including a panegyric for him sung by Britannia, two satiric portraits designed to illustrate the despicable nature of the typical grumbler against William, and poetic paraphrases of sections of Locke's *Two Treatises of Government* on the obligations and rights of kings and subjects. The most powerful appeal is to the common man who is not contending for place, but the poem draws a large circle around those able to laugh at the contradiction of tracing titles back to Norman conquerors and at the polyglot of "noble names," and able to admit that the ancestry of "a Turkish horse" is better known. In this fiction, William becomes an archetypal Englishman. He is a brave, warlike immigrant but, unlike earlier kings, has come to free Englishmen. Defoe prods his countrymen to laugh and go forward even as he praises William and makes a covert argument for parliamentary monarchy.

In addition to writing in support of William's political policies, Defoe also championed William's proclamations calling for moral reform. The pamphlet *The Poor Man's Plea* (1698) describes the futility of any reform movement not supported by the gentry: "for the Vices of a Poor Man affect only himself; but the Rich Man's Wickedness affects all the Neighbourhood, gives offence to the Sober, encourages and hardens the Lewd, and quite overthrows the weak Resolutions of such as are but indifferently fix'd in their Virtue and Morality" (17). Already Defoe is beginning to criticize the hypocrisy of society as acted out in the legal system: "These are all Cobweb Laws, in which the small Flies are catch'd, and the great ones break through" (10). The blunt, vivid metaphor is typical of his style at this time and reveals the disgust of a passionate idealist.

To look at Defoe's publications for the year 1701 is to read a sensitive gauge of the state of the nation. Even the titles of Defoe's tracts telegraph a sense of threat: *The Danger of the Protestant Religion Consider'd*; *The Free-Holders Plea against Stock-Jobbing Elections*; *The Apparent Danger of an Invasion*; *Reasons against a War with France*. It is not hard to imagine why Defoe felt as he did. In the first place, he and his contemporaries were adjusting to yet another major political change, and change is always somewhat threatening. After living under monarchies that had dismissed or dispensed with Parliament at will, England had entered an age when implementation of the sovereign's policies depended upon the *management* of Parliament. Certainly the standing army controversy is an unmistakable example of the new situation. Englishmen were certainly familiar with the continual struggle for power between Parliament and the king that was the legacy of Charles I and the Cromwell years, and they were probably accustomed to a variety of attempts to influence elections, but the three elections held in four years (1698, 1700, and 1701) revealed shocking corruption and seriously exacerbated existing divisions in the country. As Defoe had observed in *The Pacificator*, the loss would at last be Britain's.

The Whig party split into country and court factions; animosity between High and Low Church broke out again. The elections, major changes in the ministry in the summer of 1700, unmistakable signs of a new war with France, an unpopular treaty,* and increasingly overt signs of the conflicts between William and Parliament bred faction, power plays, and insecurity.[36] The country Whigs formed a coalition with the Tories, first, to oppose a standing army, for it was they who suffered from high taxes in a time of crop failures and re-coinage, and, second, to campaign for the election of men without "pension and place." *A Letter to a Country Gentleman, Setting Forth the Cause of the Decay . . . of Trade* provided a list of those who held places at court in order to warn voters against electing them.[37] Defoe and many other Englishmen reacted with shock at the behavior of their statesmen. The internal squabbling, mercenary competition, blatant self-aggrandizement, and lack of principles gave many people, including Defoe, a lifelong distrust of parties. Defoe's *The Six Distinguishing Characters of a Parliament-Man*, *The Free-Holders Plea against Stock-Jobbing Elections*, and *The Livery Man's Reasons* (all 1701) urge voting for men of experience, honesty, and good morals and describe the rivalries as "this plague." "Wherefore we the Yeomandry and poor Freeholders of *England*, having, God knows, no Hand in the Differences, tho' we have a deep share in the Damages . . . ," he writes in a typical sentence in *The Free-Holders Plea* (3). Men sit in Jonathan's or Garraway's coffeehouse and buy an election, he charges in his attack on the conduct of the East India companies (20ff.).

Defoe felt more threatened than many Englishmen because he was a Dissenter. When Anne's only surviving child, the duke of Gloucester, died in July 1700, the problem of the succession to the throne reap-

---

*The Second Partition Treaty was extremely unpopular. Having negotiated it without the consent of his English ministers, William communicated the terms to them in late February 1700. The treaty was leaked to the press in July and greeted with general resentment.

peared. In Defoe's opinion, the new animosity between High and Low Church might encourage English Jacobites. Defoe saw all eyes on the squabbling at home while Louis XIV increased his power. About some issues Defoe was never totally rational, and the "Catholic threat" was one. To the realistic tallying up of France's strengths—her king, her organized civil service, her totalitarian requisition system—Defoe added a vision of Armageddon: England, the defender of Protestantism, pitted against France, the Catholic leviathan. In such a state of mind, Defoe tended to be erratic. For example, *The Danger of the Protestant Religion Consider'd*, addressed to William, quite sanely (if unnecessarily) urged William to attend to the threat to the Protestant religion posed by continental alliances and politics, but *The Succession to the Crown of England, Considered* calls for an investigation of Monmouth's legitimacy. Defoe seems quite serious about the possibility of naming Monmouth's son, James Scott, heir to the throne. Of course, England's solution was no model of anything but expediency. Thirteen people with better hereditary claims than the Hanoverian Sophia, daughter to Charles I's sister Elizabeth, had to be passed over to assure a Protestant successor. No wonder the Jacobites, supporters of King James and his heirs, agitated anew. Real and rumored delegations to St. Germain, James's court in exile, filled the periodical press. Reports from France continued to be ominous:

17 April: king James [is] on the mending hand, and . . . the French are forming a camp near Antwerp of 30,000 men; upon which the Dutch forces are all ordered to be ready to march at an hours warning.

26 April: another French squadron is preparing for the West Indies.[38]

The great fear was that Anne and William would die in the midst of a war with France and that civil war would break out leading to restoration of the Catholic Stuarts.

In the spring of 1701 a large number of people looked past parliamentary power struggles to Europe and came to share Defoe's view that France was a serious threat. Even the imperturbable John Evelyn, then eighty years old, wrote, "The House of Commons, neglect the Affairs abroad most unseasonably, whilst the French secure themselves of Flanders &c, irreparable negligence." Burnet says that the old East India Company and "the rest of the city" "began openly to condemn the proceedings of commons."[39] M.P.'s received letters and petitions.[40]

Defoe had a passionate side, and he could be swept into extreme responses. When the justices of the peace, the grand jury, some Whig gentlemen and freeholders of Kent, the county closest to France, sent a petition to the House of Commons to be delivered by five leading citizens, Defoe became involved, and his actions over the next few months give us a revealing look at his emotional makeup.

To present the Kent petition, prepared at the quarter sessions at Maidstone on 29 April, was an entirely legal right guaranteed citizens. The British Bill of Rights stated: "It is the right of subjects to petition the King and all commitments and prosecution for such petitioning are illegal." In fact, the citizens of Kent had been careful to observe the stipulations in the 1661 act against "tumultuous petitions," which required any petition bearing more than twenty signatures to be approved by at least three justices of the peace from the county or by a majority of the Grand Jury.[41] Although the rhetoric of the request that Parliament approve funds to protect the nation was rather dramatic, it was not accusatory. The petition asked "that your loyal addresses may be turned into bills of supply." Ironically, on 8 May, the day the Kentish petitioners finally managed to get access to Parliament, William relayed a request from Holland for 10,000 soldiers as guaranteed by a 1678 treaty to repulse the French.[42] The Commons declared the Kentish petition to be "Scandalous, Insolent, and Seditious," "tending . . . to subvert the established Government of this Realm," and had the men who presented it taken into custody by the serjeant-at-arms. Five days later, after Thomas Colepeper escaped and the others became disorderly, Speaker Robert Harley had them transferred to the Gate House Prison until Parliament was prorogued.[43]

London was still a militant Protestant stronghold and deeply concerned about the effect a close alliance between France and Spain would have on trade. Defoe, always a militant defender of the rights of citizens, accordingly wrote the address to Parliament titled *Legion's Memorial,* perhaps with some encouragement from City Whigs.[44] At the time of its appearance men speculated "whether there be more signs of Legion without doors, or within [in Parliament]."[45] John Oldmixon, who knew Defoe well, said that "Foe took to himself" authorship of it in his hearing and remarked that Defoe was zealous enough, "naturally of a daring dauntless Temper," possessed of the "Spirit" "infus'd" in *Legion's Memorial,* but he went on to doubt that Defoe was then "capable of drawing up these Articles" in the form in which they appeared (235).

The closest thing to an eyewitness account of the delivery of *Legion's Memorial* tends to substantiate a collaboration between Defoe and Whig M.P.'s. Narcissus Luttrell, a not entirely unimpeachable source, writes:

A letter directed to the speaker was found in the box of the members letters at Westminster, which being opened contained 13 articles and some petitions, with threatnings and reflections on Mr. How[,] the speaker, and others: 'twas signed Legion, (for we are many). . . . upon reading it, an address was ordered to the king, desireing him to take care of the publick peace.[46]

Oldmixon says that the *Memorial* was enclosed in a letter to Harley that demanded that he read it in the Commons (235). An old legend that

Defoe delivered the *Memorial* dressed as a woman (male petitioners had to give security) comes from a letter to one of Defoe's earliest biographers, George Chalmers. According to "Mr. Polhill of Cheapstead-place in Kent," the son of David Polhill, one of the imprisoned Kentish petitioners, Defoe, so dressed and accompanied by sixteen men, presented the petition to "Speaker Harley."[47]

Defoe may, in fact, have been accompanied by "Sixteen Gentlemen of Quality" when he delivered the letter as he says, but he almost certainly did not deliver it personally to Harley when Parliament was in session. In fact, Defoe's own account says, "*If any notice had been taken of him*, [they] were ready to have carried him off" (emphasis added).[48] The difficulty the men from Kent had getting into Parliament and the heavier guard assigned after their petition would make a march up to Harley in Parliament by seventeen men most unlikely.

Whether Defoe acted essentially on his own or in a close conspiracy, and regardless of how he delivered *Legion's Memorial*, its effect was undeniable. The Kentish prisoners became heroes to visit and reward, large paper effigies of them sold for a shilling, contemporaries acknowledged that the petition and the *Legion's Memorial* were "the Voice of the People," the London Common Council came within a vote of a public endorsement of the *Memorial*,[49] and the Commons voted the king his supplies and endorsed new alliances to thwart the French. When the five men from Kent were released, Londoners collected £200 and held a banquet at Mercers Chapel for them. Defoe "was placed" "Next the Worthies."[50]

The True-Born Englishman and *Legion's Memorial* made Defoe one of the best-known men in London. His August *History of the Kentish Petition* and the late fall *Legion's New Paper* retold the events in dramatic terms. In the *History*, for instance, he says "alluding to the Words of *Luther*, to those who diswaded him from going to the City of *Worms*, [Colepeper] *told them*, That if every Tile upon the Chappel of Saint *Stephen's** was a Devil, he would present the Petition"(7). These pamphlets are full of dramatic confrontations, dialogue, and blustering claims: "From that time there was not a Word ever spoken in the House, of proceeding against the *Kentish* Petitioners"(14). Defoe lists the failings and illegal actions of the M.P.'s and ridicules their hopes of reelection. How full of himself he is when he writes "your Humble Servant the Author is to be spoken with at his House as constantly as a Quack Doctor" (*New Paper*, 4). He even proposes ridiculous penalties, such as double taxation for districts that return those he identifies as corrupt M.P.'s.

The fact that he had not only gotten away with but gained great

---

*Defoe's note reminds the reader that the Commons sat in what was formerly St. Stephen's Chapel.

success from a tract so much more inflammatory and extreme than the
Kentish petition probably misled Defoe. His position was very close to
that of the pre-Monmouth Shaftesburian Whigs, and his view of the
relationship between the people and Parliament that of a radical Lockean: "Whatever *Powers* you [M.P's] have . . . you enjoy them as . . . their
Representative"; "You may Die, but the People remain . . . Power may
have its Intervals, and Crowns their Interregnum, but Original Power
endures to the same Eternity the World endures to"; "the Center of
Power is in the People."[51] The attitude of the conclusion to *Legion's
Memorial* approaches a political philosophy. "Thus *Gentlemen*," he had
written, "You have Your Duty laid before You . . . but if You continue to
neglect it, you may expect to be treated according to the Resentments of
an *injur'd* Nation; for *English*men are no more to be Slaves to *Parliaments*, than to a King."

About this time Defoe published *The Present State of Jacobitism Considered,* in which he lectured the Jacobites to the effect that conscience
and prudence must tell them to give up the cause now that James was
dead, and *Reasons against a War with France,* in which he argues that
England should fight Spain rather than France because it will be easier
and more profitable. These tracts of late 1701 are swaggering, un-
polished, and often naive. Defoe signs many of them and deliberately
gives his authorship away in others, and his tone is often superior or
pedantic. The sense of national and specific threat that spawned them
seems to have been lost in the thrill of recognition.

Although Defoe's 1701 publications surely made some money, they
had three unfortunate effects: they gave him too high an opinion of
himself, they drew him deeply into the paper wars of the times, and
they made him a host of powerful enemies. For instance, a number of
vicious attacks followed *Legion's Memorial.* Journalists called Defoe "this
Hot-brain'd Scribler" and "Faction in a Libel." At least one even associated him and the Kentish petitioners with a traitorous club.* The food
at the celebratory banquet, it said, included "Bak'd, Boil'd and Roast,
and Cod and Calves-head in abundance."[52] Defoe came to be seen as a
dangerous spokesman for the court party, and he was never again to be
free from the suspicion of being the "tool" of a political group. In spite
of the importance of political parties, Englishmen distrusted them
deeply. "Whigs" had, after all, been Scots Presbyterian rebels and "Tories" Irish bandits. Halifax, Harley, William, all tried to maintain a
balanced government. It is almost impossible to find praise for political

---

*These clubs were rumored to meet on 30 January all over England and Scotland to
celebrate the beheading of Charles I and toast the Commonwealth. The group sang
songs and had a lavish feast, which always included calves' heads, symbolic of Charles's
followers. Traditionally, a cod's head stood for Charles, a pike for tyranny, and a boar's
head for the king preying on his subjects.

parties, but it is trivial to marshal quotations such as "party-spirit . . . [even] when it is under its greatest restraints naturally breaks out in falsehood, detraction, calumny, and a partial administration of justice" (*Spectator*, no. 125).

Besides the contemptuous label "party tool," made memorable by Butler's *Hudibras*, Defoe's opponents gave him a nickname that became so common that he could be identified by it alone: "Devil." When he concluded *Legion's Memorial* with the words, "Our Name is LEGION, and we are Many," Defoe may have intended to ally his paper with John Milton's *Animadversions upon the Remonstrants Defence, against Smectymnuus* (1641), which includes the line spoken by Remonstrant: "But could they say my name is Legion; for wee are many." Milton's essay was part of his attack upon the government of the Church of England and included arguments for the right of the "free-born people of England" to express opinions and to disobey "destructive" governments. But Remonstrant represents the enemy, Bishop Joseph Hall, and he is answered by Milton's character pointing out his affiliation with the devil. Milton's source is the story in the New Testament of the man with the unclean spirit who lived in the tombs. Jesus asks the unclean spirit its name, and, in order to protect itself, it tries to hide its own name behind the answer, "My name is Legion: for we are many" (Mark 5:30). Jesus draws the unclean spirit from the man anyway and sends it into a herd of swine which rushes over a cliff to die. In these accounts, "Legion" has many associations; the armies of Satan and God are both "Legions," and the imagery of division, strife, and unrest is in both uses. The unclean spirit is a devil and causes the man to cut himself with stones and bruise himself.

Defoe's contemporaries seized upon the traditional use of "Legion," glossing it with the character of Milton's Satan in *Paradise Lost*: a master politician and "the father of lies." A number of attacks on Defoe accused him of deliberately stirring up discord. One pamphlet was called *An Account of Some Late Designs to Create a Misunderstanding betwixt the King and His People* (1702). Another clever writer capitalized on that character and wrote, "Thou hast been a mere Devil in endeavouring to sow the Seeds of Discord among thy Fellow Subjects, and may'st well subscribe with the Name of *Legion*, which has been made use of in Scripture for a *Devil* of particular Eminence."[53] And so Defoe was accused of infusing a self-destructive spirit, a division in his countrymen, and became the "Devil" to be immortalized in a hundred vicious, doggerel ballads and caricatured in prints such as "Daniel De Foe and the Devil at Leap-frog" (1706).

Defoe began to answer some of these attacks as he did in *Legion's New Paper* and *The Original Power of the Collective Body of the People of England*. Not only did this strategy lower him to the level of the true hacks and entangle him in ephemeral, profitless exchanges, but his tracts, and especially his fearless use of names, quickly raised a rather intimidating list of enemies. For instance, nine of the petitioners satirized in Defoe's *New Discovery of an Old Intreague* were involved to some extent in Defoe's proposals to Christ's Hospital. Sir John Moore was president of the General Court of the hospital in May 1696 when Defoe first proposed building tenements. Sir Francis Child was president, and Francis Brerewood (whose satiric portrait was among the most scathing) treasurer in 1703 when the court decided to develop the hospital's land itself and to open negotiations with Lord Weymouth on its own behalf.[54] Not only had men offended by Defoe already found opportunities to disappoint him, but some of his other enemies promised future complications. Sir Charles Duncombe (satirized in *New Discovery* and *The Livery Man's Reasons*), Sir Humphrey Mackworth (answered sarcastically in *The Original Power of the Collective Body*), and the able journalists John Tutchin (satirized in *The True-Born Englishman*) and William Pittis (in *The Pacificator*) were not likely to forget Defoe.

CHAPTER 5

FUGITIVE

He was the person that wrote the pamphlet cal'd the shortest way
with the dissenters & for which he was pilloryed.

—JOHN CLERK (1706)

the same who afterwards was Pillory'd for writing an ironical
Invective against the Church, and did after that list in the Service
of Mr. Robert Harley.

—JOHN OLDMIXON (1735)

Some people said Defoe began the debate over occasional conformity. "'Twas in the memorable Year 1698 then, in the Mayoralty of Sir *H.E.* . . . that Mr. *D.F.*, a known *Dissenter*, advanc'd first in this Cause, publishing a Hue and Cry after the Purity and Sincerity of his Tolerated Brethren," a contemporary wrote, and a number of other knowledgeable people agreed.[1]

What Defoe had done was to call attention to a divisive issue in a pamphlet called *An Enquiry into the Occasional Conformity of Dissenters, In Cases of Preferments*. Defoe took the lord mayor of London, Sir Humphrey Edwin, a Dissenter, to task for attending St. Paul's in the morning and the Pinners' Hall conventicle in the afternoon. Edwin had attended both in his official robes and with the sword of his office. What made Edwin's Sunday an issue was the Test Act of 1673. It was a strange piece of legislation, and Defoe always resented it. Under this act, every holder of office—civil, military, or crown—had to take the Oath of Allegiance and communion in the Church of England within three months of taking office. Occasional conformity, a Dissenter's "occasional" taking of communion in the Church of England, was common among Presbyterians and Congregationalists and had been defended since the Act of Uniformity, when Dissenting ministers who could not take the required oaths and subscribe to the entire Book of Common Prayer were ejected from their churches.[2] However, Defoe's pamphlet called attention to what was in the eyes of some a flouting of the law, in the eyes of others a common, even "healing" practice, and to yet others religious hypocrisy.

Defoe took a stand. In fact, he may even have imitated Martin Luther by tacking his pamphlet—with a thesis for debate—on the door of St. Paul's on 2 December, the day Edwin was to attend a thanksgiving service. The *Post Man* reported a "foolish pasquil, reflecting on the Lord Mayor" posted on the door, and there was something of an English tradition of challenging authority this way.[3] Defoe consistently and strongly objected to occasional conformity. Although he could make a theological argument, he usually directed his objections to the Test Act rather than to the practice. First, he believed the act debased communion to a shocking degree. Second, he thought that the act "weakened" Dissent; it encouraged people to go to the Church of England, and those who did became less loyal to their meeting houses and finally drifted into conformity without making a considered choice. Third, the act tempted men to compromise, equivocate, and sin. In none of these objections did Defoe stand alone. For instance, Bishop Benjamin Hoadley, whose church and party were the creators of the act, opposed occasional conformity on the same grounds; communion became, he said, "the instrument of some particular sort of Christians (as well as of infidels and Atheists) getting into civil offices, and . . . the bar against other sorts of Christians, . . . debasing the most sacred thing in the world into a political tool and engine of State."[4]

Much of the emotion in Defoe's objections seems to come from his memory of the hard years, the times of persecution. The idea of men doing for office what prison could not compel them to do, and the awareness of the gradual decline of Nonconformity after the years of struggle for its survival, moved Defoe deeply. Only a decade earlier he had fought for Monmouth, seen Morton emigrate to America, and been involved in a conventicle arrest. Moreover, Defoe and many of his contemporaries had seen the Church of England's "zeal" behind the persecution of Dissenters since at least 1685. As the diarist Roger Morrice said, the Anglican justices, officers, and informers were "the visible and open agents" of the persecution, "and it must flow from their own inclinations, or from the Influence the Papists have upon them." Defoe, too, believed that the High Church extremists were Jacobites if not "tools" of the Catholics.

Moreover, Defoe had, after all, begun preparation for a career as a Nonconformist minister, and he had continued to participate in leading services at the Merchants' Lectures around the city. He was particularly prominent at Salters' Hall where a group had leased land from the company and built a chapel where services, Merchants' Lectures, and the Dissenters' Society for the Reformation of Manners' meetings were held. Here the congregation reputed to be the richest in London heard Richard Mayo, "the prince of preachers"; Nathaniel Taylor, "the Isaac

Watts of Nonconformity"; William Tong; John How; Defoe's class-mate John Shower; and even Daniel Williams. Of Defoe's participation one of his critics wrote,

> Follow him by the Scent of his Scraps of Scripture, and you'll find him at *Salter*'s or *Pinner*'s Hall . . . whether you seek for Mr. *Fo* the Hosier, or Mr. *Fo* the Preacher; 'tis all one. . . .
> . . . Mr. *Foe* may conclude with his *Salter-Hall* Prayer.[5]

His denunciation of occasional conformity was no trivial entry into a controversy but the result of deep, even emotional, convictions. Defoe explained his attack of 1697 on Edwin and why he had come to reprint his pamphlet in 1701 with an address to one of the most distinguished Dissenting ministers in London in the preface to the new edition:

> The Debate was then young, and the Practice of this Scandalous Conformity was new: Sir *John Shorter* being the first Instance of it. But it is now growing a receiv'd Custom, to the great Scandal of the Dissenters in general, the Offence of such whose Consciences forbid them the same Latitude, and the Stumbling of those who being before weak and irresolute, are led aside by the Eminency and Frequency of Examples.[6]

Edwin was well known, a devout Dissenter, a good man, and a man in a very visible office. His example had the power to influence others. "He was a strong Nonconformist, and his attendance in State, while Lord Mayor, at a Dissenting Meeting House was the origin of the Occasional Conformity Bills of Anne's reign," a standard modern reference book says.

What John Shorter, the man Defoe described as "the first instance," had done was significantly different from what Edwin had done. On 5 November 1687 Shorter heard Matthew Meade preach to his congregation at Grocers' Hall and took communion later "in a publick Church." People described Shorter's motives as "inadvertancy and want of consideration or to avoid the imputation of favoring Popery." Shorter was then living in Grocers' Hall, and he applied to Secretary of State Sunderland for permission to have both Church of England and Nonconforming divines preach to him there. According to Morrice, Shorter eventually received permission but by then realized the divisive nature of his act and never repeated it. By Edwin's time Shorter's request would have been unthinkable, and by 1701 the new lord mayor, Thomas Abney, who repeated Shorter's and Edwin's impolitic act, represented to Anglicans a mercenary abuse of law and to the Dissenters a precedent that encouraged heavy fines for those unwilling to accept public office for reasons of conscience.

Defoe, then, had first written *An Enquiry* four years before occasional conformity became the subject of wide discussion and of proposed preventive legislature. By 1702, however, in his sense of threat and outrage, Defoe was not alone. Edmund Calamy relates a story of an old woman who objected to her church's proposed call to a minister in these words: "He is a middle way man! He is an occasional conformist! He is neither fish nor flesh, nor good red herring!" Numerous anecdotes suggest growing resistance to the practice,[7] and it was like Defoe to demand deliberate, considered action of people he saw sliding into error. He knew the hope of Comprehension* and reconciliation with the Church of England was dead. What he *heard* were contradictions, equivocations, and evasions; he demanded a reasoned, theological justification.

Defoe's pamphlet, although designed to strengthen Dissent, angered and alarmed Dissenters from the beginning. The accusation that some Dissenters took Anglican communion for the sake of advancement had been around for years, but it had never been printed in such unequivocal terms. Filled with inflammatory language, Defoe's pamphlet introduced the two categories of Dissenters that haunted the Nonconformists for years. "He who Dissents from an Establish'd Church on any account, but from a real Principle of Conscience, is a Politick, not a Religious Dissenter," he wrote.[8] The Dissenter who occasionally conformed was no religious Dissenter; only Politick Dissenters conformed "to that which they refus'd" under all kinds of persecution in order to gain "Publick Advancements, and Glittering Gawdy Honours of the Age" (14). Defoe said that these people argued "this is no Conformity in Point of Religion, but done as a Civil Action" in order to serve their country. In his mind, the "Politick" Dissenter was one who set up a false distinction and "*play[ed] Bo-peep* with God Almighty." "How," he asked, "can you take [communion] as a Civil Act in one place, and a Religious Act in another?" (17)

The demand made in this pamphlet was as extreme and, in fact, the same as that of the High Church, which equally (although on opposite grounds) opposed occasional conformity (in its view, regular and conscientious conformity was called for). Defoe asked that occasional conformists be excluded from meeting houses unless they made a "Penitent Acknowledgement." He accused the Dissenting clergy of admitting Edwin "because of his Gold Ring and Fine Apparel" and Edwin of apostasy "upon the occasion of Preferment" and of making "the Sacred Institutions of Christ Jesus, become Pimps to . . . Secular Interest" (24). Defoe challenged Dissenting ministers to address the reasons why they refused to take a stand on actions like Edwin's, but the pamphlet went unanswered.

*A compromise that would have allowed some Dissenting sects like the Presbyterians to reunite with a modified Church of England. The Savoy Conference of April–August 1661 was held to effect such a settlement, but by Defoe's time, the betrayal and failure of the conference were well known, and no one thought Comprehension possible.

Defoe's language made the pamphlet divisive and memorable. Most of the other occasional conformist pamphlets written by Dissenters and Low Churchmen reflected the ambivalence people felt about the practice. Defoe, however, chose one pejorative, vivid characterization after another. "*Your Lordship* never was a Trimmer," Defoe wrote in the preface addressed to Edwin. The term came from Savile's famous essay *The Character of a Trimmer* (1688), which argued for a government composed of a balance of political parties and positions, but "trimmer" by 1697 had come to mean simply one who tacked and trimmed with the winds of change in order to reap political advantages regardless of who was in power. "The Patriot's Soul disdains the Trimmer's Art," a contemporary, Bertram Stote, wrote in his 1704 *Faction Display'd*. Among other phrases Defoe used to describe what Edwin had done were playing a "loose Game of Religion" (15), "Bantering with Religion" (18), and, of course, "*playing Bo-peep* with God Almighty." He accused occasional conformists of prostituting their religion and choosing to trespass "on their Consciences, before the hazard of their Estates" (18, 21–22).

The familiar, gibing tone that came to characterize some of Defoe's writing also made people remember the pamphlet. With tongue in cheek, Defoe "humbly crave[d] leave" to be Edwin's advocate since he had no other, and sketched in just enough of the rather comic outcome of the Pinners' Hall attendance to remind his readers of the whole story. Edwin had actually gone to both services twice—on 31 October and 7 November. After the second Sunday his sword bearer had complained to the London Court of Aldermen that the mayor had forced him to attend Pinners' Hall and that he had been locked in a pew so that he could not leave. At the hearing on 9 November, the court admonished Edwin not to compel the sword bearer or anyone else to go to meetings, and Edwin "was pleased to declare that he would forbeare it for the time to come."[9] Defoe humorously concluded that Edwin and the sword bearer were "exactly under the same Predicaments," for Edwin required the man to go to Pinners' Hall and the Test Act "oblig'd" Edwin to go to St. Paul's. Defoe jests with Edwin—and the law.

Though Humphrey Edwin was a successful and very rich man, Defoe assumed a familiar tone because he knew him. He had signed the 1691 petition regarding Boston Harbor with Defoe, and the two men had had many opportunities to meet. Edwin had been a merchant (probably in wool) in Great St. Helen's, a street adjoining the one on which Annesley lived and had his meeting house. He was a devout Dissenter and had been selected by King James to be an alderman during the time when James was courting Dissenters. Edwin was sworn in and knighted by James in 1687. In 1688 he became one of the two sheriffs of London. He supported William and captained the Yellow Regiment of city militia that rode to welcome the new king to London. Edwin was again elected alderman, was appointed to the Commission of the Excise by William, and had been elected lord mayor only that fall. When Defoe wrote in this preface to Edwin, "You never suffer'd Your Self to be abridg'd of Your Liberty," he probably knew this from years of observing Edwin.

A few pamphlets and some satirical poems appeared about Edwin's action, but the subject faded quickly. King William had, after all, come from Holland, the country James II had held up for imitation under the pretense that he believed religious toleration contributed to Holland's economic success. His chaplain was William Carstares, an ordained Church of Scotland minister and therefore a Dissenter in England. So close was Carstares to William that he accompanied him on every military campaign, was known to his detractors as "Cardinal Carstares," and may have been the only man who ever dared stop one of William's messengers and then interrupt the king's sleep to tell him he had done so.[10] William's propensities toward religious toleration were well known. In fact, Defoe chose to ignore the conflict any Dissenting lord mayor would feel. The lord mayor was expected to attend all fasts, celebrations, and special services proclaimed by the monarch; even his regalia and gown were specified at these obligatory appearances at St. Paul's.[11]

In November 1700 Sir Thomas Abney, the new lord mayor, repeated Sir Humphrey Edwin's performance. Abney attended his usual meeting house in the afternoon, that of the eminent preacher John How, and Defoe reissued his *Enquiry into the Occasional Conformity of Dissenters*. This time he addressed his preface to How and demanded that How either defend occasional conformity or declare against it. Defoe revised his pamphlet slightly in order to make it more powerful. Chiefly by breaking paragraphs into two and changing clauses into questions, Defoe strengthened the sense of the necessity for choice and of the unacceptability of compromise. For instance, he dramatically began a new paragraph after revising a long sentence with a dependent clause by recasting one clause as a pointed question: "If the Service of their Country be so dear to them, pray why should they not chuse to expose their Bodies and estates for that Service rather than their Souls?"(18). How did answer Defoe's challenge. In his stern pamphlet How reminded Defoe that the heart of Dissent was the individual conscience and admonished him not to set up as "the *Conscience-general* of Mankind" by "invad[ing] the Throne of the most High, in charging the Worthy Person referr'd to, with acting against his Conscience." How's position was that of most moderate Presbyterians, and he objected specifically to Defoe's use of the text contrasting Dissenters and Anglicans through references to Baal and God. A "prophane and impious Wit," How called it.[12]

Defoe answered How, and a heated pamphlet war broke out. It came at a very bad time; the reaction against the court Whigs had encouraged a Tory–country Whig coalition, and King William had finally been pressured into allowing the Church of England Convocation to meet. Potentially, both of these things had serious implications for the Dissenters. A bill introduced in a Commons committee to prevent occasional conformity and the anti-Dissenting feeling whipped up by the Convocation (where moderate Low Churchmen were a distinct minority) quickly turned a primarily doctrinal dispute into a political one. The bill never got out of committee, but after William died unexpectedly in early March, the Dissenters faced a very different monarch and a host of powerful men ready to capitalize on these factions.

William's death unleashed an intimidating amount of anti-Dissenting feeling. A mob celebrating William's death destroyed a meeting house in Newcastle-under-Lyme. Poets satirized mourners, who, they said, would be more sensible to "Mourn for the mighty Summs by him mis-spent" and "ten Years of War."[13] Defoe's poem *The Mock Mourners* expressed shock at actual events, and chastized those who "Insult the Ashes of their injur'd King . . . *And Drink the Horse's Health that threw him down*" (30).

The new queen contributed to the avalanche of ominous events. Almost at once she dismissed Somers, Defoe's standing army ally, and Halifax, moderate Whig and notable financial statesman, and changed six Whig colonels in the City Commission of Lieutenancy for six Tory ones. William Ashurst and Thomas Lane, both of whom had signed the Boston petition with Defoe, were replaced with old enemies of Defoe's, including Sir Francis Child, Sir John Fleet, Sir Charles Duncombe, and Sir Samuel Dashwood. When Queen Anne dissolved Parliament on 25 May 1702, her speech included an alarming statement: "My own Principles must always keep me entirely firm to the Interests and Religion of the Church of *England*, and will incline me to countenance those who have the truest Zeal to support it." The old rallying cry "the Church in danger" seemed to be gaining impetus, and in the July elections only one Whig was elected to Parliament from London.

The queen had used the word *zeal*, and there were men ready to be zealous. About the time the queen dissolved Parliament, the Reverend Henry Sacheverell preached and then immediately published a sermon called *The Political Union: A Discourse Shewing the Dependance of Government on Religion in General: And of the English Monarchy on the Church of England in Particular*. The sermon insisted upon the dependence referred to in its title and attacked the Dissenters through insinuating allusions:

reflect upon *Ahab*'s Policy, who could not be Content with the *Vineyard*, without Murdering the *Rightful Owner*[14]

and direct statements:

That Confus'd Swarm of *Sectarists*, that Gather about [the Church's] Body, not to Partake of Its Communion, but to . . . Presume to Shelter Themselves under Its Character . . . more Effectually to Undermine and Destroy it. (48)

Presbytery and Republicanism go hand in hand, They are but the Same Disorderly, *Levelling Principle*.(50)

His sermon concluded with the observation that the Church of England's "*True Sons, Pillars, and Defenders*," "every Man, that Wishes Its Welfare, ought to Hang out the *Bloody Flag*, and *Banner* of Defiance," rather than offering Nonconformists oaths and offices (59):

If therefore We have any Concern for our *Religion*, any True Allegiance for Our *Sovereign*, or Regard to the Safety and Honour of Our *Country*, We must Watch against These Crafty, Faithless, and Insidious Persons, who can *Creep* to Our Altars, and Partake of Our Sacraments, that They may be *Qualify'd*, more . . . Powerfully to Undermine Us. (61)

Sacheverell was not the only Anglican to preach and publish such sermons. The "bloody flag" became a catchword, and a number of pamphlets like Sacheverell's own anonymous *The Character of a Low Churchman* characterized the Dissenters as dangerous enemies. The historian Alexander Cunningham subsequently wrote: "At that time some of the clergy . . . exerted the utmost of their eloquence in preaching not only against the dissenters, the whigs, and the ministry, but even against the Queen herself, and the principles of moderation. . . . he who inveighed the most bitterly, and filled his flock with the most dreadful apprehensions, was the most highly applauded by his party." In describing that summer, Edmund Calamy wrote that many wanted "to bring [the Dissenters] under a Popular Odium . . . And the Populace . . . generally gave in to it."[15]

When Parliament went into session in the fall, the Commons introduced a new bill to prevent occasional conformity, and the Dissenters had real reason to fear its passage. This bill would effectively bar Dissenters from offices in cities, boroughs, corporations, the cinque ports,* and crown offices through the automatic imposition of exorbitant fines on anyone who had qualified for an office and then been

---

*A group of southeastern Channel ports (originally five) in Kent and Sussex that had officers, courts, and M.P.'s of their own.

caught in a meeting house. Although there were few Dissenters in crown offices, the borough corporations contained many, and passage of the bill would exclude Dissenters from the legislative and judiciary branches of government and prevent their having any share in the administration of laws and regulations. So inclusive was the bill that aldermen, magistrates, bailiffs, common councilmen, and even scavengers would have to conform or pay a fine. The navy, Customs, Excise, and royal household, including minor positions in the forests, would be closed to them. Some of these minor offices had been purchased or inherited, others were freeholds or the "fruits of long Service, and many of them the whole Subsistence of Families." Even contracts for supplies to hospitals, workhouses, and prisons would be forbidden (one opposition M.P. asked in committee: "What Hurt can there come from Dissenting Bread and Cheese, or Presbyterian Water-gruel?") Still in debt and struggling somewhat financially, Defoe himself would become ineligible for contracts to supply bricks such as the ones he had held with Greenwich Hospital.

Defoe and many, many others saw a crucial difference between the men and offices covered by the Test Act and those affected by the bill to prevent occasional conformity. A mayor or alderman had a separate occupation; a customs officer or a noncommissioned naval officer had nothing else. In *A Letter to a Peer* an Anglican observed, "Let any man in the World be reduc'd to this hard Choice, Either to ruine his Family, or to violate the peace of his own Mind, and He will certainly reckon himself persecuted, tho' the Doores to the Place, where he is wont to worship God, be still . . . standing open"(9).

Pessimistic interpreters of the bill saw that it could be used in ingenious ways. For example, an occasional conformist who had taken communion three times in a year in an Anglican church could be chosen for a borough office. The court of that borough had the power to impose a repressively large discharge fee or to vote down his request to be excused. Critics would later say that the Mansion House had been built with the fines imposed on Dissenters deliberately elected to City offices.[16] If the Dissenter were forced to serve, he could not go to conventicle or he risked loss of office and a £150 fine the first time he went. Defoe, after all, had paid £10 to be discharged of the friendly Butcher's Company offices and, in 1730, a Dissenter elected sheriff in London would be fined £400 for refusing to serve; discharge fees were completely discretionary. Somewhat protected for years by sympathetic magistrates, jurors, and other officials from waves of persecution instigated by the extremists, the Dissenters now feared virtual disfranchisement and crippling fines for disobeying old laws now to be rigorously enforced.

The bill passed the Commons in November and the first reading in the Lords occurred on 2 December. Defoe still opposed occasional conformity for all of the reasons he had in 1697; the bill to prevent occasional conformity alarmed him because he saw the full repressive implications and because of what it represented. He opposed the prejudices and motives of the bill's supporters as well as the bill's inclusiveness. These objections are crucial, for they explain his apparently contradictory position: to oppose occasional conformity *and* to oppose the bill to prevent occasional conformity. Even more important is the fact that they, to a great extent, explain what Defoe did and the result.

Almost every Dissenter who left a record of 1702 mentioned the sense of threat and the "rage" they felt directed at them. Many comment that their enemies must have been under "an unnatural restraint" during William's last years. Prejudice now broke out in greater vituperation because of its former suppression. The bill to prevent occasional conformity was the expression of these feelings, and the chances for its passage seemed very high. Defoe shared the humiliation and fear of his fellow Dissenters. The anonymous *The Case of Dissenters as Affected by the Late Bill . . . for Preventing Occasional Conformity* (1703) describes the psychological effect: "this Bill draws over all [the Dissenters] Heads a dismal Cloud of Incapacity. *None will* deny but a total Incapacity to serve his Prince and Country is a Mark of high Infamy, so that next to the Loss of Life it seems the heaviest Punishment" (24). The feeling lingered; years later Moses Lowman was to describe the Dissenters' situation as "a Mark of publick Infamy, and in the Sense of the Law [we] are judged Persons unfit for a publick Trust." Even a member of the House of Lords objected that "it is hard to imagine, any Offence, that is not capital, can deserve" so great a "Penalty" as "Incapacity." The *Observator* accused the bill of punishing "people who have committed no crime."[17] Defoe wrote at length about the experience. Time after time in his pamphlets and periodicals he complained about the restrictions preventing Dissenters from serving their country. In *A Serious Inquiry into This Grand Question* (1704), he defined the desire of High Churchmen to be to "[exclude us] from the Publick Trust"; "deprive us of our Birth-right, as *Englishmen*"; and "Incapacitate us for the Service of our Queen and Country." The emphatic verbs capture the stigma the Dissenters felt: *exclude, deprive, incapacitate.*[18]

Citizens of modern England and America cannot easily imagine what it was like to be a Dissenter in the summer and fall of 1702. The amount and nature of the abuse from pulpits and the press angered and intimidated even the sturdiest Dissenter. Pamphleteers traced a version of the history of Dissent in order to link Nonconformity with the Puritans who had beheaded Charles I and to preserve the idea that they were "turbulent and factious spirits," malcontents, and potential rebels.[19] They were frequently compared to vermin, reptiles, cancers, and disease. Later Defoe was to write that "*Dissenters* began to be insulted in every Place; their *Meeting-Houses* and *Assemblies* assaulted by the *Mob*; and even their *Ministers*. . . scarce admitted to pass the Streets."[20] He recalls in strings of phrases how embattled he felt: "Down with the *Whigs*, down with the *Presbyterians*, down with the *Meeting-Houses*, was such a Universal Cry, that nothing else was to be heard . . . ; Press, Pulpit, Coffee-house, all the Discourse of the Kingdom, was . . . how the Church should Triumph . . . how 41* should now be fully Reveng'd" (*Review* 2:195–96).

Defoe at this time was riding high on the success of *Legion's Memorial* but stinging from charges that he had started the occasional conformity debate and given the High Church party its most effective weapon. Many Dissenters felt he had opened the door *from within* to charges that they were guilty of hypocrisy and double-dealing. The attention Defoe's earlier pamphlets had attracted must have seemed to them at least partly responsible for the occasional conformity bills. As Mary Astell would say, if Defoe and other Dissenters "damn *Occasional-Conformity*, and have writ against it . . . what harm . . . for a poor Church-man to *Banter* it a little?"[21] The fact that Defoe was both defensive and close to the *Legion's Memorial* success helps explain his response to the bill: *The Shortest-Way with the Dissenters*. From the extremism of published pamphlets, poems, and sermons, he correctly recognized that he must try something different. His own and others' attempts to reason with the High Church zealots had been futile. *Legion's Memorial* had been a dramatic impersonation, a mock defense of repression, and it had been effective. *The Shortest Way* was a dramatic impersonation, a defense of liberty, and it surpassed the *Memorial*'s notoriety.

He chose to attack the spirit that created the bill to prevent occasional conformity rather than the bill itself as most other writers were doing. In order to expose that spirit as he had exposed the short-sightedness in the Kentish/*Legion's Memorial* incident, he took his title from a familiar proverb, "The shortest answer is doing," and ironically recommended a drastic course of action. He imitated the style of the enemies of the Dissenters and, thereby, revealed their (a) true intentions and (b) most insidious method.

Defoe was drawing on a long history of anti-Dissenting pamphlets and mingling phrases and even sentences from a number of 1701–1702 works.[22] Although it is impossible to name a single object of parody, he points a finger at some specific works and one was the

*1641: the year in which "the Grand Remonstrance," a long list of charges against Charles I's government, was brought before Parliament. Charles attempted to arrest the leaders, failed, and left London to raise support in Scotland and the north and west. Because so much of the opposition to Charles came from the City, persecution of the London Dissenters would "revenge '41."

immediate inspiration for *The Shortest-Way*. Sacheverell, of course, occupies a significant place in the pamphlet. Long known to be an enemy
of the Dissenters, he fathered a series of catchphrases such as "the
bloody flag of Defiance." But it was the anonymous *The Establishment of
the Church, The Preservation of the State: Shewing the Reasonableness of a Bill
against Occasional Conformity*, however, that directly shaped Defoe's attack. This forceful pamphlet, published about three weeks before Defoe's and planned to coincide with the November Commons consideration of the bill, furnished Defoe's subtitle to *The Shortest-Way with the
Dissenters: Or Proposals for the Establishment of the Church*. It included all of
the ideas Defoe found most offensive. Even an Anglican described it as
breathing "merciless Fury against the Dissenters." For instance, suggestions for the complete suppression of Nonconformity, usually more
veiled, appeared openly:

To tolerate their Irregularities, while there is a Power in our Hands to curb and
cure them, is so farr from an Act of Love, that 'tis rather an Indulgence of their
Disease, and a promoting of their Malady.

For is it an office of brotherly Love, to permit a man to endanger his Life by a
violent Feaver, rather than prevent it by a gentle Caustic or Phlebotomy?[23]

The tract even went so far as to say that "the most undeniable Proofs of
Reason, and that too mixt with caution and kindness, can justify severity and a penal Execution"(13). At one point the writer seems to anticipate the tone of Jonathan Swift's *A Modest Proposal*:

In kindness therefore to the Public, as well as themselves, methinks this easy
method [extermination] might be put in Practice for the effectual cure of
Differences among us, without any hardship to the present Dissenters. (16)

Defoe extends the point of view of *The Establishment* and finally en-
dorses a "penal Execution": " 'Twould be more rational for us, if we
must spare this Generation, to summon our own to a general Massacre."[24] Just as *The Establishment* had said it was kindness to cure a
Feaver, Defoe argues that it is a protective action to kill snakes:

'TIS Cruelty to kill a Snake or a Toad in cold Blood, but the Poyson of their
Nature makes it a Charity to our Neighbours . . . these poyson the Soul, cor-
rupt our Posterity, destroy . . . our future Felicity, and contaminate the whole
Mass!

I do not prescribe Fire and Faggot, but as *Scipio* said of *Carthage* . . . they are
to be rooted out of this Nation, if ever we will live in Peace, serve God, or enjoy
our Own. (126)

The Establishment is also more blatant than most pamphlets in its insistence that the Dissenters were merely enriching themselves hypocritically. "For what is the Liberty they contend for under the Pleas of

Conscience, but a Liberty to supplant the Church, undermine the State, and lastly to Establish themselves?" it asked (17). Defoe repeats the accusation that Dissenters are enemies of church and state and picks up the undertone of resentment of the Dissenters' prosperity. "THEIR Numbers, and their Wealth, makes them Haughty," Defoe writes, arguing that this is a "Warning" to England to unite and remove them. Just as the author of *The Establishment of the Church* argued that it was time to end Dissent, so did *The Shortest-Way*.

As important as *The Establishment* is for understanding the impetus behind *The Shortest-Way*, Defoe's major tactic was to collect the key phrases and major arguments of the High Church party and expose their true message.[25] He recognized their thrust and tried to reveal it to his contemporaries: "What's the Difference between Mr. *Sachevrel's Bloody Flag* and *De Foe's Gallows* and *Galleys*? Only, that . . . One is a Church-Phrase, and the Other a City-Comment."[26] Even those who attacked Defoe and called his pamphlet "this invenom'd Libel" admitted "the same Spirit, the same Notions, and many of the same Expressions . . . is to be found in most of the Pamphlets . . . against Occasional Communion, tho not always so palpable and gross." Another said, "His Title is a little more bald, and his Expressions a little more plan [*sic*] than those that have gone before him; but the Spirit, Notion and Application are the same."[27]

The Establishment's attack on the influence of the Dissenters, for instance, could be found in dozens of other publications. *The Case of Toleration Recogniz'd* (1702) threatened, "If the Strength of the Dissenting Interest is at present so considerable as to make it dangerous to provoke them, by imposing Sacramental Tests . . . it is a good Argument for having them . . . . And if they are not so terrible as they would make the World believe they are, it is prudent to prevent their being so."[28] Defoe's pamphlet parodies such lines: "They are not so Formidable as they have been, and 'tis our own fault if ever we suffer them to be so." Londoners heard sermon after sermon based on texts such as "Prepare slaughter for his children for the iniquity of their fathers; that they do not rise nor possess the land" (Isaiah 14:21). Defoe carefully used words and phrases like "bloody flag" that carried a hostile, aggressive message and had become a code. Typical of the phrases that had become part of a code were "crucified between thieves" (the thieves were the Dissenters and the Catholics, both enemies of the Church of England) and "vipers in the bosom" (the Dissenters who had been given too many rights and had enriched themselves hypocritically).[29] That these phrases were more than fifteen years old served Defoe's purposes well, because they demonstrated a history of hatred toward the Dissenters, linked present events to past persecution, and implicitly argued that readers should not be blinded by words.

What he had accomplished was to expose the rhetorical implications and actual desires of the Dissenters' enemies, to encourage Dissenters to speak out in a straightforward, forceful manner in their own defense, and to contribute to a more accurate assessment of the Dissenters' behavior and value in English society. A key word in understanding the debate and Defoe's objections is *nature,* the real issue behind descriptions of the Dissenters' history, behavior, and "danger" to society. Here we find the most insidious argument being used against the Dissenters. Many of the most crucial issues centered around the alleged "nature" of the Dissenters. In the 1705 *Consolidator* Defoe said explicitly that the High Church party propagated the idea that *"Dissenters* were *Rebels, Murtherers, King-killers,* Enemies to *Monarchy* and Civil Governments, lovers of Confusion, popular anarchial Governments, and movers of Sedition; that this was in their very *Nature* and *Principles"* (125). For that reason, an illuminating comparison exists between what Defoe did and what early feminists like Kate Millet and Betty Friedan did in the United States in the 1960s. In both cases, groups were being defined by what was perceived as their "nature" (women are emotional; Dissenters are rebels, factious spirits). What Defoe and these feminists did was to

—expose the "nature" issue;
—contest its validity;
—ridicule it by offering evidence to contradict it;
—make certain phrases and descriptions *verboten*;
—lead other members of their groups to insist upon more objective concepts of "nature" based upon an accurate account of their history, achievement, and value.

And they managed to do so at moments in history when they could influence legislation designed to institutionalize the handicaps that their opponents insisted their "natures" made necessary "for the good of society." By fostering an assessment by less prejudiced people, they were able to bring their actual behavior and value to society to public attention. That assessment probably stiffened the spines of members of Parliament already inclined against the bill to prevent occasional conformity.

Defoe undoubtedly hoped that *The Shortest-Way* would be the dramatic gesture that would hold a mirror up to men and bring them to a right perspective on their actions and the Dissenters' character. *Legion's Memorial* had been passionate, dramatic, and immoderate. It had brought ordinary citizens to express their agreement with the right to petition, the sense of threat to the nation from France, and the outrage over the violation of civil rights. Perhaps *The Shortest-Way* could evoke a renunciation of High Church extremism. Again, Defoe was seeing beyond the paper war and the rhetoric just as he had in *The Apparent*

Danger of an Invasion (1701), when he reminded his countrymen that a victory in the paper war and in Parliament might be a defeat in international relations. By drawing so many long-lived, key words and phrases together and keeping his pamphlet short, Defoe could expose the vengeful, irresponsible message beneath the apparently laudatory desire to protect church and state even as he demonstrated that *he* had not brought the occasional conformity debate into being. That attempt was fruitless, and Defoe continued to be attacked by the Dissenters. Once again he had "meddled," calling attention to the Dissenters and the bill. As a Dissenter, he might have brought official wrath down on his entire group.

It was easy to read Defoe's pamphlet rather literally. When done so, what was found was this: the speaker in *The Shortest-Way* addresses himself to his fellow loyal Britons and faithful members of the Church of England. He begins by characterizing the Dissenters as treacherous villains who took advantage of the Anglican Church's former Christian charity to place themselves in positions of self-serving power and who, now that the Anglican Church has returned to its rightful place and power, speak deceitfully of mercy and love to protect themselves. In particular, the speaker recounts their former "regicide" and argues that, since a clash between the Anglican Church and the Dissenters is inevitable, "'Twill be more Barbarous and Cruel to our own Children" not to "root out this cursed Race from the World." Fines will not turn Dissenters from their evil ways. Though he wishes that there were gentle methods, the speaker points out that these crimes "against the Peace and Welfare of the Nation, the Glory of God, the Good of the Church, and the Happyness of the Soul" demand appropriate punishment. To hang the ringleaders and the obstinate is the way to deal with the Dissenters: "*Let us Crucifie the Thieves.*" Years later the author of *An Impartial History of . . . Queen Anne* speculated that *The Shortest-Way* was "Designed to exasperate the Parliament against the *Non-Conformists.*" In other words, Defoe might be seen to represent the very factious spirit that Anglicans were attributing to the Dissenters. In many ways, of course, Defoe was a false target. It is always easier to attack those not in authority, and the Dissenters could revile Defoe more safely than they could the writers of Tory tracts, Anglican sermons, and parliamentary bills.

Defoe rightly saw that the debate over the bill was grounded in the Test Act and spawned by the hatred and jealousy of High Churchmen and country Tories. As he had in *A New Discovery of an Old Intreague*, *The True-Born Englishman*, and *The Pacificator*, Defoe perceived chauvinism and Jacobitism behind the scenes. *The Shortest-Way* is spoken by an anti-Revolution man:

And now they find their Day is over . . . and the Throne of this Nation possest by a Royal, *English*, True . . . Friend to the Church of *England*. (115-16)

where has been the Mercy . . . the Charity you have shewn to *tender Consciences of the Church* of *England*, that cou'd not . . . swear to your new *Hodge-podge of a Dutch-Government*. (116)

Sacheverell had tapped the same resentment of loss of political power: "*Comprehension* . . . would Introduce an *Heterogeneous* Breed of *Forreigners* into Both [Church and State] . . . and Drive *the Good Old Natives* out of All" (53).

Defoe even begins with a "text" for his mock sermon chosen from Sir Roger L'Estrange, not the Bible. It was Sir Roger who had persecuted and hounded the Dissenters, including Richard Baxter, in the 1680s when L'Estrange was Surveyor of the Press. By such tactics, Defoe hoped to expose the roots and motives of the persecutors of the Dissenters and bring them under the disapprobation and ridicule of his contemporaries.[30]

Charles Leslie, a journalistic enemy, wrote that he knew of no one who thought a Whig wrote *The Shortest-Way* and told how various High Churchmen were rumored to be the author. It delighted the same people who appreciated the hard line in *The Political Union* and *The Establishment of the Church*.[31] Both *The New Association, Part II* (1703) and *The Review and Observator Review'd* (1706) insisted that no one thought that a Whig or a Dissenter could have written it. John Oldmixon told how it met with Tory "Applause in our two Famous Universities" and was put beside the Bible by a Cambridge man. Lampoons laughed at the Church that had "unknowing your vile *Pamphlet* patroniz'd." The *Observator* called it "a System of the *High-Flyers Divinity* and *Politicks*" and said "herein those People are drawn to the Life." By some accounts, Defoe had the satisfaction of seeing Anglicans treated as Dissenters had been: "it stirred up the common people to that degree that the clergy were insulted in the streets and on the highways, and were in danger of being mobbed all over the nation." William King wrote that *The Shortest-Way* led "a great many well-meaning people" to believe that High Church persecution was a 'reality, "to pity" the Dissenters, and "to side in some measure with the moderate men."[32]

Had Defoe attacked the bill itself, such a result could not have occurred. In a sense Defoe put his work outside the pamphlet controversy, just as he had by locating *Legion's Memorial* outside the standing army debate. This time, however, the signals were not clear because he did not select an outside generic form such as petition. His readers classified *The Shortest-Way* as inside the controversy over the bill and assigned it to the only side such classification allowed. That is why no one thought a Whig had written the pamphlet, and why Leslie and his friends could try to guess which High Churchman had done so.

The situation was out of control. Defoe had imitated the code of the High Church too well, and, for a brief period, they quoted his anonymous pamphlet as they had Sacheverell, and the Dissenters were truly alarmed. Many, however, saw the extremism and repudiated *The Shortest-Way*—and those sermons and pamphlets like it. The pamphlet sparked a controversy about its intentions and intensified the public debate over the bill before Parliament and the treatment of the Dissenters. Some thought it was designed to give support to the bill. Defoe was known to oppose occasional conformity. If taken literally (as it had been), men might be persuaded by his arguments as they might by Sacheverell's. If understood as ironic, and if his authorship were known, men might be exasperated with the Dissenters and vote for the bill. Opinion was unanimous that the author had gone too far. Once his authorship was known, even the Whigs and Defoe's former friends thought so. The *Observator* said it was "Villany" to impose "Falshoods and Shams" on others. John Dunton accused him of teaching "us the SHORT DOCTRINE of Fire and Faggot." Many pointed out that the pamphlet raised "Jealousies and Mistrusts between Sovereign and Subject" and between the queen's "Protestant Children": the "extravagant passages of this invenom'd Libel . . . set the Nation in a Flame."

The reaction of the Dissenters surprised Defoe. He considered them the typical "initiated" in-group for whom the satire would speak and to whom meaning and method would be immediately clear. Numerous people noted that the author had grievously insulted the queen—even as he stated the position she had put herself in: "Our *Predicating Hosier* . . . [says] She must *break Her Promise to one Party* or other." To uphold the Toleration* and advance the desires of the High Church party with zeal did seem to be mutually exclusive.[33] The press asked, "If this be not blowing the Trumpet of Sedition . . . What is an Incendiary?"

When Robert Harley, as speaker of the House, persuaded the lord treasurer, Sidney Godolphin, on 14 December that the author of *The Shortest-Way* had to be discovered, no one suspected Defoe. Harley saw that the pamphlet reflected negatively on the Commons, criticized their work, and made their deliberations the subject of public discussion and controversy. On 29 December, however, Daniel Finch, second earl of Nottingham, the secretary of state for the Southern region, whom Godolphin had charged with arresting the writer of the pamphlet, issued a warrant for Edward Bellamy and by 2 January had him in custody. Bellamy was "the [Whig] Parties Agent" according to contemporary periodicals,[34] and he admitted taking Defoe's manuscript to

*The Act of Toleration guaranteed the Dissenters freedom of religion.

George Croome, the printer. The next day, Nottingham issued a warrant for Defoe's arrest with two unusual provisos—the queen's messenger, Henry Allen, was to take a constable with him, and, once apprehended, Defoe was to be brought before Nottingham himself for questioning. In the meantime Defoe's papers were to be seized and brought to Nottingham for examination.

By this time Defoe knew he was a hunted man. He eluded the messenger sent to arrest him and sent his wife to talk to Nottingham. When she reported Nottingham's cold repetition of "Let him surrender," he wrote to Nottingham. Defoe's letter reveals a great deal about him. He was completely unwilling to surrender and bargained with the Secretary of State as though he were a Cornhill shopkeeper. He asked Nottingham to write his questions down and send them to his house for him to answer. He offered to serve a year or more as a volunteer in a troop of horse in the Netherlands or, in a statement that testifies to his recovered prosperity, if granted a full pardon, to raise an entire troop of horse at his own expense and command it. So much for a guilty plea, so much more offered for a pardon.

Defoe's conception of what might lie ahead was penetrating. He speaks with dread of "the hardships of a Prison," "a Mind Impatient of Confinement," the prospect of transportation, and the ignominy of whippings and the pillory.[35] Only a few months before, another pamphleteer, William Fuller, had been sentenced to the pillory three times, to hard labor and correction in Bridewell prison until the next court term, to pay a fine of 1,000 marks and to remain in prison until it was paid. It was public knowledge that Fuller had been pelted with rotten eggs, dirt, and other things in the pillory and had received thirty-nine lashes on his first day in Bridewell. Defoe knew, too, that a man named Anderton had been executed for a seditious libel. Surely the experience of Thomas DeLaune contributed to his apprehension. In 1682 DeLaune's *Plea for the Non-Conformists* had been confiscated, then burned by the common hangman; Delaune had been convicted of seditious libel, and, with his wife and two children, died in Newgate because he could not pay his fine. Defoe knew the story and Delaune's book well; in 1706 he would write a preface to a new edition in which he called DeLaune a martyr to the faith and a monument to Dissenting ingratitude as well as to High Church persecution. The same messenger had even apprehended both. In 1686 Defoe had probably seen Samuel Johnson (not the later "Dictionary" Johnson, but the clergyman [1649–1703]) whipped at the cart for two seditious libels. Popular opinion was that Johnson had "suffered for the Protestant religion"; in prison, Johnson had been incoherent for three days after the whipping and then developed a fever. Now Defoe was being described in the same extreme terms as these men had been, and his part in Monmouth's rebellion was widely publicized. People saw Defoe's act, like Fuller's, to be unnatural, ingenious beyond the probable, perhaps even "inspired by Hell."[36]

The day after Defoe wrote his letter, the first of two advertisements offering a reward for "whoever shall discover [Defoe] . . . so as he may be apprehended" appeared in the official paper, the London Gazette. The reward was £50; rewards for detection of authors of seditious libels averaged between £20 and £50, and £50 was a notable sum for a pamphleteer when one considers that £100 was more than enough to lead a middle-class life in London for a year. It was unusual enough that Luttrell commented on it. Usually the reward was paid only upon the conviction of the author, not merely upon his discovery, as Defoe's reward would be.[37] The second notice appeared on 14 January and is the longest description we have of Defoe: "He is a middled siz'd spare man, about forty years old, of a brown complexion, and dark brown-coloured hair, but wears a wig; a hooked nose, a sharp chin, grey eyes, and a large mole near his mouth." Numerous satiric prints of the period exaggerate the nose and mole, and evidence from his grave tells us Defoe was about 5′4″ (the exact average height in 1700) and had a heavy jawbone. Dunton warned Defoe that he would soon be caught, because his chin, mole, and Roman nose were so distinctive.[38]

The advertisements include another interesting feature. In the first notice, he was "Daniel de Fooe" and "Daniel Fooe;" in the second, "Daniel de Foe alias de Fooe." How completely he had become "Daniel de Foe" rather than Daniel Foe, James's son, is clear from this ad. He would be recognized by that name, not "Foe." It seems clear that Defoe himself used "De Foe" almost exclusively by 1695, and it is not surprising that the criminal records of 1703 reflect the change. A survey of legal and quasi-legal entries from 1695 show great consistency. The 3 October 1695 Post-Boy lists "Mr. D. De Foe" as a manager-trustee of Neale's lottery; the 1695 entry of payments to accountants of the glass duty as "Daniel de Foe," and the May 1696 proposal to Christ's Hospital calls him "Defoe." His signature as seen on the Christ's Hospital document spells out "Daniel" and has a second "D" connected by the top of the letter's loop to "Foe." Defoe consistently signed what published works he did not publish anonymously with a "D.F." or, later, "By the Author of The True-Born Englishman."[39] It seems he took the name in business transactions before he used it on literary works.

Nottingham worked steadily on the case. On 14 January he ordered Henry Allen "or any other of her Majesty's Messengers in ordinary" to search George Croome's house and print shop for the manuscript of The Shortest-Way. All printed copies of the pamphlet were to be seized and marked "Sheet by Sheet."[40] The next day Nottingham ordered the arrest of the printer, George Croome, to give evidence against "Daniel

Deufoe" "ffor publishing a Scandalous Booke." On 15 January Croome was released after giving information and arranging a recognizance of £80, which bound him to appear in evidence against Defoe.[41] On 24 February Defoe was indicted in the Justice Hall in the Old Bailey; on the twenty-fifth, the House of Commons lodged a formal complaint against *The Shortest-Way with the Dissenters*.

Neither charge treated *The Shortest-Way* as irony or parody. The Commons objected that Defoe had failed to treat Parliament with respect and had infringed upon its privileges. Defoe was indicted at the Old Bailey for scheming to deny Dissenters religious toleration; the affidavits that would bring Defoe to trial there were signed by Bellamy, George Croome, and Robert Stephens, the queen's messenger. Bellamy and Croome may have felt they had no choice; both could have been prosecuted had they refused to comply with Nottingham, for the law read, "'tho printing be a trade, and selling of books also, they must use their trade according to law, and not abuse it, by printing or selling of books scandalous to the Government or tending to sedition." Under the law of the time, "contriver, procurer, and publisher" were all guilty. Bellamy's and Croome's situations are clear from entries in the Oyer and Terminer Sessions files; both were released provided they would "personally appear . . . & give evidence ag: Daniel de Foe for having writt a Scandalous Pamphlet."[42] In 1706 William Pittis's printer would be fined £200, brought to all of the courts in Westminster with a paper on his head noting his crime, and kept in prison until his fine was paid and he could give security for his good behavior for two years (*London Gazette*, 29 April).

A complaint in the House of Commons charged that *The Shortest-Way with the Dissenters* was "full of false and scandalous Reflections upon this Parliament" and tended to "promote sedition." Already concerned about their privileges and prerogatives,[43] M.P.'s chiefly objected to Defoe's portrayal of their conduct and sentiments. Among the passages cited as offensive were those implying that they were failing to execute laws meant to guarantee the Toleration Act; one read "the Face of Affairs have receiv'd such a Turn in the process of a few Months" (130). Most serious were those that suggested that the Protestant succession was threatened. "The Crowns of these Kingdoms have not so far disowned the right of Succession, but they may retrieve it again," Defoe's speaker boasted (121), but warns the audience that unless the Dissenters are eliminated the succession "has but a dark Prospect" and "our Future Princes. . . . will be Foreigners" (131).

On 25 February the House found the pamphlet a reflection on Parliament "tending to promote Sedition" and ordered it to be burned by the common hangman in the New Palace Yard, Westminster, and that "the Sheriffs of *London* and *Middlesex* do assist the Serjeant at Arms, attending this House, to see the same done." The *English Post* for 1 March reported that it was, in fact, burned on 26 February as a "seditious Libel."[44]

Significantly, the charge at the Old Bailey is different and, although excerpts from eight pages of *The Shortest-Way* are quoted in the indictment, not one of the folios to which the Commons objected is included. The Old Bailey indictment reads in part:

de Foe . . . being a Seditious man and of a disordered mind, and a person of bad name, reputation and Conversation, by a disgraceful felony perfidiously, mischievously and seditiously contriving, practicing and purposing to make and Cause discord between . . . the Queen and her . . . Subjects, and to Disunite and set at variance the Protestant Subjects of . . . the Queen, and to alarm All her Protestant Subjects Dissenting from the Church of England with the Fear of being deprived of the Exemption . . . in the . . . Act, and to persuade All the English people Conforming to the Church of England to procure the destruction of the same Protestant Subjects . . . Dissenting from the Church of England, and to prevent the union of the said Kingdoms of England and Scotland, The same Daniel on the same Twenty Second day of December . . . For the fulfilment and completion of his most vile machinations, practices and purposes, and to bring about these ends, A Certain criminal document, a Seditious, pernicious and Diabolical Libel Entitled *The Shortest Way* . . . Wrote, Composed and Printed. . . .[45]

Specifically Defoe had published "to the most evil Example of All those in like Case offending, and Against the peace of our said Lady the present Queen, her Crown and Dignity, etc." Most of the passages quoted described the behavior of the "Protestant Subjects." These passages were intended to show what alarmed the Dissenters: "But to answer *this Cavil more effectually*: Her Majesty did never promise to maintain the Tolleration, to the Destruction of the Church," (124) and what might "persuade" Anglicans "to procure the destruction" of the Dissenters: "We have been huff'd and bully'd with your Act of Tolleration; you . . . have set up your Canting Synagogues at our Churchdoors" (116).

When Defoe did not appear at the next sessions at the Old Bailey on 12 May, the attorney general began outlawry proceedings. Conviction for outlawry meant "loss of the benefit of a subject"; it was defined as "refusing to be amenable to . . . justice," "a crime of the highest nature, being an act of rebellion . . . so it subjects the party to forfeitures and disabilities." Although the terminology and the penalties were horrifying, by the eighteenth century outlawry was no more than a process to compel an appearance, because it had become easily superseded or reversed and was even bailable.[46]

Defoe continued his efforts to make terms with the government. He wrote to William Paterson, the projector and co-founder of the Bank of England, in April. In that letter, he mentions "Some Other Applications" made after his letter to Nottingham and repeats his suggestions for making reparations. Defoe's real reason for writing Paterson was to persuade him to intercede with Robert Harley in Defoe's behalf. Paterson had clearly talked to Defoe earlier about introducing the two men. Paterson was a Scot, a devout Presbyterian, and took great pride in calling himself a "merchant in London." He and Defoe had probably met around the court, city, and in coffeehouses. Defoe's *An Essay upon Projects* shows his familiarity with Paterson's work, and Paterson's respect for Defoe's can be seen in his 1703 proposal for a library on "Trade, Revenue, Navigation, &c.," in which he included a number of Defoe's publications, among them *An Essay upon Projects, The Poor Man's Plea, Reasons against a War with France*, and *The Villainy of Stock-Jobbers*.[47]

Defoe was finally caught on 21 May at the house of a Spittlefields weaver. According to the 21–24 *London Post*, two messengers seized him; the *Post Man* for 22–25 May reported that Defoe was questioned from Thursday to Saturday before being sent to Newgate under close guard. An informer who did "not care to appear himself" received the £50 reward through Thomas Armstrong, a member of Buckingham's staff.[48]

CHAPTER 6

PRISON

*He that has Truth on his Side, is a fool, as well as a Coward, if he is
afraid to own it because of the Currency or Multitude of other
Mens Opinions.*

> —DEFOE, *An Enquiry into the Occasional
> Conformity of Dissenters* (1702)

*Alas, Poor De Foe! what hast thou been doing, and for what hast
thou suffer'd?*

> —DEFOE, *A New Test of the Church
> of England's Honesty* (1704)

Defoe spent five of the next six months in Newgate Prison. The
object of the ridicule of journalists, the subject of discussions by the
most powerful people in government, the victim of legal history and
contemporary politics, he lived in an emotional tornado. He had written to Nottingham about "a Mind Impatient of Confinement," and now
he could control almost nothing in his life. For a person accustomed to
taking initiative, exercising ingenuity, moving freely, and setting his
own course and goals, prison quickly became torture. By temperament
Defoe was an active man: every day he talked to many kinds of people
and worked at different enterprises; he loved to travel around England
on horseback; the City, Tilbury, Kingsland, Stoke Newington, Greenwich, and the other places where he sold bricks and pantiles—the
contrasts between running his factory, selling his products, talking politics with friends, and writing in solitude—how varied his days and
weeks were by any measure. Even as a fugitive from January to 21 May,
Defoe led a fairly ordinary life; his writing continued, his factory remained in operation, and he had time with his wife and family. "I Do
allready Find Tis No Very Difficult Thing for me to Get my Bread," he
wrote to William Paterson in April (H 6). His capture in May ended all
of that, and the next months are an intimate picture of Defoe's resources and of the exercise of official power.

Upon his arrest by two messengers of the queen, Defoe was taken
immediately to Nottingham. Thin, tall, swarthy, serious, and by turns

brooding or prolix, Nottingham was universally described by his contemporaries as imperious, grave, and opinionated. The duke of Norfolk praised him for his "great command of the English tongue" but noted that he was habitually "too sett and formal." He went on to point out that when the government thought it in their interest to encourage the High Church party, Nottingham was "one of the ministers employ'd to please them." It was he who had introduced the bill to prevent occasional conformity through his friend William Bromley.[1] Defoe now faced this grim man who had seized his papers, spent hours examining them, and paid others to examine them. Defoe had managed to destroy some, but Nottingham received many from the messengers. The Treasury books show expenses for several meetings "for examining the many papers and libels found in De Foe's custody."[2]

Defoe would have felt resentment as well as the fear and anxiety natural to such a meeting. Not only his papers, which may have been relevant to the case, but also his books had been taken. Richard Baxter had grieved for many years over the loss of his books to such a high-handed procedure, and one of the judges in the landmark case of Entick versus Carrington described the seizure of an author's papers by order of the secretary of state as an outrage:

It is executed against the party, before he is heard or even summoned; and the information, as well as the informers, is unknown. It is executed by messengers with or without a constable . . . in the presence or absence of the party, as the messengers shall think fit, and without a witness to testify what passes . . . so that when the papers are gone . . . the party injured is left without proof. . . . if the officer should be disposed to carry off a bank bill, he may do it with impunity, since there is no man capable of proving either the taker or the thing taken. . . . Nor is there pretence to say, that the word "papers" . . . be restrained to the libellous papers only.[3]

By all accounts, Nottingham interrogated Defoe harshly. *The Reformer Reform'd* says that Defoe was "examined . . . strictly" and told he had displeased the queen; that Nottingham "laid the matter home to him." The Saturday after his arrest Defoe was sent, heavily guarded, by coach to Newgate while Nottingham examined yet more papers seized when Defoe was captured. Newgate Prison shocked any newcomer in the way Defoe would describe its effect on Moll Flanders. In his time it was in an elegant part of London but reflected its age. Built in the time of either Henry I or King Stephen, it had strangely placed windows—some without glass or casements—many bare stone floors, and primitive, stinking facilities. Defoe was lodged in the Press Yard, the most comfortable part of the prison. For about twenty guineas he secured himself space in this well-ventilated area, a space on the eastern side with prisoner access to a passage between the prison and the wall. Even here, in a place that cost him another twelve shillings per week plus the purchase of a bed and sheets, he would have been forced into the company of felons and debtors from the Masters and even Common sides of the prison who could mingle and buy beer, brandy, and wine at the "Taphouse" until "such Wickedness abounds . . . that that Place seems to have the exact Aspect of Hell itself." Defoe shared the Press Yard with at least three other men: a murderer, a felon (crime unspecified), and "a french spy."[4]

Defoe faced Nottingham's hostile questions several more times. Some people suspected that Defoe was the "tool" of a party, faction, or powerful individual, and Nottingham intended to find out all there was to know. *The New Association, Part II* called *The Shortest-Way* "a new *Engine* of the *Faction*," and, in discussing its purposes, constantly used the plural "they": "they thought," "they contriv'd . . . to *Blacken* the *Church Party*." Oldmixon's opinion that Defoe often received help from "Men of more Brains, tho' not of so much Assurance" was shared by many people.[5] Defoe devoted most of a July letter to William Penn to insisting he had "no Accomplices, No Sett of Men, (as my Lord Call'd Them) with whom I used to Concert Matters" (H 8). Defoe was trying to prepare Penn to be an effective advocate, and the detail of his discussion of this point showed the thrust of some of Nottingham's suspicions and demands.

In fact, the ministry's concerns went well beyond that pamphlet and what help Defoe might have received. The single surviving, specific question to which Nottingham demanded an answer is in a note he wrote Godolphin on 22 July: "I askt him when his advice about dissolving the Parliament was given, and he cd not at first recollect but concluded that he verily believed 'twas before the King went into Holland."[6] Defoe was being asked to talk about his role in King William's government, to describe the advice he gave on one of the vexed issues of William's last year: should the elections of November 1701 have been called. Nottingham also tells Godolphin that Defoe "Solemnly protests he knows no more of what is past than he has told." Nottingham and the others probably hoped to learn more about a Whig inner circle than about the composition of *The Shortest-Way*.

Nottingham seems to have given up temporarily, and Defoe was released on unusually high bail on 5 June. He himself made £500 of the £1,500. The rest was made by Joseph Whitaker, a "broker," Thomas Powell, "gentleman," Nicholas Morris, baker, and Defoe's favorite brother-in-law, Robert Davis, a Tilbury shipbuilder and an associate in the Christ's Hospital plan.[7] In the brief time he was free, Defoe continued to try to bargain with Nottingham, and he seems to have believed he had succeeded, for his letter to Penn said that Nottingham had agreed to "use" him "tenderly" in exchange for a guilty plea (H 7–8).

In spite of the willingness of some of those who made his bail for him to hide again, Defoe appeared in court on the first day of the new session, 5 July, and heard the indictment. He was in no position to leave. After all, he had a family, a house with a large library, a coach, and a thriving brick and tile factory that brought him a comfortable, steady income thanks to the increase in building in London and vicinity. Over the past twelve years, Defoe had gradually been paying his creditors.[8] He was the father of six children, four daughters and two sons. His oldest child, Maria, was no more than sixteen or seventeen, and his youngest, Sophia, not yet two. All but Maria had been born since 1690, and he may already have known that his wife Mary was pregnant again. At age forty and after bearing seven children, she was unlikely to be able to move with Defoe or support the children without him.[9]

His trial opened on 7 July in a setting a visitor to London described as like the "Judgment Hall of Pilate." Visitors paid a shilling for a seat and saw "a vast concourse of people who made such a din that it was often impossible to hear either barristers or judges." The prisoners stood at the bar in front of the bench on which the lord mayor or chief magistrate sat with four assessors chosen from the twelve judges of the justice of the peace.[10] Defoe did not face friends: Lord Mayor Sir Samuel Dashwood, Sir Edward Ward, Sir John Fleet, Sir Edwin Clarke, Sir Thomas Abney, and the recorder, Sir Salathiel Lovell. Sir Thomas Abney, a Cornhill resident, was the former lord mayor who had inspired the second printing of *An Enquiry into the Occasional Conformity of Dissenters*. Sir John Fleet had been governor of the old East India Company for five years (four between 1698 and 1704), and Sir Edward Ward, lord chief baron of the Exchequer, chaired the company eight times. Both must have been touched by Defoe's satiric *The Freeholders Plea* in which he accused the East India companies of trying to buy seats in Parliament and by Defoe's criticism of the company in *An Essay upon Projects*. Sir Samuel Dashwood, one "of the most pronounced Tories in the City" whom King James had displaced as alderman in 1687 for refusing to endorse the suspension of the Corporation Act, had become a London M.P. in the disputed election of 1690, and, as a new colonel in the Lieutenancy of the City, had been made a justice of the peace for his "willingness to prosecute." Salathiel Lovell, the recorder, had been attacked in Defoe's poem *Reformation of Manners* (1702) in a long satiric portrait that included the lines, "L——l, the *Pandor* of thy Judgment-Seat, / Has neither Manners, Honesty, nor Wit."[11]

William Colepeper, one of the Kentish petitioners, acted as Defoe's counsel. An impolitic choice, Colepeper was the brother of Thomas, who had recently had a second conflict with the House of Commons. Sent to Newgate for, among other things, challenging the prerogatives of the House and promoting scandalous reflections upon it, Thomas

Colepeper's election as representative from Maidstone had been disallowed. William Colepeper himself had been assaulted in an antechamber at Windsor only a few days earlier;[12] a disputed election was
the issue there, too. Colepeper faced Sir Simon Harcourt, recently
appointed attorney general for the queen, "Socinian* Harcourt" in
Defoe's *Reformation of Manners*. Colepeper entered the guilty plea and
an appeal for mercy. Harcourt responded with an eloquent speech
elaborating on the defiance and danger in Defoe's pamphlet.

Defoe was sentenced to stand in the pillory three times, to pay a fine
of 200 marks (about £134), and to remain in Newgate until he could
"find good sureties to be of good behaviour for the space of seven years
from thence next ensuing And that he do not depart from thence and
. . . be of good behaviour with regard to our Lady the present Queen
and her populace." Although a number of sentences similar to Defoe's
(such as Fuller's) could be cited, his was unusual. Each part of it was a bit
more severe than the average handed out to journalists between 1702
and 1708. Most journalists, including John Tutchin and George Ridpath, could expect to stand in the pillory once, to pay a fine of between
60 and 100 marks, and be required to find surety of good behavior for
two years. "Fines of fifty or a hundred pounds were extracted for
particularly heinous offenses," one of the foremost modern scholars
of eighteenth-century criminal procedures states. John Tutchin, no
friend of Defoe's, reported on the trial in the *Observator* and remarked
sarcastically, "The law of *England* directs that no Man shall be Fined
Ultra Tenementum, and I make no Question, but the Justice of the Court,
has Fined Mr. Foe answerable to his Estate."[13]

"Seditious libel," the crime with which Defoe was charged, was interpreted as *publication* of a writing that "scandalized" the government,
although it was described as "the intentional publication of a writing
which reflected on the government." Historically, sedition was a form of
treason, "the crime of Judas," and "seditious libel" was always treated as
a crime rather than as a tort because it allegedly threatened the security,
stability, or peace of the state or the morals of subjects.[14]

Recent scholarship on the history of the law of seditious libel shows
that Defoe had no hope of winning, but that his case illustrates important changes in the government's attempts to control the press and
remarkably anticipates the arguments for reform in the laws made in
the late eighteenth century. Defoe was one of the first men to be prosecuted after the "momentous change in the government's use of the law
of seditious libel," "probably in 1703 under the recently crowned
Queen Anne." Chief Justice John Holt had gradually been extending
the idea of libel to include reflections, not just on individual officials,

---

*One who denied the divinity of Christ.

but on institutions such as the government. Because such "libels," "diminished the affection of the people for the king or his ministers and thereby encouraged rebellion," they were seditious.[15] At the same time, Holt ruled that the actual actionable words or "the sense and substance" of them had to be part of the indictment. This requirement meant that the jury did not decide if the document was seditious because that was considered a matter of law; when the prosecution entered objectionable passages into the indictment, they thereby brought them within the cognizance of the court and made them a matter of record rather than a matter for proof. Thus, whether or not the document was a libel was in the judge's hands. A parliamentary committee in 1792 found this procedure "the unvaried practice of ages" and "a fundamental and important principle of English jurisprudence." Judges routinely instructed juries that "they have nothing to do with the Law and must be bound by the Court's Directions." A juror at John Tutchin's trial the year after Defoe's was told, "The Question is not whether the Papers are Criminal, but whether the Defendent is the Author of the Papers." Judges consistently refused to allow jurors to see the books in question.[16] At that time, juries were allowed to determine, first, if the document had been written, "contrived," "procured," or published by the accused (and Bellamy and Croome would swear to that); second, if it had indeed appeared in print (and Stephens had seized printed copies); and, third, if it included passages "referring" or "applicable" to the "present majesty" and principal officials of state (the indictment conveniently pointed these out).

Defoe admitted he had written and caused *The Shortest-Way* to be published, but he asked for mercy because his intention was not seditious and his pamphlet presented truth ironically. Because he never intended to "stir up" the Dissenters to defend themselves or to encourage others to persecute the Dissenters more severely, *The Shortest-Way* was not seditious, he said. The "seditious" remarks (and his categories match the passages quoted in his indictment) against William, the House of Hanover, and union with Scotland are part of the "irony," the imitation of "the Cant of the Nonjuring party Expos'd," he insisted.[17]

Defoe's indictment and the summary of his trial have vestiges of the older language from other laws used to control the press. For example, he is accused of "perniciously and diabolically" publishing "without lawful Authority, with force and arms." Since the Licensing Act had expired in 1695, there was no "lawful Authority." After the passage of the Treason Trials Statute in 1696, it would have been inappropriate to prosecute Defoe for treason, the form from which the language "with force and arms" came.[18] His indictment and the court's ruling, however, conform to the use that the government would make of the law of seditious libel for the next fifty years.

At the heart of Defoe's plea was the changing philosophy of the monarch/subject relationship. The court held that the ruler was transcendent and that all criticism of her was disrespectful and threatening to her authority and, therefore, menacing the peace of the nation. Defoe was a thorough "contract-theory" man, and he saw the monarch as the delegated agent of order; in his view, it was the subject's right, even responsibility, to remind the ruler of her duty, the Constitution, and the needs of the nation. Under the court's philosophy all criticism was wrong, and publication was therefore proof of seditious, malicious intent. Publication was always described as done "falsely, seditiously, maliciously, and factiously," the words Defoe complained of as "all the Adverbs" "and a Long Rapsody of . . . et Ceteras."[19] According to Defoe's interpretation of the monarch/subject relationship, there was no such offense as sedition, although incitement to riot or breach of peace was possible. When Defoe argued in 1703 that his *intention* was to expose High Church extremism, not cause unrest, he made no defense at all, because he did not address the prosecution's conception of his action.

Under the court's philosophy truth was not an issue at all. As William Bohun wrote in 1732: "It matters not whether the Thing should be true or false in a Libel. The Offense consists . . . in the Contriving . . . or in the malicious Publication." *Any* criticism, real or implied, anything that embarrassed or had the potential to embarrass the government or its officials (and bishops could be seen as "officials" since they were appointed by the monarch), was seditious libel. Delaune had argued that his only crime had been his candor and had demanded to know if "Truth be made a *Crime*." He had gone on to ask, "Ought not a Jury before they bring in their Verdict upon Oath . . . Examine and have sufficient Proof to make good those Luxuriant Cut-throat forms?" The judge responded that the "forms" were the standard words always used in such indictments and reminded the jury of their proper responsibility.[20] "Truth" was completely irrelevant to judge and jury; what mattered was possible effect and respect for the government.

In 1721 Defoe complained that no law or act of Parliament defined "libel," and, therefore, an author could not know if he were guilty or not. He called upon other writers and printers to ask for a bill to determine what a libel was under the existing statute and how it would be punished. He accurately described the situation when he summarized his experience by implication in a 1704 pamphlet on a proposed act of Parliament for the regulation of the press:

[The properest Method would be so] all Men will know when they Transgress, which at present, they do not; for as the Case now stands, 'tis in the Breast of the Courts of Justice to make any Book a Scandalous and Seditious Libel, and nothing is more ridiculous than the Letter of an Indictment in such Cases, and the Jury being accounted only Judges of Evidence, Judges of Fact, and not of the Nature of it, the Judges are thereby Unlimited.

As late as 1771 the situation was unchanged. H. S. Woodfall wrote in *A Summary of the Law of Libel* that libel was "a Crime which, is agreed to be undefinable, for it may arise from a Multitude of variable Circumstances, and no particular Words constitute it."[21]

In his own time and ours, Defoe's guilty plea has been criticized, yet history shows that it probably made little difference to the outcome. In fact, some evidence suggests that those whom juries convicted after a plea of not guilty received harsher sentences. In any event, the result of Defoe's trial was similar to those that went before a jury. For example, the next year, John Tutchin was tried for a similar offense. Lord Chief Justice Holt gave a charge to the jury that included an explanation of "the nature and consequences of such Libelous and Scandalous Papers, and what evil Effects such Libels might produce." After that, it took only fifteen minutes to find Tutchin guilty. Holt then chided Tutchin, "This is a very strange doctrine to say it is not a libel reflecting on the government, endeavouring to possess the people that the government is maladministered. . . . To say that corrupt officers are appointed . . . is certainly a reflection on the government. . . . nothing can be worse to any government than to endeavour to procure animosities as to the management of it."[22] Defoe did not seem to believe he had made a foolish mistake by pleading guilty. Years later he explained seditious libel in *Applebee's Journal* with a clear understanding of the jury's and the judges' purviews.

Harcourt received £87, a sum comparable only to that paid in state trials, for his work at the trial of "the scribbler" Defoe.[23] In fact, Defoe's prosecution was one of the most expensive in Anne's reign. In addition to the £50 reward, Harcourt's £87, and the money to be paid for Defoe's release, William Borrett, solicitor of the Treasury, submitted vouchers for £42.7.4 and requests for additional sums for "Sundry contingencies" "for which Vouchers have not been usually taken or required" amounting to approximately £12. In comparison, Borrett had vouchers in the following amounts for other libel prosecutions:

Crossfield: £14.16.10	Drake: £13.8.6
Dyer: £17.14.6	Edwards: £9.9.4.

The sum for John Tutchin, whose trial is included in all editions of *State Trials*, and, therefore, might be expected to be more expensive, was only £9.16.4. Fees for such things as drawing up indictments and affidavits for Tutchin were £2.8s. and, for Edwards, £2.11s. For Defoe, they were £3.16s. with an additional 9s. 6d. for the outlawry proceedings.

Moreover, Borrett had other categories that were given without breakdown for individual cases; for instance, in the year running from October 1702 to October 1703 (and, therefore, including all expenses for Defoe's arrest and prosecution), he spent over £30 for warrants, messengers, and searches. Thomas Atterbury, then clerk of the Cheque, received £5.15.8 for messengers and other expenses associated with Defoe's and only two other cases. Robert Stephens received a regular salary and expenses amounting to £49. Nottingham had a budget of £2,000 for Secret Service and, throughout the year, received additional grants of £50 to £150 from Borrett's account.[24]

Defoe was to stand in the pillory in Cornhill by the Royal Exchange on 19 July. This pillory was in the heart of the neighborhood in which he had grown up and reared his own children; in fact, it was almost within sight of his Freeman's Yard house and warehouse. The sentence seems to have been intended to intimidate Defoe into revealing his "Accomplices." Such tactics were familiar; the Dissenting alderman Henry Cornish was "spitefully" hanged at the end of King's Street, Cheapside, "facing his own house," in 1685, and the Dissenting minister Thomas Venner in 1661 in front of his own meeting house.[25] Defoe was examined by the Privy Council again before 12 July and again insisted he "really had No Person to Discover." Returned to the Press Yard and lodged with at least four other men, Defoe received a visit from William Penn's son William who offered him a proposal from Nottingham. Defoe made efforts of his own to avoid punishment. He sent Colepeper to Windsor with a petition for Nottingham on the eleventh. He asked three prominent Dissenting ministers to pray with him in Newgate, including John How and his co-pastor John Spademan; in addition to remembering How's part in the pamphlet exchange over occasional conformity, Defoe may have thought that they could help reconcile him to the Dissenters. Both How and the third, Robert Fleming, pastor of the Scots Church, Founders Hall, and a man with influence with King William, had preached at Salters' Hall before the Society for the Reformation of Manners where Defoe and many others heard them. Defoe may also have been challenging them; How, at least, avoided confrontation with the authorities to the point of near-cowardice. Several other ministers, for instance, had deplored How's refusal to ordain men in the 1680s; Annesley had performed the services he refused to conduct.[26]

Defoe seized upon Penn's visit to write to his famous father, a self-appointed advocate for Nonconformists in two reigns. Penn himself had been imprisoned several times, once for seven months in the Tower. However, he had been one of the Dissenters courted by King James upon his accession and soon thereafter appeared at court daily. Dissenters and others began to apply to him to be their advocate at court;

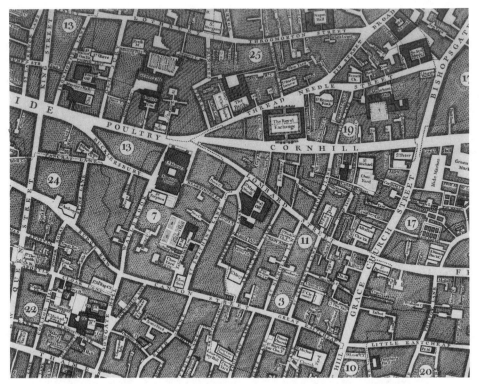

Defoe stood in the pillory in front of the Royal Exchange, Cornhill; his home
and warehouse are but a short distance to the right, off Freeman's Court, the
small street between the Exchange and the number 19.

sometimes 200 people waited outside his home. Penn was no intimate
of King William's, but upon Queen Anne's accession returned to court.
He had known Anne since her girlhood, and they resumed the friendship shared when he had visited her father.[27] Penn again took up the
causes of Dissenters in legal difficulties, and Defoe's case might have
had special appeal to him. Unbeknown to Defoe, Penn had recommended *The True-Born Englishman* to friends in 1701. Penn, too, had
published during the occasional conformity controversy. His *Considerations on the Bill Depending, for Preventing Occasional Conformity* had made
many of Defoe's favorite points, including that such a bill "infringe[d]"
upon the Act of Toleration and was "an unmerited Reflection" on the
Dissenters.[28] Penn also saw the special persecution designed for City
men: "As we are Free-men of Corporations, and Members of Companies, by the Terms of Admission, we are bound to do in our Course
the several Duties thereof; which by this Bill, we are not only rendred

incapable of, but also subject to Fines and Penalties for not doing them" (2). Penn was, however, friendly with a number of the members of the inner circle at court and may have agreed to help them find out what Defoe knew.

Defoe wrote to Penn with two purposes in mind: to explain his position and to ask "the Continuance of those Kind Offices you have So Generously undertaken for An Unknown Captive." He was quick to point out that Nottingham's proposal "of Discovering Partyes is the same which his Lordship has often Put upon me before" and that he was, in effect, being asked to "Accuse my Friends for the Freedome of Private Conversation" (H 8).

The queen herself was informed of Defoe's case on a nearly day-by-day basis. On 17 July Godolphin wrote Nottingham to tell him that William Penn had told him and the lord privy seal (John Sheffield, duke of Buckingham) that "de Foe was ready to make oath to your Lp. of all that he knew, & to give an Account of all his Accomplices in whatsoever he has been Concerned . . . provided . . . he may bee excused from the punishment of the pillory, & not produced as an Evidence against any person whatsoever."[29] It was a powerful sign of what the pillory meant that that was the punishment Defoe wanted remitted. Since the time of Wihtred, king of Kent and legal reformer, in the seventh century, the pillory had been a public means of "degradation" for cheats and tricksters. Among the offenses that sent men to the pillory in Anglo-Saxon times had been selling spoiled food, loading dice, borrowing a child with whom to beg, telling lies about people, and keeping dishonest scales. In Defoe's time the courts added perjurors, homosexuals, and rioters as frequent sufferers of the punishment. The pillory was to "stigmatize and dishonor and to mark out an offender as unworthy of trust or respect." As someone said in 1730, by making the criminal notorious and familiar, he would be marked "as a person not fit to be trusted, but to be shunned and avoided by all credible and honest men." The press used phrases such as "render'd *infamous* by *Law*" and "he is to undergo" the punishment. Judges often heeded a jury's recommendation for "the Favour of the Court" by sentencing all of the offenders in a case to the same penalties but commuting the pillory for the one shown favor. Prisoners occasionally begged on their knees to be excused from the pillory. It was, then, seen as a greater penalty than imprisonment or large fines. Pilloried men lost their right to vote and to serve on juries.[30]

The queen ordered a meeting of the Privy Council at Windsor for 18 July. On the eighteenth, Penn sent a note to "Noble Friend" (probably Buckingham) with an enclosure for Godolphin asking that Defoe's sentence "be deferr'd if not pardon'd" so Godolphin could be at the council's questioning of Defoe.[31] Nottingham deferred the sentence to

23 July and sent to Newgate for Defoe. The keeper told him Defoe could not be taken out of London because that would technically be "an escape," "a discharge of his Fine," and Defoe could not be compelled to go back to prison. On 20 July Nottingham asked Sir Nathan Wright, keeper of the Great Seal, for a writ of habeas corpus to bring Defoe to Windsor. He grumbled that to do so looked bad, like a personal convenience for himself, but it was "in many respects . . . best for the Queen's service."[32]

Defoe's appearance on 21 July at Windsor simply exasperated the queen. Defoe probably believed he could explain his actions, apologize, and show he had simply talked to private friends. Nottingham wrote Godolphin at Windsor: "De Fooe has bin with me & Solemnly protests he knows no more of what is past than he has told, and that he will by his future carriage endeavour to deserve her Majesty's favour. My Ld P[rivy] S[eal] would not speak with him again thinking it to no purpose, So I have had him alone with me & all is reduced to what I have mentioned." Godolphin described the queen's reaction: "As to *de Foe*, the Queen seems to think, as she did upon your Lps. first acquainting her with what he said, that his Confession amounts to nothing." So angry was she that she was prepared to let him stand in the pillory on the twenty-third, but left the matter up to the Lords of the Committee. As Nottingham wrote to Godolphin, the committee did not meet until 11:00 "which is always 12 at Soonest." He therefore instructed Sir Robert Bedingfield, one of the sheriffs of London:

You may expect Her Majesty's orders concerning Mr Fooe this morning but I doubt not time enough to prevent his Standing in the pillory to day if that should be her Majesty's resolution, and therefore unless you hear from me again this morning, you will do well not to execute this Sentence till Monday, by which time I shall acquaint you with her Majesty's finall determination.[33]

Nottingham and Buckingham went to Newgate to remonstrate with Defoe once more. Defoe was either unwilling or unable to satisfy them regarding his intentions and collaborators, and, on 27 July, Nottingham wrote to the sheriff: "Her Majesty does not think fitt to delay any longer the execution of the Sentence upon Mr Fooe."[34]

The end of July 1703 was not one of the best times to stand in the pillory. Three times he stood, most likely in a steady rain, in the pillory at noon in the busiest parts of London. John Evelyn remarked that "so greate & long continual Raine, as had not ben know[n] of late years" fell that day and through the end of the month (5:543). Held in the unnatural, helpless position of the pillory, the criminal's neck ached and his arms went numb. He could not wipe the water off his face or tighten his collar against the rain. Even when not particularly unpopular or guilty of a heinous crime, the criminal was a nearly irresistible target for rotten fruit, eggs, stones, dirt clods, and other refuse from the street. Offenders had had their clothes stripped off or had choked on thrown mud. Everyone could remember criminals maimed for life, and a few had been killed. Thomas Hood recalled that "a Chinaman" had paid twopence for a pipkin (a small pot or pan) to throw at him when he stood in the pillory. Hood objected to the rotten eggs most and observed that the hour was chosen "out of consideration to the innocent little urchins then let out of school, for they are a race notoriously fond of shying, pitching, . . . pelting, flinging." William Fuller, pilloried the same month as Defoe, found the pillory worse than the Bridewell whipping: "Never was Man amongst *Turks* or Barbarians known to be worse used. . . . I was stifled with all manner of Dirt, Filth, and rotten Eggs; and my Left Eye was so bruised with a Stone . . . [that] I fell down . . . and hung by the Neck. . . . I was all over bruised from Head to Heel; and on the small of my Back, as I stood stooping, a Stone struck me, which . . . weigh[ed] more than six Pounds." Hood recalled being hit by "dead kittens . . . [and] living curs" that clawed his face.[35]

By the time he stood in the pillory, everyone knew Defoe and his story. He had gone from Luttrell's unknown "La Foe" for whom a large reward had been offered by proclamation to "Daniel Foe, author" who had been examined, personally, in Newgate by Nottingham and Buckingham.[36] By all accounts, Defoe's pillory was ringed with protectors, and the only things thrown at him were flowers. Probably Defoe was protected by "the rabble," as contemporary journalists said. *Heraclitus Ridens* described "Scum" as surrounding the pillory: "His Friends, the Worthy Citizens of *London* . . . Hallow'd him down from his Wooden Punishment, as if he had been a *Cicero*." *The True-Born-Hugonot* complained that "shouting Crouds their Advocate proclaim" but said, "Nor shall his *City* Friends protect him" in the aftermath of the pillory. Others, like Charles Leslie, saw party money behind the crowd and the hawking of Defoe's books at the pillory.[37] The "scum" would have been the men most sympathetic to tracts such as *The Poor Man's Plea*, the most scandalized at the vices of the rich and the abuses of recent elections, and the first to agree with the portrait of Salathiel Lovell, who "never hangs the Rich nor saves the Poor." They had probably been delighted with *Legion's Memorial* and impressed with Defoe's behavior in Newgate. He had never brought trouble and unwanted attention on them.

A Hymn to the Pillory, one of the best poems Defoe ever wrote, was carefully composed to cultivate the ideas that Defoe was the victim of injustice and that the legal system largely ignored the transgressions of the rich. It was handed out as Defoe stood on the scaffold. The cramped, vulnerable position of the pillory, the rain, and the notoriety failed to break Defoe's spirit. Description after description echoes Alexander Pope's "unabashed on high," and Defoe never stopped insisting that an injustice had been committed. Four years later he wrote, "Would any Man in *England* but be satisfied, *however dear a cost*, that he wrote that Book. . . . Blush then, ye Tyrants of the Party, that sacrifiz'd the Man to the Lust of your Revenge" (*Review* 4:533–34).

Ugly rumors persisted that Defoe had offered to become a political writer for the men in power, that he had confessed, and that his defiant distribution of *A Hymn to the Pillory* while on the scaffold belied months of petitioning and begging. For example, *The True-Born-Hugonot* asks Defoe to explain, "How those are *Guiltless* that could *Guilty Plead*, / And ne're *Confess'd* that have *Confessions*, made"(18).

༄

Unless truly extraordinary measures were taken, Defoe had no choice but to spend the next few months in Newgate. He could not appear with sureties for his good behavior until the next session of court, which would be in October. His family had to move in with the Tuffleys again.[38] Defoe's chief debt in 1703 was the £1,050 owed to Maresco, Stamper, and Ghiselyn, but he owed money to other people as well. For instance, since his bankruptcy, he had lost a suit to Francis Annesley and become involved in a dispute with Paul Whitehurst over "small and strong drink" for the Tilbury workers. These cases show that Defoe remained less than scrupulous, continued to "borrow from Peter to pay Paul," and cast doubt on his assertion that he paid most of his creditors back in full. Since 1698, as executor of the estate of Chidley Brooke, Annesley had been attempting to collect the amount of a bond Defoe had signed on 30 July 1697, plus the penal sum now due. Defoe had instructed Annesley to draw the sum from his property allegedly held by Matthew Clarkson. In a suit in the Court of the Mayor of New York, Clarkson proved he did not owe that much to Defoe. Some time after that Defoe denied owing Brooke the money. Defoe was finally arrested for failure to appear and taken before Justice John Blencowe on 20 May 1702. An entry in the Fleet Prison commitment book reads, "Dan ffoe before Mr. Justice Blenco to Moore spirited away by ff[rancis] Southard and Mottershed." Southard was a constable or bailiff and often delivered notice of court actions to Moore who may have been a keeper for the Fleet or another prison. Adam Mottershed was Defoe's attorney. On 20 November 1702 Defoe was ordered to pay Annesley £236 and £5 damages. In the summer of 1703 Defoe told a familiar story of "differing accounts" and asked that a Chancery suit brought against him by his factory clerk Paul Whitehurst be dismissed. In his answer Defoe insisted that he should be allowed to settle claims made by Chapman, the man from whom Whitehurst had purchased the drinks. Chapman insisted that the Essex works owed him £53. 6s.[39]

In 1703, however, no one secured new contracts for the factory, suppliers feared he could not pay them, and the season for brick making continued without him. Around London workers began in late April to turn over the clay for the paste that would temper in pits through the next winter and to process the tempered clay from the past year. Defoe's workers continued to lack supervision in the critical months between March and September when bricks were molded, dried, and heated and slaked in clamps and when pantiles were made from kneaded, sieved, and precipitated clay. The process was particularly complicated in the area of Defoe's factory, for the clay had to be mixed with pulverized chalk ground to the consistency of cream. In the fall when the earth for the next year's bricks should have been dug, Defoe was in prison.[40] He employed more than a hundred workers, and the fact that he made a good profit indicates the size of his operation, for pantiles sold for fifty shillings a thousand. He lost the brick and tile factory, and, by the time he was released, feared he would need not less than £1,000 to satisfy his creditors (H 16).

During these three months, Defoe began to feel deserted and to lose hope. He had written to William Paterson asking him to intercede with Robert Harley in April; Paterson sent the letter on to Harley on 28 May. Paterson himself was making a case for his own employment rather than Defoe's during the summer. Harley had sent a man to Defoe in July who delivered the message, "Pray ask . . . what I can do for him?" Defoe replied with a letter that he later compared to the biblical quotation, "Lord, doest thou see that I am blind, and yet ask me what thou shalt do for me?" (Mark 10:51–52).[41]

Now Defoe heard nothing at all, and he surely knew that his wife was pregnant. After the excitement and triumph of his pillory experience, he had nothing to anticipate and no date set for his release. The resources of his family and closest friends probably went to support his wife and children; his brother-in-law Robert Davis's security was also threatened by Defoe's imprisonment. Davis was a shipbuilder in Tilbury and probably used Defoe's wharf. As Defoe had protested, he worked for no party and had no "accomplices," and so there was no one obligated or grateful enough to pay his fine; surety for the seven years' good conduct had not even been set. His own charges in Newgate probably amounted to six shillings a day, a sum considered so burdensome that City livery companies regularly contributed candles, firewood, and food to the prisoners.[42] And the Dissenters turned their backs on him. In *An Essay upon Projects*, Defoe had observed a man reduced by his "Errors" "to be absolutely without Three things, *Money*, *Friends*, and *Health*, he Dies in a Ditch, or in some worse place" (31). "Dies in a Ditch" was Defoe's metaphor for giving up, succumbing to a situation, and, at that time, he felt close to being without all three.

No matter how forgotten he felt, Defoe was still a very special prisoner. The dialogue about Defoe continued at court. On the thirteenth, less than two weeks after Defoe's third day in the pillory, Robert Harley received a letter from Godolphin: "I thank you for the hints about Scotland. DeFoe would be the properest person in the world for that transaction." Godolphin wondered if "the rigour" of Defoe's punishment made the plan impractical and asked if Harley had "any means of sounding him."[43] Godolphin is clearly, *replying* to a suggestion.

Despite the pillory, government interest in Defoe had continued unbroken. During the months since the publication of *The Shortest-Way*, Harley's intimacy with Godolphin, his influence with the queen, and his political base had grown. He saw Godolphin almost daily, and Godolphin's reliance on Harley increased steadily. At one point Godolphin wrote, "Besides these meetings and those agreed upon last night to be at your house, it is necessary above all the rest that the Duke of Marlborough and you and I should meet regularly, at least twice a week if not oftener to advise upon everything that shall occur."[44] Although Godolphin raised the question of the effect of Defoe's punishment and asked if William Paterson, now in their employ, would not be useful in Scotland, he was obviously prepared to accept Harley's recommendation and offered to help by sending the other secretary of state, Charles Hedges, to "sound" Defoe.

Godolphin, who had begun his service at court as a page, had a reputation for modesty, honesty, and efficiency that would stand the test of hostile times. Burnet described him as "the silentest and modestest man that was perhaps ever bred at court" and captured his strengths: "He had a clear apprehension, and dispatched business with great method, and with so much temper, that he had no personal enemies . . . his incorrupt and sincere way of managing . . . the treasury created in all people a very high esteem for him" (2:239–40). He was, however, reserved, taciturn, and unusually inaccessible. In 1703 Robert Harley had been the very powerful speaker of the House of Commons for two years. The side of his nature that people described as clear-sighted, gracious, and comprehensively informed was most evident. Godolphin surely hoped to use Harley's influence in the Commons to make financing the war easier, and Harley's "great Capacities, general Knowledge, and polite Learning, a taking and very engaging Way of Conversation," combined with his prodigious memory and fertile mind for management, fostered the rapidly developing intimacy between the men. Godolphin's own integrity and reticence probably prolonged his impression that Harley's native secrecy was simply discretion. In the years ahead Godolphin's character would stand; Harley's would strike even his closest friends as it would Defoe in one of his last descriptions of the man: "His Character was very strangely compounded of a Mixture of good and evil."[45]

By this time, the government employed many "agents," and Godolphin and Harley were two of the most ingenious users of them. Agents performed a number of services for the men in power. They sampled opinion, infiltrated different constituencies, watched the press, informed their employers about people or pamphlets that might work against their interests, and wrote periodical and pamphlet essays. The best, as Defoe could be, did all of these things. For nearly a year Harley had been on the lookout for "some discreet writer of the Government side, if it were only to state facts right, for the generality err for want of knowledge & being imposed upon by the stories raised by ill-designing men."[46] In August 1703, Harley saw a need for agents to deal with several concerns, such as the growth of the extreme branch of the Tory party; Scotland, where the Act of Security* seemed sure to pass; and continued difficulties with M.P.'s reluctant to vote sufficient funds for the war with France.[47] Not only had Defoe had extraordinary success as a pamphleteer, but he had proved himself by revealing nothing useful to Nottingham. Harley was rising, and Nottingham on his way out; Harley could do as he pleased with Defoe.

Defoe had another advocate, and this one would be Harley's instrument for Defoe's release. This participant in the saga was James Stancliffe, Defoe's childhood friend and former partner in trade. On 23 August Stancliffe had written to Harley about a private bill before the Commons that would relieve the orphan children of a Dutch merchant. At the end of this letter Stancliffe wrote, "I saw mr. ff yesterday, & he seemes to be much dejected by the deferring of Hope which the Wise man sayes makes the heart Sick; but at the same tyme he & all men must know (that know any thing) that Your Hurrys of late have been such as are not ordinarily met with."[48] Defoe might be losing hope, but Stancliffe clearly believed that Harley would take care of Defoe in the immediate future.

When Harley wrote Godolphin on 20 September, he echoed Stancliffe's words: "Foe is much oppressed in his mind." He recommended that Defoe's fine be paid and that he be told privately upon his release that it was the queen's bounty. Harley had determined that Defoe did not blame Queen Anne and the ministry but "particular persons." He guessed correctly that Defoe would feel a powerful obligation if his fines were paid and warned Godolphin that Defoe's friends were working to raise the 200 marks. A week later Godolphin reported that he

---

*An act passed by the Scottish Parliament that guaranteed Scotland the right to choose a successor to Queen Anne from the Stuart line, who would be explicitly forbidden to assume the English throne. In effect, this act would give England and Scotland different monarchs and greatly increase the threat that Scotland would form an alliance with France.

had read parts of Harley's letter to the queen: "What you propose about Defoe may be done when you will, and how you will."[49]

On 4 November Godolphin wrote, "I have taken care of the matter of DeFoe." In fact, Defoe had already appeared that day before Justice Thomas Lane with four men ready to stand as sureties for his keeping the peace. Defoe himself signed a bond for £200, and his brother-in-law Robert Davis, Charles Read, John Chase, and Thomas Fry signed for £100 each. A routine memorandum from Godolphin had probably gone to the attorney general; the formula read, "Mr. ———, now a Prisoner in Newgate . . . being represented as a a proper Object of her Majesty's Grace and her Majesty having been mov'd in his behalf by several of his Relations, who offer to give Security . . . I am commanded to acquaint you with it." With the attorney general's approval Defoe's case would have been added to the docket. Rather than paying money, the criminal and his sureties simply gave proof of an estate or goods worth £20 and pledged to pay the queen the full sum should Defoe fail to "keep the peace." Because Defoe had committed a felony against the crown, both his bail and his release required four people to make bond with him.[50]

Defoe's fine and fees due Newgate Prison remained to be paid, however, before he could be released. Godolphin, always a good administrator, had planned carefully. With the queen's approval, he wrote Harley, then went to his staff meeting in the Cockpit on 5 November and announced that James Stancliffe was to be paid £150 "Out of Secret Service money. clear of all charges." Present were William Lowndes, secretary to the Treasurer; Simon Harcourt, attorney general; and the two solicitors. That Godolphin did not discuss or explain this grant is clear from what followed.

On the fourth, the day Harley heard from Godolphin and before the meeting in the Cockpit, Stancliffe received a note from Harley written in his own hand but unsigned: "Mr. Stancliffe you are to go to Mr. Taylor at his House in Pall Mall court at eight o'clock on monday morning & there receive of him one hundred & fifty pounds which he is ordered to pay you." The note is endorsed on the back: "Received Nov 8: 1703 the contents of the within note as by order being one hundred & fifty pounds out of Her Majesty's Secret Service moneys by the hands of William Lowndes Esq. signed Ja: Stancliffe." Lowndes made a rather crotchety note in his receipt book: "My Lord Treasurer directed this sum to be paid him for Her Mats Sec: Ser: on 5th Nov & he wd give no other acq^{ce} than this."[51]

By using Stancliffe, Harley and Godolphin could hide their part from the world. This substantial London merchant and lifelong friend of Defoe's appeared in court, and those who waited for "a party" or "the faction" to arrange Defoe's release would be confused. Moreover, the "sell out" of which others accused Defoe would remain a matter of suspicion, not certainty.

Godolphin would also have spoken or written to the magistrate before whom Defoe would appear. A fairly standard form existed, which read courteously:

Mr. ——— now in Newgate having made offers of doing service to the Queen . . . I am commanded to signify Her Majtys Pleasure, that you may admit him to Bail, unless you have any objections to it, which you will be pleas'd to signify to me.[52]

Once sureties were accepted, it was standard practice for the court to continue a recognizance for keeping the peace to the next session, then to one an entire year later. If no new indictments were filed against the offender, the court could discharge him. Lane bound Defoe to appear on 14 January, the first day of the next term. Defoe appeared, and the queen pardoned him on 31 July 1704, thereby discharging him and his sureties.

With the money given Stancliffe, Defoe could pay his fine and the fees due Newgate Prison; he would then be free on the next gaol delivery day, probably 8 November. On the ninth he sent a grateful letter to Harley by Stancliffe. To Stancliffe, he wrote, "as you have Embarkt for me in the First part of this Matter, you must not Refuse to be the Messenger of my Acknowledgements" (H 9).

His reaction was everything Harley wished. His letter to Harley was embarrassing:

I think my Self bound to Own you as the Principall Agent of this Miracle. . . .

It Remains for me to Conclude . . . with This Humble Petition that if Possible I may By Some Meanes or Other know what I am capable of Doeing, that my Benefactors . . . May Not be Asham'd of their Bounty. . . .

I Can Not but Profess my Self a Debtor wholly to your Self. . . .

Most Earnestly Pray That I May have Some Opportunity Put into my hands by Providence to . . . Make Some Such Sort of Return as No Man Ever Made.

. . . A Man Ready to Dedicate my Life. . . . (H 10–11)

And the extravagant superlatives and promises went on and on. Defoe's November letter showed the surprise and joy of a man who had heard nothing after Harley's message for four months. Although Godolphin made the arrangements, Defoe knew because of Stancliffe that Harley was the instrument of his release.

To the press also Defoe was a special prisoner. He was being watched, for almost at once the press interpreted his release: "Every one is not a *Daniel de Foe* that has a Party to pay a Fine for him" and "he must have a great Interest indeed, that he could find four sufficient Bail for his good Behaviour for seven Years. It's no ungainful thing to be a *Whig*." Almost as soon as Defoe was out, efforts to prevent his return to writing began. In these efforts, it is clear that the Tories continued to suspect the Whiggish City Dissenters of paying his fines.[53] They sometimes turned in evidence about Defoe to Harley and habitually suggested that the sureties for his good behavior had been forfeited.

In less than a year Defoe had been a fugitive, pilloried, "forgotten" in prison, and the special recipient of the queen's bounty. The experience had battered him, demanded extraordinary emotional resources, and subjected him to waves of unpleasant feelings: rage, despair, resistance, helplessness, martyrdom, grief, injustice, and loneliness among others. His writing for some time after January 1703 allows us to see inside the struggling human being.

In 1703 and 1704 Defoe's writing changed in purpose, focus, and tone. On the simplest level it moved from attempting to explain and justify *The Shortest-Way*, then to understanding what happened, then to restoring his reputation and clarifying his position, and finally to earning a living as a professional, both as agent and as "free lance" writer. The 1704–1705 works often showed a merging of motives; in other words, even when he wrote professionally, traces of the first three motives appeared in the later pamphlets. On another level, dedication to "truth" was in tension with a desire to accommodate. On yet another level, Defoe revealed his personal reactions and moods in connotative words and phrases. Through it all, he believed in the importance of the issues. He saw that the Tories were bent upon emasculating the Whig party, primarily through the disfranchisement of the Dissenters, and believed that the Dissenters were finally crumbling and their numbers declining in the face of sustained persecution and benefits proffered for conforming.

The nearly two dozen publications on the subjects of the Dissenters and occasional conformity by Defoe share some major positions. In a variety of ways Defoe insists:

1. Dissenters are loyal Englishmen, not congenital rebels.

2. It is to England's advantage to let Dissenters serve their country in the military and in government.

3. The Corporation and Test Acts "are a Bait to People to Banter their Consciences"; they make "the Sacred Institutions of Christ a Drudge to Secular Interest, and a Cause of mens Sins." The Test is "an Unjust Design" and "an Unreasonable Method." An Act of Exclusion would be the straightforward way to go.[54]

4. He has always opposed the bill to prevent occasional conformity because he believes it contradicts the Act of Toleration.

5. Occasional conformity weakens the Dissenters ("prepares their Members to fall off, and Posterity to Conform totally").[55]

Defoe's position was certainly close to that of many Anglicans and Dissenters. For example, the House of Lords made the same observation about the effect on national dissent: "So the Party of all the Dissenters that came nearest the Church, and of whom the greatest Numbers have come over to it, were those that Pleaded for [occasional conformity]."[56]

The writing changed, however, as the man changed. As the shock of the experience faded, the works became less personal, less introspective, but also less intense and engaged. Smoother rhetoric, structure, and argument largely inhibited the emotional outbursts and surprising, vibrant metaphors, such as "covering too short for the Bed" as a description of many High Church explanations. The anger at the injustice and the pain lingered, but like the heroes and heroines of his novels, he refused to brood over the past, became more suave, and started a new life as a writer, not a merchant.

From the time the ramifications of *The Shortest-Way* became clear to Defoe in early 1703, he had tried to explain his publication and salvage his reputation. His first effort was to have the title page emended in a second edition published in February 1703 to read *The Shortest Way with the Dissenters. [Taken from Dr Sach—ll's Sermon, and Others.] Or, Proposals for the Establishment of the Church*. To this edition, he added the four-page "Brief Explanation of a Late Pamphlet" and mentioned the Oxford sermon by Sacheverell, the *Poetical Observator*, and the *New Association* as the works deserving censure for what he parodied. He began to sign his works "the Author of the True-Born English-man," the signature he felt was most likely to remind his readers, and particularly the Dissenters, of the times he had earned their praise and admiration. The title page of *The Shortest Way to Peace and Union* said it is "By the Author of The Shortest-Way with the Dissenters." He consistently asserted that the method and intention of *The Shortest-Way* was to expose the Tory "spirit" and desire. As might be expected in anything written and rewritten over two years, his explanation became more concise and less open to various interpretations:

'twas writ t' expose, and not excite (*Elegy on the Author*, 2:80)

[It] was wrote on Purpose to expose this *Violent Doctrine*, and fill'd with such *true* Notions of the *Party*. . . . Yet he was put in the Pillory, and *Sacheverel* had the Stamp of Authority (*The Ballance of Europe*, 8)

Multitudes of Occasions . . . convince the World, that every Word . . . was both literally and interpretively the Sense of the Party point'd at, true in Fact, and true in Representation. (*A Second Volume of the Writings*, preface)

Without exception he insists that he wanted to expose "the Cant of the Nonjuring Party"* in order for people to see their "Virulent Spirits" and actual desires; then the "whole Nation will start at the Notion."

A True Collection of the Writings of the Author of the True Born English-man came out a week before he stood in the pillory (22 July). John How had published *A Collection of the Writings of the Author of the True-Born English-man* a few months earlier, and it may have suggested to Defoe the personal and economic advantages of such a collection. How's book includes thirteen works by Defoe, but the preface is a pastiche of Defoe's sentences that reveals its unauthorized nature. In his preface Defoe complains about the pirated edition but says frankly, "I must ask leave to make some further use of the Book itself." He offers his own work, he says, to show that it has the "Spirit of Healing," not of sedition and of the "Incendiary," and has always shown great respect to the queen. He has been a "Man of Peace and Charity," except in his satiric poems, where, he admits, he may have "run at Vice with too full a Cry." Defoe is far from the entirely humble penitent, however. In the midst of this irenic volume are sentences showing that his stance on occasional conformity is as unequivocal as ever: "It is sinful against God, scandalous to the Dissenters, and will be fatal to their Interest."

Defoe chose five poems and seventeen pamphlets to reprint. He began with his great popular success, *The True-Born Englishman*. He followed that with *The Mock Mourners*, the elegy for William with its concluding tribute to Queen Anne. Generally, he included his best, most popular works and arranged them to show steady support for the Protestant religion, the Protestant succession, and moral reform. He put the occasional conformity tracts at the end, attempting to emphasize his less controversial work. Among the thirty or so works he chose to omit were the satiric poems with ad hominem attacks, *A New Discovery of an Old Intreague* and *The Pacificator*; his Exclusion Crisis tracts, which might be read as stirring up unrest; the two standing army tracts that are attacks on Somers' "club"; *The Succession to the Crown of England, Consider'd*, which suggested an inquiry into Monmouth's legitimacy; and all of the Kentish petition pieces. In other words, Defoe omitted most of those pieces with direct attacks on individuals, those most strongly "revolutionary," and those reminiscent of his defiant delivery of *Legion's Memorial*. He slanted his output toward moral reform.

Defoe, however, committed a faux pas. *A True Collection* included an engraving of himself in a full, ornately curled wig and flowing robe, and a detractor noted, "here was a lordly, full-bottomed wig . . . with

*Nonjurors were Anglican clergymen who refused to swear allegiance to William and Mary; many believed their oaths to King James prevented it.

amazing amplitude of curl. Here was richly-laced cravat; fine, loose, flowing cloak; and surly substantial citizen aspect." People remarked on Defoe's ostentatious dress throughout his life. A Bristol resident commented on his wig, lace ruffles, and sword; a coffeehouse habitué described Defoe's affected display of a diamond pinky ring. His wig, reaching nearly to his elbows, was a bit out of style in 1703, but the prosperity and foppishness it exuded in the year Defoe was pilloried made him an object of fun or annoyance. Below the picture was a coat of arms, now a sign of hard-won and fading prosperity. In order to qualify, Defoe had needed to prove to the College of Arms that he had either "lands and possessions of free tenure to the yearly value of £10" or "moveable goods" worth £300. For £30 plus the cost of stamp, writing, painting, sketches, patent case and seal boxes, and wax and ribbon, he had received his arms.[57]

The Shortest Way to Peace and Union opened with another blatant attempt to reshape Defoe's image: "It was always my Opinion, that whoever should go about to widen the Differrence, or encrease the Misunderstandings between the Church of *England* and the Dissenters, were the real Enemies of both" (439). In this pamphlet Defoe said he regretted writing *The Shortest-Way*, although it was aimed only at those who wanted to "ruin" the Dissenters; that his published works had always showed a "healing Principle"; and that he was not writing to "move the Mercy of the Government" because he had already thrown himself on the queen's mercy. Printing *The Shortest Way to Peace and Union* illustrated his sincerity, he said, because he had written it four years earlier to expound the mutual advantages of the Toleration to Dissenters and Anglicans.

What the experience was really like Defoe shows most clearly in his poetry. *More Reformation*, published only a week after his sentencing, was a grimly cynical and somber poem, attacking a number of prominent London citizens and examining, first, the perversion and wilful misinterpretation of religion and, second, the perversion and betrayal of English patriotism. Defoe put himself in the poem, and the tone became scathing, ironic, and bitter. He told his story indirectly and saw himself from a number of points of view as he reflected on the reception and consequences of *The Shortest-Way*.[58]

One of the best poems Defoe ever wrote, *A Hymn to the Pillory*, is the release of the undercurrents in *More Reformation*. Written with the reality of the pillory, the fine, and seven years' good conduct before him, the poem is a sustained cry. Designed to be handed out as he stood in the pillory, the theme is "who can judge of Crimes by Punishment, / Where Parties Rule, and L[aw']s Subservient." In this poem, specific examples and familiar names replace abstraction, and unequivocal declarations abound. He turns the scaffold into a stage and parades across it those who have committed real crimes against the nation. He sharpens reference after reference from *More Reformation*, giving each bite: "Thou like a True-born *English* Tool . . . now art like to smart for being a Fool." This line returns to the double vision of himself given in the earlier poem: even though others perceived him as a "Tool" he was actually a naive "Fool." Such a juxtaposition becomes doubly ironic when the opening reminds the reader that, contradictorily, he is the much-praised author of *The True-Born Englishman*. The poem builds to the portrait of the solitary, patriotic Defoe, "an Example made, / To make Men of their Honesty afraid."

These poems and those that follow immediately show a depressed and defiant Defoe. He called himself "dead" and named a poem *An Elegy on the Author of the True-Born English-Man*. How important it had become to express his opinions in print lay behind such fretted lines as "if being tied under Sureties and Penalties not to write . . . be not equivalent to being dead."[59] In one bleak passage he described how "if they had given me time / I might ha' hang'd my self," then rises to an expression of the Protestant work ethic: "In *Butler's Garret** I shall ne'er appear. . . . *But he that gave me Brains will give me Bread*" (2:86).

The prose echoed these feelings but in single muted lines rather than in developed passages. For example, Defoe called himself the "late abdicated Author" in *The Dissenter[s] Misrepresented and Represented* [1704] and in the same tract protested: "How can you but blush! . . . How can you be Angry at that Author [of *The Shortest-Way*], and pretend you are not for Persecuting and Destroying us, why to kill our Reputation . . . is the worst kind of Murther."[60] The mood swings at this time were great and persistent. The letters show them even though those that survive are to Robert Harley, a man he did not yet know. In a late spring 1704 letter, for instance, Defoe calls his future, "a Mellancholly prospect," compares his recent prosperity to his present destitution, writes two distressed paragraphs about his family, and observes: "The Miserable are allways full of Their Own Cases." He does, however, repeat that he has no doubt of his ability to earn his "Bread" (H 16–18):

But I was Ruin'd *The shortest way* and Now Sir had Not your Favour and her Majties Bounty Assisted it must ha' been One of the worst Sorts of Ruine. I do Not mean as to Bread; I firmly and I Thank God Comfortably Depend on the Divine Goodness That I shall Never want That, But a Large and Promiseing family, a Vertuous and Excellent Mother to Seaven Beautifull and hopefull Children, a woman whose fortunes I have Ruin'd, with whom I have had 3700*l*, and yet who in the worst of my afflictions when my Ld. N[ottingham] first Insulted her Then Tempted her, scorn'd So much as to Move me to Complye with him, and Rather Encourag'd me to Oppose him.

---

*Poets since Dryden had used Butler as an example of neglect and royal ingratitude. See Oldham's *Satire against Poetry*, Otway's prologue to Lee's *Constantin the Great*, Dryden's *Hind and the Panther*. Defoe's classmate Samuel Wesley repeats the idea in a 1721 poem.

Seaven Children Sir whose Education Calls on me to furnish Their heads if I Can not Their Purses, and which Debt if not paid Now Can Never be Compounded hereafter is to me a Moveing Artical and helps Very often to make me Sad.

But Sir I am I Thank God Furnisht with Patience. I Never Despaird and In the Worst Condition allways believ'd I should be Carryed Thro' it, but which way, has been and yet Remaines a Mystery of Providence Unexpounded.

I beg heartly your Pardon for This Tedious Epistles. The Miserable are allways full of Their Own Cases and Think Nothing Impertinent. I write This for tis too Moveing for me to Speak it. I shall attend the Ordrs and houres you Appointed To morro' Even and am

Sir, your Most obedt Servt

In scattered sentences, the painful inner life found expression. Disillusionment with people and institutions fed a growing cynicism. "By Whigs abandon'd," free to assert from his experience that Dissenters had no societies of writers, brooding over broken promises, finding law "a Heathern Word for Power," Defoe saw hypocrisy and self-interest everywhere. He described law as moving by "wild Meanders" and uses dozens of images of wheels, gears, twists, and convolutions. He saw the irony of his position because he believed that had Sacheverell been rightly understood or any number of tracts brought to the government's attention in the manner his had been, then a High Churchman would have been *justly* prosecuted. He brooded over the fact that Sacheverell deserved the pillory, while he had been "wrongfully accus'd."

Haunted by Sacheverell and what happened to himself, he repeatedly listed candidates more deserving of the pillory than himself. The parade of villains begun in *More Reformation* and *A Hymn* stretched into the next three years. For example, *A Serious Enquiry into This Grand Question: Whether a Law to Prevent the Occasional Conformity of Dissenters, Would Not Be Inconsistent with the Act of Toleration* (1704) was full of quotations from Sacheverell's 1703 publications. In it, Defoe quoted the infamous "Against whom every Man that wishes the Churches welfare, ought to Hang out the Bloody Flag" and comments, "Here comes Mr. S——ll with a Voucher from a whole University, and says, that if her Majesty wishes well to the Church of *England*, She must not Tolerate them, but hang out the Bloody Flag." Defoe compared this "Affront" to the queen with his own, which had sent him to the pillory.

With bitter irony, he says in *More Short Ways with the Dissenters* (1704) that he "was punish'd deservedly, for telling that Story in Earnest which the Church-men Preach'd, Printed, and Talkt about only in Jest" (2:274). His mistake, he said, was overestimating people's intelligence, not labeling the bear, "BEAR," and speaking "softly to a deaf Man." The High Church sympathizers in government used "Power for want of Argument," and, in the type of bitterly cynical jest he rarely employed,

Defoe added that they "supplied the place of an Answer by finding the Author a Lodging in *Newgate*."

One fascinating aspect of these personal expressions is the way they anticipate some of the key emotions of the novels. The exclamation of loneliness and distress in *A New Test of the Church of England's Honesty* is unsettlingly like the words Robinson Crusoe teaches his parrot:

Alas, *Poor De Foe*! what hast thou been doing, and for what hast thou suffer'd?

and

Poor Robin Crusoe, Where are you? Where have you been? How come you here?

At this point both Defoe and Robinson Crusoe feel sorry for themselves and puzzle endlessly over why they have been "singl'd out" for suffering. Crusoe, imprisoned and lonely on his island, searches for explanation and meaning in the experience just as Defoe does.

In a letter to Robert Harley, Defoe describes the conditions of his release exactly as he would later express Moll's and Roxana's satisfaction with arrangements made by lovers:

[Moll, after inspecting the lodgings Mother Midnight has provided for her:] Every thing was so handsome and so clean, that, in short, I had nothing to say, but was wonderfully pleased with what I had met with, which considering the melancholly Circumstances I was in, was beyond what I looked for. (2:179)

and

in the kindness the Manner is So Oblidgeing, and all the Articles of it So Generous, that as a Man Astonish't at the Perticulars, I am Perfectly Unable to Express My Sence of it. (H 11)

Just as his past had given Defoe confidence in his ingenuity and ability to recover and earn a living, it offered him bracing examples and beliefs. One of the words he used most often to describe himself was *silenced*. In *An Elegy*, he says, "What tho' to Silence they condemn thy Rhymes, / Even that Silence shall condemn the Times"(2:68). Defoe hoped his experience, too, would "preach by silence." In lines such as these and by calling himself "silenced," Defoe evoked another time, a time when Dissenters were persecuted and imprisoned: the 1660s. Ejected ministers like Annesley and Morton used the term in a special way. John Whitlock's eloquent farewell sermon explains:

God now calls us and many others to preach to you by silence. And the very silence of so many ministers, if blessed by the Lord, may prove the most powerful and effectual sermon to people that they have had.[61]

He called himself a buoy, a guide, a pointing finger, a memento mori, and described how his experience exposed, condemned, warned, and shamed others, not himself. Above all, it, too, was unjust, political, the result of hypocritical intentions, and the "use of Power for want of Argument." He hoped that, like the ejected ministers, his presence and experience would be a "powerful and effectual" enlightening for Englishmen.

The pamphlets of 1703 and 1704 include more descriptions of the persecutions of the Dissenters during Defoe's lifetime than his other writings. The specific nature and emotional content of these descriptions show how much Defoe feared the "virulent," persecuting spirit he saw in the High Church party and how much he identified with those who were hounded by the government. To a rumored plan to publish a list of Church of England sufferers, Defoe promises his own list including "3000 Ministers silenc'd and turn'd out," "500000 l. Sterling in . . . Damages," and "a Tun of Dissenters Blood."[62]

Through the winter Defoe continued to try to repair his reputation, especially with the Dissenters. Rather than remonstrating directly with them, he took a new direction in his pamphlets. Primarily he shifted the subject away from occasional conformity to popular Dissenting stances and presented the facts about the Dissenters since 1641.

After his conviction, he wrote about the contradiction a bill to prevent occasional conformity would offer to the Toleration Act and about the threat to the strength and security of the nation posed by the High Church. By doing so, he could write from an uncontroversial Dissenting position and could continue to urge the accuracy of the dangers pointed out by *The Shortest-Way*. Rather than backing down, he declared occasional conformity not the issue. In a typical passage, he says, "Whether those who Occasionally conform are Hypocrites or no, is a dispute by it self; but you cannot but own your selves to be Hypocrites . . . who having made a Law, pretending to bring us to Church, plainly now discover, 'twas only a Flam, to keep us out of the Service of our Country."[63] He admitted that the Dissenters had "publickly declar'd" occasional conformity "Lawful in it self" and recognized that there had been reasons other than preferment for some people, but there was no real accommodation in his own position. Rather he showed himself the Dissenters' advocate by asserting the rights granted by the Toleration, presenting their history, and continuing to expose those prejudiced against them: "It is now about Forty Years that the Dissenters have been treated . . . with the scandalous Titles of Factious Rebels, Traitors to Monarchy . . . favourers of Anarchy" (*Dissenter[s] Misrepresented* 2:345).

In correcting the Dissenters' history he went against the common practice of his time by giving names on both sides. He demonstrated repeatedly that Anglicans, not Dissenters, had been the "factious spirits": "Sir *John Friend*, and Sir *William Parkins* were hang'd for Contriving to Assassinate . . . King *William*, and these Gentlemen dy'd Church of *England*-men." In contrast, he named Dissenters who had served their country well, such as Thomas Papillon, first commissioner of the Victualing Office, and Mordecai Abbot in the Exchequer during William's reign.[64] More and more, his pamphlets became direct attacks on the fraud and corruption in government and on High Church extremists. No fewer than eight pamphlets written in 1704 and early 1705 attacked and quoted Sacheverell, Leslie, Stubbs, and others. He emphasized the Dissenters' loyalty, argued the advantages of "peace and union" between the Protestant sects, and insisted that the Dissenters deserved to have the odium of the Test Act removed.

The Dissenters remained cool, however, and Defoe frequently wrote that he who took up their cause must be prepared to do so at his own "Hazard" and expense.[65] They were undoubtedly confused by a man who would attack occasional conformity so violently, publish tracts against Dissenters (James Owen in *The Sincerity of the Dissenters Vindicated*) as well as High Churchmen, and involve himself in politics to the extent he did while identifying himself as a merchant. They surely resented his tendency to lecture them and his insistence that he spoke for them, representing their opinions. Defoe himself summarized their chief complaint in *A Dialogue between a Dissenter and the Observator*: "He meddl'd with that he had nothing to do with and he is the man they say who has been the occasion of all this Persecution which is coming upon us."

Consistently held up as the prototype of the "fierce" Dissenter and already being accused, if not of beginning the controversy, of introducing its most divisive arguments, Defoe had, in the eyes of the Dissenters, formulated the most damaging charge against them and refused to let the controversy die. The worst thing Defoe had done was to articulate categories that helped supporters of the bill to prevent occasional conformity equate moderation with political expediency. In *An Enquiry into Occasional Conformity Shewing that the Dissenters Are No Way Concern'd in It*, Defoe's very title divided Dissenters by saying that occasional conformists were not really Dissenters and could easily abide by the proposed bill and sacrifice attending meeting house. Defoe suggested the bill be retitled "An Act for the better Uniting the Protestant Dissenters, by preventing Occasional Conformity."

Needless to say, many Dissenters did not agree. "It seems very unaccountable that the Protestant Dissenter's [*sic*] *Moderation* towards the establish'd *Church*, which was formerly reputed a *Virtue* in 'em, should be interpreted a *Crime*," James Owen complained sadly. Another writer lamented "that Heart-breaking Division of us . . . into *Conscientious* and *Politick*" and called Defoe "Foul-mouth'd." He, like many others, saw

Defoe "At the Head of the Conscientious Gang." Calamy wrote that moderation "was now represented as Criminal, and an Evidence of an ill Design: And that was cry'd down as sinful." Writer after writer noted that Defoe "distinguishes by the Names of State or Political Dissenters, Hypocrites, &c., and is entirely for being rid of them."[66]

No matter how often Defoe argued that others found occasional conformity scandalous, that the accusations and pejorative descriptions of the Dissenters were more than fifteen years old, and that a long history of hatred toward the Dissenters existed, he could not clear himself of the association with the controversy, for his prominence in it was undeniable. His name and the titles of his works on the subject appeared countless times in periodicals, poems, and pamphlets. Even the epigraph to his first pamphlet raised dispute: "If the Lord be God, follow him: but if Baal, then follow him" (1 Kings 18:21). Pamphlet after pamphlet referred to this quotation as How and Sacheverell had, and Philip Stubbs used it as the title of an anti-Dissenting sermon, *For God or for Baal: or, No Neutrality in Religion* (1702). Without recognizing the connection to Defoe's 1697 pamphlet, the author of *Reflections upon a Late Scandalous and Malicious Pamphlet Entitul'd The Shortest Way* (1703) observed, "[Defoe's] Title is a little more bald . . . but the Spirit, Notion and Application are the same. The ill applied Text which we had not long ago from a City-Pulpit, relating to *Elijah*'s Treatment of Baal's Prophets, has the same Moral." Like those of Sacheverell, Defoe's words and phrases were endlessly repeated. Moreover, because he was a Dissenter, they were capable of being used to call the Dissenters hypocrites, and therefore deserving of such a bill, or to describe them as already separated from the church and unconcerned with the bill. Defoe's pamphlets so overshadowed others that reminders about the history of occasional conformity were necessary. "The Moderate *English Presbyterians* have all along declared against *Total Separation*, and practiced *Occasional Conformity* without any Prospects of Temporal Advantage," James Owen protested. No wonder the House of Lords reminded the Commons that occasional conformity was "no New Practice invented to Evade a Law."[67] Already embroiled with the factions raised by the standing army and *Legion's Memorial* controversies and the object of the most distressed and furious protests by the Dissenters, Defoe understandably multiplied the images of himself as a hounded man.

Prison and its aftermath left Defoe with an uneasy peace with the Dissenters. He never trusted them again, never felt himself truly one of them, and they returned the feeling. Although he continued to write in their interest, he often slipped into making a wry, slightly bitter comment and consistently recognized that he could expect no gratitude.

The names of his City friends and acquaintances gradually dropped out of his life, and he became a man who largely worked and traveled alone, rather than one immersed in the vigorous community exchanges of the tight neighborhood of the ancient Corporation of the City of London.

PART II

1703-1714

CHAPTER 7

FOUR HUNDRED
THOUSAND WORDS

*Seaven Children Sir whose Education Calls on me to furnish
Their heads if I Can not Their Purses. . . .*

*. . .I Never Despaird and In the Worst Condition allways be-
liev'd I should be Carryed Thro' it, but which way, has been and yet
Remaines a Mystery of Providence Unexpounded.*

——DEFOE TO ROBERT HARLEY, Spring 1704

*[Writers' earnings are the] Reward of Industry, the Prize of
Learning, and the Benefit of . . . Studies.*

——DEFOE, *An Essay on the Regulation
of the Press* (1704)

Defoe left Newgate expecting government employment and obsessed
with the desire to demonstrate his gratitude to Harley. He knew that
hundreds were employed in the offices of commissioners, auditors,
diplomats, and chief ministers. He knew men employed as agents,
press spies, and writers. In London, Scotland, Ireland, and on the
continent the queen's servants thrived while he faced a pregnant wife,
six children, an elderly, straitened father, his ruined Tilbury factory,
the impossibility of getting credit for a new business, large debts due
immediately, and galling ridicule in the press. Among the names he
had been called, he listed "Prostitute," "Hackney," "Tool," "Foul Mouth,"
"Insolent Scribler," "Scandalous Pen," "Rash," and "Immoderate." Even
as the attacks acknowledged his journalistic successes, they kept alive
his humiliation:

the *Dissenters* will not give us an Inch of the Advantage, while their Secretary is
able to hold a Pen in the *Mint*,* and plays at Hide and Seek with the Messengers
of Parliament [sent to arrest him]. . . . this Reprobate stands in open Defiance
against Parliamentary Authority. (*Heraclitus Ridens*, 4–8 January 1704)

His previous recovery from bankruptcy, he always implied, had been
based upon a gift from King William,[1] and it is no wonder that Defoe

---

*The area in which debtors were free from the threat of arrest.

turned to Robert Harley to find out what the government wanted him to do.

The answer was not immediately forthcoming, and, by midwinter, the relief and optimism of November became confusion, cries for mercy and "fair play," and a growing sense of what the pillory meant. In 1692 he had managed to hang on to some income-bearing property and had had enough capital to start the Essex factory. In 1703 he had nothing left and knew it took capital to get credit. Moreover, the sentence of seven years' good conduct largely disqualified him from any kind of political writing. He could not afford to publish another "seditious" pamphlet, and politicians and booksellers were naturally wary about employing him.

The few letters written between November and June that survive recite the needs of his family, express acute anxiety, and beg Harley for employment:

> I Impatiently Wait to Reciev your Ordrs . . . Wishing if Possible the Time May Come, that you May find this Neglected fellow servicable, or at least Make him So.

> I Entreat to as speedy an Audience as possible that I may at last Enter into your Intrests and Service. (H 14, 15)

He remained a "Neglected fellow," clearly underemployed and unable to support his family.

Defoe was never one to remain less than fully occupied or to put his hopes for the future in one enterprise. Scarred by his first bankruptcy and miserable over his "distressed" family, he vividly imagined debtors' prison for himself and destitution for his children. Certainly the meager legacies left by Defoe's father two years later suggest that even the extended family was feeling strain; the largest bequest was £100 to his grandson Daniel. The more obvious it became that Harley and the government would not provide a comfortable living, the more specific Defoe became in his requests to Harley and the more ingenious he became in his efforts to support himself. Just as in 1692 he had begun to work at his economic recovery with a variety of new projects and in a number of ways, so now he tried in several ways to put himself on firm ground again in 1704.

With trade and manufacture closed to him, he turned back to his pen. At first he concentrated on trying to repair his reputation and, incidentally, capitalized on his notoriety by writing almost exclusively on Dissenting issues. As his discredited and desperate situation became clear to him in early spring of 1704, he began to exploit what he knew of the London book trade. For the first time in his life, he earned almost his entire income as an independent writer. (He would do so again ten years later.) Now, at forty-four, he elbowed for room in the company of people like Charles Gildon (writer of translations, essays, plays, poetry, collections of tales, criticism), Delarivière Manley (plays, several issues of the *Examiner*, pamphlets, scandalous memoirs, novellas), and William King (issues of the *Examiner*, essays, poetry, translations, travel books, pamphlets, collections of stories, even a cookbook).

The second period when he depended entirely upon his pen produced his best works—the novels, the beautiful *Atlas Maritimus*, and popular works of practical divinity such as *The Family Instructor*. The first time produced nothing of that quality, but they reveal a great deal about the relationship between Defoe's life and his writing, about his method of composition, and point to some of his future literary work. In 1704 he published more than 400,000 words, including pamphlets, poems, some occasional pieces, and an "instant book" on a natural disaster; he began two periodicals, an allegorical book, and a major philosophical poem. His first long, unified, imaginative works—*The Storm* and *The Consolidator*—were born in that year.

This enormous output derived from two pressing, highly emotional sources: his need to support himself and his family and his need to demonstrate his gratitude and usefulness to the government. The simultaneous existence of these motives makes it impossible to separate the political from the economic and the political from the personal impulses that produced most of the works of that year. Defoe continued to write many of the kinds of things he had written before. For instance, he continued to write about current controversies and bills before Parliament. In these tracts he "answered" a few more people, obviously hoping that the popularity of, for example, Charles Davenant's *Essays* would help sell his *Some Remarks on the First Chapter in Dr. Davenant's Essays* (1704).

Some of his work, however, is clearly aimed at a more general market. The *Second Volume of the Writings of the Author of The True-Born Englishman*, published with a second edition of *A True Collection*, offered some of his satiric, personal, and patriotic poems with nine pamphlets on Dissenting issues, another on King William, and a final one against a parliamentary bill to set up parish industries to employ the poor. It was an obviously commercial venture. In contrast, *The Consolidator*, *The Storm*, *Jure Divino*, *A True Relation of the Apparition of one Mrs. Veal*, *The Master Mercury*, *A Review*, and a few other pieces were written in forms already greatly in demand, and yet Defoe dared to add strong elements of political propaganda. A few works should be regarded primarily as attempts to strengthen his position as a government writer with ambitions. Yet even the items in this category are not obvious. For instance, much of Defoe's poetry belongs here, but for most of it he had high literary standards and aspirations.

Pressing as these needs were, Defoe had yet others. He was notorious, destitute, and disqualified forever from his chosen occupation of merchant. One of his first subjects holds an important key to Defoe's thinking about his vocation and reveals some of the ways he was coping with the traumatic collapse of his settled life. Soon after he was released, one of the most destructive hurricanes in its history hit England. The storm began shortly after midnight on Thursday, 26 November, and grew stronger until Saturday night. Narcissus Luttrell called "the damage incredible . . . a great many people killed, and many wounded; . . . we are apprehensive we shal [sic] hear of great losses at sea." In the next few days, Luttrell described the damage he saw and records reports from England, the continent, and the fleets.[2] Periodicals, sermons, and correspondence continued the awestruck tallying of damages, and soon books such as *An Account of the Sad and Dreadful Accidents . . . about the Cities of London and Westminster . . . the 27th of November, 1703* (1703) and *A Wonderful History of All the Storms, Hurricanes, Earthquakes . . . That Have Happen'd in England for Above 500 Years Past. With a Particular . . . Account of the Dreadful Storm . . . of November 1703 . . .* (February 1704) appeared. Defoe started to work on his book *The Storm* at once. Its subtitle, *A Collection of the Most Remarkable Casualties and Disasters*, related it to innumerable collections of stories, anecdotes, historical episodes, and maxims. Defoe hoped to take advantage of the popularity of examples of "remarkable" events, coincidences, and "providences" and of the current interest in the storm. He had contributed to John Dunton's *Athenian Mercury*, which answered questions on religion, apparitions, and providences, and to William Turner's *A Compleat History of the Most Remarkable Providences, Both of Judgment and Mercy . . . Extracted from the best Writers, the Author's Own Observations, and the Numerous Relations Sent Him from Divers Parts of the Three Kingdoms* (1697).[3] This latter work, also published by John Dunton, included material quoted from "authorities" and their published works and from solicited letters, just as Dunton's *Athenian Mercury* and *Post Angel* had done. Dunton's invitation to would-be contributors to Turner's *Compleat History* is very much like Defoe's advertisement for contributors to *The Storm*:

We do hereby invite all men, especially DIVINES to impart unto us any such Remarkable Providences as they have recorded, or remember to have befallen themselves, or others either in *Mercy, or Judgment.*

   . . . we desire the ingenious Reader . . . to send us accounts of as many . . . as fall under his *own proper Experience and Knowledge,* directed to *John Dunton,* at the *Raven* in *Jewen-street*; whence, with all convenient speed, they shall be transmitted to the Press. But always remember, that what you send be circumstantiated with the Name of the *County, Town, and Place,* you send it from . . . they shall be received with all *Candor and Gratitude* imaginable, and the *Names of the Authors* published, if permitted, that the publick may know to whom they are indebted for the promoting of such an *useful Work*. (*Athenian Gazette*, 22 May 1695)

Defoe's advertisement was nearly as long and explicit. Although he did not enumerate the kinds of providences he wanted contributed, he did include the other parts of the invitation:

To preserve the Remembrance of the late dreadful Tempest, an exact and faithful Collection is preparing of the most remarkable Disasters which happened on that Occasion. . . . For the perfecting so good a Work, 'tis humbly recommended by the Author to all Gentlemen of the Clergy, or others, who have made any Observations of this Calamity, that they would transmit as distinct an Account as possible . . . to the Undertakers, directed to John Nutt near Stationers hall, London. All Gentlemen . . . are desired to write no Particulars but what they are well satisfied to be true, and to set their Names to the Observations they send, which . . . shall be faithfully Recorded, and the Favour publickly acknowledged. (*London Gazette*, 2–6 December 1703; a very similar notice appeared in the *Daily Courant*, 2 and 4 December 1703)

Quotations from clergymen and the preservation of the varying epistolary styles of those who responded were intended to give the work authenticity. The circulation of the *London Gazette* at that time was nearly 9,000, that of the *Daily Courant* about 800, and answers began to arrive in less than a week.[4] Defoe included about sixty letters or excerpts. Like Dunton and Turner, Defoe also quoted such respected sources as the *Philosophical Transactions of the Royal Society* and Ralph Bohun's *A Discourse concerning the Origine and Properties of Wind*[5], and gave his own experiences with comments and reflections. He remarks, for instance, that "the Mercury sunk lower than ever I had observ'd . . . which made me suppose the Tube had been handled and distur'd by the Children" (25).

In publishing a pamphlet, *The Lay-Man's Sermon*; a poem, *An Essay on the Late Storm*; and a book on the storm, Defoe began what became a common practice for him. Throughout his writing career, he would quote himself either in long identified passages or in phrases, analogies, and well-turned sentences repeated from work to work. Moreover, with *The Storm* he began writing for different audiences or in very different modes on the same event. He would, for example, get *Due Preparations for the Plague* (for the pious), *A Journal of the Plague Year* (for the modern skeptic), and several periodical essays from the 1721 threat of plague. This stratagem to exploit the different markets for books and pamphlets became more frequent, calculated, and obvious. It appeared in a growing variety of "voices" in which Defoe wrote his pamphlets and in the forms of prose in which he dealt with the same subjects. In later years Defoe's tracts would be written from the points of view of an Anglican, a Dissenter, a Quaker, a Scot, a leader of the mob, a Whig, a Jacobite, and others; he would produce thousands of pages on the Great Northern War (between Sweden and a coalition consisting of Denmark, Poland, and Russia) in the shape of "lives," histories, periodical essays, news items, and a novel, and he would quote other sources, both with and without acknowledgment, as he does Bohun in *The Storm* and would John Perry in his Great Northern War writings.[6]

More significantly, however, the prefatory materials for the storm publications show us Defoe coming to terms with and accommodating himself to his new life. Statements of defiance and of hope often occur simultaneously in his writings, as in "He who gave me Brains will give me Bread." He expresses impatience often, but never despair. He had rejected a "calling" as a youth when he decided against the ministry; now he was deprived of his chosen calling of merchant. His surviving letters return and return to the idea that some divine plan, some hand of Providence, must be behind his ruin.[7] *The Lay-Man's Sermon*, published in February 1704 while he was still gathering letters for *The Storm*, connects the life of a clergyman, rejected in his youth, and his present writing. "The Term Sermon . . . is but *Sermo*, a Speech," he wrote, explaining that although his pamphlet does not treat the subject as seriously, it has one of the primary functions of a sermon: to explain a message from God. In the preface to *The Storm* Defoe wrote, "I cannot be so ignorant of my own Intentions, as not to know, that in many Cases I shall act the Divine, and draw necessary practical Inferences." In late spring he characterized his "present Useless posture" as his most pressing "affliction" (H 14). The self-consciousness of "cannot be so ignorant of my own Intentions" signals the fact that Defoe has adopted a role for himself.

In *The Lay-Man's Sermon* Defoe began by explicating a text from the Bible in exactly the way Dissenting ministers did exegesis and moved to interpreting the storm as God's condemnation of the immoderate behavior of parties of his contemporaries. This text, Nahum 1:3, was the same one he used as epigraph to *The Storm*: "The Lord hath his way in the Whirlwind, and in the Storm, and the Clouds are the dust of his Feet." Both works drew analogies between their own forms of discourse and sermons, and both emphasized the "speaking" element. He once described the perfect prose style as an address, a form of speaking. "In publick Callamities, every Circumstance is a Sermon, and every thing we see a Preacher" (5); "We ought dilligently to observe the extraordinary actings of Providence,"(4) he wrote, and we see the inspiration for *The Storm*, and the promise of the mind of Robinson Crusoe and of H.F. in *A Journal of the Plague Year*, as well as a man exploring the ways life as a writer might satisfy him. Both storm works draw attention to the writer's greater audience: "Preaching of Sermons is Speaking to *a few* of

Mankind: Printing of Books is Talking to *the whole World*" (preface to *The Storm*; emphasis added). Defoe even talks of the "tenfold Obligation" of the person who publishes. Not only is he linking his work as a writer to his youthful ambition, he is raising the status of the writer's occupation and finding a comforting reason for his personal disaster. By the spring of 1705, he could thank God for allowing him to be useful and say of his writing: "I am still farther delighted in observing by what secret steps in his providence he has furnish'd me with or directed me" in that work "which I believe I was brought into the world and am suffer'd to live in it only to perform" (H 84–85).

In light of this rhetoric, the fact that three of Defoe's works written shortly after this are apocalyptic is not particularly surprising. His third publication on the storm, the poetic *An Essay on the Late Storm* appended to his *An Elegy on the Author of The True-Born English-Man*, begins dramatically by asserting that "every Blast" of the storm said "*Reform*" and every falling timber "*Repent.*" "The Storms above reprove the Storms below," he says and returns to his familiar catalogue of public corruption, immorality, faction, and Jacobite plots. *The Consolidator*, published seven months later in March 1705, is a 360-page "allegorick Relation" of political, religious, and other recent events and controversies. *The Dyet of Poland: A Satyr*, begun in late spring 1704, casts London as Dantzick (Gdansk today) and Parliament as the Diet. Both of these latter works repeat the ideas and opinions of Defoe's 1704 works, but they present them in very different ways. Both give lightly veiled histories of recent events with highly similar accounts of William's reign, his people's ingratitude, corruption in high places, High Church extremism and the occasional conformity bills, and election abuses. Avaricious statesmen, hypocritical noblemen, and a fractious people populate these works; in them England is her own greatest enemy. Because Defoe gives both a sweep of history and many developed, individual anecdotes, the portraits of England are devastating, prophetic condemnations. The very rhythm of English history and the character of her citizens are established in the periodic repetition of sentences such as "This Peace was no sooner made, but the Inhabitants . . . , according *to the constant Practice* of the Place, fell out in the most horrid manner among themselves . . ." (*Consolidator*, 192). Within the accounts of war and controversies are stories of individual victims. For example, Abraham Gill's unjust imprisonment and impressment* illustrate the results of Church of England factions and sharpen a picture of pettiness, injustice, and persecution.[8]

The Consolidator is nearly a compendium of the subjects on which

---

*Because of his conversion to nonconformity, Gill was accused of forging his ordination papers and imprisoned on that and other trumped up charges. It took two years for him to clear himself.

Defoe wrote in 1704 and 1705. Loosely motivated by an initial analogy between the narrator and Peter the Great of Russia (both are travelers seeking knowledge) the book quickly becomes a static dialogue rather than a fictional travel book. Peter's visit to England in 1698, his eagerness to learn, and the differences in cultures had fired the English imagination, and Defoe capitalizes on that. As his traveler listens and compares, Defoe gives his own position on the state of the fleet, the War of the Spanish Succession, the succession to the English throne, the need for better relations with Scotland, and many other pamphlet and *Review* subjects.

Like so much that Defoe wrote at this time, *The Consolidator* is deeply pessimistic and shows considerable independence. In a kind of psychomachia, he recreates an English mind made of, among other things, a "Retentive Warehouse for Conscience" ("the Locks are very Rusty" and seldom opened but in sickness, jail, and near death) and another for the devil (always open and displayed with pride) (19–20). In other places, he comments that those willing to listen and use reason to make decisions are the least likely to succeed (342). In a truly subversive section, Defoe recommends that the Dissenters unite and bring England to her knees economically. This section contemptuously ridicules the stupidity of the Anglicans and weaves a vindictive fantasy of their tradesmen "at their Wits end," sitting in their shops with "little or nothing to do"; their Bank of England dissolved, and their Companies taken from them by Dissenters' guile (245–56). But, Defoe concludes, English Dissenters are "Narrow, mean-Spiritied, short-Sighted, self-Preserving, friend-Betraying, poor-Neglecting People" and will never unite (271).

Just as his writing about the Dissenters suggests independent thought, so does the fact that *The Consolidator* is unusually pro-Scotland for a work of 1705. It repeatedly describes the Scots as clear-sighted and reasonable in their demands. His metaphors for the Scots/English controversy are among the best in the book; and his condemnation of the English unequivocal. The Scots, he says, have as much right to make themselves secure as a householder does to bar his windows (103). "Poverty and Weakness is not a sufficient Ground to oppress a Nation" (104), he observes. In this strongly anti-Anglican book, Defoe finds the religion of the Scots at the core of the hatred and resentment many Englishmen direct at them. All of his sympathy is on the side of the Scots, who want a Union "upon just Conditions." In a time when England was furious at Scotland for defying the queen and Parliament by passing its 1703 Act of Security, legislating that, after Anne, the same person could not be sovereign of both countries unless trade inequities had been resolved, Defoe's advocacy of Scottish measures and insistence upon English religious bigotry went beyond any party line.

Not only was *The Consolidator* composed in pieces over some time, but three separate publications came from it. *A Journey to the World in the Moon*, *A Letter from the Man in the Moon*, and *A Second and More Strange Voyage to the World of the Moon*, each only four pages long, may have been puffs for *The Consolidator* or intended to reach a larger audience with propagandistic sections. For example, the first, *A Journey*, had only one paragraph and a doggerel poem not in *The Consolidator*. The poem and a final "Advertisement" identified the notorious author and promised "Diverting News," "Comical Intreagues," and more. *A Letter from the Man in the Moon* is addressed "To the Author of the True Born *English-Man*" and condenses the *Consolidator*'s interpretation of the actions of the principals in the War of Spanish Succession. This account satirizes the irrational behavior of the allies in the face of Louis XIV's violation of the Treaty of Partition* and questions England's involvement in the war. If Defoe were not the author, then someone who knew the contents of the *Consolidator* in remarkable detail was. *A Journey* draws from several parts of the longer book and rearranges the pieces freely, and *A Letter* reduces the thirty-page text "to the Author of these Sheets" in the *Consolidator* to four pages, primarily by reducing print size and by omitting paragraphs. The new transitions preserve Defoe's arguments carefully.

Despite the fact that it came out over a year after its spring 1704 conception, *The Dyet of Poland* seems highly unified. The structure obviously derives from Dryden's *Absalom and Achitophel*; the divisions and internecine destructiveness of recent times depicted in the narrative part of the poem give way to a vision of harmony ushered in by the queen's selection of Godolphin and Harley as her chief ministers. The poem exhorts,

> If there's a States-man honest and upright,
> Whom neither Knaves can bribe, nor Fools Invite
> . . . .
> That loves the People and obeys the Crown,
> And seeks the Nations safety, not his own
> . . . .
> *Court him, Let Great Augustus Court him to't.*
> (*Poems on Affairs of State* 7:128)

Godolphin and Harley answer the summons, and a new time of peace, prosperity, and happiness begin. This poem not only attempts to build support for the Harley-Godolphin ministry and its policies, but also encourages Englishmen to select a "Dyet" of the best men in their districts in the upcoming elections.

*The treaties of 1698–99 that divided Spanish possessions in order to prevent the union of France and Spain under a single monarch.

The Consolidator had required a second edition eight months after it was published, and *The Dyet of Poland* was a great success. This poem is one that rises from the tangle of works motivated by political, literary, and personal needs as identifiable as written specifically to improve Defoe's position and value to Robert Harley and the ministry. Circulated in a limited edition in May, Defoe gave the poem to John Barber to print for general sale in mid-July. John Darby, whom Tutchin said printed the spring edition, had just inherited his father's shop. The elder Darby often printed "for liberty and religion" and had published *The Succession to the Crown of England*, Defoe's 1701 pamphlet asking for an inquiry into Monmouth's legitimacy. *The Dyet* attacks the Dissenters' enemies and the injustice of the occasional conformity bills and would have fit in with other Darby publications. The poem would have appealed to Harley because of its plea for moderation and attack on some of the men Harley hoped would not be reelected.

In contrast to small presses like Darby's, Barber and the big publishers Defoe came to use could turn out 250 pages an hour. Barber was quickly becoming one of the ministry's favorite printers and would do many of Swift's and Prior's works, the *London Gazette*, the *Examiner*, and even the votes of the House of Commons. His printers worked in relays and kept four presses (two for each side of a page) going continuously. They could, therefore, produce large editions very quickly. *The Dyet of Poland* went through three editions in six months (one pirated by Bragg), and Barber said he made £100 "clear of all Expence" on it.[9] William Pittis answered it in the carping *Dyet of Poland: A Satyr. Consider'd Paragraph by Paragraph*, and even that had two editions. The *Whipping Post*, a periodical that ironically imitated many of Defoe's Scandal Club conventions, conducted a mock trial on 10 July of the "Common Incendiary" who did "Compose, Print and Publish a certain Lying, Traiterous, Villanious and Scandalous" work. This pamphlet accused Defoe of selling the poem "by means of the Porter, who bag'd them about, and left them at the Booksellers Shops, and Whig-Coffee-Houses" and of leaving Newgate richer than when he was arrested because of "the Contributions rais'd at *Jonathan's* Coffee-House and elsewhere." Part of the sale undoubtedly came by way of copies bought to be distributed in the country.[10] As he said, Defoe would never starve as long as he could write.

Several poems can be interpreted in no way other than as "public poems" intended to bring Defoe the rewards writers of such poems expected in 1704. Taught as schoolboys to write poetry, Defoe and his contemporaries understood that to accept an office appointed by patronage was to accept an obligation to write about political events. Defoe saw poetry as a way to escape the namelessness of ordinary press spies, subordinate accountants, and minor customs collectors, and the English victory at Blenheim provided him with a chance to distinguish himself.

A Hymn to Victory took less than two weeks to write, for it was published only sixteen days after the news of Marlborough's victory at Blenheim reached England on 29 August. The fifty-seven pages of verse showed real insight into the realities and tactics of modern warfare. By reminding his readers that victory was now "A Prostitute to Stratagem and Art" and "The longest Purse subdues the longest Sword," Defoe encouraged the funding of Britain's army and navy, thereby working for Godolphin's chief concern.[11] Defoe was particularly good at contrasting Marlborough's style to that favored by continental generals. He noted accurately that "*Long Campings, Dodgings and Delays*" (25) were not Marlborough's way and found the English temper behind Marlborough's ability to force lines and avoid sieges.[12] Parts of the poem are dark and repeat Defoe's familiar ideas about England's ungrateful treatment of William and her reluctance to fund his army, about graft and fraud by men in power, and about the destructive nature of parties:

> Parties decide the Nation's Doom;
> Fighting abroad's a Jest, *The War's at home.*
> (16)

Such couplets required neither originality of thought nor technique; they revealed haste and Defoe's continued depression. As additional evidence of his state of mind, the poem included attacks on Nottingham, Defoe's *Shortest-Way* persecutor (15, 17), and on the "deep Designs" (18ff.) of factions.

Only eleven days after publication Defoe's poem merited a large second edition, but it quickly became a galling reminder of the limits of his personal possibilities. Defoe was preparing *The Double Welcome* to celebrate Marlborough's triumphant arrival in London when Joseph Addison's *The Campaign* and the duke appeared simultaneously on 14 December. Addison had been commissioned to write the poem, had been made commissioner of appeals in regulating excises, and profited from knowing the date of Marlborough's arrival and from the government's careful puffing of his poem. For example, the *Diverting Post* of 28 October reported, "We hear that shortly will be publish'd a Poem upon the Signal Battel of Blenheim; wrote by Joseph Addison . . . It's believ'd that this Piece will be perform'd with that Spirit and Fire, even to reach the Glory of that Celebrated Action, in its highest and most exalted Perfection."[13]

Defoe's *The Double Welcome* came out in early January and shows spleen. He attacks Addison and writes some of the most bitter, self-pitying lines of his career. Defoe calls Addison "our modern *Virgil*," then sneers that "he had never sung" without pay—"till he had 200 l. per Annum secur'd to him," the exact income from Addison's office of commissioner. Defoe describes himself as "Abject and low, and *scorch'd by Party-Fire*" and compares himself to Addison:

> Envy and Party-Spleen h'has never known,
> No humbling Jayls has pull'd his Fancy down:
> The Towring Youth with high Success aspires,
> And sings as one whose Song the World admires.
>   (12)

With his untroubled life, appreciated art, and youth, it is easy for Addison to sing. In contrast, Defoe is "*Supprest* by Fate, and humbl'd with Disdain." Defoe's mood motivates another nostalgic, poignant account of William's career with strong, vicious descriptions of the king's detractors ("Ingrateful Devils," 7). His poem soon descends to a long attack on those he associates with *The Shortest-Way*; the conclusion, asking Marlborough to work to bring domestic as well as foreign peace, is brief and unconvincing.

Defoe's place in the eyes of the ministry can be seen in part by its treatment of Addison, and the fact that several other men, including Matthew Prior, John Dennis, and even the forgotten John Philips, were encouraged to write Blenheim poems and rewarded for them. Dennis, for instance, received a hundred guineas for *Britannia Triumphans* and, in 1705, became a royal waiter in the London Customs House. Philips wrote his poem while a guest in Bolingbroke's house. Outmatched in classical education, poetic ability, and patronage, Defoe persevered. The strengths of these and *A Hymn to Peace, A Hymn to Thanksgiving, On the Fight at Ramellies [sic]*, and other public poems published in periodicals are in their narrative vigor, allegorical abstraction, and the evocation of England's noble, historical character rather than in grace or metrical beauty. Defoe does occasionally rise to above-average poetry. For example, in *A Hymn to Victory*, Defoe wrote in praise of Marlborough:

> See how *Britania* leads him to the Field!
> Valour his Guide, and Providence his Shield!
>   See on his Right *Victoria* stands,
>   Receives his high Commands;
>   She serves *Cadet* and *Voluntier*:
> Attended thus, What shou'd the Hero fear?
>   (48)

His allegorical, mercenary lady Victory is a fine device by which to elevate Marlborough's accomplishment through an account of England's long years of courting her.

In prose Defoe had more success. At the time of the standing army controversy, Defoe had once noted that men he knew were thinking of hiring better journalists to serve their party's ends.[14] A number of periodicals were flourishing in 1704; De Fonvive, for instance, made £600 a year from his *Post Man* and even the poorly written official *London Gazette* supported itself entirely on sales and advertising. Reading such papers had become a major part of the coffeehouse society in which Defoe moved. His favorite coffeehouse—the one where he received messages from Harley—was located a few blocks from Guildhall, conveniently between Cheapside and St. Lawrence Jewry Church. At "Jones's in Finch Lane," run by the recently widowed proprietor Ann Jones, the war and England's financial problems, local and court politics, and reports from the papers sparked endless discussion.[15] And so Defoe began the *Review*, the periodical he wrote singlehandedly for over nine years. Defoe himself always denied that the *Review* was a subsidized party paper. He described its creation "in *Tenebris*" as part of his divinely guided recovery. "He who gave him brains" gave him the idea along with the inspiration for the Scandal Club, he wrote in the preface to volume 1 of the *Review*.

The first number of his first periodical, *A Review of the Affairs of France: And of All Europe, as Influenc'd by That Nation . . . with an Entertaining Part in Every Sheet, Being Advice, from the Scandal Club . . . in Answer to Letters Sent Them for That Purpose*, came out on 19 February 1704. The *Review* promised a "History" of France emphasizing that nation's rise to military greatness, its treatment of its Protestants, and its conduct of the present war with England. Obviously designed to answer the kinds of questions raised in coffeehouse debates, the *Review* seldom included "news" as we know it. The early *Review* especially was highly narrative, and, throughout its tenure, the paper would announce a series of essays on a specific topic. The "Scandal Club," a "Corporation" of self-appointed moral legislators, gave the *Review* a lighter side designed to attract more readers. This "*Mercure Scandal*" he described as "A Weekly History of Nonsense, Impertinence, Vice, and Debauchery." In addition to rival journalists, Defoe's tribunal considered the problems and behavior of a very wide cross section of London citizens. They ridiculed justices who became drunk in public, offered young men advice about avoiding duels, and told matrons how to break off with undesirable neighbors. Defoe's love for jests enlivens his answers; for instance, he tells the matrons to send the chambermaid in to drink tea with the offending neighbors. Soon readers began to send questions, and Defoe added the popular question-and-answer form to the summons and proceedings of the club. His mixture of familiar situations, firm morality, common sense, and biting satire made the club so popular that Defoe would complain that it threatened to swallow the paper.

Although the *Review* had political motives from the beginning, was seen from its inception as Harley's "discreet" voice "to state facts right," and its first paragraph bore significant resemblance to Harley's idea as he stated it to Godolphin in August 1702,[16] there is strong evidence that Defoe acted independently in starting the *Review*. In studying ways by which he might support himself and his family, Defoe at some point would surely have thought of starting a periodical. Just as his association with John Dunton influenced *The Storm*, so it could have encouraged the creation of the *Review*. Dunton's *Athenian Mercury*, a twice-weekly publication, was, like Defoe's, more magazine than newspaper and used the question-and-answer format of the Scandal Club. In fact, Dunton accused Defoe with some heat of costing him £200 by stealing his "Question-Project," and Defoe would bind his *Reviews* with a preface and index as Dunton had the *Athenian Mercury*.[17]

Whatever the judgment is on Defoe's own disclaimers, the best evidence for Defoe's initial independence is the paper itself and, specifically, its June and July numbers, which Godolphin asked Harley to investigate in order to identify the author. From February until 4 July the paper was made up of one essay after another which set the French "in a true light." Defoe describes their army, its administration, its present deployment, and recent campaigns, and harps on "the unhappy Temper of the *English*," which is their most dangerous weakness (cf. *Review* 1:26). Primarily the paper gives the previous year's campaign in a highly narrative style: "Thro' all these Difficulties and Hazards they mov'd on with incredible and unparallel'd Expedition" and so the "history by inches" goes (1:45, 53). The information in the paper was available in De Fonvive's *Post Man*; in Abel Boyer's *History of the Reign of Queen Anne, Digested into Annals*; in *The Compleat History of Europe*; and in pamphlets such as *A Short, but Impartial Account of the Most Remarkable Occurrances and Transactions of the Two Last Campaigns*, but Defoe's narrative style and acute commentary set the *Review* apart.

The *Review* is so critical that it is surprising that it was suspected of being a government tool. "Whence is it that we being every where Masters of the Sea, are yet not able to prevent the *French* carrying their Arms into the remotest Parts of *America*?" Defoe asked on 11 March. "Some Articles in this *Portuguese* War,* had neither Honesty nor Ra-

---

*In 1704 most of the English troops in Portugal were captured and made French prisoners of war.

tional Prospect in them," he complained on 24 June. Burnet, too, complained that English expectations were sadly at odds with the results; he lamented the loss of "Our expedition . . . and our armies there, which cost us so dear." "The Scandalous Club's" unrelenting attack on the official *London Gazette* must have made its editor Charles Delafaye ridiculous. The club would summon a fictional "Delafaye" week after week, demanding, for example: "Read your own paragraph and tell us how many were taken Prisoner." Or: "How [could] one of their Comrades be taken in two Villages?" The *Review's* Delafaye could never answer any of the questions. At this time the club was a major part of Defoe's effort to correct "the wrong Notions of Things." He pointed out errors, obscure prose, and dubious sources in almost every contemporary paper: "They write from *Tunbridge*, by way of *Edinburgh*, that the Duke of *Ormond* was safe arrived at *Dublin*" is a typical club parody and exposé of the circuitous and improbable routes by which reports arrived. By discrediting the other papers Defoe puffed his own, and his unified, apparently information-filled essays gave the *Review* additional credibility. His examination of the French continued, and his catalogue of their strengths grew. Even when he enumerated weaknesses, he took little away: "It must be necessary . . . to look into [weaknesses] . . . tho' God knows they are very few" (1:37).

Signs that the *Review* would survive came early. By 11 March Defoe's printer Matthews was accepting advertisements, which rapidly increased in number. On 1 April Defoe announced he would publish twice a week instead of once, and at the end of May he answered apparent requests that he publish three times a week with gratitude and willingness but insisted he could not afford to: "He has all along wrote it without Profit or any manner of Gain whatsoever; so he is not able to spare so much more of his time from other needful Studies" (*Review* 1:116). Had the *Review* been subsidized, Defoe surely could have agreed to increase its frequency and would not have had to reduce its size from a whole to a half sheet (1:33). Circulation then stood at 400 copies, but estimates are that five to ten people read each copy. One contemporary wrote that the *Review* was "the Entertainment of most Coffee houses in Town." Charles Leslie, a rival journalist, complained that "the greatest part of the *people* . . . cannot read at all, but they will gather about one that can *read*, and listen to . . . [a] *Review* (as I have seen them in the streets)."[18]

It was 29 June 1704 when Godolphin demanded that Harley "find out the author" of the *Review* and take action, for his "magnifying of France is a thing so odious."[19] Defoe's rhetoric was, after all, more appropriate to Parliament's recalcitrance during the standing army controversy than it was in 1704. Defoe had detailed the impotence of the British navy. He had said of the recent campaign: "They taught us last Year, that with about 50000 Men . . . they cou'd keep the Confederates with above 80000 from Attempting any Fatal Enterprize" (1:113). He habitually used descriptions of the French such as "prodigious Strength" (1:118) and referred repeatedly to French power, wisdom, policy, greatness, and efficiency. Defoe was not being deliberately provocative; rather he was using the style that had earned him praise in King William's time. A rival journalist described Defoe's style as "Oracular" and commented, "To make this Allusion plain, / The Poet had suited it more, / If apply'd to the Rebels of *Charles* his reign."[20]

Finally, Defoe went too far. His language was far from current journalistic practice, and his point dressed in memorable phrases. On 24 June he said he would be glad to buy the reversions of military men's commissions* at seven years' purchase because he knew it would take England at least that long to beat France, for "That Nation that has *Bullyed Europe* for 30 Years past, and now threatens the Gates of *Vienna*, will not be so easily brought down." And he catalogued the number of their "Impregnable Fortifications," their "Disciplin'd Soldiers," "Experienc'd Officers" and "Bottomless" supplies (1:143). On 27 June he said it was universal knowledge that English folly had contributed more to French greatness than anything else. Such words outraged and shocked some readers. One pamphlet pointed out that "nothing but a perpetual War, can make his Purchase [of reversions of military commissions at the rate he named] valuable" and concluded by humbly leaving "the Construction of such injurious Amusements, to those Honourable Gentlemen, whose proper Businesse" it was to prosecute such "Incendiary" work.[21]

Harley obviously reached Defoe. In the 1 July *Review* Defoe had expressed boredom with the charge that he favoured the French too much and referred the reader to earlier numbers of the *Review* rather than repeat his position. Because of this assertion, the fact that the 4 and 8 July *Reviews* are devoted to clearing himself of the charges of magnifying French power is extremely significant. These two essays are carefully written; they include several extended, entertaining stories to serve as analogies, supporting examples for his method from the classics, history, and "our Saviour," and numerous compound sentences joined by "but" ("the *French* are strong . . . *but I never said they were invincible*"). Defoe's letter to Harley on 7 July says, "I Confess my Self also Something Impatient to have it from your Self, that I had Explain'd the Review to your Satisfaction" (H 26), adding that he hopes he has disguised the social rank of those who objected. On 11 July he

*Defoe speaks of the practice of buying the right to succeed to a commission upon the retirement of the present holder for a sum equivalent to seven times the annual income of the appointment. In time of war the perquisites and captured booty made such commissions highly lucrative.

apologizes yet more: "He has been told" that he wrote with "too much Contempt of the Objectors." He insists he directed no criticism at Queen Anne and King William, or at the present controversial movement of Marlborough's troops.

In this paper he turns the attention of his readers to Charles XII of Sweden whom he charges with "Ambition, Injustice, Ingratitude," and "Impolitick and Immoderate Fury" (1:163). Not only is the change of subject prudent, but it also signals the beginning of the *Review*'s dedication to propagating the central policy line of the Queen Anne ministry. Even though Defoe had worried *before* offending Godolphin that he was following history "too close at the Heels" (a phrase he borrowed from Sir Walter Raleigh), the *Review* now becomes even more topical. The first numbers after the explanation describe the progress of the Great Northern War, with specific emphasis on the ways that war affects England and on the War of the Spanish Succession. Here Defoe is producing propaganda directly in line with a current government position. By maintaining Swedish neutrality in the War of the Spanish Succession and invading Poland, Charles XII had angered England, which wanted Charles to join the Grand Alliance to defeat France. His refusal to do so deprived England not only of a great ally but of a number of highly skilled mercenaries (many of them Scots) who were fighting with Charles; moreover, Charles seemed disloyal to the "Protestant cause."

As secretary of state for the Northern Division, which included northern Europe and Scotland, Robert Harley had special knowledge and interest in the progress of the Great Northern War. At a time when even Charles's most trusted advisers were urging him to join the Grand Alliance against France or at least to avoid aggression in order to "encourage a better press in western Europe," Defoe's position was uncontroversial and solidly "party line."[22] From this point on the *Review* followed history "close at the heels," and the course of its essays generally paralleled the ministry's central policy line on one major issue after another. The relationship of this policy line to Harley's positions was not nearly so constant; sometimes he and Defoe appeared to be in complete agreement; on other occasions Defoe stayed in the center of the position when Harley was known to disagree with a specific policy. References to the *Review* continued to argue its relative independence from Harley. On 6 May 1706, for instance, Defoe wrote to Harley: "You Were pleasd to Tell me you Desir'd to speak with me on Account of The Review &c. I have Often Endeavour'd to have the like honor and began to hope Some thing might Offer" (H 119).

This crucial period of the *Review*'s life helps pinpoint the beginning and nature of Defoe's employment by Harley. Secretary of State Nottingham had become increasingly unhappy with the Whigs in the ministry; he had offered the queen the seals of his office three times before Anne accepted them on 22 April. Harley was added to the Privy Council on 27 April and offered a secretaryship. After hesitating for nearly a month, he agreed to become secretary of state for the Northern Division while retaining his position as speaker of the House. From Harley's notes it is clear that he lacked a compelling interest in foreign affairs and worried about the work load. One note reads, "how are the letters answered? al by the Principals own hand?" He took the oaths of office on 18 May. He now drew the salaries and allowances of both offices including £5 per day as speaker, a salary of £1,850, and £2,000 for secret service as secretary of state.[23] About the time Nottingham resigned, Defoe wrote Harley a letter about a meeting he had missed with Harley because he had not received Harley's message until the day after the proposed meeting. Defoe explained that he would have gone to Harley at once and waited indefinitely, but for his awareness of the need to conceal "your Admitting a Man Lately Made Despicable" and for his chagrin at being confronted only two days earlier by someone who knew "when, where, and How often" they met (H 12, 13).

This letter and those immediately following show that Defoe and Harley met but make clear that Defoe's work was evolving, not established. Harley had always met people secretly at his back door. For example, no less a power than William Carstares, King William's "Cardinal Carstares," habitually saw Harley this way; in a typical note, Harley wrote, "I will be ready upon your giving three knocks at the back-door, to let you in." Harley seems to have been attempting somewhat indiscriminately to win journalists over; for instance, William Pittis wrote in a request for money, "You were pleas'd . . . to tell me that rathar [sic] than my Necessitys should make me Comply with Booksellers Requests in writing what they should put me upon, your Honour would be assistant to me your self."[24] On 16 May Defoe had not heard from Harley and wrote to see if his first letter had been received. Here he says he "Impatiently" waits for orders and hopes "you May find this Neglected fellow Servicable, or *at least Make him So*" (emphasis added). Were Defoe already Harley's agent, he would surely not have used these phrases.

The next few letters reinforce the sense of a tenuous and undefined relationship. Although he mentions "short Interviews," he offers in a single letter to do several different kinds of work: "The Voyage you propose is Very Acceptable to me" *and* "Either That One Branch of the Auditors office . . . May be bestow'd on me . . . Or That his Ldship will appoint me a Convenient Private Allowance for subsistence On which I might Comfortably Depend." Over and over he repeats that he will be "Glad to Distinguish my Self in any Thing and at Any hazard," and "Entreat[s] to . . . at last Enter into your Intrests and Service." When he

Robert Harley, first earl of Oxford.

and his family receive yet another generous gift, he writes, "I am Impatient to kno' what in my Small Service pleases and Engages" (H 14, 15, 16).

Defoe's confusion soon gave way to a sense of engagement and purpose. In early June,[25] he wrote to Harley full of plans for a trip he had evidently agreed to take on government business, asked for a pass, and a leave for Christopher Hurt, a minor customs employee who was to go with Defoe. He also promised a plan for a spy network, mentioned his work on the political poem, *The Dyet of Poland*, and strongly recommended the dismissal of Sir George Rooke, Commander of the Fleet. After Harley became Secretary of State in May, he clearly moved to use Defoe more extensively and rapidly defined Defoe's work. On 31 July Godolphin wrote Harley: "I return You the blank warrant signed by the Queen for D——'s pardon. Her Majesty commands me to tell you she approves entirely of what you have promised him, and will make it good." As secretary of state for the Northern Division, Harley would have needed more information about matters that might affect government policies, especially about Europe and Scotland. Once again the queen and Godolphin were fully informed about Defoe's affairs. Records show that as speaker, Harley received money from Godolphin for his agents.[26] Now he had direct access to budgets from which he could pay Defoe.

CHAPTER 8

THE LITERARY EFFORT OF
A LIFETIME

His Body shou'd not be confin'd
Who's a true Monarch in his Mind
One who with his Majestick Pen
May give the Law to other Men.
— JOHN DUNTON

Not so inconsiderable neither,
the Famous Mr D F—
— CHARLES LESLIE

At last Defoe felt he had work to do for Robert Harley. With characteristic rash confidence, he appointed himself Harley's adviser. Although his letters included extravagant gratitude, fawning compliments, and melodramatic pleas for money or a secure position, his self-assurance dominated. He wrote papers not only on controlling the ministry and queen, on winning the loyalty of various groups of Englishmen, and on influencing elections, but also on how to manage Poland, Hungary, and Sweden. His effrontery extended to repeating highly personal, insulting remarks to Harley. Always introduced with shocked dismay, apologies, and protests of their inaccuracy, these statements were clearly intended to suggest the wisdom of following Defoe's advice about "managing" people and affairs. As early as midsummer 1704, Defoe's letters included such "common opinions" as:

You are a Man wholly Resolv'd to Make your fortunes and . . . will Sacrifize your Judgement as well as your Friends to your Intrest [*sic*]. (39)

[You have] Trim'd So Long On both Sides, and Cares't both Partys, Till . . . Neither Side will stand by [you]. (67)

Harley controlled people by rewarding what he liked through compliment or cash and by ignoring what another person might rebuke as impertinent. By the end of August Defoe's discourse to Harley had acquired the tone it would have for the rest of their relationship. He generally limited himself to reporting his observations, interpreting them in a sentence or two, and slipping brief recommendations into the reports. His letters remained manipulative, and his psychological astuteness about causes, motives, and means of influencing opinion and action became increasingly impressive and integrated into the flow of prose.

Harley believed in a secret service, and he, Godolphin, and the queen knew that the problems caused by political factions were becoming extremely serious. Harley already had numerous agents in England and on the continent who relayed information on individuals, on such bodies as the Scottish Parliament, or on port activities. Defoe, an avid reader of Jean Le Clerc's *Life of the Famous Cardinal, Duke du Richelieu* (trans. T. Brown; London, 1695) and a strong believer in "intelligence," had flooded Harley's mail basket with suggestions. Beginning in early summer 1704 Defoe became a spy, and he himself had laid the design for his work. With Harley's acquiescence, he traveled, took note of opinions, reported objections and reservations about the ministry's actions, infiltrated groups, identified influential men and faction leaders, and wrote pamphlets and essays designed to reassure and win over the suspicious or uncommitted.

His work followed the pattern of the Whigs' network in the 1680s, described by George Speke in *The Secret History of the Happy Revolution in 1688* (1715):

[Speke] travelled several times through England, to inform himself with the greater certainty of the state of the kingdom, and to know the inclinations of the people, and by frequenting all public companies, had obtained such a perfect knowledge not only of the general bent and turn of the minds of the commonalty, but of the temper and disposition of the most considerable gentry. He did not neglect . . . to inquire who were the most considerable and leading tradesmen in boroughs and corporations, and to take down their names and dwelling places.[1]

Defoe surely knew about men like Speke, and the Whigs he met in the 1690s would have told him anecdotes about their work. In fact, he may have done such work himself, for he said in 1711 that he had traveled to "every Nook and Corner of . . . England, either upon Publick Affairs, when I had the Honour to serve . . . King *William* . . . Or upon my private Affairs (*Review* 7:570).

In early summer 1704 Defoe traveled in the southeast; in late summer he made an extended tour of the eastern counties north of London. The September reports to Harley were specific, detailed, and shot through with useful observations and advice. Even the earliest reports were concise and expert. From the center of Hertfordshire he reported that the counties to the west were generally Whiggish, with many Dissenters, and those east more High Church. He noted the importance of the Royston Club and identified Ralph Freeman as a particularly influential person. Defoe began to love this work and feel its importance. In an October *Review* he wrote that he was still "in the Country, upon his Extraordinary and Lawful occasions." He saw himself writing and talking "to furnish our Friends with arguments to defend the cause against a clamorous noisy Enemy" and was proud to be establishing a network to distribute his pamphlets and poems "amongst Friends all over England."[2]

Something else was on Defoe's mind, too, however. He was writing a major poem, one that had great importance for him. *Jure Divino* would be his defense of the Revolution that his beloved King William exemplified, the argument that proved absolute monarchy a specious, outmoded idea, and the literary work that established his reputation as a poet. It was the work of a man confident of an audience for his writing. An ambitious undertaking by any measure, *Jure Divino* would satirize the idea of the divine right of kings in a twelve-book poem in heroic couplets with Defoe's portrait, a dedication to Reason, a preface, a poem to the author, an introduction, a conclusion to the queen, and copious notes. The folio edition, sold by subscription, would be more than 375 pages long. On nothing else he wrote did he spend so much time—not on any of the novels, not on his long, universal history, not on his 1,200-page *Tour thro' the Whole Island of Great Britain*. Even his longest works were usually written in under a year; on *Jure Divino*, he would spend five. In it he left a record of those years, of his literary models and ambitions, and of his dedication to his subject.

Already the author of at least thirteen substantial poems, Defoe probably began the poem around 1701, the same year he named his daughter Sophia after the electress of Hanover, the year the Act of Settlement passed. In that year, too, his *The True-Born Englishman* sold as no poem since Dryden's *Absalom and Achitophel* had. Defoe's prose writings showed that he shared the outrage of his countrymen when King Louis XIV of France promised the exiled James II on his deathbed in September 1701 that he would acknowledge "James III" king of England, and he shared their concern over the childless state of Queen Anne, whose only surviving son had died in 1700. The English people faced an emotional choice for Anne's successor: a distant German cousin or a Catholic nephew. Defoe's writings around that time, especially *The Succession to the Crown of England*, *The Apparent Danger of an Invasion*, and *The Present State of Jacobitism Considered* had suggested several courses of action and argued the need for national unity. *Jure Divino* broadened their purpose: "To open the Eyes of Mankind to the true Interest of their Native Country" (*Review* 1:49).

Defoe, the "True-Born Englishman," therefore, began a new poem to support the Protestant succession. The nucleus of *Jure Divino* can be found in *The Original Power of the Collective Body of the People of England*, a

pamphlet dated 1702, but largely written before King William dismissed Parliament on 11 November 1701.³ Similarities between this
tract and *Jure Divino* strengthen the case for dating the beginning of the
composition of the poem to 1701.

The Original Power was a forceful, theoretical attack on hereditary
monarchy. At the time when William's popularity and power were at
their lowest ebb, Defoe had hoped to bolster William's position and
presented the king's decision to call for new elections as a response to
his subjects. Thus he portrayed William, not Parliament, as listening to
the people, who had "recourse" to the king "to depose *for them* a Power
which they saw going to be misapplied to the Ruine of those from
whom and for whom it was appointed"(24). The final phrases unequivocally located the supreme power in the people, whose petitions
for new elections, Defoe said, had been appropriate and effective and
recognized as such by the king's action.

The Original Power, like *Jure Divino*, "vindicates" the "Original Right of
all Men to the Government of themselves." The pamphlet, dedicated to
the king and the members of both houses of Parliament, tells them,
"you may Die, but the People remain . . . Original Power endures to the
same Eternity the World endures to . . . Nor have I advanced any new
Doctrine, nothing but what is as ancient as Nature, and born into the
World with our Reason" (dedication). The pamphlet discloses the ideas
underlying Defoe's *Legion's Memorial*, the notorious document delivered to Harley as speaker of the House of Commons soon after the
imprisonment of the "Kentish petitioners" in May 1701. The basic
premise and some of the assumptions and implications are startlingly
like parts of the *Second Treatise* in John Locke's *Two Treatises of Government* (1685). Both locate the supreme power in the people and assert
that the origin and purpose of government is "public good," that the
"chief end" of government is the preservation of property (which they
define as life, liberty, and estate), and that the people have the right to
armed defense of their rights against a government that tyrannically
transcends its limits.⁴ Locke's preface had given the purpose of his
essays to be "to establish the throne of . . . King William . . . and to
justify to the world the people of England whose love of their just and
natural rights, with the resolution to preserve them, saved the nation
when it was on the very brink of slavery and ruin." In 1701 Defoe
wanted to justify the actions of men like the Kentish petitioners and to
strengthen William's position as the king attempted to get additional
funds from Parliament to protect England from France. Defoe always
equated Catholic France with "popery" and popery with slavery; Louis's
action and the Tory resistance to William put England once again on
the brink of "slavery and ruin," he believed.

Defoe quoted several lines from *The True-Born Englishman* in *The*

Original Power. These lines carried Lockean ideas, too. For instance, Defoe asserted, "That Kings when they descend to Tyranny, / Dissolve the Bond, and leave the Subject free" (6). *The True-Born Englishman* sold out nine editions in the year it was published; it seemed that everyone had heard of the poem and could quote lines from it. Defoe turned again to poetry to propagate his ideas and began *Jure Divino*. Even the similes of *The Original Power* were carried over into the poem. In the pamphlet he had said that "Reason governs Men when they are Masters of their Sences, as naturally as Fire flies upwards, or Water descends" (8). In *Jure Divino* he would write, "As fire ascends, and Waters downward flow . . . Men opprest resist" (8:30).

Defoe chose a deeply traditional form for this important poem. His choices of poetic types were already becoming increasingly ambitious. Among the poems after his elegy for Samuel Annesley (1697) had been *The Pacificator* (1700), part of the Garth/Blackmore paper war; *Reformation of Manners* (1702), a formal satire; and *The Spanish Descent* (1702), a panegyric on the victory at Vigo. Before *Jure Divino* would come out, he would publish a panegyric welcoming Marlborough back from the Battle of Blenheim.

Defoe chose the verse essay, then a respected species of didactic poetry. The greatest poets of Defoe's age classified the form as "heroic" or "Greater Poetry," the category to which epic and panegyric (or the "great ode") belonged. And they used it for some of their most serious works: Dryden for *Religio Laici* and Pope for *An Essay on Man*.[5] Springing from the poetry of Persius, Juvenal, and especially Lucretius, the verse essay had developed formal expectations. The form had become the standard one for the presentation of a system designed to increase order, wisdom, and human happiness. Its architectural structure depended upon an examination of a subject and its principles; its movement flowed from statements about the nature of man and existence through cumulative examples, images, polemical antithesis and rejoinder, and exposition to a celebration of an organizing conclusion. The poet self-consciously worked with humankind within society within a providential world, and therefore always moved diachronically and synchronically to expound his philosophy. Like the prose essay, the verse essay was a *personal* form—a form giving pleasure not so much from conclusion as from the contemplation of the mind in motion.[6] These poems usually sprang from deep feelings about crucial human uncertainties, perhaps the most profound of all human questions: about reality and man's nature, soul, source, destiny, and end.

Poets writing in this form ruthlessly subordinated beauty to clarity and argument. In the preface to *Jure Divino* Defoe called it "the Reasoning Stile" and admitted he "often sacrific'd the Poet" to it (xxvi). In spite of this controlled rhetoric, the form depended more fully than other kinds of poetry upon levels of style and diction and even varieties of poetic kinds. Rosalie Colie's term *florilegium* describes the poems well, for they routinely included narrative, allegory, panegyric, hymn, satire, polemic, and exposition.[7] Just as Pope selected the form for the heart of his magnum opus, so it was programmatic for Defoe to choose it at that moment in his poetic career for a subject in which he believed so passionately.

Defoe began *Jure Divino* with an introduction establishing the usual model of the universe and advancing an organizing principle for human nature: "All Men *would be Tyrants* if they cou'd." From that premise, the poem asserts, "All wou'd be Kings, *all Kings would Tyrannize.*" By the end of the introduction the rest of the poem is set up: "*Satyr*, the Grand Inquiry now begin, / Describe the Mortal, and describe the Sin / . . . paint the Man that *thinks himself a God* . . . and teach Mankind the horrid Plague to cure" (vi–viii). The contents of the twelve books of the poem may be sketchily outlined as follows:

1–2: the origin and evolution of kingship

3: tyranny and the appropriate purpose of kings defined

4: an inquiry into the origin of the idea of the divine right of kings

5: "Property prov'd the true and only Original of Power"

6: further definition of tyranny and a defense of the right to resist it

7–10: a historical survey demonstrating that resistance to tyranny is natural and universal and that no nation, including England, has ever had a purely hereditary monarchy

11: a panegyric on the English Constitution

12: a panegyric on the queen, her government, and selected noblemen who preserve the Constitution, which defines and limits the monarchy

The single poem that Defoe cited as precedent was one written somewhat later than the great Renaissance verse essays but always cited among them by Defoe's contemporaries. Abraham Cowley's *Davideis: A Sacred Poem of the Troubles of David* (1656) used the story of David to present philosophical ideas. Cowley, like Defoe (and Spenser before him), divided his poem into twelve books, "after the Pattern of our Master *Virgil*" and willingly sacrificed some of his poetic strength to his message, for he wished to "teach that *Truth is truest Poesie.*" At the time Defoe wrote *Jure Divino*, his contemporaries ranked *Davideis* with *Paradise Lost* and *The Faerie Queene*. Samuel Wesley, a former classmate of Defoe's, acknowledged the influence of *Davideis* in his *The Life of our Blessed Lord & Saviour Jesus Christ* (1693). Defoe, a very close reader and great admirer of Dryden, may have recognized the echoes of *Davideis* in Dryden's *Annus Mirabilis* and his translation of the *Aeneid*.

By choosing the verse essay, Defoe allied his poem with all of the poems that advanced serious, unified philosophies. By clothing abstract ideas in incidents (often historical or biblical exempla) and characters, he, like these other poets, believed ideas could become perceptual and then cognitive, be made images and vehicles of knowledge. At one point Defoe said tyranny cannot be described but must be experienced, and he multiplied example upon example until repression and suffering seem physical. In short, the poem becomes experience, and its cumulative methods more persuasive than argument.

Defoe hoped to exploit the strengths of the form which used familiar, concrete figures of speech, analogies, and traditional commonplaces in order to free ideas from complexity, to be absolutely lucid, to clarify rather than innovate or explore, and to touch readers. Poets employing the verse essay hoped that drawing upon a collective moral past would create a shared assent and commitment. Defoe, for instance, used the unfolding Augustan style to encourage people to examine the source of tyranny:

> Fear not the untrod Path of endless Thought,
> This straight to those *vast Seas of Light* lead out.
> The bright pacifick *Sea of Knowledge* stands,
> Behind these tow'ring Clifts, those threatning Sands.
> And if with steady Sail thou canst but pass,
> *Time* will present thee there with Nature's Glass:
> The bright transparent *Miror* will unfold,
> Such Truths as *Pen ne'er wrote*, or Story *told*.
>   (7:13).

This passage, reminiscent of lines by Milton and Dryden, relies upon expansive images of space and time. As so much early eighteenth-century poetry does, it strives to move beyond the historical moment to an overarching perspective. Phrases like "endless Thought" and "vast Seas of Light *lead out*" (emphasis added) move deliberately to passage beyond "threatning Sands" to a place where Time herself "will unfold / Such Truths as *Pen ne'er wrote*." Defoe's intention is to encourage his readers to share his explorer's spirit and join him in recognizing and revealing the ways tyranny perpetuates itself. Because the verse is leisurely rather than concentrated, dedicated to plain diction rather than rhetorical power, the reader is meant to find honesty, personal seriousness, and finally "completeness" and "incontrovertibility" in it.[8] Combined with the couplet as used by Dryden, Defoe, and Pope, this cumulative method allows memorable summaries that appear to grow almost inevitably from long passages. When joined with biblical and historical anecdotes and exposition, lines seem to affirm a truth rather than fix a meaning, as does "As Fire ascends, and Waters downward flow . . . Men opprest resist" (8:30).

꿏

A few months after Defoe began the poem, of course, King William died, and then *The Shortest-Way with the Dissenters* appeared. These events significantly changed *Jure Divino*. When Nottingham issued the warrant for his arrest, Defoe made numerous efforts to explain his pamphlet. Above all, he insisted that *The Shortest-Way* parodied the language and goals of some of the sermons and pamphlets published to encourage the passage of the bill to prevent occasional conformity. Among those named in *A Brief Explanation of a Late Pamphlet* (1703) was Charles Leslie's *The New Association* (1702), and Leslie profoundly influenced the composition and publishing of *Jure Divino*.

Leslie was the premier High Church political propagandist. Former chaplain to the earl of Clarendon and an active controversialist since 1691, Leslie would be praised by Samuel Johnson as "a reasoner, and *a reasoner who was not to be reasoned against.*"[9] The pamphlet that provoked Defoe was his *New Association*, which accused Nonconformists and moderate Church of England men of uniting in order to restore commonwealth principles and bring down the Constitution and the Church of England. Leslie insisted that it was sensible and just to deny Dissenters the vote and all civil or crown offices, asserting: "They are not so *Capable*, because not so fit to be *Trusted*" (10). He recited their "history" of faction, rebellion, ingratitude, and unrest, ridiculed their claims of goodwill, loyalty, and the need for national unity, and denied that the bill would "persecute" them or deny them rights. The idea that the right to vote was a birthright he called a "pretence" "upon that *Whig-Principle* . . . That all Men are Born *Free* . . . and Consequently cannot be obliged but by their own Consent." He went on to accuse the proponents of these opinions of having "designs," and exposed what he saw as their efforts to intimidate by exaggerating their numbers: "And their *Strength* lies in their *Legion*, for *they are Many*," he mocked. This final quotation came from Defoe's *Legion's Memorial*. Defoe's suspected authorship of the memorial and his prominence at the dinner for the petitioners allowed Leslie to strike against him through this quotation.

Defoe's *Shortest-Way* indisputably reflects his objections to *The New Association*. Just as Leslie ridicules the Dissenters' goodwill, Defoe satirizes the High Churchmen's charity. Defoe specifically engages a number of Leslie's topics including Scotland, the meaning of the Toleration, and the need for unity. In places Defoe parodies Leslie's exact words. Leslie writes,

But if they were now as *Considerable* as they would make themselves; The *Government* is then in the greater *Danger*, and have the more Reason to *Begin* with them, to take Power out of their Hands in Time, before they Grow too Strong for it. . . . they must have *All* or *None*. (15)

Defoe says,

The more Numerous, the more Dangerous, and therefore the more need to suppress them; and God has suffer'd us to bear them as Goads in our sides, for not utterly extinguishing them long ago. (122)

At present, Heaven be prais'd, they are not so Formidable as they have been, and 'tis our own fault if ever we suffer them to be so." (130)

Leslie describes barring the Dissenters from employment and voting as "a *Kindness* to them, to keep them from *Mischief*, like taking a *Sword* from a *Mad Man*, or a *Knife* from a *Child*, who cuts his *Fingers* with it" (8–9). Defoe transforms Leslie's idea into saving "Millions of future Souls" "from Infection and Delusion." Leslie accused the "faction" of publishing "Poyson" and compares them to vicious dogs and poisonous creatures; Defoe's pamphlet is notorious for its images of vermin, reptiles, and contagion. Leslie had begun with a reference to Herod and Pilate, and Defoe ends with one to Barabbas. Leslie concludes by saying that his intention is "to shew thence the *Spirit*, the *Principles*, and *Designs* of the *Faction*," the same purpose Defoe was to claim for *The Shortest-Way with the Dissenters*.

Defoe had seen the threat to the Hanoverian succession in the bill to prevent occasional conformity, and some of the passages in *The Shortest-Way* were designed to reveal that threat:

The Crowns of these Kingdoms have not so far disowned the right of Succession, but they may retrieve it again, and if *Scotland* thinks to come off from a Successive to an Elective State of Government, *England* has not promis'd not to assist the right Heir, and put him into possession, without any regard to their ridiculous Settlements. (121).

Your Mercy to [the Nonconformists] proves Cruelty to your poor Posterity. How just will such Reflections be . . . when our Government shall be devolv'd upon Foreigners, and our Monarchy dwindled into a Republick.[10]

Phrases such as "Successive to an Elective State," "the right Heir," "ridiculous Settlements," and "Monarchy dwindled into a Republick" unmistakably opposed the hereditary against the parliamentary ideas of the monarchy, with the stance and rhetoric of the speaker making clear the preference for hereditary monarchy. No one could read anything other than the Pretender and the House of Stuart into "right Heir" and the House of Hanover into "Foreigners."

Just as the Whigs hoped to expose the Jacobite face behind the Tory mask, so did Leslie and the Tories hope to reveal a commonwealthman behind the Whig façade. Again and again, Leslie and the others insisted, "There is a Sett of Men . . . who are Visibly Driving on . . . the Ruin of these *Nations*; by setting up the *Principles*, and carrying on the same *Pretences*, which began and at last Compleated the Bloody *Revolution* of *Forty One*, with the Destruction of the *Church*, the *King*, and the *Laws*."[11] Leslie and other Tory writers emphasized Queen Anne's hereditary right to the throne and gradually began to deny her any parliamentary right. With a possible succession crisis ahead because of Anne's childlessness, Defoe and others saw this movement as extremely dangerous. Were Anne seen to govern because she was the daughter of James II and therefore a Stuart and not because Parliament had confirmed her accession, the case for the Hanoverian succession would be weakened and that of the Pretender, "James III," strengthened. The most extreme Whig position, the position Leslie called "revolution principles," held that King James had been deposed—his "desertion" or "abdication" had been forced—and that the Convention that made William king had acted when the government was "dissolved" and had established a parliamentary monarchy with the supreme power vested in the people. The Whigs tried to make the Tories full partners in the Revolution of 1688, and the High Church Tories insisted upon the dangerous and "fatal" consequences of "revolution principles." They cleverly stigmatized these principles further by identifying them with the Dissenters and by predicting anarchy. In this scenario the Dissenting academies became "nurseries" for "New *Schemes* of *Government* out of their own Heads" and for wild, impractical ideas that would turn the country into a "confused," "tempestuous" sea. Children scrambling for apples and jealous lovers with a mistress were two of Leslie's analogies.[12]

Although Leslie mentioned Defoe and *The Shortest-Way* in his 1703 publications, his attention is upon the principles he finds behind the pamphlets written by the Whigs, and, in *The New Association, Part II*, he undertakes a refutation of "The Great *Lock* in his *Two Treatises of Government*." Leslie chose Locke not because he was already the great spokesman for Whig ideology[13] but because he was easily associated with the most extreme radical causes since Cromwell, and because some of his propositions could easily be parodied and ridiculed. Locke had, of course, been political secretary and intimate friend to the earl of Shaftesbury and could thus be associated with Monmouth's rebellion. In more recent times the *Two Treatises* had been used to argue that Ireland had a right to an independent parliament. In addition to being associated with this separatist stand, *Two Treatises* had been prominently cited by men such as the radical Whig Walter Moyle and the Deist Matthew Tindal. When Locke's work was praised, the praise was often qualified in the way William Atwood did when he observed that the "Ancient Constitution" might be endangered because of the people's right to form a new government.[14] Leslie could point out the impractical extensions of some of Locke's ideas: "The Great *Lock . . .* makes the *Consent* of every *Individual* Necessary. Which is only *Impossible*. For then every one must, at least, *Vote* for his *Representative*. Which is not *Practicable* in any one *County*, much less a *Kingdom. . . .* then the whole *World* must Meet to *Canton* it self out by *Plurality* of *Voices*" (42).

Leslie's beliefs in a hereditary monarchy, non-resistance, and monarchical prerogatives animate his entire series of 1702–1703 pamphlets, but especially this discussion of Locke. Most abhorrent to him are the ideas of limited monarchy and the "natural rights" of liberty and property—all ideas Defoe had championed as early as 1689 and as vigorously as he had done in *The Original Power of the Collective Body of the People of England* and in *Legion's Memorial*.

Leslie's *The Rehearsal* attacked "revolution principles" in a long series of essays. In this periodical, he ridiculed Defoe and several of his publications and included nine numbers aimed at refuting Locke's *Two Treatises*. Leslie's status as the premier High Church propagandist and his attack on Defoe not only assured that Defoe would engage him, but kept Locke in Defoe's mind and helped focus his arguments against the High Church view of monarchy as he wrote *Jure Divino*. So much was Leslie on Defoe's mind in these months that even in *The Storm* he directed a gratuitous political analogy at Leslie. He compared absolute monarchs with the plunderers of wrecked ships who "flatter themselves with the Lawfulness of this Kind of Theft, plead a Property in it, and call it *God's Good*":

Mr. *Rehearsal* must pardon me, if the Similitude of Cases almost makes it natural to call it by a Name he is mighty fond of, I mean, DIVINE RIGHT. These Sort of Thieves, and those he calls Monarchs, but in right speaking Tyrants, happen to be in the two Extremes of Wickedness that Mankind is capable of, both claim from the same Original, and I think, it is easie to prove, they do it with the same Authority.[15]

Defoe intended *Jure Divino* to be *the* great defense of revolution principles and the heart of his argument is Lockean. He hoped to discredit ideas of absolute monarchy, the divine right of kings, and passive obedience for all time. The essential question had been posed in Parliament's statement about the Civil War: "The question in dispute is whether the King should govern as of God by His will; or whether the people should be governed by laws made by themselves and live under a government derived from their own consent." On 4 January 1648 the Commons had resolved "That the People are (under God) the Original of all just Powers." The trial of Henry Sacheverell would be another forum for the same debate. In the body of his poem Defoe argued that property precedes government and comes from the right people have to subsistence and comfort; society always precedes government; in the beginning, societies are naturally patriarchal, choosing a superior man as leader; as a society evolves, it establishes rules; societies join together to defend against invasion and arbitrate disputes in the interpretation of the exercise of natural rights; and the superior's right to rule is joined to the property to be protected. Therefore, the notion of the divine right of kings is absurd, and when superiors "break the Laws, trample on Property, affront Religion, [and] invade the Liberties of Nations," they may be resisted by force. The poem supports a Polybian mixed government, grants considerable power to monarchy, and finds the origin of authority to be divine and vested in the people and their property. "I esteem the Liberty of Estate and Religion, equally with our Lives," Defoe asserts. Furthermore, he finds these liberties "every Man's Birthright by Nature" (preface, xxv).

Throughout Defoe reasons from a theory of the nature of man and a deeply Protestant belief in every man's ability to test law and legal authority (synonymous with the conduct of the monarch) by his own reason. Combining his own basic Calvinism with some Hobbesian thought, Defoe portrays men as proud, headstrong, depraved, and foolish—in a word, fallen. Unlike Hobbes, however, Defoe finds humankind social and believes war to be the result of periodic corruption rather than the "state of nature." Defoe argues from Scripture and from empirical deduction. For example, the truth of authority from property comes from the creation story, specifically from God's giving Adam dominion over Eden. In book 7, Defoe shows that all nations in all times have finally resisted tyranny and that even English Jacobites fought with William against the Catholics in Ireland at the Boyne;* thus, resistance to tyranny rather than passive obedience is a divine law "written within Man's breast."

None of the ideas in *Jure Divino* is new. Algernon Sidney, for example, had believed that government derives its power from the people and insisted in *Discourses concerning Government* (published 1698) that they had the right and ability to evaluate their rulers and hold them accountable. Defoe quotes him approvingly and says that Sidney was beheaded because it was the only way his argument could be defeated (4:217–28). In fact, Defoe had been steeped since his youth in such ideas. Charles Morton's lectures on government, for instance, granted great respect and power to the monarch but gave preeminence to the English Constitution and "the liberties of the subject." Significantly, they argued "a right to the *ordines regni* to restore the constitution, by the extraordinary call of some person to the throne" in the event of violation of the constitution or "failure" of the government. At Mor-

---

*The 1 July 1690 battle at the Boyne River where William defeated James. Both were present and commanded international armies that included their major allies. The battle crushed the Jacobite rebellion.

ton's school, too, Defoe may have read books such as George Lawson's *Politica sacra et civilis* (1660), an assertion that the government had been dissolved in 1642 and its powers returned to the "general community," and *An Appeal from the Country to the City, for the Preservation of His Majesties Person, Liberty, Property, and the Protestant Religion* (1679), an early defense of a Protestant succession to the English throne.[16] Morton's system, like most of these, presented limited monarchy as the best form of government. Defoe mentions that among the school papers that he had saved was "a Declamation" in which, by "History and Reason," monarchy was proved the best government.[17]

By 1700 Defoe (like Locke) knew Grotius, Pufendorf, Hooker, Sidney, and the other major anti–divine right theorists, and he refers to them in *Jure Divino*. It is Locke's *Two Treatises* that his poem most closely resembles in thought, however, and Defoe seems to be drawing inspiration and even phraseology from Locke.

The points of comparison between *Jure Divino* and Locke's *Second Treatise of Government* are extensive, major, and extend the arguments of the earlier writers in the same ways that Locke had done.[18] Faith in Reason, the fiduciary conception of monarchy, consent of the governed, the central significance of property, the long-suffering nature of a people who will inevitably rebel against tyranny, the supremacy and binding nature of laws on monarchs, and the fact that government was "dissolved" when it acted contrary to its trust comprise the backbone of both men's theories of the origin and nature of political power. As Leslie had seen, the conception of man as essentially, permanently free stood behind their arguments. Both believed that men acted against nature when they "enslaved" themselves. Locke argued that a man could not surrender this freedom "but by what forfeits his Preservation and Life together," and that he therefore had no more right to "give another power" over his life than he had to commit suicide. Defoe, too, saw these limits upon the rights a subject could surrender: "'Tis Bantring God Almighty as well as the Prince, to swear to pay a larger Obedience to Princes than the Laws of Nature have furnish'd the Man to perform; Mankind can't" (4:24), and "*Nature directs*, as God himself design'd, / What *once he gave them*, they should now defend" (5:24). Putting their trust in man's long-suffering nature, Locke and Defoe denied anarchy, chaos, or nearly continual unrest to be the consequences of their position. Both saw resistance as inevitable: "how they will be hindered . . . I cannot tell," Locke wrote, and Defoe gave nearly two full books of his poem to historical examples of nations finally driven to resistance after years of persecution and suffering.

Some of the smallest touches also argue Locke's immediate influence on Defoe. The use of the same words with the same implications and of the same examples can be multiplied many times over. For instance, both writers remind their readers that many of the first leaders were military generals (and therefore chosen with a very specific, limited "end"). Both use analogies to the conduct of mistreated animals to reinforce their arguments about the rational interpretation of resistance to tyrants. The fact that Defoe uses such relatively obscure sources found in Locke's *Second Treatise* as King James I's 1609 speech to Parliament points especially to direct, major influence.[19]

In spite of this influence, however, Defoe mentions Locke's name but once; his references to Grotius, Pufendorf, and even Milton are more frequent. Works by all of the men cited were paid more ideological respect in the early 1700s than Locke's *Second Treatise*, and none were as closely associated with recent party causes as Locke. To be a political philosopher, even a radical one, was better than to be of a "party" in the time when "political parties" and "faction" were synonyms and most upperclass men resolutely resisted party labels.

⁓

Thus, the quiet and security of 1701 gave way to the maelstrom of 1702–1703. According to Defoe, he never published most of the part of *Jure Divino* composed before 1703. Rather, the "greatest part" of the poem released in 1706 was written in prison (fall 1703).

Defoe tells us in the preface that he did not publish "the second Part," which was "the first in Action," because he feared that, "*coming from him*," it would "give Offence." This preface is very much a document of 1704–1705 and hints at the struggle publication would be. From the time of his release in November 1703 until the publication of the poem in July 1706, Defoe's life was one of hardship, distraction, and insecurity. In his preface Defoe described himself as being under "intolerable Pressures" and subjected to "the constant ill Treatment of the World" (xxv). He mentioned "the little Composure" he had felt, and the book shows that it was printed in sections at different times and was never adequately corrected. Defoe speaks of those eager to misconstrue his work and those who watch "for my Miscarriage." To those people, he says, he "sacrifices" part 2 of *Jure Divino*.

Almost from the time Defoe was released from Newgate, he had been scrutinized and harassed by those who wanted him silenced or who thought others might pay to have him so. Robert Harley received several "tips" about Defoe's activities. In early March 1704 a Tory press spy submitted a report on Defoe. "A Character of Daniell de Foe writer of the Pamphlet calld the Review" identifies him as a Whig, a dangerous hired pen, and presented evidence intended to allow the government to start legal proceedings against him again. In April "R.A." smugly reported that he had by chance been present at a secret meeting of Dissenters who "imagined me to be one of their own dissenting sanctified fraternity." They gave him a copy of a short pamphlet that presented a High Church character ranting that the press must be controlled to save the Church of England. This informer said that he was told Defoe wrote it. *To the Honourable the C——s of England Assembled in P——t* does repeat Defoe's ideas about the High Church as stated in *The Shortest-Way with the Dissenters* and in a number of his post-pillory publications. R.A. concluded his report with the evil suggestion that Defoe had forfeited the sureties for his seven years' good behavior.[20] Both of these reports use sarcastic, pejorative adjectives such as "sanctified fraternity" and "purified party" to describe the Dissenters, identify Defoe entirely with the City Whigs, and have silencing him as their objective.

In June 1704 Defoe was in some danger and had little time for *Jure Divino*. Persistent, numerous rumors that he was author of the four-page tract *Legion's Humble Address to the Lords* refused to die. In fact, Defoe had written the mock appeal and commendation to the House of Lords. In it, he continued his attack on the Commons by accusing them of infringing upon the rights of citizens and neglecting their duty to the extent that they had become "an Unlawful Assembly" that "may and ought to be . . . Dismist by the same Laws of Nature . . . that Oppressed Subjects may, and . . . have, Deposed Bloody and Tyrannick Princes" (1–2). The pamphlet complained of election abuses the Commons tolerated, and congratulated the Lords for upholding the rights of the Aylesbury freeholders. It undeniably insulted the Commons and fit any contemporary definition of seditious libel. On 14 June another informer, "J.W.," wrote Harley that "Dan Foe," "supposed author of the libel," could be arrested "at Captain Roger's" in Canterbury.[21]

On 27 September Secretary of State Charles Hedges issued a warrant for the arrest of Nathaniel Sammen, the weaver at whose home Defoe had been apprehended. On the twenty-eighth Hedges wrote Harley that "one Sammen a weaver" had been arrested for distributing *Legion's Humble Address* and that Sammen was "a tool of De Foe's."[22] Sammen admitted delivering a bundle of papers to the bookseller Lintot but said he did not even know if they were printed or written. The bundle came, he said, from "one John Pearse, his acquaintance, who is a Broker on the Exchange, and was primarily a Silkman." Hedges forced Sammen to admit that he had returned to Lintot's to see how many more copies Lintot wanted. Sammen either could not or would not give more information, and Hedges sent him to Newgate on the twenty-ninth. Hedges complained that he could "get no more out of Sammen" and when notified on 5 October that Chief Justice Holt had taken bail for Sammen, sent the attorney general the evidence of those who would testify against Sammen, Thomas Smith and Joseph Chamberlain.[23]

At first, Defoe was annoyed. Upon hearing reports that he had hidden from the law, Defoe joked in the *Review* that "he has some Thoughts of exposing himself to their View, and for Two Pence a time, *the Price of seeing a Monkey*, they shall have the Satisfaction of seeing him like a Quack Doctor, from 8 in the Morning to 12; and from 2 till 9 at Night" (1:120). Matters became more serious, however, and attacks on Defoe increased. Leslie's *Rehearsal*, originally entitled *The Rehearsal of Observator, &c.*, took discrediting Defoe as a major objective. On 26 September Narcissus Luttrell thought that a warrant had been issued to arrest Defoe for his remarks about Admiral Rooke. A manuscript newsletter of 30 September says that Defoe has been "silenced for a Blasphemous Expression" and will be prosecuted for it and his ridicule of Admiral Rooke; both offensive pieces had appeared in the *Master Mercury*.[24]

The *Master Mercury* is the perfect example of the kind of distraction that, first, delayed Defoe's work on *Jure Divino* and, second, complicated its publication. The *Review*, like Godolphin and Harley, was committed to moderation and avoidance of ad hominem exchanges, but Defoe had some personal scores to settle and believed that some battles had to be fought with weapons inappropriate for the *Review*. The *Master Mercury* may have done more than anything else to exacerbate the Tories' resentment of his work, and certainly it was an entirely typical example of the kind of many-pronged attack he could sustain for months. The first *Master Mercury* ridicules almost all of the newspapers in London in sharper terms than even the first numbers of the *Scandal Club* had. He hopes, Defoe says, that the papers will "mend," and he demolishes each in a few words. The *Daily Courant* "picks our pockets" because it has so little news; Abel Roper stretches the truth in the *Post Boy*; and Defoe questions the intelligence of those who "can bear to read the *London Post*" and the judgment of those who "believe the *Flying Post*."

The second number introduces the actual subject of his new paper. Defoe reports the capture of a single Swedish ship and, with heavy sarcasm, describes the event as proof that "the English Captains will fight, and so will their Seamen too." He continues,

We cannot but give a just Encomium to our Admiral, who when he perceived the audacious Boldness of this obstinate *Swede*, laid about him for the Honour of the *English* Nation, and the Dominion of the four Seas, and after a very obstinate Fight, took him Captive, with all his Men, Guns, &c.

Nor let any man object the Disparity between one Ship [the Swede's] and a whole Squadron [the English]; for we can tell him when some Commanders less brave and daring . . . let the Enemy pass unfought with, tho't odds have been as great. (6)

Defoe's target is Sir George Rooke, admiral and commander of the Grand Fleet, and his motives were many. Rooke, a High Church Tory, represented the kind of person Defoe felt had no place in English government. Defoe had been working to persuade Harley that England could have only one great war hero: Rooke or Marlborough. In June Defoe had said that Rooke "Fill'd the Fleet" with the "high furious Jacobite Party"; in September he said, "The high Church Party look on him as Their Own. The Victory At sea they look upon as Their Victory Over the Moderate Party." Defoe manipulatively presents Rooke as an enemy to Harley's party and policies: "The Sea Victory Set up against the Land Victory, Sir Geo: Exalted above the D of Marl" and "I leave This to your judgemt" (H 60–1).

It was Rooke who had made Marlborough's plan to establish Cadiz, Spain, as a base in 1702 a farce. With a remarkably large force of fifty English and Dutch ships, including twenty to thirty frigates, fire ships, and bomb vessels, and nearly 16,000 soldiers prepared to land, Rooke finally began attacking towns and forts around Cadiz on 12 August. After ingloriously plundering undefended towns and making almost no progress toward Cadiz by 5 September, Rooke rejected the advice of other commanders who wanted to attack in places closer than the forts chosen by him which were several days' march away, and, on 15 September, withdrew and sailed for England. One of Rooke's own admirals said, "If we ask why [the expedition] was abandoned, we can but be answered that it was not persevered in."[25] Rooke was lucky, though. On the way to England a Captain Hardy heard by chance that the Spanish silver fleet lay in Vigo Bay, and the commander of the Dutch troops demanded that they ambush it. Only seven of the galleons were actually captured, but the English got a million pounds and destroyed the French men-of-war guarding the galleons.[26] The drama of the capture and the magnitude of the prize largely compensated for the mishandling of Cadiz, but most shrewd Englishmen knew Rooke had been more lucky than skilled. Defoe's *The Spanish Descent* (1702) catches the character of Rooke's campaign well. Of Cadiz:

> The Unattempted *Town* Sings Victory
> And scar'd with Walls, and not with Men, we Flye,
> ....
> And thus we Quit the *Andalusian* Shores
> Drencht with the *Spanish* Wine, and *Spanish* W[hore]s.
>   (10)

Of the fleet:

> How oft have they been fitted out in vain,
> Wasted our Money, and destroy'd our Men,
> Betray'd our Merchants, and expos'd their Fleets,
> And caus'd Eternal Murmurs in our Streets?
>   (17)

Of Vigo:

> The Nation's Guardian Angel has prevail'd.
> (18)

The capture of the Spanish treasure had great popular appeal at home and did much to encourage Portugal to join the Grand Alliance. However, the Mediterranean campaign had been completely ineffectual in 1703, and in 1704, when Rooke left with orders to capture Toulon or Cadiz and, above all, to defeat the French fleet, England wanted results. What they got was another debacle and another lucky accident. In May 1,500 seamen and marines landed at Barcelona, but they withdrew three days later without results, and the fleet spent six weeks sighting and ineffectually pursuing the French fleet. However, in the course of carrying out a "diversionary action," the English captured Gibraltar.

Rooke's clumsy 1704 campaign coincided with the early months of the *Review*. Defoe had said in 1701 that "every Barber" followed the news of the fleet,[27] but, in addition to his desire to increase readership, Defoe had a personal motive beyond his religion and politics, as he so often did when he mounted a sustained campaign. Rooke had been the occasion for an assault on his friend and counsel, William Colepeper. While Colepeper waited in an antechamber at Windsor to hear the effect of a petition he had presented to Nottingham in Defoe's behalf in July 1703, one of Rooke's friends assaulted him. Later Colepeper was repeatedly challenged to a duel in Rooke's behalf and was finally waylaid and assaulted on the street. The trial of Rooke's friends at the Queen's Bench began on 14 February 1704, and Defoe not only reported on it but, in an attempt to influence the court, described at length French penalties for issuing threats and challenges and told anecdotes that obviously paralleled the Rooke/Colepeper altercation.[28]

Although two of Rooke's champions were convicted, Defoe was outraged at their light sentences—a fine of 200 marks for one and 100 marks for the other. Soon afterwards, Defoe sent Harley a position paper entitled "Of the Fleet and Sir Geo: Rook." In it he pretended to be repeating "the wholl Nation's" opinion that "The Nations Safety, the Publick Reputation, and the Creditt of the Ministry, Calls for a Suspension at least of this Obnoxious Suspected Man" (H 20–25). "The People hate" and "decry" Rooke, who has brought reflections and suspicion on the ministry, Defoe asserted. Reviewing Rooke's recent failures, he concluded that Rooke should be removed from command and investigated. No response from Harley survives, but Defoe ridiculed the fleet in the *Review*s of 13, 17, 20 and 24 June. He quoted the *Paris Gazette* report that when Rooke had forty-five ships and the French Count de

Toulouse twenty-nine, Rooke avoided a fight, and yet "most Men say, 45 is more than 29."

Forced to label these attacks on Rooke as satires on the *Paris Gazette*, Defoe shifted ground (*Review* 1:155–56). The part of *A True State of the Difference between Rooke . . . and Colepeper* that shows some signs of Defoe's collaboration jibes mercilessly at Rooke: "If any Man should enquire where the Duke of *Marlboro* was on the 3d of *July*," [Marlborough] "would not be stung at such a Question" and surely would not "stoop to employ Murderers on the Occasion" (44). This pamphlet appeared about 18 August, ten days after Defoe's new periodical the *Master Mercury* first appeared. Defoe consistently reported the news in both papers with deft slices at Rooke: "Sir *Cloudsley Shovel* [commander of the Channel fleet] had received Orders from *Lisbon*, to . . . joyn . . . *Rook*, who not being able to fight the *French* Fleet, nor to take *Barcellona*, as was expected, was sailed out of the *Straits*."[29] With such a beginning, Defoe gives the Prince of Hesse, Shovel, and two English captains credit for taking Gibraltar. After Malaga, a battle in which England garrisoned Gibraltar but lost 2,700 men, Defoe undercuts the English success by quoting the *Paris Gazette*, the *Observator*, and other papers. He emphasizes contradictions in English and French accounts over claims of victory and the number of casualties, and can ask damaging questions about such specific matters as the English lack of ammunition. Alternating reports of Marlborough's incontrovertible successes with descriptions of Rooke's actions, Defoe hardly needs to diminish Rooke's achievement by his repeated criticisms beginning, "Yet perhaps some People may say" and the refrain "If this was not a Victory. . . ." The 22 August *Review* speculated about what England's position would now be had Rooke taken Cadiz and Barcelona, beaten Toulouse, and, in short, "done all that a Fleet could do, or that we expected"(1:211).

Defoe's Scandalous Club had announced the *Master Mercury* with a delightful series of autobiographical admonitions to its author: "Newgate hath many Mansions" and "have always . . . ready for the Press, a HYMN " (like that on the pillory) (1:200). They proved prophetic. By September 28 Defoe had to write a pleading letter to Harley. Not only did he assert his innocence in ridiculing Rooke "because I Saw you Dislik'd another man upon that head" and ask for Harley's protection from prosecution, but he was skilled enough to continue his most clever maneuver against Rooke. No mere explanation to Harley with a change of focus was enough to save the *Master Mercury* as it had the *Review*. The 25 September number appears to have been its last. In January Rooke was removed from command and a committee of the House of Lords appointed to investigate his conduct.

This 1704 saga illustrates why Defoe was such a feared writer. His campaign against Rooke is sustained, varied—and effective. He writes in several modes, and his weapons include sober historical account, statistics, raillery, innuendo, ridicule, mock dialogue, and light-hearted fantasy. His insight into broad political realities occasionally surpasses that of the best of Queen Anne's statesmen. He was correct in seeing the Tories' use of Rooke as a threat to "the Triumvirate's" war effort and as exacerbating party differences. As if to fulfil his prophecy, the nation saw rival congratulatory resolutions to Marlborough and to Rooke introduced in Parliament that fall.[30] The ability to analyze Harley and his readers, touch the springs of their actions, and manipulate them were talents that would make Defoe a fine novelist, but in 1704 they were beginning to make him the most feared journalist of his generation. The High Church writer Charles Leslie, always one of the first to recognize Defoe's work, wrote: "Defoe may change his name from *Review* to *Mercator* from *Mercator* to any other title, yet still his singular genius shall be distinguished by his inimitable way of writing."[31]

The Rooke writings also show that Defoe was no alienated, isolated, friendless exile after his release from Newgate. Although his resentments (Sacheverell, Rooke) sometimes seem to live longer than his friendships, his loyalties are always strong and fearless. He does not blame Colepeper for his own harsh sentence. More important is the fact that he continues his efforts in behalf of the Dissenters' interests as he sees them. Political faction and wars abroad are often integral parts of the most important struggle in Defoe's landscape: that of protecting the Protestant interest. The various reports of clandestine meetings and privately circulated poems and pamphlets lead to the inescapable conclusion that Defoe still had close friends among the Dissenters and even suggest that Nottingham may have been right to accuse Defoe of having confederates.

The few intimate, personal comments that survive give a completely consistent picture of a charming, stimulating companion. John Barber, the printer of *The Dyet of Poland*, would never apologize for his friendship with Defoe even in the face of his friends' strong disapproval. His biographer reported that once, after being criticized, Barber said that he "never should have been sorry for Printing that Poem, 'tho he had lost, instead of getting Money by it, since 'twas the Work of a Person, no Man ever could converse with, without being wiser and better for that Conversation, unless it was his own Fault." The bookseller John Dunton, who had known Defoe since youth and had far more dealings with him, assessed Defoe's character a number of times over a twenty-year period. Agreeing that Defoe "is a Man of good Parts, and very clear Sense," Dunton goes on to join in the praise of Defoe's conversation: "His Thoughts upon any Subject, are always *Surprising, New*, and *Singular*"; "*Foe* has Piety enough for an Author, and Courage enough for a

Martyr . . . if ever any, [he] is a TRUE-ENGLISHMAN; and for that Reason, he's more respected by Men of Honour and Sense, than he can be affronted by Alderman B———." In other places, Dunton described Defoe's conversation as "ingenious," "brisk enough," and "enterprizing."[32]

The same consistency appears in the surviving letters of two friends. The Norwich linen-draper John Fransham and the Edinburgh writer* John Russell both join wholeheartedly in assisting Defoe. They disseminate his opinions, give him information they believe useful, worry about him, and refer to happy, social times with punch and good talk. In regard to the *Consolidator* Fransham wrote, "You have follow'd the Heels of Truth so close in your Consolidator that the danger of a kick gave some pain to [me]." The two men mention visits, and Fransham occasionally looks forward to discussing one of Defoe's ideas. He calls Defoe "friend" with no self-consciousness at all. Russell jokes that Defoe will be glad to share a bottle in Scotland when the High Church faction makes "home too warm" for him, exchanges family gossip, and passes along messages and information about political affairs.[33] Letters from Defoe to them, both those surviving and those merely alluded to, are sometimes long, newsy, and intimate. It is clear that Defoe wrote honestly about personal experiences and showed these men the depths of some of his feelings. One letter to Fransham asks if he's been forgotten or was not worth the postage and shows nostalgia for times together. Another friend made about this time became godfather to one of Defoe's grandchildren born more than twenty years later.[34]

John Dunton and a number of other men praised Defoe's courage publicly. One of them, "J.L.," supplied a Latin poem in honor of Defoe for *An Elegy on the Author of the True-Born English-Man* (1704). In it the poet writes,

> Gaudeo Te Daniel, Legis sub mole sepultum,
> Carminis aeterni vivere jure tui.

[I rejoice that you, Daniel, buried under the mass of the law, / Live by the justice of your eternal song.]

. . . .

> Mortuus interea vivis super aethera notus,
> Et moritur fato gens inimica tuo.

[Meanwhile, dead you live known above the ether, / And the clan unfriendly to your fate dies.)

. . . .

> Delius obscuro respondes Phæbus ab antro,
> Atque timet vatum turba togata deum.
> Heu frustra foetus asinus tibi ponit in umbra,
> Quicquid agit titulus, noscitur ungue Leo.

*Scots for lawyer, factor, or "man of business."

[You, the Delian Phoebus, answer from the dark cave / And the togaed
crowd fears the prophet bard. / Oh! also in vain the idiot puts your
offspring in shadow, / Whatever the label represents, the lion is known by
the claw.][35]

Dunton, too, saw Defoe as a man who could never "be hir'd to disgrace
the *Quill* or . . . wrong his Conscience." Such men believed in Defoe's
work and often did what they could for him. Dunton, for instance, says,
"He REVIEWS without Fear, and acts without fainting— He is not
daunted with Multitudes of Enemies; for he Faces as many . . . as there
are Foes to *Moderation* and *Peace*." "Whatever he says upon . . . PEACE
and WAR , is so True and Correct, that . . . it might almost stand for an
Infallible Rule."[36]

These friendships and Defoe's steady love and respect for his wife
somewhat soften the reality of the Defoe who used powerful contacts
and his art to settle political and personal scores and would even prepare manipulative position papers for Harley, such as "Of the Fleet and
Sir Geo: Rook" and, later, "Methods of Mannagement of the Dissenters." He was haunted by the needs of his "Vertuous and Excellent" wife,
who had brought him £3,700 as a dowry. He always spoke of her in
respectful, affectionate terms, and his appreciation for the way she
encouraged him to adhere to his principles, his sense of obligation to
her, and his trust in her stewardship of the family resources seem to
grow rather than merely remain constant. He refers to his own "ill
husbandry," but Mary is always his "faithfull Steward." When he traveled, he wrote her several times a week (H 53–56, 62, 96).

~≈~

In fact, family affairs were much on his mind and drained away the
composure he needed to complete *Jure Divino*. His financial affairs
were in "Unsufferable Disorders," he said. He described his children as
"Beautifull and hopefull," constantly worried about their educations,
and knew that it was time to be deeply concerned about his sons' future
occupations. In asking Harley for a position in a branch of the Auditors' Office, he implicitly asked for a place for his son. "I Sollicit [this
position] . . . Because Twill be a Certainty in which I may bring my Sons
up Under me to be in Time Servicable to Their Fathers Benefactor"(15). At that time many administrative positions all over Europe
carried the expectation that space in the department would be made
for children or even other relatives and that some offices would be
almost automatically inherited.[37] By getting such a position Defoe
would almost guarantee positions for his sons. Although Defoe's letters
and the *Historical Collections* indicate that Mary Defoe was entirely capable of educating her daughters, the sons needed more, and Defoe
would soon send one to university.

The loyalty of his family and friends may have actually made Defoe's life harder. He could no longer afford a house in the City for them, but his work increasingly kept him away from home. While they continued at Kingsland, Defoe appears to have had to stay in the City, sometimes with his sister and brother-in-law Davis in Essex Court near the Middle Temple and sometimes as a roomer of Sammen's, the Spittlefields weaver.[38] After Defoe began traveling as Harley's agent, he would spend more time away than with his family for the next five years. Not only was his absence from the family he loved so deeply painful, but he missed some of his children's most formative years. The effects of their separation colored his marriage and relationship with the children for the rest of his life.

How hard life seemed to Defoe creeps out in a few scattered sentences marked by powerful nouns. In an early letter to Harley he apologizes for reciting his recent history, saying, "The Miserable are allways full of Their Own Cases." In May 1705 Defoe tells Fransham that God has led him "through Wildernesses of Troubles." The preface of *Jure Divino* probably exaggerates a little in order to excuse the time between subscription and publication, but the stress of the months since Newgate cannot be denied: "It has been wrote under the heaviest Weight of intolerable Pressures. . . . Let any Man, under Millions of distracting Cares, and the constant ill Treatment of the World, consider the Power of such Circumstances."[39] Even the hours Defoe proposed to be on display "like a Monkey" to prove he was no fugitive convey the struggle in that they suggest extremely long working hours: 8 to 12 and 2 to 9. Not only was Defoe writing thousands of words, absorbing personal abuse, and worrying about his finances and the attempts of the Tories to have him prosecuted again, but his trips for Harley exposed him to new suspicion and insult, even as they made him less able than ever to manage his London affairs and finish *Jure Divino*. The *Review* and Defoe's correspondence include several references to times when he had to hurry back to London, when he worried about details beyond his reach, and when he felt his life to be no more secure than it had been in the winter of 1704. Any thought of completing *Jure Divino* had to be put aside.

The Defoe that emerges in this period is not an attractive one. His self-importance and assurance jar with embarrassingly obsequious intervals, and his biblical allusions seem at odds with his Machiavellian advice to Harley. For instance, very soon after he began to see Harley regularly, he proposed a "supreme ministry" and ways to "reconcile" the nation to it. He asks rhetorically, "How shall you Make your Self Prime Minister of State, Unenvy'd and Unmolested?" And answers, "'Tis very feasible with an Accurate Conduct." Among the directions for such conduct, Defoe includes plans for finding out all "private affaires in the Court," winning over enemies with favors, and taking completely undeserved credit for the defeat of the occasional conformity bill in Parliament in order to garner favor with the Dissenters. In another proposal, "Methods of Mannagement of the Dissenters," Defoe betrays five years of lobbying for the restoration of the Dissenters' civil rights: "'Tis Not Necessary in the present Conjuncture to Restore The Dissenters to Offices and Preferments"; "They are Better kept at a Due Distance." Although many of the ideas in this paper are the same as those in the *Consolidator*, the context changes the meaning enormously. The lament over his divided and "impolitic" people in the *Consolidator* appears to be an opportunity for the statesman to keep them so and lull them into satisfaction with the government by words rather than by liberalizing restrictions. The emphasis upon secrecy and comprehensiveness in these documents is quite remarkable. Over and over he stresses these things: "Yet the Persons Entrusted Not kno' who they Serv Nor for what End"; "have a Sett of Able heads, Under a Secret Management . . . from whom to Recieve Such Needfull Informations . . . & yet These Secret heads Need Not Correspond" (43). His ambitious "intelligence" plan had as its goal no less than assuring that "the Affaires [of] all Europe may Lye Constantly before you in a True light" and in advance of every important event (20). In July Defoe envisioned himself as the head of a new government department overseeing the gathering and collating of correspondence from "Every Part of England, and all the World beside" (28). Once in place, "All the Leading Men of all Sides, would be Influenc'd . . . by a . . . Secret Mannagement. They Should Never Stir or Speak as a Party but it Should be known" (45). Harley would know "what Every body Said" of him (67). Defoe's plan may have been based, at least in part, upon Richelieu's and especially upon the sophisticated political network organized by the Whigs in the 1680s. His ideas match the descriptions of that time's opinion gathering, influence, and pamphlet distribution remarkably well.[40]

It is not impossible to see why Defoe was willing to sacrifice so much dignity and integrity. In the first place, he believed he had family responsibilities he could not meet. He was candid enough to say that he was able to supply his family's necessities, but he believed he had other important obligations to them. Because Defoe had been an imprisoned bankrupt before, he could easily imagine being returned to Newgate, and so he reacted more emotionally to his economic situation than to anything else. He had almost nowhere to turn but to Harley:

My Own Pressures which are Sometimes Too heavy and Apt to Sink the hopes I Conciev'd [*sic*] from your Goodness Force me to Importune you. (H 14)

I Refer . . . to your Goodness that . . . I may be Delivered from the Unsufferable Disorders of my affaires. (H 15)

The Gulph is too Large for me to Get ashore again. . . . Not less Than a Thousand Pounds will Entirely Free me. (H 16)

As time passed, the metaphors and the sums of money needed pile up.

Second, Defoe felt the deepest gratitude and obligation to Harley. His letters repeatedly ask for a chance to undertake such service as to "be Usefull to So bountifull a benefactor" and "Discharge My Self of the weighty Debt of Gratitude." He tells Harley, "You have bound a Gratefull Fellow So Close to you that Nothing Can be too great for me to attempt in your Service." Years later he would excuse himself in *An Appeal to Honour and Justice* by explaining his obligations "of honour and gratitude" to Harley and the queen in these terms: "Let any one put himself in my stead!" [and consider] "what must my own heart have reproached me with" [had I been ungrateful to] "Him that saved me thus from distress" [or to] "Her that fetched me out of the dungeon, and gave my family relief."

Finally, Defoe was, as he said, "by Inclination and principle heartily in the Intrest of the Govermt [*sic*]." He really was a strong believer in the monarchy and a patriot, and he shared many of the opinions and goals of the Triumvirate. Like Harley, he firmly believed in power being in the hands of moderate men without strong party sentiments. Over and over he repeated that extremists would eventually fall and that the moderates, the great majority, were the only safe governors of the nation (H 52–53). Furthermore, he believed in the necessity of the war to restore the balance of power in Europe and protect the Protestant interest and knew that the Tories did not support it. He wrote Halifax that his reason, principle, inclination, and duty to his country were in "Exact Unison" with his work to promote "the Generall Peace and Intrest of this Nation" and to oppose the High Church Tories (86). In a July 1705 *Review* he explained that working to make the nation "at Peace with One Another" was a "Publick Service" and "Doing Good." He consistently saw himself as a patriotic citizen, using his talents in his country's best interests.

The difficulties of Defoe's life, and his energy and dedication, become a subtext for his reports, and all hope of uninterrupted time for *Jure Divino* faded. For instance, on 16 September he was in Cambridge, then hurried to London to appear to confront the press spy Robert Stephens, and was back in Bury St. Edmunds, 65 miles from London and fewer than 30 from Cambridge, by 28 September. To do this he was forced to travel in a V, going some 110 miles out of his way to end the rumor that Stephens had a warrant for his arrest.[41] In order to move about freely and efficiently, Defoe had to be sure he would not be detained, even on a misunderstanding, in some small town. The fact of his pardon was not generally known, and he did not yet carry a pass from Harley.

The next year Defoe left London on 16 July, traveled through the southwest of England through Reading, Salisbury, and Weymouth as far west as Bodmin in Cornwall, then north through Bridgewater, Bristol, Worcester, and Shrewsbury as far as Manchester, Halifax, and Leeds, southeast through Sheffield, Nottingham, Leicester, and Coventry, finally to Cambridge and Colchester and back to London by 6 November. His reports follow the form of the previous summer's. Concise, specific, and to the point, they describe each area's predominant stance as Whig, moderate, Tory, or High Church; identify leaders; and report on elections for, although the vote on the Tack* had identified the Tory moderates, more information was needed in order to identify the Whig factions.

From maps, correspondence, and Defoe's "abstract" of his trip, his method emerges. He would travel five to seven hours on horseback during the day and then spend his afternoons and evenings in each town talking politics in coffeehouses and with Dissenting ministers or one of Harley's agents. In most places, he established correspondents who agreed to distribute some of his publications and to write him the kinds of letters John Fransham and John Russell did about local events and the reactions of people to national news.

Some of the men with whom Defoe stayed must have been business contacts and friends; others were simply names given him as he worked his way through England. Nearly as many were solid merchants as were Dissenting clergymen. In Tiverton, for instance, Francis Bere (or "Bear" as Defoe spelled it and Devon people pronounced it) was a prosperous merchant and brother to Thomas Bere, who had represented Tiverton in the Commons since 1690 and would be elected again. Whigs and active Presbyterians, the Beres owned the pleasant manor of Huntsham, four miles from Tiverton.[42] Samuel Elisha of Shrewsbury was an attorney and burgess.[43] Nathaniel Priestley, a well-to-do Presbyterian minister, had purchased land and built a Presbyterian chapel at Northgate End, Halifax, where he earned a reputation for moderation, piety, and learning. Defoe's friend John Dunton knew him, and people praised Priestley for "ingenuity," the quality often recognized in Defoe himself.[44] In Leeds Defoe visited James Ibettson, a wool trader, "one of the most prominent" merchants of the city.[45] Nathaniel Kinderley was a bailiff in Wisbech. The "Mr. Jardin" of Cambridge was either Richard, a linen draper, or Alexander, a wool comber; both were Independents and may have been brothers. So wealthy was Alexander that, upon his death, a thousand guineas were found concealed in his bed.[46] Yet another typical contact was John Morley,

---

*The land tax provisions had been "tacked" onto the bill to prevent occasional conformity, thereby assuring its defeat.

The Itinerary of 1705

Defoe's 1705 travel for Robert Harley.

grocer in Bury. Defoe knew him well enough to have mail sent there. Morley was a dedicated Presbyterian who had been fined for refusing to attend the Anglican Church and often took responsibility for obtaining licenses for meeting houses.[47] Such prosperous, moderate, dedicated Whigs could give Defoe good advice and information and lived in comfortable houses spacious enough to allow his visits.

Defoe often asked Harley for news "Other than the Prints Informe." Settling convivially in a coffeehouse with a tankard, he would then swap his news for their explanations of the past election and of the local situation. In a report to Secretary of State Hedges, Hugh Stafford, the justice of the peace who tried to arrest Defoe, gives a picture of Defoe telling lively stories in various towns, including one about "the young parliamt men." Defoe allegedly described these men drinking in the Fountain Tavern until time for a vote, then pouring into the House to vote as "Sir Edward, Sir Humphry, or Sir John" did without thought or integrity."[48]

In most cases Defoe spent but a single night in each town. For example, on 21 September he was in Rochdale; on the twenty-second at Halifax, twenty-five miles away; and on the twenty-third at Leeds, about twenty miles away. Traveling first with Christopher Hurt and then with his brother-in-law Robert Davis, Defoe developed a highly effective system of information gathering.

His visits attracted attention, however, and resentment often greeted him. Most people saw him as a potential troublemaker who might heighten bitter divisions. On 25 September, for instance, a Liverpool citizen named Thomas Johnson wrote a friend, Richard Norris, "We have had mr Defoe here[.] I did not see him—mr Done [Samuel, a Dissenting physician who owned a fine house with stables on Castle Street] was very busie and invited him to his house—which in my opinion had been better let alone." Yet another Liverpool resident wrote Norris that Defoe had been there and that his visit had been "the great Subject talked of and been a great matter of Speculation." On the twenty-eighth, Johnson wrote Norris again and observed, "I cannot be of the opinion that mr Done did well in takeing mr Defoe to his house—I do not like such men let them be of what side they will—it's those creatures endeavours to influence us." Some towns even passed ordinances to "forbid Strangers intermeddling in the Election." The fact that at least one township coupled the ordinance with one forbidding "Voters carrying Clubs, sticks or weapons" suggests the atmosphere in which that year's elections were held.[49]

Only rarely did Defoe detail the difficult experiences his unwelcome visits provoked. In July Mayor Edward Tucker of Weymouth attempted to prosecute Defoe and several others for plotting against the government. The problem began when Defoe's letters were collected by the wrong James Turner. Turner thought that the letters contained confusing sentences, elliptical but suggestive phrases, and many political comments. The puzzled recipient showed them to a number of people, and an investigation ensued. A series of entries in the minutes of the Weymouth borough court quote several witnesses called to give information. James Turner explained how he came to connect Defoe with the letters and how Defoe's friend the Dissenting minister John Fenner had tried to defuse the situation by joking that the letters "came from some wenches." The Weymouth schoolmaster Peter Johnson described his efforts to help Turner understand the letters. Four others, including Fenner, were summoned. Fenner alleged that the letters made no sense to him either and quoted Defoe as saying he "cared not who saw them or if they were set up at the Market Cross."

This investigation provided enough evidence for Judge Robert

Price, sitting at the Assizes then meeting in Dorchester, to issue a summons addressed "to the Mayor, Baylliffs, Constables and other Officers of W[eymouth] and M[elcombe] R[egis] and every [*sic*] of them." Fenner, both Turners, "Mr. Daniel Dufoe," and "Mr. Jonathan Edwards" were accused of corresponding "with severall disafected persons to the Government and have received Letters of Trayterous designs" and were to appear before Price on 27 July. Judge Price dismissed the charges.[50]

Defoe remained relatively unmolested until Hugh Stafford, justice of the peace at Pynes, Devonshire, issued a warrant for his arrest "for spreading and publishing divers seditious and scandalous Libels and false news to the great disturbance of the Peace of this Kingdom." Defoe detoured again but finally appeared openly at church, walked around the green at Excester, and confronted Stafford. Once Defoe had to show his pass to hearten his friends, and he alluded to it in a letter to Stafford intended to end Stafford's harassment. Stafford wrote to Secretary Hedges, whom he assumed Defoe meant, to complain that Defoe "pretends he has Authority, and license . . . from your Honour." In his haste Stafford forgot to enclose Defoe's letter. Hedges wrote on 14 September, "I desire you will please to send it me, that I may take such Meaures as are fitting for Suppressing these Proceedings."[51]

By avoiding one town and remaining carefully among friends in others, Defoe finished his work in Devon and moved on to Bath. No part of his travels was uneventful, however. Sometimes he was horrified by the heat of opinion: "All the Gentry of the high party [in Chipenham] . . . act like Devills more than Men," he wrote (H 103). Sometimes his distinctive kind of love for the land would creep into the letters; in September, for example, he traveled in "that Great Vale of Trade Extending from Warminster . . . to Cirencester in Gloucester shire."

All through this period Defoe's personal problems continued. Although he seemed confident about money from Harley, he was completely unable to reduce his debts. In July he described himself as beleaguered by "Crowds of Sham-Actions, Arrests, Sleeping Debates in Trade of 17 Years standing Reviv'd; Debts put in Suit after Contracts and Agreements under Hand and Seal; . . . Writs taken out for Debts, without the knowledge of the Creditor, and some after the Creditor has been Paid." Ten days later, he listed three actions for debts totaling £2,800 begun against him but insisted he did not know to what debts they applied.[52] Writing to his Coventry friend Edward Owen in October, he did not deny he owed £3,000.

Defoe saw party malice behind the attempts to have him arrested for debt or libel—the Tories, in his opinion, seemed delighted to try both.

"This is all for the Party," he writes, and, in a typically witty sally at his persecutors adds, "A Gaol would not Check [the *Review*]. Perhaps . . . it might furnish me with Leisure to perform it better" (2:214). While press spies dogged him, the Tory writers devoted increasing amounts of energy to discrediting him. *The Review Review'd* identified him with the "Violent, Arrogant, Implacable Spirits" of the Cromwell era and carefully condemned him of forfeiting his recognizance by producing another seditious libel: "Are things come to that pass, that such a Scribler as thou art dares abuse, banter, and ridicule some of the most considerable . . . Gentlemen of our Nation? Thy former Papers show thee to be . . . a perverter of some scraps of History, a malicious Incendiary." *The Moderation, Justice and Manners of the Review* accused Defoe of ridiculing the laws, legislators, and queen and, to make its point, printed fifteen pages of quotations from the *Review*. Such invitations for the government to prosecute him usually taunted him with being a hired pen. In a typical attack *The Republican Bullies* accused him of receiving £100 from the government for the first volume of the *Review*, and *The Reviewer Review'd* became a periodical with no purpose but to counter the *Review*. The bishop of Chester took out an advertisement to refute part of Defoe's *The Experiment; Or, The Shortest Way with the Dissenters Exemplified*. These publications stigmatized Defoe as a representative of "the Violence of his Party."[53]

❧

All this time, Defoe continued to try to work on *Jure Divino*. On 26 September 1704 the *Review* had announced that subscriptions for it would be taken at sixteen London locations and in "most of the Principal Towns in *England*" (1:251–52). Subscribers were to pay half a crown down (one quarter of the promised price) and would receive the twelve-book poem "near 100 Sheets in *Folio*, with Large Annotations, Printed on the finest Paper" for a total cost of ten shillings. This advertisement gives some clue to Defoe's progress, for it estimates the length at 100 sheets in folio. In fact, the published work would be nearly double that. In October Defoe wrote to friends that *Jure Divino* "goes on" and is "near putting forward." Some of these men, including John Fransham, were encouraging their townsmen to subscribe with mixed success. Fransham catalogues the difficulties with some humor: the number of subscription books never published made men wary, "the greatest part of this City would have subscribed for the contrary subject," and most people prefer their money to books, he wrote (H 63, 64).

Defoe, however, delayed publication because the Tories were then strong enough in the House of Commons to pass a warrant for his arrest for seditious libel and the Rooke essays were fresh in their minds. About the time Parliament sat, Defoe removed the ad for *Jure Divino* from the *Review* (from the 2 December issue). They could, he wrote in the preface to *Jure Divino*, have suppressed "both it and me" (xxvii). As the general elections of February 1705 approached, attacks on Defoe and the *Review* grew in vehemence. The circulation of the *Review* had doubled to 400 copies sold per issue,[54] and Defoe's arsenal of verbal weapons was hard to counteract. Election results came in slowly, and interest in who had been elected remained high. According to him, his paper of 17 April sold 5,000 copies: "some People . . . gave me publick Thanks for my sincere Endeavours . . . and made me print five Thousand . . . to be sent all over the Nation to move us to [domestic] Peace, and paid me very frankly for them" (*Review* 5:414).

When the queen dismissed Parliament in the spring, the Triennial Act decreed new elections. The 1 May 1705 *Review* carried the announcement that *Jure Divino* was being printed "with all Expedition," invited people to go to John Matthews' shop to see the sheets, and asked that all subscription money be turned in (2:100). This notice, with its invitation to see the printed sheets "as they come out of the Press," was repeated in several issues of the *Review* in September and October.

It was over a year later on 24 May 1706, however, before Defoe wrote Fransham that *Jure Divino* "at last is finished" (H 124). It appears that the proofs were done in early summer, but that Defoe did not have a chance to correct them until November when he returned to London. "Millions of distracting Cares" and "Interruptions of private and publick Hurries" delayed publication until 20 July 1706. Defoe described himself as living "very remote from London" in the first *Review* after his journey (a *Review* published late because it arrived in London late). Kingsland was ten miles from his printer's, and this distance undoubtedly retarded correcting proofs. In addition to writing the *Review*, the *Supplements*, and *The Little Review*,* Defoe also published a sixty-page poem, *A Hymn to Peace*, and wrote pamphlets on various bills before Parliament as well as defenses of himself and his opinions. The folio edition has an embarrassing number of oversights. The running head for the preface is "Peeface" on page xxv; a few pages are misnumbered; some footnotes do not match the letters in the text; book IV once appears as VI; grammatical and printing errors mar every book. The poem is more repetitious in some places than cumulatively powerful, and the verse approaches the worst Defoe ever wrote.

Jure Divino may also have been delayed because of cost. Defoe complains in both the *Review* and the preface to the poem that subscribers failed to pay even the half crown. He says that "not half" have paid the

---

*When questions continued to pour in to the *Review*, Defoe found that even the monthly *Supplements* were inadequate to satisfy the demand. On 6 June 1705 he began *The Little Review; or, an Inquisition of Scandal: Consisting in Answers of Questions and Doubts, Remarks, Observation and Reflection.*

Portrait by Taverner, engraved by Vandergucht,
prefixed to Defoe's 1703 *Works*.

author, and that without the generous assistance of friends and other
subscribers, he would not have been able to pay for paper and printing.
One satiric attack, *The Proceedings at the Tryal . . . Of a Certain Scribling,
Rhyming . . . Hosier* (1705), says that Matthews held back publication for
a while for fear he would lose money on the poem.[55] As further proof
of his lowered status, some time before publication Defoe's subscribers
refused to have their names listed on the pages usually reserved for this
purpose.

The worst was yet to be, and Defoe's impotent distress and outrage
showed that no pleasure or even profit would ever come from the
major literary effort of his life. Benjamin Bragg, a former printer of

Engraving made from copper plate taken from portrait in
1703 *Works* for the pirated edition of *Jure Divino*.

Defoe's, began to sell a pirated edition of the poem for five shillings,
half the price of the non-portrait, legitimate folio edition. Bragg had
been able to get a copy and print his cheap edition by 19 July, one day
before the thirteen-shilling subscription copy with Defoe's portrait became available. Defoe called it "Forgery," "Robbery," "base," and "vil-
lainous," and labeled Bragg "Publisher in ordinary to the Pyrates." His
lengthy advertisement in the *Review* is a jumbled appeal for men to do
the right thing—buy his edition. He insists Bragg's book has "Corrup-
tions, Errors and false Representations" and promises to print an oc-
tavo edition for less than five shillings (3:347–48). A week later, on 27
July, Defoe claimed he had found nearly a hundred errors in the first

The *Jure Divino* portrait.

DANIEL DE FOE

The Defoe portrait from the chap book, a pirated edition
published section by section and without all but a few of the notes
in the other editions of *Jure Divino*.

half of Bragg's work alone and complained that the "Sense" and design were altered and "the Understanding of it render'd impossible." Moreover, the portrait, recut (and thereby coarsened) from the portrait in the 1703 *True Collection*, looked "as much like the Author, as Sir *Roger Le'strange* [*sic*], was like the Dog *Towzer*" (3:360). Soon a pirated sixpence abridged chapbook version went on sale. Henry Gaudy quickly wrote an answer to prove that "Paternal Power" was the foundation of all civil government, *Jure Divino: or, An Answer to All that Hath or Shall be Written by Republicans against the Old English* (1707). Defoe later claimed that he had lost £1,500 because of the pirated editions. A rapidly pirated edition by a former publisher; a chapbook—not even Dryden received such tributes. But with *Jure Divino* in hand, the interest seems clearly to be in Defoe. By that time *Jure Divino* was a poem on a highly charged current issue by one of the most notorious political criminals in England. His dreams of establishing himself as a major poet could never be realized; his past, not his poem, drew the attention.

Perhaps nothing measures the change in Defoe's hopes and status as well as *Jure Divino*. The man who had the leisure, confidence, and fame to follow *The True-Born Englishman* with a philosophical verse essay had experienced three devastating years, years in which he endured the pillory, prison, harassment by press spies and periodical writers, debts becoming so serious as to threaten another imprisonment, and travel in a dangerous role to places where party feeling ran high enough to lead to violence against men far above him (the lord mayor of Canterbury had been clubbed and hit in the face with a stone).[56] His disorganized reaction to the collapse of his attempt to gain significant profits from *Jure Divino* and his weary responses to attacks such as *The L——d H——'s Vindication* suggest uncharacteristic discouragement.

His reply to *Haversham's Vindication* describes yet again the shock and unhappiness of recent months:

I had the Honour to be Trusted, Esteem'd, and . . . value'd by the best King, *England* ever saw . . . But Fate, that makes Footballs of Men, kicks some up stairs and some down . . . and no Man knows . . . whether his Course shall issue in a PEERAGE or a PILLORY; and time was, that no Man could have determin'd it between his Lordship and this mean Fellow. (8).

John Thompson had served King William when Defoe had; created Lord Haversham in 1696, he had become a lord of the admiralty in 1699. In this paragraph we see that Defoe remembered the young man who could dream of becoming an alderman or even lord mayor and the adult who had worked beside other promising men and could imagine serving his king and rising as Haversham had.

In the struggle to find the time to finish and publish the poem, his glorious dreams for *Jure Divino* had faded until he held on to the memory of the dream rather than to the dream, and finally that dream became the experience of the poem as an exhausting, imperfect, even forced act. Enthusiastic hope gave way to grim determination to silence his critics by fulfilling a burdensome obligation to his subscribers; publication problems and piracy tarnished whatever remained of his dreams.

CHAPTER 9

NEW LIFE

*I'm not very timerous and yet I tell you that every day here wee are
in hazard of our lives.*
—THE EARL OF MAR, 1706

I have run as much danger as a soldier on a counterscarp.
—DEFOE TO ROBERT HARLEY, 1706

There are times when success means nothing, and the summer of
1706 was one of those times for Defoe. The fruits of his hard work were
all around him, but he saw only prison ahead.

In the two and a half years since his release from Newgate, he had
become a successful writer. In March 1705 Defoe had expanded publication of the *Review* from two to three times a week. Sales continued to
climb, and interest in the Scandal Club section had led first to the
monthly *Supplement* begun in October 1704 and then to the *Little Review*, begun in June 1705. The Club had gone far beyond the early
satires on the press. In some ways, it became more like Dunton's *Athenian Mercury* and began to answer questions about the immateriality of
the soul and about science, such as whether glass was "a body" or "a
quality." In other ways, however, it expanded in directions prefiguring
Defoe's conduct books and periodicals like the *Tatler*. For example, the
number of questions and full-blown stories about marriage and manners increased every year. Dialogue, dramatic irony, and families of
characters became regular delights of the Club sections. And Defoe
received gratifying letters such as one dated 29 August 1704 that said,
"I prefer your Club much before the *Athenian Oracle*." (1:219). Attacks
on the *Review* increased, and in February Defoe even accused Charles
Leslie's High Church "Brethren" of stealing the 26 February *Review* on
the parliamentary bill "An Act to Prevent Frauds Committed by Bankrupts" from coffeehouses all over the city. Pamphlet after pamphlet
abused the "mercenary Scribler," "broken Hosier," and "Incendiary."
Such attention testified to his success as a journalist to be reckoned
with. Whatever he wrote sold well, and booksellers looked to him for
new works, pamphlets on controversies, and introductory material for
reissued books. For example, Charles Drelincourt's *The Christian's De-*

fence against the Fears of Death, originally published in English in 1675, sold vigorously after it was joined with Defoe's *A True Relation of the Apparition of One Mrs. Veal* in 1707.[1] Defoe wrote "Truth and Honesty" for the *London Post*,[2] a paper that had been a rival. Booksellers were so eager for his work that they had openly threatened to pirate *Jure Divino* and "sell it for half the Money."[3]

Moreover, he had proved his usefulness as a government agent. A small-town politician, Roger Coke, wrote, "Moderation was . . . the passe partout, that opened all the place-doors between the Lizard Point in Cornwall and the town of Berwick-upon-Tweed,"[4] and Defoe's reports helped Harley know whom to reward and whom to pass over. The intelligence system was in place and functioning. Reports came in to Defoe in such numbers that he persuaded Harley that he needed an assistant. His correspondents assiduously distributed Defoe's works. Fifty copies of *A Hymn to Victory* had gone to Samuel Elisha in Shrewsbury in August 1704, and evidence of scattered dissemination of other works exists, but nothing earlier compares to the 5,000 copies of the 17 April 1705 *Review* sent all over the country, Fransham's May order for 100 copies of each *Review*, or the spring 1706 list of sixty-three men responsible for distributing nearly 2,000 copies of one of Defoe's pamphlets. The growth in the size and activity of his network suggests remarkable diligence and persuasive power.

The rewards for such service were considerable. Besides the generous payment for the April 1705 *Review*, Defoe was now receiving regular "hints" from Harley and payment for distribution copies. Nearly 50 were placed in coffeehouses around the city, and estimates that some numbers sold 1,400 copies are probably correct.[5] The duchess of Marlborough had sent Defoe a sizeable monetary gift for his 1705 writings in praise of her husband, and he undoubtedly received other such gifts. The duchess's gift had been sent anonymously through Charles Montagu, Lord Halifax, who had given her a number of Defoe's works, including the *Consolidator*, some *Review*s, and the two poems praising her husband, and identified their author. Halifax had known Defoe since King William's time, had encouraged Defoe to write in favor of a bill introduced in Parliament on currency and the regulation of promissory notes, and practiced what he recommended to the duchess: "A little money can not be better placed by those who are in Power, than in obliging and engaging those who have Wit, and Storys, that may be turned on them, or the Enemy."[6] Montagu continued to have some contact with Defoe until the earl's death in 1715.

Defoe could also have pointed to signs that he retained his ability to pique interest in "projects" to improve fiscal administration. In November 1704 the House of Lords appointed a committee presided over by the duke of Bolton, incidentally one of the guests at the banquet for the

Kentish petitioners, to consider "the state of the nation in relation to naval affairs." Specifically it was to examine "victualling and manning" the navy, smuggling (called "the clandestine trade" by the committee), and Rooke's Mediterranean campaign. On 14 January the three greatest military leaders of the time—Marlborough, Shovel, and Byng— appeared before the committee and underscored the difficulties in attracting sailors. "We first try Bounty money, then we presse, but neither will doe," they agreed. On 20 January 1705 the committee ordered the printers of the *Review* to "give notice to the author of the said paper to attend the Committee." Defoe appeared before it on the twenty-fifth, and Bolton asked him to submit his proposal for manning the fleet by 30 January. As it had been in King William's time, it was still common for parliamentary committees to consider "projects" from citizens. Defoe had published a sketchy version of his proposal based on the 1697 *Essay upon Projects* in the *Review* beginning on 13 January. On the sixteenth he had declared himself ready to accept exile if his proposal could not bring to pass the improvements in manning the fleet that he described (1:378). The committee summoned him to hear the details of how he "pretends he can save the Kingdom great sums."

Defoe did not appear on the thirtieth. On 3 February he was ordered to meet with the duke of Bolton before the next meeting of the committee. Bolton brought Defoe's proposal to it on 10 February, where the members liked it well enough to ask Defoe to appear in person. On that Committee were Somers and Halifax, as well as a number of former enemies of Defoe's, including Buckingham. The committee asked Defoe if he had presented his proposal "to the Secretary or any other" and, assured that he had not, wanted details and procedures for putting the plan into effect, but Defoe had not yet written them. Because Parliament was to be dismissed in a few weeks, he was asked to write up his entire proposal in detail to present directly to Prince George, lord high admiral of the fleet, "when required." Later Defoe asked for more time, and on 3 March Bolton's committee agreed to give him until the next session of Parliament.[7]

Defoe was always better at conceiving plans than at working out details and carrying them through. Even the flattering attention from a parliamentary committee could not overcome this characteristic problem. He did present his plan to Prince George, however, and much later wrote that "it was at last declined only upon some Scruples about Liberty and Compulsion."[8] In truth, his proposal severely restricted the rights of merchants and sailors. Defoe wanted all the seamen in England in the navy; once under public jurisdiction, they could be assigned to military or merchant ships, prevented from entering foreign service, and required to accept a fixed wage scale. All hiring and payment would be done by the government. Typical of Defoe's authoritarian, centralized schemes, the proposal identified real problems (large wage discrepancies—23s. per month for naval men versus 55s. for merchant sailors—and lack of provisions for families left at home) but gave unacceptable solutions.

Though not immune to carping criticism—malice still spoke of his large wig, his posturing with his blue cape, and his flashing a diamond pinky ring in coffeehouses—Defoe was a success in the eyes of the world. He repeatedly reveals, however, the distance between perception and actuality. He had, for instance, added an epigraph below his portrait for *Jure Divino*. Below the arms appeared the words "Laudatur & Alget." In the preface to *Jure Divino* (xxvii) Defoe commented that they came from an appropriate motto for him:

> Aude aliquod brevibus Gyaris* & Carcere Dignum,
> Si vis esse aliquis: *Probitas* laudatur & Alget

from Juvenal's famous *Satire* I, the satire that influenced Defoe's *Reformation of Manners* and *An Elegy upon the Author of the True-born Englishman* and included the much-quoted "Difficile est Satyram non scribere." As Dryden translated them, Juvenal's lines read:

> Wou'dst thou to Honours and Preferments climb,
> Be bold in Mischief, dare some mighty Crime,
> Which Dungeons, Death, or Banishment deserves:
> For Virtue is but dryly Prais'd, and St[a]rves.[9]

Charles Leslie had used the key phrase in the 6 November 1703 *Heraclitus Ridens* to *contrast* the fate of most writers to Defoe's. "Every one is not a *Daniel de Foe* that has a Party to pay a Fine for him," Leslie sneered; instead, he observed, writers too often learn the truth of "*Probitas laudatur & alget*." Defoe turned the words, "Honesty is praised and starves," to his own use, for they harmonized well with his repeated assertions, first made in *A Hymn to the Pillory*, that he suffered unjustly for speaking the truth. Even the "three griffins passant counterchanged" had more significance now. The griffin, mythical guard of hidden treasure, lived in perpetual strife with the one-eyed Arimaspians who sought to seize its treasure and, thus, had obvious associations with Defoe's embattled position and state of mind.

To read the personal statements scattered in Defoe's printed works and correspondence is to see how little his very considerable successes meant to him. In 1706 the scramble for money and self-respect blotted out all sense of accomplishment. Defoe believed he was on the verge of going back to prison for debt. On 6 May he wrote to Harley to explain that he was hiding from his creditors, that he desperately needed help

---

*Gyarus, a barren island in the Aegean that symbolized banishment.

and saw his carefully built correspondence network disintegrating. He tells Harley that, if he has anything specific in mind, now is the time to give it to him. So close to imprisonment is he that he asks for £200 or £300 at once and to be sent "Somewhere Abroad, Out of The Reach of Their hands." In *A Reply to . . . The L——d H——'s Vindication* published before this letter was written, Defoe mentioned that, were the war over, he might settle in Spain where he could earn a good living (7). Defoe also told Fransham that he believed he would have to leave England unless his case was covered by the recently passed Act for Preventing Frauds Committed by Bankrupts (H 123–24).

Although some of Defoe's debts may have been bought up and pressed by his Tory persecutors, he had spent a considerable amount of his own money printing and distributing his works and traveling, and some long-standing debts remained. In 1706, however, he tended to blame everyone but himself for his predicament. In the May letter to Harley, he said he had been "Unjustly Ruin'd and that in her Majties Name." In the Haversham tract he accused everyone of mistreating him and concluded, "with a Numerous Family, and no helps but my own Industry, I have forc'd my way with undiscourag'd Diligence, thro' a Sea of Debt and Misfortune . . . in Gaols, in Retreats, in all Manner of Extremeties, I have supported my self without the Assistance of Friends, or Relations." He complained of the ingratitude of those whose cause he championed, the "betrayal" of friends, and the "abuse" of "Barbarous and *Unnatural Relations*."[10] When hard pressed, Defoe often came to cast himself as the mistreated stepchild and direct the harshest words at his own family. The demands of his large family and his extended absences made Defoe feel his inadequacies and led to misunderstandings. In one of his last letters, written some twenty-four years later, he used the same rhetoric: "Looking on myself as Abandon'd of Every Comfort, every Friend and Every Relative . . . . the injustice . . . [and] inhuman dealings of my own Son . . . has broken my Heart" (H 474).

In fact, some of Defoe's relatives were in no position to help him much. His father, now seventy-six, had left his Throgmorton Street house to move into rented space at the Bell on Broad Street in the autumn of 1705 and, in December, his second wife, Elizabeth, died and was buried in Bunhill Fields. James and Elizabeth had lived on Throgmorton Street for over fourteen years and had had at least one child.[11] Now, when Defoe needed him, James was moving out of a long-established home and burying a wife, and there was no sign that Defoe's stepbrother or sister was alive to help him. In March 1706 James Foe made his will. From the will, it seems unlikely that Defoe could include his father among those he called "Barbarous and *Unnatural Relations*." James's piety and common sense were the same in 1706 as they had been in the 1670s when he chose Morton's Academy for Defoe. He thanked God for his sound mind and committed his soul to God and his body "to the earth from whence it came to be decently interred . . . not exceeding the charge of twenty pounds Sterling." In setting a limit on his burial expenses, James was allowing enough to cover them respectably. Scattered records show that the average funeral of a tradesman such as James would have required about £5 for a coffin, 10 shillings in cemetery fees, including grave digger, 5 shillings for the wool garment required by the 1678 Burial in Wool Act, and a few shillings more for the burial tax calculated on the rank of the dead. James provided £20 because his funeral would be well attended and therefore expensive. The Butchers' Company would come as a group in their livery, and friends, neighbors, and his Dissenting meeting house group would be there as well. The company would even provide the pall, which others had to rent. Mourning clothes for the family and rings for them and the closest friends had to be provided by the deceased's family. In addition, the family had a "drinking" (usually beer, cakes, breads, and coffee) or a full "funeral meal" after the burial for everyone where gifts such as ribbons, hatbands, and gloves were given to many of the guests. Those who attended James at the end, such as the nurse and apothecary, would expect small monetary gifts.[12]

James's bequests reflect his modest circumstances. He left his married granddaughter, Elizabeth Davis Roberts, £20, and her younger sister, Anne Davis, furniture to be claimed when she married or reached twenty-one. His older grandsons, for whom their fathers could be expected to provide, each received a watch—Francis Bartham the silver and Benjamin Defoe the gold. To Defoe's younger son, Daniel, he left £100 to be paid when he was twenty-one; in James's practical mind this money would presumably help Daniel establish himself in a trade. Except for bequests to his cousins John Marsh and John Richards, the rest of the estate was to be divided equally among the sisters of Daniel and Benjamin. James made Defoe his executor and included a provision allowing Daniel or Mary to use their children's legacies for their "Subsistence, Education or Clothing" should the family "be at any time distressed." This clause suggests either that James did not anticipate his death a few months later or that, in his opinion, Daniel and Mary were not seriously distressed at that time. The phrase, "for the Subsistence, Education and Clothing of their said children" was added, however, and the addition testified to by the witnesses, thus showing James's strong desire that the legacy be used for the children.[13] Even if Defoe knew the terms of the will, he could hardly have thought such an estate would have made much difference to him. In fact, the terms of the will protected James's legacy from the creditors to whom Daniel owed £2,000.

At least one member of the family chose to share Defoe's new life as an employee of Robert Harley. Robert Davis, husband to Defoe's second sister Elizabeth, had been a partner in the Christ's Hospital plan in 1696. He may have let Defoe stay with his family in the four months before his capture for *The Shortest-Way*,[14] and he had stood for £250 of Defoe's bail in 1703. Davis was a shipwright with skill at building mills, waterworks, and docks. He may have helped Defoe design and operate parts of the brick and tile factory. From the 1700 court judgment we know that Defoe's Tilbury land had a wharf he could use to ship his bricks and tiles on the Thames and that Davis could use for shipbuilding and repairs. At the time he paid Defoe's bail, Davis was described as a shipwright of Tilbury. Unlike Defoe, Davis seemed to have financial good luck. He had recovered a number of silver bars when he went down in a diving bell off the coast of Cornwall, and in September 1704 he received £147 from the Treasury for "Discovering a great Quantity of Timber" in Rockingham Forest, worth about £5,000, which belonged to the queen and would be useful for shipbuilding.[15] Davis's first direct involvement in Defoe's new work seems to have been in April 1705 when he carried an oral proposal from Halifax to Defoe, but his involvement became absorbing. By the summer of 1705 he was carrying messages to and from Harley, but without Defoe's full trust. In August Defoe asked Harley to give Davis "any thing you please to Convey to my Wife . . . But Rather by Bill than in specie, and Seal'd because Sir I have learnt . . . to make Agents without Accquainting them with Perticulars." In September Davis joined Defoe at Bath and finished the circuit with him (H 81–82, 92, 100, 103–4).

In spite of these clear signs of family support, in the early summer of 1706, Defoe was feeling mistreated and abandoned by his family. If even a few letters from his English correspondents were like the ones that provoked the tangled explanations of his affairs he gave in his letters to Fransham, Defoe only felt his reputation sinking and his plans disintegrating. "I am sorry to see you assaulted about my Integrity," he wrote to Fransham. By the end of June, in the hope that he would qualify for protection under the 1705 Act for Preventing Frauds Committed by Bankrupts, Defoe submitted his case to a Commission of Bankrupts. The commission, appointed by the lord chancellor, had the power to examine the debtors' "goods, books, and effects." The debtor was allowed to keep 5 percent of his estate if it did not exceed £200, discharged from all debts owed at the time he became bankrupt, and could be issued a certificate promising him relief from future prosecution for his present debts if he met the terms of the act and if the commission found "no reason to doubt" the debtor's accounts.

After meeting with Defoe the commissioners set up meetings to which Defoe's creditors could come to present their cases. Advertisements in the *London Gazette* show that by 22 July the commission had met twice and would meet twice more within a month. These meetings were held in Davis's Middle Temple, Essex Court, lodgings.[16] Defoe was unable to put his problems to rest. Two judges of the Queen's Bench Common Pleas and Court of Exchequer at Westminster had to "allow and confirm" the commission's conclusion and issue the certificate. Their failure to do so may have resulted from any of several reasons. One of the conditions was that the bankrupt had to make a full "Discovery of his Estate and Effects" and give no "reason to doubt the Truth of such Discovery." In Defoe's case damaging accusations of secret resources had cropped up several times over the summer. His own pamphlet *Remarks on the Bill to Prevent Frauds Committed by Bankrupts* (1706) may have compromised his veracity enough to leave "reason to doubt." In that tract, he wrote, "Men whose Affairs are declining, are not always *the exactest People* in their Books . . . ; Omissions, Mistakes, and forgotten Articles are never so frequent, as when Men, knowing they are *playing a losing Game*, grow desperate" (26). Given Defoe's initial elation, however, the most likely surmise is that he simply foresaw no lasting difficulty, even when creditors appeared at the required Queen's Bench hearing and presented substantive objections. By the time the case came to a decision, Defoe was probably out of the city. In a *Mercator* Defoe mentioned a "malicious Slander" falsely reporting that he had given a deficient Account and explained that, when he left London in 1706, he intended to complete getting the certificate on his return (12–14 January 1714). The lord chancellor, William Cowper, could have validated the certificate, but he was, after all, a Whig given office to please his party and probably knew that he was not Harley's first choice. In 1707 the Commons "negatived" the Bankrupts Relief Bill, and the Act to Prevent Frauds was amended so that Defoe had no chance to qualify. Seven years later a Yarmouth man was still pressing his suit, and as late as 1728 others would renew their cases against Defoe.[17]

At the time, however, Defoe was pleased with the result. On the day of the settlement, 21 August, he wrote Harley that "God almighty . . . has given me at last a Compleat Victory Over the most Furious, Subtill and Malitious Opposition That has been Seen in all The Instances of the Bankrupts act." He promised to give diverting details and gloated over his triumph. It appears from the 20 August 1706 *Review* that he might have exposed someone who owed him money and was attempting to conceal the fact. The settlement may have come about in part from the evidence from his earlier agreement to surrender all of his assets to Samuel Stancliffe, a friend and former partner, who had acted as a trustee-negotiator.[18] This time James Stancliffe was trustee.

Whatever the details, Defoe was finally free from the threat of debtors' prison. He had a new plan in mind, too—one that capitalized on groundwork laid over several years. On 23 July Lord Keeper William Cowper for England and Lord Chancellor James Ogilvy, first earl of Seafield, for Scotland presented the proposed Treaty of Union to Queen Anne. Most of the Scottish commissioners left for home at once, and Defoe intended to follow them.

After all, Robert Harley was the secretary of state responsible for Scotland. Harley's attitude toward Scotland was complex. In 1703, he had told William Carstares, "indeed, to say the truth, I think it very unfit for any one here to meddle with Scotch affairs, which are so much out of the way of our comprehending. . . . I do not find one person who pretends to understand the proceedings [of the Scottish Parliament]. To say the truth, very few speak at all about them. . . less than they do of the King of Sweden and the Pole." He nevertheless told Carstares that he saw "a cloud gathering in the north." Even after he was secretary of state, Harley said in Parliament that "he knew no more of Scotch business than of Jappan" and "avoided even the conversation of those of that country."[19]

The queen wanted Union. She wanted the succession settled, and her general, Marlborough, wanted to be sure Scotland would neither rebel nor send soldiers to Louis XIV. At this time, both Godolphin and the queen had better information and more influence than Harley. They managed the very powerful Queensberry and Argyll firmly, received good intelligence from Stair and Mar, and provided positions and even money for useful men at critical moments. Marlborough, with whom many Scots had fought, could be counted on to write well-timed letters to powerful Scots. Allegedly one directed to the right person united the Squadrone,* the chief opposition's "former friends," behind the treaty. Harley could not make up for those years of familiarity and political business. He could, however, help the effort and prepare for the time when his influence would be greater than Godolphin's: when the treaty came before the English Parliament and, if things went as hoped, when he would be responsible for putting the treaty's stipulations into effect. Harley began to influence whomever he

*The "Squadrone" (or "New Party," as they called themselves) broke away from the Cavalier party dominated by James Douglas, fourth duke of Hamilton. When the Cavaliers believed an incorporating treaty was too great a national price to pay for Union, Tweedale, Haddington, Marchmont, Johnstone, Roxburgh, Rothes, and Baillie of Jerviswood disagreed. Called the "Squadrone Volante" after the military term, they became a compact group whose swing votes decided a number of questions as early as 1704–1705.

could in favor of the Union and to improve his propaganda and intelligence efforts.

No one was confident that the Union would pass. On 31 July Queen Anne ordered Queensberry, her lord commissoner, in the strongest possible terms to adjourn the Scottish Parliament rather than allow it to amend the treaty to create a federated union* or to defeat it. Somber reports from the Scottish commissioners began arriving in London. Some effective anti-Union propaganda had been published during the summer, and now George Lockhart made the terms of the treaty public. Armed with this evidence that an incorporating Union was proposed, opponents of the Union began to organize resistance all over Scotland. James Erskine told his brother, the earl of Mar, "There are certainly a great many violently against it, & though there are severals [*sic*] for it too yet they don't seem to be half so zealous for it as the others are against it."[20] Mar wrote Godolphin that he had "converse[d] with a great many and I found most of them prepossest against the Union." He identified the lord advocate, Sir James Stewart, as an agitator against the Union and suggested that Godolphin write Queensberry that those who failed to cooperate would "lose favor"; Queensberry would be instructed to show the letter to those who needed to be influenced.[21]

In August Defoe had sent Harley a sample of the kind of propaganda being produced, but Harley was already aware that he was stumbling about. Harley wrote to William Brenand that he understood "he had been too forward" in trying to "serve" Queensberry.[22] He was also aware of the inadequacies of his reports from Scotland. Of his informants, John Forster was in bad health, provided apologies and vague reports of Jacobite activity, and made such useless suggestions as that men and money be sent to Scotland "to breed a broil."[23] John Ogilvie wrote tantalizingly frustrating reports: "I had almost forgot to tell you that there was two Scotchmen at St. Germain just come over and was to return back immediately . . . they have been both of them trusted with letters formerly to my knowledge; but as to that I shall say no more." He gave no clue as to who they were or for whom they delivered letters.[24] William Paterson had been sent to Edinburgh around 26 August, but no one had full confidence in his reports. At one point Godolphin said of Paterson, "His notions seem to me for the most part very confused." Moreover, Paterson's letters reveal a tendency to tell Harley what he thought Harley wanted to hear. For instance, when Scots were telling Harley that resistance to the Union was increasing, Paterson wrote him that Queensberry and others "appear very hearty and unanimous,

---

*A federated union would have left the legislative and judicial systems of the two countries intact; an incorporate union would make them one country.

which gives those . . . for the Union great encouragement."[25] William Greg, whose 1705 reports were among the most valuable sent to Harley from Scotland, now worked as a clerk censoring letters written by important French prisoners of war. A number of powerful men including William Carstares, the earls of Leven, Mar, and Stair, and George Lockhart wrote to Harley, but their information could hardly be disinterested, and some were quite irregular correspondents.[26]

Sometime between 24 August and 13 September, Harley decided to send Defoe to Scotland. According to Defoe, both the queen and Godolphin knew about his mission, and discussion had advanced to the point where Defoe could review his assignment:

I beg leav . . . to Set Down how I Understand my present bussiness—as foll.

1 To Inform My Self of the Measures Takeing Or Partys forming Against the Union and Applye my Self to prevent them.

2 In Conversation and by all Reasonable Methods to Dispose peoples minds to the Union.

3 By writeing or Discourse, to Answer any Objections, Libells or Reflections on the Union, the English or the Court, Relateing to the Union.

4 To Remove the Jealousies and Uneasyness of people about Secret Designs here against the Kirk &c. (H 126)

Defoe's language makes it clear that he is rehearsing what he believes to be an agreement. In addition, the last item on the list suggests intelligence passed to Harley from some of his Scottish correspondents who knew that the opinion that England wanted to weaken the Kirk was common.

In fact, Defoe most likely had maneuvered Harley into doing what he wanted. Harley still had provided no regular employment or stipend for Defoe. After all, as recently as 6 May, Defoe had written Harley that he had "Often Endeavour'd" to have a proposed talk about the *Review*; on 21 May he sent verses he'd written with a blatant appeal for reward ("Perhaps you may Make Use of Them to my advantage") and proposed to write an essay on the victory at Ramillies. The letter Defoe sent to Harley on the day he left for Scotland shows that Harley had told him he would be supported in Scotland out of Harley's private money rather than from government funds; internal correspondence, however, shows that Defoe was paid by the crown. Harley gave Defoe a mere £25 to provide for his entire traveling needs—from which Defoe had to buy two horses, a saddle, bridle, and pistols.

The primary impetus for Defoe's trip probably came from a circle of Scottish friends made after his release from Newgate. Since then Defoe had spent hours discussing Scottish politics with Scots merchants in London. These conversations, the treaty negotiations, and Harley's office provided Defoe with a better opportunity than anything London had to offer him. Defoe's writings suggest his growing familiarity with

Scotland. His 1705 *Consolidator* includes some startling discussions of the current animosities between the "Nolunarians" (Scots) and "Solunarians" (English). Throughout he represents the Scots as having just grievances and realistic fears. The English, he says, "were for declaring War immediately upon the Northern Men, tho' they cou'd show no Reason at all why, only because they would not do as they would have 'em" and call them "*a parcel of poor Scoundrel, Scabby Rogues . . . a pack of Crolian Prestarian Devils . . . .*" Defoe sees both class and religious prejudice behind England's actions, and presents the Scots as upright and sensible: "It was easy to see . . . that their Design was *not a War, but a Union* upon just Conditions."[27] In 1705 his remarks are dramatically at odds with those of his contemporaries. Frances Phillipson, sent to Edinburgh as a government accountant, wrote, "I am come . . . into a Strange place and amongst a strange sort of People yet I find them much civiller and regular than I expected." Even Burnet talked of "great heat and much vehemence" and "violent motions," and described Scotland as "strangely inflamed"; Queen Anne called the Scots "unreasonable" and "that strange people." A typical description called Scotland "a Country almost inaccessible and unknown, inhabited by men of a different habit, of a different language."[28]

Scattered sympathetic remarks about Scotland appear in Defoe's writing throughout 1705 and begin to figure prominently in his vision of the future. The concluding address to the queen in *Jure Divino*, for example, portrays an England so blessed by God that apparent evil works for good: "*Cadiz* repells your Troops, that they may fly, / To *Vigo* Spoils, and Golden Victory" and, parallel:

> *Scotland* rejects our Settlement and Crown,*
> That Two vast Nations may unite in One;
> And all the threatning Clouds of Northern Night,
> Assist to make that Union still more bright;
> . . . .
> And all the Men of Plot, and vast Intrigue,
> While they inflame the Nations, press the League.

A Reply to . . . The L——d H——'s Vindication is a full-scale attack on Haversham's recommendation of policy toward Scotland: "A Law to force them to declare the Succession of their Crown with Ours, *Only because we think we can do it*," he says, "has no Maxim of State in it. . . . The Justice of Government, has no manner of Dependence upon the Power of it."[29]

Defoe had seen the future of English/Scots relations aright. On 16 April 1706 commissioners from Scotland and England came to Lon-

---

*Defoe refers to England's Act of Succession, which would give the crown to the House of Hanover rather than to the Catholic Stuart.

don to negotiate the Treaty of Union between their countries. This attempt was not the first at Union. In 1603 and 1702 serious efforts had been made, but this time each country had pressing reasons, and the "treaters" had been carefully selected. Scottish trade with France—a nation to which Scotland was historically and culturally close—and the recent Scottish Act of Security seemed ominous signs to the English of a potential French ally on their own island. The Scots seemed to them ungovernable and continually in turmoil. By late 1705 the Scots could hardly doubt that the English would invade them to prevent Scottish independence. The Aliens Act, passed in answer to the Act of Security, would make all Scots aliens in England (barring them from owning or inheriting land), forbid imports from Scotland, and prohibit the selling of weapons and horses to Scotland after March $17\frac{05}{06}$. This act also empowered Queen Anne to appoint commissioners to negotiate a Union *if* the Scots also did so. The Scottish economy was in desperate trouble, and religious and family factions crippled the government.

Queen Anne appointed both commissions, thereby assuring a majority of solid unionists. The English group included Godolphin, Harley, Charles Hedges (the other secretary of state), nine other high-ranking court appointees, two archbishops, and such Whig stalwarts as Bolton, Halifax, Charles Townshend, and Wharton. The Scottish commission was even less balanced than the English. Only one known anti-Unionist was appointed, and those recommended by Seafield, Queensberry, and Mar came to London to negotiate.[30]

The Scottish commissioners had friends and relatives in London. Among them was George Scott, merchant brother to an Edinburgh University professor of philosophy. Sometime in early May, Scott introduced Defoe to the brothers John, Hew, and David Dalrymple, members of the duke of Queensberry's circle. All three were commissioners, and their family's connections and power were great. John, earl of Stair, had been Scotland's lord advocate, then one of her secretaries of state and a minister in King William's court; he was a member of Anne's Privy Council. Hew had taken his grandfather's place as lord president of the Court of Session in 1695, and David, the youngest brother, was Solicitor-General to Queen Anne.[31] On 14 May George Scott wrote his brother,

I supose you expect I shou'd say some thing concerning our union, the only thing talk of here[.] sentiments are very different about it, most people talks as the[y] wou'd have it . . . I must tell you that having the Honr: to converse with some of our great folks viz: Lord Stairs, Lord president, Sir Dav. Dalrymple, Lord Roseberry & others, I did bring them aquainted with one Mr Deffoe who seeing to understand trade & the interest of nations very well, he was the person that wrote the pamphlett cal'd the shortest way with the dissenters & for which he was pilloryed[.] at our request he has wrote, an essay at removing nationall prejudices against a union with Scotland, it is very well done & is only the introduction to 2 more books he designs upon the union before the Commissioners have done. others have wrote upon the Subject, a Collection of all I shall send you with the first oportunity.[32]

"At our request," Scott writes. In this scribbled, personal letter is the information that the Scots in London engaged Defoe in their cause. Choosing him at least in part because he seemed to "understand trade & the interest of nations very well," they, not Robert Harley, pointed him toward the work of the next three years of his life. Pleased with the result, George happily tells his brother that Defoe plans "2 more books" on the Union before the treaty negotiations end. Defoe's *An Essay at Removing National Prejudices against a Union with Scotland. Part I* had been published on 4 May, and *Part II*, the second essay, would appear on 28 May.

Defoe published nothing else on the Union that summer, but his friendships with the Scots commissioners grew. Besides the Dalrymples, Defoe came to know John Clerk well. Clerk was a young man on his way up. He had been educated at Glasgow and Leyden, been a student of the Italian composer and conductor Arcangelo Corelli, and a correspondent of the Dutch physician and professor of medicine and chemistry Hermann Boerhaave. He was a Scots M.P. by 1702 and in 1705 was part of a commission to investigate proposals for currency reform and a member of the Council of Trade. The duke of Queensberry's son-in-law, Clerk was ostensibly selected for his usefulness in negotiating the economic clauses in the treaty. He was widely described as "a very pretty gentleman," a phrase indicative of his youth, learning, cultivation, and promise.[33]

By 13 July Clerk knew Defoe well and could enthusiastically tell his father that Defoe was coming to Scotland:

receive a paper written by De foe upon our equivalent & coyn. he has another essay upon the union of about 5 or 6 sheets to come out this day, but I fear it will not be come out before Gill [his servant] go off. he promises to go out with Robin & me some day to Newbiging [the Penicuik great house] to teach us some improvements, in which he is very knowing, but he wou'd come with the better will if he was first acquainted with you here. he goes with the Precedent to his house some spare day & afterwards having considered our ground & grains, he is to write about the improvement of Scotland; he says the East country cannot be much improv on he makes himself believe he cou'd improve moorland grounds to double their rent.

The "5 or 6 sheet" essay would have fulfilled Defoe's promise to Scott and his friends to write three essays on "Removing National Prejudices" before the treaty negotiations ended. The essay may never have been released, however, because about this time the Scots in London would have heard from Edinburgh that parts 1 and 2 had been reprinted together there as propaganda *against* the Union.

Clerk's letter shows that Defoe made his decision to go to Scotland at the height of his negotiations with the commissioners of bankruptcy. Moreover, it outlines the methods and subjects of Defoe's earliest Scottish pamphlets. Relying heavily on his friends, Defoe would adopt their opinions and begin immediately to write persuasively on the affairs of a country in which he had probably never been. Clerk's letter supports Defoe's own account of his decision to come to Scotland:

My Curiosity prest me to take a Journey thither, and being by all my Friends, to whom I communicated my Design, encouraged, to think I might be useful there to prompt a Work that I was fully convinced was for the general Good of the whole Island; and particularly necessary for the strengthning the Protestant Interest.[34]

Defoe did believe wholeheartedly in the Union. He saw a "manifest destiny" for his island and consistently argued military points on the basis of protecting Protestant nations all over Europe from possible Catholic encroachment. That summer the *Review* characterized England as fighting with God on her side "to Muzzle" the "French Tyrant" "for the Liberty of Europe." "I applaud as much as any Man the Bravery of our Army, the Conduct of our Generals, and the Goodness of our Troops; But they that cannot see distinguishing Providence cutting out Victory, and preparing Causes . . . must be blind" (3:258). To unite England and Scotland came to be, in the *Review*'s vision, but another sign of God's allowing Anne to preside over the fulfillment of England's destiny.

◈

On 13 September 1706 Defoe left for Edinburgh, 372 miles by the Berwick route. The trip usually took ten to fourteen days, and a series of inns was well known to travelers. Defoe might have stayed, for example, at the Swan in Welwyn, the Cock at Eaton, the Bell at Carlton, the White Hart at Bedford, and the King's Head at Darlington at a charge of about a crown a day before he reached John Bell, one of Harley's agents, in Newcastle.[35] Defoe complained that it rained every day until 28 September; the weather slowed his trip by several days, and he arrived in Edinburgh with a severe cold.

Defoe always regretted that visitors did not arrive in Edinburgh from Leith on the north because the eastern view as he came from North Berwick gives "but a confus'd idea of the city . . . under the greatest disadvantage possible" (*Tour* 2:298). At that time, Edinburgh was "*one Fair Street* from West to East, about a *Mile* long from the *Castle* to *Halirood-House*." To Defoe, High Street seemed "perhaps the largest, longest, and finest street for buildings and number of inhabitants, not in Britain only, but in the world" with buildings "surprizing both for strength, for beauty, and for height." At the east end was Holyrood

The Castle, From the Mound, Edinburgh, by Shepherd.

House, the royal palace of Scotland that had been razed by Cromwell's army and recently restored. At the west end of the street stood Edinburgh Castle, 450 feet above sea level and cut off on three sides by "a frightful and impassable precipice." The castle, built before the Norman Conquest and capable of accommodating a thousand men, was commanded by William Carstares' son-in-law, Major James Coult, who served under its governor, the earl of Leven.[36] Visitors to the city believed that *Edinburgh* was a compound of the "British" *Adain* and the "Saxon" *Borough* and meant "City near the Winged Castle" because the castle, the "eagle's head," was between "wings"—the beautiful Corstorphine Hills and the Salisbury Crags.[37]

Moving to Edinburgh from London called for some adjustment. The buildings, called "lands," were comparatively tall; five or six stories (called "houses") were usual, and twelve and fourteen not unheard of. The older lands were wooden with oval windows cased with doors and having no glass; the newer ones were stone with "modishly framed" windows. Unlike London lodgings, the stairs were outside the houses so that renters did not have to use a common entrance, and each floor might have a separate landlord. Although High Street was clean and pleasant, the little streets were "very steepy and troublesome, and . . . nasty." Defoe excused the Scots from the charge of delighting "in stench and nastiness" by describing the natural "disadvantages" and "inconveniences" of the "rocky and mountainous situation" and lack of water. Less charitable visitors complained of the lack of sanitary facilities and of offensive habits of sanitation, for each family kept its "excrements and foul water" in large vessels until 10:00 P.M., when the bells of St. Giles signaled that it was time to dump them into the open street.[38]

Edinburgh was a frightening city in the autumn of 1706, and Defoe was in a dangerous position. The fact was that the Scottish people were largely opposed to the Union; Jacobites, Highlanders, seamen, and "the rabble" joined ordinary Church of Scotland rank and file in hopeless opposition to the parliamentary coalition. As one contemporary said, "There are scarcely so many Unioners to be found in any one . . . Burgh or Shire, as there are sitting in Parliament-House." Defoe joined one of the strangest pilgrimages in British history. As the M.P.'s and their entourages slowly moved into Edinburgh for the last session of their Parliament, so did large numbers of ordinary citizens. Some came as lobbyists and probably aimed at concessions. Others hoped to find a way to voice their opposition. The Highlanders, exotic even to Scots, walked through the streets fully armed with broadswords, shields, pistols, daggers, and staffs. One witness described their clothing as "very pretty; he wears a Scotch [plaid] over his Shoulders, like a Scarfe, and a great Basket hilted Sword by his side, a Pistoll tuck't into his Belt, a Bonnet with a Bunch of Ribbons on his head, and a pair of pumps on

The Parliament House, Edinburgh, by Shepherd.

his feet; with which hee'l travell 6o miles a day." Defoe described the incongruity in their "Insolent" and proud mien as they drove cows through the streets in their "Mountain habit." Curiosity seekers moved in with relatives.[39] Peddlers and other opportunists swelled the population yet more.

By the time Defoe arrived, the Scottish Parliament had already opened with the traditional "Riding," a procession from Holyrood House to Parliament, then held in what is now the great entrance hall of the Court of Session. Less than a century old at that time, Parliament House had cost the Scots £11,000. A troop of grenadiers led the "riding." They were followed by the parliamentary representatives of the burghs dressed in black, then the representatives of the shires, and finally the representatives of the first estate (barons, viscounts, and earls) in scarlet robes. Each representative was accompanied by liveried servants, their numbers indicating their master's rank. The Lyon King-at-Arms, with trumpeters and pursuivants, preceded three noblemen chosen to carry, respectively, the crown, scepter, and sword of the king of Scotland. The queen's commissioner, Queensberry, and other crown and Edinburgh City officials followed with their pages and servants. Finally came a squadron of the Royal Horse Guards.

Once at Parliament House, each of the 314 members had an assigned seat in a symbolic place. For example, the nobles sat on tiered benches to the right and left of the ancient throne. A few seats behind a bar allowed spectators with passes to observe, and other nonmembers could be present if they were willing to hold the batons, the long white sticks given by the marshal and constable "to priviledge people to come in as their Guard."[40] Surely the sense that this might be Scotland's last Parliament hung over the members as they began to play their parts.

Quite simply, the Union treaty meant an end to Scotland as an independent nation with its own Parliament. A proud and ancient people, the Scots reacted with outrage as they came to understand that they would be "incorporated" rather than joined by negotiated, give-and-take clauses of a treaty. This emotional point united Scots of all classes, who would chant "No Union" outside Parliament, threaten the commissioners, and talk of the "obliterating Union." Among the surviving papers from this last Scottish Parliament are anti-Union petitions from twenty-two counties, twenty-five burghs, thirty-four parishes and royal burghs, and two presbyteries. Major opposition came from the churches; Catholics, Jacobites, and most Episcopalians opposed the Hanoverians in favor of the Pretender, and the Church of Scotland noticed that the treaty lacked a clause protecting their church and its form of government. So strongly did these people feel about their government that Patrick Hume, earl of Marchmont once sniped that they would "suffer as much for it, as, I think, they would for Christianity itself." [41] "Treaters," the way the Scots abbreviated "Commissioners to negotiate the Treaty," when pronounced with a good Scottish accent sounded like "traitors," and the commissioners were reviled, cursed, and sometimes threatened.

Approval of the treaty in Scotland would result from a determined, concerted effort by a relatively small group of men.[42] Some of them knew they would profit substantially from the Union, but others believed idealistically in a prosperous future for their country. Some had fought abroad with Marlborough and understood the crisis their island faced. Years later John Clerk would write that no one could understand the Union without knowledge of the "miserable circumstances" in Scotland that meant that "our nearest and dearest Relations with tears [were] obliged to part with their Native Country through meer Necessity."[43] In 1706 the dukes of Argyll and Queensberry had been brought to favor the Union; the earls of Mar and Seafield were already committed to Union; Montrose, recently appointed president of the Privy Council, had begun to work quietly to persuade others to support the Union, and the "Squadrone," identified as led by Rothes, Jerviswood, Haddington, and Tweedale, reluctantly agreed that these united interests were strong enough to pass the Union, and feared being on the losing side. None of these groups alone had the power to control the Scottish Parliament or to oppose the Union. Partly because some men believed in it and partly because some wanted to be sure to be included in the inevitable payoff after Union, a coalition formed that augmented itself by persuading some and purchasing others. Queensberry, who had delayed coming to court in 1705 in spite of the queen's requests because he was, he said, short of money, received at least £10,000 between 28 August 1706 and 17 February 1707; Rosebery, whom Defoe had met at Scott's in May received the chamberlainship of Fife and a £300 pension; the earl of Glasgow distributed £20,000—an impressive £264,200 in Scots money.[44]

The opposition in Parliament, small in numbers and suspicious of one another, hoped to get an adjournment designed to force attention upon the popular opposition to the treaty. Unfortunately, they faced united, skillful parliamentary management, and most of them had too much to lose to be entirely effective. The duke of Hamilton, the most powerful of the opposition, was typical. Like most of them, he admitted that a union was essential in order to prevent "Blood and Confussion upon the Death of the Queen." Like the others, his English connections were strong; for instance, when he wrote to Harley, he addressed him warmly as "honest Mason," perhaps an indication that both of them were Masons. Though in favor of many of the concessions granted in the treaty, Hamilton felt that the cost of an incorporating union was too

great a price. He might have wielded somewhat greater influence had
he not been so deeply in debt and, therefore, dependent on such things
as the horse trade with England. He was related to Queensberry and to
two of the most determined anti-Union magnates, John Murray, first
duke of Atholl, and John Hamilton, third Baron Belhaven, but he and
Atholl had often been competitors for power, and any alliance between
them was likely to break down at crucial moments. Furthermore,
Hamilton's manner often disguised his pragmatic insight and worked
against his interests. Queensberry once remarked that he did not act
"like a man of business." When he surprised his party by moving to
allow the queen to choose the Scottish commissioners to negotiate the
treaty, he did so with his "usuall haughty and bant'ring Ayr" and managed to insult both the Scots and the queen. An eyewitness reported
that he said "that the [Scottish] Parliament was too much in heats and
feuds, and could never agree upon proper persons, but the Queen,
who was free from partiality, might doubtless make a good choice, but
. . . if she should make a bad one . . . they might send the Act back to
the place from whence it came." This blunt speech had not even gotten
him membership on the commission, and such a sign from the English
throne was not lost on those who might have been his allies.

   In any event, the Hamilton family had found out that there was no
hope as early as the first week of October. Hamilton wrote his mother
on the eighth:

My heart is Broke for the Buisness of this nation . . . The Squadrone have keept
up ther sentiments with great cautiousness till this day they have declared them
selves all as one man for the union . . . they say mr. Johnston upon a letter
written to him by the Duke of Marlborough to negotiate with them Rox[burgh]
is to be a Duke of Brittan immediately[.] what tweedall and the others are
behence I know not. It's wonderfull men should goe soe much against their ain
Light . . . had it not been for this I think wee meight have gained a delay . . . my
heart Bleeds to see what I doe[.] but what remedie.[45]

The naked weapons of the two sides came into play at once. Hamilton
asked for a recess in order to inform Queen Anne of the extent of
popular resistance to the treaty. Belhaven asked for eight days' recess
"to consider more deliberately the Articles." Another moved that consideration of the articles be delayed until the English Parliament considered the treaty. Yet another motion for a recess to allow the Scottish
M.P.'s time to consult their constituencies was defeated. The reading of
the treaty and the debate on Article I proceeded inexorably. Hamilton,
Atholl, and others raised objections and entered protests. Everyone
knew that a favorable vote for Article I would effect an incorporating
union. As Hamilton rightly observed, "the first Article . . . is . . . to fix
uss into the Incorporating union . . . wee must be fors't into the conclu-

sion befor we take . . . the grounds of it into consideration."* By hold-ing firm to consideration of Article I first and by resisting all efforts for a recess, the pro-Union forces assured that only an extraordinary event could prevent the ratification of the treaty. On 4 November, Article I carried by a vote of 116 to 83. Soon Hamilton and the others saw that there were not to be real but "sham alterations" in the rest of the articles. The speeches and letters of the opposition repeat the lament for "our ancient mother Caledonia" and label the treaty "ane Eternall surrender of what air forefathers have maintaine'd with honor & reputation these two thousand years." As Defoe wrote,

Like true Souldiers, tho in a Bad Cause, they fought their Ground by Inches.
　From Article to Article, they Disputed every Word, every Clause, Casting Difficulties and Doubts in the way of every Argument, Twisting and Turning every Question, and continually Starting Objections to gain Time; and, if possi-ble, to throw some Unsurmountable Obstacle in the way.[46]

When it became clear outside the House that the M.P.'s would stead-fastly refuse to delay considering the treaty long enough to consult their constituencies and would continue to ignore the petitions and protests delivered daily, the people took to the streets in mobs. Defoe was correct to observe that "the Difficultys are Many and the People Obstinately Averse." The commissioners became targets of frightening abuse. Hard words were spoken in Parliament and transformed into physical abuse in the streets. Belhaven called the treaters "Patricides," and Fletcher of Saltoun was nearly summoned to the Bar of the House for accusing them of betraying the nation's trust. Outside, feelings were even more violent. The end of each day's session meant a parade of triumph for Hamilton and the opponents of Union. The Union sup-porters, and especially the treaters, came to expect taunts and threats. Sometimes the mob threw garbage and stones at their coaches, and the mail often contained vicious comments and threats of assassination. Once a mob attacked Queensberry's coach when he, Argyll, and Sea-field were leaving Parliament. The mob threw stones into the coach, knocked the coachman down, allowing the horses to run away, and beat and robbed several of their servants.

　On the night of 23 October a full-scale riot occurred. So severe was it that the Privy Council ordered the earl of Leven, "Commander in cheif [sic] of her Majesties forces in Scotland" to "take possession of the Netherbough Port," the Weighhouse, and the entrance to Parliament,

*Article I read: "That the Two Kingdoms of *England and Scotland* shall upon the First Day of *May*, which shall be in the Year One Thousand Seven Hundred and Seven, and for ever after, be United into one Kingdom by the Name of GREAT BRITAIN. And that the Ensigns Armorial of the said United Kingdom be such as her Majesty shall appoint, and the Crosses of St. *George* and St. *Andrew* be conjoyned in such manner as Her Majesty shall think fit, and used in all Flaggs, Banners, Standards and Ensigns, both at Sea and Land."

and to "disperse the mob by force." The mob had attacked the house of one of the treaters, had been routed by the town guard, and then had begun roaming the city, breaking windows and assaulting pedestrians. Leven's troops gained control of the city and restored order, but riots occurred again and again. Clearly the intention was to intimidate the pro-Union M.P.'s. "We are threatened every day that we shall be murdered," Mar wrote in late November, commenting that they could not go into the streets without being insulted.[47]

As an Englishman and one whose presence was a matter of speculation, Defoe himself ran a fair amount of risk. Scarcely two weeks after arriving in Edinburgh, he tells of hearing someone yell, "There was one of the English Dogs" as he hurried from a friend's coach into his lodgings. On another occasion stones were thrown at his lighted window. Before the treaty passed Defoe would write Harley that Scotland was "a Nation . . . in a Terrible Ferment," that "Insurrection" "is Not Unlikely," and even "the war here is begun." A contemporary wrote of "the whole Country run to Arms," and several described the plot to use mobs to break up the parliamentary session before it could ratify the treaty.[48]

⁊₰

As soon as he arrived Defoe set to work explaining the benefits of Union, softening resistance by the Church of Scotland, and keeping Harley informed of events and opinions in Edinburgh. He quickly found his notoriety a benefit. John Bell, Harley's Newcastle agent, had complained to Harley that Defoe "is not nice in telling his name, and will own it at Edinburgh."[49] In any event, the existence of Defoe's Scottish acquaintances prevented using an assumed name, but Defoe's past was, in fact, an advantage in Scotland. He had, after all, suffered for the same Dissenting church that was the Church of Scotland.[50] His notoriety made his ability as a writer common knowledge, and his imprisonment and the subsequent, widely publicized (although exaggerated) accounts of his being a fugitive from creditors and from messengers sent by the government to arrest him for one or another pamphlet made people ready to believe his explanation that he was considering moving to Scotland to start a new life.

Defoe made friends quickly. Even the skeptical John Bell wrote Harley four days after meeting Defoe: "I have had the favour of [his] conversation for two or three days and find him to be a very ingenious man . . . . I wish him good success."[51] The Scots Defoe knew were active in the most influential groups in Edinburgh and were probably eager to persuade him to settle there.

Defoe's move into Edinburgh life began at once. With the help of his friends he began to write his third *Essay at Removing National Prejudices* and a series of *Review* essays. Within weeks he had published his third

Essay, had the fourth in press, and was preparing to print attacks on several opponents of the Union. He was quick to see that improvements in the economy through trade were the clearest benefits to the Scots and that the lack of guarantees for religious toleration was one of the most serious stumbling blocks. He therefore, addressed these two points in his first Edinburgh *Essay*, which he also used to introduce himself to the Scots. He presented himself as a firm believer in the Union who had written his first two essays in an attempt to win over his fellow *Englishmen* who believed that the Scots would receive many benefits and the English few. He insisted that the treatment "I have met with from Parties and Power in my Native Country. . . . will Secure me from the Scandal of being an Emissary." He said, "my Bussiness [*sic*] is known here . . . tending to Trade, Settlement and general Improvement"(34). Other families like his own, he argued, would come to Scotland once the Union revived trade. He said, as he did in his third *Essay*, that he had "always Profest a more than Common Regard" for Scotland (33). He could say with rhetorical indignation that he was in Scotland, "pursuing my private, lawful and known Design of settling my Family abroad" (*Review* 3:547).

John Clerk, Hew Dalrymple, and other acquaintances gave Defoe access to each day's parliamentary debates and votes. Perhaps one of the happiest times of his life, the fall of 1706 found Defoe, the Scottish M.P.'s, and their friends caught up in fourteen- to sixteen-hour days. Parliament sometimes met until 8:00 P.M., and committee meetings and strategy sessions brought men together day after day. Defoe, like other nonmembers, could always hold one of the batons and be admitted to the debates. He and his friends sometimes met at the traditional gathering place for Scottish M.P.'s and the inner circle of the Commission of the General Assembly of the Church of Scotland: Fortune's. This coffeehouse was in Old Stamp Office Close and was affectionately called "Sue's," because it had been the town mansion of the earl of Eglinton's beautiful wife, the Countess Susannah.[52] Comments in the journals and letters of Scots and in Defoe's letters to Harley capture the excitement, the dedication, and the kinds of efforts made to assure approval of the treaty.

On 23 October Parliament appointed a committee to examine the calculation of the Equivalent* and the clauses regarding imports and exports. By 5 November Defoe was meeting regularly with this committee which included Alexander Campbell of Cessnock, Montrose, John Areskine, and Gilbert Elliot—men who would be part of his life in Scotland. Because so much of their work involved comparing English

---

*Because Great Britain's taxes would go in part to reduce English debts contracted before the Union, Scotland would receive £398,085.10s. as compensation, or "equivalent," for the amount alleged to be involved.

and Scottish values, weights, and measurements, the committee found Defoe's knowledge of trade and accounting useful. For example, Scotland produced a "two penny ale" that was not easily compared to either small or strong beer in England, and coal was sold in different ways in the two countries. Defoe soon became a kind of secretary to the group, using his facile pen to write up their "explanations" and even suggesting amendments (H 144).

Hew Dalrymple was a powerful member of the presbytery of North Berwick, and Defoe already knew other members of the Commission of the General Assembly of the Church of Scotland, appointed by the General Assembly to "advert to the intrest of the Church on all occasions." This group had begun meeting daily in Edinburgh in order to protect the "security" of the Church as the Union deliberations progressed. Defoe managed to insinuate himself into this important group and spent hours defending England. He told Harley that he worked "incessantly" with them and described numerous meetings with individuals who "go from me seemingly Satisfyed" but reverted to their former "mad" behavior as soon as they were with other clergymen. On 8 November the commission approved and delivered *The Humble Representation and Petition of This National Church*, a petition asking that the Scottish Parliament protect the "doctrine, worship, discipline, and government" of the Church with a list of seven "difficulties" presented by the Union treaty. A group of commissioners was appointed to lobby Parliament members. About the same time, Defoe called the commission a "mob," and on 29 October he told Harley of a sermon at "high Kirk" on the text, "Let no man take thy Crown." All of his letters express dissatisfaction with his success with the clergy, yet he was admitted to their debates, their dinner tables, and was able to send Harley copies of their work.[53]

Defoe's explanation of his visit made his consideration of various occupations quite reasonable. He talked to merchants about trading, to manufacturers about wool and linen, and to others about such things as newspapers and fisheries. He widened his circle of friends and solidified a number of special friendships that led to evening after evening of punch and good talk.

Defoe soon established himself as the writer the pro-Union men had been looking for. He was doing just what his Scottish friends wanted, even as he followed Harley's orders. From the time they arrived back in Scotland, the Scots saw the need for writers to counter the anti-Union propaganda being produced by a number of able writers. Patrick, earl of Marchmont, said he saw "a secret influence set up, and moving to alienate the minds of the people from the [Union] . . . putting strange and terrible shapes upon every remote consequence . . . ." One of William Paterson's correspondents referred to "a parcel of Scriblers, who made it their business to perplex, Confound, or if possible, make the Union to Shipwrack." Even Queensberry noted the need for "the Queen's servants" to answer recently published pamphlets against the Union. Mar took a more active part; he asked Nairn for pamphlets printed in London with an eye to having useful ones reprinted. At the end of November he complained how little the local merchants knew, and now and then (as on 2 December) he told Nairn that he was printing tracts sent by him from London.[54] Even in the first of the Scottish pamphlets, the third *Essay*, Defoe spends a few pages refuting one of the best anti-Union pamphlets published, Andrew Fletcher's *State of the Controversy betwixt United and Separate Parliaments* (1706), an argument for a federated Union with a Scottish Parliament to protect Scottish interests.

The earl of Mar wrote to Sir David Nairn on 14 November, "I have sent you Defoes 4th Essay[.] he is still here[;] I'm not acquainted with him but he really takes a great deal of pains in this affair."[55] The signs that hostile pamphlets including attacks on Defoe were in preparation had to be evident in such a small town. Defoe's pamphlets began to draw the rage of the anti-Union writers. Over the next few months, they were answered by the ablest Scottish pamphleteers including Andrew Fletcher, William Black, James Hodges, James Webster, and William Adams, but by engaging them in answering his points rather than producing new arguments against Union, he did the pro-Union forces his greatest service. Defoe addressed a varied audience in his works. *A Letter from Mr. Reason* and *A Short Letter to the Glasgow-men* chided the mobs and repeated the advantages of the Union in simpler, more immediate terms. For instance, Defoe told the mob in *Mr. Reason* that many more people would be hired in the fish, linen, and wool trades and that they would soon eat like the English—beef and cabbage, pork and pudding rather than a "Nogan of Pottage" or salt herring. A pamphlet and a poem ridiculed Lord Belhaven's emotional speech calling for the preservation of "our ancient Caledonia."[56]

Defoe's work pleased Harley. In the earliest known letter to Defoe in Scotland, Harley wrote,

I received Yesterday Your Letter of November 14th and this day that of the 13. from your Brother; By last Post I wrote to You the Cautions I thought necessary, Since you are intrusted in that affaire, that you may discharge Your Self, as becomes a lover of both Countryes. I was not then approzed of the particulars proposed for your consideration, but I have now obtained a Paper of Observations which were to be sent in answer to the Memoriale come from Scotland that will sufficiently informe You of the State of this matter, and your own Prudence will conduct You in it; But I must add this Caution, that You do not by any means ever suffer this Paper to be seene therefore pray transcribe the substance of it in other forme—and return me the Originall, and be cautious, not to let the similitude of Phrases ever discover that you have seen it.

I very much approve your writing to the Lord You mention [Halifax] he is
one I have great respect for, and have longd [sic] served; But I desire You will
not by any means let him imagine, You correspond with any one here, or have
any motive beside Your selfe for your going thither; and then you may continue
writing to him, and I will find a way to make it usefull to You.

The Ballad is the best answer to that stuff.

The letter Harley had just received from Robert Davis explained specific problems and asked for directions. Defoe intended to "lead" the
committee to propose only such amendments to the treaty as England
could "comply with." Harley replied by enclosing an official document;
on the twenty-eighth, Defoe dutifully returned the original copy of
Harley's paper.[57]

Although Defoe had known Halifax, the great leader of the Whig
party, longer than Harley and had benefited from Halifax's friendship
in various ways, including the receipt of the gift from the duchess of
Marlborough, he asked and received Harley's permission to carry on
the correspondence. Harley's motives for keeping his relationship with
Defoe secret from Halifax are not clear; Harley had great respect for
Halifax and even when he was part of the Tory ministry continued to
confide in Halifax and ask his advice. Both men discussed their most
important ideas with each other, and each frequently assured the other
that he was willing "to be an Instrument under your Direction to bring
your Schemes to bear."[58]

Defoe's special usefulness to Harley came from his pen, and here
Harley approves Defoe's method of answering John Hamilton, Baron
Belhaven, who had given an emotional, anti-Union speech in the Scot-
tish Parliament. Defoe had written a "Ballad," "The Vision," to counter
Belhaven's beautifully rhetorical, "I see a *Free and Independent Kingdom*
delivering up . . . Power to Manage their own Affairs. . . . I see *the
Valiant and Gallant Soldiery* . . . sent to learn the Plantation Trade
Abroad. . . . I see *the Honest Industrious Tradesman* loaded with new
Taxes. . . . I see *our Ancient Mother* CALEDONIA . . . breathing out her
last."[59] With jocular ridicule Defoe's poem, like Harley's letter, rejected
the sentimental appeal to preserve "our ancient Caledonia." He began:

> Here's a Lord in the North,
> Near *Edinburgh* Frith;
> . . . .
> He's seen such a Vision, no Mortal can reach it.
> I challenge the Clan of *Egyptians* to match it.

In his next letter, one answering Harley's, Defoe described the mood
of the Scots and their resistance to the Union. He counseled Harley to
allow some amendments and promised, "they shall be Triffles." In a
postscript he enclosed Belhaven's poetic answer to "The Vision" and
chuckled that Belhaven had blamed it on Thomas Hamilton, sixth earl

of Haddington. At this point, the mutual confidence and close working relationship between Defoe and Harley was at its zenith.

Throughout this time Defoe had the encouragement and, probably, direct help of Scots like John Clerk and Alex Campbell, Marchmont's son. Both Clerk and Campbell served on the parliamentary committees charged with evaluating the articles of Union and the calculations in them. In letters to Harley, Defoe mentioned being called to Campbell's house and, on occasion, dining with him. Defoe and Clerk had much in common. Both were intensely interested in politics and economics, read history avidly, and were active men whose health and temperaments supported their work on causes in which they believed. Deeply religious, they thought of God and invoked his name as easily as they breathed.

Defoe's tracts written during these months show his affinity to Clerk. They repeat the advantages of the Union to Scotland and address the nation's anxieties about their trade, religion, civil government, and the succession to the English throne. The larger part of the writing, however, is about economic issues. Defoe calculates Scotland's probable advantages, projects the new balance of trade, explains the ramifications of individual articles of the treaty, and justifies the Equivalent. These calculations are identical with John Clerk's as found in his 1706 journal, his published *A Letter to a Friend, Giving an Account How the Treaty of Union Has Been Received Here*, and *An Essay upon the XV. Article of the Treaty of Union*.[60] The information Clerk had and his knowledge of Scotland's resources and trade were invaluable to Defoe.

Soon after Defoe arrived in Scotland, his pamphlets became more specific and more effective. George Ridpath, a prominent, prolific controversialist and determined opponent of the Union, had written of Defoe's first London *Essay*:

You will . . . hear of [a tract] call'd an Essay upon the Union, by an unknown hand. It is writt with strength and judgement, and his sentiments are exactly mine, except for some matters of fact wherein he is misinform'd, and that I perceive him to be a cavaleer: but his scheme is right, and had he produced authoritys to justify his proposition, it would have been a finished piece.[61]

Nothing Defoe would write in Scotland could be mistaken as the effort of a cavalier, a royalist.

The writings after the summer of 1706 present the figures, information, and arguments found in the papers of the Queensberry circle and the committees on which Clerk served. As Defoe came to know Scots and Scotland, he increasingly addressed the problems and doubts that Union advocates in the north saw.

How close Defoe and Clerk could be can be seen from a comparison of Clerk's *A Letter to a Friend* (significantly a tract William Lee assigned to Defoe) and Defoe's third and fourth *Essay[s] at Removing National Prejudice*. One of Defoe's essays was published immediately before and one within days of Clerk's. These essays make many of the same arguments, and attack the most articulate of the anti-Union writers. Both the third *Essay* and Clerk's pamphlet, for example, insist that the Church of Scotland will be safer after the Union, which will guarantee its independence and sovereignty. Clerk compares Scotland to a bride who sees her vulnerability and marries before she can be conquered, and Defoe uses the metaphors of marriage ("Love, Peace, Charity and Mutual Assistance") to describe the post-Union situation, says the Scottish Parliament will not be "seduced" into a treaty that does not protect the Church, and continues to talk in terms of mutual affection. Both discount the disadvantages of the loss of the Scottish Parliament and insist that improved trade will increase the prosperity of the country. They refute other pamphleteers and argue that the treaty will be advantageous and inviolate. Clerk is much more specific in his tract, especially regarding the financial aspects of the treaty, but both pluck some of the same emotional strings. Some of Defoe's sentences echo Clerk's emotional description of "our nearest and dearest" forced to leave Scotland to earn their bread. From Defoe's third *Essay*: "The Misery and Hardship which now makes your People fly from their Native Country, and makes you the Nurses of *Europe*, that you have the trouble and expense of your Children till they are grown up; and then other Nations reap the Profit of their Labour" (9–10).

Defoe's fourth *Essay* answers Hodges, the primary target of Clerk's *Letter*. Defoe again argues that the English Parliament will keep its word and the treaty, but the major part of the pamphlet discusses the value of Scottish land, the salt and malt taxes, the fishing trade, and the calculation of the Equivalent; these topics are those of Clerk's *Letter*, and the figures are the same. Clerk concludes his *Letter* with a list of "queries" regarding the Equivalent, and Defoe concludes with his own list of Equivalent issues. In this *Essay* and in a series of *Review* articles (cf. nos. 148, 149, and 151 for 12, 14, and 19 December 1706), Defoe engages Hodges and other Union opponents mentioned in Clerk's *Letter*. Occasional references to requests that he write additional pamphlets appear in his correspondence, as they do in late November. Now and then he mentions that his friends believe his work has some good effects (cf. H 154).

Caledonia, the "Poem in praise of scotland" that Defoe had described to Harley on 2 November, is the most eloquent testimony to Defoe's support in Scotland. The sixty-page poem came out with a grant from the Privy Council and a subscription list more prestigious than that of any other work in the century. Determined not to repeat the experience of the pirating of *Jure Divino*, Defoe had petitioned the Privy

Council for the "sole privilege" of printing, vending, and selling the poem. On 30 November the council, presided over by the marquis of Montrose and attended by many of Defoe's subscribers, approved it. In the preface Defoe mentioned that he had special obligations to the Forbes family, and Sir Robert Forbes, friend of John Clerk and Hew Dalrymple, was the clerk of the Privy Council and may have suggested Defoe's petition. Agnes Campbell, printer to the crown, brought out a folio edition soon after. The London edition printed the subscription list that had been withheld in the highly charged political atmosphere of Edinburgh. Eighty-four names appeared, almost all of the pro-Union and Squadron M.P.'s and a handfull of prominent citizens.[62] The names of Queensberry, Seafield, Montrose, Argyll, and both secretaries of state led the list. If Defoe knew half of these men, he was well connected indeed. Certainly he knew seventeen of them reasonably well by then and may have already known others, such as John Russell, soon to be one of his lawyers. The poem itself celebrates a number of Scottish families and shows a knowledge of their history and family relationships impossible without the assistance of native Scots.

Defoe had more trouble with Harley's orders than with the Scots' requests. Harley had cautioned him to be sure no one knew he was an agent and had instructed Defoe in strong terms to insist that amendments to the treaty might determine its defeat in England. To conceal his connections *and* to appear to have special knowledge made Defoe's task more difficult; he had to persuade people that he was reading the English mood and character accurately. Defoe found this assignment troublesome from the beginning. He told Harley that he had repeatedly said that "if they broke in Upon the Articles to alter the Terms of them, they Unravelled the Treaty" and a new commission would be necessary. Day after day he asked Harley whether small changes—many of which he personally found justified—could be tolerated. He sent copies and asked which were not acceptable. Soon he realized some amendments would be made, and his concern increased.

In fact, there were many things Defoe did not know. Stair, Montrose, and Mar shared Defoe's concern about amendments, wrote their powerful friends at court, and had been partially reassured. Among the ministers who had taken the Scots' concerns to English M.P.'s were Godolphin, Sunderland, Halifax, and Somers. Some letters included words to use in order to prepare to bring about what the Scots' calculations showed without "breaking into the Articles." By the end of November word came from court that the Scots' "explanations" and additions would not be a problem. Even less did Defoe know about the court's behind-the-scenes efforts to control the actions of the Church of Scotland. The Church was a matter of grave concern to everyone in favor of the Union, and many people besides Defoe were working "incessantly" with the clergy.[63] Mar had written Godolphin in October that "the Ministers preaching up the danger of the Kirk is a principle cause of increased resistance to the Treaty," and Seafield told Godolphin that the address from the commission of the Assembly "troubls me most."[64]

Unbeknownst to Defoe was Queen Anne's permission for Queensberry to "give Our Assent to any condition, Article or provision that shall be voted by Parliament for the security of the government of the Church . . . within the limits of Scotland."[65] Moreover, the moderator of the General Assembly of Scotland that year was William Wisheart, an Edinburgh clergyman and an admirer of William Carstares. Carstares was therefore in a position to influence the Church's actions strongly. Queen Anne's chaplain for Scotland and a believer in the Union, Carstares was in frequent correspondence with members of the court, with Harley, and with both Scottish secretaries of state, Mar and Loudoun.[66] In early October the commissioners from the General Assembly voted a fast, but Carstares led the Assembly to reject it and went on to direct the ministers to pray for the success of the Union. On hearing that news Halifax wrote, "I can now tell you very confidently that the Union will be agreed to in Scotland."[67] On 16 October Carstares led the commission to apply to Parliament for protection of the Church and its government. When Parliament incorporated the Act of Security into the treaty on 12 November and the queen ordered the royal assent, effective Church resistance within Parliament ended. In fact, some violent reactions to the perceived inadequacies of this act broke out, and the Presbytery Commission held a new series of emergency meetings, some at 7:30 A.M. With one final, mild address on 16 January asking for protection of the Church, the threat of a united official Church of Scotland opposition ended.[68]

It had been clear by early December that the treaty would pass easily. The opposition votes decreased slightly on key points, and the leaders surrendered to what had been inevitable since the selection of the commissioners to negotiate the treaty. In fact, Hamilton's brother, the earl of Selkirk, had written his mother on 14 November, "Their is now no dout of their carieing the union through as they please . . . I reekon the union concluded." On 4 December Atholl also wrote Lady Hamilton, his former mother-in-law: "I spent so much time, mony & prejudiced my health, & after all coud not bring things to a good issue for this nation."[69] On 4 January Defoe wrote, "I believ the bussiness as good as Over here," but he had been writing about his future for several weeks. On 9 January he wrote, ". . . I may Now give you Joy of the Union, The 22d Article haveing past." On 16 January the final vote carried, and Queensberry touched the treaty with the ancient Scottish scepter.

CHAPTER 10

A TERRIBLE PEOPLE

I Resolve to Omitt Nothing I Can do . . . to push the Great work of
Reconciling the minds of this People to One Another and to the
Union.

— DEFOE TO ROBERT HARLEY, March 1707

The ratification of the treaty of Union in January 1707 left Defoe unemployed again. Three years' experience with Robert Harley had taught him to take the initiative, and he began to send Harley a steady stream of hints and direct suggestions about his future. Even as he carried on what would become a tense, involved negotiation with Harley, he was deeply engaged in Edinburgh. He had found good friends, respect, and a full life. He worked with men he admired and in a cause he believed important. Even after the treaty ratification, they requested that he stay "to quiet peoples minds" (H 191), and they made him feel useful and respected. Defoe, however, needed a way to support his large family, and 1707 brings out his complex personality and desires and makes clear his complicated situation.

Although Defoe frequently expressed his willingness to work in England or Scotland, his proposals are for positions in Scotland. In early January, he had written Harley, "If nothing better Can be found Out for me I Could Wish you will please to Settle me here after the Union" (H 188), and his suggestions show that, if he did not actually prefer to remain in Scotland, he believed his opportunities to be greater there. At one time or another, he mentioned employment as a Customs House official, surveyor of any of the major ports, comptroller of accounts, inspector to prevent "the clandestine trade," and even a "Generall Survey such as Dr. Davenant* has." Ironically, Defoe was undercutting suggestions of these secure administrative positions even as he made them. In the first place he continued to demonstrate that he still had plenty of work to do in Scotland by sending useful, information-packed reports. Both the work he was doing and the paragraphs (prob-

*Author of political and economic tracts, Davenant had been appointed inspector general of imports and exports in 1705; he had served as secretary to the commissioners negotiating the treaty of Union in 1706.

ably designed to argue that he could be profitably employed in Scotland) describing what could be done worked against any urgent, determined effort to find him a place.

Moreover, Defoe's letters communicate deep ambivalence about an administrative post. Above all, the letters show a desire for challenge and variety. He designs work for himself and encourages Harley (and by extension, Godolphin and the queen) to do the same. Clearly drawn more to the novel than to the predictable, to the mission than to the routine, Defoe usually closed his reminders of his desire for employment with expressions of willingness to serve in whatever way Harley and Godolphin wanted and to live in either England or Scotland.

Giving Defoe a position in Scotland might have been a problem for Harley anyway. Considerable resentment of Englishmen in addition to the aggressive demands for places for themselves, their relatives, and friends by all of the Scots who had contributed to ratification of the treaty complicated Harley's decision. On 30 April alone, Godolphin received eleven petitions from men who wanted positions in the Customs Office.[1] To give Defoe too high a post would have aroused Scottish jealousy even as it focused attention on Defoe's past and on his suspected connection to Harley in England. Like Adam Smith, Defoe's contemporaries felt that a pilloried man was "irrecoverably degraded by the punishment, though not by the crime," and, although Defoe had recovered better than anyone else in history, there were still innumerable positions irrevocably closed to him.[2] Yet to offer Defoe too low a position would have been ungrateful and insulting.

Defoe's letters also express anxiety and resentment toward Harley. In early March he wrote, "Everybody is Gone [to London] to Sollicit their Own Fortunes, and Some to be Rewarded for what I have Done." At the end of April he added a postscript: "My Friends Write me word I shall stay here till I am Forgott." His strongest protest came on 21 May: "I am Inform'd Sir the Custome house is Settled for this Country. Is there No Room for an Absent Servant?" And again three weeks later: "Absent and Forgotten are frequently synonimous. I have no Dependence but on your Self, but Sir while I see Men as *Rigby* . . . in Commission, I Can Not but hope you will Cause me to be Remembred." "I look Now as One Entirely forgott," he complained in July and noted that the commissioners of customs were rapidly filling all positions there. Even as Defoe saw neglect and procrastination, however, he was blind to the effects of his own indirection and ambivalence. His "hints" about positions were not in harmony with his reactions to news of others receiving them. For instance, he recommended that those "sent Down to the Customes and Excise" should be patient, civil, calm people able to "draw" the Scots, because the Scots are a "surly, Haughty" people and cannot be compelled. Nowhere in this letter does Defoe recommend himself, and his friend John Clerk did not think to suggest him when his advice was solicited about these same positions by the Queensberry circle. Queensberry, to whom Defoe had gone to congratulate and say good-by before the nobleman left for London, did nothing for Defoe when Godolphin asked him for the names he "and the rest of her Majesties Servants of Scotland" had agreed upon.[3] Yet what Defoe wrote about the news of the next set of appointments shows that he believed he had given Harley and Godolphin clear hints that he wanted one of the jobs.

Godolphin and Harley were not indifferent; they were trying to find a place for Defoe. "There is not much to be said upon your Scotch letters more than to ask you what should be given to DF," Godolphin had written Harley as early as 4 January. In May Godolphin told Harley that he had left a blank for Defoe's name as the secretary for the Custom House. Godolphin, however, saw a problem. He believed that William Lowndes, secretary to the Treasury, might resist the appointment, "unless it bee recommended from" Harley.[4] Lowndes' dislike for Defoe could have come from several differences in opinion. Defoe had criticized Lowndes' re-coinage plan and had perhaps angered Lowndes again in his writings regarding the two competing South Sea companies. Certainly Lowndes had acted in ways that were nearly the opposite of Defoe's printed recommendations in both instances. More recently Lowndes, as M.P. for Seaford, had introduced a bill in the Commons that would have prevented the mass importing of duty-free goods being stockpiled in Scotland. The Scots were furious about the bill, and Defoe wrote he was "Exceedingly Harrass't and Fateagu'd" with the questions and insults directed at him because of it. "[T]hey say [it] is Directly Against the Union, and they talk of Meeting," he wrote. As well as opposing the bill in letters, Defoe did so in pamphlets and the *Review*.[5] The bill was defeated in the Lords, and Lowndes was probably in no mood to accept Defoe's appointment. Harley, too, supported the bill and may have seen Lowndes' objections to Defoe. Certainly his stern letter of 12 June to Defoe gives a view of the Scots' plans to export their stored goods to England that contrasts sharply with Defoe's:

> I will add but two things more; those Goods (tho' they should come in quickly) will come to no market, And the next thing is that the Wine, Brandys & other Goods of the Growth & Manufacture of the Kingdom of France are intirely forbidden here, and can no way be brought in either before or since the Union but as Prize Goods, & then the Duty is fixed high, and this is as plain as A.B.C. (H 228–29)

In the same letter Harley calls what the Scots are doing "Cheat & Knavery."

Even as the Custom House position closed, Harley and Godolphin went on to consider other possibilities. In that 12 June letter Harley

Sidney Godolphin, first earl of Godolphin.

encouraged Defoe to propose specifically "Your own Service & where You can be most usefull." Harley told Defoe that Godolphin thought "surveyor of one of the Ports" might be the best position. This suggestion shows that Defoe's requests had been considered. As a surveyor his accounting skill as well as his ideas for reducing the "clandestine trade" and for dealing sensitively with the Scots could be put into practice. Harley asked that Defoe let them know if the surveyor's position met with his approbation, and, if not, that Defoe propose "any other Alternative; the Sooner the Better." Included in this letter was advice: Defoe was to address Godolphin, the higher ranked statesman, in a letter enclosed in his next to Harley, and Defoe was to continue to foster the idea that Queensberry was his soliciting angel to the ministry.

By 9 August Defoe had made his decision. "[I] Doubt not but My Ld Treasr Will be pleased with the Choice I have Made, of being Servicable Rather Than Proffiting of his Ldships Goodness," he wrote. Later he would say he had turned down "a Very Good Post in Scotland." Defoe and those of his time with a Puritan conscience had a pressing desire to be "servicable." Defoe had chafed at his uselessness to Harley upon his release from Newgate, frequently asked how he had been or might be useful, worried about events or circumstances that might make him useless, and filled his letters with biblical allusions to usefulness: "The night cometh when no man can work"; he wants to be sure Harley's money is "faithfully Applyed and not Intrusted with an Unprofitable Servant."

For Defoe to have taken a routine administrative post when he could have done something more valuable to his religion or country would have been, in his opinion, irresponsible and perhaps even sinful. In February 1707 he had concluded a *Review* essay with the remark that he desired "no better an Inscription on my Grave, than that I was honour'd by the invisible Hand of Providence, to be in the least Instrumental to so glorious a Work" as the Union (3:678). Moreover, Defoe and many of his contemporaries believed themselves to be involved in a national and European conflict between the Protestant and the Roman Catholic religions. For Puritans like Defoe, to serve their country would be to participate in this struggle and to be instruments of truth. Still insisting that his work was "to tell things aright," Defoe believed that he worked for moderation and national harmony.

Defoe took no easy path. Working for Robert Harley had often been frustrating. At the height of the final voting on the treaty, he mentioned that he had not heard from Harley in eight weeks. For the next four months Defoe asked repeatedly whether he should return to London or not, for new instructions, and for information he definitely needed in order to talk and write accurately and constructively. "Without your Directions I am a meer Image without life, soul or Action," he once wrote. Sometimes he worried about money. On 19 July he wrote Harley that he could not afford to print a pamphlet he had written on the worth of the Exchequer bills the English had sent to Scotland as part of the Equivalent.

Surely Defoe had had enough experience with Harley to suspect that neither money, instructions, nor appreciation would be regularly forthcoming if he did not accept a regular civil service appointment. However, to reject the offered position was to choose the life style he seemed to like best. When he could, Defoe always combined travel and writing with his work. As a merchant in the 1680s and 1690s, as Harley's agent in 1704-1705, and again in Scotland, Defoe had made sure his days were filled with varied, not routine, activities. In these times he took a keen interest in politics, legislature, and the opinions of average citizens. He had been drawn to controversy and written in what he considered the public interest over and over. No one who did not like to write would have done so much of it, and Defoe's decision assured that he would continue the kind of life he had already chosen three times. Even as he waited for Harley's orders in the spring of 1707, he took a few weeks' trip through Glasgow, Sterling, and western Scotland. The vigorous *Reviews* and letters and the occasional enthusiastic comments testify to Defoe's preference for this work. In a typical sentence, he writes about several hard weeks of work with the clergy: "I am pleased to Tell your honour I am heard in it."

Although Harley and Godolphin heard regularly from a number of Scots—for instance, Montrose's letters arrived most quickly and were very full—and had other agents whom they paid better, they definitely valued Defoe's work. They exchanged his reports, commented on them, and took his recommendations seriously. For example, Godolphin wrote Harley on 16 January, "De Foe's letter is serious and deserves reflection. I believe it is true and it ought to guide us very much in what we are doing here, and to take care in the first place to preserve the peace of that country."[6] Godolphin probably referred to Defoe's common sense thoughts about the Oath of Abjuration; Defoe pointed out that, as things stood, the Scots would have to "abjure a prince for being of their Own perswasion," and that Quakers in England did not have to take the oath (H 192–93). Later, when Defoe was traveling through Scotland, Harley apologized for having to send Godolphin a report about Edinburgh events from another agent. Occasionally the two men made haste to get information to Defoe. Near the beginning of April Godolphin suggested a flying packet (the fastest mail service and one that could reduce the time for a letter to Edinburgh to a few days) for a letter Harley had already dispatched. In this letter Harley asks Defoe to send a plan for preventing "future frauds in the Customs" without inflaming the Scots "as soon as you can in writing."[7] Defoe's steady stream of reports were concise, clear, and informative. He listed the Scottish people's discontents, evaluated their justice and their gravity, and summarized what needed to be done as well as what was being done.

In addition to the pamphlets and poems written in Scotland, Defoe continued the three-day-a-week *Review*. The essays in it were useful to Godolphin and Harley. "I endeavour . . . to put the best Face on the proceedings . . . in order to prevent the ill use . . . made . . . in England," Defoe wrote, and he insisted that the Union was an "absolute and mutual Necessity" that he would "defend, explain and describe."[8] In February he encouraged the two nations "to study reciprocal Acts of Kindness." His essays tirelessly enumerated the advantages of Union, explained the objections of each side to the other, and took up each controversy as it arose. For example, in the autumn of 1707 he warned both sides of the dangers of extreme, non-negotiable positions in the controversy over duty-free imports, and throughout the year he wrote a number of papers on the anxieties of the Church of Scotland. His method is consistently irenic if not entirely truthful. He habitually defines, isolates, and reduces the numbers of opponents to the Union. His arguments tend to be aimed at political or economic "mistakes" made by men whom he describes as largely well-intentioned. In the *Review*, too, he avoids bringing divisive events to the reader's attention unless the publicity and controversy make it necessary for him to discuss them. For example, we look in vain in the *Review* for a report of the mobs in Edinburgh in June. The August *Review*'s report of the mob of five hundred in June in Dingwall in northern Scotland makes the jocular observation that not all of the riots in the world are the work of Presbyterians, prints an "Information" allegedly by an eyewitness who makes a strumpet, "Isbel Macka," the leader of the mob, and never mentions the crowd's intention to join "king James the 8th, whom they soon expect."[9] So valuable were Defoe's reports and *Review*s that Godolphin finally told Harley that Defoe should be paid from his accounts rather than Harley's (H 229).

Edinburgh remained in a turmoil. The Commission of the Church of Scotland felt it necessary to address the Privy Council to ask for more attention to the disorders "through the Country." James Erskine wrote his brother the earl of Mar that "town & country, continue still to have a disgust at the Union" which "is (I'm afraid) losing ground evry day," and the earl of Rothes described how he avoided his family chapel because the minister described the Union as God's judgment on Britain. Seafield's letters to Godolphin described "tumults" in the evenings and the "fears and discontents" of the merchants.[10] At this time in 1707 Defoe's activities and contacts in Scotland were astonishing. His power to penetrate diverse groups ranks him among the greatest spies of all time, but his motives in 1707 were not simple. For example, it is clear that Defoe formed genuine, mutual friendships with some Scots. His private hours, his investments, his travels around Scotland, and his publications portray a full life with complex, intertwined relationships and a number of loyalties.

Because the men Defoe knew in Scotland played parts in so many aspects of his life, some of them must have known he was, in some way, working for the English government. His 27 January letter tells Harley that he has "Caused it to be spread that I am fled hither for Debt and

Can not Return." However, the information and solicitations from various people that he passes along to Harley bear out the idea that a few knew his secret. In May, for example, Sir John Clerk had arranged to let Defoe know about a vicious pamphlet that accused Defoe of telling the Scots that he had been sent there "by *Somebody*." By 1708 a satiric poem could describe him as Harley's "chosen Friend sent forth / So privately to spy" and identify John Bell: "And what great Sums the needy Vassal / Receiv'd at Post-house in New Castle."[11] In his *Memoirs* John Clerk wrote that Defoe "was sent to Scotland by the prime minister of England, the Earl of Godolphin, on purpose to give a faithful account to him from time to time how every thing past here. He was therefor [*sic*] a Spy amongst us, but not known to be such, otherways the Mob of Edinburgh had pulled him to pieces."[12] Since these *Memoirs* were written from journals some of which are now lost, it is impossible to determine when Clerk knew that Defoe was "to give a faithful account" to Godolphin. There is no reason to think Clerk did not know from the beginning, and Clerk says the *mob*, not Clerk or his acquaintances, would have "pulled him to pieces." To work for the Union with England was no shameful act among Clerk's friends. They, too, corresponded with English ministers, tried to win over opponents in conversation and print, and identified those who might be bribed or intimidated into supporting the cause. Scots displayed interest in Defoe's writing and often acknowledged his relationship to Harley in neutral tones as Robert Wodrow does in 1712: "I hear [from] some private letters . . . that . . . the Treasurer called for De Foe, and told him he heard of ane insurrection in Scotland . . . and ordered him to write to Scotland, and inform himself about it, and write some reveues [*Reviews*] upon it. I'le be fond to see them, when they come out." That Defoe had English connections gave them proof that England wanted the Union badly and raised Defoe's stature in their eyes. It would be like Defoe, too, to name Godolphin rather than Harley, either out of a desire to exaggerate his own importance or to obey Harley's injunction to secrecy. Clerk may not have known about Defoe's assignment until 1708, when Godolphin did send Defoe to Scotland. Other evidence that Defoe's contacts were known exists. For instance, Defoe participated in the effort to help Major James Coult retain the governorship of Edinburgh Castle and have his pay restored to its pre-Union rate. Had his Scottish friends not known of his connections, Carstares, Russell, and others certainly would not have asked his help.[13]

Defoe's Scottish friends continued to encourage him to write about the economic articles of the treaty, the Equivalent, and the transition period as it would affect imports, exports, and the monetary system, and their help was still apparent. Three more *Removing National Prejudice* essays, *Observations on the Fifth Article of the Treaty of Union, Considera-*

tions in Relation to Trade Considered, An Enquiry into the Disposal of the Equivalent, and other pamphlets by Defoe elaborate on the Queensberry circle's points and, as in his first group of Scottish pamphlets, show close similarities to the work of John Clerk.[14] For example, *Observations on the Fifth Article* is a discussion of ships owned jointly by Scots and foreigners, the subject of one of the sections of Clerk's *Letter to a Friend*. Other essays review the calculations that led to the malt tax and Equivalent, point out the specific advantages to merchants and interests such as those of fishermen, and explain the proposed re-coinage of Scottish money. These topics were all treated similarly by Clerk in his pamphlet and are frequently mentioned in his letters and journal.

With the knowledge of some and the innocent help of others, Defoe constructed a fairly convincing set of reasons for staying in Scotland. He proposed a new edition of the Psalms to the Commission of the General Assembly. Some of his youthful meditations had included lines from the Psalms, and his poetic publications might have appeared to some to qualify him. The beauty of this plan of Defoe's was that he would "lock my Self up in the College . . . for the performance." Not only was William Carstares the principal of the College, that is, president of the University of Edinburgh, but Agnes Campbell Anderson's print shop was there.[15] As printer to the crown and the best known printer in Scotland, she received manuscripts Defoe would like to see, and see before they were printed.

A second scheme involved the Edinburgh Town Council and the Privy Council; through them, Defoe got warrants to search the registers and parliamentary minute books in order to write a history of the Union. Under this guise, he got "Every Thing told me" and "rummag[ed]" "among old Records" to his heart's content.[16] The idea of writing a history was particularly inspired because the Scots felt the need for one. The Edinburgh Town Council voted several small amounts of money to would-be historians, and even ordinary people felt the need for a history of their own. For instance, after seeing an advertisement in a newspaper for information for a history, Andrew Colquhoun of Garscadden wrote a friend, "It is the duty of all good Scotts men to assist in this work if they are able . . . . I shall wish the work may be well done, to the honour of the nation." As late as 1773, however, the perceptive Samuel Johnson made the same observation: that Scotland was "a nation that has no historians."[17]

In addition to the two writing projects, Defoe began to talk more concretely about investments. Over the next two years, the number and variety of his investments and projects rivaled those of the 1690s. He made a contract with a master weaver for the manufacture of linen tablecloths. He went back to wholesaling wine, especially claret and canary. He sold horses. In a March *Review* (4:82) he said he was investing in salt, only to be ridiculed promptly by *The Review Review'd* for pretending to set up as a salt factor without the credit needed to do so.

Defoe described his linen manufacturing project in his letters and *Reviews*: "I have now above 100 poor Families at Work . . . for the making such Sorts of Linen, and in such Manner as never was made here before, and as no Person in the Trade will believe, could be made here," he wrote.[18] In fact, Defoe was probably still in the "talking stage" of this project with John Ochiltree, former Deacon of Crafts for the weavers, although he had designed the tablecloths, one of which he offered to Harley on 7 December 1706. In 1705 Ochiltree had received a contract to instruct poor boys in the art of weaving. In the spring of 1707 Ochiltree was preparing to move from Paul's to the Potterrow in order to supervise linen manufacture in New Greyfriars. In September the Edinburgh Town Council gave him 100 merks (about £6 sterling) to pay for his moving expenses and the damages to his personal effects caused by the move. It was not until 30 November 1710, however, that Defoe and Ochiltree registered the contract that bound Ochiltree to furnish a loom and workers to produce linen damask tablecloths with Defoe's design of the new arms of Great Britain in exchange for yarn and, upon delivery, payment of 7s. sterling per eln* of finished cloth. Ochiltree may have moved in part in order to gain more space for Defoe's subcontracted work. The linen trade had been singled out as one of the industries to be encouraged by the Union, and Defoe may have believed his investment a timely one. His statement in the spring of 1707, however, is obviously an exaggeration. Ochiltree was a master craftsman to whom Defoe could have contributed little knowledge of weaving, and it is unlikely that he and Ochiltree together employed "above 100 poor Families." A December 1711 report to the Edinburgh Town Council lists six men, twenty-nine women, and eighteen boys and girls as the poor at New Greyfriars.[19]

Ochiltree was one of a number of merchants and middle-class citizens whom Defoe had come to know well. From scattered remarks it is clear that Defoe continued to visit his friends' homes and to develop firm friendships. He shared bowls of punch and hours of talk with a group of Edinburgh professional men and merchants who were less prominently connected than John Clerk.

Sometimes these friends worked together. They brought Defoe into their groups, and he became a willing, if somewhat sporadic, worker. For example, he joined the Society for the Reformation of Manners in April 1707. "Baillie" John Duncan, a merchant burger and one of the founders of the Edinburgh Society for the Reformation of Manners,

---

*A linear measurement of 37.059 inches. By an act in 1617 the City of Edinburgh became the keeper of the elnwand, an ancient iron rod that was the standard eln.

put Defoe up for membership on 7 March after explaining his idea for a correspondence with the London societies.[20] Defoe, he said, was already a member in London. At that time two members had to propose a man, and the vote to admit him had to be unanimous. Among those who supported Defoe then were Dean of the Guild* Adam Brown, soon to be lord mayor, and Nicol Spence, Edinburgh writer and Clerk† to the Edinburgh presbytery.

Once a member, Defoe worked with George Drummond, former lord provost, and Gilbert Elliot of Minto to establish an exchange of edifying books and pamphlets. Defoe and his committee succeeded and, for the rest of the year, he was as faithful as the average member of the group. According to the minutes, he led prayers just as the others did. Meetings were held every Tuesday afternoon at three, and sometimes the committee met at Defoe's lodgings. The societies were small neighborhood groups, but they had close ties to one another and held "Correspondent meetings" that, in turn, initiated committees of members from several societies.[21] Through his chapter, then, Defoe would have met an ever-growing circle of prominent Scots.

Defoe probably had told the truth to Duncan when he said that he was a member of a London Society for the Reformation of Manners. In 1698, one of the busiest years of Defoe's life in the City of London, the societies were very active, and many had existed since 1691. The second oldest society numbered fifty "Tradesmen and others." King William encouraged the societies in his address to the Commons in 1697, one of the years Defoe worked most assiduously for him. Josiah Woodward wrote that "near 20 *Societies* of various *Qualities* and *Functions*" existed in London and thanked God for "the Brotherly Assistance . . . given us by some of our *Dissenting Brethren* (especially those of the *Presbyterian* Perswasion)."[22] Woodward mentioned the schedule of the Sunday evening lectures at a number of churches, including some very close to Defoe's house. For example, two Sundays a month the lectures were held at St. Giles, Cripplegate, the church in which Defoe's sisters had been baptized, and one of the sample warrants for apprehending those guilty of immorality published in *A Help to a National Reformation* came from the Cornhill society. Defoe's acquaintance John Dunton was active in the Tower Hamlet society and published several works for the society in 1694, the year Defoe's classmate, John Shower, preached before it. In addition the Dissenting societies met at Salters' Hall, the place mentioned by a rival journalist as the site of Defoe's "sermons" in 1704.[23] In 1703 the London societies were described as "now expiring," but the same writer made clear that the Dissenters "contributed their best En-

---

*The elected head of the court of the Edinburgh guilds.
†The chief administrative officer of a presbytery; he was elected by the members.

deavours" to the societies, which were still "the *brightest Constellations* of the *English* Church."[24] In its first year the *Review* included a number of anecdotes about the Society for the Reformation of Manners. Some of these stories are of the novel kind that people like to repeat, such as the one of the coal merchant rebuked for saying, "God Almighty had not dealt fairly" in sending an early spring (1:60). Others suggest personal rather than hearsay knowledge. For example, several numbers give specific details and criticize magistrates for refusing to prosecute the rich (1:132 and 1:271).

The goal of the societies was to discourage "public vice," especially drunkenness, swearing, "bawdy houses," "lewd behavior," and "profaning the Lord's Day." The ways of carrying out their work, however, varied from society to society. Some recruited and paid large numbers of informers; others walked with constables on their regular routes; some put pressure on parish officials to have constables and magistrates enforce the laws strictly; a few confined their activies largely to preaching and distributing tracts. Generally, the societies defined offenses carefully and focused on clear-cut cases. For example, several limited drunkenness to being "unable to stand on his legs" and went on to caution members to use care in labeling people drunk when illness, a blow to the head, or old age might be the cause. All distributed books and tracts: "Many Thousands of Books have been dispersed by these Societies throughout the Kingdom, and put into the Hands of Lewd and Profane Persons," one manuscript tells us.[25] In fact, the societies distributed books throughout the world. As early as 1699, books went to the colonies to be handed out by the American equivalent of the society, the New England Company. Defoe may have been involved in that too. The first two students of his old schoolmaster Charles Morton had been educated at the expense of the New England Company to be missionaries to the Indians. By 1705 the society in Cambridge, Massachusetts, where Morton had lived, had grown so large that it had divided into two groups. Cotton Mather, minister of Second Church of Boston, overseer at Harvard College, and one of the most energetic members, corresponded with Defoe.[26]

In Edinburgh society members took turns walking the streets, usually with a constable. Defoe's group, known as "Society Number Two" because it was the second oldest, was the acknowledged leader of the other dozen or so Edinburgh societies. Soon after Defoe joined, this group, so rich in leadership, turned its energies from patrolling and book-swapping to a bigger project: the formation of the Edinburgh Society for the Propagation of Christian Knowledge (SPCK). The initiative for the Society for the Reformation of Manners (SRM) had come from the General Assembly of the Church of Scotland and, once again, the Church was leading a reform movement. Throughout the winter, the Church built support through the presbyteries and synods, for the General Assembly did not meet until April. Only fragments of the records of their activities appear to survive, but those fragments testify to a well-coordinated effort. Church and Commission minutes show careful planning and systematic involvement of synods and presbyteries from September 1707 until long past the granting of the queen's patent on 25 May 1709. Collections for the work were continuous; by October 1710, for example, Greyfriars Church alone had raised £962. The membership of "Society Number Two" determined that its members would be in on the initial stage before the General Assembly, and they shared the responsibility for gaining support and raising money to start an SPCK chapter.[27]

When the General Assembly commission met, it defined the goals of the Edinburgh SPCK to be to found charity schools and to bring "the Protestant religion and morality to the Highlands."[28] The timing of this effort hardly appears to have been free from political considerations. Resistance to the Union came in large part from the Catholic Highlands. William Carstares, the shrewd old politician who had never ceased his efforts to bring about widespread acceptance of the Union, saw the SPCK as a way to use the Church to begin making inroads into the Highlands. The founding of charity schools probably grew in part from the new economic ambitions of the Scots. A number of Scots worried in print about their countrymen's inability to speak or write southern English comprehensibly. Members of the SRM and Edinburgh Town Council were already deeply involved in education at, for example, the Merchant Maiden Hospital, a boarding school for girls.

On 7 October 1707 the SPCK was an agenda item at a meeting of Defoe's Society for the Reformation of Manners,[29] and the SRM's leadership ability was evident from the start. Part of a "scheme" to increase subscriptions addressed to the lord advocate outlines their first plan of action: it asks that he endorse their efforts. He would be an example, encouraging others to join, they argue. Their plan was to enlist influential, admirable people first and to target "several particular States of persons Such as Lords of the Councill, Session Members of Parliament" and others: "Such as are acquainted with the Design at Edinburgh are to divide the Several parts where they have Influence & induce one or more in each shire or Burgh to Agent the affair among their Neighbours as they are here Marked." What follows are lists of people who will be approached in London, other towns and cities, synods, and military commissions with the names of those to contact them on the right. The London entry begins with the annotation: "Our members of parliament who go thither who are to be well Informed of the Deseyn," and continues with the list. Prominent on that short list of ten lines is "Mr. Defoe," who is to contact "Mr. Allen" in London. The other names, including that of Sir Walter Pringle, are those of solid Edinburgh citizens. Since Defoe is included on this list, he was surely still working with his SRM friends. In the *Review* he praised their plans to "plant" schools and ministers in the "Northern Part of Scotland" where "no such Thing as Religion of any Kind whatsoever has ever yet been heard of, no more than was found in the *Northern* Continent of *America*, indeed not so much."[30]

A few partial lists of subscribers to the Edinburgh SPCK survive, and among them are Defoe's friends John Russell, Gilbert Elliot, John Clerk, and John Duncan (who pledged a hundred pounds). One thousand pounds was raised in a year, and a draft patent sent to the Church of Scotland and Hew Dalrymple for the Lords of Session's endorsement on 25 November 1708. The careful work to involve church and civil powers laid the groundwork for the rapid formation of the society. A petition to the queen must have included the names of almost every prominent Scot with Edinburgh connections: among Defoe's closest acquaintances listed on a surviving fragment are John Russell, John Duncan, Adam Brown, Nicol Spence, Hew Dalrymple, John Clerk, and even Agnes Campbell, his printer.

On 25 May 1709 Queen Anne signed the patent to incorporate the Edinburgh SPCK, and as soon as the seals were passed in Edinburgh the society developed rapidly. In November the first Committee of Managers included Defoe's friends Queensberry, Buchan, Cessnock, and Adam Brown. The Edinburgh Society had already published two books; in January 1710, the *interest* on the £3,000 it had collected was substantial enough for it to begin opening schools. By 1713 twelve existed. The investment and managerial skills of the Scots as well as their Church of Scotland affiliation led to a series of rebuffs by the London SPCK, concluding with, first, a decision not to seek a similar patent from the queen and, second, a decision that correspondence between a "free, voluntary society" and an incorporated one was inappropriate.[31]

Defoe had heard about the plans for the SPCK from the church before the SRM chapter was involved. On 29 September 1707 he wrote Harley: "I am Invited to Dine with The Presbytry [*sic*] of *Kircaldy* to day, being the Day before the Synod, And shall have the honor to sit in The Synod the Next Day and Hear all their proceedings; and which is More Than Ever was allow'd to a stranger, have Liberty to give my Opinion in any Case." The synod of Fife met at Kirkcaldie the next day, and among the agenda items was a General Assembly letter expressing concern for the spread of popery and the need for education in the Highlands with the suggestion that an Edinburgh SPCK be formed.[32] Defoe was not the only English Dissenter admitted as an observer with permission to speak. Edmund Calamy wrote on 16 April 1709 that he "had liberty to attend [the General Assembly] from day to day and hear all that passed, making my remarks and observations. To get the better insight into their affairs, I [went to committee meetings and met] . . . every evening over a glass of wine."[33]

For the next few years, the names of those involved in the SPCK continue to appear in relation to Defoe. Adam Brown helped Defoe get support from the Edinburgh Town Council for his *History of the Union*, John Russell managed many of Defoe's financial affairs, and the names of other SPCK supporters such as James Hart, John Flint, and James Grierson reappear in connection with Defoe's activities. Rather than breaking with the SRM, Defoe, like his fellow members, turned his energy from one Christian outreach activity to another.

The connections between Defoe and these men were numerous and varied. For example, John Russell, a writer to the Signet (able to plead cases in the Court of Session), was one of the men approached by Defoe's chapter of the SRM regarding the exchange of tracts with the London societies and one of the earliest supporters of the Edinburgh SPCK. By the time he met Defoe, he was prosperous enough to have bought two farms and respected enough to handle the affairs of men like the earl of Leven. He soon became Defoe's friend and chief "writer." A member of the influential Merchant Company, the group of merchants, burgesses, and guild brothers elected to protect the trading interests of the city, and, incidentally, who also led the city in educational and philanthropic endeavors, Russell could introduce Defoe to other leading citizens.

Russell's acquaintances included a number of Defoe's. As factor for the earl of Leven—the commander-in-chief of the queen's forces in Scotland and pro-Union M.P., whom Defoe had met in the summer of 1706 in the company of George Scott—Russell would have known James Coult, governor of Edinburgh Castle and son-in-law to William Carstares. His membership in the SRM, SPCK, and Merchant Company overlapped with Adam Brown's and John Duncan's. John Sandilands, a neighbor who had sold Russell two farms, was a frequent visitor to Sir John Clerk and was the man who had told Defoe of the libellous pamphlet *The Review Review'd*, which Clerk had received from his son. It was Russell who represented Defoe at the drawing up and signing of the contract with Ochiltree and it is his correspondence that revealed Defoe's investments in wine.

The connections to the Clerks' acquaintances were equally numerous. Besides the obvious ones to the Queensberry and economic commissions circles, the Clerks were friendly with some unlikely people as well. James Hart, the Greyfriar's minister who belonged to both societies, was one of the most persistently outspoken critics of the position in which the Union put clergymen because of the oaths, yet he often visited Penicuik. Hart came to know Defoe well enough to spend money from drafts drawn on one of Defoe's accounts. Defoe's printer, Agnes Anderson, was notoriously litigious and unpleasant; so illiterate and careless that the Bibles she printed were a scandal, she hardly seemed the kind of person who would have known Sir John well enough to have had a passkey to the "Fountain at Penicuik."

During this time Defoe's friendship with the Clerks grew. He became a frequent visitor to Penicuik and to John's pious father, Sir John. The estate was an easy seven miles from the city, and the house was, in John's words, "ample rather than magnificent, useful and convenient rather than sumptuous or splendid, . . . clean and bright." The gardens, apiary, fountain, caves, and especially the fishponds made Penicuik a delightful and restful place. According to his son, Sir John was "every way well qualified for business & spoke very fluently & accurately," was a frugal, good manager, and "was both wise & sagacious." At 5'8" he was a little taller than Defoe and a far more imposing man; he was "thick & strongly built of an Herculean shape . . . his limbs muscularly & finely shaped, the calves of his legs about 17 & some times 18 inches round clean . . . his Anckles small & feet little—one of the best made Little men" in Edinburgh. Like Defoe, he was an active man with a keen interest in horses and improving land. Sir John would have appreciated Defoe's piety, economic acuity, diligence, and dedication to the Union.[34] He recorded some of Defoe's visits, and his son began to collect Defoe's works in the winter of 1706–1707. The Clerks sometimes shared the expense and occasionally asked for works back to reread.

The respect he had for Defoe's political insight can be seen in the Clerks' correspondence about Defoe's published works. John Clerk had sent the early *Removing National Prejudice* essays and other pro-Union tracts to his father as they were published. On 7 January he paid £14.4s. for a "defoe poem," probably a bound copy of *Caledonia*.[35] On 10 February Clerk wrote to Penicuik:

I left the consolidator with you, which was only sent me, the Author has gotten doun 20 Setts of his works, wherof I wou'd fain put you to the expense of one, which in my opinion will be very well worth buying. They are as follows
    The jure divino a book in folio price 10 lb. (scots)
    his miscelany works in 2 voll octato [sic] 12 lb.
    a volume of his potical [sic] Reveus 9 lb. in quarto,
    the consolidator 4 lb.
    5 pamphlets upon different subjects about 8 sheets each.

Defoe seems to have been selling the "20 Setts" of his works himself, and the prices were negotiable. Queensberry, for instance, paid 12s. 6d. for the bound volume of the *Review*, 16s. for the two-volume *Works*, 3s. 6d. for the *Consolidator*, and £1 for the folio edition of *Jure Divino*, for a total of £2.12 sterling, or about £33 scots.[36] Clerk had paid "about" £40 scots. On the seventeenth, Clerk asked his father to share the cost of the works: "If you contribute 1 guinea & a half for Defoes works, I shall contribute the rest, for they will be useful to me, because you must know I am chosen one of the 45 to represent in the first Parliament of G.B." Coincidentally, Sir John had written to his son the same day requesting more Defoe books:

send me per Gill of Mr. D'foes books well bound to the valoue of one & a half & I shall send the same per next to you, I'll certainly be rich for thou[gh] I admire poesie I'm neither a poet nor am I fond to spend my time that way or on mathematicks, for both these will be satisfied with nothing less than the wholl man: let me have chiefly then his works in prose & as few of his poetrie as possible. & so I keep the consolidator as one of them send me back again D'foes 6th essay agts Mr Webster

On the eighteenth, John noted in his account book that he paid £29.5 s. scots for "De'foes works." A few days later, he wrote,

Receive De foes jure divino in folio the 2 vollum of his revisions, & the first vollum of his works, I have the 2nd vollum of his works here & 6 pamphlets.
I have bought them & payed for them, because of their being absolutely necessary to let me know a littel of the bypast transactions of the house of commons, however this will not free you to bear a part of the expense as you promised. in the first volume of his works, you'l find his Satyre of the Treu born-Englishman, which is much esteemed.

The Clerks were not mere admirers, however. At one point John describes one of Defoe's *Review* essays as "impudent."

Most of Defoe's work as an agent throughout 1707 was with the Church of Scotland. Resistance to the Union from the church had been a serious concern to all Union supporters from the beginning, and, after the ratification of the treaty, unrest in the church grew rather than diminished. Defoe was clever enough to see that the chief danger to the acceptance of Union was the church,[37] and that the chief beneficiaries of resistance would be the Jacobites, the supporters of the Catholic Pretender, James. In early July Defoe wrote, "The Intollerable boldness of the Jacobite party . . . is Such Now . . . that Unless Some speedy Care is Taken to prevent Their Disorders The Consequences Can not but be fatall [to the Union]." He understood that a serious matter of conscience was at issue for many. For these people, like many of Defoe's own elderly friends, had taken the National Covenant and Solemn Oath in the 1640s which bound them to work to reform the Church of England and disallowed the civil power of the clergy by removing those bishops who held seats in Parliament by virtue of the office from Parliament. Even if they could reconcile themselves to an oath of allegiance to the English monarch (and head of the Church of England), they found it impossible to take the Oath of Abjuration that would, in Defoe's words, "Joyn [them] in Excluding their Own Church from the succession." Moreover, some of the clergy sincerely feared that the English M.P.'s would use their superior parliamentary representation to impose the episcopal form of government on the Scottish church, especially since English bishops were not excluded from Parliament.

Defoe understood many of the clergy's reservations, but he believed them wrong. Although he published extensively on church issues and entered into long controversies with a few clergymen in attempts to soothe the Church of Scotland's concerns, he expended his major effort on visits. He met frequently with Edinburgh and provincial clergymen, tirelessly attended synod and presbytery meetings, placed spies in commissions,[38] and tried not to miss any General Assembly meetings. He traveled as far as Glasgow, Sterling, and Wemyss and offered to go into the Highlands. He explained in February that he was "at present Entirely Taken up in Meer Cavil and Continuall Dispute with the Clamorous Clergy," and noted in June: "I am Travailing thro' the Towns and Disputeing with The Rigid and Refractory Clergy who are the worst Enemies of the Union." Time after time Defoe described how he had left a minister reassured about English intentions, only to find the man a day later repeating the same "wild chimeras" he had held when Defoe met him. His frustration with the clergy began early and grew over the year: "I Find there is Bigotry without popery," he grumbled more than once.

Defoe's work with the Church of Scotland took on a more personal aspect in January when the Reverend James Webster accused the London Dissenters of collaboration with the Church of England and, therefore, of lacking fidelity to their religious principles. Defoe immediately protested that Webster "grossly wrong'd" the English Dissenters, who "never have deserv'd this Treatment . . . *much less Now.*" He reacted with special outrage to the charge that his people had embraced King James's Act of Indulgence. His *The Dissenters in England Vindicated* is mild enough; in restrained prose, it gives a list of factual objections to Webster's generalizations. *Passion and Prejudice*, printed within days of *The Dissenters . . . Vindicated* is another matter. The epigraph begins, "These Six things the Lord hates . . . A False Witness that speaketh Lies . . . ." He quotes lines from his own poetry: "As Disputants, when Reasons fail, / Have one sure Shift, and that's to rail"; and he accuses Webster of raillery, passion, unfair argumentation, lying, scurrilous language, nonsense, sophism, equivocation, and "barefaced" slander. If he reasoned as Webster did, he could prove him "a Horse, a Woman, a Turk, a Thief." Of this pamphlet, in which vituperation multiplies page by page, Defoe wrote, "I had printed a Replye to him Bitter

Enough, But when I Considred my bussiness here was Peace, Reconciliation and Temper, I thought it better to use him Gently. . . . So I
supprest the book and wrott another."[39]

This substitute pamphlet, *A Short View of the Present State of the Protestant Religion*, is a 48-page history of denominations on the island of
Great Britain concluding that English Dissenters "have suffered all
Severities for their Consciences, and cannot . . . *be distrusted* . . . as
Episcopally inclined" (40). Its language is dignified, formal, and biblical. Tedious in its desire to forestall every possible objection, the pamphlet often repeats itself; for example, Defoe sets the following in an
indented extract on page eleven: "Note, for I desire to be rightly understood, I do not say it was their Duty not to separate, but they were
convinc't of its being their Duty." A final section makes an emotional
plea for peace and charity between England and Scotland and offers
himself as a model, for he has "quitted the just Resentment at unsufferable Insolences" by publishing this pamphlet instead of *Passion and
Prejudice*. Even here, though, how deeply he felt the aspersions cast on
the English Dissenters can be seen. Webster and those who agree with
him "Preach up distrust between a Society of Brethren" and "their
Principles are Abominable, their Ways of Propagating them . . . Un-
Christian . . . their Methods . . . Detested" (48). Of the Dissenters of
King James II's time who were optimistic or naive enough to accept the
Act of Indulgence temporarily, Defoe writes, "It cannot but be *out of
Season*, to rip up the Follies and Mistakes of Men who are dead, and
cannot answer for themselves, especially of Good Men, whose shining
Patterns deserve better Treatment" (41). Defoe's "rip up" suggests vio-
lence to the corpses, and he is obviously still alive to these "shining
Patterns'" suffering; in another paragraph, he calls them "that Glori-
ous Body of Protestants" (43).

Defoe told Harley that the moderate clergymen "Come Every Day to
thank me for [the pamphlet]" and it "has gotten me a Compleat Victory." In fact, Webster had since published *The Author of the Lawful
Prejudices . . . Defended* and *A Second Defence of the Lawful Prejudices* but
had turned his wrath on the Reverend William Adams, who had written *A Letter from the Country Containing Some Remarks concerning the National Covenant and Solemn League* (1707) in order to contradict Webster's interpretation of the oaths. Adams was a renegade with Episcopa-
lian sympathies; Defoe told Harley that he had been able to turn the
radical clergy against each other, "like Sathans [*sic*] kingdome Divided
against it self the Furious Temper Can not stand." With Adams attacking Webster, Defoe could leave the battlefield.

In this controversy, too, Defoe had the encouragement and help of
local Scots. He told Harley that he had been asked by several clergymen
to explain that most of them were innocent of "the scandal Raisd on

them by Webster."[40] These pamphlets contain a number of anecdotes that could only have come from long-time residents of the country. In *An Historical Account of the Bitter Sufferings*, for example, Defoe says, "I have not only searched into all the publick Records of this Matter, which I could have Access to, but have made as strict Enquiry, as possibly I could, of the most Impartial and Unbyass'd Persons" (17). This pamphlet reveals its anecdotal sources, too, in the way it mixes loose quotations from the acts of the Scottish Parliament, rather rambling accounts of the lack of enforcement of these acts, and statements of outrage, such as "The persecuted Episcopal Clergy-man insults them from the parish-Church, and keeps both the Pulpit and the Stipend, in spight of them all" (16).

Throughout the rest of the year Defoe visited the clergy, attempted to reconcile them to the Union, and used the *Review* to explain and excuse Church of Scotland actions to the English. Sometimes he noted that his Scottish friends had asked him to tell their London "brothers" that the extremists rather than the majority of the clergy were responsible for hostile sermons, pamphlets, and mobs. *An Historical Account of the Bitter Sufferings . . . of the Episcopal Church in Scotland, under the Barbarous Usage and Bloody Persecution of the Presbyterian Church Government* has some interest because, in it, Defoe once again attempts to make the point of *The Shortest-Way with the Dissenters* through irony. Rather than describing what the title promises, the pamphlet portrays the Church of Scotland as moderate, tolerant, and reasonable, especially in comparison to the way the Church of England has treated the English Dissenters. In this case, however, only the title is ironic; the text is in fact a straightforward examination of the treatment and situation of Episcopalians in Scotland.

৵৶

Godolphin's recognition of his value and his own decision not to accept a civil service position did not improve Defoe's lot. In fact, by September Defoe worried about money as he had not done since he left London. On 11 September he described himself as holding a letter from Godolphin that promised "an Allowance for Subsistence," "Offring me Comfortable Things," but being like a besieged town, heartened by the promise of relief but overwhelmed nonetheless. Days passed, and Defoe brooded and worried: "When I Read Over Sometimes My Ld Tr . . . s Letter which I Carry in My Pocket, I Think 'tis Impossible I should be in the Case I am." In London, his brother-in-law and companion Robert Davis wrote to Harley,

I crave leave to remind your honour of your promise that you would not only take care that my brother D F should be supplied, but also spur my Lord T——r to settle that affair on him before your honour goes in the country.

I hope that [neither of you] will not now neglect him while all the world sayeth he hath been very serviceable, and will so continue both in private and public (if he be not too much neglected). . . . I beg your honour's pardon for this trouble, and hope his condition with his sickly, large and needy family here may be sufficient motives to move you.[41]

When paid by Harley, Defoe seems to have had problems caused by a lack of anticipation of expenses on both sides and by irregularity of payment rather than from stinginess on Harley's part. Through John Bell, Defoe received at least £129. 8s. between October and mid-April in addition to the horse he had had to replace in October at a cost of £14. At first the general postmaster in Edinburgh supplied Defoe with "what he has Occasion for" but requests for larger sums soon went to Bell as Defoe began to distribute his writings. The fact that £10 would make Defoe "Easy for some time" suggests costs in Edinburgh and Defoe's modest needs. From other letters, it is clear that Defoe's family in London received money from a separate source. Since even the most expensive lodgings in Edinburgh cost only £20 a year, and Defoe lodged at a "good friend's house,"[42] it seems he was generously supplied.

But in the fall, week after week passed without word or money. Defoe continued to send reports, but the strain of preserving a matter-of-fact tone showed. He continued to compare himself to a failing garrison and contemplated what he considered a dishonorable "retreat"— departure from Scotland without orders to do so. His sense of alienation and distress grew, and he began to call Scotland "remote," "distant," and "strange." He had been away from home almost exactly a year, and the news from his family had not always been reassuring. His father had died the past December. From Defoe's reaction to the news of his burial in Bunhill Fields on the twenty-fourth, it seems he did not expect the death. In a rather distracted letter to Harley, Defoe said, "I Confess myself in Some Disordr to night, The Account of the Death of my Father Comeing just as I was writeing this." Now his daughter Martha was seriously ill, and in mid-October she died.[43] This child, born while Defoe was in prison, must have been almost a stranger to him, yet his letters telegraph the agitation he felt, because, ironically, they grow calmer again after her death even though he still had nothing but promises to live on.

Finally, in late November, Defoe received £100 through John Bell with permission to return to London.[44] The money appears to have come from Harley in spite of the June arrangement that Godolphin should pay Defoe. Defoe's letters to Godolphin and his references to him are far more formal and deferential than those to and about Harley. Contemporaries found Godolphin to have an "awful serious deportment," to be "of very hard access," and to give answers that were "commonly very short and shocking." His age, long-held position, and forbidding manner kept Defoe at a distance. In contrast, Defoe's letters to Harley show that Defoe grew to believe he understood Harley. Although the two men make almost no personal statements except as apologies for delays and almost never give personal news, the letters come to share a revealing biblical idiom. In a passage that begins like many that Defoe wrote, Harley writes, "I hope I have not been an unprofitable Servant." In this letter, he reflects that "it has been often so" that good servants "bear Reproach for doing what others could not, or would not do." He goes on to tell Defoe that he has now taken a stand, hopes to frustrate his enemies, but is prepared for the consequences, regardless of what they may be.[45] The use of biblical language as a shorthand to convey position and feeling and the metaphors for servant, lonely warrior for right, and defender of truth testify to the common Dissenting backgrounds of the two men and the temperamental bond between them. Defoe often fell back upon allusions to such New Testament stories as the cripple at the pool when he began to describe feeling rather than fact.

Defoe wrote this way to everyone, but Harley did not. Harley's letters to the Presbyterian minister Carstares are most similar in language to his to Defoe. Perhaps, like Defoe, Harley believed in taking St. Paul's advice: "I am made all things to all *men*, that I might by all means save some." Rather than changing the message, they meant to assume the terms and point of view of their readers so that they would be understood and persuasive. Defoe, of course, had moved as close to the Scottish perspective as he credibly could in order to answer the objections to the Union, and Harley tended to encourage his employees' efforts by talking about his work in the terms he believed they saw as their own.[46] Yet there is no question that Harley was a Christian, and his biblical allusions were knowledgeable, resonant, and sincere. For instance, in a letter to an apparently unlikely recipient, the earl of Leven, he compared the Scottish anti-Union clergymen to "the Jewish Zealots" of the epistles of Peter, James, and Jude. Moreover, Harley's speeches often used biblical language, and he wrote notes to himself with moral injunctions. Almost everyone who knew Harley well commented on his piety. The man who wrote Defoe that he had set his course was the man Swift, Pope, Dartmouth, and a host of others saw. As Pope said of Harley,

> A Soul supreme, in each hard Instance try'd.
> Above all Pain, all Passion, and all Pride,
> The Rage of Pow'r, the Blast of publick Breath,
> The Lust of Lucre, and the Dread of Death.[47]

No matter what happened, Defoe saw Harley as one who understood him and was willing to help him out of difficulties. In the fall of 1707, however, Harley himself was in trouble. Caught in the power struggle between the Whigs and the Tories, he angered former friends. Godolphin's daily meetings and intimate notes filled with respect for Harley's judgment changed, and soon Harley was forced to plead his loyalty repeatedly. On 2 September he had written,

I desire your lordship will permit me to trouble you . . . with what I did intend to have spoken to your lordship . . . if I had met with a proper opportunity at Windsor. I desire only to assure your lordship most sincerely, that I am resolved to do everything to the utmost of my power (if required) to make the Queen's service and her ministers' easy, and I will be under your lordship's directions and be active or passive, to do anything or nothing, to meddle with business or let it alone, as your lordship shall think best and shall be pleased to let me know your pleasure.[48]

Such a letter would have been unthinkable in 1705, but Harley was rapidly losing ground to intrigue, faction, and suspicion. In January 1707 he collapsed at his desk, but he appeared in the House the next day to assure the passage of a crucial bill on financing the war, and then took until well into March to recover enough to resume business. Quarreling, competing for places, and rumor-mongering immobilized the court and Parliament, and, on his return, Harley tried to effect a reorganization of the ministry. He wanted moderates who would exclude the extreme Whigs to whom Godolphin felt indebted. The struggle would continue until February, when Marlborough threatened to resign if Godolphin left the ministry; even Harley realized that the country could not lose its great general at that moment and persuaded the queen to accept his own resignation instead.

꧁꧂

In many ways, the year in Scotland had not been good for Defoe. He had written nothing first-rate and may have committed a number of demeaning acts, including stealing a horse. Indeed, he had compromised his principles at least twice. Apparently forgetting the courage and glory of *Legion's Memorial*, he attacked the anti-Union Scottish petitioners and, in doing so, contradicted his own earlier position. In 1701 the proud phrases asserting the citizens' right and duty to demand that Parliament listen to them flowed easily:

We do hereby
    Claim and Declare.
    1. That it is the Undoubted Right of the People of *England*, in case their Representatives in Parliament do not proceed according to their Duty, and the Peoples Interest, to inform them of their Dislike, . . . and to direct them to such things as they think fit, either by Petition, Address, Proposal, Memorial. (110)

In 1706 Defoe took a very different stance and made every effort to discredit the Scottish petitioners in order to diminish the impact in England of reports that anti-Union petitions were "pouring" into the Scottish Parliament. Day after day he asserted in the *Review* that few signatures appeared on each petition. His most common attack was to insist that he and others who examined the petitions quickly saw that the signers were primarily Jacobites. Even with a petition from so important a group as the Convention of the Royal Burroughs, he isolated the petitioners. He pointed out that twenty-three of the sixty-seven burroughs were unrepresented and that twenty of the forty-four in attendance refused to sign. In the sixth *Essay*, probably published in January 1707, Defoe specifically addressed petitioning. In *Legion's Memorial* he had used verbs such as "command," "compel," "claim," "require," and "demand." In this *Essay* he defines petitioners as "supplicants" and petitions as "prayers." In fact, he states explicitly that those who "demand" are not petitioning (5–6). The interpretation that he or the Kentish petitioners were "praying" and were willing to "Submit to the Wisdom and Authority" of Parliament would have been ludicrous, but in 1706 Defoe was attempting to teach Scots that "duty."[49]

This sixth *Essay* reflected the sting he felt from a strong, clearly written pamphlet published at the beginning of 1707. *A Reply to the Authors of the Advantages of Scotland by an Incorporate Union; and of The Fifth Essay, at Removing National Prejudices* accused Defoe of undermining the very "Revolution Principles" he had defended in England. In a telling section this author chides Defoe for saying that even if the majority of Scots were against the Union, they had no right to restrain Parliament. "Who, by his Principles, is Judged Competent in this Matter?" he then asks Defoe, and answers with Defoe's own ringing words from *Legion's Memorial*: "The People or Parliament; The Representatives, or the Represented; the Fountain or the Stream. . . . Thus, Sir, you see, what it is to set up for a Time-Server."

Another vicious satire, *The Albanian Animal*, responded to Defoe's *A Scot's Poem: Or, A New Years Gift, from a Native of the Universe, to His Fellow-Animals in Albania*. In it Defoe had praised Scotland, complimented individual Scots, and tried yet again to enumerate the advantages to Scotland of Union. The forty-page poem is, however, pedestrian and as pretentious as his title with its claim to being a "Native of the Universe." Quick to exploit weakness, the author of *The Albanian Animal* pricks his vanity and likens him to slinking, groveling animals.[50]

Indeed the mediocrity of Defoe's work now threatened the *Review*. Because Defoe was so far away, the *Review* was more like "history writing by inches," the reflective historical essays typical of the first year of the periodical. The issue for 19 November was probably written on 5

November, for *Miscellanea* sounds like Defoe's letter to Harley of the same date and reports news of the parliamentary debates over the treaty as a tribute to King William, whose birth date happened to coincide with the date on which Parliament was to consider Article I of the treaty. After that date, the *Review* continues to address Scottish fears more than England's objections. Never a newspaper anyway, the *Review* lost its immediacy, its harmony with the ephemeral interests and curiosities of the man on the street.

Beginning on 15 February 1707 Defoe made concerted efforts to respond to criticism and boost circulation: "Nothing but Union, Union! says the Publisher of this . . . they want a little Diversion, they want something about the rest of the World, how Affairs go abroad, and Affairs at home, who and who are together, and what is a doing in the World" (4:9). From then until 11 March the *Review* followed the Great Northern War in the first part and considered domestic trade in its *Miscellanea*. Defoe tried to add variety in a number of ways. For instance, he quoted lines from his own poetry in a number of issues, included "projects" for financing the war, and increased his use of anecdotes and dialogue. He asked his readers to send him more questions. Some of his material lightened the tone considerably; he explored "What makes a bad Wife?" and "What is the worst sort of Husband?" as he had in the Scandal Club pieces and as he would in his conduct books and novels. Now and then, he noted that a paper was entirely "for your Mirth" and printed jokes, riddles, and bizarre solutions to riddles.

He also began to make more extreme statements. For example, he compared Lord Haversham's most recent speech to Belhaven's emotional "dream" speech and chided Parliament on its duty. He continued to write on two subjects in each *Review* and worried about its appeal. In January of 1708, he wrote in *Miscellanea*, "I have had frequent Notices sent Me of late, that I have left off diverting the World in the *Review*. . . ." Some of these subjects Defoe had tried to give up before, and it was unlike him to be deliberately sensational. In the fall both the Swedish and Russian ambassadors officially complained about Defoe. Few journalists in less than a month offend both sides in a war, but Defoe had. On 20 September he had accused King Charles XII of Sweden of assisting France; on 16 October he had remarked that money "hirest Servants to the Devil, nay, to the very Czar of *Muscovy*."[51] Later Defoe was to write sympathetic lives of both Charles and Czar Peter I, of Russia; after 1707 Defoe found it easier and easier to write on both sides of a question.

The second time Defoe compromised his principles was when he lost his temper and descended to the vituperative ad hominem attack upon Webster in *Passion and Prejudice*. Throughout his life Defoe prided himself on his moderation, restraint, and refusal to descend to "Billingsgate."* Not only did he believe personal attacks un-Christian, he thought them ineffectual and sure signs that the writer had been bested in argument. Yet even in *A Short View of . . . the Protestant Religion* he broke out in a passion to exclaim, "Their [Webster and his party's] Principles are Abominable . . . and to me they merit the utmost Contempt" (48).

Indeed, Defoe had struggled through the entire year for patience and Christian charity. He found the Scots stubborn, irrational, violent, refractory, susceptible to rumor, and fickle. His impatience, frustration, and anger broke out time after time. Hardly a month passed that he did not use the word "recalcitrant" to describe the Scots. He seemed to offend them repeatedly when he, in his opinion, had only the best of intentions, and he reacted by calling them haughty, insolent, proud, positive, and surly. By fall, when he was tired of Scotland and anxious over finances, his impatience and resilience give way to resentment, hurt, and even vindictiveness: "I have quitted the just Resentment at unsufferable Insolences." "How will you regret the unkind Treatment of your Friends, who will thus requit you Good for Evil, and heap Coals of Fire on your Heads." At his best he saw that the Scots were "a Sober, Religious and Gallant Nation," but he often struggled to hold that opinion.

Defoe believed firmly that Scotland could bloom as London had after the Great Fire. His faith in the possibility of economic development never faltered, and he tirelessly exhorted Scots to give up their foolish prejudices and join together to build a new Scotland. His descriptions of what their nation could become are the descriptions of what London became after the Great Fire. What Scotland needed to prosper, Defoe wrote, was "English Stocks, English Art and English Trade." He had left England with that idea, and he continued to hold it. His language often became elevated and prophetic. In his first *Essay at Removing National Prejudices* he told the Scots that with "Application to Manufactures, Encrease of Trade, Fishing, Shipping, and the like" their people would become a kind of wealth and they would not have to emigrate to eat. "There wants nothing but Liberty and Industry to recover *Scotland*, and make her quite another thing," he insisted over and over.

After fifteen months Defoe went home. The Union was a fait accompli, but both "nations" were in turmoil, and his family accustomed to living in Kingsland without him. A great deal was happening that must have caused him anxiety. Political journalists had been arrested and

*Coarse, vulgar, abusive language. The name arose from the kind of language heard at the Billingsgate fish market.

punished harshly. In September John Tutchin, the Whig *Observator* writer, had died after being cudgelled by unknown assailants,* and nearly every week reports of journalists sentenced to the pillory appeared in the papers.[52] Divisions and conflict in Queen Anne's ministry kept the nation in suspense. From his 5 January letter it was clear that Defoe felt himself to be Godolphin's employee, but his loyalty and hopes were with Harley. "I have No hand to Act or Tongue to speak Now but by his Ldpps Directions," he wrote Harley in a letter asking for help in arranging a meeting with Godolphin. This letter suggests that Defoe was under stricter orders regarding his writing, unsure of his next work—and out of touch with the irreparable breach between Harley and Godolphin.

For the next month, rumor put first Harley, then Godolphin, then Harley out of power, and tales of intrigue and schemes scarcely exaggerated the maneuvers at court. The debates over the bills of supply for the next campaign deepened the crisis, and the discovery that a spy had worked for months as a trusted interpreter in Harley's office further undermined confidence in the ministry.[53] Defoe, like so many other government servants, waited anxiously and tried to prepare to stay afloat regardless of the outcome.

*Political writers were frequently threatened and beaten during the century. Both Pope and Johnson were threatened and Dryden was assaulted, for instance.

CHAPTER 11

༄ ྅ ༅

POLITICAL MAELSTROM

destitute between two Parties, & not able to restrain either of them.
—ROBERT HARLEY, August 1710

Robert Harley resigned on 11 February 1708. The Pretender attempted to land in Scotland in March, and at the end of that month the
earl of Godolphin sent Defoe back to Scotland.[1] Defoe probably had no
objections to going north again. London was an inhospitable place for a
party journalist that winter, and Harley's fall had left Defoe depressed
and somewhat at loose ends. "I Sir Desire to be The Servant of your
Worst Dayes," he wrote to Harley on 10 February; "I Entreat you Sir to
Use me in Any Thing in which I may Serve you." In this letter Defoe
mentioned that he had been to Harley's home and would be back the
next night "as by your Ordr." His affectionate admiration broke
through in the closing, "I believ you Unshaken by This storm."

To Godolphin, Scotland had always been a burdensome source of
administrative problems. His predominant attitude could be summed
up in a remark he made in late spring 1707 to Harley: "I foresee a
thousand difficulties and inconveniences." Now he had Scottish prisoners from the unsuccessful invasion on the way to London, and some
of them were from Scotland's chief families. In spite of Edinburgh
officials' efforts, "tumults" continued and mobs fearlessly drank the
Pretender's health and cursed the Union.[2] Competition for places continued. Problems with the Equivalent money persisted, and the need
for a new revenue system seemed urgent. Dozens of major decisions
and hundreds of minor details required attention. The Scottish elections scheduled for June provoked, in Defoe's words, "perfect novelties
of conduct" as new resentments and maneuvers surfaced.[3]

And Godolphin had his hands full in London. The Junto* Whigs
believed Godolphin in their debt and were making demands that
Queen Anne opposed.[4] Bills of supply had to be voted; the war had to

---

*The name comes from the Spanish *junta*, meaning "council," and refers to a group of
Whigs, including Wharton, Somers, Orford, Halifax, and Sunderland, who set themselves in opposition to the Court Whigs. Because of the amount of land they owned, they
wielded considerable influence at elections.

be carried on. Just as in their passion for power and places the members of rival political parties had neglected the war with France in 1701, so they seemed about to do so again in 1708. Godolphin had little time for Scotland, yet he chose to oversee it himself when Chancellor of the Exchequer Henry Boyle became the secretary of state for the Northern Department. Boyle, a moderate Whig, was a friend of Harley's, and Godolphin suspected Harley of continuing to meddle in government affairs. Indeed, Defoe's report on February 20 to Harley on the Scots' resistance to the part of the Equivalent paid in Exchequer bills tends to confirm Godolphin's opinion.[5]

Defoe saw his job in Scotland to be to provide "plain, naked, and unbyasst accounts both of persons and things." He sent reports both to Godolphin and to the earl of Sunderland. Sunderland, a Junto Whig and son-in-law to the duke of Marlborough, had been secretary of state for the Southern Department since December 1706. In his youth he had called himself a republican and insisted that he thought the House of Lords should be abolished. Highly intelligent, handsome, wealthy, and member of a powerful family, Sunderland also had a violent temper, an autocratic personality, and a reckless spirit. Above all, he was a restless man who seemed to enjoy causing turmoil. He seems to have contacted Defoe before he left London, for Defoe says that "According to Orders," he had gotten in touch with John Shute, one of the commissioners of the Customs, as soon as he had arrived in Edinburgh.[6] Defoe was receiving money from both Godolphin and Sunderland, and he made a point of explaining to Sunderland that he feared that if Godolphin knew about Sunderland's "favours," Godolphin would feel less inclined to support Defoe and to keep his promises to "do something" for him. Defoe may have felt more in harmony with the politics of the Junto, now moderate Whigs, who were allying themselves with the Squadrone in Scotland. The Squadrone included Defoe's friend Montrose and was speaking out more vigorously against the Jacobites, now open in their support for the "Pretender," James, than the court party, the extreme Whigs, loyal to Godolphin. Moreover, Defoe had long known and respected other members of the Junto, including Somers, who had defended King William in the House of Lords and been impeached for his part in negotiating the Partition Treaty, and Halifax, who had recommended Defoe to Godolphin, the duchess of Marlborough, and others on several occasions.

When he arrived in Edinburgh on 17 April, Defoe found he had less work to do with the Church of Scotland than he had anticipated. William Carstares had been elected moderator of the General Assembly, and Defoe correctly interpreted that as a sign of the new pacific spirit in the church. The upcoming elections provided him with plenty of work, however, and both Godolphin and Sunderland were deeply interested in assuring the election of as many Whigs as possible. Godolphin believed the key to managing Scotland to be clear indications of who enjoyed court favor, and he allied himself with Seafield and Queensberry.[7] He had sent Defoe north with a letter of introduction to the earl of Leven, one of Queensberry's circle. Defoe, of course, had met Leven with Scott in May 1706 and knew Queensberry personally. In fact, part of the motive for writing his *History of the Union* may have been a desire to "do his Grace Justice." Several 1706 *Reviews* praised Queensberry for his steady courage in the face of threats, insults, and angry mobs and especially for the way he continued to act with "Tenderness and Gentleness, to an insolent but deluded People."[8] Queensberry was John Clerk's father-in-law and even after his daughter's death had continued to be, in Clerk's words, his "good friend" and "patron."

Sunderland played a more dangerous game for the Junto. He struck a bargain with his brother-in-law, the duke of Hamilton, who was imprisoned in the Tower with the other Scots suspected of encouraging the Pretender's invasion. In elation, Sunderland wrote Montrose,

> Before this Comes to your hands your Grace will hear of Duke Hamilton's being at Liberty, this as it was dexterously manag'd so it has produc'd such an Union, as will in all probability carry the Election of the sixteen Peers, in the manner your Grace & all of us wish I can only say, that the whole squadrone is in the List agreed on, & as I am sure you may depend upon Duke Hamilton, & his friends to a man, so I beg you would shew the same Confidence towards him & his.[9]

The released Hamilton would join with the Junto and Squadrone to help elect Whigs, but not necessarily those chosen by Godolphin and Queensberry. Furthermore, a number of Jacobites would be added to the Squadrone list in order to secure men's commitment to voting for the entire list. Elections likely to be lost would be disrupted in order to provide grounds for protests.[10]

Defoe, who had always written against election abuses, found the machinations and crass alliances beyond anything he had ever witnessed in England. He compared some of the things he saw to episodes in his satirical *Consolidator* and, when the Scots complained, asked if such things could happen anywhere but on the moon, the setting for most of the *Consolidator*. Godolphin wrote Marlborough that his mail from Scotland was "full of the heats and animosity of that country about the election of the peers" and called the complaints "endless."[11] Some of the most notorious abuses were laid at the door of Defoe's friend the earl of Leven. Among the accusations against him was that he had had Alexander Mackey arrested on suspicion of treason and imprisoned in the Castle in order to help Mackey's opponent, an army man under Leven's command, win a seat in the Commons. Reports of

Leven's enforcement of his "Interest by promises and Threatenings" came from a dozen sources scattered throughout Scotland. Even those in the center of the struggle sometimes expressed distress at the actions they felt they had to take. Lord Loudoun, keeper of the Great Seal of Scotland, wrote numerous letters to the Dalrymple family about the elections and the need to secure proxies to carry their list. In May Loudoun wrote with some distress that Hamilton had been released: "Be warned," he said, Hamilton was intended to unite the Squadrone and the Tories.[12]

A few days after the election, Defoe reflected soberly in the *Review*: "I have been among a great many of your Elections my self: I have been an Eye-Witness to many of the most fulsome and lothsome [*sic*] Stories. . . . I have seen the Possibility, ay and too much the Practice, of Men's voting implicitly, here for Ale, there for Influence, here again for Parties, and there by Perswasion." It was common knowledge that the Squadrone tricked some of the army peers into giving them their proxies, that four earls had joined the Squadrone because they were given places on the list of nominated men, and that deals had been made among the greatest families. The dates of local elections were juggled, unqualified people voted, some votes were counted twice, and money and ale flowed plentifully. Among those receiving complaints and attempting to keep the elections respectable was Defoe's friend Alex Campbell, Lord Cessnock, who heard complaints about Leven. Defoe—and almost everyone else in Scotland—knew Sunderland's remarkable part. "[The Squadrone] exposed my lord Sunderland's Letters about here very strangely," one Englishman in Scotland wrote, and Queensberry complained to Godolphin and the queen about the use of her name. Sunderland seemed to have no fear. On 7 June he had written to Montrose to say that he had sent a letter to Roxburgh "to be shewn publickly . . . I have no reserve." Even after being summoned by the queen, he persisted. The queen, who had objected strenuously to his appointment, found she had been prophetic: "He & I, would not agree long togather [*sic*], finding by experience my humour & those of a warmer will often have misunderstandings." Defoe wrote, "GOD knows, I speak it with Regret . . . it is not an impossible thing to debauch this Nation into a Choice of Thieves, Knaves, Devils Shock-Dogs* or any thing comparatively speaking"; "you are ruining your Country. . . . you have sold your Nation, your Birth-right, your Chil-

---

*Usually a lady's lapdog. The word may be a corruption of "shough," a lapdog originally imported from Iceland. From the time of Queen Elizabeth I lapdogs were partially shaved, and some lapdogs were "lion-dogs" because they were clipped and shaved to resemble lions. The allusion is to an instructive tale in Defoe's *Consolidator* in which an influential man is able to get his dog elected to office. See also, *Review* 5:69–71 and 81–84.

dren, to a Pack of Thieves."[13] The fact that the election results should have pleased Defoe underscores the amount of corruption he had seen. After all, twenty-seven of the forty-five newly elected men were clearly part of the Queensberry-Seafield-Argyll-Mar coalition, and eighteen or nineteen were Squadrone Whigs. "There are not six that will think themselves scandalized at the name of a *Whig*," Defoe said of the peers elected.[14]

Defoe wrote a number of *Review* essays and a pamphlet, *A Memorial to the Nobility of Scotland, Who Are to Assemble in Order to Choose the Sitting Peers for the Parliament of Great Britain*, specifically as election propaganda. Scots continued to be concerned about inflammatory pamphlets; in order to exert some control, the Edinburgh Town Council, the governing body in the city where all but one or two Scottish print shops were, passed an act requiring printers to affix their names to everything they printed.[15] Unusually lively, these *Reviews* ironically urge everyone to vote for the Tories. For example, Defoe asks them if the peace with France that the Tories promise would not be worth their "Liberties, Religion, Posterity," and Trade. Over and over he asks where Scotland learned to divide itself by parties and calls "Bribing, Treating, making Parties and Interests" "a wicked English Custom" (*Review* 5:118). Although he attacks the Jacobites, his primary target came to be the Squadrone, the loose alliance of men whose naked move to gain more power at Queensberry's expense became more obvious every day. Years later he would write that "as I always thought it my duty to oppose Jacobites and all that joined in their interest, I oppos'd them with all my might, altho' I knew them to be *Whigs*, and in other Cases, very honest Gentlemen; . . . if I had been guided by my Interest against my Judgment, I ought to have acted for [them], being under Obligations enough to have them expect it of me" (*Review* 9:25–26).

A Memorial to the Nobility of Scotland is a very different document. The restrained, dignified prose reinforces its serious appeal asking the peers to unite to make the Union an advantage to Scotland, since the Union is now a fait accompli. He depicts the Scots as having gone to London "with Zeal and Love to their Countrey" but returning with "the Contagion of *England*'s Divisions" (5–6). The peers have a choice, he says; they can choose "Men of Capacity and Merit" who would "raise and maintain the Reputation of *Scotland*" or they can continue to strive to raise "the Reputation of Party, in the hopes of a share in the Spoils of the Nation" (15). The ugly term *Spoils* hangs in the air as he concludes with a warning that they risk making Scotland powerless in Parliament and themselves contemptible.

Defoe had seen the wagons bringing the Equivalent to Scotland stoned by the common people; he had seen Exchequer bills treated as nearly worthless paper; he had watched party fury lead to the death of a journalist he had known personally and to the fall of a statesman whom he believed exemplary. He had characterized his own time as one in which it was a "Sin against Custom to do [our Superiours] Justice"; "unhappy is the Time . . . that nothing, the Government can do, must be own'd, much less defended as well done" (*Review* 4:371). Now he had seen men he had admired stoop to bribery, apostasy, and begging.

Through all of these shocking and disillusioning events, he held on to the idea that the Union was "God's Providence," a great blessing to England and the Protestant religion, and one of the most significant acts in English history. He turned from the election storm to writing *The History of the Union.* In doing so he continued some of the efforts all of his Scottish writings share. He hoped to reconcile people to one another and to the Union. He wanted the divisions and resentments put aside in order to begin the work necessary to realize the benefits he believed the Union offered. In both his life and his novels Defoe was one to get on with things. In *A Memorial* he had written: "It is no matter who were for, or against the Union, that comes not in Consideration now . . . ; you are all now equally concerned to . . . make it an Advantage"(4). *The History of the Union* would remind the Scots of the patriotism and nobility displayed in their nation's last Parliament, proclaim the Union a providential blessing, and reiterate its benefits.

After the elections Defoe was relatively on his own, though at no time had he been anyone's sole observer, agent, or correspondent. His great narrative gift, the ease with which he wrote long letters "to the moment," his eye for detail, and his perceptiveness about human motivation combined with the keen economic sense that Harley trusted had given his letters great interest in 1706-1707. Over time, however, Godolphin and others had ceased to trust many of these very qualities. Defoe, Godolphin once wrote, "gives you the worst side of the picture." Sunderland had what he wanted, and Godolphin's preoccupation with the war and his conviction that "nothing is more certain than that generally the people of Scotland are dissatisfyed" promised neglect. Indeed, by August Defoe had to beg Godolphin to pay him and to provide for his distressed family. Even as Defoe pleaded, Godolphin was paying the native Scot John Ker of Kersland generously—at least £300 in 1708 and £700 in 1709.[16] Through the lovely Scottish summer that he described as warm, "clear and calm," Defoe worked on his history, kept up the *Review*, and relaxed with his friends. He and the Russell family in particular came to share jokes and private family news. Warm letters and thoughtful shipments of wine, china, plate, and even pickles continued after Defoe left Edinburgh.

Just before Defoe left for London in late fall, a controversy erupted over *The History of the Union* which he had just delivered to his printer, Agnes Anderson. Defoe had suffered increasingly vicious personal attacks since the beginning of 1707, and the pre-publication attack on his *History* and his response capture the nature of the nearly two-year-old conflict. The Reverend James Clark in *A Paper concerning Daniel De Foe* accused Defoe of giving a biased, erroneous account of his responsibility for the Glasgow riot of 7 November 1706. In a second publication, *Rabbles and the Author of Rabbles Condemned*, Clark again accused Defoe of writing bad history. Here Clark objected to the way Defoe would "comment," "reflect," and "expatiat in opprobrious Invective." Not only does the *Paper* make the most damaging charges that could be made against a historian, it summarizes the "Information anent* Mr. *De Foe's* Morals and Politicks." The author shows himself to be an observer of Defoe and a collector of printed attacks on him. He describes Defoe in Glasgow "procuring Subscriptions" for the *History* and depicts him as subject to flattery. By "caressing" him and filling his time with social invitations, the enemies of Clark had been able to keep Defoe from enquiring after the truth, the writer alleges. Defoe's enemies were again portraying him as pretentious and even foppish. According to the *Review Review'd*, at age forty-seven, Defoe still wore a long wig, now with tassels at the end of it, and the diamond pinky ring that he flashed ostentatiously in coffeehouses. Such behavior and the company the "broken Hosier" kept irritated a good many people, and they kept the memory of the pillory before the public's eyes. So notorious was Defoe that a Sidbury, Devon, clergyman complained to the London SPCK and then to Offspring Blackall, bishop of Exeter, about a pamphlet he wrongly assumed Defoe had written. He asked both if they did "not think it worth their while to have it answered." Defoe's own words were often turned against him. Samuel Wesley used a quotation from the *Review* as the epigraph for his 155-page assault on the Dissenters, *A Reply to Mr. Palmer's Vindication of the . . . most Christian Behaviour of the Dissenters towards the Church of England* (1707).[17]

James Clark referred with approval to the *Review Review'd* and other attacks such as that in the 1705 *Compleat History of Europe*, which had described Defoe as rash, impudent, and a "Hackney Tool."[18] Such aspersions on Defoe's source of income were common; for example, in *A Paper concerning Daniel De Foe* Clark offered a new motto for Defoe's picture: "To get my Bread no other way I ken, / But by the Clatter of my Tongue and Pen." Some went on to scoff at the idea that Defoe would settle in Scotland: "You think none of your base Treach'ry smells: / You in each Company are pleased to cant, / 'Tis here to Live, and here to Dwell, you want." Others ridiculed his writing style; "Doggerel *Caledonia*," they mocked, and they quoted particularly infelicitous lines or observed that "neither Sense nor Grammer [*sic*] can confine him." The

*Scots for "about."

most vicious accused Defoe of cheating and defrauding others, of living "by Defamation," and even of getting the wife of the Spittlefields weaver Sammen pregnant.[19] James Clark shamelessly recalls all of the accusations and offers Defoe advice aimed at putting him in his social and occupational place, "Ne sutor ultra crepidam" (The shoemaker should stick to his shoes).

In the spring of 1707 Defoe had been stung to answer some of these attacks. He usually insisted upon his moderation and honesty, but sometimes he attempted to clarify his point or refute the other side's argument. He always jeered at the idea that he was being paid, and his best responses were often satirical jibes at his tormentors' contradictions: "If I lay before them the Advantages of Union and Peace . . . lo, the Man is an Emissary, . . . an Envoy of the *Presbyterians,* . . . an Emissary of *France,* . . . a Tool of the State." His most common remark was to say that their insults were like dust thrown against a wind—"It all flys back in [their] own Eyes." In *A Short View of the Present State of the Protestant Religion,* however, he admitted the sting of their strategy of "reproaching the Man, to weaken his Discourse" and demanded, "I challenge them to bring the Man . . . that ever saw me drink to Excess, that ever heard me swear . . . can charge my Conversation with the least Vice or Immorality, with Indecency, Immodesty, Passion, Prophaneness" (45). Discouragement and weariness crept into this tract as Defoe reflected on his life: "The Party . . . mistake me [that think] I avoid Reflecting on their Follies . . . for any Value or Fear of their Resentment, they must be little acquainted with the Scenes I have acted in the World . . . and I refer them to the Resentments of Men much more Capital than their Ambitious Thoughts can pretend to" (47–48).

When *A Paper concerning Daniel De Foe* appeared, Defoe countered with *An Answer to a Paper Concerning Mr. De Foe,* a pamphlet allegedly written by his Edinburgh friends.[20] Defoe, it said, "has on many Occasions in his Writings very well deserved of this Nation" (1). Here is the defense of 1703; just as he had written effectively in the Dissenters' behalf before *The Shortest Way* and been rewarded with criticism and misunderstanding, so he saw ingratitude again. Once again an ambitious subscription project was foundering.[21] In the advertisements Defoe had identified himself only as "the Author of the *True-Born Englishman,*" a reminder of his greatest patriotic literary success. In fact, Defoe's qualifications as historian were at least as solid as his poetic ones. His first substantial manuscript was the *Historical Collections,* he had called the *Review* "history writing by inches," and nearly every pamphlet he had ever written relied at least in part upon historical knowledge. He always said that fine literature was his "constant study and ambition," but now, when he believed *A History of the Union* a credit to him, he faced disappointment again. At the urging of his friend the

Glasgow merchant, James Montgomery, and Clark's friend, John Spreul, he met Clark, and they agreed to end the controversy. Defoe would revise his report of the Glasgow riot, and Clark would not publish additional complaints against Defoe.[22]

Unfortunately Defoe had to work hastily and soon afterwards from an awkward distance to get Mrs. Anderson to reset part of his finished, partially printed manuscript. He instructed her to remove Clark's name and make a number of small changes intended to give a more polite if not substantially different account of the instigation of the Glasgow riot:

ORIGINAL VERSION	REVISED VERSION
I shall convince the Gentleman concerned, that this Account is not made for a Satyr upon him . . . and when both he, and those who heard him reflects on, how much more his Unhappy Temper, at that time forc'd from him, than I set down here, all which I have by me *verbatim* . . . he will . . . be convinced, that I talk no more, than, in the Obligation of a Historian to Truth of Fact, I am bound to do.	This Account is not made for a Satyr upon any particular Person, . . . Nor shall I say any thing more than in the Obligation of Historian to Truth of Fact I am bound to do.
. . . this was the full Purport of the Expression, without the least Variation; as to the Weak Good Man that spoke them, I will not suggest, that he foresaw the Consequence of them, . . . tho it calls for some Charity to guess his Meaning; The kindest thing I can say of them, is, that he did not mean at all what followed, but spoke in his Haste.	. . . this was the Purport of the Expression, without the least Variation; as to the Gentleman that spoke, them, I will not suggest, that he foresaw the Consequence of them, . . . The kindest thing I can say of them, is that he did not mean at all what followed. . . .

By eliminating phrases such as "the Weak Good Man," "his Unhappy Temper," and "spoke in his Haste," Defoe gives a picture of Clark as a naive speaker rather than as a hot-headed, passionate rabble-rouser. Either because Defoe's instructions came too late, the binder erred, or Mrs. Anderson's well-known avarice took over, many copies of *A History of the Union* with the original account were sold. Clark published *A Just Reprimand to Daniel De Foe*, which attacked Defoe's accuracy and methodology and accused him of "shamefully" failing to keep their agreement. Later Defoe wrote that Mrs. Anderson and Mr. Campbell, her "Corrector," admitted that they were to have suppressed all of the original sheets. Defoe himself had contracted to pay Mrs. Anderson for the revisions, but he ended up removing some of the books on which she could not bear to lose the profit. He did, however, insist upon the accuracy of his account of Clark's sermon and asserted that he could name five men who "remember the very words."[23]

⁂

In December 1708 Defoe was back in London and less creative and less committed to anything than at any other time in his life. The *Review* meandered among a number of familiar topics, and his pamphlet output dropped to nearly nothing. In April he started the Edinburgh edition of the *Review*, and by early June he described the *Review* as "publish'd in all principal Towns and Cities of *Scotland*." Generally the same paper appeared in both cities, the Edinburgh one about twelve days late. According to Defoe, he was encouraged to start the Scottish *Review* in discourse with friends and by "generous" subscriptions raised in Scotland. The first numbers explain that the Edinburgh *Review* can be bought only at Mrs. Anderson's shop; people could subscribe there and at Adam Blackadder's Coffeehouse, and their papers would then be delivered (*Review* 6:108). In a series of essays Defoe explained his conception of the paper. Above all, he intended to "Represent *Scotland* right in England, and Represent Things in *England* right to *Scotland*" (6:3). He and his Scottish friends felt that "North Britain" suffered "in her general Character Abroad" and that the misperceptions damaged her trade, decreased interest in investments and immigration, and motivated unbeneficial legislation and harmful prejudices. His vision of Scotland's potential and its subjects were those explained in *Caledonia*; for instance, he believed the Scots could "Better your Land, Enrich your Tenants, and Encrease your Rents."

Defoe had moved his family to Stoke Newington and, as was characteristic of him throughout his life, may have begun to take an active interest in the administration of his parish. In August the parish decided "to settle ffour families of the Palatines to the number not exceeding twenty persons at the rate of ffive pounds per head" there.[24] That action was at odds with the opinion of most of the rest of the country and came in the same month that Defoe published *A Brief History of the Poor Palatine Refugees Lately Arriv'd in England* (1709). Nearly 14,000 "Palatines," German refugees from the area between Mannheim and Cologne, arrived in London between May and October 1709. To Defoe they were the victims of the war with France; they had been "plundered," "their labour devoured, their properties taken from them by violence, . . . oppressed and devoured." The nation had to cope with these thousands living in tents outside London, and Defoe tried to foster sympathy for these fellow Protestants. Some people believed that the Palatines were responsible for outbreaks of disease. Although most of his contemporaries wanted them sent to the colonies, Defoe argued that they could be beneficially settled in England, and the queen seems to have concurred, for Sunderland had reported so to the Council of Trade on 11 June.[25]

For all the satisfaction of championing such unfortunates, Defoe's mood was probably no better than it had been since the letdown after his decision to turn down an administrative appointment and Harley's subsequent fall from power. A poem he wrote in the summer of 1708 captures the emotional struggle that was draining his energy. In "Resignation," Defoe wrote:

> Happy the Man Confirmd above,
>   And t' Heavens Dispose resign'd,
> That by his Rule Directs his steps,
>   And On him stays his Mind.
>
> Can on his Various Providence
>   With Satisfaction Rest,
> That Unexalted Can Enjoy,
>   And Suffer Undepress't.
>
> Boldly he steers thro' storms of life,
>   And shipwreck of Estate:
> Without Inheritance he's Rich,
>   And without Honours great.
>
> When the World Trembles he's Unmov'd,
>   When Cloudy he's Serene
> When Darkness Covers all without,
>   He's Allways bright within.[26]

Good Puritan that he is, Defoe begins with a reference to salvation, but his own suffering is the "besetting sin" of his 1681 *Meditations*: he is decidedly not to "Heavens Dispose resign'd." How unfortunate and unappreciated he feels surfaces in every verse of the twenty-four stanza poem. He is "Unexalted," he suffers, he is "without Honours," he fears "Scarcity" and want. He writes feelingly about envy, slander, impertinence, and "Fierce Afflictions," a term he had used in 1704. It is clear that he is trying to come to terms with a "Low Station" and lack of "Opinion-fame" (respect and good reputation). Other stanzas show the waves of tempestuous emotions revealed in the *Meditations* and the post-pillory poems:

> Ambition, Mallice, Pride, and Hate,
>   Are strangers to his Soul,
> . . . .
> He Seeks the Merit, not the Name,
>   The Virtue, Not the Praise.

At this point Defoe was describing the happy man from without, and the fact that he returned to this poem to revise and publish versions of it three times between that summer and the summer of 1712 underscores its personal power for Defoe. Years later Defoe has Robinson

Crusoe's happiest time be an interval when he finds his mind "entirely composed" by resignation "to the Will of God."[27]

In line 65 of *Resignation* Defoe had mentioned malice and hate, and these emotions, not submission to Providence, roused him. On 5 November 1709, the anniversary of King William's landing in England and Guy Fawkes Day, the Reverend Henry Sacheverell preached a sermon at St. Paul's called *The Perils of False Brethren*. Sacheverell said that the Dissenters' "*Obedience* is *forc'd*, and *constrained*, and therefore so *Treacherous* and *Uncertain*, as never to be *Trusted*, because proceeding upon . . . meer *Interest* and *Ambition*" (18). He excoriated not only the Dissenters but all those who recognized the Toleration. Here was the "bloody flag of defiance" again. The recollection of the mood of 1702, the memory of Sacheverell's sermons, and the aftermath of *The Shortest-Way with the Dissenters* assured that Defoe would not remain "Serene" in the face of this particular strife.

Defoe had returned to Scotland in the early fall, taking his son Benjamin with him. Edinburgh still offered more to Defoe. His son could join other sons of English Dissenters at the University of Edinburgh; so well educated was Benjamin that he was able to join the second-year class. Defoe's credit was better in Scotland, and he had more of the respect he craved. For example, on 19 October, the Town Council had voted him the unusually large sum of fifteen guineas, probably to reward him for writing *The History of the Union* and to compensate him for some of the expense. He was expanding his trading interests and beginning to take a more active part in the Edinburgh press. In December Defoe gained control of the *Scots Postman*,[28] but the Sacheverell sermon turned his attention back to London.

Because he was still in Scotland, Defoe's first mention of the sermon was late, not until the 3 December *Review*. Here he casually noted that Sacheverell's sermon belonged in the list of failed attempts to divide the nation: "The Honest, Wise, Judicious Gentlemen that heard him, would not . . . thank him for his . . . Endeavours of inflaming the Nation." He did, however, immediately make the connection to Sacheverell's earlier sermon, for Defoe said that Sacheverell "lifted up his bloody Flag" (*Review* 6:414). Less than a week later, however, Defoe devoted an entire essay to Sacheverell's sermon. Defoe accused him of attacking "the Government, the Parliament, the QUEEN, the Bishops, in short every Body, but the Papists," but he recommended that they laugh at Sacheverell, for he would soon wear himself out. This amusing *Review* had a light tone and a number of funny, visual comparisons, such as that of Sacheverell to a horse and then a barking dog. The people in the anecdotes were calm and in control, certain of their course of action. Sacheverell, as horse and dog, was headstrong and silly: "See how he flies, champs, foams, and stinks" (6:422). The fact that Sacheverell was a large man—both tall and heavy—with a "livid" complexion and did yell, foam, sweat, and turn red in the pulpit added to the delight the contemporary reader would have found in the description.

After this, one essay after another and a stream of pamphlets followed. Defoe's arguments show how vividly he was recalling 1703–1704, for he uses again many of the lines, arguments, and allusions from his writing during that earlier time. He says, "Would all the *High-Flying* Clergymen preach at that extravagant Rate . . . they would every Day lessen the Number" of their followers; he demands that Sacheverell reconcile the Battle of the Boyne to the doctrine of Non-Resistance; he retells the stories of Darius and Sardanapalus from *Jure Divino*; he quotes lines on Sacheverell from his *Hymn to the Pillory*, and he says he will not "beat a Man when he is down"—the words of his own cry for fair play in 1704. He describes Sir Simon Harcourt "bullying" him at the Bar and even recalls some of Harcourt's rhetorical lines. He tells again the story of the Dissenting ministers who refused to pray with him. The depth of his feeling breaks out most unguardedly in the 27 December *Review*:

> You may bear with me Gentlemen, for being warmer in this Case than in another, *my Part in it has been very hard*: I adore the Wonders of Retaliating Providence that has suffer'd the Wicked thus to fall into their own Snare, and that has from Heaven given a Testimony greater than I could ever have hop'd for, to the Justice[,] the Reasonableness, and the Seasonableness of those fatal Observations I made on this Man's Preaching and his Party's Practice, for which . . . I suffer'd the Overthrow of my Fortune and Family, and under the Weight of which I remain as a banish'd Man to this Day.

In another *Review* he calls Sacheverell the "Foundation of my Destruction" (6:462). Here we have one of the few acknowledgements of the meaning of the pillory. In his fiction Defoe always insists banishment is the greatest penalty a society can impose; here he names that as the price he paid. The Dissenter who adored the "Retaliating Providence" behind the news of the indictment of Sacheverell for seditious libel continues in the same vein to pledge, "No Fear has deterr'd me, *tho' often threatned*, bully'd and insulted. No Favour has withdrawn me. . . . Am I better than *Delaun* . . . or D[ewitt]* that hang'd for you?" (6:455) As he celebrates Sacheverell's indictment for the very charge for which he was convicted, Defoe places himself among the martyrs of his faith.

Defoe's personal animus breaks out repeatedly. In analogy after analogy he says that Sacheverell "stinks" and calls him a beast and "Dr. Firebrand."[29] Defoe's malice goes beyond gloating and name-calling. He attempts to define Sacheverell's crime and show him to be an enemy

---

*Cornelius De Witt, probably falsely accused of plotting to assassinate William of Orange while he was still in Holland, was dragged from prison with his brother, who had been tricked inside, and both were killed and mutilated by a mob.

to the Act of Settlement. The *Review* had always addressed M.P.'s, lectured them on their duty, and offered them advice.[30] Before Sacheverell's trial Defoe lost the measured, rational tone that might have been effective and became one of the railers. Too often he stated the case in extreme terms; for example, on 3 January he wrote that Sacheverell had "taken away her Majesty's Parliamentary Title to the Crown, and cloath'd Her with an Hereditary Geugaw [*sic*]" (6:462). In his defense, it might be said that he saw Sacheverell's impeachment as a chance to affirm the most important tenets of the Protestant succession and English liberty. But even in saying that, Defoe errs in tone. In the 10 January *Review*, written perhaps to encourage the members of the Commons who were then considering the articles of impeachment prepared by their committee, Defoe sets up the rhetorical pattern, "Now is the Time. . . ." Unfortunately, he follows each clause with more rash diction:

> *Now is the Time*, when the illigitimate spurious Birth of these Monsters. . . .
>
> *Now is the Time*, when you shall declare it Criminal. . . . for ever silence this wicked Party, strike dumb . . . and blast. . . .

The language of annihiliation and of complete absence of charity which he had parodied in *The Shortest-Way* now flows from his own pen.

Defoe went yet further. The prosecution presented its case first, of course, and from 27 February until 2 March, argued the four articles of impeachment: that Sacheverell had condemned the Revolution of 1688, had attacked the Toleration, had falsely said that the Church of England was in danger (thereby accusing the queen of maladministration), and had suggested that enemies of the Constitution were tolerated in the queen's administration. The prosecution's case had been interrupted by the discussion of the mobs that had rampaged through London burning meeting houses and threatening the Bank of England on the evening of 1 March. Because of this situation, its summary was a brief, disorganized mess, and Sir Simon Harcourt was able to maneuver an adjournment until Monday.

Harcourt, thus, would make his opening speech for the defense at a time when people were rested and calm restored. He would have attentive listeners. Defoe had not forgotten Harcourt's eloquence and power. He was, in the words of a contemporary, "the most eloquent lawyer of the whole profession," and Defoe had been impotent before him in 1703. On 8 March Harcourt lived up to his reputation. That day Defoe decided to give what help he could to the prosecution. He knew that James Stanhope, one of the managers appointed by the Commons to present the prosecution's case, had sent for some *Reviews*. This fact gave Defoe an opening he could use. Stanhope had argued article 1 (on the Revolution), and Defoe wrote a petty, smarmy letter to Stanhope offering evidence pertinent to that charge. Defoe said that he would "at any time appear and produce sufficient testimony" to the truth of his information. He then gave Stanhope the names of men who had drunk with Sacheverell and knew that he had pledged King James's health and King William's destruction. In Defoe's opinion this evidence would help prove that Sacheverell was guilty of calling the Revolution "odious and unjustifiable" and would damage Sacheverell's character, which "is part of his applause among this rabble."[31] His letter flatters Stanhope ("you are managing [this affair] with so much applause"), apologizes repeatedly for his boldness in writing ("asking your pardon for the rudeness of this"; "chose rather to be impertinent") and, after the vicious *Reviews* and pamphlets of the past two months, contradictorily presents himself as having refused to "blacken and expose" "this insolent priest" on a "nicety of honour."

On 23 March Lord Chancellor William Cowper pronounced the "derisory sentence" to Sacheverell at the Bar. His sermons "The Communication of Sin" and "The Perils of False Brethren" were to be burned by the Common Hangman, and Sacheverell was forbidden to preach for three years.[32] Immediately celebratory bonfires burned in nearly every London street, crowds of people drank Sacheverell's health, and rowdy processions burned effigies of the Reverend Daniel Burgess.* Even "young ladies" gave twelve pence each to dress an effigy of him. All over England church bells rang and Dissenting meeting houses were defaced or destroyed, and Sacheverell, purportedly on his way to Selattyn, North Wales, to take up a parish,† toured the country and enjoyed parades, banquets, and receptions in his honor. He traveled with a crowd of admirers that sometimes swelled to over two hundred people. Many tributes were extravagant. For example, at Bridgenorth two miles of hedges were decorated with flowers and flags; at Shrewsbury five thousand mounted men escorted Sacheverell into the city.

Sacheverell's trip from London to Selattyn should have taken three days, but extended over four weeks. He remained in Selattyn long enough to be inducted into his living of £200 per year and to lead one service. He could not give the sermon, of course, because he knew no

---

*A distinguished and unusually dynamic Presbyterian minister; one of his famous witticisms was that God had called his people Israelites because they could never be Jacobites. It was his new meeting house near Lincoln's Inn Fields that the Sacheverell mob gutted on 1 March.

†Sacheverell could do so because the living from that parish was held along with a university fellowship and was the private gift of the lord of the manor. The Lords had voted not to bar Sacheverell from preferments during the three years of his sentence. This "right of property" took precedence over ecclesiastical or royal patronage until 1986.

Welsh. After this two-day residence in his new parish, Sacheverell returned to Oxford, this time taking three weeks to make the two-day trip. Defoe and many other Whigs were frustrated and furious. M.P. John Smith called the sentence "a ridiculous judgment"; Richard Onslow, speaker of the House of Commons, and a group of Whigs tried to send Cowper back to the Lords to reconsider the sentence and "what was due to the dignity of the Commons."[33]

Defoe's first public statements about Sacheverell and the verdict were as moderate and guarded as those immediately after the 5 November sermon. He insisted that the important thing was that Sacheverell *had* been convicted and gently ridiculed the Tories for celebrating. In a dialogue between "Whig" and "Cousin Tory" in the 28 March 1710 *Review*, Whig asks, "Are you making Bonfires for Joy that he is . . . found guilty?" When Cousin Tory explains that the mild punishment is the cause, Whig snaps the trap and asks, "Then you expected it, *Cousin*, to be heavier?" (7:2) Soon, however, the strain on Defoe's temper shows, and he ridicules the Sacheverellites more sharply. For instance, among the "Extravagancies of the poor deluded People," he reports "the honest Bone-Lace Pedlar . . . aged beyond Sixty, fat as the White Elephant, and beastly as a She-Bear; dancing round a Bonfire, and singing to the Mob, to the Immortal Honour and Glory of the Famous Dr. *Sacheverell*" (7:11).

Just as Defoe argued more strenuously and attacked more viciously in anonymous pamphlets than in the *Review* before the trial, so he did after it. In *A Speech without Doors** he began by remarking that all who had read any of Sacheverell's sermons might "easily know" he was not the author of the speech he gave at the trial.[34] *Instructions from Rome*, also in 1710, is a mock letter from the Pope calling Sacheverell the Pope's son and recommending hypocrisy, rabble-rousing, and debauchery like Sacheverell's as means to advance the Catholic Church.

As Sacheverell's popularity persisted and violence toward the Dissenters and their meeting houses continued, Defoe wrote his most popular satire of Sacheverell, *The Banb[ur]y Apes*. This pamphlet begins with a procession modeled on a popular custom Defoe had seen many times in London and Edinburgh. In Defoe's "procession," after the bellman and sexton of the town came, pursuivants carried the crest that Defoe had designed for Sacheverell (Pope Clement XI's head)† and the motto "Unlimited Passive Obedience." Others in the

---

*"Speech without Doors" meant outside of Parliament.
†Pope 1700–1721. Although popular with Protestant countries at the time of his election, he had supported Philip of Anjou's claim to the Spanish throne, thereby allying himself against the English side in the war. After Joseph I conquered Naples and threatened Rome, Clement was forced to support Charles VI's claim to the Spanish throne.

procession included an old lady with "on her Bum the Effigies of *Ben H——y** with his Head downward," twenty-four tinkers beating kettledrums, and "a vast Mob, hollowing, [and] hooping." Sacheverell is likened to an ape shown by a trickster in Queen Elizabeth's time. In this tale the monkey makes a face at a lord mayor's wife. Here, in yet another attempt to discredit Sacheverell and his followers and separate Queen Anne from the attacks on the Toleration of Nonconformists, Defoe reduces Sacheverell and his sermons to making a face at the queen. He shows the mistaken thinking of those officials who entertain the monkey and the drunken revelry of the lower classes who toast their "idol." This pamphlet saw four editions, and most of it was reprinted in Defoe's *A New Map of the Laborious and Painful Travels Of Our Blessed High Church Apostle* (1710).

Through late spring and early summer Defoe devoted many *Review* essays to topics of interest to his City tradesmen readers, covering, for example, news about the bakers and coal traders, but he also used the *Review* to satirize the growing party animosity. In late April he created two "dreadful Armies," one attacking and the other defending liberty, property, and the Constitution. Already he was advising "the Friends of the Consitution" to prepare for the election that would come if Parliament were dissolved. Some of his rhetoric is that of all propagandists. For instance, he asserts that before any elections will be called, "the Eyes of the Country People will be open'd" (7:47). And he was carefully watching Harley's recovery of power. Even if he did not know the full significance of the coalition formed in the closing days of Sacheverell's trial, he could not miss the implications of Sunderland's dismissal on 14 June. Sunderland was the first of the old "Court Whigs" to go, and his demise was a clear sign of loss of influence by Godolphin and Marlborough.[35]

On 17 July, Defoe wrote Harley an optimistic letter about the immediate future prospects of England and presumed that he could "Renew the Liberty of Writeing to you" "without the Least View of private advantage." He reminded Harley that he felt great personal obligations to him and concluded, "It would be a Double honour to Me to have my Gratitude Mixt with the Service of My Country." Here as elsewhere Defoe stated that, above other things, he hoped to "Make The End of all my Actions" "the publick advantage." The patriotic assertion and the warmth and respect for Harley were to be expected, but he also showed a strikingly buoyant attitude about his country at a time when Dissenters were being physically threatened, when Sache-

*Hoadley was a Low Church Anglican and chief defender of that point of view and the Dissenters.

verell was still growing in popularity, and when addresses against the Toleration were pouring into Parliament. He wrote,

> I kno' Sir you are blest with Principles of Peace and Concern for your Country and a True Tast of its Liberty, and Intrest, which are Now Sadly Embarrast.
> I can Not but Think that Now is The Time to . . . Improve Those blessed Mediums of This Nations happyness. I can Not but hope That Heaven has yet Reserv'd you to be the Restorer of your Country.

Within a week Defoe had seen Harley and had an assignment very much to his taste. Back with his fellow "servant in the vineyard" who he knew shared his commitment to moderation and balanced party representation, Defoe wrote relaxed, happy, purposeful letters that stand in sharp contrast not just to his letters to Godolphin but to everything he wrote in 1709. He felt confident of Harley's principles and regard and could in good conscience begin to reassure the Dissenters that "They are Not all to be Devoured, and Eaten up" and that they could trust Harley to uphold moderation, "Tolleration, Succession [and] Union." The *Review* had come to address the Dissenters more particularly in the spring of 1710, and now it was in a good position to carry Defoe's message. If such an outspoken, even rabid, enemy of Sacheverell said that there was nothing to fear and took a restrained, moderate tone, then others might take their cue from him.

Defoe knew how to do his job. He apprehended the nature and depth of the Dissenters' and Whigs' fears. When he used the phrase, "Devoured and Eaten up," he communicated his understanding, for these are the words Robinson Crusoe would use repeatedly to express his fear on the island. The verbs suggest loss of identity as well as loss of life and property, and the attacks on the meeting houses and schools of the Dissenters threatened his people with extermination. In 1714 he opposed a bill designed to forbid these places by promising that martyrdom would result before the Dissenters would give up their "natural right" and "religious duty" to educate their children in their faith. Here and in his earlier tracts, Defoe recognized the threat to education as an attempt to absorb the Dissenters into the Anglican Church.[36]

With Harley Defoe felt free again to take the initiative and make ambitious suggestions. The number, confidence, and happiness of his letters to Harley grow as the weeks pass. In mid-June, the governor, deputy governor, and two other Whig directors of the Bank of England visited Queen Anne to ask that she not dismiss Parliament or make further changes in her ministry lest there be a disastrous fall in credit. Defoe had started a series of *Review* essays on credit, and in his 28 July letter to Harley he offered to discuss some ways to support credit. The queen did, of course, make additional changes in her ministry, including dismissing Godolphin on 8 August and making Harley chancellor of the Exchequer on the tenth. In his letter to Harley Defoe exulted, "It is with a Satisfaction . . . I can Not Express, That I See you Thus Establish'd Again. . . . Providence Sir Seems to Cast me back Upon you (I write that with Joy)." "I shall Serv . . . with Principle, and Inclination."

Once again Defoe gave a virtuoso demonstration of how prolific and powerful his pen could be. Stocks did indeed fall; on 1 July Bank of England stock was 119¾; on 3 August when Godolphin's fall was anticipated by a great many people, Bank stock was 112¾, and by 3 September, it had risen to only 114¼. The United Company fell from 133 to 125 and rose to 126 in the same period; the Million Bank fell from 74¾ to 73¼ to 71. A change of even one point was significant, and the declining confidence of people in their investments threatened a panic. When the news of the British defeat at Brihuega came on 27 December, Bank of England stock fell to 100¾ and that of the Million Bank to 67.[37] Defoe, however, was not discouraged; he worked to reassure people, especially the Dissenters, about the change in the ministry in order to prevent the further fall of the government's credit, and to discredit the rising tendency to claim hereditary right for Queen Anne, a claim that might weaken the Protestant settlement of the throne. Within a few pages Defoe could give a clear, forceful argument, shift to playful satire, marshal telling analogies, and then construct a sustained allegory.

What he could not do in the *Review* because of space limitations or audience, he did in one of the finest groups of pamphlets in his long career. *A Letter from a Dissenter in the City to a Dissenter In the Country: Advising Him to a Quiet and Peaceable Behaviour in This Present Conjuncture* is clear, pragmatic, and dignified. On one hand he reassures the Dissenters that the new ministry has the interests of the nation at heart; on the other he asks the Dissenters to live up to their professed superior "Conformity to the Law of Christianity" by maintaining their dignity and discipline in hard times (11). In contrast, *A New Test of the Sence of the Nation* is full of fun. It is a satire of language like so many of the political writings of Defoe's contemporaries, most notably Swift. "Nothing seems more remarkable, than the frequent Alterations made in the Meanings of the same Things . . . by which it is grown preposterous to expect, that Men shou'd be suppos'd to mean the same Thing to Day, that they meant yesterday by the same Words," Defoe writes (2). He goes on to concentrate on how "the sence of the nation" (a phrase much used in pro-Sacheverell addresses to the queen) allows people to understand the contradictions in the Sacheverellites' discourse; his parodies of the transmogrifications of their words end with the image of them as asses "mumbling" thistles. For this work he received £150 for "special services," and the money came from the Exchequer endorsed by William Lowndes.[38]

A few years later Defoe would say that trade was the "whore" he could not resist, and it was in his tracts on credit, "that [which] gives Life to *Trade*," that he was most creative. For the *Review* he created the emblematic Lady Credit, and in his *Essay upon Publick Credit* he argued that Credit was the child of Trade, and therefore the product of English history and achievement. In both types of work he tried to explain credit to a population that was still becoming accustomed to it. He demonstrated the relationship between credit and economic prosperity and between credit and England's ability to carry on and end the war with France. Above all, he defined credit by nature and manifestation as a national, rather than party, concern; because credit is not "pinn'd to the Girdle" of one man (Godolphin), he says, it is not at the mercy of a man, a party, or an event. The strength and good sense of the English people themselves can be depended upon to support credit. Within a few paragraphs Defoe could use irony, satire, analogy, allegory, and parody and then switch to his best middle style to employ historiography, polemics, and journalism.[39]

If the deposed Godolphin had a sense of humor, he must have found the autumn of 1710 highly entertaining. In August Harley wrote, "I cannot see but the continuing this Parliament, must leave me destitute between two Parties, & not able to restrain either of them." The emotional force of the word "destitute" captures the frustration Harley felt as circumstances drove him to make appointments and compromises he disliked. Parliament was finally dissolved on 21 September, and the ensuing elections made the abuses and excesses of the 1708 Scottish elections appear quotidian. Harley, who had once divided M.P.'s into Whigs, Tories, and the "Queen's servants,"[40] saw the High Tories, and especially their clergymen, campaign as if the Kingdom of Heaven were at stake. Burnet described months of "inflaming sermons" and clergymen who "went about from house to house, pressing their people to shew, on this great occasion, their zeal for the church, and now or never to save it" (6:13–14). Candidates carried Sacheverell's picture on banners, and throngs chanted, "For the Queen, the Church, and Sacheverell." The results were overwhelmingly Tory. Modern estimates conclude that 332 Tories and 181 Whigs were elected in England, and many of these Tory members were hot-headed, inexperienced extremists. Out of the 92 county members, fewer than a dozen were Whigs. Men like James Stanhope, hero of Minorca and numerous other battles, and Robert Walpole, who was pelted with dirt, were humiliatingly defeated. Harley, who had worked so patiently and effectively to secure a moderate, less partisan ministry, faced a Parliament he could scarcely understand, let alone control.[41]

Defoe found himself at the center of a press maelstrom as violent, complex, and partisan as Harley's world. His *Review* and powerful tracts had caught the opposition a bit off guard, and his early perception of the changes in government and of issues had kept him out of the periodical debates of early summer. Now, however, a number of publications such as *A Late Dialogue Between Dr. Burgess, and Daniel d'Foe, in a Cyder-Cellar near Billingsgate* and *An Epigram on Dan. de F——* appeared. They used the familiar terms of abuse: "incendiary," "devil," "source of lies and rudeness," "broken hosier." Satiric prints portrayed Defoe as part of a monster and associated him with the symbols of rebellion. As Defoe was quick to point out, they did not refute his points but resorted to ad hominem attacks. Moreover, the High Church party had begun a concentrated policy of harassment intended to silence the *Review*. The 21 March *Review* carried the first of many advertisements that read: "Whereas great Industry has been us'd to suppress this Paper, by several Members of a Party, to whom it is particularly Grievous to hear too much Truth—By whose Art the Publication of it has so far been stop'd, that none have been to be had, either of the Hawkers, or Shops where other such Papers are sold." His printer, John Matthews, was kidnapped and threatened by a mob, and on 25 April Defoe announced that John Baker, who would not be "bias'd, terrify'd, or any way prevail'd upon to keep it back," had become the *Review*'s printer.[42]

By late summer the most distinguished group of journalists in the eighteenth century were at work. Richard Steele's *Tatler* became increasingly political; Joseph Addison began the *Whig Examiner*; the classically educated Kit Kat,* Arthur Maynwaring, wrote most of the *Medley*, and, of course, Jonathan Swift took over the *Examiner*. These papers joined such long-term political commentators as the *Rehearsal*, the *Observator*, and the *Flying Post*. The government lost control completely; perhaps one of the best signs is that almost every journalist in London would be arrested at least once in the next two years. London was inundated with partisan periodicals, and the papers themselves make witty observations about the press's activity. For instance, the *Tatler*'s fictional upholsterer complains that he has been studying the pamphlets and papers since Sacheverell's trial "night and day" but, because they are so numerous, he is now a fortnight behind (no. 232). Because the competition was for readers as well as between Tory and Whig papers, derogatory sniping might be addressed to any paper by any other. Although Defoe was nominally engaged on the Tory side because Harley was now a Tory, the Whig character of his *Review* opened him to attacks by Tory papers supported by his patron. He might be assailed as "grown insipid" one day, called an "ignorant Fanatick scribbler" the next, and then ridiculed for the "nonsense" or bad

*A distinguished literary club.

logic of individual phrases by any one of the rival papers.

Secure in his relationship with Harley and happy with his work, Defoe met these attacks with authority and even humor. In contrast to the offended, nearly whining tone of the previous year, he could quote back his adversaries' insults and refute them by action rather than by protest. For example, in *The Sence of the Nation,* he quoted a list of what his critics found wanting in his style and then gave a demonstration of what he could do:

The Wisest Men in the Nation . . . that are Masters of the Tongue, and other Tongues too; that write a Fluent, Easy, Copious Stile, Strong in Sence, Flowing in Eloquence, and Rich in the Beauties of Conception, when they come [to explain Non-Resistance] . . . how do they chew it, and mumble it like an Ass upon Thistles; and when it is ingested with all the Art and Cunning they can employ upon it; behold it comes out most Incomprehensible Nonsense. (75–76).

Here Defoe takes the phrases hurled at him and pits his lack of "a Fluent, Easy, Copious Stile" against the clarity of his vivid metaphor. His adversaries are asses mumbling thistles. Thistles, of course, have little nourishment, and Defoe catches the fruitless effort with "mumbles," a word suggesting toothlessness, futility, and even old age. The archaic doctrine of Non-Resistance, even when mixed with "Art and Cunning," must finally be expelled, not swallowed and digested, and then it is but a disgusting mess. Even as Defoe is attacking and arguing, he is participating in the language controversies of his time. Against the classical grace of Maynwaring and Addison, he offers "plain English." Dryden, in the Preface to the *Sylvae,* had explained what Defoe's chosen style meant to their contemporaries: spirit and artless truth (3:18).

Unlike so many of his recent works, the *Reviews* and pamphlets of 1710 sold briskly and were filled with memorable epithets. *The Ban-[bur]y Apes* required four editions, *An Essay upon Publick Credit* three, and *A Supplement to the Faults on Both Sides* five. Rival journalists seized upon his images and phrases and came to react rather than control debate. For instance, the first issue of the *Medley* quoted Defoe extensively, jibing at his "quaint . . . ingenious" idea of a pope judging "what is, or is not Reason," his "Piece of *Clockwork* . . . wherefore you may well be giddy," and his "something" that "is the essential shadow of something that is not." A number of pamphlets with titles such as *Dissenters Self-Condemned* and *An Impartial Survey of Mr. De Foe's Singular Modesty and Veracity* (both 1710) did little but call Defoe names and dispute individual, often minor, points in his works. One of the most subtle of such strategic publications reprinted portions of *Jure Divino* with a woodcut of Defoe in the pillory on the first title page. Defoe still represented radical Whiggism to many people. William King remarked that he'd never seen a Whig "with Satisfaction" "unless it was *D——l d'Foe* in the Pillory" and went on to use him and *The Shortest-Way with the Dissenters* as evidence that the Dissenters were capable of burning their own meeting houses in order to gain sympathy and political advantage.[43]

In the midst of this excitement Defoe suggested that he go back to Scotland to work in Harley's behalf before the elections in Scotland. He saw important work for himself to "Calm and Make Easy The Minds of people," "In Matters of Election . . . to forward the Intrest and Choice of Such Men whose Tempers are Most Moderate and best Enclind &c . . . to give Such Intelligence of Things and Persons . . . for her Majties Service . . . [and] To Settle and Continue Such Correspondence in Every Part . . . as May be proper, for an Exact Intelligence in all parts after this Journey May be Over" (H 291). Here he combines the work he had designed for himself in 1705 with the work he had done in 1707. Not only did he hope to continue to reconcile people to the Union, but he hoped to establish the kind of network of observers that he had had in England after his summer travels.

Harley's concerns about Scotland appear to have been different from Defoe's. A number or Scots had helped Harley during the closing days of the Sacheverell trial, and Harley needed to keep their support. Mar had persuaded the earls of Northesk and Wemyss to join him and the earl of Poulet and the duke of Hamilton in the "Not Guilty" vote; Argyll became one of the chief proponents of the mild sentence, and his brother, the earl of Islay, and the earls of Rosebery, Loudoun, Queensberry, and Orkney joined that vote. In the elections the entire list of men prepared by the Scottish lords loyal to Harley was elected to the Lords, but only twenty-five firm supporters out of forty-five were returned to the Commons.[44] Harley had hoped to have a solid block of loyal, moderate men from Scotland to balance the High Tories elected from England. In Scotland "Tory" nearly always meant "Jacobite," but he could count on most of the men elected from Scotland being opposed to the English Jacobites. After all, these Scots were Tories because of the Union, not because they were Church of England men. In fact, however, more Jacobites than any one wanted had been elected in Scotland.

Just as Godolphin had had to reward the Whigs who had supported his policies, so Harley was expected to take care of the Scots in 1710–1711. For instance, he gave Hamilton the lucrative lieutenancy of the County of Lancaster. One of Defoe's services was to characterize the Scots and help Harley do what was necessary for them in the ways most beneficial to his ends. Edinburgh alliances were very different when Defoe returned there, and his old circles were now divided in complex ways. Gilbert Elliot, Defoe's friend from the Society for the Reformation of Manners, for example, was now a determined opponent of Harley's because of his strong Whig sentiments. Queensberry was nearly without influence. The Squadrone, which included Montrose, supported the Whigs identified with Godolphin and allied with the Junto. However, the Squadrone found themselves excluded from the list of peers to be elected and stayed away from the election of peers. Among those so alienated were Montrose, Roxburgh, Tweedale, Rothes, Buchan, Marchmont, and many more.

The earl of Stair had been excluded from the list of those to be elected, and the entire Dalrymple family had therefore to be considered soft support for the Whigs. Leven, as a strong supporter of Marlborough and Godolphin, was in trouble but finally agreed to vote for the list. Defoe hardly knew Mar and Argyll, the new powers. Defoe's Church of Scotland and merchant friends could only look on the change with trepidation because they were the "Dissenting Church" and because the Tories were the traditional conservatives toward trade. As Defoe himself said, the "Scenes here have as great a Variety as can be Imagin'd, differing not Onely from themselves but from things of the like Nature in England in a most Extraordinary Manner." As early as August Hew Dalrymple wrote Loudoun, "All hands will be at work about our elections in which there is no tyme to be lost." For months after the election complaints of irregularities and "gross practices" accompanied official protests against the results.[45]

Nevertheless, Defoe seemed glad to be back in Scotland, and he did his work with vigor. A large number of his closest associates had been elected magistrates for Edinburgh, including Adam Brown and John Duncan (H 290), and he had business enterprises under way that he cared about. His reports and letters showed a combination of pragmatism and opportunism. To some extent he managed to reward his Scottish friends, yet he was honest about them to the point of near disloyalty. For instance, he worked to help Leven keep his position, but he wrote Harley that Leven and Hyndford had helped assure the desired election results through "Cowardice, not good will." When asked to comment on men who might be appointed the queen's commissioner to the General Assembly of Scotland, he suggested, among others, Hyndford, calling him "a person without Exception"; Buchan, a man Carstares cared deeply about; and John Dalrymple, earl of Stair, his friend Hew's brother. About these men, too, Defoe was honest—Buchan, he admitted, was hot-headed, although "of Great Integrity and Understanding." Harley gave Buchan a £200 per year "pension" and Defoe's old friend Alexander Campbell, Lord Cessnock, received £100.[46] Stair, of course, had flirted with the Squadrone when he discovered his name missing from the list of peers to be elected.

In at least one case Defoe used considerable guile to help a relative. His brother-in-law Robert Davis had continued to go back and forth between London and Edinburgh and, in addition to helping Defoe with his work, had begun to develop an independent livelihood in his old trade as a shipbuilder. From 1705 on Defoe refers to Davis as with him, as carrying messages, or as a safe person to whom to address letters. Nothing, however, indicates that Davis understood Defoe's work any better or was trusted with more information than he had been in 1705. In 1710, however, Defoe became actively engaged in helping his brother-in-law. Davis was already established in Leith, a beautiful town about a mile outside Edinburgh. In 1707 Davis had formed a partnership with a man named John Heislop to build a watermill "for cutting and sawing of timber," and in 1709 he became a burgess and guild brother of the City of Edinburgh by right of his new wife, Janet Livingston, whose father was a merchant burgess and former session clerk. In 1710 Davis wanted to build larger docks and expand his operation to include work on larger ships. A contemporary described Leith as "the Ware-house of Edinburgh . . . a thriving Town, having a double advantage, the Sea-Trade and the Citizens Recreation to inrich it; for thither they flock by foot or in Coaches to divert themselves." Docking more ships and boats than any other Scottish city at that time, Leith was the hub for sailors from Queensferry, Musselburgh, Preston-pans, Burntisland, Kinghorn, Kirkcaldy, Wemyss, and other towns.[47]

In 1710 Davis had powerful competition. In April the Corporation of Edinburgh had petitioned the queen to order, and therefore pay for, wet and dry docks at Leith. In May a report from the Admiralty Office recommended Leith "as most useful to the trade of North Britain." Many of the most powerful Scots joined in lobbying for the docks; the earl of Loudoun, for example, wrote Harley to argue that the docks would be tangible evidence to the Scots of England's desire "for advancing their trade & well being and would remedy the Disagreeable decay that appears at Ed[inburgh] since the Union, because of . . . removing the parlia[ment] and privie Councill." In August Secretary of State Boyle sent the papers for improving Leith harbor to the commissioners of the Treasury with the message that the queen's pleasure was they "give such orders and Directions concerning the necessary Expences for carrying on the works at Leith" for she felt "well dispos'd to encourage any thing that may be to the Advantage of the Trade . . . particularly of . . . Edinburgh."[48]

Once well established in Harley's employment, Defoe wrote against the idea. On 5 September he called it "the Pick-Pocket proposall" and, in his position paper for Harley, "Of Improvemts in Scotland," he argued strenuously for building the dock on the Firth above Queensferry. Some of his arguments show considerable understanding of economic and military affairs, but others exaggerate or even strain the truth. He makes much of the physical disadvantages of Leith and repeats several times that the Leith proposal is "Calculated Onely for the private Advantage of the City of Edinburgh, without any View of the Public Good." At one point he alludes to Davis as "a Workman (I carryed down there and) who has Since built them Severall Smaller Boats." Sir Patrick Johnson, then lord provost of Edinburgh, in London on the council's behalf, wrote on 23 May, "That ane paper I formerly mentioned . . . insisting upon the [cost] . . . alledgeing the want to water has done us in part a diskindness." Johnson said he was told that a Scot named "Captain Mudie" had written it, but he seemed unconvinced.[49]

On 13 December the Edinburgh Town Council granted Robert Davis, "shipbuilder in Leith," a 29-year lease for land and space in Leith to build "more Convenient places or Docks for dressing & repairing of Large Ships," including small men-of-war.[50] Davis did expand, and records of further building and contracts for work appear infrequently in various Edinburgh records. For example, the contract with Heislop was registered in 1712 and shows Davis to be responsible for building and staffing the mills. Once Davis had paid off Heislop's £120 investment, he would be an equal owner. In 1712 he contracted with the City of Edinburgh to furnish two ballast boats* for £35 sterling per year. Because of more urgent projects rather than because of Defoe's urging, no dock was begun in Leith by the English until 1717.

About the same time Davis moved his diving bell closer to Scotland. The next year, 1713, he offered to sell "one of the best daving Engins that ever was med" to Harley, whom he had heard had been granted a patent for diving for wrecks off the coast of America. This letter and its enclosure show Davis's affection for his Scottish wife, reveal information about his past, and perhaps explain why Defoe did not find Davis an altogether ideal messenger:

> The experience I had of your Lordships generosity & goodness, encurages me to presume. . . . I have latly brought [the bell] from Leizard, to the hous of Mr James the berar, in order to have brought it hear, for the Erall of Mortown† profer'd me very good encuragment, to have gone alongst with him to Zeatland, & dived upon some Dutch East India ships. . . . But I setled hear in my tread of Ship bulding, & maryed to a very tender loving wife, who will on no account submite to my going any more in the Engine, tho I might have the Indias for going one fathom under the watter, so I am resolved I will doe nothing that will be such a trubble to her, tho she ware not my wife She is a gentelwoman & a very desirving person.

Davis offers it to Harley for £50, because his wife will not allow him to bring it to Scotland where it would bring a better price

---

*Boats that carried ballast for ships that needed to augment or reduce their weight as they entered or left the harbor.

†The earl of Morton and "severall Merchants and others of London" had petitioned the queen in February 1712; they asked that a fort be repaired to protect their fisheries around the Isles of Zetland and Orkney (PRO SP 34/13 [14]).

least I should be tempted to goe down in it my self, & inded if I ware to Divie any more I would not part with it for ten times what I demand for it, for I am very scerten it is the best ever was maed, it cost some hundreds pounds, dowing & undowing, making and maring, befor it was brought to that perfection, there are many pretends to be Enginears: but have given litell proofe of ther Skeill.

As an afterthought, he concludes: "I hope your Lordship has not forgott me I had the honor to attend your Lordship on Mr. Alexander Goldsmiths account."* A certificate signed by some of the leading citizens of Lizard parish testified to the fact that Davis had gone down "severall ffathom deep" in several places along the Cornish coast, had brought up bars of silver, and had once sung Psalm 100 while below.

By the time the new dock at Leith was built, Davis was listed as a carpenter rather than a shipbuilder and had married the very wealthy, widowed sister of Defoe's friend John Russell.[51] Helen Russell Hamilton Davis died soon after the marriage, and Robert married yet again in 1718. This fourth wife was Mary Fullerton, daughter of the collector of Customs at Kirkwall, Orkney.[52]

By lobbying against the Leith docks Defoe was working secretly against the proposal of his Edinburgh city friends and acting disingenuously toward Harley. Because he hides his brother-in-law's plans and identity from Harley, he gives the impression that he is a disinterested observer giving Harley objective advice. Although there can be no question but that he preferred Harley to Godolphin, Defoe was more independent, and perhaps disaffected, than ever before. He could hardly have been inspired by Harley's dependence on the High Tories and the double game Harley was having to play in a dozen ways. The long periods of silence and neglect that Defoe had experienced in 1707 began again, and Defoe wrote about several matters just as he had then: "[I] Wish I knew what Answer to Give, but it is My Misfortune to act wholly by my Own judgement."

On 26 December he wrote to Harley in mock outrage about a pamphlet called *Atalantis Major*, which ridiculed the part Argyll and Mar had played in the election. On 1 January he said he had not been able to get a copy to send Harley but had "with some Difficulty and meerly by force prevented its goeing to the press." He himself had in fact written this pamphlet which described Godolphin and Marlborough, the men Defoe had called Harley's enemies, as "Men of the greatest Eminency in their Station that the Age had produc'd . . . their Country had no Error to find in their Conduct except it were that it was so much in debt to their Services, that they could not be capable of rewarding it. . . .their very Enemies had not been able to assign any Reason" to dismiss them (13–14). Argyll is quoted as having said that only men willing to im-

---

*"Alexander Goldsmith" was one of Defoe's code names.

peach Marlborough regardless of the evidence would be on the list of peers to be elected (27, 29). Excluded men like Montrose and Stair are described as noble and patriotic, in direct contrast to the petty, dictatorial, pretentious Argyll. In light of his letter to Harley describing his employment by Godolphin as carried out "Allways with Regret," Defoe can only be seen as hypocritical.

This pamphlet shows loyalties and opinions far different from Harley's. In describing the change of ministry that brought Harley to power, Defoe not only praises Godolphin and Marlborough as "faithful Councellors" who "had raised . . . the Honour of their Country, to the greatest Pitch the Age has ever seen" but lists deleterious effects, including the fall of credit and the prolongation of the war with France. As is so common in his work, Defoe asserts that he writes to open the eyes of his countrymen. "Especially" those "who *have been already so delighted*" with the Scottish election news, he says, need to be told the true story. This tract includes examples of Defoe's strongest propaganda skills. It uses the kind of allegorical travel narrative found in *The Consolidator* and sets up a devastating contrast between the patriotism and dignity of Montrose and the imperviousness, irrationality, and peevishness of Argyll. Defoe also uses an anecdote to compare the earl of Islay, Argyll's brother, to a hypocritical, slick-tongued hangman and gives thinly disguised summaries of events to show how Argyll and some of his followers failed to profit from their actions. Perhaps because the Argyll-Mar list had included some Jacobites, Defoe makes statements, extreme even for Hanoverians, about the succession to the throne. Queen Anne, Defoe asserts, was "plac'd upon the Throne by the Suffrage of the Nobility and People, without Regard to her Father or his Male Children" (7). Whether Harley guessed the true authorship of *Atalantis Major* is not known, but Defoe left one strong clue to its authorship—he gave the *Review* credit for making Islay a laughing stock and thereby rendering him useless to the cause (23).

In this pamphlet Defoe praised some of his Scottish friends and released the antagonism he felt toward Argyll and Mar, who had set up "like royalty" in Edinburgh and let all of the other Scots come calling, hats in hand, asking for places on the "Queen's list" of peers to be elected. Some of his own opinions about English politics invigorate his portrayal of Godolphin and Marlborough and the way they had been carrying on the war. He was too astute an observer not to know that Harley would have to preside over a "Tory peace" or resign, and that no Tory peace would humble the king of France as Marlborough wanted to.

Even as he sent Harley reports, visited people and argued the moderate principles "at bottom" in the new ministry, and wrote thousands of words in pamphlets and the *Review*, he expanded his own business interests. He went back into the export-import business, at least on a limited basis, and shipped wine, china, plate, and even pickles. In addition to his investments in salt and in the linen factory,[53] Defoe began to expand his control of local newspapers. He received a grant to print the *Edinburgh Courant* "in place of the deceast Adam Bog" on 1 February and became part owner of the *Newcastle Gazette*. At this point Defoe was close to controlling every newspaper in Edinburgh and was trying to recruit staff from as far away as Newcastle. He tried to get exclusive privilege of printing news for Edinburgh, but the Town Council would only grant exclusive days of the week.[54] Although this dominance served his political ends well, it also held the potential for giving him— or one of his sons—an independent income.

No one, not even Robert Harley, could win a struggle for moderation in the face of the Tory majority then in Parliament. From the time Parliament convened, the Tories were headstrong, unpredictable, and closed-minded. They met together frequently, glorying in their ability to use their numbers at will. As an observer wrote the elector of Hanover's adviser, the question was whether the ministry could "govern them . . . and restrain them from unreasonable demands," not whether Harley favored the Hanover succession or was "zealous" to support the Alliance and pursue the war. Harley struggled to be able to continue to employ moderate Whigs and men relatively independent of party, but the newly elected Tories considered themselves to have been elected on a popular tide of disapproval of Whig policies and patronage and felt their duty to be reform. One Whig observed that the Tories saw their duty as "to inquire into . . . mismanagements . . . and punish the offenders to the terror of others."[55] To this end, they quickly introduced bills aimed at reforming elections, at investigating all grants made by the crown since 1688, at preventing occasional conformity, and for building 150 new Anglican churches. By January the "October Club," as the Tories who met weekly had begun to be called, numbered about 160 M.P.'s. They pushed through their resolutions to investigate the government accounts of 1710 and the navy debts and to revoke King William's grants. People were beginning to criticize Harley and his ministry openly and to say that he was incapable of restoring public credit.[56] The Tory M.P.'s attacked Harley by name in Parliament on 17 February.

Just as Harley was telling Swift that he might have to resign,[57] an alleged French spy, the marquis de Guiscard, stabbed Harley with a pen knife during his interrogation by the Cabinet Council on 8 March 1711. Suddenly Harley was a hero. Crowds accompanied the hackney chair carrying him home and became a gullible market for the numerous periodical and pamphlet accounts of the stabbing. Letters, condolences, prayers, and gifts poured in to Harley's house. For months after his recovery, crowds waited to see him enter or leave the Treasury.

Moreover, during his recovery, several events occurred that highlighted his effectiveness. The Commons descended into acrimonious, ineffectual debate. The leather tax, intended to finance supplies for the war, was defeated. Furthermore, Harley's slow work to undermine the October Club by encouraging older, more moderate Tories to join it in order to soften its position and by making carefully chosen appointments from its ranks began to weaken and divide the club and consequently the entire Tory party.[58] On 24 May Queen Anne made Harley earl of Oxford and Mortimer, and on the twenty-ninth he became lord treasurer. Over the next three years Harley punished the chief schemers against him (Nottingham, Somerset, and Walpole), maintained the Tory majority in Parliament, established the South Sea Company as a Tory rival to the Bank of England and the East India Company, and secured the peace with France that his country wanted so badly.

Harley's success, however, came at the expense of some actions repulsive to Defoe. Harley would obtain his peace through the betrayal of the allies and the sacrifice of Marlborough, the general who established England as a great modern military power. And he would trade his support for the detested occasional conformity bill and Toleration bill* for bills of supply for the war. Defoe had no illusions about what happened. He wrote that the policy had been to "abandon" the Dissenters and described their treatment as "like *David*'s Heifers, first to draw the Cart, and then to be burnt with the Wood of it."[59] Defoe, who had emerged from Newgate in 1703 as a solitary keeper of his own counsel, had flirted again with being a joiner of prestigious groups, an invester, and an adviser to a government, but his experience had only confirmed his alienation and his dependence upon his own resources, and chiefly upon his pen.

*This act extended the Toleration Act to the Episcopal Church in Scotland.

CHAPTER 12

THE GOLIATH OF THE PARTY

*In pursuing an Enemy, that has neither acted the Gentleman or
the Christian, methinks no Man ought to expect my keeping the
rules.*
> —DEFOE, *The Scots Nation and Union
> Vindicated* (1714)

*they adventure upon the meer Guess at Language, to call me the
Author of any thing they do not like.*
> —DEFOE, *Some Thoughts upon . . . Commerce
> with France* (1713)

Queen Anne died on 1 August 1714. Her ministry and the Tory
party, still an overwhelming majority in Parliament, were in shambles.
Divided on almost every issue, the Tories were as leaderless as they had
been in 1710 when they rallied to the Sacheverell banners. Robert
Harley could never change himself or them enough. His preference
for solid administrators rather than articulate, visible leaders preserved his position and power but fostered such dependence on him
that weaknesses were exaggerated and problems remained beyond the
address of those who might have been in the position to help another
man. Harley had always been a master at analyzing situations and
exploiting them, but he had never mastered thinking beyond the next
few months, nor had he developed any kind of foreign policy beyond
securing peace with France. He himself often said that "policy" was not
"as is commonly supposed, the forming of schemes with remote views,
but the making use of such incidents as happen."[1] The years of struggle
with the Tories and with the temperamental Anne, the death of his
beloved daughter, bad health, and the workload had worn Harley
down, and, in the last years, he became procrastinating, sporadically
apathetic, and even prone to drunkenness. He could rouse himself to
suppress challenges to his authority, but he was physically and emotionally unequal to the need to prepare for the transition after Anne's
death to the Hanoverian monarch. Bolingbroke's* attempt to oust

*Henry St. John, Viscount Bolingbroke, had been secretary at war but resigned with
Harley in 1708; in 1710 Harley reluctantly appointed him secretary of state for the

283

Harley in 1714 further divided the Tories and the ministry, brought yet more extremists into the range of gaining power, and increased resentments between Tories and Whigs.

The fatal mistake that Harley, Bolingbroke, and the Tories had made was alienating George Ludwig, elector of Hanover. He was one of their allies in the War of the Spanish Succession who had been betrayed by the Tory Peace of Utrecht; his European interests had been ignored, and his *solicited* suggestions for better guarantees of the Hanoverian, Protestant succession in England were neglected. Near the end of the war he dissociated himself from the British and fought on with the Dutch and the Empire at his own expense. He joined Austria in refusing to sign the treaty at Utrecht in 1713. Upon the death of the Electress Sophia in June 1714, he became heir to the British throne and sent his sealed list of regents to England, and this augured solid Whig control of the transition administration. In London communications from him and the actions of his envoys unmistakably revealed his distrust of the Tories.[2] Within a year of Anne's death Bolingbroke had fled to France, fellow Tory cabinet members the duke of Ormonde, the earl of Strafford, and Lord Lansdowne had been impeached, and Harley was in the Tower.

Defoe's position, though far more obscure, was equally precarious. Because he had been so prominently linked to Harley and his policies, Defoe stood to lose more than his primary source of income. In the last frantic months of the Harley ministry, he had worked loyally for Harley and the Peace of Utrecht. In the very months since George had refused to sign the treaty, Defoe had written the strongly pro-treaty *Mercator* and several pamphlets pressing the despised postscript to the Treaty of Utrecht, the Treaty of Commerce and Navigation;* he had attacked Steele and the Whigs repeatedly and written the most discussed contemporary defense of Harley ever published, *The Secret History of the White Staff*. His authorship of most of these works was known and some, including *Some Thoughts upon the Subject of Commerce with France*, he boldly labeled "By the Author of the *Review*." To George I and the Hanoverian interest, he had given scarcely a nod. In fact, Defoe already had a bad name with the new king. A report sent to Jean de Robethon, private secretary to George, reported the contrast in the ministry's treatment of journalists, specifically between that of "insolent" "Foe, qui

---

Northern Department. Known as the "man of mercury," he was a great speaker, a gifted negotiator, and a diligent worker, but he was almost as famous for his debauchery as for his genius.

*The Treaty of Commerce and Navigation would have given France most favored nation status, primarily at the expense of Portugal. Many Englishmen believed that it would adversely affect the balance of trade, and the treaty was defeated; it was omitted from the Treaty of Peace.

dans son ecrit a si male parlé de la Maison de Hanover" and William Hurt "qui a si bien defendu Cette illustre Maison" "que le meme gouvenement [*sic*] a fait punir si severement."[3]

Knowledgeable people in the Treasury office could tell that Defoe had received at least £400 a year from the government since 1707; by at least February 1711 a regular quarterly payment had been arranged, and between January 1714 and the queen's death he had received at least £500. The day before Harley left office he paid Defoe £100.[4] With the collapse of the Tory party, Defoe found himself without advocates in high places.

Defoe would be lucky if he were labeled merely a mischievous party scribbler. As early as 2 June 1710 the *Moderator* had called Defoe the "Goliath of the Party," and the seventy or more pamphlets he had written since then assured that he was the most prominent political writer in England. Shortly after the new king's arrival in London, the government undertook an aggressive campaign against the press. In November the attorney general was ordered to apprehend and prosecute a number of writers. Even lowly hawkers and delivery persons were caught. The number of press spies and government agents increased as payment to them rose. Rewards far greater than the £50 offered for Defoe in 1704 show the government's determination to control the press; for instance, £1,000 was offered for the author of *English Advice to the Freeholders of England*.[5]

By this time nearly every journalist in England had attacked Defoe. He had been lambasted by the Whig *Medley* one day and the Tory *Moderator* the next; he had been rebuked in a list with the Whig *Observator* one day and cursed with Swift's Tory *Examiner* the next. Even his former friends joined the chorus that damned him as an utterly unprincipled mercenary. Defoe could expect people to come forward with evidence against him and the press to celebrate should he be sent to prison. Even the sympathetic might hesitate to employ him.

The way Defoe came to this unenviable position illuminates not only his talent and ingenuity but also his sense of mission and his position vis-à-vis Harley. History's legacy is wrong; Defoe was not an unprincipled weathercock, but he was deeply human *and* one of the best propagandists and fiction writers who ever lived. Defoe had a sense of mission and a number of firm opinions, but he also had strong loyalties and a pessimistic opinion of some of his countrymen's ability to understand England's best interest. The consistency of Defoe's major arguments and objectives may be obscured, but it is never wholly absent. At one point in 1711 Defoe had listed the issues of the Tory years of Anne's reign as "Affairs of the State [foreign diplomacy], Management of the War, Modelling of the Court [composition and balance of the ministry]," the economy ("the Credit, the Bank, the Funds"), and "above all the War."[6] On these issues Defoe's principles and Harley's objectives were close together, but some of Harley's policies troubled Defoe deeply.

Defoe's writing during the last three years of Anne's reign fell easily into the categories determined by the issues he listed in 1711, with "Affairs of State" largely inseparable from the management of the war. The business of the Tory government was to make peace. The nation's desire for peace had brought it to power, and the ministry's survival depended upon achieving it. Defoe, like his contemporaries, was decidedly tired of the war, aware of the negative effects it was having on trade, discouraged by recent losses, and confused by the current situation. The cost of living had risen 30 percent between 1700 and 1710. Malplaquet in September 1709 had been a pyrrhic victory—the allies had suffered at least 16,000 casualties—and Spain was lost with the defeat at Brihuega in December 1710.

Even before Brihuega virtually took away the British sticking point, "No peace without Spain,"* Englishmen wondered why the successes of 1706 and 1709 had not brought peace and, whether, in light of France's obvious weakness and the victories that had secured territory adequate to protect the allies' interests, it was really necessary to continue the war at all.[7] After the breakdown of peace negotiations in 1709 Defoe had written, "What particular Evil Planet influenced the Affairs of the Confederates at that time, that they should shut their Eyes against such Proposals as these, I am not Conjurer enough to determine" and "Providence . . . closed the Understandings of the Polititians. . . . Heaven . . . Infatuated them to reject Peace."[8]

Whatever the Whigs, the Whig press, or history has said about resentment toward the Tory peace, the nation was very tired of war, and the signs were everywhere. Parliamentary records bear out the newspaper reports of desertions in the army. The queen had to appeal to her subjects to return to their regiments. After the publication of the preliminaries, crowds gathered to cheer Matthew Prior, the ministry's negotiator recently returned from France, and some witnesses compared them in size and enthusiasm to the mobs for Sacheverell. On 4 December 1711 the *Daily Courant*—the paper that had Whiggishly leaked the preliminary articles—observed, " 'Tis inconceivable what Joy the Appearance of Peace causes among the People of this Country." Defoe was always out and around London, and he could not have missed the mood of his countrymen. Some of them expressed ideas

---

*The War of the Spanish Succession was so called beause England and the allies were fighting partly to prevent a union of Spain and France under Philip V of Spain, grandson of Louis XIV of France. As late as March 1709 Parliament passed yet another resolution affirming "no peace without Spain." Defoe's first use of the term seems to be in the 29 May 1707 *Review*, 4:188.

Defoe would soon print, and they used the same words. "The last years campaign has showed us the folly of a fflanders warr, and has demonstrat [*sic*] to us that our purse will be empty before wee can reduce Spain. . . . We are very hopefull of a speedy peace," one wrote a friend.[9] Defoe's own inclinations, a realistic view of the nation, and his work for Harley came together.

Because of Robert Harley's personality and Parliament's composition, the peace negotiations make one of the most erratic chapters in British history. Regardless of the nearly universal desire for peace, almost no one found the way it was brought about easy to explain or pleasant to contemplate. Defoe was no exception; the ways he carried out his work and balanced his principles and Harley's needs tell a lot about Defoe and the peace itself.

Even though Harley was not appointed Chancellor of the Exchequer until 10 August 1710, as early as 10 July the French had been in contact with his most intimate cronies, and by 1 August Harley's secret negotiator, the earl of Jersey, had begun negotiating with the French.[10] Jersey, Harley, and Shrewsbury began the work on the treaty, often called pejoratively England's "separate peace" because it was conducted largely without England's allies and with less attention to their interests than some thought desirable. By December Jersey had agreed to let Philip keep Spain, but it was 26 April 1711 before the rest of the cabinet knew and June before the queen gave Parliament the principal provisions of the treaty that the ministers had endorsed on 5 May.[11] The Dutch had been told in April, but when they expressed resentment and asked for additional conditions, Harley excluded them again. At this point the ministry set in motion a concerted effort to discredit the allies, justify the separate negotiations, and prepare the nation for a peace British historians still call "dishonorable." Marlborough, who would not collaborate in such a treaty, denounced the proceedings as "directly contrary to her majesty's engagements with the allies"[12] and had to be discredited as well.

After the vituperant reactions to the treaty at home and abroad, negotiations became secret again. They continued throughout the summer, and on 27 September the two secretaries of state for England, Bolingbroke and Dartmouth, signed the agreements—one document for the allies' scrutiny and the other containing the concessions France and Spain were making to England. By this time even Shrewsbury's conscience troubled him; "something in them looks so like bargaining for yourselves apart, and leaving your friends to shift at a general treaty," he complained. Later he refused to sign the preliminary articles.[13]

Harley's confidence in Defoe and his need for support led him to tell Defoe about the terms of these double "preliminaries" somewhat before the ministry's other premier propagandist, Jonathan Swift, who was not informed until the end of September. In May Defoe was still working out ways to prevent the succession to the Spanish throne from destroying the balance of power in Europe. In July he discussed in the *Review* and in his letters to Harley the impossibility of ever obtaining free trade with the Americas from the Spanish, although this privilege, including the Asiento* for thirty years, was part of the treaty.[14] A month later, however, he discussed such trade as feasible and even provided for under the terms of the 1701 Treaty of the Grand Alliance. His subject here was really the South Sea Company, and, since May when Parliament had passed the act creating the company, the terms Harley demanded for England were heavily influenced by his plans for the South Sea Company. Quite simply, the South Sea Company was Harley's way of financing the war by setting up a rival economic source to the Whig Bank of England and the East India Company. The idea had another advantage: the Tories who invested in the South Sea Company became as dedicated as the Whigs to gaining trade concessions from Spain and France. The plan was for the people who had made short-term loans to the government to finance the war to exchange these notes for stock in the South Sea Company. The government guaranteed the company a monopoly on English trade to the Spanish ports in South America and granted it an annuity of £558,678, which provided a payment of 5 percent interest on the stock.[15]

This shift in Defoe's position indicates that he had been told of the negotiations for territorial concessions in South and Central America. At this point Harley and the English were confident, and these provisions would resolve most of Defoe's objections to the South Sea Company. The plan for the company, largely designed by the wealthy City men John Blunt, George Caswall, Jacob Sawbridge, and Elias Turner, had struck Defoe as unfortunate, and he had told Harley and his *Review* readers so. Defoe had argued that it would be both more practical and more effective for the company to finance an English settlement from which it could open a trade with the Spanish and "improve" the "native Fruitfulness" of its territory. He did not believe that France or Spain would allow English trade if they could help it, but he believed the Spanish settlers would come to the English settlement to buy what they needed. He envisioned the new English colony as "a declar'd Free market over the whole Dominions of the Spaniards in America" and an

---

*A highly lucrative term contract for a slave-trading monopoly granted by the king of Spain. The holder of an *asiento* could have facilities in the Spanish colonies in the Americas where they could sell slaves (and usually other goods). At the time of the Peace of Utrecht the contract holder was bound to deliver 4,800 slaves per year to Spain's American possessions.

attraction to all who lived in the New World. Defoe also objected to linking the war debt and the company.

Defoe had not needed to point out the problems with the scheme. A controversy broke out at once over the prospects of the company, based on predictions regarding England's likelihood of receiving significant concessions from the Spanish when peace was made. In a series of *Review*s and pamphlet references Defoe tried to explain the idea and defend the South Sea Company in principle, and his remarks make clear how inseparable the campaign for peace and the provisions for the company had become. What he wrote in an August *Review* reveals his new knowledge of the negotiations and lays the groundwork for these special English provisions by criticizing the allies:

> As we Zealously and Vigorously assert the Interest of the House of *Austria*, and are not only at the Expence of great and powerful Succours and Assistances to the War, but *as it were*, wholly carry on that War at our own Expence of Blood and Treasure, so it is but reasonable . . . that some Consideration should be made to the *British Nation*, for all that Expence (8:234).

But an unexpected event changed the negotiations again. Defoe had begun to write cheerfully about the South Sea Company and the soon-to-be-improved trading conditions in the Spanish West Indies, but England gave up its demands for territorial concessions in South and Central America before the *Daily Courant* published the treaty preliminaries, which unmistakably contradicted the expectations Defoe had been led to print. England had held firm until mid-August when its negotiator, Matthew Prior, was stopped at Customs in Deal with the French diplomat Nicolas Mesnager. This embarrassing discovery of Prior's stay in France and his companion's identity assured that the Dutch would know that separate negotiations were in progress. England compromised in order to rush the treaty through, and the secretaries of state signed the completed, revised preliminaries on 27 September.

Defoe found out about the preliminary articles in September. On 1 September he was still ridiculing the idea that England would make peace "without Spain," and on 8 September he laughed at the notion that England desperately needed peace. "Will you *beg Peace* with Victory in your Hand?" he asks (8:290). His *Essay on the South Sea Trade*, published 13 September, also denied that England would make a hasty, weak peace and give up Spain.

On 6 October Defoe published *Reasons Why This Nation Ought to Put a Speedy End to This Expensive War*; on 9 October, a *Review* specifically acknowledged what was going on: "If you dislike the Treaty; If you suspect the Conditions; If you think the Peace now Treating of Unsafe,

Dishonourable, and Clandestine, and not lasting, Why do you buy Stock?" (8:343) By referring to "the Treaty," Defoe admitted its existence days before the *Daily Courant* published the preliminary articles on 13 October. *Reasons Why This Nation* expresses deep war-weariness and assesses England's situation in such a way as to leave the impression that England has little choice but to make peace. This position is exactly that ridiculed in the 8 September 1711 *Review*. The pamphlet is a masterpiece of propaganda. Defoe argues that the nation has but three choices: impose a general excise (tax on food and clothes), stop the funds (pay no more interest on loans to the government), or end the war.[16] The first two choices were obviously unacceptable and outrageous. He describes the common people "crying" for peace, quotes the *Post-Boy* as saying "The Desertion of the Infantry is Great to Astonishment," and says trade withers. He insists that the "true Ends and Designs of this War" are within reach, an advantageous peace treaty possible, and additional gains unlikely to compensate for the inevitable losses of men, money, and trade.

"The Case is alter'd Now" becomes a refrain emphasizing the contrast between the past ("when our Youth first felt their own Strength") and the present ("the whole Kingdom sold to Usury"). Throughout, the language is emotional and manipulative: "But how lie the Bones of 22000 of the best and bravest Soldiers in Christendom sacrificed . . . to decide . . . who should possess the Hedges of *Taniers*"[17]; "35000 of our boldest . . . Troops lie buried in the Ditches of those paltry Places"(7). The relentless tallying up of gain and loss, the amassed effect of words like "hedges" and "paltry Places," and the insinuations that the allies gain more than England and should, like England, be able to make advantageous peace, have the cumulative effect that Defoe wanted. From his emotional, biblical opening to his concrete ending, Defoe puts together a tour de force of propaganda. Here is Defoe at his best. Here is the Defoe who could draw all of the other journalists to attack him, thereby depriving them of initiative and originality.

Reasons Why This Nation required three editions in October: *Reasons Why a Party among Us, and Also the Confederates Are Obstinately Bent against a Treaty of Peace*, *Armageddon*, *The Ballance of Europe*, and *An Essay at a Plain Exposition of That Difficult Phrase A Good Peace* all went through three editions, and all appeared before the end of the first week of November—232 pages arguing that it was time to make peace and that *the* peace the nation wanted was in sight.

In the eighteen months after the publication of the preliminaries in the *Daily Courant* and Swift's *Conduct of the Allies*, seven controversial events occurred:

—31 December: Twelve new Tory peers were created in order to end the Whig majority in the House of Lords.

—4 January 1712: The *London Gazette*, the official paper, announced that Marlborough had been dismissed.[18]

—29 January: The treaty negotiations began at Utrecht.

—10 May: Bolingbroke sent Marlborough's replacement, the duke of Ormonde, the infamous "restraining orders" that commanded him to avoid engagements with the French army but to do so without informing his allies of these orders.

—July: British troops under the Empire's command were no longer paid by England; thereby, they were separated from the allies despite treaty agreements.

—9 April 1713: Queen Anne announced signing the treaty at the opening of Parliament.

—18 June: The Treaty of Commerce and Navigation was defeated in Parliament.

Throughout this period Defoe worked to make the treaty and its articles acceptable in a variety of ways. At first glance it appears that he repeatedly committed apostasy. For example, just two months after the publication of pamphlets like *Reasons Why a Party among Us, and Also among the Confederates Are Obstinately Bent against a Treaty of Peace*, which attacked the allies and strongly advised England to make peace, he published *A Defence of the Allies*, in which he presented the Dutch as maligned and the English as foolish and perhaps dishonorable in their dealings with their allies.[19] In the same month he wrote *No Queen: or, No General*, which defended the dismissal of Marlborough; and *The Conduct of Parties in England* and *Peace, or Poverty*, which attacked those who opposed the peace and answered objections to the treaty, including complaints about the treatment of the Dutch.

In fact, Defoe was doing what the best propagandists always do: he argued from different points of view and in different ways in order to support a single objective. Defoe believed that peace should be made. His consistency may be somewhat obscured by his deliberate shifting of point of view, and the way he took a pragmatic, rather than idealistic or theoretical stance, may further complicate interpretation. Moreover, a number of his—and his countrymen's—opinions had changed; for example, as the implications of the death of the emperor Joseph became clear, he gradually eroded the very important idea of "no peace without Spain" that he had originally supported. He was not at odds with many of his countrymen. As early as 1706 Shrewsbury, always a shrewd and powerful politician, starkly captured the conflicting demands in a letter written to Charles Delafaye: "To speak between you and I, to go no further, a Peace is much wanted and desired in the Countrye . . . money is so scarce . . . I speak the general voice thou' at the same time if the Peace be not good any warr is better than a Peace that doe not settle King Charles in Spain." By 1712 the balance of opinion was even greater. On 6 June, in the midst of the controversy over the restraining orders, the Edinburgh Town Council addressed the queen with approval: "It hath pleased Almighty God to prosper your armes . . . as to Give us the Joyfull prospect of ane approaching safe and Honourable peace . . . [which] Cannot but be most acceptable . . . to all good men."[20]

⁂

As he wrote about his issues of the Tory years of Anne's reign, Defoe remained true to several principles and developed two major themes consistently. First, he insisted it was time for a "safe and honourable Peace," and his definition of "safe and honourable" remains the same. Second, he introduced and developed the idea of "Tempora Mutantur, nos & Mutamur." Translated literally, it means, "The times are changed, and we are changed," and Defoe harmonized his works by emphasizing how circumstances made change wise, not traitorous. Passages such as the following one from *The Validity of the Renunciations of Former Powers* (1712) repeat like a sounding bell:

Time has taught us to see, that neither the Opinion of Princes, or Parliaments, are so infallible, as not to be Subject to the Mutations . . . which the Accidents of Government . . . bring upon them; and that which may to Day be esteemed dangerous and impracticable, to Morrow becomes not only safe but necessary . . . for as Circumstances alter, the Judgments of Men will and ought to be altered.[21]

Not only does he use the idea to help justify the end of the demand for "no peace without Spain" after the death of the emperor Joseph, he calls upon it repeatedly to argue that England and the allies have already won what they began fighting for. Even in small points he uses it effectively. He could call William's solution to the problem of the Spanish Succession as it existed in the Treaty of Partition an "exploded Notion," but he is always careful to contrast William's circumstances to the present ones.

Defoe never wavered from his position that England was now much stronger than France and could negotiate a good peace, that the war had achieved England's objectives and those of the Grand Alliance,* that any treaty should have considerable territorial and commercial advantages and safeguards, and that continuing the war was not only pointless but was weakening England and damaging her trade in significant ways. In all of these tracts, but especially in those associated with the *Review* by the fact of their being published by John Baker, Defoe is strongly Hanoverian and can even seem paranoid about Jacobitism. The memories of King James's rule seem to linger behind

---

*The alliance made by England, Holland, and the Empire in a series of treaties signed between 1689 and 1701. Later Prussia, other German states, Portugal, and Savoy joined.

much of the prose of 1712. Defoe always had a chauvinistic streak, and he was as willing as any of his countrymen to be sure England gained the most from the war, to pressure the allies, and to insist upon England's prerogatives. Nowhere does he have much praise for the Empire, and his attacks in pamphlets like *Imperial Gratitude* are therefore not surprising. The Dutch are to him, as they were for many of his contemporaries, England's great trading rival. Dutch success, however, determined that English people would feel respect and would recognize the nations' economic dependencies even as they simultaneously felt jealous and competitive.

In these things Defoe was consistent. Certainly, however, he was willing to stretch the truth and engage in special pleading. For instance, anyone who knew the ministerial rage at all of those responsible for the publication of the preliminaries in the *Daily Courant*, let alone England's duplicitous and piecemeal communications with the allies, would have laughed at Defoe's statement in *The Ballance of Europe*: that "just hearing the Proposals which *France* has made, and communicating them to be consider'd of by the Allies . . . and this is done so publick and so above-board, that not only the Allies have them, but every Newspaper has printed them." (34).

In taking different stances Defoe was sometimes willing to contradict himself. He could call the Dutch "the best of Friends that ever *England* had" and characterize them as "cunning," while at the same time excoriating them for wanting the lion's share of the spoils of the war and for retarding the peace negotiations. He could insist that the queen had no intention of negotiating without the Dutch and yet insist that she had that right and might do so. He tended to take his old stance as a casuist and gloss over theoretical issues, and, by writing about the European nations as if they were individuals, he transformed principles of diplomacy and international relations and the terms of treaties into the psychology of human beings with their inconsistencies, complexities, and deficiencies. Like people, the nations in his works reacted to circumstances, to historical experiences—shared and separate—and to perceptions. They could act from pride, anger, self-interest, or loyalty, and motive and circumstance took precedence over strict principle. As he would do in novels, Defoe explained, if not excused, them by placing them in a world of conflicting ethical and practical imperatives. England and her people needed peace; they had fought long and deserved a good treaty; they believed they had carried the chief burden for their side. What exactly did they owe the allies? How much ought they to delay or compromise the settlement for them? Just as opinions about people and their actions may vary, so, within a range, do Defoe's. One day he may excuse the Empire's natural desire to see its archduke Charles on the Spanish throne, and the next he may lash out at it for its deficiencies in the Spanish campaign. His pragmatic outlook never falters, and he summarizes his own position in sentences such as, "We were none of the Forwardest for a Peace . . . yet . . . Peace is always desirable to trading Nations. . . . always allowing the Queen had an undoubted Right by the Constitution to make Peace and War."

When there are true contradictions, they are often shocking but rhetorical rather than substantive. For example, in *A Further Search*, Defoe writes that the reception of Swift's *Conduct of the Allies* "must be acknowledged to be all owing to the Truth, coming with an irresistible Force upon the Minds of Men, and which always carries its own Evidence along with it." (3). A few months earlier, in *A Defence of the Allies*, Defoe had written of *Conduct of the Allies*: "When an Author purposely Voluminous, seeks to make his Argument good, rather by drowning his Meaning in a Torrent of Words, than by Clear and Intelligible Expressions," that author either lacks evidence or is taking advantage of the "present" temper (1–2).

In this same pamphlet, Defoe ridicules Swift for the very case he himself already made in *Reasons Why This Nation* and *Reasons for a Peace*: "The great Weight he puts upon our Mortgageing [*sic*] the Funds, and Entailing long and large Debts upon Posterity . . . is the Thing by which he enforces his Flegmatick Thoughts about carrying on the War; and that we have nothing left . . . but the Land-Tax and Malt-Tax" (43). Early on he may have written that the Dutch were never obliged by the Grand Alliance "to keep up any certain Number of Men or Ships, but it was left to themselves to send a Supply of as many as they well could," and, considering the size of their country, they always sent more than England. Later he would publish a balance sheet showing that the Dutch had quotas and failed to meet them year after year, supplying, for instance, twenty-seven instead of forty-three ships in 1707.[22]

A more painful case for Defoe than the shift in portrayal of the Dutch was the need to justify the dismissal of Marlborough after he refused to cooperate with the separate peace. Defoe knew that Marlborough was the greatest general in England's history, that he had established his country's military superiority, and that the dismissed Godolphin had given England "the longest purse" (the phrase that Defoe used repeatedly when he explained modern military superiority: "'Tis the longest Purse Conquers the longest Sword"). Through Halifax, the duchess of Marlborough had rewarded Defoe for his tributes to Marlborough, and he knew that the gathering criticism of the duke was aimed at making him a sacrifice to expediency. In *Atalantis Major*, the pamphlet about which Defoe lied to Harley, he described Marlborough as a "victorious," "most glorious" commander now treated ungratefully (7–8). *A Short Narrative of the Life of Marlborough*, published two months later, called Marlborough "a Great Captain, equal no doubt to any in all Ages" (4), summarized the highlights of his military career, and concluded with an extravagant comparison of Marlborough to Moses. Defoe used a long list of adjectives such as "temperate," "courageous," "politic," "skillful," "affable," and "humble" and may have collected some of the flattering, personal anecdotes from his Scottish friend the earl of Leven, who knew and admired Marlborough. As late as 1712 Defoe reminded his countrymen of the victory at Blenheim and described Godolphin as so honest and prudent that his "Ministry appeared beyond the Power of all these Attempts to lessen it."[23]

As time passed, he simply avoided mentioning Marlborough and the campaign in the *Review*. In pamphlets like *The Conduct of the Parties in England* and *No Queen: or, No General*, however, he could not spare Marlborough entirely, yet he could not bring himself to perjury. Marlborough becomes a character in the foreground of a story of Whig ingratitude, shortsightedness, and error. The Whigs cast Harley out, split their party, alienated the Junto, and made enemies. *Their* papers, such as the *Observator*, criticized the ministry and the management of the war as harshly as the Tory press. Moreover, Marlborough ignored complaints of the duchess's avarice and his own exorbitant profits. Marlborough's downfall, Defoe says sadly, was "Coin'd in this Mint, Forged in this Furnace." Marlborough becomes the victim of his party, his friends, and his family. As these people challenged, undermined, and angered the queen, Marlborough stood back, and a reluctant queen had no choice. In every case Defoe carefully maintained his position. By blaming others, by depicting Marlborough as unwilling or unable to change things enough to stop criticism, and by reminding his readers that such things as Marlborough's profits were merely alleged by enemies, not proved, he managed to avoid contradicting his earlier opinion of Marlborough as a great general, even as he justified the queen's action.

From these examples, it is clear that some were apparent, not real, contradictions and that Defoe did come to some new opinions as did his countrymen. For instance, opinion changed drastically about the original treaty of alliance with the Dutch, especially after the Commons' resolutions* were published in February 1712.[24] That actual contradictions can be found that reflect upon Jonathan Swift may be more indicative of Defoe's deeply ambivalent attitude toward Swift and Swift's propagandistic techniques than symptomatic of Defoe's dishonesty.

Swift was Defoe's only serious rival for the place of premier propagandist, and as early as 1704 he and Defoe had been opponents on the issue of religious toleration. The ministry had other writers in its

---

*The Commons passed eleven resolutions based upon an Admiralty report that documented the discrepancies between the allies' treaty commitments and their actual supplies.

service, of course, and some wrote works that rivaled or even surpassed Defoe's in popularity. Charles Hornby's *A Caveat against the Whigs* and Joseph Trapp's *The Character and Principles of the Present Set of Whigs* went through multiple editions just as some of Defoe's pamphlets did, and, of course, Swift's *Conduct of the Allies*, with its six editions between 27 November 1711 and the end of January, holds a unique position in the history of propaganda.

The greatest difference between the two men was in their strategies, and Defoe surely believed Swift's wrong. They were certainly unlike his own and those of men such as Richard Steele, whom Defoe praised. Swift used invective, ad hominem attacks, and satiric exaggeration to inflame and polarize, while Defoe constantly said, in letters and in print, that he wanted to open people's eyes and bring them to temperate behavior.[25] A 16 October letter captures both propaganda methods and implies his judgment: "Now is the juncture; when The Minds of The People, Fluctuating and Stormy like The Sea, Listen to Every Wicked Inflamer and Would Listen also to Calm and Cool admonitions if Given with Temper and Sincerity" (24). What may be his earliest comment on the *Examiner* comes in a *Review* essay that sets out his principles of journalism and recalls his comment that the "weakest Step the *Tatler* ever took" was to take notice of "the Barkings" of the press. In this essay Defoe says it is "absurd" to call a man names such as idiot and "pretend" to enter a debate with him. He chides the *Examiner* for "Billingsgate" language and lack of manners, and says he refuses to fight at the *Examiner*'s level (7:450). In another place, he distinguishes between name calling or "railling" and debate or "arguing," and his training in disputation at Morton's school stands behind his precepts. Once he observed that upon "Corrupted, False, [*sic*] Foundations [Swift] erects a Fabric as Corrupt."

In some ways Swift's success reveals Defoe's superiority as a propagandist. Swift had spent many months on *The Conduct of the Allies* and while working on it had written little else.[26] Defoe seems to have had no trouble sustaining the *Review* and publishing more than twenty tracts on the negotiations (plus half a dozen pamphlets on other subjects) in twelve months. The signs of haste in Defoe's work are usually as minor as a few awkward sentences and some "afterthought" structures, such as "*Flanders* is not the Place where he, the King of *France*, is best able to keep us at Bay."[27] Swift's exuberant rhetoric and personal opinions sometimes caused trouble as his snipes at the Scots in *The Public Spirit of the Whigs* did. Swift's pamphlet was printed by John Barber, who did most of the government's work, was advertised in a large number of London periodicals, and was widely distributed by the Tories to their constituents in the country.[28] Defoe usually made his own arrangements with printers and inserted a "This Day Publish'd" in the *Review* and perhaps another periodical or two. Although the government distributed some of Defoe's work, most of it had to make its own way on its merits.

Defoe tended to attack those who attacked him primarily when he thought they might influence others or when he believed them mistaken and their mistakes useful to correct or dangerous to his point of view. Some scholars have seen Defoe as restrained about the *Examiner* because he knew that it, too, was one of Harley's papers. In fact, Defoe treats it as he does almost every opponent in his long journalistic career. His compliments on the *Examiner* essays on the Greenshields' case* are as typical of his fairness and opportunism as are his objections to Swift's "blunders" about the history of the Toleration. Such neutral statements as the following are typical of Defoe's equal treatment of the *Examiner* with other papers: "Whether the *Observator* then, or the *Examiner* since, has rail'd most at the late ministry, I leave to [you]." Except for the rare instances when a personal attack could lure Defoe into defensive autobiography, he responded to other journalists almost solely when it served a propagandistic end. Often he shows that he knew that engaging a journalistic opponent called attention to that paper and increased its influence.

Most of the exchanges with the *Examiner* and Swift's tracts are part of the ordinary Whig and Tory ways of seeing the world. As Defoe once put it, the "Whigs are for carrying on this War till they may obtain a safe and honourable Peace" and the Tory ministry is "for ending this War by a safe and honourable Peace."[29] Swift's rhetoric always offends Defoe, though. In *A Defence of the Allies* he calls Swift's stance that of a "Gladiator at the *Bear-garden*" "blustering upon the Stage, shouted in by the whole Tory Mob" (2–3). A typical complaint is that he works by "Calamy" and "flings at those he rather would have us think Guilty than be able to prove it." Moreover, he believed that Swift "nowhere bound himself up to any Rules, or [took] any Care to quote Impartially." Now and then there is a resonance to his prose that signals an unusual personal intensity. In part 2 of *The Secret History of the October Club* (1711), for instance, Defoe places Swift in the company of "a Drunken Lord, a Gamester and a Popish Priest" and lists the *Examiner* superior "for unintelligible Jingle, fine-spun Emptiness, and long-winded Repetition, without truth, without evidence, and without meaning."[30]

Swift, however, could sting even the most hardened man. He had a gift for sensing the vulnerable points in the psyches of the victims of his

---

*The Reverend James Greenshields had opened an Episcopal meeting house in very close proximity to St. Giles, Edinburgh, and flaunted his use of the English liturgy. The Scots prosecuted and imprisoned him; Greenshields appealed his case to the House of Lords; Scotland denied the Lords' jurisdiction, but in 1710 the House decided in favor of Greenshields.

satire. So good is he at these insights that his thrusts often seem off-hand. Once the impact is clear, however, he is merciless and tenacious. Defoe had nearly ignored the *Examiners* until 16 November 1710 when one of these deft thrusts hit him squarely. Defoe was accustomed to being called a devil (by implication an acknowledgement of his skill) and a mercenary, but he was also used to respect. When the *Examiner* called him "illiterate," Swift made Defoe defensive not only about his own learning but about Dissenting education, which had been under attack since Defoe's childhood. His response to Swift rehearses the major points in the debate over the value of the Dissenters' emphasis on English, modern languages, science, geography, and the "mechanic arts." Clearly infuriated, he insults Swift with a series of exemplary stories that compare what Swift has done to invitations to box with a chimney sweep, scold with a fishwife, and duel with an adulterer (7:450–55). For the next few years, he will occasionally refer to the insult.[31]

As the months passed Defoe continued occasionally to lash out at Swift. When Swift gratuitously insulted the Scots in his *Public Spirit of the Whigs* (1714), Defoe responded with a full-scale refutation and his most direct attack on Swift. In *The Scots Nation and Union Vindicated* he called the pamphlet a "foolish Lybel," "preposterous," and "plain Lyes," likened the author to a ravenous beast and a cruel monster, and challenged England to match the nobility and bravery of the Scots, especially on the field of battle. Knowing the small London publishing world as well as he did, Defoe must have been able to identify almost all of Swift's work as it came from the press. Not only did John Morphew, publisher of the *Examiner*, do pamphlets for him, but its printer, Swift's friend John Barber,[32] also did Defoe's *Mercator*. Defoe had known and worked for years with the people now being coached to serve the Tory party's ends.

From the end of the Sacheverell trial until the death of Queen Anne, Defoe's productivity was astounding and his efforts in behalf of the peace simply unparalleled. No one else even vaguely approximated the quantity and quality of Defoe's work. His was the work of a man who believed in his labor and in the major arguments he made. In accounts of battles, treaties, and public offices, the nation's war-weariness can be overlooked, but it was unavoidably, strikingly obvious to Defoe's contemporaries, and Defoe shared their weariness and wholeheartedly believed it was time to make peace.

Defoe often quotes the lines from St. Paul's description of his ministry: "I am made all things to all men, that I might by all means save some." Paul means that he preaches in the terms of and from the point of view of his audience. By assuming a voice, he assures himself of being understood and becomes more convincing; he sounds like one who understands rather than like a foreigner. Paul does not mean that he changes or that his message does. In fact, the idea is common in the eighteenth century. Samuel Johnson's *Idler* no. 85 reads, "Truth like beauty varies its fashion, and is best recommended by different dresses to different minds." Defoe often uses the line "all Things to all men" as he tries to bring others to his opinion. His pleasure in assumed voices comes from what he believes is the skillful performance of his job: to bring the mistaken to truth.

Defoe also explains his dedication to opening the eyes of the deluded in letters, the *Review*, and pamphlets. A cluster of these images appears in the late winter of 1712 when the Utrecht negotiations were beginning and the need for peace and the relinquishment of "no peace without Spain" most obvious. For example, Defoe rejoices that he has laid "the Truth Naked before them, that it may be out of the Power of Wicked Men to do harm, by placing false Lights before them." He complains of the abuses of the press and the dangers of believing their false rumors and asserts his duty to reveal the truth. The Bible is full of references to eyes opened to truth; one of the most striking is in Paul's defense before Agrippa. Paul explains that the voice on the Damascus road changed him to minister and witness to the people, "To open their eyes, *and* to turn *them* from darkness to light, and *from* the power of Satan unto God." Defoe finds his sense of danger and duty embodied in Paul's story.

Only rarely does Defoe seem aware of the elevation of his model in comparison to his own situation and existence. Later in 1712 he writes, "I Endeavour to practise The great work of Resignation Under the Injurious Treatmt I Reciev, Submitting it to his Disposall who in a like Occasion (Tho' of higher Moment) Bad Shimei Curse." The phrase "Tho' of higher Moment" shows Defoe identifying with the emotions of the incident while recognizing the distance between David's struggle for a kingdom and the participation of a journalist in efforts to attain a peace and assure the Hanoverian succession. In Defoe's time such distortion of significance was expected in personal uses of biblical analogues. The Bible offered types, and people were to find parallels, not duplicates, of their emotions and situations in them. In fact, the difference in degree suggested the significance of the individual's experience; his own opportunity for service was a silhouette of the biblical event.

In this light, Defoe probably saw his contradictions as unimportant and *felt* them as assumed stances.[33] As he took on the voice and point of view of one pamphlet, he wrote what he believed such a person would believe and say. Sometimes when he felt the significance of the Protestant succession for his country and his religion, he must have thought of himself as helping to save a nation. And surely over four years some of Defoe's opinions did change.

❧

Defoe's output was particularly astonishing because he had a full life in Scotland for part of this time. In December 1709, when the Sacheverell crisis took Defoe away from Edinburgh, he was building business investments and maintaining his wide acquaintances. The outcome of the trial may have reminded Defoe of the precarious nature of political employment even when it benefited him financially during Harley's rise in power. When he returned to Edinburgh he expanded his commercial investments.

Most of Defoe's major business activities seem to have been handled by John Russell. Their surviving correspondence shows that Defoe went back into the liquor trade on a small scale and began to sell horses. Using experience gained in the 1680s, Defoe shipped canary, ale, and wine to Scotland.[34] By 1711 he had entered the lucrative and active horse-trading business. The earl of Hyndford, commander in chief of the forces in Scotland and an avid horse trader, bought from Defoe and arranged for his officers to give Defoe a commission to buy horses for them. Major Coult, governor of Edinburgh Castle, paid Defoe at least £85 for horses in the summer of 1711. References to sizeable notes and bills of varying denominations in Russell's letters testify to Defoe's steady, if modest, trading (167).

In November 1710 Defoe and John Ochiltree finally formalized their agreement for the manufacture of linen tablecloths decorated with the new arms of Great Britain. The Treaty of Union and subsequent acts of Parliament had provisions for making Scottish linen and wool more profitable, and the Corporations and Royal Burghs continued to subsidize factories that employed the poor.[35] The contract obligated Ochiltree to set up a broad loom to work the linen damask tablecloths before 31 March 1711. Defoe paid Ochiltree £10 towards mounting the loom and promised to pay 7s. per eln for each completed tablecloth. Defoe was to supply the thread, and, should he be unable to furnish enough work, Ochiltree could use the loom for his own work after giving sixty days' notice. Defoe had exclusive right to the design as long as he supplied work. The penalty clause named the modest sum of £10 sterling.

The contract suggests that Ochiltree knew Defoe well; written into the contract is a lengthy clause regarding the requirement and responsibilities of a factor. Because of Defoe's long and rather unpredictable absences, he needed a reliable person to act for him. On 30 July 1711 he made Hanna Goodale his factor. The deed, written in Edinburgh by

John Russell's clerk, had been signed in London and was registered in the books of the Scottish Court of Council and Session on 7 August 1711. Defoe granted Hanna Goodale the full right to "manadge and negotiate all affairs of mine whatsover within Scotland . . . receave and discharge and if need bee pursue for all sums of money principals and rents."

Defoe was also involved in a proposal from a company of brass man-ufacturers, who offered to save the government money by selling it brass, rather than copper, "Ready wrought" for coining farthings. On 8 June 1710 Russell wrote Defoe that he "doubt[ed] not but it will answer your expectancies but I am inteerly a stranger to that affair" and could do nothing "to forward your design." Defoe also wrote Harley to en-courage the contract, but it was refused.[36]

Partly as good business and partly to further his work for Harley, Defoe began to buy Edinburgh newspapers as they became available. He had begun printing the *Review* in Edinburgh as well as in London in the spring of 1709. On 13 December 1709 Defoe contracted with David Fearne to publish the *Scots Postman* for a year, beginning on 27 Decem-ber. On 9 January the Edinburgh Town Council transferred Fearne's rights to Defoe.[37] A year earlier Fearne had gone to the Faculty of Advocates, a prestigious professional and learned society to which he belonged, to report to them that "he at the earnest desire of several noblemen and other worthy persons had undertaken to publish" the paper and had already set up foreign and domestic "intelligence" for that effect, and he asked them for their support. The advocates recom-mended that all their members "and such as depend on them" buy his paper and "allow him the benefit of publishing all advertisements they may be any ways concerned in." On 17 August the Edinburgh Town Council gave Fearne the exclusive right to print news on Tuesday, Thursday, and Saturday.[38]

The Faculty of Advocates did support Fearne. For example, on 16 December they paid him £4 sterling for "furnishing the news to the magistrates" and for advertisements. Part of the contract between Fearne and Defoe addressed Defoe's obligation to continue to supply Fearne with copies of the papers for the faculty and their circle. For £10 a year, to be paid quarterly, the paper became Defoe's, and he would receive four shillings for each subscription Fearne sold.

A few weeks later Defoe took over the *Edinburgh Courant* when its proprietor, Adam Boig, died. At that time, the *Courant* was the city's best paper. In a format much like the London *Post Man*, the paper printed foreign and domestic news, the queen's speeches and procla-mations, reports from ports, ships' orders, notices about the chief fam-ilies of Scotland, and even serialized pamphlets of special interest. Among these had been Defoe's *Review* for 4 December 1705 (no. 120) on the reasons for the Union and Charles Gildon's 1705 *Letter from Sir Gwynne* (1706), the pamphlet that sent Gildon to Newgate.[39] Boig held a copyright to print special news from Scotland, including the exclusive right to print the lists of newly elected members of the British Parliament. He received support from the Edinburgh Town Council and even from the Convention of Royal Burghs.[40]

In fact, Defoe may have written for the *Courant* before Boig's death. Some of the 1709 articles are on topics of special interest to Defoe, and a proposal to the Royal Burghs to subsidize setting up "Correspondence with severall parts of the Kingdome" sounds like Defoe's idea. Boig died on or immediately after 27 January, and on 1 February Defoe received the patent to print the *Edinburgh Courant* from the Town Council. Defoe received exclusive right to the name, thereby forcing a rival to become the *Edinburgh Evening Courant*. Some of Defoe's plans for his new acquisitions can be inferred from a letter Russell wrote Defoe on 14 March:

I have been with the Magistrates anent what you propose & they tell me they cannot Grant ane exclusive privilledges as you desyre but if you will choice three dayes in the week to publish your paper upon they will dyscharge any others to be printed on these dayes[.] I refer you to Mr. Goodale who will write you more fully[.] all I shall say is [that] had the affair been my oun I wuld not have presst it more warmly.

In June Russell wrote again to tell Defoe that Adam Brown, lord provost of Edinburgh,[41] had agreed to "authorize & protect" Defoe's "printes" if Mr. Goodale would hire four boys to distribute them.

Defoe seems to have let both papers lapse—only two numbers of the *Edinburgh Courant* have been found. In fact, Defoe's business dealings are more interesting for what they tell about his friendships than as commercial ventures. Negotiations and deliberations about the Treaty of Union had artificially united Scots. Family and class barriers faded in the efforts to pass the Union and gain as many advantages for Scotland as possible. Once ratified, the Union became a source of deep divisions and fierce competitions. As Scots scrambled for seats in the Parliament of Great Britain, for civil and crown appointments, and for Equivalent dollars, and as competing commercial interests surfaced, former allies became vituperative enemies. Men who had found Defoe useful and his information gathered from diverse sources interesting turned their attention to those who knew Scotland's ancient family histories and to the Scots now in position to help them at court. Defoe might know English economics and politics, but he could never maneuver the intricate, centuries-old history of, for instance, the relationships between the Hamilton and Dalrymple families well enough to influence elections.

Resentments and suspicions about Defoe were inevitable. Some things he wrote caused embarrassment or discomfort, and objectionable pamphlets that he had not written were ascribed to him, as *An Historical Account of the Elections in North Britain* (1708) was. In a typical incident Mungo Graham wrote Defoe's old friend Montrose that the book was by Defoe, that it accused Junto Scots of being Jacobites, and "is no ways yr freind [*sic*]."[42] Defoe's circle shrunk to the Edinburgh merchants, men like himself who had achieved what Defoe had wanted twenty-five years earlier. John Russell was burgess and a guild brother of the City of Edinburgh. Elected to the prestigious Merchant Company when he was only twenty-four, he had quickly risen to Writer of the Signet, a promotion that allowed him to argue cases before the Court of Sessions.

John Ochiltree, with whom Defoe contracted to make tablecloths, belonged to the Company and was a former dean of the Guild. The dean of the Guild, like London's lord mayor, held a court to settle disputes between merchants or between merchants and mariners. Adam Brown was a burgess, a former dean of the Guild, and a member of the Company as well. In the eighteenth-century, membership in the Company, which had been founded in 1681 to protect the trading rights of Edinburgh granted by King Charles, was limited to "Merchants, Sellers or importers of cloths, stuffs and other merchandise for the apparel or wear of the bodies of men and women" who were both burgesses and guild brothers.[43] As a former hose factor Defoe would have shared many of their interests and concerns.

Russell had conducted business for the earl of Leven and Major James Coult and was related to Coult by marriage.[44] This fact and Defoe's letter of introduction to Leven brought him into contact not just with them but with the earl of Hyndford and, at some distance, William Carstares. Russell's letters to Defoe indicate that Leven intended to write Defoe and that Hanna Goodale had written; they also mention the names of half a dozen other middle-class Edinburgh citizens. This connection involved Defoe in efforts first to restore Coult's pre-Union salary and then to help Leven and Coult keep their commands when the Tories came to power. Carstares asked Defoe to work in Coult's behalf and sent him messages through Russell. In August 1711 Russell wrote to tell Defoe that Carstares was on his way to London: "I doubt not youll have occasion to see [him] And he will commune with you anent the affair. I am sure I need say nothing to you in the Majors favour." Coult's letterbook shows that he sent at least a dozen letters to Defoe between June 1708 and November 1711, and the accounts of Edinburgh Castle record a few payments to Defoe.[45]

Defoe's brother-in-law, the Leith shipbuilder, married Russell's niece Helen, and Defoe's factor, Hanna Goodale, was the daughter of a Leith wright. Hanna's brother often attended meetings and represented Defoe's interests.[46] This brother may have been John Goodale, professor of Hebrew at the University of Edinburgh. This position was usually given to young native ministers since students were not required to pass exams in Hebrew but merely to attend lectures during the year devoted to the study of ethics and natural philosophy.[47] Benjamin Defoe boarded with a Mrs. Goodale; if John were the brother, Benjamin probably lived with Hanna rather than with John and his wife, for he had a family and only four rooms in the college. Both John Goodale and John Ochiltree had seats in Lady Yester's Kirk.[48]

In addition to these people, Defoe continued to see local churchmen. The letters from Russell as well as Defoe's reports to London show that he kept in contact with at least a half dozen prominent clergymen. Some small business transactions occurred between them, and he continued to work to reconcile the anti-Union ones to the Union. Russell mentions "a kind letter" to James Hart, minister at Old Greyfriars, in October 1712; in this letter Defoe probably urged Hart to take the Oath of Abjuration, the oath Scots objected to so strenuously because it pledged them to uphold the provision that the British monarch must belong to the Church of England. When Hart came to London in 1714, he drew his bills on Defoe.[49]

The most intriguing business contact may be David Fearne. Fearne had taken a law degree and become secretary to Lord Stair, the father of Hew and David Dalrymple, when he was lord president of the Court of Session. When Stair was forced out of office in 1681, Fearne opened a private practice and became known as "the Whigs' lawyer." In 1705 he began to solicit the government for employment, for he was, he said, "reduced to embrace the first honest employment that God sends me." He represented himself as able to help bring about the Union because he knew "the people's constitution, tempers, estates, powers, and weaknesses" so well. He said that there was "not one county" in which he did not have relations or former clients. He began to work for Harley for the Union and received money through John Bell in Newcastle just as Defoe did. In November 1706 Bell wrote Harley that Defoe and Fearne knew nothing of each other. Payments to Fearne were always quite small in comparison to those to Defoe, and Fearne's surviving reports suggest that he reported events rather than circumstances and opinions. Harley defended him as "a formal fellow, but very faithful and in credit with the Kirk."[50] Whether Defoe knew that Fearne also reported to Harley is not clear, but Defoe would have known him as a pro-Union man and would have seen his contacts and his paper's audience as useful and as a desirable acquisition.

By this time Defoe undoubtedly knew that Harley had many other correspondents in Scotland and that he paid some of them. With none of them does he seem to have collaborated. The mysterious "J. Pierce," perhaps the same Pierce involved in the publication of *Legion's Humble Address*, traveled and made reports for Defoe. This Pierce seems to have been a Scot, because of Defoe's repeated comments that no one else he knew could have gone in safety to the people in Scotland that Pierce did. Of John Ker, another of Harley's agents and one often given very large sums of money, Defoe says nothing at all.[51] Two other prominent Londoners in Scotland to work for the Union were Barrington Shute, sent to work with the nobility and gentry, and Christopher Taylor, a Presbyterian minister. Defoe mentioned Taylor and another London minister, Samuel Roswell, as having tried to answer the Church of Scotland's objections to the Union. He seems genuinely sorry that they had not succeeded. In 1708 Sunderland instructed Defoe to communicate with him through Shute, but Defoe wrote that Shute never answered his letters.[52] That Defoe knew Shute is clear, but his interest in him seems minimal.

In contrast, William Paterson, a Scot he had known since the 1690s and appealed to for help in 1702, could arouse rivalry and resentment. In March 1707 Defoe wrote Harley, "I Can Not but Observ that a Motion was Made to Recomend Mr Paterson to her Majtie" (H 212). Only a month after he began to work in Scotland, he seems to think that Paterson might be trying to discredit him, and he undercuts Paterson in turn. He notes that Paterson seems to think that Defoe "had started" the idea of demanding a drawback* on Scottish pork, a troublesome idea to the English, and he denies it cleverly by saying that such an allegation "Onely Serv'd to Convince me he Converst with but few, Since The Merchants Concernd are Many" (H 157). Paterson, too, received large sums of money from Harley.

Defoe continued to see John Clerk and the Scots he had met in London, but their membership in the British Parliament and their return to the occupations and friends of ordinary life reduced Defoe's contact with them. Of one of the Clerks' acquaintances, however, Defoe saw quite a lot. Defoe's first Scottish printer, another person whose reach in Edinburgh extended like an octopus's tentacles, was Agnes Campbell Anderson. She had printed John Clerk's work, was printer to the crown,† had her press in the library of the University of Edinburgh, and maintained a paper mill at Penicuik, the Clerk estate. Mrs. Anderson was a tough, litigious, and fairly unpleasant person. For forty years after her husband's death, she terrorized the other Edinburgh print-

---

*Percentage of a tax to be paid back when the commodity was exported; in this case, the proposal was for Scotland to receive part of the export tax its citizens paid on pork back as a lump sum at the end of each fiscal year.

†A royal warrant gave her exclusive right to print and import Bibles and to print all royal proclamations, speeches, and lists, as well as all books of psalms, and of law, divinity, and medicine.

ers. She jealously guarded her printing rights and by 1706 had made a large personal fortune. Allegedly an ignorant woman who could hardly spell, she handled criticism in a cavalier manner. For example, when a delegation from the Church of Scotland spoke to her about her "erroneous" Bibles, she cheerfully said she would let anyone the General Assembly appointed "revise and correct" them at her press—unpaid, of course.[53] She was infamous for her efforts to destroy her competition. A contemporary described her as falling "Tooth and Nail upon the Booksellers." In 1680 she had a former apprentice declared a rebel and imprisoned in the Tolbooth shortly after he opened a rival print shop. In 1682 she went to court to oppose an Aberdeen printer's royal patent "on the ground that one press was sufficiently able to serve all Scotland." In 1696 she hurriedly produced an almanac to compete with John Man, another rival printer. Man complained to the Town Council that she did more than reduce his sales to the point of near bankruptcy: her almanac was so bad that it prejudiced people against almanacs in general.[54]

Just as Mrs. Anderson had been careful to keep her patent as printer to the crown, she alertly applied for other exclusive privileges whenever she could. She carefully cultivated powerful men and used her personal wealth to great advantage. For instance, she agreed to print "the monthly disputes" at the university in exchange for free space for her press, and then resisted all of the college's efforts to evict her at least until 1713. She became the printer to the Church of Scotland by purchasing the set of acts of the General Assembly from their former printer, George Mosman, for over £3,300. James Watson, perhaps the best printer in Scotland, complained that "No other printer in Edinburgh could afford to make this purchase," noting that part of the money went to persuade Mosman's heirs not to bid against her.[55] Time after time Mrs. Anderson went to the Edinburgh Town Council and the Scottish Privy Council for exclusive rights to print orders, proclamations, and other writings. The payments to her were large, and more noticeably so because of the straitened economic circumstances of Scotland in those years. Year after year she received an average of £200 from the Edinburgh Town Council for work done for it or books and papers supplied to it. According to the inventory submitted by her executors, she was worth £78,197 at her death.

Mrs. Anderson printed Defoe's early work, his *Caledonia*, his Edinburgh *Review*, and his *History of the Union*. All of his life Defoe read and corrected his own proofs carefully; therefore, the advantages of using Anderson as his printer outweighed the risks of her bad spelling and careless work. As early as 1678 she had sixteen employees and several presses.[56] She could produce large numbers of copies very rapidly when necessary, and the official documents received for printing could be made available to Defoe before publication. In spite of Defoe's dissatisfaction with the printing of *The History of the Union*, he tried to help her keep her patent to be printer to the crown. Beginning in August 1711, Mrs. Anderson campaigned relentlessly for its renewal. Ironically, her work for Defoe became one of her rivals' weapons against her. In 1711 John Baskett, one of the crown's London printers, joined with two Edinburgh printers, Robert Freebairn and James Watson, and agreed to act together to try to replace Anderson when her patent expired on 12 May 1712. They put together a memorial, and Freebairn went to London to argue their case with Bolingbroke, then the secretary of state with power to grant the patent.

On 7 June Defoe wrote to Harley to tell him that some ministers were uneasy about the three applicants, none of whom belonged to the Church of Scotland. He mentioned a few unfortunate consequences that might result should they get the patent, but only after an agreement had been reached with Freebairn did Defoe send a strong, detailed letter. On 20 July Defoe asked Harley to put a stop on the grant. He, like most Scots, might have assumed that the patent would not be decided so long before Mrs. Anderson's grant expired. The patent was awarded to Freebairn, however, and Defoe wrote to protest on 7 September.[57] Mrs. Anderson first protested the award as illegal because it had been given before her patent ended and because Bolingbroke had completely ignored Scottish requirements for qualification of the printer.

When this tactic failed, Anderson lured Basket and Freebairn away from Watson and began a suit based on the contention that the patent had been issued to Freebairn and that Watson had no right to it without him. Watson responded with a countersuit arguing that the idea, initiative, investment, and subsequent improvements to the print shop had all been his and that Mrs. Anderson had bribed Basket and Freebairn, had acted as she had "to ruin him," and that she had even stated these intentions. In the effort to gain the patent and win this suit against Anderson, Watson and others used the fact that she printed Defoe's *Review*s as a charge equal in seriousness to the allegation that her Bibles were corrupt and error-marred. As one contemporary wrote, "in the very Time she was solliciting for the renewing her Gift of being the Sovereign's Printer," she continued to print "the seditious Reviews of Defoe . . . containing unparalled reproaches against the Queen and her present Ministry; and who lately printed the seditious seasonable Warning." In his deposition, Watson mentioned the printing of the *Review*s in the same paragraph with an account of Anderson's "refusal" to put "one Candle" in her window on the queen's birthday "tho' her House be in the chief Part of the City."[58]

Defoe had begun using other Edinburgh printers before 1711. John

Moncur, a Presbyterian and a Whig, opened a print shop at the end of
Bull Close in 1707, and in 1710 printed "A Reproof to Mr. Clark." Since
that tract reflected on Anderson's work, the choice of a different
printer was tactful. In 1711 Moncur printed the Edinburgh edition of
The Representation Examined. Watson had printed some of Defoe's work,
but it may not have been authorized. In 1705 he had done the short
excerpts from the *Consolidator* and in 1713 a pamphlet called *The Trade
of Scotland with France*, which was merely *Mercator* nos. 19 and 20
printed together. There is no doubt, however, that Defoe continued to
give Mrs. Anderson work as long as he printed in Edinburgh.

Defoe's representation to Harley that the Scots largely supported
Anderson's petition for the renewal of her patent is correct. A number
of them went on record in her favor, and the Scottish court decision is
in harmony with that opinion. In 1715 David Dalrymple wrote the
English court what might stand for common opinion. He mentioned
Watson and Freebairn's inviting promise to print Buchanan and their
hopes for better-quality work but concludes, "I doe wel remember that
Freebairn's grant was under great observation when he got it . . . and
Mr. Freebairn was known to be at hart what he now appears [a Jac-
obite]." Dalrymple speculates that opposition to Mrs. Anderson at
court in 1711 came from men like Bolingbroke who resented her open
espousal of Whig principles, including hearty support for the Protestant succession.[59]

Some Scots had feared that this controversy would result in the
award of the warrant to an Englishman. Dalrymple, for example, had
included a paragraph about the danger of the decay of "our printing
(as many other things)" in his letter. The citizens of Edinburgh particularly feared this "decay" and made vigorous efforts to stimulate the
economy and compensate for the loss of the court and Parliament.
Among the minor schemes was one to bring more English Dissenters,
then barred from English colleges, to the University of Edinburgh.
Defoe joined Carstares and others in what became an acrimonious
competition with the University of Glasgow. Prominent English Dissenters including Daniel Williams, Edmund Calamy, and Joshua
Oldfield received honorary degrees from both universities, Edmund
Calamy was made a burgess and guildbrother of the City of Edinburgh,
and the universities exchanged insults. Glasgow questioned Edinburgh's right to give degrees and Carstares and Robert Stewart, the
Edinburgh philosophy professor and nephew of Sir James Stewart,
lord advocate of Scotland, protested in the strongest terms to John
Stirling, principal of Glasgow. The Glasgow men complained that their
city had been unjustly branded as one of riots in contrast to Edinburgh,
the city of "that peace and that moderation which are not in Glasgo."
Daniel Williams lamented that five of the eight students he had hoped

would go to Glasgow had chosen Edinburgh instead and blamed it on "a certain person (not a Scotchman or student)" who, he implied, knew Scotland firsthand.[60] This person could well be Defoe, for his *Review*s had reported several riots in Glasgow and had included reflections on the temper of Glasgow citizens in *The History of the Union*. As a prominent English Dissenter, well known to have spent a considerable amount of time in Scotland, Defoe would be a person whom Londoners might have consulted about the best university for their sons.

Edinburgh began its effort to increase the number of Dissenting English students with several disadvantages. For years these young men had gone to universities in Germany and Holland and to the University of Glasgow, and these places had reputations and a kind of familiarity that the University of Edinburgh did not. Daniel Williams' outspoken advocacy of Glasgow was so strong that some London ministers feared "a rupture" that would divide them from Williams and, therefore, divide the London Dissenters, should they champion Edinburgh. The college itself presented a rather ramshackle appearance in comparison to Glasgow. A visitor praised Glasgow's "neat Quadrangle," its "stately" front entrance on the main street, its large garden, and its harmonious chapel, common hall, and "several" schools. The University of Edinburgh was well away from the main street, and the same visitor remarked that it consisted "of one small *Quadrangle*, and some other Lodgings without Uniformity or Order, built at several times, and by diverse Benefactors." He found the arrangement of books in the Edinburgh library strange, for they were "marshall'd . . . according to the Benefactors" rather than arranged by subject matter. Edinburgh's library did have, however, the skull of the great Scottish humanist George Buchanan, "very intire, and so thin that we may see the Light through it."[61]

At the height of the effort, in the winter of 1709/10, Carstares received a paper entitled "Considerations and Proposals for Encouraging Parents in Sending their Youth to the University of Edinburgh." Many things suggest that Defoe was the author. It was like him to court a powerful man with a proposal. A number of his oldest friends, including George Drummond from the Society of Reformation of Manners and the Scots Parliament Committee, were helping Carstares, and, of course, Defoe's son was a student at the university.

The paper is without Scottishisms except for one reference to Edinburgh as the "good town" and shows many characteristics of Defoe's style. He almost invariably wrote in "sentence paragraphs," paragraphs each composed of a single sentence. These paragraphs vary considerably in length, primarily because of his habit of stringing ideas together with "and" and with subordinate clauses designed to clarify his points. The paragraphs consistently begin with subordinating elements that note the relationship between paragraphs. The proposal closely resembles Defoe's most formal essay style and calls to mind the style of the "Observations" in his *History of the Union*. The careful attention to the details of the plan, typical of similar sections in *An Essay upon Projects* and the later *Religious Courtship*, appears not only in the well-thought-out lists of duties of the tutor and his assistant, of the dangers to the student, and of the advantages to Edinburgh and Scotland, but in specific references always associated with Defoe's fictional style ("every night betwixt the hours of four and lighting, students . . . prepare their lesson").[62]

During the time Defoe was establishing Benjamin in Edinburgh, it would have been natural for him as a father to consider what he needed to provide for his son and characteristic of him to turn these ideas into a formal proposal. He had bombarded Harley with "proposals" and "schemes" when he thought he might be helpful, and this memorial for Carstares has many of the same qualities. Just as some of his ideas for Harley involved presentation and implementation at the cabinet level, this one directs its argument beyond Carstares to the Town Council, the group Defoe saw as having the means to set up boarding houses for English students. His final paragraph echoes the language of council minutes: his plan "must contribute to the honour and advantage of the University and good town, in particularly drawing strangers to the place and laying a strong obligation on parents to wish it well for their childrens sake, and on youth to do it all the service afterward they can" (345). Here he captures the city's concern with its future and its failing economy, which had been based on the periodic influx of people drawn by the meetings of the Scottish Parliament. The educational aims and details, the dependence upon central authorities, and the rather heavy-handed explanation of civic benefits might have come from *An Essay upon Projects* and look forward to *The Family Instructor* and *Augusta Triumphans*.

Defoe's participation in efforts to help Scotland benefit from the Union took on more personal overtones when the Scots felt the treaty violated. Defoe had been the most prominent English apologist for it in Scotland, had interpreted the articles, and vouched for the English character. In the years immediately after the passage of an indisputably unpopular Union, Scots jealously watched England and were ready, even eager, to find their reservations about the treaty confirmed.[63] The crisis over the shiploads of wine and brandy in the spring of 1707, in the continued resentment of the oaths, the slow payment and form of payment of the Equivalent, the abolition of the Scottish Privy Council, the bill introduced in Parliament to tolerate Episcopal communion in Scotland, the Patronage Act, the Greenshields case, the peerage bill, and the decision to impose the malt tax on Scotland when the peace with France was made[64] all kept Scotland in agitation. So loyal a Union man as Mar wrote Harley in 1711 that he feared for the Union "shou'd that hardship of the Peeradge be putt upon us So contrair to all Sense, reason and fair dealing, and if our trade be no more encouradg'd than yett it has been, or indeed is like to be, how is it possible that flesh and blood can bear it and what Scots man will not . . . do all he can to get quit of [the Union]?" In 1713 a motion to dissolve the Union, initiated by the Scots in Parliament, failed by only four proxy votes. Several Scots outlined their country's dissatisfactions, and Englishmen as well as Scots admitted that animosities between the two countries were greater than before the Union. That so many Englishmen voted with the angry Scots shows how seriously endangered the Union was. On the eve of the debate Defoe published a *Review* defending the Union, primarily in terms of its necessity for the Protestant succession. Here he made no claim to economic advantages and listed no benefits that Scotland had received. In fact, he confessed the Scots' situation when he said, "Let the Gentlemen be never so angry at the present hardship they are under, (I wish they had no cause to complain)."[65]

Defoe's daily contact with the Scots subjected him to their complaints and chidings, and his letters argued tirelessly in their behalf even as a string of *Review*s and pamphlets presented their side to the English.[66] As early as April 1707 he was telling Harley that the actions of Parliament would mean there "will be No Staying here for me nor hardly any Englishman"; here he acknowledges that his position is especially uncomfortable. He quotes the Scots, "Now you see how we are to be served . . . what we Are to Expect from a Brittish Parliament." He says that he is "Exceedingly Harrass't and Fateagu'd" and that his reputation is suffering badly (216–17). Even after Harley's fall, when he had to address the more unfamiliar and intimidating Godolphin and the unpredictable Sunderland, he continued to insist bluntly upon the injustice of the oaths and even to assert that the treaty had been broken. In February 1708 he reminded his employers that the Equivalent was to have been paid promptly in sterling so that the Scots would benefit from the circulation of the money. A contemporary quotes one of Defoe's "seditious" statements to be, "Parliament can make an Oath to Day, and punish a Man for keeping it to Morrow."[67] Now and then, he even uses "us" and "our" to refer to the Scots as though he were really one of them.[68]

Many Scots continued to appeal to Defoe for advice or help. The ministers of the Church of Scotland could be the most certain of his loyalty, and Defoe received and used papers like the one sent him on 24 March 1711, "Memorial Anent the Power and Privelege of Presenting Ministers in Scotland," on the patronage bill.[69] Defoe continued to lose status in Edinburgh, however. More and more people came to resent his English connections. When they had wanted Union and favors, those contacts were an advantage. In a time dominated by resentment of England and disappointment in the anticipated benefits of Union, however, Defoe could expect to be a scapegoat. His former hopes and rosy pictures became jokes. Always a proud and sensitive man, Defoe felt his own helplessness. His acquaintances among the nobility and gentry largely forgot him. His familiarity with English politics and his pen no longer interested them, and his circle dwindled. As Oldmixon said, Defoe became "an Author *once* very much in the good Graces of the Scots" (emphasis added).[70]

Scotland became a faded dream for Defoe, and the end of the Sacheverell trial in 1710 marked the turning point. Before that he expanded his commercial investments; after it some of the patterns of overextension and neglect that had led to his bankruptcy in 1691 reappeared. His son began to neglect his studies at the university; in September 1711 Defoe ordered Benjamin home, and in August 1712 he enrolled him at the Inner Temple in London.[71] Defoe continued to work closely with a number of prominent Scots, but there is a marked contrast in the projects and people with whom he was involved. Rather than being concerned with the establishment of anything like the SPCK, with parliamentary elections, or with plans to improve the economy of Scotland, Defoe was involved in small trading ventures, a petty dispute among Edinburgh printers, and an unsuccessful attempt to increase the number of English Dissenting students at the university. Above all, the outcome and aftermath of the Sacheverell trial threatened Defoe's most cherished political ideals. The desire to defend religious toleration and the Protestant succession called him back to London, and 1712 saw his last visit to Scotland.

CHAPTER 13

A TEAM OF WRITERS

This Day . . . 13 Persons, who were taken up for printing and publishing Books and Pamphlets against the Government, appear'd in the Queens Bench Court.
—*The Evening Post,* 23 October 1711

If Truth be his Foundation, if his Countrys Good be his clear disintrested View; Gaols, Pillories, Gibbets, and Death, have nothing in them to terrify him.
—DEFOE, *Review,* 7 May 1713

Even at fifty Defoe could commit acts that became chains of consequences beyond his power to escape or break. His sense of mission and belief in the tactic of "being all things to all people" held the potential for misunderstanding and resentment. As *Realpolitik* increasingly controlled the actions of Robert Harley, the distance between Harley's decisions and Defoe's opinions increased. For a long time what Defoe wrote was pitched somewhere between Harley's most extreme Tory actions and Defoe's most radical Whig opinions. As the Harley ministry came into a crisis, Defoe's loyalty pushed him away from his moderate, balanced position, and he half-heartedly defended some extreme Tory policies and procedures. At that moment, Defoe's own reservations— both moral and political—and resentments broke out in a few publications that diverged from his middle position in the opposite direction.

A simple but detailed analysis of Defoe's peace pamphlets shows a virtuoso propagandist at work, able to write from a variety of points of view, to make the same points repeatedly and yet hold readers' interest, and to respond quickly to events and rival publications. Harley and the entire ministry—and the journalists who supported it—had had to follow what has been called Harley's "double game."[1] This policy reflected the necessity of (1) satisfying the Tory M.P.'s that peace would be made, and (2) continuing to prosecute the war vigorously enough to satisfy the allies and to force the French to make an advantageous treaty. Even the queen had to contribute to this effort. In her speech at the opening of Parliament in the fall of 1710, she expressed the war-weariness of the nation, her awareness of the sufferings of "this long and expensive war," and her hope of bringing the war to a "speedy conclusion," but also pledged herself and urged her legislators to continue the war "with the utmost Vigour."

A closer look at Defoe's work reveals a man struggling to reconcile conflicting loyalties and competing strategies. Step by step, he was drawn into being "the Goliath of *a* party," even as he—and others— knew that it was not his party. Perhaps he underestimated the dangers and consequences. Certainly he worked so hard and became so absorbed in the issues that the personal and professional costs, when they came, were the greater and the more disconcerting. At a time when Swift was withdrawing, first psychologically and then physically, Defoe was increasing his output and arguing more intensely. Once again, his actions contributed to circumstances beyond his control, and he found himself misunderstood and further isolated.

⁂

Defoe has been called a team of government writers by himself;[2] until the last few months of Anne's reign, his pamphlets are from the points of view of, and addressed to, groups ranging from the most opposition Whigs to the most moderate Tories. He did not develop his various stances and angles; he used them from the moment it was clear that the Sacheverell trial meant a Tory government. In 1710–1711 Defoe's Sacheverell papers evolve into his attacks on the October Club and other Tory extremists as he attempts to encourage the election of moderate men and to reassure the Whigs and Dissenters that Harley meant to make few changes. *Review* essays on credit and pamphlets such as *An Essay upon Publick Credit* and *An Essay upon Loans* explain the nation's economic system, praise its advantages, and give nonpartisan reasons to support it. A few essays and pamphlets discuss the change of ministry, and here Defoe usually limits himself to characterizing the new leaders favorably and arguing again that no radical changes in policy would be made, especially as regards the succession and the Dissenters. Not only can he not bring himself to attack Godolphin's administration, but he often compliments or defends it. In *The Re-representation: Or, a Modest Search after the Great* PLUNDERERS *of the* NATION (1711), for example, he takes to task those who describe the Godolphin ministry as dishonest; it is guilty, he says, of no worse than deficit spending, which it could not avoid because of the necessity of carrying on the war (32–39). However, Defoe always supports the monarch's right to change ministers, and his access to Harley made the 1710 change, on balance, desirable to him.

From beginning to end, the Harley ministry rested upon the High Church Tory landslide that followed Sacheverell, and neither Harley nor Defoe could ever feel anything but aversion for most of the party.[3]

Out of expediency as well as principle, Harley attempted to hold as moderate a course as possible and to maintain, at least with the Dutch, a working relationship with the Allies. By so doing, he enraged the extreme Tories who wanted faster and more decided action.

The Sacheverell trial had polarized Englishmen more than Harley and Defoe realized. The name-calling and divisions that had begun over the trial persisted; in fact, divergent groups became more insular and demanded more conformity from their members. Everything and everybody came to wear a label—Church of England clergymen, politicians at every level, merchants, and even printers. People refused to eat with "enemies"; women wore "party patches" and men colored scarves;* Whigs avidly read Whig papers and Tories Tory ones in order to collect support for their opinions and to hear the latest insults aimed at their rivals.

Whether from necessity or cleverness, Defoe used the reputations of booksellers to help reach his chosen audience. For example, he addressed his established Whig audience through the *Review* and several pamphlets carefully labeled "By the Author of the *Review*."[4] These essays purport to weigh and balance how much changed circumstances—the death of Emperor Joseph, France's visible weakness, the allies' diverging interests, England's economic problems—justify the renunciation of "no peace without Spain" and the present negotiations. They repeat that England (and Defoe) are neither pusillanimous nor dishonorable; circumstances have changed and England has attained her ends, they say. Defoe repeatedly quotes speeches and documents. He reminds his readers that Parliament voted, and, *at the time*, the queen agreed, that Louis XIV's grandson must not rule Spain. The demand was, however, no part of the Grand Alliance, he argues, and suggests that the same Parliament faced with Spain's union with the Empire would probably vote against the same resolution.[5] He points out that the "exorbitant power" of France is gone, the balance of Europe established, and enough territory taken to assure the security of England and the allies. These works sometimes praise King William's concept of barriers and interpret the war as efforts "to secure the Liberty and Religion of the Protestants" in Europe, both extremely distinctive, long-term characteristic ideas in all of Defoe's essays.[6]

Most similar to the *Review*, these pamphlets are chiefly those published by the printer of the *Review*, John Baker.[7] The most numerous group of Defoe's tracts, they include *Reasons Why This Nation Ought to Put a Speedy End to This Expensive War, Reasons Why a Party among Us . . .*

---

*Perhaps more in satires than in fact, women wore beauty spots as described in *Spectator* no. 81 (2 June 1711), and both sexes wore party colors (yellow being the color of the House of Hanover).

(advertised as by the author of the first tract), *A Defence of the Allies, An Essay on the Treaty of Commerce with France, An Enquiry into the Danger . . . of a War with the Dutch, And What if the Pretender Should Come?* and at least a dozen more. Except for the earliest of these, the pamphlets are solidly Whig and often attack Tory publications or writers by name. For example, *Armageddon* attacks the *Post-Boy*, the paper universally acknowledged to be "the ministerial paper."[8]

These essays are Whiggish in their concern for trade, their general support for the allies (especially the Dutch), their passionate opposition to the Jacobites, and their insistence that the Whigs are not opposed to peace. They warn against party extremism, against anything less than than a vigilant, full commitment to the Hanoverian succession, and against settling for disadvantageous peace terms. For example, *An Enquiry into the Danger . . . of a War with the Dutch* (1712) begins by stressing the negative effects such a war would have on trade, mentions the "Protestant interest" and the Hanoverian succession, and concludes, "the present Popular Cry against the *Dutch* is a sad Token of the Growth and Encrease of *Jacobitism* among Us" (40). Such gathering of the watchwords and interests of the Whigs in a single pamphlet came with reassurances that it was "obvious" "that it is not the Inclination of the Ministry to break with the *Dutch*" (32) and that the long-desired, good peace was within reach. These pamphlets frankly lamented past failures to make peace but cautioned against too much haste and willingness to compromise with the French, thereby modifying Harley's "double game" for the Whigs. In stressing the discussion of trade, Defoe could point out what England would gain, how her interests were different from those of the allies, and could strengthen his arguments for giving up demands to put the archduke Charles on the Spanish throne by explaining that Spain and France were natural trading rivals and therefore unlikely to hurt English interests.[9]

In harmony with his moderate stance, Defoe frequently derides critics of the ministry as extremists and dishonest alarmists. In tones of reason and faint condescension, he explains that the preliminaries are "no more than . . . Proposals from the Enemy" and insists that they were communicated to the allies promptly and properly. He reviews English history in order to affirm his belief that the nation always "awakes once more" out of its credulity and shakes off those who would impose on the people.[10] He reminds readers of the strength of the English constitution and national character and recommends fortitude, patience, and common sense. Some of these pamphlets are light in tone and use an amusing news story to advance a propagandistic point. For example, at the height of the campaign to get the Dutch to cooperate in the peace negotiations, Defoe examines the reports of quarrels among the footmen at Utrecht and complains that the Dutch and French cannot be very concerned about peace if they are willing to disrupt the negotiations over trivialities.[11] Some of the Baker pamphlets rise to emotional exclamation, pulpit oratory, and exhortation. "O thou Nation famous for espousing Religion, and defending Liberty," he begins *A Seasonable Warning . . . against the Insinuations of . . . Jacobites*. "Let us reason a little together," "For God's sake *Brittains*! what are ye doing?" and "*O Jerusalem! Jerusalem!*" he writes and conjures up an image of "Swarms of Popish Priests from Abroad, and *Jacobite* Emissaries at Home . . . busily employ'd to carry on these wicked Designs; how in Disguise they run up and down the Countries, mingling themselves in all Companies, and in Coffee-Houses, and private Conversation . . . to prepare you for receiving [the Pretender]" (15).

These pamphlets published by Baker use a rich variety of tones, rhetorical strategies, and satiric techniques. Sure of their audience and familiar in address, they badger, cajole, and instruct their readers. Defoe is never far beneath the surface. He will quote his own work, recommend it, and make tongue-in-cheek comments such as "For we are told by the Author of the *Review*, and that is an Authority not to be question'd."

By January 1710 pamphlets like the *Reasons Why* ones were published by "The Booksellers of London and Westminster" or simply labeled "Printed in the Year. . . ." Among these were *No Queen: or, No General*, which explained why Marlborough had to be replaced, and *The Present Negotiations of Peace Vindicated*, which answered procedural objections to the negotiations. These pamphlets, too, attacked Swift and other Tory writers, but they also criticized the Junto specifically and took a harsher stand on the failure of the 1709 peace talks, on Marlborough, on the critics of the new negotiations, and on the Whigs in particular. For instance, *The Conduct of Parties in England* accused the Whigs of introducing all of the charges against Marlborough that the press now reported; Defoe traced them to the Junto struggle for power against Godolphin and concluded with a rapier thrust at the Whigs' recent alliance with the Tories to pass the occasional conformity bill: "The Dissenters cannot wonder that these Men have delivered them up . . . the Dissenters . . . ought to wonder at themselves, that they should put their Confidence so far in Men, who had but a Year or two before testified so plainly they could join with any Body . . . to get themselves into the Publick Places, Profits."[12] These tracts stated bluntly that things had gone so badly for the English military in Spain that there was no hope that Spain's Philip could be forced to give up his throne. While the Baker pamphlets argued that England should no longer want Philip to abdicate, these stated coldly that Spain had been lost on the battlefield. Now and then, these pamphlets "correct" the *Review*: "Let us expostulate a little with the *Review*, or his Party," one says.

These pamphlets, like some of those done for Baker, often carry an insidious, artfully disguised second message. For example, *The Conduct of Parties*, even though the old Whigs and extreme Tories are Defoe's purported subject, repeats all of the pejoratives spewed at Marlborough ("Insatiable, Tyrannical Tory in Disguise, Ambitious" [19]) and repeats the opinion that his profits reach £80,000 a year. Similarly, Defoe had reminded England of the costs of the war, the meager gains, and the advantages to the Dutch even as he declared his purpose to be to defend the Dutch against Swift's *Conduct of the Allies*. Moreover, simply by refuting Swift's assertion in *Conduct* that England was not the "Principle" [*sic*] but only an "Auxiliary" in the war, Defoe strengthened the ministry's case for making a separate peace. Sometimes the implications of a sentence expand and expand under analysis. In *Reasons against Fighting* Defoe projects what the duke of Ormonde (Marlborough's replacement as captain-general of the allied army) might have answered when questioned about his orders not to fight. He might, Defoe says, have been justified in replying, "They were there to fight when Probable Occasions presented . . . but not *Alamode de Blaregnies,** to sacrifice the Lives . . . of Men to the Glory of a General . . . for the meer Name of a Victory, as was done at *Malplacquet*" (18). With the allusion to Malplaquet, Defoe reminded England of the cost of the last big victory, tarnished Marlborough's reputation again, and aroused England's war-weariness.

Yet another set published simultaneously approximated some of the Tory arguments for carrying out separate negotiations. These were published by John Morphew, the Tory *Examiner*'s chief bookseller, and, as his, could be advertised where they would be sure to attract the same readers as Swift's. At first these pamphlets drew upon themes from Swift's *Examiner* as *A Further Search* had, but they came to be another means for Defoe to explain and champion the terms of the Utrecht treaties. By then a group of Tories called the "whimsicals" and led by Sir Thomas Hanmer had begun voting occasionally with the Whigs. Both more solidly Hanoverian and more moderate than most of the Tories then in Parliament, they were a natural group to whom Defoe might address propaganda. This group of pamphlets included *Peace, or Poverty*, *A Further Search into the Conduct of the Allies*, and the allegorical *Memoirs of Count Tariff*. The most quotable anti-Dutch statements appeared over and over: "We have been greatly Impoverish'd, and they exceedingly Enrich'd by the War"; "[the] North Seas Service [was]

---

*The British and Dutch encampment at the battle of Malplaquet where so many of their men died. The crack Dutch infantry was all but destroyed, and the British counted 600 of their men killed and 1,300 wounded.

wholly and solely a Work of Interest, Protecting their own Commerce [and] Fishing."[13]

Defoe's vicious ridicule of the Whigs extends the themes of his attacks in other pamphlets. They say they will ruin credit, he jeers, "yet they can no more forbear, than a Vulture can forbear his Prey; the Funds are the Carkass [*sic*] they feed on . . . in spight of their Faith, often Pledg'd to their Party and Friends, . . . to . . . lend no Money, let but the Ministry find a Fund, and the Parliament establish a Lottery, or Subscription, or Loan, and they are ready to trample one another to Death to get in their Money."[14] The fact that the Whigs had traded the Dissenters' interests away and gone in league with Nottingham to pass the occasional conformity bill makes the writing of such attacks easy for Defoe. Since *The Consolidator* in 1705 Defoe had tried to get his people to unite and impose economic sanctions, and he had suggested it again in 1712 in *Wise as Serpents*. Surely Defoe still identified with the Whigs and Dissenters, but now he expressed the angry side of his ambivalent feelings about their recent behavior in the abusive "like vultures unable to forbear their prey."

౷

That Defoe would become the object of attacks by every segment of the press was inevitable. During the Sacheverell prosecution both Whigs and Tories recruited able writers and a variety of hacks. As time passed both sides drew additional writers, and politicians and gentlemen who had never thought of publishing propaganda did so. Defoe, first caught in Harley's position as a moderate between the impatient Tories and the displaced Whigs, and then as the "team of writers" publishing from several points of view, found himself attacked as never before. On a single day he might be skewered as a Tory and roasted as a Whig. For instance, the Tory *Moderator* accused him of sowing sedition and "ripening" a fruitful harvest of rebellion. The Whig author of *Two Letters concerning the Author of the Examiner* put him in a "class" of writers who "tend to the Corruption of our Morals, the Subversion of Religion, the enslaving of the Nation, the betraying of our Constitution, the ruining of our Trade, and the slandering of Men of Merit"; in this group he included the authors of *A Tale of a Tub*, the *Examiner*, *The Conduct of the Allies*, the *Review* and the *Mercator*. "The *Review*, who was last Winter an Eminent Jockey at *Utrecht*, now (like Prince *Almanzor*) attacks sometimes his Foes, and sometimes his Friends," the author of *The Infernal Congress* complained.[15] Defoe protested "almost every Book being called mine, as well one Side as the other" forced him to defend himself repeatedly. The *Review* and some of his pamphlets challenge his readers to find contradictions, and he explains the principles behind his positions endlessly. Time after time he repeats the equivalent of these sentences from *Some Thoughts upon . . . Commerce with France* (1713) and the last *Review*s:

These are my Reasons . . . and I have set them down with as much Clearness and Impartiallity as I can. . . .

I have here given my Reasons for my present Opinion . . . which I have done rather as a Testimony to future Times of the Foundation upon which my said Opinion is grounded, and to Answer the Calumnies . . . than from any prospect I have, that the soundest Reasoning will allay the Ferment which the Parties . . . have unhappily put the Nation into.

Find any Change of Principle in all I have written. . . .

Let no Man say this is a new Thought of mine, imposed upon the World just now, or written to please anybody.

Defoe had more to fear than slanderous statements. By his account, he received threatening letters and had trouble publishing and distributing the *Review* on schedule. In the preface to volume 6, he calls his would-be "assassins" cowards and chides them for naming the day and the "very Manner" by which they intended to kill him, "yet not one of them has been so good as his Word." The letters and coffeehouse threats could not be entirely dismissed, however; some of them named other journalists as precedents, including John Tutchin, who had been beaten to death. The 21 March 1710 *Review* carried an advertisement explaining that the "Industry . . . of a Party to whom it is particularly Grievous to hear too much Truth" had suppressed the paper, but that in future *Review*s would be available at two bookshops as well as at the regular places. Very shortly after that, he had to transfer the *Review* to Baker: "Behold a Party of the Run-aways of the defeated *High-Church* Army falling upon Mr. *M* . . . the honest Publisher of this—have taken him Prisoner of War, and the Man being entirely in their Custody, and consequently not *sui Juris*, you are to expect no more *Review*s from his Hand." This essay and a long advertisement printed in the 14 March 1710 Edinburgh *Review* listed other attempts made by "the party" to suppress the *Review*. Defoe portrays "the Courts of Justice, Benches of Justices, Grand Juries, and Superior Powers" as teased and importuned by dishonest complaints against him. Even foreign ambassadors have been incited to complain,[16] he says.

Defoe's family had to be concerned over the way things were. His brother-in-law fought with a pewterer and muster master named Silk over one of the *Review*'s columns. Defoe had written that an "Impudent Officer . . . a Scandal to the Lieutenancy, and a Reproach to the City of *London*; who Marching through the City on his gew-gaw Cavalcade, at the Head of the *London* Trained Bands, caus'd his Haut-Boys to play the Tune of *The King shall enjoy his own again*" and thus insulted the queen far more than the woman who had presented a medal of the Pretender to the Scottish Faculty of Advocates (8:283). Samuel Tuffley and Silk happened to be in the same place, exchanged insults over the column, and ended up fighting a ludicrous duel. According the local papers, both were rather drunk, Tuffley slipped during the fight, and Silk took his sword and gave it to an onlooker. Tuffley was enraged by that action and hit Silk over the head with a cane. The papers disputed who won the fight that resulted.[17]

From his youth, when he carried a "Protestant flail," Defoe himself never lacked physical courage, and all of his responses to threats are consistent. He says his assailants would dare not attack him except at night or from behind; he tells anecdotes of confronting men even as they amused themselves with fantasies of beating him; and he insists that, on all occasions, he "has appear'd, whether in Courts of Justice, or at the respective Offices of Her Majesties Secretaries of State, or at any Place where any of these pretended Complaints have been made." In the first *Review* after the kidnapping of Matthews, he attacked the High Church party in one of the most imaginative satires of his career. Uncharacteristically fictional and witty, this paper describes the outcome of the victory of the Constitution over High Church in an allegorical battle. Some of the High Churchmen are depicted in retreat by quoted verses, "Still as he run he curst, but as he curst he run"; others as following the scriptural admonition "Master, save thy self." Many were wounded in the *back* of the head, and, he says, had they had brains, they would have been killed. The satiric density is unusual for Defoe. For instance, he could count on his audience to recognize the context for "save thy self" and to remember Christ's response. He explains changes in city politics by the "Astronomical and Geographical Position or Situation of the L[ord] M[ayor']s Horses Tail," an accurate forecaster because of the "exact Communication" between the mayor's brain and his horse's "farther End." He concludes the essay with the promise of fifteen new volumes from the author of the *Consolidator* that will explain such things as new inventions (devised to serve the queen by destroying meeting houses, to increase trade by tumult, and to aid the City by undermining credit) (*Review* 7:53–56).

Defoe's defiance came partly from Harley's backing, his own experience, and his natural courage and partly from his convictions about his mission. He often quoted the maxim "The Cur that barks is not the Cur that bites." More significant, however, is his faith in his place in a providential world:

I firmly believe, it will not please GOD to deliver me up to this bloody and ungodly Party; and therefore I . . . shall still go on to detect and expose a vicious Clergy, and a bigotted Race of the People, in order to reclaim and

reform them, or to open the Eyes of the good People of *Britain* . . . whether in
this Work I meet with Punishment or Praise, Safety or Hazard, Life or Death,
TE DEUM LAUDAMUS

Here he affirms his belief that all things happen at God's will; only if it
"pleased God," if God took action, would Defoe be "delivered up." He
could admit in the same preface that he and the *Review* were insignificant, but his cause, the defense of the Protestant religion in England,
was one God would defend (*Review* 6: preface). To these defiant statements, he consistently affixed his initials, "D.F."

In 1703 Defoe had confessed he lacked "passive courage," and 1713
almost tested it again. In March 1713 one of his creditors began an
action against him for an old debt of £1,500. The debt went back to
Defoe's 1691 bankruptcy and seems not to have been adjudicated to the
creditor's satisfaction then or in the summer of 1706. Defoe explained
that the debt, contracted to a Yarmouth citizen, had not been settled
because the man believed others had been paid a higher percentage
than he. On 23 March Defoe was arrested on an escape warrant and
sent to prison. At first he tried to negotiate a settlement on his own. A
week later, however, he appealed to Harley for help, and, after eleven
days in prison, came to terms with the creditor, paid his fees, and was
released. Defoe insisted that the Yarmouth man had been set on him by
his journalistic rivals and that he had agreed to 10 percent of the debt,
but stories circulated that Harley had paid the entire £1,500 for him.[18]

Only a few days later his journalistic rivals finally managed to have
him arrested for something he had written. Defoe had just published
three pamphlets with eye-catching titles: *Reasons against the Succession of
the House of Hanover, And What if the Pretender Should Come?* and *An
Answer to a Question That No Body Thinks of, viz. But What if the Queen
Should Die?* Since the Jacobites seemed to be increasing daily, since
many people feared a successful invasion by the French-supported
Pretender, and since the ailing queen might die at any time, these
pamphlets sold vigorously. Their titles were but bait to attract Tory
readers, for all three urged people to unite to assure the Protestant
succession. The first two included heavily ironic rhetorical questions
such as, "Had we not much better deny our God, our Baptism, our
Religion and our Lives, than deny our lawful Prince, our next Male in a
Right Line?"[19]

Just as *The Shortest-Way* had mimicked High Church rhetoric in 1703
in order to attract Tory readers, so the title of the first, *Reasons against
the Succession of the House of Hanover*, and the subtitle of the second, *Or,
Some Considerations of the Advantages* . . . seemed to be theirs. The other
title was absolutely comic, for *everyone* was thinking of the question.
Defoe described his method as giving "a Turn in all I Wrot, which

should gratifye Some of the Weaknesses of those poor people, to Detect the Rest" (H 407). Unlike *The Shortest-Way*, however, these pamphlets made no attempt to imitate the language of the High Church writers. In irony so blatant as to approach sarcasm, they argued that the Pretender would teach them the meaning of slavery and would bring tranquillity to England with such remedies as "easing them of the trouble of chooseing Parliaments."

A minor Whig writer, William Benson, in collaboration with two other Whigs (Thomas Burnet and George Ridpath), filed a complaint against Defoe before Lord Chief Justice Thomas Parker. All of them under prosecution for seditious libel, they resented the ministry's protected writer and hoped to embarrass him and his patrons by putting him in the position they were in. At Benson's suggestion, Parker issued a warrant for the printer, Richard Janeway. On 10 April Janeway not only cooperated but brought in his own workers and implicated the publisher, John Baker. On their evidence, Parker issued a warrant for Defoe, which was executed on the eleventh, a Saturday morning. Defoe was forced to remain in Newgate until Tuesday, when he was able to appear to post bail. On 15 April Parker sent Bolingbroke copies of the pamphlets and the "informations" (statements made by witnesses) with the suggestion that it would be "for the Honour of her Majesty and the Ministry" for the attorney general to prosecute the case at the queen's expense.[20] Bolingbroke took the information to the queen, but she had already ordered Dartmouth to have Defoe prosecuted. On 20 April Bolingbroke wrote Parker to tell him that and to thank him for bringing pamphlets that he had not seen to his attention. On the same day Dartmouth informed his cabinet of the prosecution.[21]

At first Defoe was highly incensed. The arrest came as a complete surprise to him, and everything about it seemed infuriatingly orchestrated. At that time Defoe spent many nights of the week in an apartment in the Temple, but he was arrested on a peaceful Saturday morning at his home in Stoke Newington, then a suburban retreat for successful City merchants. In fact, he was in the middle of a report to Harley.[22] What infuriated Defoe was that Janeway's messenger boy had led the tipstaff to his house the night before so that they could recognize it and him when they came back the next day with a "cavalcade" and as much "clamour" as possible (*Review* 9:169). Moreover, Defoe believed that Benson had tricked Janeway into revealing himself to be the printer by pretending he wanted a large enough number of the pamphlets to warrant another printing. Because Benson kept talking of a charge of treason, Janeway and others were intimidated.

Defoe wrote to Harley to let him know what had happened and was careful to mention the possible charge of treason, for it was not bailable. In fact, Benson tried to have Defoe's sureties disqualified, and the bail was set at an unusually high £1,600. Fortunately, William Borrett, solicitor general of the Treasury under Lord Treasurer Harley, appeared and asserted firmly that the sureties were adequate.

Ridpath immediately published a sensational account of the arrest.[23] In his version, the officers had had "to take Constables and a great many other Persons to their Assistance" in order to break Defoe's door down and take him by force. Only "with much Difficulty and Hazard" had they succeeded, the paper read. Instead of being proud that a fifty-three-year-old man with a severe chest cold could put up such resistance, Defoe's outrage increased. Not only had he opened the door, he said, but he had been allowed to ride his own horse to Newgate while the tipstaff walked. "Nothing had been easier than for me to have rid away from them all, if I had thought of it; but I had not Guilt enough to make me think of an Escape," he sniffed (9:170).

Defoe soon realized what kind of opponents he had. Benson was a member of the Hanover Club, the Whig propagandists' club for men "of Figure and Fortune," which included Steele, Addison, Horace Walpole, and Ambrose Philips. He was under prosecution for *A Letter to Sir Jacob Banks*, an enormously popular pamphlet that had sold 60,000 copies in London and been reprinted in Dublin, Edinburgh, France, Germany, and Holland. His bail was set at £4,000, and the government harassed him by calling him to frequent court appearances but, allegedly, lacked evidence to convict him. Burnet, the son of the bishop, was under indictment for a pro-Marlborough tract called *A Certain Information of a Certain Discourse*, and Ridpath for several numbers of *The Flying Post*. As one contemporary said, they spared neither pains nor expense. In fact, Benson allegedly offered Attorney General Edward Northey ten guineas as a retainer to prosecute Defoe.

Defoe wrote Harley on 19 April that he believed that the government should move to prosecute when he appeared in court to answer on the first day of term (H 409-12). Should the government not, Benson could then bring in an information and do it himself. Should this happen, the ministry would be embarrassed, the prosecution would be hard to stop, and he, Defoe, would be ruined because his authorship could not be hidden.

When he appeared at the Queen's Bench on 22 April, the first day of Easter term, Northey entered the crown's intention to prosecute, and Defoe was continued on his recognizance until the next term. Before he left the court, however, Parker asked Defoe if he were the author of the *Review*s for 16 and 18 April, the ones carrying his enraged description of his arrest. Defoe admitted authorship, and Parker turned them over to the other judges who ruled them insolent to Parker and "a notorious Contempt" to the court and the nation. They committed Defoe to the Queen's Bench Prison for publishing them. Defoe petitioned Parker and the court for pardon and, after publishing an apology and his petitions "at their command" in the *Review*s of 28 April and 5 May, he was fined the token fee of 3s. 6d. and released.[24]

Defoe's indignation never died, and the situation became more serious. The indictment read when Defoe appeared at the opening session of Trinity term might have angered him further had consternation not been foremost. After the usual string of phrases labeling him "a seditious and malicious man" and a "disturber of the peace and tranquillity of the realm," Attorney General Northey began quoting the obligatory string of seditious sentences into the record:

containing among divers other scandalous and malicious materials, to wit in one part according to the following tenor videlt: The Author of the Review one of the most furious opposers of the name and interest of the Pretender . . . openly grants his legitimacy and pretends to argue against his admission from Principles and foundations of his own forming[.] we shall let alone his Principles and Foundations here as we do his Arguments and only take him by the handle . . . that he grants the person of the Pretender . . . legitimate.[25]

Defoe had written that sentence to expose the dishonest methods of argument used by his Jacobite adversaries. His point had been that, because of the Revolution settlement, the Pretender's legitimacy did not matter at all—what mattered were "principles and foundations" the Jacobites had to "let alone" or undermine their position by admitting. Moreover, to hear his description of the *Review* as "one of the most furious opposers" of the Pretender—a description he was proud to own—used against him as though, among other things, the *Review* were also being slandered in the pamphlets at issue, must have struck him as mad.

The indictment accused him of being a Jacobite intent upon casting doubt on Anne's title and "subverting" the Protestant succession. By operating within a very short historical context, by omitting Defoe's explanations, and by quoting topic sentences without their ironic, "supporting" examples, the attorney general made a devastating case against Defoe. In fact, English law had established long ago that irony was no defense. For example, the indictment quoted a section on Scotland from *And What if the Pretender Should Come?*

We shall begin with our Brethren of Scotland and there we may tell them that they of all the people of this Island (meaning the Island of Great Britain) shall receive the most evident advantages in that the setting the Pretender (meaning the said person etc.) upon the throne (meaning the throne of Great Britian) shall effectually set them free from the bondage they will groan under in their abhor'd Subjection to England by the union which may no question be declared void and dissolv'd as a violence upon the Scottish Nation.[26]

Because the Scots M.P.'s had introduced a bill to dissolve the Union that very spring, it was easy to interpret Defoe's sentence as sowing sedition

and working against the harmony of Great Britain. The facts that the
desire to settle the succession on a Protestant heir was a major reason in
1707 for support of the Union in Scotland as well as England and that
the bill introduced in 1713 to dissolve the Union had a forceful clause
guaranteeing the succession were ignored. In another place, the indictment merely quotes a summary sentence from *Reasons against the Succession of the House of Hanover*: "These are some good reasons why the
Succession of the House of Hanover . . . should not be our present . . .
view." Immediately before, Defoe had criticized the divisions among
Englishmen as crippling their ability to defend the Protestant succession should they need to. Without their context within the pamphlet,
other sentences were alarming in themselves. For instance, one from
Reasons against the Succession says, "After soe long and so cruel a war
none can think of entring upon a new war for the Succession without
great regret and horror." Another from *And What if the Queen Should
Die?* remarks upon "what a state of Confusion distress and all sorts of
dreadful Calamitties they will fall into at her majesties death." The
indictment neglects to add that Defoe says this situation will occur only
if people are not prepared and united. In some cases the recommendation of protective measures or explanations of English patriotism have
been omitted; in others the ironic sentences that precede or follow
them.[27]

The case was bound over again, and Defoe assumed it would be
dropped. In October, however, he received notice to appear and plead.
The evidence that he had indeed written the pamphlet and "caused it
to be published" was conclusive. Solicitor General Borrett advised him
to petition the queen for pardon, and with obvious chagrin he did so.
His petition states his intention as "to Propagate The Intrest of the
Hannover Succession and to Animate The people against The designs
of the Pretender" and quotes a number of sentences to illustrate his
ironic mode. Throughout October Defoe found himself harassed by
the prosecution. Borrett continued to warn him that he needed the
pardon before he had to plead on the first day of term.[28] On 26 October Defoe quoted Borrett as saying that Northey was "Timerous and
Cautious to a Fault" and that Defoe needed the pardon; on the twenty-
eighth, he reported that Borrett had said, "If it be Delayed a Very little
longer It will be my [Defoe's] Ruine." That fall Harley, devastated by
the death of his daughter, drank heavily, and seemed to put everything
off. Finally, on 18 November Defoe thanked Harley for his deliverance
but had to remind Harley that he could not afford the fees for the
pardon and to ask that Borrett be empowered to take care of the
expense. Northey's draft of the pardon, dated 17 November, had gone
to Bolingbroke, who was with the queen at Windsor. On 20 November

11.

To The Queens Most Excellent Majesty

The Humble Peticõn of Daniel de Foe

Sheweth

205

That yor Peticoner wth a sincere design to Propogate The Intrest of the
Hannover Succession and to Animate The people against The designs of the Pretender
who he allways look'd on as an Enemy to yor Maj:[ties] Sacred Person and Government did
Publish severall Pamphlets Perticularly One Intituled Reasons against The Hannover
Succession, what if The Pretender should come, and Others

In all which books altho' The Titles seemed to look as if written in favour of the
Pretender and sundry Expressions, as in all Ironicall writing it Must be, May be
Wrested Against the True Design of the whole; and turned to a Meaning quite different
From y[e] Intencon of the Author; yet yo[r] Peticoner Humbly Assures yo[r] Maj:[tie] in The
Solemnest Manner Possible, That his True and Onely Design in all y[e] said books was by
an Ironicall Discourse of Recommending The Pretender, In The Strongest and Most forcible
Manner to Expose his designs, and the Ruinous Consequences of his Succeeding Therein.

And yo[r] Peticoner Humbly hopes The Truth of this will appear to yo[r] Maj:[ties] Satisfac
:tion, by The books Themselves, where The following Expressions are Very plain (Viz)
That The Pretender is Recomended as a Person proper to Amass The English Liberties
into his Own Soveraignty; Supply Them wth The privileges of wearing Wooden shoes,
easing Them of The Trouble of Choosing Parliaments, and The Gentry and Nobillity
of The hazard and Expence of Winter Journeys; By Governing them in that More
Righteous Method of his Absolute Will, and Enforcing his Laws by a Glorious standing Army,
Paying all The Nacons Debts at Once by stopping the funds, and Shutting up the Excheq:
easing and quieting Their Differences in Religion, by bring them to The Union of Popery
Or leaving Them at Liberty to have no Religion at all: and The like

These May it Please yo[r] Maj:[tie] are some of the Very Expressions in y[e] said Books, w[ch] yo[r] Peticoner
Sincerely desired to Expose and Oppose as far as in him lyes The Intrest of the Pretend[er] and with No other
Intencon; Nevertheless yo[r] Peticoner to his great Surprize has been Misrepresented, and y[e] said
Book Missconstrued, as if written in favo[r] of the Pretender and yo[r] Peticoner is Now Under
Prosecucon for The same, w[ch] Prosecution if farther Carryed On will be The Utter Ruine of
your Peticoner, and his Numerous Family.

Wherefore yo[r] Peticoner Humbly Assuring yo[r] Maj:[tie] of the Innocence of his
Design as Aforesaid, Flyes to yo[r] Maj:[ties] Clemency, and most Humbly Implores
yo[r] Maj:[ties] Most Gracious, and Free Pardon.

And yo[r] Peticon[er] shall Ever Pray &c.

Defoe's petition to Queen Anne, in his own hand.

Bolingbroke signed a copy and sent it back to Northey with directions that the pardon be dated 27 November.

Defoe had cautioned Harley at least twice regarding the pardon. He wanted to be sure it was so full that Benson and his confederates could not assume the prosecution. As drafted, the pardon was to include the offense and "all Indictments, Convictions, Pains, Penalties, & Forfeitures incurred" with "such apt & beneficial Clauses" necessary to make the pardon "more full, valid & effectual." The Queen's Bench records show that the attorney general duly entered the Noli Prosequi, and Defoe received the pardon with the royal seal on 3 December.[29]

~❧~

Some of the personal consequences of the years of journalistic controversy unfolded gradually and without the drama of an arrest but may have had deeper resonance. For instance, Defoe came to be in conflict with men whose writing he had always respected. The eighteenth century is unique in that almost every major writer wrote political propaganda. By 1710 London supported some twenty political periodicals with a weekly output of 44,000 copies; by 1712 total sales of newspapers alone were between 67,000 and 78,000 copies per week.[30] Between 1710 and 1714 such writing absorbed the major efforts of Defoe's greatest contemporaries, among them Richard Steele. In 1710 Defoe openly admired Steele's work; by 1714 he had cooperated in the effort to oust Steele from the House of Commons.

When Steele started the *Tatler* on 12 August 1709, Defoe's *Review* was the English paper most like it. Both were essay periodicals that absorbed other forms of writing like poetry into their content. Steele's Bickerstaff, like the voice of "Mr. Review," gave the paper unity and a stance carefully designed to appeal to readers. The essays from St. James (those on foreign and national news) dominated the early numbers of the *Tatler*, and Steele felt as free as Defoe to discuss politics, recent events, and his own personal experiences. Bickerstaff once remarked that he "had settled a correspondence in all parts of the known and knowing world,"[31] a close approximation of the sentence Defoe had used occasionally since his travels for Harley in 1705. Both the *Review* and the *Tatler* were clearly influenced by the French *Mercure Galant*, the *petit journal* published by Donneau de Visé in collaboration with Thomas Corneille. At first in the form of a letter to an imaginary woman, the paper presented in a familiar manner the "inside story" from court and literary circles. Steele imitated more of its light material and its confident, familiar tone;[32] he began at once to appeal to the ladies, to depict the beau monde, to set himself up as a literary critic, and to include such amusements as anagrams and riddles. Steele imitated Defoe's old *Mercure Scandal* with its authentic-sounding idiomatic name, too, by including frequent censures of other periodical writers. He and Defoe rebuked other journalists for errors in grammar, syntax, and information—"the tautology, the contradictions, the doubts, and wants of confirmation," as Steele put it. Defoe was more likely to complain about nonsense and impossibilities—how could one man be taken in two towns? Steele's sentences were often more polished, "Where Prince Eugene has slain his thousands, Boyer [editor of the *Protestant Post Boy*] has slain his ten thousands." Both men were also deeply concerned with morals; in its earliest numbers, the *Tatler* included stories aimed at encouraging domestic tranquillity and respect, ridiculed a rake drunk at the theatre, and instructed men on what to value in women. Later Defoe would recognize their shared method in a *Review* comment on the *Spectator:**

I must ask the Readers leave, to reserve a small part of this Paper, to Moralize a little upon such Subjects as come in my Way, both for his Profit and Delight.
 Not that I purpose to put in for *Spectator.* (9:80)

Defoe enjoyed the *Tatler* and even learned from it. His earliest mention of it seems to be on 30 March 1710, when he ends a *Review* with an anagram, "which (as the *Tatler* says) I insert for the Benefit of the Female Readers" (7:7). He began to include more riddles, "énigmes," and fables. He occasionally entered into big-brotherly badinage with Steele:

I have always thought that the weakest Step the *Tatler* ever took, if *that compleat Author may be said to have done any Thing Weak*, was to stoop to take the least Notice of all the Barkings of the little Animals, that have *Condol'd him, Examin'd him*, &c. He should have let Envy bark, and Fools rail, and according to his own Observation of the Fable of the Sun, he had nothing to do but to SHINE ON. (7:449)

Defoe seemed to feel no rivalry and, at the height of the Sacheverell trial, used the *Tatler*, which he had obviously read carefully, as one of the signs of the change in the city: "Nay, the *Tattler* [sic], the Immortal *Tattler*, the Great Esq; *Bikerstaff* [sic] himself, was fain to leave off talking to the Ladies."[33] These witty and unusually strong compliments to a contemporary's work put Steele in a special category.

 Around 20 September 1710 Defoe published *A Condoling Letter to the Tattler: On Account of the Misfortunes of Isaac Bickerstaff, Esq.* The form and tone of this essay are very much like the *Tatler*'s. It begins with the kind of general observation so common in the *Tatler* essays: "Nothing is more remarkable in the Nature of Man . . . than that he never Fails to commit that Crime himself, which he reproves in another." Defoe's

---

*The paper that Steele began in collaboration with Joseph Addison soon after he ended the *Tatler*. Less political, the *Spectator* was a less dangerous paper and an immediate success.

premise is that the *Tatler* would have satirized one who did what Steele
had done: with a "Plentiful Income, no great Family . . . [he ran] himself in Debt, meerly by Luxury, and Profuse Living." Because Steele
called himself the "Censor of Great Britain," Defoe finds his habitual
financial problems contradictory. In October 1709 Steele had begged
Halifax for £150 until his hearing in Chancery because he was in "danger of being torn to peices" by his creditors. Now Steele's recent imprisonment for debt seemed to be a good occasion for Steele to reflect
upon the opening observation and repent.[34] Defoe next moves
through a series of examples from the *Tatler* and concludes by asking if
Steele can "pretend" to honesty or "expect" pity.

As harsh as the content sounds, the tone largely offsets it. Defoe
intended, I believe, to be witty, to imitate Steele, and, above all, to give
him a timely warning. The longest example in the pamphlet draws a
parallel between the hoax Bickerstaff had played on the almanac writer
John Partridge and Steele's imprisonment for debt. In the hoax perpetrated by Swift, Bickerstaff had predicted Partridge's death, then described it, and finally accused Partridge of continuing to publish after
death. Steele had brought the hoax to mind as recently as 26 August by
referring to it in a fictitious advertisement ending, "Beware of counter-
feits" (4:113). Moreover, Defoe may already have been at work on his
British Visions, to be advertised as "Isaac Bickerstaff's 12 Prophecies for
the Year 1711"; the antiwar pamphlet recalled Swift's hoax and deliberately imitated Swift's tone and style. In his *Condoling Letter* Defoe observed that a jail—as he says Steele was in—is "that worst of Graves" and
jokes that Partridge "had a Death without a Grave" and Bickerstaff "a
Grave without Death" (7).

In the second example Defoe argues that George Ridpath's *Flying
Post*, not Jacques de Fonvive's *Post Man*, should be the object of Steele's
ridicule. In echoes of the *Review*'s Scandal Club, the August *Tatler* and
several other recent issues had asked the *Post Man* to explain "dubious"
phrases. The third example remarks that the *Tatler* "has been very
diverting of Late, in the Account he has given us of his *State-Barometers*,
and his *Church-Thermometers* . . . but, I wonder, how he came to make
no Mention of a certain *Oeconomical Barometer*" brought back from
the Moon by "the Author of the *Review*."[35] Defoe points out what he sees
to be a great similarity between his barometer and Steele's Church
Thermometer and comments that it was unlucky that Steele had forgotten that the economical barometer existed and therefore neglected
to use it.

In many ways the pamphlet gives contradictory signals. It is highly
critical of Steele, yet it imitates his distinctive essay style and tone,
participates in the Partridge joke, reminds the reader in two unmistakable ways that Defoe and Steele have written highly similar things, and

even includes an admission that Defoe has committed Steele's error: the narrator of the pamphlet remarks that Defoe "does not seem to have made much Use of [the economical barometer] himself" and Defoe thus becomes a joint object of satire with Steele, for both have "committed the crime they reprove in others." Moreover, in 1704 and 1705 Defoe had written extensively about how unreasonably strict the world was with satirists and reformers whose faults and mistakes are discovered.

Defoe's intention seems to have been to warn Steele about the true nature of pamphlet warfare. At the time he wrote his pamphlet, the *Tatler* had been in a series of exchanges with several Tory papers including the *Moderator* and the *Examiner*; was being harassed by De-larivière Manley in "scandalous chronicles" such as *Memoirs of Europe*; was suspected of depicting Harley as "Polypragmon," who "makes it the whole business of his life to be thought a cunning fellow," and had published two strongly worded papers satirizing party passion. Many of the gestures he described as characteristic of Polypragmon were Harley's. For instance, Cowper said his "humour" was "never to deal clearly or openly, but always with Reserve, if not Dissimulation, or rather Simulation; & to love Tricks even where not necessary," and Swift complained, "an Obstinate Love of Secrecy . . . seems . . . to have some Resemblance of Cunning; For, he *is* not only very retentive of Secrets, but *appears* to be so too." Even Pope, who did not deal with him officially, said that he was "huddled in his thoughts, and obscure in his manner of delivering them." Only a month before, Bolingbroke had sniped at the *Observator, Review*, and *Tatler* in a single sentence in his *Letter to the Examiner*, but he had saved the most cutting remark for the *Tatler*.[36] Defoe could surely see the gathering clouds, and he knew from experience that Steele could expect no pity. Defoe had referred to his own imprisonment as a death and Newgate as a grave, and poverty had put Defoe in prison far more often than seditious libel.

If *A Condoling Letter* is intended as warning, it is not nearly obvious enough. Once again Defoe parodies a form (the *Tatler* essay) so well that his intention is obscured as it was with *The Shortest-Way with the Dissenters*. Moreover, the subject is too personal and moral, the examples too diverse and obscurely related. Steele certainly saw nothing instructive about the tract. In no. 229 for 26 September he alludes to it in a witty essay on how the *Tatler* provides "food" for numerous writers; the *Tatler* is the fox and the oak, while the writers who "annotate," "examine," and "condole" are the fleas and the ivy. In Defoe's mind he was *condoling* because he had been in Steele's position, but on paper he appeared to be like the *Examiner*, hitting Steele at a vulnerable point and criticizing his work as tactless, wrongly directed, and imitative. Steele's reaction is not only understandable in light of Defoe's text but also a sign of Steele's current vulnerability. When Cowper published his *A Letter to Isaac Bickerstaff* praising the *Tatler* as the work of a true patriot and an honest, loyal subject of his queen, Steele responded by dedicating volume 3 of the *Tatler* to Cowper.

Defoe's unique praise for Steele and his publications continued. On 19 May 1711 Defoe described him as "that Universally, and indeed Deservedly approv'd Author"; on 14 August as having "Beauty, Strength, and Clearness"; on 24 January 1712 as "that happy Genius."[37] He begins, however, to find fault and to stake out trade as his own province. Several times he corrects the *Spectator* and insists upon his superior knowledge and understanding. Once, for instance, he refutes the *Spectator*'s picture of England's agriculture, and he remarks in a *Mercator* dig at the *Guardian* that "Knowledge of Trade was not of the Number of his Acquisitions."[38] Increasingly critical of the *Spectator*'s judgment, Defoe will agree, for instance, that the *Spectator* is right to praise Czar Peter I for visiting other countries to learn modern methods but wrong to see him as "a true Hero."[39] He explains that the London ruffians called "*Mohocks*" are named for American, not Asian, Indians (8:613). Around the same time, the *Spectator* (in an essay by Addison) alluded to "the many Discourses . . . [on] Credit," all "defective" because all came from "Party Principles" (1:14).

Perhaps related to Defoe's growing rivalry with Steele is a verse lampoon Defoe wrote to satirize George Plaxton. Party rumor and periodical rivalry increased; Steele began a new periodical called the *Guardian* in March 1713 which he soon used to attack the Peace of Utrecht, the Tories, the *Examiner*, and Swift—and in no. 53 for 12 May, he signed his name and claimed authorship of no. 41, thereby admitting authorship of the two most extreme numbers of the paper. Defoe, who had occasionally criticized the *Examiner* and Swift, might have been expected to remain neutral, and he did until the 7 August *Guardian* when Steele added to the paper's long list of objections to the treaty and the ministry a diatribe against the government's failure to demand that France raze Dunkirk as specified in the treaty. Defoe's anonymous, twenty-page reply, *The Honour and Prerogative of the Queen's Majesty Vindicated . . . in a Letter from a Country Whig to Mr. Steele*, was out only six days later. Introducing himself as an Old Whig and using a good-natured, moderate, somewhat detached tone, the fictitious letter writer began with graceful compliments on the "Charm of your Pen," the "Musick of [the *Guardian*'s] Tongue[,] like *David*'s Harp . . . allay'd the Storm . . . and the Evil Spirit of Contention went out from among us." But now, he continued, "We Whigs" feel "Shame and Grief, in your behalf" because of the 7 August paper (4–5).

The sting of the pamphlet comes from the contrast between the *Guardian*'s achievement—to be recognized as the premier Whig paper—and the offending paper, which, in Defoe's opinion, has made all Whigs vulnerable to the old accusations that they are ungrateful, antimonarchical, rebellious, and rash. Defoe addresses Steele as "you that had obtain'd the good Opinion of both sides . . . who our affected Wits and Polititians stood in awe of" (8) and accuses him of speaking to the queen as "an Imperious Planter at *Barbadoes* speaks to a Negro Slave" (10). He condemns the paper to "the House of Office" (the privy) and tells Steele that, had he been present, he would certainly have been told he belonged there with his paper. One of the few scatological insults in all of Defoe's work, it concludes that Steele belongs in an outhouse rather than in Parliament and warns the voters of the town of Stockbridge, where Steele was running for election to the House of Commons, to beware. Defoe concludes, "Pray, Mr. *Steele*, be so Ingenuous as to tell me whether this be Parliamentary Language?" (16)

The objectionable part of Steele's essay had been a letter addressed to the persona of the *Guardian*, Nestor Ironside, from "English Tory." The letter was obviously fictitious, however, and Defoe and others were correct to sweep aside the interpretation that Steele intended his English Tory to condemn himself out of his own mouth. Indeed, Steele did the same in *The Importance of Dunkirk Consider'd*. The demolition of Dunkirk, promised in the Treaty of Utrecht, was an election issue for Steele and the Whigs. The Dunkirk magistrates were petitioning the queen to save the harbor, and only a few months before the razing was to be completed, none of the work had been started. The Whigs saw Dunkirk both as a notorious harbor for pirates and French privateers and as a gauge of France's intentions to comply with the treaty articles—and England's willingness to insist that it do so. As Steele's letter said, "The *British* Nation received more Damage in their Trade from the Port of *Dunkirk*, than from almost all the Ports of *France*," and its destruction would move France "several hundred Miles further off of *Great Britain*." Robert Walpole's campaign speech similarly linked Dunkirk and the peace treaty: "Her Majesty has been pleas'd to tell us . . . that Dunkirk should be Demolish'd, but not one stone is remov'd . . . And as to the Terms of Peace I dare be bold to affirm that had the King of France beaten us, as we have done Him he would have been so Modest as to have given us better Terms than These we have gain'd after all our Glorious Victories." Defoe himself had called Dunkirk "a Pledge from *France*, That he will not . . . go back from his Offers of Peace."[40]

Defoe pointed the way for the sustained campaign against Steele that would conclude with his ejection from Parliament. Seizing upon Steele's "the British Nation expect," Defoe repeated it often, pointed out its inappropriateness as an address to the queen, set it in several contexts to emphasize its outrageousness, and managed to dramatize it in such vivid ways that it would be long remembered. For example, he translates it into "Madam! WE EXPECT, and we would have you take Notice that we expect it, that *Dunkirk* be Demolish'd" and compares it to "I expect this Sugar to be ground, and . . . that it be done forthwith" (10). Because Steele's tone is so peremptory, it is hard to know exactly when Defoe is quoting Steele and when he is modifying or parodying Steele's sentences. Even this pamphlet might be taken as warning and advice to Steele. Defoe recommends that Steele ask the queen's pardon or identify the author if it were not he. Here "your Practice," Defoe says, "is just the reverse of your Instructions" (22).

Unrepentant, Steele published *The Importance of Dunkirk Consider'd: In Defence of the Guardian of August 7th.* In it, he repeated that the nation did expect the demolition of Dunkirk and portrayed himself as a brave public servant following the "Dictates" of his conscience.[41] He insisted that "laying before her Majesty's Ministry, that the Nation had a strict Eye upon their Behaviour with relation to *Dunkirk*" was done "from a true Grateful, and Loyal Heart" (109). He contrasts what he has done to the "true and real Danger to the Queen's Honour" that those who tolerate abuse of "such Instruments of Glory . . . as . . . *Marlborough*" and "such wise and faithful Managers as . . . *Godolphin*" (110). He called Defoe and Swift "prostituted Pens." Steele ended the *Guardian* on 1 October and began the more flamboyant *Englishman.* This periodical provocatively repeated the motto of the 7 August *Guardian*, "Delenda est Carthago,"* on its first number and often spoke in tones reminiscent of Defoe's own *Legion's Memorial.* As the *Englishman* moved to the subject of the clauses of the commercial treaties ("shall the Crown . . . deliver its self up to the Vanquish'd") the periodical war intensified.

Defoe finally engaged the *Guardian* at the end of September in his periodical, the *Mercator.* In doing so he said he was maintaining his refusal to engage with the "little barking" pens but had joined "Issue with a Man whose Sense and good Manners qualifies him to be a Match for any Man."[42] Purporting to be confident that the *Guardian* would "handsomely yield" when proven "mistaken," Defoe spent four numbers correcting Steele's theories of trade and opinions about such commodities as cloth and wine. These papers occasionally called Steele or his calculations about French trade mistaken, unreasonable, or improbable, but they were never satirical, contemptuous, or abusive. Extremely detailed in their figures and explanations, these *Mercator*s concentrated on what Defoe knew best from his own experience: wool,

---

*The title of a famous speech delivered by the first earl of Shaftesbury at the opening of Parliament in February 1673. The phrase is Cato's and implied that the rivalry between the English and the Dutch was as fundamental as that between the Romans and the Carthaginians. Shaftesbury's speech helped move Parliament to vote supplies to fight the Dutch.

wine, and linen. Only when Steele encroached into Defoe's province, trade, did he criticize the *Guardian* and then only in polite terms.

Steele continued to publish periodical essays and pamphlets under his own name and to develop and heighten his contrasts of the old ministry to the present one. "The Minds of the People, against all common Sense, are debauch'd," Steele says, and goes on to depict post-Marlborough Europe: the French no longer have to bother with "strong Garrisons and Fortify'd Camps," the emperor and Empire fight on alone, the Dutch and Catalonians are betrayed and at risk, the House of Bourbon is more likely to "engross the whole Trade of *Europe*" than before, and Dunkirk is still largely intact. Some of his sentences are almost unbelievably provocative considering the political climate. From evidence such as the government's conduct in making peace and its toleration of "Treasonable Books," Steele concludes that the Hanoverian succession is at risk: "We cannot help it, if so many Thousands of our brave Brethren, who laid down their Lives against the Power of *France*, have dyed in vain; but we may value our Lives dearly, like honest Men. . . . let us struggle to the last Drop of our Blood for its Religion and Liberty."[43]

As Defoe said, if that were not seditious libel, then nothing was, for if, as Steele said, the Protestant succession, guaranteed by law, was endangered, it implied that the queen's government could be charged with maladministration. For months the ministry had been planning Steele's ouster from the Commons, and now it moved quickly. Steele had been associated with the Junto Whigs since the very earliest *Tatlers*. By the time he published *The Crisis* in January 1714, Steele's journalism had added the support of the Hanover Club, the envoy of the elector of Hanover, and the future hopes of the Whig party, Walpole and Stanhope.[44]

Defoe had been urging Harley for months to exert pressure on the Whig press, and when Steele published *The Crisis* and then, a month later, an *Englishman* satirizing Harley by emphasizing that he was a Dissenter supported by a High Church political party, Defoe wrote Harley a strong warning: that "New Champion of The Party," he wrote, is planning to make speeches in Parliament and then print them in order to "bully" the ministry "in as Publick a Manner as possible" (H 429–31). Defoe argued that a move against Steele would be a much-needed check on a political party grown insolent. Within a few weeks Defoe sent Harley a list of legally actionable statements from Steele's recent work. The indictment, issued two days after Harley received Defoe's list, used some of his subheads and was decisively carried 245–152. Steele was expelled from the Commons.

Defoe's action was almost certainly the result of his analysis and, he insisted in his letter to Harley, not primarily expression of personal resentment. His perception of Steele as the "new champion," and his respect for Steele's ability and readership led him to conclude that Steele must be driven from his most influential forum and intimidated if possible. "Who shall be able to stand before the *Guardian?*" Defoe had asked in his first *Mercator* about the *Guardian*. In another place he had referred to "the Witchcraft of his Perswasions." He noted that the Whigs "could not have taken a cunninger Step than . . . to put the Reputation of [Steele] into the Scale with the Argument." In an exceptionally clear-sighted paragraph Defoe asked Steele, "And what is this Dispute for, but to form Interests for and against Persons and Parties, to the Destruction of the publick Peace?"[45] Although Defoe had been quibbling with Steele for a week, sometimes over as little as two pence in their calculations, and taking the propagandist's line that Steele's sums were wrong, his fears groundless, and his effect to be stirring people up "against the best Measures taken to enrich" them, he could stand back and describe exactly what he and Steele were really doing.

As the best-known spokesman for the Whigs against the Treaty of Commerce and Navigation and as a pawn in their efforts to destroy Harley, Steele's influence had to be limited. Defoe respected him as a man of unusual ability, "sense," and "manners," and nothing shows the lamentable effects and contradictions inherent in the party warfare of the last years of Anne's reign so much as Defoe's *A Letter to Mr. Steele*, published in June, just three months after his letters to Harley about Steele. Writing as a Tory in this pamphlet, Defoe seconds Steele's *A Letter to a Member of Parliament concerning the Bill for Preventing the Growth of* SCHISM. Defoe says that he intends to give his reasons for holding, in this one instance, the same opinion that Steele does. This pamphlet shows Defoe still reading Steele with attention and approval, granting him his reputation, and even taking advantage of it in order to attract readers for his own pamphlet. So sure is he of Steele's popularity that he does not bother to print the schism bill but merely notes that it is in Steele's pamphlet (6–7). Here again Defoe refers to Steele as the "Champion of the *Whiggish Cause*" and says he has the reputation "as to stick at nothing . . . to support . . . it." In one of his last periodical essays, the introduction to the *Universal Spectator* (1728), Defoe paid a final tribute to Steele by asking, "Is there no Wit or Humour left . . . ? Is the Spirit of the SPECTATOR all lost, and their Mantle fallen upon no Body?" (Lee 3:466) Defoe never deviated from his estimation of Steele's abilities in 1714 either, but he came increasingly to the opinion that Steele did not always see his actions in a large enough ethical perspective and should "stick at" some things.

☙

As disillusioning as Defoe's changed feelings about Steele were, they could not compare to his fluctuating fortunes with Robert Harley and his progressive disillusionment with the Whigs. From the time of his release from Newgate in 1704, Defoe had felt himself under special obligations to Harley and, as his letters show, had come to believe that he and Harley shared principles, objectives, and a special understanding. His pleasure when Harley regained power and the relief in his first letter seem genuine and even unguarded. When he wrote that he could serve Harley with "Joy" and with "Principle and Inclination" in 1710, he was sincere (H 273, 275). Soon he had nearly daily contact with Harley and almost unlimited chances to influence him. In February 1711 he wrote, "Tho' I Confess the honour you are Pleased to do me in Frequent and long Audience is Very Great, yet Sir, . . . I thought it my Duty to Save as Much as possible of your Time and Trouble by Minuting Down Thus the heads of Things [to be discussed]." Through the spring of 1711 Defoe continued to write reports, answer questions, and meet with Harley. "In Obedience to your Ldpps Commands I have here Enclosed an Abstract" and "I Shall attend On Monday Evening According to your Ldpps Ordr" are familiar sentences. On 19 June, however, he writes, "I am Very Unhappy Not in My Private Affaires Onely, which are . . . Ruinous, from the Discontinuance of your Favor, But in Not haveing The Occasion . . . of Layeing before your Ldpp Severall Matters of Importance Relateing to the Publick."

By this time Harley was busier than ever, was in the midst of complex negotiations, and had other writers, including Jonathan Swift, working for him. Defoe's concerns were not always Harley's. In his letter of 7 June Defoe seems to be becoming aware of some of Harley's dissatisfactions. "I kno' the Inconvenience of Troubling your Ldpp with Tedious preambles" from Scotland, he wrote and offered a list for efficiency's sake, including things that must have seemed completely trivial to Harley at that time: the cases of Mrs. Anderson's printing monopoly, of "Dalziel the Privateer," and of the earl of Hyndford's dragoons.

In early July, however, Defoe was back in frequent contact with Harley and "Putting My Thoughts into writing" as requested. Harley needed him to write about the South Sea Company, and in Defoe's 13 July letter he appears to summarize one of Harley's directions: "How [the South Sea Trade] May be put in Terms not to Give The spaniards any Umbrage and yet carry as good a Face and be as Effectuall at home as if it were otherwise."[46] Here the doubleness of Harley's policy and its reliance on deceptively reassuring appearances are obvious. The frequent contact and familiar correspondence resume. For example, at the end of August 1711 he writes that he will explain something in full when he sees him, "which I Shall attend for as usuall Every Evening."

By 16 October, however, he is saying, "I have My Lord Humbly

addressed your Ldpp and Constantly attended . . . yet hitherto I go
Unsent; your Ldpps Leisure Not Permitting my Audience." The significant thing about the date is that it is only three days after the *Daily
Courant* published the peace preliminaries. In this case Defoe's impor-
tunity comes not from genuine neglect but from other causes. First, he
sees the significance of the preliminaries and the public reaction and
wants to begin his work. "Now is the juncture," he writes, saying he
wants "your Approbation of my thoughts on This head." The lack of
surprise or need for interpretation upon the publication of the preliminaries as well as his late September–early October pamphlets such
as *Reasons Why This Nation*, argue that Defoe knew about them and their
official status. What he wants appears to be permission to "calm" people
in certain ways and with specific explanations and information. Second, he realizes that he is in trouble. The Whigs are now alarmed and
infuriated, and he reminds Harley that he has already "Irritated and
Exasperated" them. "Unless your Ldpp pleases to Take me into your
Protection . . . *I shall One day Fall by The hand of This Saul*," he writes.

Finally, Defoe's tone may come from his awareness of Jonathan Swift
as a rival. His letter also promises effective service and concludes with a
postscript reminding Harley that he "had Success in as hard a Case in
Scotland." Against Swift's satiric power Defoe could offer experience
and proven success. Believing that Swift's tactics would inflame people
and become counterproductive, he may have wanted to employ his own
kind of persuasion as early as possible. Defoe here does speak of his
"Missfortune" and his "Low Station," and there is something abject in
his reminders that he has waited for Harley and will wait again that
night. Harley, of course, wanted Defoe's pen, and Defoe wrote far
more in the cause of peace than Swift. Most of Defoe's anxiety came
from his own feelings rather than from Harley's actions. After all,
Defoe had persuaded Harley to let him continue to meet him secretly at
night rather than publicly in the mornings as Swift did.

Certainly it would have been as disingenuous for Defoe to say of
Swift, as Swift did of him, "I have forgot his name," but Swift, who had
taken the High Church line since 1704, never became a central part of
Defoe's consciousness. Robert Harley was. Again in January 1713, De-
foe wrote, "The Affliction it is to me to have Lost the Favour of being
Admitted to your Ldpp as Usuall I can Not Express." By this time
Defoe had been in and out of close contact with Harley several times.
Whether Harley saw Defoe or not, he could trust him to write what
Harley needed. Although he was capable of bringing Defoe into line by
withholding attention, he usually neglected Defoe when he was busy,
moody, or not in need of special services.

Still, Harley shows some concern for Defoe's feelings and loyalty. At
first he seems to have tried to dissociate himself from actions he knew

would be distasteful to Defoe. In late November 1711, in order to force the renegotiation of the peace treaty with France, the Whigs agreed to support the occasional conformity bill in exchange for Tory votes. This scheme, devised and orchestrated by Defoe's old nemesis Nottingham, worked.* Harley made it a point to tell Defoe about it on 18 December, the day the bill passed in the Lords, and to dissociate himself from it. Defoe confessed himself speechless and distracted by the news and said he looked upon the Dissenters as ruined (H 363–64).

Defoe appealed at once to Harley to try to influence the queen to refuse to give the royal assent to the act and begged the queen to do so in the 22 December *Review*. His outrage toward the "chameleon" Whigs and their "mean" "sacrifice" of the Dissenters to pass Nottingham's amendment knew no bounds. He accused the Whigs of buying peace at the cost of fetters and chains and alleged that the act took "Native Liberties," civil and religious, from the Dissenters; the act was an "Invasion of Property" and "Persecution." He proclaimed himself ready to go to jail again: "God forbid I should cease . . . to Complain of the Injury . . . , if they make it Criminal, I am ready to suffer; but I will never lose my little Share in the Liberties of my Country, without Crying out." "Et tu Brute!" he says to the Whigs and accuses them of selling their friends "for a single worthless Voice, that will desert you." They have "Ruin'd your own Interest, and have lost the Honour of your former Integrity," Defoe tells them, piling up images of the betrayed, sacrificed Dissenters.

Within days of hearing about the deal from Harley, Defoe published *An Essay on the History of Parties, and Persecution in Britain* and circulated "A Speech of a Stone Chimney Piece" in manuscript.[47] The first begins with the Test Act and the rest of the Clarendon Code, records the times "sacred promises" have been broken, and concludes with a summary of the destructive consequences of the Act of Occasional Conformity for the Whigs and the nation. The speech is an effective personification of the chimney in the old House of Lords; the stones, not the Whigs, can weep: they have softer hearts than the Lords.

Similarly, his reaction to the schism bill, which would forbid Dissenting educational academies, was outrage and depression. One contemporary labeled the bill "more like a decree of Julian the apostate, than a law enacted by a Protestant parliament" and compared its sponsors to heathen emperors and the Inquisition.[48] In *A Brief Survey of the Legal Liberties of the Dissenters*, Defoe compared the liberty of teaching one's children to the right to get up in the morning and predicted that the bill would produce martyrs (7–8). By now he expected little from the

---

*The amendment read in part: "No peace could be safe or honourable to Great Britain, or Europe, if Spain and the West-Indies were allotted to any branch of the house of Bourbon."

Whigs, "vultures" willing "to trample one another to Death" to make money, who "could join with any Body . . . to get . . . Profits." And he had learned to be circumspect with Harley by now too; "Last Nights Conversation Could not but afford Many Useful Remarks to Me," his letter on the subject of the bill begins. He adds pacifically, "It is True My Lord The Conduct of The Dissenters has call'd for More Than this" and suggests very indirectly that the bill might be amended to allow the "Common Introduction," the teaching of elementary subjects to young children. In fact, the bill that passed would be amended in just this way. In *The Weakest Go to the Wall* Defoe observes, "If the Tories have led [the ministry] on farther than they intended to go, it must have been because the Tories are become more necessary than they were before. . . . and has [*sic*] driven the Ministry from their first Measures" (40). Defoe believed Harley to be driven, but he obviously lamented the exigencies to which Harley submitted.

By 1714 Defoe called "Our old Friends" the Whigs "pretended Friends" and told Harley flatly that he expected them to "give up" the Dissenters as they had in 1711 when the occasional conformity bill passed. Since 1703 he had universally described the Dissenters as a "People, some of whom would not pull me from under a Cart-Wheel, if they saw me in the Danger of it" and a people unwilling to unite for their own benefit.[49] The growing virulence of his descriptions of the Whigs shows his disillusionment with men with whom he had placed himself since King William's reign.

His association with Harley entered its final scene in the spring of 1713. Twice in a very short time Harley saved Defoe from prison and helped him pay an enormous sum to a creditor. Defoe's gratitude to Harley, perhaps tempered by the nine years of faithful service he had given him, again blazed extravagantly and became a pressing sense of obligation. On 14 April he wrote:

This My Lord is The Third Time I am Rescued from Misery and A jail by your Ldpps Generous and Uncommon Goodness; and This is the goodness for which the Gratitude of This Age Would have me, Against principle, Conscience, Honour, and Gratitude, Maltreat and Abuse you. . . . Unless God and Nature Abandonne me together, it is Impossible I can forbear to Serv your Ldpps person and Intrest, while I live; at what Hazard Soever. (408)

Just at this time Harley's ministry was in crisis. Undermined from within by the disaffected Bolingbroke, Harley's leadership faltered, and few felt much loyalty for the increasingly isolated, secretive, drunken, and erratic Harley.[50]

At this point the Whigs saw that a defeat of the detested Treaty of Commerce and Navigation might be the means to bring down the Tory party as the Sacheverell trial had the Whig one.[51] Defoe joined the battle on Harley's side, and some of their closest collaboration took place over the next few months. Defoe soon realized that the *Review* could not serve his purposes, and in the next few months he invented one propaganda vehicle after another. Beset by one illness after another, hobbled by the gout that would plague him for the rest of his life, Defoe nevertheless published a steady stream of essays.[52]

First he tried to use the *Review*. Paper after paper answered the objections based upon concern for the wine and wool trades.[53] On 21 and 23 May he attempted to reduce the entire controversy over the Treaty of Commerce and Navigation to "Whether it be worth our while to open a Trade with *France* or no?" (9:196). On the twenty-sixth he complained that he had tried to write impartially but had inadvertently embroiled himself in destructive party politics again. The next numbers discuss the less charged move to dissolve the Union, but on 6 June he concludes he must give up the *Review*. He has again displeased "the Legal Authority," he says, and offers his future silence as "Penance." In fact, the *Review* had lost all credibility by its stance as a moderate Whig paper trying to support a Tory trade treaty. In *Some Thoughts upon the Subject of Commerce with France* Defoe explained that he "lay'd down the *Review*, because my thoughts of things did not agree with the present Opinion of those People for whom I had so much Respect, that I was weary of differing with them" (46). In addition, readership had declined considerably.

This 6 June *Review* is a harbinger of what Defoe was to become in the next few months. The paper reveals conflicts, ambiguities, and lies. As he had done so often before in hard times, Defoe appeals to "him, who knows better than all of us" to witness and to corroborate Defoe's version of matters. God, he says, knows that he "opposed, with my utmost Skill, cool Argument, and calm Reasoning . . . Party Rage, Personal Prejudice, and Universal Clamour." And God alone can understand the purpose of the situation that Defoe has described for people's enlightenment: "fatal" divisions. Dramatizing himself through metaphors and biblical allusion, he comes back to a familiar image of himself as innocent sufferer, sacrifice, martyr. He has, he says, been like the man who steps between duellers and loses his life: "*Alas!* I have seen no Gain, but Enemies; and these I have increas'd without Number" (9:210).

After this outpouring of sanctity and his vow of silence, however, he says that he might have turned to writing on trade, but the *Mercator*, a paper with government encouragement in the form of original papers, documents, and access to authorities "which I never pretended to," has completely usurped that opportunity. The *Mercator* was his paper, too, and he had named it with the common word for "merchant" in Scotland, a word that was becoming rare in England. In it he could support the treaty and the ministry without the mask of the moderate Whig Mr.

Review, and he could sell 1,600 copies per issue instead of the few hundred the *Review* managed.[54] With a few final criticisms of the clergy, the Whigs, and the Dissenters, Defoe ended the *Review* after nine unbroken years of publication. Perhaps this paper had been his obsession, his mistress, his love, as he says, but, in the next sentence, he praises the *Mercator* again.

The resilient realist went on to other work and left no record of nostalgia. On 23 May he had published *An Essay on the Treaty of Commerce*, and on 26 May the first *Mercator* had appeared. The defeat of the treaty on 18 June did nothing to diminish the attacks on the ministry; in fact, in October, Defoe could still describe the Treaty as "an Arrow Shot at The present administration" rather than a "Dispute about Trade" (H 418–19).

Halifax, Stanhope, and others had started the *British Merchant* as an opponent to the *Mercator* in August, and Defoe had taken on yet another literary power in his defense of the ministry. Joseph Addison's *The Late Tryal and Conviction of Count Tariff* retold the story of the defeat of the treaty as an allegorical trial of a suit brought by Goodman Fact against Count Tariff. In a work as good as any of his *Tatler* or *Spectator* pieces, Addison made his satiric points through artful descriptions of Fact and Tariff, through the familiar tactic of characterizing opponents by their followers, and by the creation of a kind of Greek chorus of delighted citizens who cheer Fact and light bonfires to celebrate his victory. The brevity, unity, and careful repetition of major, memorable images assured the allegory's popularity and effectiveness. For instance, Goodman Fact wore a rich, plain English broadcloth and "cuts down the finest orator" with his natural, straightforward, honest eloquence. Tariff wore brocade embroidered with fleur-de-lys, and his speech "abounded in empty phrases, superficial flourishes" and "feeble proofs" accompanied by "gesture and grimace." Addison's cleverest trick was to expose the Tory propagandists' methods through Tariff's presentation of his case. As a comment on the amount of Tory propaganda published, Tariff himself was loquacious and repetitious. He accused his adversaries of actionable seditious libel and labeled everything they said as "faction." So pleased with the modification of "Goodman Fact" into "Goodman Faction" was he that he repeated it for an hour. Defoe and many others had, of course, been accusing the Whigs of acting from no motive but party prejudice; even the defeat of the treaty had been an act of "faction" and not conviction. Tariff's witnesses were the *Mercator*, the *Examiner*, and the Asiento. The *Mercator* is a "shuffling, prevaricating rascal" who will not give his name or address but says, as Defoe often did in his periodicals, that the people "were resolved to be as arrant fools as all their forefathers."[55]

In less than a month Defoe answered with the *Memoirs of Count Tariff*, a 95-page "secret history" of Addison's Tariff. Where Addison's character had accused Goodman Fact of being Dutch by birth and at heart, Defoe's Goodman Fact is really Sir Politick Falsehood in disguise. In his version, the treaty was defeated because of self-interest and gullibility. Clever people banded together to trick Harry Woolpack (English manufacturers) into opposing the interests of Alderman Traffick (merchants). Mynheer Coopmanschap (the greedy Dutch) has every reason to want the treaty defeated and joins the caballing club of villains. Defoe's characters owe more to Bunyan's and the seventeenth century than Addison's, but he, too, can transform what had become a repetitious party exchange into a coherent allegory with memorable exchanges.

Harley, always aroused by threats to his position, agreed with Defoe's advice to delay additional parliamentary debates on commerce, and it was February before Parliament convened again. In the meantime Harley began to work more actively with Defoe. Surviving correspondence shows that Defoe had regular meeting nights scheduled with Harley. On 31 October Defoe sketched out a new theme for the *Mercator* and let Harley know that he had written *A Letter to the Dissenters* based upon "a hint" Harley had given him. He and Harley worked together to increase the free distribution of pamphlets,[56] and Harley increased the sums paid Defoe to make publishing and distribution easier. Most of Defoe's work warned his countrymen of the dangers of divisions in a time when unity might be required to settle the Hanoverian succession. By concentrating on this line he was largely able to avoid apostasy and contradiction.

Agitation increased, as did Bolingbroke's efforts to force Harley out. When Harley was forced to speak in favor of the schism bill, hostile journalists had a field day, and everyone knew that Harley, a member of a Dissenting family, had been brought reluctantly to support the bill. When things looked hopeless for him in late spring 1714, he rallied. By introducing a proclamation setting a huge bounty on the Pretender should he land in England and by cooperating wholeheartedly in the parliamentary investigation of the Asiento contract, he weakened Bolingbroke enough to save his position a little longer.

Defoe had directed most of his energy into the *Mercator*, for which he had been solely responsible since 25 March 1714,[57] and to opposing the schism bill. He was thoroughly depressed and angry over what he saw as wholesale betrayals of the Dissenters and had even published some anti-administration pamphlets such as *Considerations upon the Eighth and Ninth Articles of the Treaty of Commerce*. This pamphlet displays the energy and command of Defoe at his best while those in support of the treaty, such as *An Essay on the Treaty of Commerce*, often seem defensive and mired in technicalities. Later he was to imply that he had "had a bad Case to handle" in helping his "Clients" with the treaty.[58] His defense of Harley had been clever, developing minor themes rather than full-scale discussions of the controversial politician. In the *Memoirs of Melfort*, for instance, he had the Jacobite Melfort say, "But one Man in Britain . . . gave me much Uneasiness, and that was the T[reasure]r" and that the Chevalier never talked of Harley as friend although he frequently mentioned all of his other friends (33–34). By implication, then, many others, but not Harley, were Jacobites. In *Reasons for Im[peaching] the L[or]d H[igh] T[reasure]r*, Defoe encouraged the procedure, for it would vindicate Harley.

Harley's resignation and the death of the queen drew Defoe back to a new commitment to Harley. "I Think it my Duty to Repeat my assurances of my following your Worst Fortunes," he wrote the night before Harley resigned. On 3 August he wrote Harley that the queen's death had made it necessary to stop the printing of "what I was upon for Vindicateing your Ldpps person and Conduct and Exposeing your Enemyes as I had proposed to your Ldpp" (444). This pamphlet was probably *The Secret History of the White Staff*, and here and elsewhere Defoe makes Harley's knowledge of it clear. Unlike almost every other contemporary, Defoe never complained that Harley spoke obscurely or indirectly, and the pamphlet contains information and interpretations that Defoe could not have got anywhere else. On 26 August Defoe sent Harley a copy and explained the method. Because of the mood of the people, he says, he has decided he must "Talk with them" "by Little and Little, gaining upon their Furious Tempers by Inches." Eventually he intends to base his defence of Harley upon a dramatic contrast between Harley's ministry and the one Bolingbroke might have led (445); to that end, he published the *Secret History* in three parts.

One of Harley's last acts on the night before he resigned was to pay Defoe £100. This consideration stands in sharp contrast to the neglect of others' claims. The earl of Mar, for instance, wrote that Harley "had done more like a friend by me had he left me less in arier [arrears], but I do not take it that his doing so proceeded from unkindness to me in particular & he did no otherwise by me than he did severall others of his friends."[59] Defoe kept in contact with Harley as long as he could and even tried to diminish periodical attacks on Harley at some risk to himself (H 447–48). Once George I arrived in London, however, Harley met an angry king and began to move his household and huge library to the country. As Matthew Prior wrote years later, Harley's character was so suspect to many that "his sickness is all counted for policy, that he will not come up, till the public distractions force somebody or other . . . who will oblige somebody else to send for him in open triumph, and set him in *statu quo prius*. That, in the mean time, he has foreseen all that has happened; checkmated all the Ministry."[60]

The last few years had been a maelstrom for Defoe. His enormous effort had concluded in alienation from almost everyone. Isolated at the end as Harley's champion, he could not even claim to be a party writer. He watched other writers receive rewards for their loyalty to the Protestant succession—Samuel Buckley became the editor of the lucrative *London Gazette* with a grant for forty years; Steele received several sinecures and grants, one as early as 18 October, and was knighted in April 1715; even Ridpath was offered the place of Treasurer to the King's Kitchen.[61] A comment Defoe made to Harley captures his uncharacteristic mood: "I hardly could Tell which way to direct words . . . as Not to do harm instead of Good" (H 444). After eighteen months of nearly continuous illness, he must have felt all of his fifty-five years as he faced a new world.

PART III

1714-1731

CHAPTER 14

SIX HUNDRED
THOUSAND WORDS

The chief Leader of the Scribbling Troop is now said to keep Five
Presses Employed, and to be Author of three single Itinerant
Papers, besides Occasional Pamphlets.
                    —*Monitor*, 1 May 1714

The uniform constant and uninterrupted effort of every man to
better his condition.
          —ADAM SMITH, *The Wealth of Nations*

In the aftermath of Queen Anne's death Defoe faced a painfully
familiar situation: he was once again without a source of income. For
many of Robert Harley's circle, the great issue was to come to terms
with Harley's ouster in the final days of Anne's life and his party's utter
disintegration after her death. Defoe felt some of that need, too, but he
had a more compelling need to come to terms with his own actions.
Defoe was basically an idealist. Faced with the long-pent-up criticism of
the last years of Anne's reign and numerous, scathing periodical attacks, he was confronted by the discrepancies between his opinion of
himself and that of a very large number of Englishmen, many of them
Whigs and Dissenters like himself.

Defoe's reputation had never been worse. He looked like a thoroughly discredited hack, and his character had been destroyed by reports of such base actions as horse theft and cuckolding a friend. According to journalistic gossip Defoe had failed to return a hired horse
to its owner in Coventry on one of his trips north and had even fathered
a child by the wife of his friend Nathaniel Sammen.[1] Even contemporary personal notations on his works show the effects of the Queen
Anne years. For instance, a note on a copy of *The True-Born Englishman*
preserved in the University of London Senate House reads, "Writ by
Daniel D'ffoe. a mercenary Fellow that writ for and against all parties."
His reputation as an unprincipled writer-for-hire had been fixed. The
kind of abuse directed at him in *Judas Discuver'd* [*sic*] could be repeated
endlessly: "Of all the Writers that have Prostituted their Pens, either to

encourage *Faction*, oblige a *Party*, or for their own *Mercenary Ends*; the *Person* here mentioned is the Vilest. An *Animal* who shifts his Shape oftner than *Proteus*, and goes backwards and forwards like a Hunted *Hare*; a thorough-pac'd true-bred *Hypocrite*." The publication of his *A Letter to the Dissenters* (1713) had harmed him immensely. This pamphlet argued that the Dissenters enjoyed many privileges and should be grateful and submissive; it labeled as manipulative troublemakers those who represented their civil rights as threatened. Reprinted at the time of the debates over the schism bill, the pamphlet seemed to call the Dissenters gullible and misguided. In one place it promised that they would be "like *David*'s Heifers, first to draw the Cart, and then to be burnt with the Wood" (26). The hurt that the Dissenters felt comes out in the way Edmund Calamy described it as insulting the Dissenters "in a cruel manner." He, like many others, believed that it came from Harley or, "at least," had been published "under his direction." Another pamphleteer characterized it as a transparent, knavish attempt "sometimes by Sophistry, sometimes by Flattery, sometimes by Reproaches, and sometimes by Threats," to persuade the Dissenter to change "from the *Country-Party* to the *Court-Party*." When his authorship was known, Defoe heard himself called "Wretch," "hireling Scribler," "this Mercenary," "broken hosier," and "Profligate." *Remarks on the Letter to the Dissenters* characterized him as "render'd *infamous* by *Law*" yet loading himself with "greater Infamy . . . in the Service of *France* and her Friends" and as "hired" in the way "*Conjurers* set *Devils* to work, to pick up Cockleshells, to prevent their doing Mischief to themselves." As a "tool" and a "fool," the pamphlet continued, Defoe was "hated by those he serves, and despis'd by those he has deserted."[2]

In a deeply human way Defoe tried to affirm what he believed himself to be. What he did testifies strongly to the kind of man he was and provides insight into the needs and ambivalences driving him. To his credit he continued to defend Robert Harley when the risks were clear and even after Harley had repudiated Defoe's work in an advertisement in the *London Gazette* (9 July 1715). Just before that John Dunton's preface to *Queen Robin*, the postscript to the anonymous *A Speech Design'd to Have Been Spoken in the House of Commons on the Resolution concerning the Terms of Peace*, and other pamphlets had accused Harley of writing *The Secret History of the White Staff* and described the excuses and explanations as confessions. His defense of Harley therefore forced Defoe to spend more time reviewing his strategies and his own recent past and provoked still more journalists to offer Defoe a mirror in which to see him as they did.

Even as he struggled to come to terms with himself, his need to support himself and his family grew. The new king's calculated snub when the earl of Dorset introduced Harley to him in effect exiled

Harley, and Defoe appears to have lost touch with him soon after. Since Defoe's bitterest attacks in recent months had been against the Whigs and Dissenters, he could find no resort with them. Scotland and his friends there seemed far in the past. During the hard months of 1703 he had learned that "the God that gave me brains will give me bread" and that earning a living, "'Tis No Very Difficult Thing." His conduct between August 1714 and the end of 1715 makes clear how well he had absorbed the lessons of 1703. Without hesitation he picked up his pen, exploited what he had learned about the book trade, and published over six hundred thousand words.

⁊ℛ⅋

His first publication after George's landing on 18 September was *Advice to the People of Great Britain*. A cautious, temperate essay, it begins, "The publick peace is justly the concern of every true lover of his Country," and urges people to "cease that foolish strife, forget the Wrongs done to one another, and bury the Resentment of past Follies" in order to enjoy the new reign in harmony.[3] As he had when Harley returned to power in 1710, Defoe assures his countrymen that they can expect moderation, steady principles, and experienced, competent administration. Just as he did then, he tells people that their first duty is to "Study to be Quiet, and do our own Business" (1 Thessalonians 4:11) (40). The pamphlet also quotes several other passages of Scripture. In *Advice* Defoe projects his conception of himself as a man devoted to opening the eyes of others to truth.

Defoe concludes the pamphlet with a timely parallel to the Israelites' rejection of Saul when he was first appointed king; by doing so, he promises George I's patience and the people's ultimate acceptance of their king. In fact, compared to his 1713–1714 work, the writings of 1715 are full of scriptural quotations and hortatory expressions. Many pamphlets conclude with biblical passages. Time after time Defoe uses biblical passages to summarize or advance a typological parallel. Some of these quotations seem inharmoniously fervent. In *A View of the Scots Rebellion*, for instance, he contrasts the fighting styles of the Highlanders and the British and concludes that, unless Mar has been able to change them, "which he will find very difficult to do," the king's army will win, even if outnumbered three to one. Then, in a remarkable passage, made more striking by the fact that it follows such a specific, detailed analysis, he says:

Wherefore to encourage ourselves also, *on a yet surer and stonger Foundation* [emphasis added], I conclude this Part in the Word of the *faithful Spies* to the Children of *Israel*, when the wicked Spies terrified the People with the Multitude and Strength of their Enemies, *Fear ye not the People of the Land for they are but Bread for us, their Shield is departed from them, and the Lord is with us*, FEAR THEM NOT. (26)

That this prophetic quotation from Numbers 14:9 seemed more reassuring to Defoe than the twenty-five preceding pages is inseparable from the role he had assumed. His years in Scotland now miraculously—or at least providentially—seemed to have prepared him to be the "faithful spy" for his people. Because of his tone and his propensity for predicting the outcome of events and implications of personalities, as he had in his *Review* essays on Charles XII, many of Defoe's journalistic critics already scoffed at him as "Daniel the Prophet."

Now, however, the variety, number, range, and relative obscurity of his biblical allusions suggest a Defoe trying to return to his deepest sense of himself. Phrases such as "Some will have it . . . that we have nothing to do but to sit down under our Vines," offhand references to such things as Joshua's oath with the Gibeonites and to people like Hasaell, the piling up of allusions as he does to show the persecution of good priests and prophets even in the Bible,[4] and quotations such as the one in *A View of the Scots Rebellion* show that Defoe had been actively and seriously rereading his Bible.

Within *Advice* are other signs that Defoe was doing more than explaining a familiar, pragmatic position. As he does so often, he includes brief historical passages, and here he blames the nation's tumult and divisions not on the Sacheverell trial but on the "Breach at Court" when Parliament was dissolved in 1710. At that time, he says, one group raised fears about religion and the other group destroyed faith in the management of the war, and the nation never recovered its confidence. Because the two sides were so obstinate and irreconcilable, both were forced to do regrettable things, and any chance of cooperation, and, therefore, of moderation, disappeared. The results were extremism in government and lingering fears and divisions about religion and economics.

Here, too, he begins what will be his major defense of Harley: "There were yet a Body of Men, even in the new Ministry, *and at the Head of it too*, who tho' they made use of Instruments for their Convenience, yet saw with other Eyes than those Instruments saw with, and pursued other Ends than they pursued" (7). The product of Defoe's need to understand Harley's policies rather than a need to come to terms with the events immediately before and after Anne's death, this explanation carried obvious dangers. In effect, it admitted a lack of integrity and candor for, at best, pragmatic, political reasons and, at worst, for personal gain. Defoe attempted to create a lonely, moderate, patriotic Harley opposed by scheming, secret Jacobites, who inflamed both parties in the hope of driving out all who stood in the way of their plan. They worked to make Harley "suspect" and uneasy, "reproaching him with being a Presbyterian in his Heart, inclin'd to the Whigs, and having taken secret Measures to betray them all to a new Scheme of Moderation" (9). After tirelessly but vainly endeavoring to bring the schemers to a sense of their duty to their country, Defoe said, he finally "left them to try their own Wisdom" and withdrew voluntarily from government. In his fable their "new Model" fell "asunder" immediately, and everyone set up for himself to the confusion of everything. Just as honest men were coming to see Harley's virtues and merit, the queen died. Defoe went on to interpret her deathbed appointment of Shrewsbury as a repudiation of the schemers.

This five-page "history" presents a concise, neat explanation of events. Its oversimplifications and distortions pit patriotism (and necessity in the use of imperfect "Instruments") against ambitious Jacobite self-aggrandizement.[5] Defoe conveniently omits to note that Harley's withdrawn and irresponsible behavior and his real shortcomings as a policymaker contributed to his fall and that Queen Anne was all but comatose when the Privy Council persuaded her to appoint Shrewsbury.

Significantly, the Dublin edition has a different title page, including the words, "With a Vindication of the Earl of Oxford." The first part of *The Secret History of the White Staff*, published nearly simultaneously with *Advice to the People*, develops the story and extends it back to the time when Harley was displaced in 1708 and forward to an imaginery scene of a group of thwarted schemers swearing after the queen's death. The language is more abusive and provocative. For instance, Abigail Masham is called "That Female Buz" and some of the courtiers accused of thinking fit "to plough with the Heifers of the Court" (42). Throughout Harley appears as a long-suffering, forgiving, moderate, dedicated, patriotic statesman who chose to resign with an eloquent, high-minded speech. The queen is moved by the resignation and plans to return the staff of office to him after an interval designed to cool tempers. Unfortunately, "something which affected her Heart was supposed to occasion her Death" although an autopsy showed the rest of her body "sound and perfect, suited to a long Life and good Constitution" (62). This fanciful description of a queen the nation had expected to die for at least a year shows Defoe's uncharacteristic lack of attention to what might be credible.

Throughout the next year Defoe adhered to this story. He added more details, included more specific dates and events, and defined Harley's opinions, but he varied the account only in emphasis, not in substance. Years later, Harley's long associate Dartmouth described his ministry as "four years cessation from plunder,"[6] and, in Defoe's pamphlets, Harley's scruples and integrity are most obvious on this count. According to Defoe, Harley began by alienating people by reducing or cutting off commissions and bounties; he made trouble for himself by insisting that his office assume the war debts run up by his predecessor;

he opposed the expensive, futile Canadian expedition,* and he worked to prevent the "criminal Intreagues" others set in motion to enrich themselves.[7] Consistently blaming party divisions for limiting Harley's options, Defoe develops the picture of a man baffled in Parliament and thwarted at court.

These pamphlets serve more to provide an explanation than to defend successfully. By repeating that Harley was willing to use the Jacobites, Defoe makes him seem callous, scheming, and unprincipled: "The *Staff* . . . ever thought that *Jacobites* might be made Instruments, &c. yet was of the Mind also, that they should never be longer imploy'd than while the Necessity remain'd."[8] That he was forced to use the Jacobites because of "the Rage of Parties" merely reinforces the sense of Harley's helplessness. Defoe insists repeatedly that Harley was without power as much as a year before the queen accepted his resignation. Because Defoe offers no guiding policies and no goal other than making peace, he offers nothing that might justify Harley's actions. Those parts that should have worked to Harley's advantage with his critics— his overtures and leniency to the Whigs, for instance—were overlooked or dismissed.

It was unlike him to be such an inept defender, to open so many new lines of attack to his opponents, but for Defoe the idea of lingering in the hope of serving his superior or of regaining influence made sense. He had done just that for years and seen himself rise and fall. His faith that Harley's absence would be felt and his merit rewarded was part of his personality. Moreover, he had adapted a series of reasons for his time in Scotland for a variety of groups, had "been all things to all men" in order to get his pamphlets read, and had certainly obtained useful information from people he did not like. Analogously, he saw that Harley had come to believe that the ends would justify the means. By the time he wrote part 3 of the *Secret History*, he would say that both sides "set aside the known Christian Rule, not to do Evil that Good might come" (21). Occasionally, he harshly and coldly stated what might have motivated Harley: "The Principle which leads States Men to get into Places by any Means they can, leads them to make use of all possible Measures, to keep themselves in the Possession of that Power they got." In 1718 he mentioned Harley's "indolence" and concluded "for certainly had the Earl applied himself with the same Vigor to the last . . . his Enemies had never been able to supplant him."[9]

Most of the time, however, Defoe depicts Harley as patriotic and

---

*Bolingbroke pushed through approval of the expedition to take Quebec while Harley was recovering from stab wounds (1711). Abigail Masham's brother, General Jack Hill, received the command, but he and the strongest force ever sent to the colonies up to that time returned after eight ships and more than seven hundred men were lost in the mouth of the St. Lawrence River because of a navigation error.

well-intentioned but forced to compromise. Almost as though he were persuading himself, Defoe distances Harley from the events that drew the most criticism: employment of Jacobites, Ormonde's restraining orders, the creation of the twelve new peers, the means of making peace, and the passage of the occasional conformity bill. In the fall of 1714 he tended to stop at insisting that if left to himself Harley would not have done things as they were done. By early summer of 1715, however, he insists that Harley took no part in the peace negotiations, then did so only at the queen's orders, and repeatedly found Boling-broke and others taking unauthorized action. In another place he says that the vote on the peace had carried by one more than the twelve created peers and that Harley had therefore been correct in believing that the queen had not needed to take such drastic action.[10] Even in the case of the Occasional Conformity Act, his anger is directed not at Harley but at his own people:

Neither the E. of N[ottingham] insisting on such high Terms for so mean an Advantage, as the best Service he could do them, nor the Easiness of the Whiggs at that Time, to part with the Dissenters on such cheap Terms, were, by far, so wonderful, as the Satisfaction with which the Dissenters stood and lookt on while the Fetters and Mannacles of this new Law were fastened upon them. . . .[11]

That Defoe includes such passages and gradually brings in all of the actions he had had the most difficulty accepting gives away how person-al the pamphlets really were. When, for instance, he represents Harley as being always in favor of retaining Marlborough, he indicates yet another part of the past that disturbs him.

Nearly universal outrage greeted these pamphlets and especially *The Secret History*. Defoe was treated as Harley's "hireling" and "scribe," and the pamphlets were interpreted as a base attempt to blame others for mismanagement. John Oldmixon, William Pittis, and others combed *The Secret History* for contradictions. To the assertion that Harley had not profited from office, one jeered, "Your L——p made one Cousen a P[ee]r, a second a Coadjutor, a third an Auditor . . . got Preferments for all your poor Relations, and an Heiress for your Son." The selection of Prior as negotiator, when "a Person of Quality or Distinction" might have been chosen, became evidence of Harley's lack of zeal for the Hanoverian Succession.[12] As Defoe persisted, the attacks became more pointed:

What a world of Contradiction and Inconsistency shall we ever find in the Writings of a guilty Person strugling against Fact and Conviction. The Histo-rian set to work by *Staff*, pretends in answer to all this, that his Patron did the most Meritorious Thing he could think of.
He acknowledges every where, that the *Enemies* to the House of *Hanover* were

got into the *Ministry*, and that he himself was the occasion of bringing them in to, [*sic*] maintain his usurp'd Authority.[13]

The scurrility heaped on Defoe knew no limits. The pent-up venom of journalists who had dared not strike the ministry's writer too often spewed out: "For was ever a Man bearing the Character of a Gentleman, so reduc'd, as to employ a Wretch to defend him, who wants Probity and Manners as much as Grammar and good Sense." Defoe was accused of telling incredible lies and of working for the worst of the booksellers. Oldmixon and others accused him of writing the last part of *The Secret History* primarily to take advantage of the booksellers. Even satires of other men reminded Defoe of others' profits; a typical one regarding Swift's appointment to the deanery of St. Patrick's, Dublin, read, "Two famous Divines, *Sacheverell* and *Swift*, were advanc'd, the one for Beginning, the other for Compleating . . . the Ruin of the WHIG Party."[14]

Defoe never slunk away from abuse. Once he devised explanations for the policies of Harley's administration, he repeated, defended, and explained them ad nauseum. Very rarely did Defoe do more than repeat the same story of Harley's last four years, but it is clear that he found more and more decisions with unfortunate results to brood over. At one point, for instance, he mentioned affronting Scotland by forcing twenty-two of its most prominent men to come the length of the country only to be bailed in London. In another, more extended passage he criticized the formation of the South Sea Company.[15]

Working on these pamphlets and reading the answers they provoked drew out the defensive, self-righteous Defoe of 1703. His loquacious, detailed accounts of his conduct, arranged not by a list of reasons but by a chronological list of events and his thoughts, prefigure the "reasonings" of some of his ensnared but guilty fictional characters. He explains and explains those statements that appeared to be contradictions or apostasy. He quotes himself to prove his consistency or his virtue. He even asks his readers to look for the man behind the pen as he had not done since the publication of *The Shortest-Way with the Dissenters*.

∼≈∽

In the fall and winter of 1714, Defoe wrote *An Appeal to Honour and Justice*, his most famous *apologia pro vita sua*. The essay is a sketchy account of his life, an explanation of his conduct since 1704, and, more significantly, a denial of a few of the charges being made against him by the press. Staggered by the virulence directed at him now that the government that protected him was out of power, Defoe asked to be judged as a human being. He gave three reasons for writing *An Appeal* at that time, and the first two concern his family:

1. I think I have long enough been made *Fabula Vulgi*, and born the Weight of general Slander; and I should be wanting to Truth, to my Family, and to my Self, if I did not give a fair and true State of my Conduct. . . .

2. By the Hints of Mortality, and by the Infirmities of a Life of Sorrow and Fatigue, I have Reason to think that I am not a great way off from, if not very near to the great Ocean of Eternity . . . Wherefore, I think, I should *even Accounts* with this World before I go, that no Actions (Slanders) may lie against my Heirs, Executors, Administrators, and Assigns, to disturb them in the peaceable Possession of their Father's (Character) Inheritance. (192)

In spite of his long absences in Scotland and his immersion in politics, Defoe had never ceased to worry about his family. He never referred to 1703 without mentioning how he had "ruined" them, and the guilt he felt never seemed to die.[16] Both his mother-in-law Joan Tuffley and his old friend Samuel Stancliffe were recently dead, and both were reminders of past reprehensible acts. His worried comments about his children's educations and the concern about his elder son, Benjamin, implied by Russell's letters to him increased as the children matured. In 1714 Benjamin was at the Inner Temple, close to the heart of political publishing and controversy. His youngest child, Sophia, was a sensitive thirteen year old. His other children were young adults and sure to be hurt by the things said about their father. For at least the past year, Defoe had involved both of his sons in his publishing, and this fact undoubtedly gave them added exposure to published statements about their father.

Defoe's family could not but be drawn into arguments. In 1715 Dudley Ryder, an acquaintance of Benjamin's, recorded a conversation with him "about the behavior of the late ministry." Ryder concluded, "He did not say much to justify them." Ryder's general opinion was that Benjamin "does not seem to have very good sense . . . and talks the notions he has had from his father."[17] Before their fight in 1711 Samuel Tuffley reportedly told Captain Silk to address Defoe, for he could take care of himself, but Silk continued to bait Tuffley and finally followed him down a public street. Such public taunts that Defoe was a hireling scribbler and a government tool occurred often.

In *An Appeal to Honour and Justice* Defoe laid his start in government work to chance—the publishing success of *The True-Born Englishman*, written because he took offense at another poem—and explained his continued political work as the result of gratitude and the collapse of his business interests. His most emotional appeal asked that his obligation to the queen and to Harley be accepted as an honorable motive: "Gratitude and Fidelity are inseparable from an honest Man. . . . let any one put himself in my stead, and examine upon what Principles I could ever act against either such a Queen, or such a Benefactor; and what must my own Heart reproach me with?" (201) He presents himself as employed by the queen. He says that both Harley and Godolphin have told him to consider himself so engaged, both introduced him to the queen, and it was she who gave him the only "appointment" he ever had. Throughout the essay, he denies that anyone, and particularly that Harley, directed, ordered, or paid him to write anything.

At first glance this statement seems to be a shocking lie. Defoe dates the queen's "appointment," however, to the time when he worked in Scotland and when Godolphin and Harley were corresponding about "what should be done for Defoe" and when their correspondence acknowledged the queen's agreement to some of their arrangements with Defoe. If his quarterly payments were established then, as Treasury records suggest that they were, the money he received would be rather like the annual sums paid the Scots who had done the most to help the passage of the Union. Harley's and the secretaries of states' grants to people for "special services" were far from uncommon and usually came *after* the publication of useful or pleasing pamphlets. In some cases they reimbursed writers or provided for the disbursement of pamphlets. If Defoe received his money in all or some of these ways, he was guilty of special pleading, not lying. A few lists of periodicals sent gratis to M.P.'s and officeholders by the secretaries of state do survive. On none of these—not even the longest of ten papers—does the *Review* appear.[18]

In his argument for the obligations of gratitude, Defoe compared those he served to a parent and offered a set of rules that can be summarized as defending what he thought could be defended and keeping silent about everything else. He continues, "suppose a Man's Father was guilty of several things unlawful and unjustifiable, a Man may heartily detest the unjustifiable thing, and yet it ought not to be expected that he should expose his Father. I think the Case on my side exactly the same" (205). As he had done so often, he then offered a list of ways he had offended the Dissenters and a list of positions upon which he had been consistent.

According to a postscript allegedly by the publisher, Defoe fell ill before he completed the essay, and "his friends" decided it should be printed. In many ways it is a troubling document and seems less candid than, for example, the preface to volume 8 of the *Review* (1712), which makes several of the same points. In this preface Defoe had reminded his readers of some of his past actions that ought to have prevented their accusing him of apostasy and "prostitution." For instance, his conduct in 1702, he says, should have convinced them that he "could neither be *Brib'd* from the Truth, or *Threat'ned*, or *Terrified* from my Principles." This preface speaks often of his "quiet Conscience" and reflects metaphorically on his life:

I have gone through a Life of Wonders, and am the Subject of a vast Variety of Providences; I have been fed more by Miracle than *Elija* [*sic*], when the Ravens were his Purveyors. . . .

In the School of Affliction I have learnt . . . Philosophy. . . . I have seen the rough side of the World as well as the smooth, and have in less than half a Year tasted the difference between the Closet of a King, and the Dungeon of *Newgate.*

An Appeal to Honour and Justice is one of the most stark, unadorned pieces Defoe ever wrote. The reader cannot but pause over some of his statements: that he received no money, that he wrote nothing except the *Review* for nearly a year (he undoubtedly meant 1709, when he did, in fact, write far less than most years), that he was not the author of the *Mercator.* Even the postscript forbids credibility; that Baker, the publisher with whom he had the longest and closest relationship, would have published *An Appeal* without his permission cannot easily be accepted.

The few pages before the essay breaks off contrast to the bare account that goes before and seem to reveal deeply personal things about Defoe. He writes that he "concludes" "this Part in the Words of the Prophet" and quotes Jeremiah 20:10 in full. Moreover, he follows that rather long verse with a lengthy paragraph from Matthew Poole's *Annotations*. In Poole he finds an exact representation of his own position which the second (and unpublished) part of *An Appeal* will describe:

The Prophet . . . here rendreth a Reason why he thought of giving over his Work as a Prophet; his Ears were continually filled with the Obloquies and Reproaches of such as reproached him; and besides, he was afraid on all Hands, there were so many Traps laid for him, so many Devises devised against him. They did not only take Advantage against him, but sought Advantages, and invited others to raise Stories of him. Not only Strangers, but those that he might have expected the greatest Kindness from; those that pretended most courteously, they watch . . . for opportunities to do me Mischief, and lay in wait for my Halting, desiring nothing more than that I might be enticed to speak, or do something which they might find Matter of a colourable Accusation, that so they might satisfie their Malice upon me. (236)

Defoe's complaints against the Whigs and Dissenters, against those ascribing radical pamphlets to him, and against those who made him fear prosecution and prison again resonate remarkably with this passage. His next two paragraphs, although they depict him as the severest sufferer, describe how his children and Harley are insulted on his account. In this place, too, he writes, "A constant, steady adhering to *Personal Vertue*, and to *Publick Peace* . . . will AT LAST restore me to the Opinion of Sober and Impartial Men, and that is all I desire" (237). This part of the pamphlet exposes a Defoe who returned to Scripture for comfort. He does not merely quote a verse he remembered or a passage he habitually printed; the epigraph to the essay (Jeremiah 18:18), the quoted verse, and Poole's interpretation show Defoe not just reading Scripture but reading commentary as well. Other writings done that year draw upon Jeremiah, too; for example, the minister who preaches to the family in *The Family Instructor* chooses Jeremiah 10:25. Feeling as he did about his mission in publishing, he would find the prophets fitting. Knowing the Bible as he did, he could select the suffering, derided, scorned prophet Jeremiah* and find typological comfort. "My Case may . . . be likened to that of the Sacred Prophet," "excepting only the vast Disparity of the Persons," Defoe writes.

This conclusion, with its implied call for a return to "personal vertue" and "public peace" and its extended reference to Jeremiah, suggests why the essay went unfinished. Too much in the first part lies inharmoniously beside virtue and peace.[19] After casting himself as Jeremiah, he could hardly proceed to work on a guileful, distorted document. Defoe habitually published, however, by sending his manuscript to the printer in sections of some eight to sixteen pages. These pages would be set, and he would correct them even as he delivered subsequent sections.[20] Once the early part of the essay was delivered, Defoe may have been reluctant to withdraw the pages. Self-pity or vanity might have urged their publication—he *had* suffered, and the account given in the beginning of *An Appeal* presented him well. Every author hates to destroy his words, and this reluctance, or simply the expense of giving up already-printed pages, could have helped Defoe decide to consent to, if not encourage, the publication of the first part.

Defoe had been seriously ill in the fall. That and the change in his fortunes helped awaken his spirituality. He believed, as he would write to a friend, that "the Time of Sorrow is a Time to reflect, and to look and see wherefore he that is righteous is contending with you" (H 449). Affliction for Defoe was a providential hand calling back or pointing a new direction. Like most Puritans Defoe felt that works were the evidence of a living faith. As William Perkins said, "The main end of our lives . . . is to serve God in the serving men in the works of our callings." Another conduct book writer explained the publication of his book in these terms: "Men can't be Indifferent to such useful and necessary Service, without proclaiming their Neutrality in the Cause of GOD."[21] In that spirit Defoe began *The Family Instructor*. Both to follow the injunction not to let the right hand know what the left performed when doing good and to avoid the deluge of skeptical ridicule such a book from his hand would provoke, he went to considerable lengths to hide

---

*Jeremiah, hated by his kin and countrymen, was imprisoned (once in a cistern) and his life was in danger several times. He gave warnings against turmoil and division and wept over his people and his country.

his authorship. He had his Newcastle publisher, Joseph Button, print it and the Dissenting bookseller Emmanuel Matthews distribute it in London.[22]

Although Defoe had shared his generation's periodic concern with the reform of manners, he had never before written a conduct book.[23] Such books enjoyed enormous popularity; seventeenth-century works such as Richard Allestree's *The Ladies' Calling* and *The Gentleman's Calling* (1660), Francis Osborne's *Advice to a Son* (1656), and Obadiah Walker's *Of Education* (1673) had attained the status of classics. Recent books such as *The Necessary Duty of Family Prayer, A Present for Servants*, and William Fleetwood's *Relative Duties of Parents and Children* had sold well. His Morton school classmate Timothy Cruso had written *God the Guide of Youth* (1695), and in 1714 Richard Steele had published a very successful conduct book, *The Ladies Library*, which was an unabashed compendium of earlier works.[24] Moreover, lists of recommended books appended to the annual edition of *An Account of the Society for Promoting Christian Knowledge* included many of these books and promised additional sales.

Defoe's *Review*, like the *Tatler* and *Spectator*, had included lively, moral domestic tales. They had shown families in action, turned relationships into dialogue, and believed in their power to reform. In a *Review* of 2 October 1711, for instance, he debated the *Spectator's* interpretation of a father's conduct (8:329–31). His own work had always been full of domestic examples and in recent times had drawn out many more of these analogies into full-scale fictions. In *Union and No Union* (1713), for example, he gave two pages to a dying father's admonitions to a son engaged to a worthy but poor woman. *The Scots Nation and Union Vindicated; From . . . The Publick Spirit of the Whigs* (1714) had five pages of realistic dialogue between a husband and wife who might have been the engaged couple in *Union and No Union*.[25] He shared the common opinion of his time that private morality provided the foundation of public strength and that the family was an emblem of the nation, and he exploited the metaphoric possibilities for clarity and instruction. His interest in the illustrations themselves and in fictions developed rapidly and found expression in *The Family Instructor*. In the year after Queen Anne's death he wrote secret histories, memoirs, histories, and epistles and called his works "accounts," "reflections," "considerations," "reasons," "expostulations," "replies," "appeals," "rebukes," "apologies," and half a dozen other forms of address.

The debates over education occasioned by the schism bill, the excessive celebrations of George's accession, the king's irregular conjugal arrangements, his love of the theatre, and the card games and balls held by Caroline, Princess of Wales, seemed to call for additional literature of reform. In *Fears of the Pretender* Defoe specifically mentioned masquerades, balls, and gaming "advanc'd at Court."[26] Many conduct books were written by fathers for their children, and Defoe's children were at critical ages. His oldest daughter, Maria, had probably just married Henry Langley, a Queenhithe salter.[27] The other children were all under twenty-five. Like Benjamin, they would be restless, occasionally rebellious, and concerned about their futures. Hannah and Henrietta would have been thinking about marriage, and Daniel as well as Benjamin choosing an occupation. Because of his residence in Scotland and busy London life with frequent short absences, Defoe would have faced fitting in to a family used to making rules without him. Their established habits and his attempt to lead a more regular, godly life undoubtedly caused friction.

The Family Instructor, then, was probably written partly as a guide for his own children, and some parts of it may record some of his own experiences. Part 1, for example, includes sections on parents' attempts to discipline older teenagers, and part 3 offers advice to parents whose children are about to marry and to young couples regarding their obligations to each other. The son's faults are bad company and idleness, and Benjamin could be accused of both.[28] In another place Defoe warns readers against leaving estates to children who could then be "entirely independent of the Parents." The £100 James Foe had left Daniel might have enabled him to set up a very modest business, but it hardly seems to qualify as giving independence. The will of Mary Defoe's brother, Samuel Tuffley, makes clear, however, how immediate the concern was to the Defoe family. He signed his will on 22 October 1714 and included a strongly worded passage intended to direct Mary should she decide to give any part of her inheritance to her children:

My will and desire is that in such Case she would give the greatest Share of such part as she will be pleased to give to her said Children to such of them as behave with the greatest tenderness Duty and affection both to their father and to her self—declaring that if any of the said Children shall behave undutifully disobediently or disrespectfully either to their said Father or Mother and continue obstinately to do so without humbling themselves to their parents and obtaining their pardon that it is my declared will and resolved desire and I hereby make it my request that to such not one shilling of my estate shall be given my desire being as much as in me lyes that the said Children should be kept in an entire dependence upon the said father as well as their Mother.[29]

The father of Defoe's friend John Clerk had experienced a number of the family problems dramatized in *The Family Instructor*. His daughter had been rebellious, finally eloped, and continued in a stormy marriage. John himself had been extravagant and then tried to deceive his father about his debts. Sir John worried about the disobedience of John's brother William. In fact, he feared that William would become a "profligate soldier" and never return home. Sir John's fears recall the conclusion of the elder son's story in Defoe's book, in which the young man, now maimed, comes home to die.[30]

Defoe called *The Family Instructor* "a Toy, a Novelty" and explained its dialogue form as an "entirely New" method, one "mean and familiar," but designed to appeal to a generation delighted by "a different colour'd Coat" or "a new Feather." In fact, the dialogue form was not entirely new; a few other conduct books, such as Richard Baxter's *The Poor Man's Family Book* (1674), Eustace Le Noble de Tennelière's *The Art of Prudent Behaviour* (translated by Abel Boyer in 1701), William Darrell's *A Gentleman Instructed* (1704; sixth edition 1716), and James Puckle's *The Club: Or, A Dialogue between Father and Son* (1711), had used it.[31] Defoe also drew upon a method he had used in *The History of the Union*; he followed each dialogue with commentary. What was original about Defoe's conduct book was his fully realized, even leisurely narration, the individualized characters, the realistic dialogue, and, above all, his analytical interest in relationships. In a time when conduct books employed summaries, excerpts, and even lists of maxims, Defoe definitely moved against the trend.

Even when the conduct books were cast as letters or addresses to an individual, the style tended toward the epigrammatic, relied on exhortation, and lacked familiarity and personality.[32] The Reverend Samuel Wright, who wrote the prefatory letter to the first edition, commented somewhat critically on Defoe's unusual method: "The *Dialogues* are sometimes longer (in my Opinion) than was needful to the Design; and there are now and then some Expressions that may seem . . . not perfectly suitable to the Circumstances . . . But I think there can be no Disgust which will not quickly be taken away, if a Dialogue be read over. . . . Let but the several main Strokes be carefully observed, and the lesser Incidencies may be hastned over." Here Wright remarks on aspects of *The Family Instructor* that Defoe would use—and defend—in his novels, most notably in the preface to *Moll Flanders*. Wright also testified to the truth of *The Family Instructor*: "The Substance of each Narrative is *Real*. And there are some whole Dialogues to which, with very little Alteration, I my self could put *Names* and *Families*." In the notes to the first dialogue, Defoe said he had hidden the true identities of the characters, for the book will serve future readers as parable rather than history anyway, and he means the book to be "general, not a particular Reproof" (221). In this insistence upon a kind of "private history" as opposed to "made up stories," Defoe drew upon a well-established convention in prose fiction and moved closer to the novels he would write.[33]

Defoe, like William Darrell, called his method "a Religious Play." He was aware of the ways in which he violated readers' expectations, and some of his notes provide the most detailed information available about his theory of composition: "There seems to be more Circumlocutions in this Dialogue . . . and some may suppose them unnecessary, but . . . [they are] not useful only, but necessary; the last to preserve the Cadence of things, and introduce the Substance of the real Story by necessary Gradations" (273). The remarkable thing about this statement is Defoe's desire to include a new kind of realism in his work. An awareness of the relationship between temporal and fictional time and of the pleasures of a good story artfully told so that character as well as theme emerge and develop sets Defoe dramatically apart not just from the writers of conduct books but also from most of the writers of prose fiction. Thus Defoe takes the time for the husband to coax the wife into telling him what troubles her, for the brother and sister to complain to each other about new restrictions, and for the father to question the children at length about actions the reader has already seen performed. Another eighteenth-century reader recognized this originality and attributed the continued great popularity of *The Family Instructor* to its "dramatic forms of dialogues, supported with so much nature and feeling, and the interest which his manner of writing has thrown into the familiar stories and incidents of domestic and common life."[34]

Some of the dialogue is hopelessly stilted and reminiscent of the worst of Bunyan. For instance, the husband says, "Tell me, *my Dear*, what afflicts thee; if it be in my Power to relieve it . . . *as in Duty I ought*, so in Affection I am inclin'd to give you all the Comfort . . . Advice, and . . . Assistance I am able" (68). The psychological insights, however, seem strikingly astute. As the parents discuss the reasons for their neglect of religious instruction and the difficulties and humiliations of trying to institute it with grown children, they seem perfectly plausible and the products of penetrating, detailed analysis. When Defoe recounts conversations rather than giving them in dialogue, he is idiomatic and assured: "[She] told her Mother *in plain Words* she would not be hinder'd, she was past a Child, she would go to the Park, and to the Play . . . ay that she wou'd" (85). When he came to write novels, Defoe tended to use such lively narrative paragraphs rather than direct conversation. Once into a situation, Defoe could create realistic, even slangy dialect as he does when the children talk to each other.

⁂

Most eighteenth-century people believed that human beings were more alike than different, but 1715 impressed Defoe with the significance of personality, and *The Family Instructor* is partly a deliberate study of the consequences of "Temper and Constitution" (84, 111). He presents how differently people respond to the very same situations. When faced with restrictions one child burns her own romances and play-books, and two others leave home; one of these two sincerely repents in adversity, and the other continues a dissolute life.

A series of pamphlets explore the personalities and interactions within the Harley ministry, and they, rather than events, come to determine what happened. Particularly with the queen, Defoe depicts "constitution and temper" as fatal to the nation's interests. Time after time he excoriates the queen for weaknesses often assigned to her sex. In *Memoirs of the Conduct of Her Late Majesty* (1715) he shows her weeping over the war's fatalities, imagining men dragged away from their families to fight, and, in an excess of sentiment, ordering her ministers to make peace, then pushing them into a precipitate, unsatisfactory treaty, and exerting her "Womanish Reasoning" to determine such decisions as Ormonde's restraining order. She is alternately too easily persuaded and too peremptorily jealous of her power.[35] He blames her for falling under Abigail Masham's influence and makes Masham representative of "the subtle Sex, Cunning" who took advantage of the abuses of Sarah Churchill, duchess of Marlborough. Just as Masham could manipulate the queen, so others, too, could "impose" on her. Like Eve, the queen lacks the intellectual ability and independent principles to resist specious persuasion. Occasionally Defoe opposes her affections and her reason, and affection consistently determines her actions. When the affection is misplaced, as it is with Masham, the queen errs and then bitterly regrets; when the affection is justified, as it is with Harley, it acts as a magnet, albeit a weak one, to pull her back to right action. She is so merciful as to be too weak to punish those who take advantage of her or who abuse the freedom she has given men like Sacheverell. Her basic desire is to be "the general Mother" of her people, and, like many a foolish literary mother of the period, she fails to educate her children and even prevents the deserved correction that might save them.

Defoe comes to the opinion that the queen surrendered the scepter, the symbol of the power to administer the civil government. By doing so, she gave up her power to assure justice, redress public grievances, encourage commerce, lead Parliament to make beneficial laws, control foreign policy, protect religious toleration, and uphold the constitutional rights of her people. In England's recent history he finds the scepter, "the most essential Part of the Monarch," too often given over to the monarch's ministers. The result, he says, is faction, intrigue, plunder, and the destruction of public peace.[36] The queen watches helplessly as the scepter changes hands over and over and even cries helplessly over the unfortunate consequences. With her scepter out of her possession, her ministers, after all, can do many things she does not approve and that cause unrest and even misery for some of her subjects.

Defoe uses *The Secret History of State Intrigues* (1715) to warn George I to control the scepter. In a surprisingly critical description of William III's inability to hold the scepter, Defoe implies that George is a contrast to William. In fact, Defoe may have received the information in this section directly from William. In a memorandum to George, Count Johann von Bothmer quotes William as saying that "having made a wrong choice of Ministers at the outset, [he] could never afterwards work well with either party."[37] George, Defoe says, is entirely capable of managing crown, sword (which Anne also surrendered), and scepter. William, also from abroad, could not overcome a disadvantage that George shares: the necessity to "see with other Men's Eyes" when administering domestic affairs (12). The "Ignorant or Indolent Prince" who allows himself to be persuaded that he has nothing to do "than enjoy his Ease and Repose" and mindlessly signs warrants and orders deserves the hatred subjects usually reserve for tyrants, Defoe argues. Defoe, then, offers the prescription that could make George a great king: "But if he hears all Sides, and judges impartially, he then becomes thoroughly inform'd, is no longer a Stranger to his People, and puts himself in a Capacity to be the King of all his People, as effectually, as if he had been born among them: And such a King alone is able to make his People Happy" (67). Defoe seems aware here of George's limitations and tendency to isolate himself.

In these pamphlets, too, Bolingbroke is the ambitious, jealous, erratic man; Francis Atterbury the treasonous, irreligious, subtle puppeteer; Simon Harcourt a spineless dupe, and the earl of Nottingham, "Dismal," passionate and vindictive. Just as Defoe used dialogue as well as narration to delineate the characters in *The Family Instructor*, so he does in the pamphlets. When the thwarted men meet after the queen's death, their words symbolize their characters (pt. 1:71). Atterbury becomes Milton's Satan and proposes "desperate measures." The others play the parts of Satan's despairing, venomous followers. "Did I not warn you from breaking with him?" Harcourt asks. Atterbury begins to rave, swears, and then explodes, "We have but one way left, *France* and the Lawful Heir." They give their "full Consent" to "Treason against both Queen and Country."

A more extended study of personality and its effect on public and personal affairs is *The History of the Wars, of his Present Majesty, Charles XII, King of Sweden*, a work perhaps commissioned by the emperor's staff.[38] Rather than finding a hero in Charles XII, Defoe found a fascinating example of a man at the mercy of his faults. As early as 1704 he found Charles guilty of "Ambition, Injustice, Ingratitude, and above all, an Impolitick and Immoderate Fury" (1:163). Over the years Charles confirms rather than outgrows these characteristics. What Defoe deplores in Charles—his sacrifice of his Livonian subjects, his campaign in Saxony, his execution of General Johann Reinhold von Patkul, his invasion of Russia, his willingness to go beyond neglect of the Protestant interest to threaten it in new ways—became evidence for Defoe's interpretation of Charles's motives. He provided an analysis of a personality and an interpretation of current events.

In Charles, Defoe saw a man blinded not only to Europe's interest but also to his own and his country's. In some of his best writing, he captured the qualities that made Charles a great subject for later writers of the caliber of Samuel Johnson and Voltaire:

Unhappy Ambition! . . . when it once flatters Men with the Glory of Conquest, blinds them with Mists and Shadows of imaginary Glory, in Pursuit of which they precipitate themselves into the deepest Gulphs of Human Misery.

What could it be to the King of *Sweden* to reign over abandon'd Deserts, and to govern barbarous Nations . . . What greater would he be for Hoards of *Tartars*, or Swarms of *Cossacks* . . . ?

is not the King of *Sweden* now a *Memento Mori* . . . to set Bounds to . . . Appetites, and not to let the Lust of Conquest lead . . . beyond the Bounds of Justice?[39]

As Defoe said in his preface to *The History of the Wars*, Charles XII rivaled "the Caesars and Alexanders of Antient Story" and resembled the heroes of *romans courtois*. He promised this fascinating hero, the "Glorious Actions, Battles, Sieges, and Gallant Enterprizes" of the war, and clear explanations of the background and events of the war.

In his *Review* Defoe had said that Providence had punished Charles for being an overreacher, for carrying the war beyond reasonable objectives in order to gain personal glory and revenge. Here, too, Defoe occasionally drew attention to the workings of Providence in Charles's life. For example, the execution of Patkul immediately preceded the defeat at Poltava. In both are the signs of Charles's arrogance and belief in his own omnipotence. The narrator says, "But Heaven had other Designs, and the Lawrels his Majesty had Gain'd in a Series of uninterrupted Victory, were now to be snatch'd from his Head by the Barbarous *Muscovites* in one Day" (283). For instance, at a battle Defoe sees as provoked and defensive, he shows Charles encouraging his men with the words, be not "daunted at the great Number of the Enemies, but rather . . . be convinced, that God the Protector of Right, and Avenger of Justice, would not fail to Strengthen them" (88). Defoe tells how the clear morning became a foggy, snowy day that allowed the Swedes to advance undetected to within fifty feet of the Russians and win a great victory. Later, the fictional Scottish narrator criticizes Charles for keeping his men in small troops in Livonia while he took the bulk of his army in pursuit of the Muscovites and goes on to describe its gradual decimation (148–52). In addition to its other satisfactions, then, Defoe offered the pleasure of popular fiction's promise of virtue rewarded and pride punished.

Although the book reviewed the past, its focus was the immediate future. George I's accession brought the Great Northern War to the attention of Englishmen, and Defoe knew more about it than all but a few of his countrymen. One of George's last acts in Hanover had been to give orders that any request by Charles for passage through his country be denied, for it would be "hostile" "and their passage should therefore be resisted, be it by force."[40] Felicitously for Defoe, Charles XII had finally managed to return to Sweden from his refuge in Turkey, and the heroic king who ascended the throne at fourteen and at seventeen had led Sweden's armies to victory over Denmark, Poland, and Russia before he lost the decisive battle of Poltava ten years later in 1709 was back in time to oppose the new alliance of Hanover, Denmark, and Prussia that George had joined in order to obtain Bremen and Verden.* This alliance and Russia had declared war on Sweden in 1714. Even Charles's return had been characteristically prodigious. He had ridden more than nine hundred miles on horseback in fourteen days; when he arrived at his palace, his feet and legs were so swollen that his boots had to be cut off.[41] With George's accession, the Great Northern War became a matter of intense interest and serious controversy among Englishmen.

Defoe's preface speculated that "the Second Part of [Charles's] History, may render him more Glorious than the First." By selecting as narrator a Scot in Charles's army, Defoe could give a sympathetic portrait of the king. He could invest infrequent sights of Charles with an aura of wonder. Charles, he says, was "smiling and beautiful," "Youthful and yet Grave" (88); "his Figure . . . was their Terror . . . he always look'd like a King whatever his Dress was" (137), and "the King with his usual Intrepidity advanc'd to the Charge" (295). As a soldier, the narrator could describe the ways the armies prepared for battle, the fighting itself, and explain the aftermath. Moreover, he could develop themes that moved the book toward its conclusion. *The History of the Wars* as Defoe structured it is the story not only of Charles's loss of perspective but of the development of the Russian army, another new rival to English power. In the course of the narrative, the army that the Scot had called the worst strategists in the world became "another kind of Man in the Field," an army now able "to Fight [the Swedes] upon equal Terms."[42] Faced with new difficulties and new enemies at the end of the book, Charles stands poised to "write" the "Second Part of his History,"

---

*Bremen and Verden controlled the mouths of the Elbe and Weser Rivers, now more valuable to George because they were convenient for sailing to Great Britain.

and Defoe's readers are prepared to observe, understand, and evaluate.

This book illustrates yet another of Defoe's attempts to affirm what he believed himself to be. In it he could unite his desire to inform his countrymen, "to open their eyes," and his literary ambitions. History was the genre Defoe read with the most enjoyment and respect and, since he had laid his poetic ambitions aside, the one to which he aspired. His book seemed especially promising because Englishmen had not followed the Great Northern War and might be expected to feel a need to bring themselves up to date. The fact that the *Review* reported far more foreign news than any other London paper suggests just how little reached the British public. Defoe would complain that the reason was lack of reader interest; he said that his countrymen "neither value or understand the Intelligence Abroad" and choose "the Contention of Parties, and the Interests of Persons." In fact, it was not easy for journalists to get reliable news from abroad. Foreign news at that time was reported to the British public by the official *London Gazette*, which was supposed to receive weekly reports from the government's ambassadors and consuls, who were responsible for gathering news and collecting newspapers, newsletters, and information from their correspondents. More foreign news appeared in several other newspapers, such as the *Daily Courant* and *Post Man*, which took their news from the Dutch and French newspapers, scheduled to arrive in London twice a week, from the *London Gazette*, and from private letters or even information given by ships' crews.[43] Early in the reign of George, at least one of the ambassadors to a northern country had to be urged officially to send information by "every post" "supported and fed by the fullest and best intelligence of historical occurences."[44] By 1710 immigrant journalists like Jacques de Fonvive and Abel Boyer had "correspondents" on the Continent, primarily in France, Holland, and Flanders.[45] The most common source of all foreign news, however, was plagiarism from other newspapers.

Whereas the crucial battle of Poltava had received almost no serious press attention, by the summer of 1715 when Defoe published *The History of the Wars*, northern affairs had begun to receive prominent, extensive coverage.[46] The British navy, allegedly sent to the Baltic to protect the merchant fleet, left England on 29 May, and war-weary Englishmen began to ask if George had violated the Act of Settlement.* In this climate, Defoe's book appeared, and a typical contemporary reader, his Scottish friend John Clerk, left a record of its appeal; he

---

*One clause forbade England's participation in a war not involving British possessions without parliamentary approval.

recommended it "For understanding the rise of the warrs in the north" and described it as "very diverting," "as full of variety as any . . . written."[47]

The History of the Wars is an uneven book. Vivid descriptions and tightly written anecdotes alternate with pages of summaries and quotations from dozens of documents. Like so much that Defoe wrote that year, wishful thinking mingles with factual reporting. As he had done in the *Review*, he imagines Charles as a potential peacemaker and defender of the Protestant faith. Yet he can give cogent demonstrations of the ways Charles's actions hindered the allies' fight against France. Although he manages the stories of each nation well most of the time, there are lapses in which he says, "as I have said" or "as above mentioned." The same kinds of narrative problems can be found in *The Family Instructor*, in which he uses such clauses as "as will be seen in the last Part of this Work" (189) and says, "The two last Dialogues are to be understood to be a Recapitulation of what had been acted" (358).

In *The History of the Wars*, however, Defoe begins to use such statements to direct his reader's attention to process. Rather than an admission of inability to handle simultaneity and multiple plot lines, they become a means of firm guidance with clear didactic ends. For instance, the narrator says ominously, "but it was from this time we found the *Muscovites* another kind of Men in the Field" and then goes on to explain the defeat at Poltava (277–311). In Charles's life, as in his shorter accounts of his own and Harley's lives, Defoe would study courage, fortitude, and responses to adversity. Just as he had prepared the reader to analyze the slaughter in Livonia and the change in the Russian army, so he uses such transitions as a kind of division. At one point, he writes, "But this Year 1710, was a fatal Year to *Sweden*" and the plague, the losses at Riga, and other disasters follow (347–51).

By focusing on process Defoe also underscores personality. The Great Northern War, he points out, was a conflict entirely among non–Roman Catholic countries

begun in a manner that no Protestants ever used to begin their War . . . carried on as no War since the Ages of Christianity . . . was ever carried on. . . .

The . . . Extremities they seem to tend to . . . as if . . . Men were turn'd Ravenous Beasts, Monsters and Devils. . . .

What the Wise Ends of Providence may be, in thus letting loose the Passions of Men, and suffering them to run on to such Rage, Fury, and Inexorable Barbarity, as no Christian can read without Horror; and, as I confess Chills my very Blood when I write it.[48]

Again and again, he would write about Charles and his great adversary, Peter I of Russia. Their personalities stamped their extravagant campaigns. Compared to the administrator kings of England and France,

Charles and Peter seemed elemental and even primitive, and they fought in a vast, sublime land.

Part of the unevenness in the quality of this book and some of Defoe's pamphlets probably resulted from the method of publication he had developed during the time of his greatest productivity in the reign of Anne. He had divided the work and begun to use both of his sons. Benjamin lived in the Inner Temple and seems to have enjoyed the rather idle, sociable life for which its students were known. Defoe seems to have stayed there often; in fact, he may have been the renter of the rooms himself, for his printer Richard Janeway specifically calls them "Mr Daniel De Foes Chamber in the Temple."[49] From this convenient place close to the booksellers, Defoe could easily see several forty- to fifty-page pamphlets through from conception to publication in three to four weeks.

Defoe would contract with a publisher and then begin delivering pages to be set in type within a few days.[50] He had a standing arrangement with John Baker that allowed him two guineas on every five hundred six penny pamphlets printed. Editions varied from 1,000 to 3,000 copies, with the most promising propaganda tracts averaging 2,000 copies. From others, like Janeway, Defoe usually received four guineas plus twenty or twenty-five copies of the pamphlet for every thousand sold. Defoe was unusually well paid; another writer, one definitely above average, received but fifteen shillings for the same sized pamphlet.[51] As the pages were set by half-sheets, one of the printer's boys would bring them to Defoe at the Temple or at his house in Stoke Newington where he would correct them. Sometimes Benjamin would proofread them, and sometimes he or Defoe would do so while the boy waited. At other times one of the sons would return the proofs later. Young Daniel, who wrote in a distinctive italic hand and had easy access to his father's library, sometimes wrote in passages copied from other books, such as that of the resignation of King Richard in *Reasons against the Succession of the House of Hanover*. Benjamin, who became a journalist, may have done more creative work. *A Letter to a Merry Young Gentleman* (1715), a pamphlet that ridicules Defoe's work as well as Thomas Burnet's, satirizes a young law student who has begun to be a "hackney" and write pamphlets (4–5). Almost six pages of the manuscript of *Reasons against the Succession* is written in a third hand, described as "after the Swedish manner." Soon after this Defoe compared the writer to a "Master Workman" who "assembled" works. By 1720 he saw himself as part of a group of "Masters and Undertakers in *the Pen* and *Ink* Manufacture."[52] Defoe would send his complimentary copies as well as additional purchased ones to Newcastle, to several places in Scotland, and even to rival London booksellers.

Throughout the year the press continued to attack Defoe, and Defoe found himself continually confronted with skepticism, ridicule, and vituperation. "A Health to be Sung and Drank by all Honest Britons" made no distinctions between Defoe and the impeached peers and other "traitors" including Prior, Roper, Swift, Sacheverell, and Leslie. *The Golden Age* called him a tool of the Jacobite party, hired to ruin his country.[53] Yet he continued to publish. The years during which he rapidly wrote hundreds of pages had established the habit, and he published too many long, mediocre pamphlets. The defenses of Harley, for example, average seventy-four pages. Sometimes Defoe set himself an impossible task, and sometimes his anger and resentment take over a pamphlet.

As part of his effort to return to his position as moderate man, voice of reason, and opener of people's eyes, he tried to revive the themes of his 1710 work. For instance, *Some Methods to Supply the Defects of the Late Peace* (1715) asks for "a compleat Union at home, a chearful supporting the Government, an universal Adherence to . . . our King . . . [for then] we shall . . . be very rich, strong, and happy" (40). With George as king, Defoe saw the possibility, not just for peace during his lifetime, but for "our Children being blessed with it when we are gone."[54] Just as he had when Harley returned to power, he relied primarily on promises that no drastic changes would occur and that a stable, competent administrator was in charge.

In truth, none of these reassuring pamphlets of Defoe's is very good. George I was an enigma to his new subjects, had not even bothered to learn fluent English, and kept his former wife imprisoned in the remote Castle of Ahlden in northern Germany.[55] He was a short man with protruding, striking blue eyes, heavy lips, and the long, pointed family nose—completely wrong for an age that favored an elegant, slender man with patrician features. Although his arrival in England on 18 September had been greeted by enthusiastic crowds as large as a million and a half, scattered Jacobite riots occurred.[56] Coronation Day and every holiday and election day thereafter brought unruly mobs into the streets. Over thirty Dissenting meeting houses were wrecked on James's birthday, and the Riot Act made such destruction a felony. Some people began to wear oak leaves, symbol of the Stuarts, on public occasions, and many of them did so to the end of George's reign. Even in the city of London, still a Dissenting stronghold, military intervention and "calculated acts of legal terror" had to be used to keep order. For instance, the London militia shot several rioters on 10 June, the Pretender's birthday.[57]

Feeling as he did about the Protestant succession and the end of the war, Defoe needed time to understand his Tory countrymen. He had admitted to Harley that he needed time to understand "which way to direct words So . . . as Not to do harm instead of Good."[58] To him the end of the war meant the recovery of trade and the promise of English prosperity; to his contemporaries the heavy taxes and high prices that the unpopular war had occasioned were far more prominent. Many of them felt themselves threatened by competition as never before; Scotland, Ireland, and France could now compete as Holland and Portugal already did, and the Whig immigration policy that had let twelve thousand Palatines, among others, into the country, left the merchants, tradesmen, and farmers assailed at home as well as abroad. The Whigs were associated with money, trade, and the city; many Englishmen still valued land and traditional, even isolationist, values. Finally, George I had been a Lutheran, and Defoe and the Dissenters had celebrated the death of the Schism Act on the very morning they were supposed to pray for Anne's soul. Sacheverell's mobs had not died with Queen Anne; their hatred for "the new association" of Low Church and the Dissenters blazed, and they burned meeting houses and effigies of clergymen again. These people believed that schism threatened their country's welfare as passionately as Defoe believed in religious liberty.

Many of Defoe's pamphlets in 1714 and 1715 worked by negatives, focusing on what the English should not expect rather than on what they could anticipate. For instance, in *Some Methods*, he asked if it could be probable that George could be ignorant of the English Constitution and its guarantees to the Church of England as safeguard for his own crown (26–27).

Defoe's tendency was to present George as a type of King William, as he sometimes had Anne as a type of Queen Elizabeth. When Defoe reeled off praises that he habitually used in his memorials for William, they ring hollow:

A Prince who comes, like King *William*, fill'd with Resolutions to make us Safe, Rich, Easy and Happy; willing to do all that lies in him to contribute to our National Felicity, and to hearken to all good Council for his Direction, inspir'd from Heaven with a Zeal for Religion; a Passion for his People's Liberty; Charity for the Miserable and Unhappy.[59]

To ascribe eagerness for "all good Council" and charity for the miserable to the king flirted with the ludicrous. George was remote and seemed suspicious and even indifferent. By universal account he was shy and cold; combined with his awkward French and inability to speak good English, this manner isolated him and alienated people. Satires began to appear; a typical one read,

Behold he comes to make thy People groan.
And with their Curses to ascend thy Throne;

> A Clod-pate, base, inhuman, jealous Fool,
> The Jest of EUROPE, and the Faction's Tool.

It was June before he appeared to review the troops in Hyde Park and admitted people to kiss his hand, and he seemed to show no interest at all in his subjects. Even more ridiculous were Defoe's attempts to depict George's face as an "Indix" of his honor, probity, faith, and goodness. In one place Defoe went so far as to say, "His Person is Comely and Grave" and "his Countenance has Majesty and Sweetness."[60]

Most commonly Defoe presented George as a vigorous, experienced administrator, and here he was correct and, in fact, ahead of many English courtiers. George had been one of the most powerful men in the Empire and continued to manage Hanover throughout his reign. He was methodical, deliberate, and, in a time when the country needed these qualities, economical and cautious about making commitments. Defoe was correct to perceive in him a confident leader who had effectively led an army, a man highly knowledgeable in the affairs of Europe, and a person familiar with the duties and prerogatives of a king.

When he was not reassuring people about George's good intentions and moderate policies, he used his predictions to give George and his counselors thinly veiled advice. Throughout his life Defoe wrote in the literary tradition that allowed subjects to educate their monarchs and to try to improve them through praise of qualities to which they might aspire if they did not already possess them. In this hope Defoe endlessly praised George for moderation, for being above party politics, for refusing to gratify party desires for revenge, and for protecting the rights of his subjects. In a few places he called the king's imagined policy of moderation "extensive, *Godlike*," thereby echoing the most famous contemporary example of such writing, Dryden's *Absalom and Achitophel*.

Defoe's hopes, no matter their reason for presentation, clearly mingle with his responses to the catastrophic divisions within the queen's ministry that had led to Harley's fall. Here his anger at the ministers and especially at the queen breaks out increasingly clearly. A typical passage from *Strike While the Iron's Hot* reads:

Whoever he be, that promotes the fatal Experiment of Governing this Nation by a Ministry, especially at a Time when we have not a Woman on the Throne, but a vigorous and magnanimous King; a Prince experienc'd in Government Equal, to the Weight . . . as able to handle the *Scepter*, and wield the *Sword*, as he is to wear the *Crown*. (18–19)

Above all, in these pamphlets Defoe expresses reservations about the strong influence of advisers or a ministry; he makes some of his strongest statements in favor of the legitimate powers of the executive and legislative branches of government.

In the events that crippled the Harley ministry, Defoe also finds weaknesses in the Revolution settlement. Just as William's accession had occasioned these parliamentary acts, so George's might allow some "improvements" that "Six and Twenty Years" suggest to be needed. Among the deficiencies that Defoe sees are inadequate preventives of the exercise of arbitrary power, the failure to "suppress the stupid Notions of Divine Hereditaty [sic], Indefeazable Right, &c.," and an undefined, unsatisfactory establishment of religious toleration.[61] In these complaints and suggestions Defoe makes a covert case for additional powers for Parliament. On the queen, who let her scepter be a prize to be squabbled over by a few contending men, and on the idea of government by a strong cabinet, he heaped abuse and rewrote history in order to recommend his vision of the best form of government.

Perhaps more than his outbursts of anger, his anxiety about earning a living was a greater obstacle to his desire to show that he was the man he believed himself to be. When in trouble Defoe always tended to over-invest and overcompensate. In 1714 he was a master at manipulating the press and had established himself as a writer who could make a profit for a bookseller. Defoe continued to publish his best and most clearly Whig work with John Baker, but he also began to cultivate the large, ambitious booksellers William Taylor and James Roberts and to place particular kinds of pamphlets with several fairly specialized printers.

At that time booksellers, often called "publishers," purchased manuscripts from authors, employed printers, and then sold the published copies in their own and other shops. They commonly exchanged books or made agreements to share profits.[62] By that time, too, they owned periodicals and supplied them, often in bulk, to subscribers. In 1708 Defoe had reported to Godolphin that "a Club of 20 Booksellers" managed the *Daily Courant* for profit (H 263). In *The Secret History of the Secret History of the White Staff*, Defoe described the practice of booksellers who hired writers, sometimes the same person, to write on both sides of a question, "causing the deceiv'd People to Dance in the Circles of their drawing" (8). Such booksellers, he continued, kept "Clubs, or Setts of these Men . . . in constant Employment" and "joyn together their Stocks, when such Books are written, to pay as well the Charge of Writing as of Printing the same, and then unite their Interest . . . for the more effectual vending the said Books" (18). Here Defoe explains the practice that Baker and Janeway recorded in their 1713 informations. Although the practices of keeping "stables" of writers is associated more with London in the time of Fielding's *Author's Farce* (1730), it had rapidly become well established in the last four years of Anne's reign. A contemporary commented humorously: "I can assure you this sort of Business goes on so very briskly, that I fear even Quills, in a little time, will be a scarce Commodity; and that a Flock of Geese will yield more, than a Flock of Sheep."[63]

In addition to employing his sons and perhaps a hack or two of his own, Defoe had begun to repeat himself frequently and to borrow more freely and heavily from books by others. From the beginning of his career, he had quoted himself approvingly, and he had often repeated a few paragraphs or more in several pamphlets. Sometimes he had published the same material in the *Review* and in individual pamphlets. Now he began to use his own material more often and began to fall back on clichés and repeat himself without the kinds of self-conscious, often amusing, admissions of his practice of quoting himself. He began to rework historical anecdotes like the one about the Queen Mother in the reign of Louis XIII of France in *The Secret History of the White Staff, The Minutes of Monsr. Mesnager* (1717), and *The Memoirs of a Cavalier* (1720). He even allowed one of his 1715 pamphlets to be issued twice almost simultaneously with two misleadingly different titles.[64]

Soon after being deprived of his income from Harley, Defoe made his strangest liaison and one that contributed in peculiar ways to his development as a fiction writer. Samuel Keimer, who published his *Secret History of the Secret History of the White Staff, Memoirs of the Conduct of Her Majesty* by "the Right Honourable the Countess of ——," and perhaps as many as eleven other pamphlets, had just opened a print shop.[65] More sensational and base than almost anything he had written earlier, the pamphlets Defoe gave Keimer often seemed to exist parasitically on Defoe's work for other publishers. *The Secret History of the Secret History*, for instance, consisted primarily of a dialogue between a Quaker and a curiosity-seeker in which Defoe's authorship of *The Secret History of the White Staff* was denied even as Defoe was depicted as "the poor Man in a very Dangerous Condition, having had a Fit of an Apoplexy . . . insomuch, that his Life was despair'd of " (16), the same story given by the publisher of *An Appeal to Honour and Justice. Memoirs of the Conduct of Her Late Majesty*, with its portrayal of the weeping, maudlin queen, would be worthy of the worst of Delarivière Manley's scandalous memoirs.

Defoe's enemies were quick to harass him for going to Keimer, whom they compared to "*John Dunton* of Raving Memory." The pun on the sign at Dunton's shop, the Raven, associated Keimer not only with madness but with scavenger-printers. Keimer had opened his printing house in 1713, but he was best known for his membership in a charismatic religious sect, the Camisards. In 1708 he had become a "Minister Extraordinary," and his sister would achieve some eminence as a prophet. He wore several pieces of yard-long green ribbon and grew a beard in a time when men were nearly universally clean-shaven. The ribbon, "the livery of the Lord," had his Camisard name, "Jonathan, of the Tribe of Asser," written on parchment, sewn inside. These distinctive marks would allow God to recognize his chosen people on the day of judgment. Keimer frequently printed the Camisards' books at his own expense and occasionally libeled the government; he was arrested in June 1715 for seditious libel and went bankrupt in 1716. Two of the prophets in his sect ungratefully seized his effects while he was in prison.

Keimer may have encouraged Defoe's fictional experiments, for he specialized in fantastic reports, and he seems to have introduced Defoe to the Quaker persona. Keimer greatly enjoyed verbal sparring and dispute. He created Quaker characters and gave them some of the same witty, argumentative mannerisms that Defoe began to use in his own pamphlets. In the year he began to write for Keimer, for instance, Defoe used the Quaker in *The Secret History of the Secret History* and *A Friendly Epistle by Way of Reproof from one of the People called Quakers*.[66] Keimer seems to have had a gift for persuading far abler men than himself to come into his projects. Later he employed Benjamin Franklin several times, but Franklin, who once pretended to help him found a new religion, remarked quite accurately that Keimer was profoundly ignorant of the practical ways of the world.

Defoe also began to sell a few pamphlets to two printers whose small shops also soon went out of business. Both J. Moore (or Moor) and R. Burleigh had taken over part of the business of one of Defoe's former Dissenting printers, Ann Baldwin. To Moore, for instance, he sold anti-Jacobite pamphlets of a more fictional nature than his customary work. His *Memoirs of John, Duke of Melfort* (1714) had required two editions, and, therefore, he found a ready market with Moore for other defenses of Harley and *An Account of the . . . Actions of James Butler* [1715]. He also went to Ann Dodd, an often arrested "mercury"* who was best known for keeping a large supply of books and pamphlets in stock in her shop outside Temple Bar. To John Morphew, the favorite printer for Anne's Tory ministers, he continued to give work such as the defenses of the ministry like *Some Reasons Offered by the Late Ministry in Defence of their Administration* (1715). He also began to sell work to James Roberts, an excellent printer who had rented Ann Baldwin's shop. To Roberts, a publisher worth cultivating, he sold several attacks on the clergymen who continued to provoke unrest through sermons and tracts emphasizing the schismatic possibilities of George's Lutheranism.[67]

Besides their number and mediocrity, the works of these seventeen

---

*People, mostly women, who bought newspapers and pamphlets wholesale and then sold them to hawkers or out of a small shop.

months are notable for their experimentation with fictional techniques, especially dialogue. In addition to his first sustained work in a woman's voice (*Memoirs of the Conduct of Her Late Majesty*), he developed the voices of the witty Quaker that would be so important in *Captain Singleton* and the soldier of fortune who would animate *Memoirs of a Cavalier*. Moreover, he continued to develop his repertoire of sectarians. These pamphlets often include long, obviously made up speeches, personal even eccentric details about the narrator, dialogue, and unusual attention to details such as dress or setting. *The Candidate*, another Keimer production, even includes an entire act from an allegedly unacted, unpublished play.[68] Propaganda had failed to save the Treaty of Commerce and Navigation and the Oxford ministry; it was proving ineffective if not counterproductive in the defense of Harley, and every scribbler now used the tactics Defoe had pioneered. Obviously seeking new ways to influence public opinion, Defoe, even as he wrote in great haste, experimented with point of view, character, and literary form as he had never done before.

Immediately after Queen Anne's death, one of Defoe's most serious problems was legal. He was again under indictment for seditious libel. George Ridpath, the editor of the *Flying Post*, had become a fugitive from arrest the previous April, and the men he had engaged to continue the paper replaced the printer William Hurt with Robert Tookey. Hurt tried to continue the *Flying Post* himself, and Defoe helped him. Hurt explained that "malicious people" had turned Ridpath against him and that he had continued the paper because he could not afford to lose that part of his income. According to Defoe, his own plan was to drive Harley's critic, Ridpath, out of business. The confusion and competition caused by publication of two papers with the same name and the "softened" Whig news in the Hurt/Defoe *Flying Post* would make the papers unprofitable.[69] On 19 August Hurt's paper published a letter that began,

Sir, You cannot be ignorant of the late Journey of a No[ble] Pe—r to Ireland . . . part of the Design of which we are assur'd was, to new model the Forces there, and particularly to break no less than 70 of the Honest Officers of the Army, and to fill up their Places with the Tools and Creatures of Con[stantine] Phi[pp]s, and such a Rabble of Cut-throats as were fit for the Work that they had for them to do.

The "Noble Peer" was Arthur Annesley, fifth earl of Anglesey, and, unfortunately, one of King George's regents.* The letter was danger-

---

*As determined by the Regency Act of 1706, the seven great officers of state and nineteen men chosen by George Ludwig assumed the executive functions of government until George arrived in England. Shrewsbury was in both categories.

ous because it was true—Anglesey had gone to Ireland on Boling-broke's orders to help the Jacobite Phipps crush the Whig Corporation of Dublin.[70] This action could have been part of a far-reaching plan to make an invasion by the Pretender easier. The *Flying Post* letter drew attention to Anglesey's trip and to his associates and all but called him a Jacobite.

By the twenty-first the ministry had issued a warrant for Hurt's arrest, and by the twenty-third John Baker, Defoe's loyal publisher, had been arraigned. On the twenty-fourth Baker's and Hurt's papers were seized.[71] On the twenty-seventh Secretary of State William Bromley wrote to Attorney General Northey to tell him that the regents wanted his opinion regarding "who may most properly be prosecuted." The regents suggested Hurt, Baker, and Defoe. Significantly, Bromley added,

There is no positive Proof who writ the Ms, nor is De Foe yet apprehended, tho' a Messenger has been employ'd to make diligent Search for him.

The Lords Justices are further pleased to order, that you lay before them an Account of the last Prosecution against Defoe.

On the twenty-eighth Bromley wrote to say that Hurt, already in prison until he paid a fine, was not worth the cost of prosecution. He continued, "As to Deffoe, there is no Evidence against him, but Hurt's saying he believes the Letter . . . to be his hand writing, which I doubt is an Evidence not to be depended upon."[72] Later that day, however, Bromley had Defoe in custody, brought Baker back in for questioning, and obtained the manuscript copy of the *Flying Post* letter about Anglesey—in Defoe's unmistakable hand. He interrogated Defoe again on the thirtieth, and on the thirty-first Defoe appealed to Harley for help. He was being accused, he said, of insulting Anglesey at Harley's direction. According to Defoe, Hurt had received the letter from an unknown person, and Defoe had "softened" it by removing "Severall Scandalous Reflections" on Anglesey and then copied out the revised letter. Defoe asked Harley to intercede for him with Anglesey and "assure" Anglesey that he knew nothing else and "did nothing . . . but with Design to Serve his Ldpp."[73]

A number of things about this letter do not ring true. By suggesting that others saw Harley behind his work, Defoe hoped to engage Harley, but at this point Harley was still in London and had not yet given up his hopes of an accommodation with George. He certainly would not have allowed the insult of one of George's regents. Moreover, the man leading the investigation was one of Harley's most loyal followers, Bromley, who would refuse an office under George,[74] and Bromley would have been careful to keep Harley's name out of the case. Defoe, moreover, would certainly not have been trying to "serve" Anglesey. Anglesey had made one of the strongest speeches in favor of the schism bill, and his characterization of the Dissenters as dangerous surely rankled. Earlier Defoe had blamed Anglesey and the earl of Abingdon for the defeat of the Treaty of Commerce and Navigation and described Anglesey in terms that showed complete disrespect for his ability: "Now being unfortunately come to have a Seat in [the House of Lords] . . . he sets up for a deep Politician . . . and fancies himself equal to the first Posts in the Government, though nothing can be more apparent, than that . . . let the Waters . . . be ever so shallow, he always contrives to get himself out of his Depth in them, and plunge some few of his implicit Followers along with him."[75] Anglesey's mission to Ireland and the sudden death of the queen offered Defoe a chance for revenge. He probably hoped to prevent any permanent appointment and influence for Anglesey, and, in fact, the investigation of Constantine Phipps that the regents launched simultaneously with the prosecution of Defoe resulted in the dismissal of Phipps as lord justice and lord chancellor of Ireland.

On 3 September Bromley sent Attorney General Northey the depositions and evidence he had and ordered him to prosecute Defoe in the name of the regents. On the seventh Baker, Defoe, and Beardwell, a printer, made bail and were released.[76] Defoe again fruitlessly appealed to Harley to persuade Anglesey to drop the prosecution. Near the end of the Michaelmas session, Defoe had to enter a plea of "not guilty" and was bound over "to answer the King concerning certain trespasses, contempts, and misdemeanors." The indictment presented in Hilary term accused Defoe of "being a seditious and malicious man and plotting and intending evil to the . . . Queen . . . and to scandalise and vilify the memory of . . . the Queen . . . and cause to be believed that [she] intended . . . that wicked and dishonest reports and reputations be created of the Officers" in the Irish army. It quoted only the opening sentence of the *Flying Post* letter and complained that Defoe was in contempt of the law, causing "the perturbation" of George I's country and setting a bad example.[77]

In spite of this prosecution and the end of his government employment, Defoe approached the future confidently. One of the first things he did in August 1714 was move from one Stoke Newington House into another.[78] This second house stood on four acres of land, and he had space to expand the house and plant pleasant gardens. He selected a large room in the newer part of the rambling house for his study and made plans for a life of relative retirement. He believed that the queen's sudden death had prevented the vindication or even restoration of Harley, and, surrounded by his large library, he began to support himself with his pen. The Queen Anne style house has been called a "gloomy and irregular pile of red brick," but it had thick walls, lovely large deep windows with pleasant window seats, and plenty of space. In

DANIEL DEFOE'S HOUSE AT STOKE NEWINGTON. 1724

Defoe's home in Newington, 1724.

Scotland Defoe had presented himself as something of an expert on gardens, and at this house he planted and improved several kinds of gardens, including a "pleasure ground," an orchard with walks and convenient seats, and a kitchen garden. He planted lime trees, so beloved in Scotland.

The rigors of 1703 had confirmed Defoe's somewhat bluffing "The God that gave me brains will give me bread." In 1714 he knew that as long as he could write, he could support himself and his family. To move into a larger home within weeks of the fall of Harley shows how independent and capable he felt himself to be. Years later he said that most authors considered themselves good writers, "for if a poor Author had not some good Opinion of himself, especially when under the Discouragement of having no Body else to be of his mind, he would never write at all." Certainly in 1714 as he faced the verbal and printed insults now freely hurled at him, he needed a hearty dose of such self-confidence. A good writer, he believed, wrote to "PLEASE and SERVE."[79] He could count a number of items that fit that description, and he had completed two works more substantial than anything he had done since *The History of the Union* in 1709.

Eleven months after he moved into his new house, Defoe came to trial at the Guildhall. Persecutions of journalists had been vigorous in George's reign, and that month alone the government moved to prosecute Robert Thompson, printer of *English Advice to the Freeholders*, and Charles Hornby for *A Letter to Steele*, and had ordered the seizure of Charles Leslie and his papers.[80] The jury found Defoe guilty of writing and "causing" publication of the *Flying Post* paragraphs about Anglesey. By that time, however, the regents had found a core of truth in Defoe's statements about Anglesey and the army in Ireland, and Defoe appeared before Chief Justice Parker, the judge before whom he had argued his loyalty to the House of Hanover in 1713. Parker deferred sentencing Defoe and the other two men convicted that same day on unrelated charges until Michaelmas term.[81]

The months between conviction and sentencing worked to Defoe's advantage. The Lords voted to impeach Bolingbroke, Harley, Ormonde, and Strafford, and troops had to be moved into London to keep order. After moving Harley's impeachment, the Lords debated sending him to the Tower. During that debate Anglesey made a speech that seemed to expose his Jacobite sentiments, and he had been forced to apologize upon threat of the Tower.[82] Suddenly the "crime" of calling Anglesey a Jacobite in print seemed no libel. Defoe's case became absolutely insignificant as national turmoil grew. On 6 September the earl of Mar raised "James III's standard" in Scotland. James Butler, duke of Ormonde, tried to invade the Devonshire coast twice, and a third group of Jacobites harried northern England. England was alarmed enough that the Dutch were asked to send the 6,000 men guaranteed by treaty to protect the Protestant succession.

Once the rebellion broke out Defoe used his knowledge of Scotland to discredit Mar and any threat his troops might be. He knew that no one wanted to join a doomed rebellion. His method and his familiarity with Scotland are obvious in *A View of the Scots Rebellion* (1715). Here he describes the Highland rebels, gives detailed information about the geography of Scotland, and outlines the means to defeat them. He implicitly discouraged those who might join them with specific, telling details that predicted their defeat; for example, he found their fighting strategies old-fashioned and ineffectual and their supplies and money easily cut off. Although he allows 50,000 fighting men in the Highlands, he predicts that but 10,000 to 12,000 will fight for the Pretender—a figure corroborated by every modern historian.[83] Once the rebellion was crushed, Defoe worked to place the blame almost wholly on Mar and to reconcile the nation to the Scots, whom he portrayed as deluded, betrayed, but brave. *A True Account of the Proceedings at Perth* and the introduction to *A Journal of the Earl of Marr's Proceedings* ridiculed the leaders of the Scottish rebellion and prepared the way for the relatively lenient treatment of the rank-and-file rebels.

Much of Defoe's 1714–1718 writing was directed at preventing the growth of Jacobitism. He continued to deny James Edward's claim to the throne by casting aspersions on his legitimacy, by arguing vigorously against "divine indefeasible hereditary right," and by asserting the validity of the constitutional monarchy. He reminded his readers that much of the turmoil was being caused by Tories who lost their places when George arrived, and distinguished between "honest Tories" who were "friends" to the Tory ministry but supported the Protestant succession and the "distracted" Tories who were willing to break the laws of their country and violate their own Abjuration Oaths.

Even before the rebellion Defoe was writing against the Jacobites without reward from the government. He detested them and needed no commission once Sacheverell and other High Churchmen began inflaming the people and using their pulpits to influence elections. His *Pernicious Consequences of the Clergy's Intermedling with Affairs of State*, *The Immorality of the Priesthood*, and other pamphlets assembled a vicious history of the results of clerical involvement in politics. From the Spanish Inquisition to the 1714 riots, he says, injustice, faction, fanaticism, and suffering have come when the church forgets Christ's admonition, "My Kingdom is not of this World." By January Sacheverell's sermons were being subsidized so that they could be sold for a penny, and attempts to influence elections in the manner of 1709 angered Defoe.[84] In a series of ugly metaphors, he compares the offending preachers to festering wounds, gangrene, and bleeding sores.

A royal proclamation had gone out in December directing the clergy not to discuss politics but to use their sermons to appeal for unity. Defoe also engaged vigorously on the side of the government when a pamphlet called *English Advice to the Freeholders* appeared and created an immediate sensation. *English Advice* purported to expose the Whigs' plan to renew the war with France, to increase taxation and the size of the standing army, and to repeal constitutional limits to George's power. In addition, the pamphlet presented George's Lutheran background as a threat equal to the Pretender's Catholicism. Even as a private citizen, Defoe could not let the pamphlet go unanswered. His beloved King William had been attacked on many of these same counts. Defoe accordingly began to revise his *True-Born Englishman*.

English Advice had been written by Francis Atterbury, the man Defoe had depicted in *The Secret History* as the master schemer ruthlessly manipulating Bolinbroke and Harcourt in order to prevent the Protestant succession.* Defoe answered Atterbury's pamphlet with *Treason Detected* and *A Reply to a Traitorous Libel*.[85] His outrage is most obvious in

*It is not entirely certain that Defoe knew the author was Atterbury.

Treason Detected in which he refutes each point so briefly as to be dismissive. In January the government had offered £1,000 for information leading to the apprehension of the author of *English Advice* and £500 for the printer. In *A Reply to a Traitorous Libel* Defoe continues to devalue the pamphlet. It is nothing but party fury and Billingsgate, he says, written to deceive and alarm the voters.

Moreover, Defoe had been addressing the mobs and discouraging riots. In all of these pamphlets, whether addressed to the readers of Atterbury's pamphlet, to the clergy, or to the mob, he finds folly and delusion everywhere. In *Hanover or Rome*, for instance, he calls the Jacobite mobs "rabble" and evidence of "the imposter's" desperation, for riots are not the tactics of a strong king or a good general. By harping on delusion and foolishness, he can discredit the Jacobites even as he absolves the people whom he is calling back to sanity and moderation.

Defoe, however, had every reason to fear another large fine if not a prison sentence as well. As late as 25 October the Treasury book records £7.19.0 spent on his case and the decision to proceed with the prosecution. His old persecutor from the time of the *The Shortest-Way with the Dissenters*, Nottingham, was present at that meeting. The *Weekly Packet* announced 21 November as the date for sentencing but noted, "Mr. Defoe is said to have withdrawn himself."[86]

Defoe avoided a sentence by accepting government employment. According to his account, he had written to Chief Justice Parker who interceded for him. Parker, one of the managers of the prosecution of Sacheverell in 1709, was a solid Whig. Immediately after Sacheverell's trial he became lord chief justice for the Queen's Bench. George I confirmed his appointment and promoted him to lord chancellor in 1718. By all accounts Parker conducted his court "with discrimination and learning" and would have wanted to be useful to the government as well as to assure justice. Secretary of State Townshend agreed to employ Defoe. In exchange for his freedom Defoe was to keep his connection with the government secret, was to continue to appear to be alienated from the Whigs and disaffected on Harley's account, was to begin a new moderate Tory paper called *Mercurius Politicus*, and was to infiltrate as many Tory presses and periodicals as he could in order to reduce their impact on the public and to inform against the Tory writers when necessary.[87] Defoe had retired to Stoke Newington with visions of repairing his reputation in peace in a new home; sixteen months later he was the mercenary writer, the duplicitous protean his enemies had accused him of being. Once again his large family, his marginal finances, and his fear of prison turned the idealist into an opportunist. Defoe became what he had spent more than a year trying to deny he was.

CHAPTER 15

A DISCONTENTED PEOPLE

*A discontented Nation, and by far Harder to rule in Times of
Peace, than War*

—DEFOE, *The True-Born Englishman* (1716)

Now too experienced to be a tool of government, Defoe took advantage of fortunate circumstances to shape his work to please himself. Events in the first years of George's reign gave him the chance to write about issues of perpetual interest to himself with little need to trim his views to fit the political aims of others. He now earned only one-quarter of his former stipend, and Secretary of State Townshend had less interest in his work than Harley, but these circumstances contributed to Defoe's independence, and his writing began to change significantly.

The nation was tearing itself apart. Dislike for George increased, and a subtle propaganda campaign tried to justify resistance to George on moral grounds. The kinds of entertainments enjoyed at court, satires of the king's mistresses, innuendoes regarding his "abominable purposes" in keeping his two Turkish servants, and his quarrel with his son became the daily fare of the reading public. George's foreign advisers, his desire for a large standing army, and his Baltic military ambitions stirred resentment and added to the people's grumbling over high prices and taxes. Defoe said, "We all know, that ever since the Rebellion [unrest] has been daily increasing instead of abating in any measure." Some modern historians believe that as many as two-thirds of the nation were hostile to the new king.[1]

The bitter party divisions of Anne's reign continued and became even more desperate as the Tories gave up or lost their places at court and the Whig factions began to compete against each other for power.[2] As George rapidly appointed Low Church bishops and Whig magistrates and judges, the Tories saw power draining out of their hands. Each side revived the most damaging accusations and stereotypes about the other; the Tories went back to the rallying cry of 1709 by insisting that George's Lutheranism put the "Church in Danger" even as the Whigs conjured up visions of "Arbitrary Government" and "Popery" as they had done in 1686. The riots and Jacobite rebellion, the Riot Act and the suspension of habeas corpus, the trials and seizures of the estates of the rebels, the impeachment of the Tory ministers, the imprisonment of Harley in the Tower, and the news of intrigues between the Pretender and both Sweden and Russia kept the nation in turmoil and further polarized the people. When the British were not complaining about politics and economics, they were quarreling among themselves.

On a number of previous occasions Defoe had described people as running mad, but he had always thrown himself into what he called opening their eyes to their best interests. By 1716 he expressed little surprise and seemed far less engaged with the issues. He had hoped for great national prosperity at the end of the War of the Spanish Succession, and watching the nation tear itself apart frustrated him. He responded to this national folly in two ways: he met his obligations to Townshend and his Whig employers, and he became more selective in order to satisfy himself. A spirit of detachment characterized work that a few years earlier would have called forth more ingenuity, more variety, and, above all, more thoroughness. In his earlier participation in controversies over public credit and the Peace of Utrecht, for instance, he had covered every angle, reached out toward every audience and every viewpoint, and employed a stunning arsenal of propaganda methods. After 1714 Defoe never again acted as a one-man team of writers.

In some ways Defoe was like a man catching his breath after a long struggle. His stipend from Townshend was only £100 per annum,[3] and he needed to write a great deal in order to support his family. A few years earlier his friend John Clerk had concluded that publishing pamphlets was largely futile, and Defoe seems to have come to a similar conclusion, for he wrote fewer and fewer of them. Out of his turning away from some of his propaganda strategies, out of his detachment, and with the release of his imaginative impulses came an amazing second wind.

⁓

Once in the service of the government Defoe played his part conscientiously. In his mind he associated George with William and held some of the hopes for better days that William's reign had encouraged. His pamphlets echoed the content and tone of his early Williamite and Harleyan statements. For instance, *Some Thoughts of an Honest Tory in the Country* (1716) offered a model for loyal conduct, attacked the High Churchmen, and enumerated some of the benefits of George's reign. Nothing could have been more congenial to Defoe than the need to support George's treatment of the Jacobites and to condemn the rebellion. The young man who fought for Monmouth had never wavered

in his energetic commitment to the Protestant succession, and he endlessly explained its benefits. Many of the arguments that he had mar-
shaled for William's accession could be repeated, and the prosperity he
saw ahead seemed delayed by malicious or mistaken people. Thousands of words in his periodicals and pamphlets urged national harmony and the complete repudiation of Jacobitism. His appeals for moderation had changed little if at all.

He even revised *The True-Born Englishman*, the popular poem that
had ridiculed his countrymen for their rejection of King William. The
current reaction to George did indeed show "the same unsufferable
[*sic*] Manner as it did then against King William,"[4] and Defoe recognized the grumbling spirit and certainly had not forgotten that the
poem had made his fortune with William. The revision sharpened the
satire's main thrust—that it is the Englishman's "nature" to be contentious. "Strife's the natural Physick to their Phlegm" and beggars will
"spend the Parish-Alms at Law," he laughs. The 1716 poem concludes
in a more pessimistic way than the 1700 version that had left a consola-
tion and a challenge with his readers: "'Tis Personal Virtue only makes
us great." That poem had laughed at those who forgot their immigrant
past. Regardless of ancestry or opinion, the reader could have personal
merit. In 1716, Defoe ended, "We act what we intend." Here he repeated his belief in personal responsibility, but he implicitly dismissed good
intentions as an excuse for deplorable conduct. Actions, he said, relia-
bly reveal the character, the nature, the true essence of a person, and
the prognosis for a tranquil England appeared gloomy unless his countrymen came to their senses.

Defoe's specific charge when he went to work for Townshend had
been to edit the periodical *Mercurius Politicus* and to emasculate the
Tory press. His first number of *Mercurius Politicus* appeared in May
1716 and gave the ministry a steady, reliable Tory mouthpiece even
after Defoe's authorship was recognized a few months later. Purporting to be an impartial historian of public affairs, "A Lover of Old England," rather than a party journalist, Defoe drew upon the strategies of
the *Review*. The early numbers of *Mercurius Politicus* gave the history of the Jacobite conflict, just as the *Review* had begun by tracing the
roots of the War of the Spanish Succession. Defoe set almost every item
in context, concisely giving some background and spelling out implications. Just as the *Review* had maintained a moderate Whig position
through most of its life, *Mercurius Politicus* struck a Tory note from the
beginning. For instance, Defoe's introduction reflected on the "scandalous" treatment the church received in the press: "It is . . . time that
some Body began to do Justice to Truth and the Church of *England*," he
wrote. His statements about the church, however, contrasted sharply
with those of true High Church writers. Defoe's praise most often went

to those who demonstrated tolerance and charity. The introduction to the second number commented on the favorable reception of *Mercurius Politicus* as a sign of the nation's awareness of its need for "an Impartial Relation of things" and observed that it was surprising how little people knew about what was done at their own door.

Mercurius Politicus was a lively paper. Each month began with a major news story, then reported on the business of Parliament, the courts, and foreign diplomacy, and included many items appealing for their novelty or general interest. The first story selected usually had wide popular appeal, narrative potential, and diverting angles. For instance, Defoe began May and June 1716 with accounts of the Scots rebels, including a few escapes and dialogue from some trials; in July he described the king's preparations for his visit to Hanover and made this titillating comment: "We must do justice with respect to the Rumours rais'd of stripping *Hampton-Court, Windsor*, and other Pallaces, of a great deal of the Royal Furniture to be carried with the King" (82). News from Parliament, except for the officially printed votes, was still rare, and Defoe's rather full reports with occasional comment provided people with the records they desired in a convenient form. He and a few other journalists took advantage of a loophole in the Standing Orders that allowed reports of divisions. In 1738 an act to prohibit such reports would be passed.[5]

Because *Mercurius Politicus* was a monthly, Defoe had a large number of horrifying, amazing, and singular events to choose among. His prose was concise, clear, and sprinkled with single sentence reactions that must have given his readers a sense of the personality behind the print. "Nothing more horrible can be thought of," he said of an accident with molten metal, and of a lady shooting her attacker, he concluded that she would be much celebrated "for this rare, but too violent instance of defending her Chastity." Anecdotes from the streets, the docks, and the courts captured personality as well as social history. One Samuel Kempton, offered the chance to sign an indenture in exchange for his life, boldly told the judge that he "had rather be Hanged than sold for a Slave." Over the months, a person could learn that dried walnut leaves were being sold for tobacco, that "Francia the Jew" had been acquitted, that the soldiers sent to put down a riot at Oxford were pelted with "dirty turnips," and that Jacob Rowe had invented a device to take "altitudes at sea." Reports on the Scottish outlaw Rob Roy became a near-serial adventure novel.

Defoe's mastery of propaganda makes *Mercurius Politicus* a fascinating document. Every issue has touches of Tory bias. His most common strategy is to make brief editorial comments, many of which sound like the ejaculations a reader might make. In April 1717 Defoe mentions riots at Oxford, notes the pamphlets that seized on them as "excuses" to reduce the university's privileges, and calls it a plot to "bring the Colleges into an entire Subjection to their worst Enemies." In August he prints the list of Lords who voted to acquit Harley. These small touches, appearing comfortably after the event or made about events of relatively limited impact, give the paper its Tory bias without actually helping Tory causes. At the same time *Mercurius Politicus* carefully supports the government on substantive issues. It reports the king's leniency to the rebels month after month and uses such specific information as number of pardons and percentage of the condemned actually executed. Changes at court would be reported, but the reassuring information that business continues uninterrupted followed immediately. Defoe gradually establishes the picture of a well-run, moderate, wise government functioning smoothly, unshakably, and impenetrably.

In June 1716 Defoe saw his first chance to invade the existing Tory press. *Dormer's News-Letter* became available. George Dormer had taken over the very popular Tory *Dyer's News-Letter* after the death of John Dyer in September 1713 but had attracted Stanhope's unfavorable attention early in George's reign. In October 1715 Dormer had been arrested for "seditious and dangerous" practices and remained continuously under suspicion or on bail.[6] Defoe began to write this paper too.

At the same time Defoe was writing parts of *The Annals of King George, Year the Second*. This book competed with other annals such as *The Compleat History of Europe* and *The Political State of Great Britain*. As *pièce de résistance*, Defoe promised "a compleat *History* of the *Rebellion*." In many ways, his 450-page *Annals* sounded like the other yearbooks. It listed without comment acts passed, quoted official exchanges between king and Houses of Parliament, and often used rough and ready transitions such as "But to leave this Part of the Story for a while . . ." and "We are now at the latter End of *October*." In parts of the book, however, he produced highly unified, lively narratives that gave the mood and therefore something of the experience of the people. He alternated accounts of the actions at court, the vacillations of Mar, and the movement of the armies, presenting them smoothly and in considerable detail. Inclusion of such things as descriptions of Leith, the numbers of the king's soldiers in Scotland, and an inventory of the Pretender's ships and supplies suggests personal experience as well as official sources. "It is now Time to look a little into *England*," he says at one point, and describes his method of tracing the rebellion and the year's "publick Transactions" as going on "by short Periods as they went" hand in hand—"history writing by inches" (58–59). Such breaks emphasize the contrast between the laconic recital of parliamentary proceedings and the dramatic accounts of troop movements and individuals' actions. The ceremonial language used to introduce official communications between the monarch and Parliament and to explain bills underscores how free the story of the rebellion is of formulaic language.

Here, too, Defoe promised to be the impartial historian, but a slight Whig bias is unmistakable. For example, in a description of the rampant disaffection in England he noted that much of the blame had been laid on the clergy, but reported fully on the Whiggish archbishop of Canterbury's declarations against unrest and even quoted his most important ones in an appendix. In another paper he reported the addition of five items to the impeachment articles against Harley and commented that "his evil Council" regarding the Canadian expedition became another charge against him. Not only was it uncharacteristic of Defoe to call Harley's advice "evil," but he surely knew that Harley had been recovering from stab wounds at the time of the expedition and may have known that Harley had opposed the venture and then discovered that Bolingbroke and Arthur Moore had skimmed off £21,000 to enrich themselves personally.

By this time Defoe had probably discovered Harley's correspondence with the earl of Mar and the Pretender. Harley's 1709 agent John Ogilvie served as their trusted messenger, and Harley had begun to offer the exiled court of the Pretender advice. The exiles sought his opinions and discussed his letters so freely that his collaboration could hardly be secret. That a number of Scots still in Great Britain wrote unguardedly about Harley suggests that someone must have told Defoe. English Jacobites like Bishop Atterbury, who detested Harley and felt undermined by Harley's assessment of him, could also have let the information become common knowledge. Even Secretary of State Craggs may have been aware of the situation, for the abbé Jean-Baptiste Dubois, chief minister for the regent of France, mentioned Harley's help in planning a Jacobite invasion.[7] Defoe described the Jacobite as the traditional emblem of Obstinacy: "a strong middle-aged Man, grasping his Head with both his Hands, the Palms of them covering his Eyes, and the Thumbs thrust in his Eyes; and in this Posture plunging himself into a deep Bog" (*Commentator*, 18 March 1720). Perhaps that is how Defoe saw Harley. In the *Memoirs of Major Ramkins* he could write that the Pretender had the English "Generalissimo and his Arms, the Secretary, The Treasurer [Harley], &c. all at his Devotion." He could not, however, bring himself to expose Harley in a full-scale attack. Because of loyalty or mourning for weak human nature, he kept his counsel.

These papers came to bear the major burden of Defoe's work of explaining and supporting George's policies. Defoe still wrote pamphlets, however, and he used them to complement and reinforce the periodicals in the same ways he had in the Queen Anne years. One of the major victories in the Whigs' efforts to maintain and consolidate their power was the passage of the Septennial Act, and Defoe's publications about it reveal his principles and methods.

Quite simply, the Whigs sought to delay the 1718 elections mandatory under the Triennial Act. They argued, generally, that elections every three years encouraged parties, factions, and corruption and, specifically, that elections so soon after the Jacobite uprisings and rebel trials might result in widespread unrest and even violence. In support of the change, Steele, again an M.P., quoted Sunderland as saying, "The first year of a Triennial Parliament has been spent in vindictive decisions . . . about the late elections; the second session has entered into business, but . . . with a spirit of contradiction . . . [and] the third session [has] languished" as the members prepared for new elections. In fact, George and his policies had never been less popular, and the Whigs feared losing control of Parliament.[8]

Even some of the Whigs felt that the Tories had the best side of the septennial argument. Only a few months earlier, after all, they had offered £1,000 for the author of *English Advice to the Freeholders* for saying that they would repeal the Triennial Act. As one peer said, for members of the Commons to continue themselves beyond the term for which they were elected made them "a House of their own making," not "the representatives of the people."[9] However, the Whigs wanted to hold their slim advantage in parliament in order to establish the changes just begun, and pragmatism won out over principle. The septennial bill passed both houses and, on 7 May 1716, received the royal assent.

Defoe's opinion of the Triennial Act was that it was an essential protection of the people's liberty and an important hindrance to corruption and sinecures, but he had believed at least since 1705 that such frequent elections fostered factions and parties. "All our Burroughs in *England*" became "the Scenes of Contention, Party Strife, and . . . Separate Interests," he wrote; "it has this fatal Consequence in it, which all *England* feels." Like most of his generation, Defoe distrusted and even disliked political parties; frequent elections encouraged interest groups, and the consequence of them, parties who "contend on every Occasion, choosing their Parish-Officers, their Recorders, their Magistrates . . . all . . . by Parties."[10]

When the septennial bill was proposed, Defoe published at least two pamphlets in favor of it, *Some Considerations on a Law for Triennial Parliaments* and *Arguments about the Alteration of Triennial Elections of Parliament* (both 1716). His close observation of several especially bitter and dishonest elections, his recognition of the revived Tory tactics of the Sacheverell years, and his honest belief that passage of the bill would calm national turmoil by discouraging the Pretender's followers at home and abroad led him to support it. He argued for the legality of the action in the same terms in which he would later argue against "unredeemable" notes held against the government as part of the national debt: every parliamentary action could be repealed. In this case, *repeal* seemed too strong a word to him, and he pointed out that a new requirement for elections was being firmly set. In *Arguments* he went so far as to say that the septennial bill restored the intention of the Triennial Act (4–5). Since the autumn of 1714 Defoe had consistently written about a "conspiracy" of men, a "set" of men, who were working to spread disaffection and rebellion. In these pamphlets, too, he erects this shibboleth and asks for the defeat of their "Hellish Design of spreading" poison.[11]

In *Mercurius Politicus* Defoe dared to report on the Whigs' motives and the best of the speeches in opposition. He even called the speakers against the bill those "who appeared for [Posterity's] Liberties" (134), but he argued that the results of the act would justify it and smoothly reminded his readers of the amount of current national turmoil and of the danger of Jacobite ambition. By separating his Tory readers from the High Church faction, he subtly made the Septennial Act the lesser of two evils. In the *Annals of King George*, published in 1717, he described how the hope of winning the triennial election served to encourage the Jacobites and High Churchmen, increased the number of their followers, and kept disaffection and the spirit of rebellion alive. Here Defoe makes his strongest statement: "For this Reason, it appear'd not only reasonable, but just, and very necessary, that . . . the Hope of the Party be thereby defeated." At this time, he said, the Whigs were the "Bulwark of the Crown" and its "Stay and Support."[12] This forthright statement, made after the passage of the act, suggests that Defoe did support it wholeheartedly, for he was capable of reporting past actions without comment or with equivocal statements. Here, as in the Queen Anne years and despite the political orientation of his writing, certain consistent principles and opinions emerge.

⁂

Defoe had been fortunate in being recommended to Charles Townshend by Justice Parker. Townshend was an easy man for Defoe to serve. He had been one of the thirty men to sign the protest against the Schism Act in June 1714, and he had never wavered in his support for the Protestant succession. The Whig negotiator of the Barrier Treaty, the treaty that had brought the Dutch into alliance with England in 1709, he was known for his dependable administrative skills. Scrupulously honest, he believed it his duty to speak his mind when the nation and its interests were at stake. It was he who read the objections to George I's proposed trip to Hanover in a cabinet meeting in June

1715, and he opposed some of the most Hanoverian of the king's northern European policies.

Discontent soon infected the innermost circle of the king's advisers, however, and Defoe again found strife as "natural" to English ministers of state as to ordinary citizens. During the time the other secretary of state, Stanhope, was in Hanover with George, Townshend's conduct regarding the treaty with France was misunderstood and the king came to see that Townshend would continue to disagree with his northern policy. Sunderland, desirous of a secretaryship, misrepresented some of Townshend's actions and did all he could to prevent reconciliation. In December George dismissed Townshend but persuaded him to accept the position of lord lieutenant of Ireland. By April Townshend's obstructionist actions in Parliament and cabinet forced George to dismiss him; Robert Walpole, Townshend's brother-in-law, resigned along with several others, including John Methuen, who had been authorized to act for Stanhope during the time he was in Hanover with the king.

At first Defoe loyally defended Townshend and Walpole. His *The Quarrel of the School-Boys at Athens* and *An Impartial Enquiry into the Conduct of . . . T[ownshend]* (both 1717) reminded readers of Townshend's ability and loyal service to his country and tried to reduce the gravity of the division. In the first he suggested that the return of the "schoolmaster," the king, had restored order, and in both he blamed jealousies and faction for Townshend's fall. *The Conduct of Robert Walpole* reviewed Walpole's service as glowingly as he had Townshend's in *An Impartial Enquiry*. These tracts included a number of powerful reflections on the psychology of administrators. In *The Quarrel*, Defoe wrote, "It is certain, that in most Governments, it is sometimes a Crime to excel; Moderate Merit gets many Friends, but uncommon Merit raises invincible Enemies, and Opposition" (29). "*Fear* and *Hate* go much together," he observed in *The Conduct of Walpole* (5).

Townshend's removal increased Defoe's distance from court. Between December and April Stanhope took over the Northern Department and Methuen the Southern. After the resignations in April, Stanhope became chancellor of the Exchequer, and Sunderland and Addison were appointed secretaries of state. Defoe became the employee of the scheming, mercurial Sunderland (H 452–53). Resentful of Sunderland's part in the fall of Harley in 1708 and his meddling in the Scottish election, convinced of Sunderland's selfishness, ambition, and limited ability as a statesman, Defoe might dislike his position, but he could count on the fact that he had appeared to work with Sunderland effectively during the Scottish years. When Sunderland had been dismissed in June 1710, Defoe had even praised him in two numbers of the *Review* for refusing the pension that Queen Anne offered. Defoe focused on Sunderland's gallant words, and Sunderland must have felt some gratitude for being portrayed as a hero who said that "if he could not have the Honour to SERVE his Countrey, he would not PLUNDER IT" (7:143).

Less than a year later, Stanhope returned to his secretaryship, and James Craggs became secretary for the Southern Department. In March 1718, then, Defoe began to work for Stanhope. In some ways the changes did not affect Defoe greatly. He seems to have had contact with Samuel Buckley and then with Charles Delafaye rather than with the secretaries. Both of these men were experienced with the press; Buckley had written the Whig *Daily Courant* for years before becoming the editor of the *London Gazette*, and Delafaye had written the *Gazette* from 1702 until the time Steele became editor. Moreover, Delafaye had been Sunderland's secretary from 1706 until 1710 and had managed finances; he would, therefore, have been responsible for paying Defoe whatever Sunderland ordered. In 1717 he had become Sunderland's undersecretary of state and would keep the same position under Stanhope and then Townshend. Defoe had had his differences with both men; he had ridiculed the style of the *Daily Courant*, and Buckley had attacked the *Review* repeatedly. Delafaye had been Nottingham's secretary at the time Defoe was prosecuted for *The Shortest Way with the Dissenters*, and Defoe had satirized Delafaye's slips in the *Gazette* just as he had Buckley's. Delafaye, however, was a Huguenot, had served under William at the time of the Treaty of Ryswick, and was a steady civil servant whom Defoe could respect.[13]

❧

When changes in Queen Anne's ministry had required Defoe to shift from Harley to Godolphin, then back to Harley, he had insisted that he was the queen's servant and that she had the right to change her cabinet. Defoe's praise and support for King George came more easily than affection for Anne, and one reason for his early enthusiasm was the hope he shared with a large number of Dissenters that their years of loyalty would be rewarded by the repeal of the Corporation, Test, Occasional Conformity, and Schism Acts. Both the king and Stanhope were behind the idea, and the Dissenters held large meetings among themselves and with their supporters in order to increase support. Like all good politicians of the time, they mobilized a press effort. Some were set to write about the Dissenters' loyal service, others about their rights, and others about their ability to help the country in the future.[14]

The issue was close to Defoe's heart. In *The Question Fairly Stated* (1717) he wrote, "There seems Room to hope, and Reason to expect our Deliverance from these Burthens . . . of persecuting Laws, and of unrighteous Distinctions." The Dissenters, then, would "be restored to that Freedom which as *Englishmen* they have a Native Right to, and which as Christians they have a Divine Right to" (4–5). Since October 1716 Defoe had been repeating that forty years of loyalty, the present unrest in the kingdom, and the shared political interests of the Dissenters and the Church of England argued that it was time to reward England's "faithful Friends." They are "the most Sober, the most Industrious, the most Thriving, and the most *Loyal*" subjects of the king, he insisted.[15]

He threw his entire repertoire of persuasive arts into the fray. He appealed to history, to natural and divine right, and to justice, but as is typical of his mature propaganda, his hope seemed to lie in appeals to pragmatic self-interest. In this time of economic trouble, he made much of the fact that George needed soldiers, although Dissenters, now barred from service, wanted to fight for their country. Jacobite rioters were being discharged by magistrates, but loyal Dissenters could not serve in office. Moreover, the wealth of the Dissenters made them desirable "brothers." Defoe was not alone in his impatience. Groups of Dissenters of all ages, including one to which Benjamin Defoe's friend Dudley Ryder belonged, met regularly and discussed ways to encourage the government to restore their rights.[16]

On 13 December 1718 a bill "for strengthening the Protestant Interest in these kingdoms" was introduced in Parliament. Anti-Dissenting propagandists were already at work, and again Defoe was one of their first targets. They represented Defoe as a typical Dissenter and accused him of writing seditious, republican pamphlets, representative of the Nonconformist temper. *A Presbyterian Getting on Horse-Back: Or, the Dissenters Run Mad in Politics* (1717) sneered, "He thinks himself incompass'd with *Drums*, and *Musquets*, with *Fire* and *Smoak*." The writer trotted out all of the old accusations against the Dissenters: "It's the darling Principle that the People are the Fountain of Power; that Government is a Trust, which the People . . . have a Power to take away . . . it's but reasonable to suppose that they would act . . . as they did in the days of King Charles" and "he [Defoe] finds nothing but . . . *Destruction* and *Desolation*, to befall the *Inhabitants of Earth*, except they be instantly *Converted* and become *Righteous Saints*, that is Dissenters" (34).

The parliamentary debates reminded Defoe of the times the Dissenters had been disappointed in the Whigs and recalled the painful days of 1714 when the Dissenters had been sacrificed to political exigency. Now he saw William Wake, archbishop of Canterbury and a reputed Whig, lead the fight against repeal.[17] Moreover, their opposition to Stanhope and the king's party led both Townshend and Walpole to vote against the bill to repeal the limitations on the civil rights of Dissenters. After that Defoe's statements about them cooled. In *The Defection Farther Consider'd* (1718) he raised questions about their motives for resigning, pondered the specter of resentment and "impatience at repulse," and commented that past service can never excuse present disloyalty: "History is full of greater Heroes than ever R—— W—— can pretend to be . . . who have been led to Execution for their Undutiful Behaviour to the same Princes" (13–14). That he used Ezekiel 18:24 as epigraph and then repeated it prominently in the pamphlet spoke volumes. Significantly, Defoe quoted only the first part of the verse: "But when a righteous man turns away from his righteousness and commits iniquity and does the same abominable things that the wicked man does, shall he live?" The second part of the verse, which used the words Defoe would probably have chosen to describe Townshend's and Walpole's votes on the bill to restore the Dissenters' civil rights, but that were too provocative for safe use, read: "None of the righteous deeds, which he has done shall be remembered; for the treachery of which he is guilty and the sin he has committed, he shall die." Yet both *The Defection Farther Consider'd* and *Some Persons Vindicated against the Author of the Defection* (1718) defended their right to resign and deplored recent efforts to tarnish their records. Of Townshend, for instance, Defoe asserted, "they neither have been able to charge him with any Omission of his Duty to his Country, or to his Majestie."[18]

Committees and debate pared clauses away, and the Occasional Conformity and Schism Acts alone were repealed. In the same session, however, Parliament provided some relief from the Test and Corporation Acts by guaranteeing that those who had not complied with these acts but who went unchallenged for six months were automatically confirmed in their offices.

Defoe reacted with disappointment and anger. He saw clearly that the Dissenters were still second-class citizens and those who felt as he did about communion still barred from civil, military, and crown offices and from the universities. Before and after the pillory Defoe consistently affirmed his duty and courage in speaking out when an important principle was at stake. In a typical statement he affirmed that "The Day being yet to come that I ever withheld Speaking what I thought was needful to say, and what I knew I could Defend the Truth of, for Fear of any Man's Face or Power in the World. Upon which Principle I still act." Of Parliament's refusal to repeal all four acts, he said,

Lest . . . it should be alleg'd, that our patient Submission to the Discouragement of Penal Laws, is a silent Acknowledgment of Guilt, or that we forfeit our Rights and Privilege, by ceasing to claim them; we judge it very proper to declare publickly our own Sense of the Hardships impos'd upon us, as Fellow-Protestant Subjects and Free-born *Englishmen*.
The Truth is, thru' the Hatred of our Enemies, and the Fearfulness and Indolence of our Friends, we have suffer'd so long.[19]

Here is the voice of *Legion's Memorial*, of *The Original Power of the Collective Body of the People of England*, of the lifelong believer in the fundamental rights of humankind. When he reported the events in the *Annals* as the "impartial Historian," he introduced the topic as a discussion of the Dissenters and their hopes for "Liberty from Limitations which they expected" (286). Even here, in this paper carefully slanted toward the Tories, even the High Church ones, Defoe's disappointment and outrage find expression. He presented the Dissenters as thinking that

the healing Spirit should have diffused it self to all those honest and deserving People called *Dissenters*, who, after the Testimonies they had now given of their Loyalty unshaken, and Zeal indisputable, to the Interest of the Royal House of *Hanover* . . . after all this, they could scarce conceive, that the modest and just Request of being allow'd . . . to have a Liberty given them of serving the King, at a Time when there was good ground to accept of all the Services that could be found ready, should be disputed. (286–87)

After outlining the Dissenters' hopes and their realistic reasons for holding them, he reported, "On a sudden, a Mine prepar'd for other Uses, blew up this and many other good prospects of the Nation's Felicity and Peace" (289). That mine would be called the Bangorian controversy.

⁊⧵⧽

A number of factors made the complete repeal of the acts unlikely. The Church of England was deeply divided, and the fact that King George had carefully chosen Low Church clergy alone for appointments contributed to the polarization within the church and therefore to High Church agitation over "the Church in danger."[20] To alienate more Tories and High Churchmen in favor of the less numerous, long-suffering Dissenters would have been bad politics. Moreover, Englishmen's fears of dissent went very deep. Even John Locke discussed schism with heresy in his *Letter on Toleration*. Locke had begun by saying that "mutual toleration among Christians" is "the chief distinguishing mark of a true church," for lack of toleration is "more likely to be signs of men striving for power and empire than signs of the church of Christ," but he concluded with the statement: "Now let us consider schism, which is a fault akin to" heresy.[21] In 1986 a British intellectual defended eighteenth-century feeling and then asked, "Is that not what Ireland is about—schism?"

The Bangorian controversy, the "Mine prepar'd for other Uses," contributed significantly to the climate that determined the defeat of total repeal, and Defoe's writing about the controversy can be understood only in relation to the Dissenters' failure to regain their civil rights.[22] Benjamin Hoadley, bishop of Bangor, one of the first bishops appointed by George, had answered *The Constitution of the Catholic Church and the Nature and Consequences of Schism, Set Forth in a Collection of Papers Written by . . . George Hicks* (1716). Hicks, an inflammatory non-juror, left this work in manuscript at his death and, published posthumously, it caused more trouble than he had while alive. Hicks called the Low Churchmen as well as Dissenters "breakers of the bond of peace . . . and all charity in the city of God." The book was a sensation and drew attention to Hoadley's *Preservative against the Principles and Practices of the Non-Jurors both in Church and State*. His position was Erastian and claimed that Christ was "Sole *Law-giver* to His Subjects . . . Sole *Judge* of their Behaviour, in the Affairs of *Conscience* and *Eternal* Salvation. . . . He hath . . . left behind Him . . . no Judges over the Conscience or Religion of His People." Not only did this position undercut the power of the Church of England, but it made all sincere Christian believers, Conformist and Nonconformist, equal before God.

When Hoadley presented the heart of his argument in a sermon before the king on 31 March 1717, the Bangorian controversy became a full-scale, vituperative paper war. George had allowed a Convocation* of the Church of England, and a committee of the lower house of it officially condemned Hoadley's sermon and his book. The Convocation committee then saw their resolution through the lower house, which passed it on to the Bishops with a recommendation for action. The Convocation reflected unfavorably on the king's promotion of Hoadley to his bishopric by taking such action, and the government realized that a similar vote by the Bishops in the assembly's upper house and any subsequent action would increase Tory criticism of the king. On 17 May 1717 the king prorogued the Convocation by withholding the royal license authorizing its houses to proceed to business. Shortly afterwards four of Hoadley's opponents—Thomas Sherlock, Francis Hare, Andrew Snape, and Robert Moss—lost their positions as royal chaplains.

The Bangorian controversy focused England's attention on schism, on the Dissenters' dependence upon "sincerity" as an explanation for their Nonconformity, and on increased reservations about King George as head of the Church of England. Without the controversy, the bill to repeal the acts might have escaped the kind of intense scrutiny, heated debate, and splenetic defections that determined its defeat.

Defoe had to treat the controversy as news, and his readers expected reports. When he first reported on it in *Mercurius Politicus* in May 1717, he predicted that it would be "a very tedious Dispute" and promised to produce monthly abstracts "By which the Reader may be eased of the Trouble and Expence of Reading or Collecting all the Tracts upon that

---

*The Convocation, composed of a lower house (the general body of the clergy) and an upper house (the Bishops), was a gathering of representatives of all ranks of the Anglican clergy for the purpose of deliberating upon matters concerning the Church of England. The Act of Supremacy in 1534 gave the monarch the power to convene and prorogue Convocations.

Voluminous Quarrel." In the *Annals* he numbered the published tracts at sixty-seven.[23] These reports quoted from some of the pamphlets written by the most prominent combatants and reprinted verbatim most of the numerous advertisements placed in the newspapers by Hoadley, White Kennet (the bishop of Carlisle), and others. Defoe confined his comments to remarks on how regrettable the situation was, how contemptible it made the participants, and how scandalous some of the events were. He seemed to take some pleasure in reminding his readers that this dispute was wholly within the Church of England and among "the Dignifi'd Clergy of the Church, Bishops, Deans, Doctors, &c."[24] In this coverage, he did not discuss the doctrinal issues; nor did he bring in some of the very best pamphlets, such as William Law's *Three Letters to the Bishop of Bangor*, when they were written by less well known men.

As a pamphleteer rather than as a journalist, Defoe has appeared enigmatic to some people. It would seem that a number of Hoadley's opinions would have appealed to him. He would have agreed entirely with the assertion that Christ had left no "visible" church behind. In fact, he notes that none of Hoadley's critics ever contradicted this statement. He would certainly have sympathized with Hoadley's attempts to come to terms with sincerity and the individual conscience and approved Hoadley's *The Original and Institution of Civil Government Discuss'd* (1710) in which he found no scriptural support for indefeasible hereditary right and endorsed the contract theory of government.[25] But Defoe was no uncritical admirer of Hoadley, who was well known for his efforts to persuade the Dissenters to conform. His arguments in favor of "complying" for the sake of peace had been satirized by Defoe, Calamy, and other Dissenters.[26] Defoe's first entry into the controversy, *An Expostulatory Letter, to the B[ishop] of B[angor]* [1717], objected to Hoadley's book and was published several months before the sermon.[27] In it Defoe strongly condemned the idea that James's religion—as opposed to his maladministration, tyranny, or abdication—had "incapacitated" him and brought about the Revolution. Defoe thought that Hoadley's stance falsified history and, worse, cast in doubt the Revolution principles affirmed by the Convention Parliament.

That Defoe's deepest feelings about the controversy came from its effects on the national temper and the resulting defeat of the repeal of the parliamentary acts can be seen in his statements in works such as the *Annals*. Here he described it as putting an end to restoring the Dissenters' civil rights and to "many other good prospects of the Nation's Felicity and Peace" (289). Strong expressions of rage and disappointment were far from uncommon. One pamphlet writer asked angrily, "What Occasion was there for this Sermon at this Time?" He went on to call it "very *unseasonable*," to blame it for cheating the Dissenters out of their deserved release from unjust laws, to call it "the Ax to the Root of the Tree" of their hopes, and even to raise the possibility that Hoadley intended this effect.[28] To embroil the nation in a conflict that increased disaffection with George and tended to identify the king with a party seemed unfortunate. Defoe was eager for peace and the prosperity he believed it would bring. Scattered throughout his Bangorian pamphlets are statements endorsing such official actions as the proroguing of Parliament and defending George's ability to head the Church of England well.

That he recognized immediately that nothing could keep the controversy from running its extensive course in part determined his response. No group wrote more in the eighteenth century than clergymen, especially Anglican ones, and this controversy drew responses for years. Nowhere did Defoe bother with the kinds of clarifications of issues typical of his other pamphlets; in none did he offer a resolution or "the last word." What drew him in were the consequences for the Dissenters, the aspersions cast on the government, and the way the controversy evolved. In *A Reply to the Remarks upon the Lord Bishop of Bangor's Treatment of the Clergy and Convocation* (1717), he called one of Snape's expressions "a *sly Insinuation* against the Government" and agreed that it appeared to support Hoadley's complaint that he was being hounded because of his "affection" for the government. When the principals began using advertisements in the newspapers to answer each other, Defoe recognized the novelty of this turn in the controversy. He saw that information on the controversy was becoming more widely available than on any before it and reaching kinds of readers different from pamphlet purchasers.[29]

Most of Defoe's pamphlets on the controversy merely demonstrated the uncharitable, undignified, and unchristian tactics used by the disputants. He pointed out that they made the clergy and the Church of England objects of ridicule and even contempt. Lower-class readers of papers were likely to be influenced in ways that pamphlet readers might not be. Defoe and many of his generation felt that increasing materialism and secularism threatened England and that anything that reduced respect for religion could encourage these tendencies. Over and over Defoe asked if the clergymen involved were displaying the Christian virtues they had spent their lives teaching. In pamphlets such as *The Conduct of Christians Made the Sport of Infidels* (1717) he could express appalled astonishment at the behavior of some of the highest-ranked churchmen in England.

Throughout his life, and most notably in *The Shortest-Way*, Defoe had insisted that Anglicans lacked charity and benevolence. To him they always seemed closed-minded, vindictive bigots. The Bangorian controversy appeared to make all of these traits obvious, and Defoe delighted in their bungling. It was just like the Church of England to try to use a body like the Convocation to crush someone who differed with its most extreme faction, he thought, and for Anglicans to treat one another as they had him and other Dissenters opened them to ridicule. In one place he reduced the motives of Hoadley's critics to their reluctance to lose the power to "oppress and persecute" the Nonconformists. He collected their "gibes" and "taunts" and pointed out how they were unbecoming to the writers' characters "and the Gravity of a Divine." He quoted them and asked if there could be any intent except to bait and insult. He analyzed their rhetoric and pointed out exaggerations, wilful misrepresentations, contradictions, and special pleading. He referred to their earlier works and said they had once written just what Hoadley had preached. In all of them, Hoadley included, he found a tendency to rely on eloquence, wit, and "Satyrs and Sarcasms" rather than upon clarity and honesty. Mock amazement emphasized his point:

The most astonishing Thing in all this, seems to me to be, that this should be Dr. *Sherlock*! And I find Abundance of People surprized at it; thinking Dr. *Sherlock* had been a Man of better Breeding, and of better Principles. . . .

Hadst thou seen . . . how furiously these People call'd *Christians* opposed one another, how scandalously they treated the personal Characters of their Opposers.[30]

Defoe always loved to point out that he had been right, and the Bangorian controversy gave him a wealth of opportunities. Unfortunately Defoe soon had cause to admonish his own people. The Salters' Hall controversy became a bitter paper war carried out among the Dissenters; they, too, used advertisements in the newspapers, thereby spreading the news of their undignified squabble "to all parts of city and country." Just as the accusations of the bishops of Bangor and Carlisle had contradicted each other, so did the statements by the Salters' Hall disputants. As Edmund Calamy wrote, "Yet were facts . . . so very differently represented, that people were, generally, rather amazed and confounded than satisfied."[31]

The Salters' Hall controversy was in many ways a variant on the Bangorian controversy. It arose over the ordination of Hubert Stogdon of Devon, who held unorthodox views on the Trinity.[32] The General Body of London ministers meeting at Salters' Hall quickly agreed that there were some errors of doctrine so serious as to disqualify a person from the ministry. The dispute arose over the test of the truth of whatever doctrine might be at issue. One group of representatives insisted the Bible alone should be used, while the other wanted the confessions of faith as well as the Bible. For some, the idea of using the confessions of faith implied that scripture alone was inadequate. Scriptural authority carried by four votes, and a group of ministers withdrew from the meeting. Because they insisted upon the subscription to the doctrine of the Trinity as stated in the fifth and sixth answers to the 1643 Westminster shorter catechism and the first article of the creed of the Church of England,* they were called the "Subscribers" and those who remained in the General Body "Nonsubscribers." The Protestant Dissenters, like the Anglicans, now engaged in a bitter dispute over the authority of the church and the sufficiency of the Scripture—by implication, of the sufficiency of reason and conscience.

As Calamy said, pamphlets in great abundance poured from the press. In May 1719 Defoe published *A Letter to the Dissenters* in which he urged an end to the public discussion of the issues and recommended a second Salters' Hall meeting. "Hell and the Booksellers are the chief Gainers in the Quarrel," he commented (24). Not only did Defoe deplore the way the ministers were carrying on the debate, but he believed that the dispute reflected upon the church to the extent that the common people would feel free to skip public worship and that error and even atheism would result. A contemporary agreed and, as late as 1723, cited the controversy as a cause of the decrease in the number of Dissenters. Defoe also felt strongly that the conflict should have been kept within Salters' Hall and not allowed into the public papers. He was particularly chagrined that it broke out at a time when the king and many others were favorably inclined toward the Dissenters. He would have agreed with Strickland Gough's assessment that the dispute "injured the dissenting interest more than all their enemies together."[33]

Defoe, like many of his contemporaries, saw that the doctrine at issue in Stogdon's case was particularly unfortunate, and he recognized the implications of the Subscribers' stand fully: "How have ye by so scandalous a disagreement in the very first and principal Article of Faith, *viz.* The Union of the Godhead . . . brought the Truths of God declar'd in his Word to be doubtful, inextricable, and past our Understanding."[34] In *Mercurius Politicus* Defoe had stated unequivocally that the opinion held by Stogden and others was the same as that of "*Arius, Socinius*, and other Antient, or indeed Primitive Hereticks."[35] Among the contemporary apologists for this heresy he identified the Anglicans Samuel Clarke, William Whiston, Thomas Emlin, and John Toland.† That this "scandalous disagreement" should have spread outside the Church of England to involve the Dissenters, and that it should be reported as being over the Trinity in the latter's meeting rather than as

*Question 6 reads: "How many Persons are there in the Godhead?" "There are three Persons in the Godhead: the Father, the Son, and the Holy Ghost; and these three are one God, the same in substance, equal in power and glory."

†The Trinitarian controversy in the Church of England began over Clarke's *Scripture Doctrine of the Trinity* (1712) and Whiston's *Primitive Christianity Reviv'd* (1711) and included a movement to relax the requirement that Anglican clergy subscribe to "all and every statement" in the Book of Common Prayer, Articles, and Ordinal.

a question of imposing dogma, did not surprise him, but it reinforced his conception of the Dissenters as inclined to self-destruction. In *Mercurius Politicus* he quoted the statements signed by both groups, some orthodox discussions of the Trinity, and some of the advertisements written by the disputants and reported briefly on the unfortunately personal turn the controversy was taking: "Thus they stand divided, one against another, not in Opinion only, but in Charity" (285).

☙

All of these controversies and the press and pamphlet wars that followed increased Defoe's interest in how people were persuaded to believe as they did. His work shows increasing analysis of others' rhetorical strategies and experimentation with methods intended to make his own writing more credible.

Partly because he had lost the respect given "Mr. Review" and the impact of "the Goliath of his Party," he needed new voices "to open the eyes" of people. By 1715 every periodical point of view triggered a political identification: "A Lover of Old England," the sobriquet for *Mercurius Politicus*, signaled "Tory." Moreover, the Queen Anne journalists, in spite of determined hounding and prosecution by the secretaries of state, had learned to use news, even foreign news, as a means of discrediting the ministry's achievements.[36] At the beginning of the reign of George, the way as few as two or three events were reported marked a paper as Whig or Tory; this association worked even in papers with as little editorial comment as the *Daily Courant* and Defoe's *Whitehall Evening Post*.

Sometimes Defoe took advantage of his readers' conditioned interpretations of party affiliation in his pamphlets, and his personae in these years include "Honest [read, 'old' or 'Revolution'] Tory," Low Churchmen, and Protestant laymen. Increasingly, however, Defoe wanted to free his work from party labels. Only by doing so would he attract a wide variety of readers and assure his work an attentive, open-minded reading. In fact, party was not as important to Englishmen as Defoe's difficulties with party politics might suggest. The term remained one of opprobrium throughout the century, and many writers used it as a synonym for "faction." Even Bolingbroke said, "Faction hath no Regard to national interests," and Harley had attempted to maintain power without strong party alliance; Halifax, Shrewsbury, and a number of the greatest statesmen in England did everything they could all their lives to resist absolute identification with a party.[37] The great majority of Englishmen associated parties with special interests, "causes," and competition for appointed offices. Just as few American voters would ever subscribe to every plank in the Democratic or Republican platform, few of Defoe's contemporaries were pure "Whigs" or "Tories"—if such existed except as stereotypes. Except to stigmatize others, Defoe seldom used the terms; he did not, for example, call himself a Tory when in the service of Harley's Tory ministry or of Mist's *Weekly Journal*.

Although Defoe continued to rely heavily on the reasonable, moderate voice of the *Review* and hundreds of his pamphlets, he began to move decisively away from the pamphlet form in 1714. Many of these first efforts experimented with the "secret history" or "scandalous memoir," made both popular and effective by Delarivière Manley before 1710. Her novels evoked an "essentially fictional world whose inhabitants were not so much real persons as they were embodiments of popular concepts," and her *New Atalantis* had helped discredit the Whigs and make the 1709 fall of the Godolphin circle palatable.[38] Manley cleverly transformed contemporary charges against its individual members into existing myths of class prejudice and, by doing so, fixed the names of her characters upon Sarah Churchill, duchess of Marlborough, and others. Manley's fictional world was one of luxury, decadence, selfishness, sexual and political intrigue, and alliances based on personal lust for power and wealth. The unrealistic, overwrought plots with their extravagant settings combined with the transparently allegorical characters to allow shocking insinuations and interpretations.

When Defoe began writing secret histories to defend Harley, he retained the world of intrigue and self-interest but eliminated the decadent settings and artificial prose. Somehow his characters' avarice seems more sordid because they have no taste for satin sheets, jasmine and orange scent, and beautiful women. They are misers and power-mongers, not hedonists. That the women are sexless schemers—heifers and plow oxen, in Defoe's words—heightens the sense of a group devoid of human qualities. Manley's characters could feel lust, jealousy, and loneliness; Defoe's jockey for the ear of the sovereign, for the most powerful office, and for sinecures for undeserving relatives. *The Secret History of the White Staff* publications form a group with the *Memoirs of the Conduct of Her Late Majesty* (1715) and *Memoirs of Some Transactions during the Late Ministry*. In all of them the narrators presented themselves as insiders, people in positions to hear private conversations and to observe the principals consistently enough to know their true characters. By speaking as a woman, the "Countess of ——," in *Memoirs of the Conduct of Her Late Majesty*, Defoe could give a more intimate picture of the queen and her women and purport to describe the queen in circumstances in which she became a weak woman without the public trappings of a queen. In all, he selected the point of view in order to reveal the subject most dramatically.

In fact, readers had slightly different expectations of secret histories and memoirs. Both were expected to reveal a kind of truth, to let readers in on behind-the-scenes secrets. Traditionally, secret histories told more about people, memoirs more about events. When Harley's character was the issue, the secret histories could set him in a favorable light in contrast to his scheming, discontented colleagues. When specific charges had been made in the impeachment proceedings, memoirs provided a better vehicle for assigning Harley's part in specific actions. Readers expected secret histories to reveal character and memoirs to provide interpretive commentary on actual events. Both provided explanations for events (perhaps explanations that would be politically dangerous to express) within a highly fictionalized narrative.

Just as Defoe had written a few secret histories before 1714, so had he written propagandistic memoirs.[39] Now, however, he published a cluster of memoirs, and they show deliberate experimentation with the range of the form. *Secret Memoirs of the New Treaty of Alliance with France* (1716) was a creative piece of propaganda allegedly written by a hanger-on at the French court. Like so many memoirs, it used a middle-class narrator, cast a skeptical eye on the nobility, and praised shrewdness and practicality. Set free by class and position to observe with a measure of disinterest, such a narrator could "reveal" what the French had given up and even defend the use of commoners like Matthew Prior in the negotiations.[40]

Memoirs of the Church of Scotland (1717), a book of more than four hundred pages, came out in April to support the parliamentary presentation of a delegation from the Commission of the General Assembly of the Church of Scotland. Two Edinburgh clergymen were again appealing the imposition of the Oath of Abjuration, the oath that required them to aid in barring all members of their own Church from the throne of Great Britain.[41] Because Jacobites in England refused to take the oath, some people, especially after the rebellion of 1715 in Scotland, confused the Scots' objections to the oath with the Catholics' loyalty to the House of Stuart. In his book Defoe began with the Reformation and dramatically and rather sensationally recounted the Church of Scotland's courageous resistance to Roman Catholicism. He hoped to show his countrymen how much the Scots had suffered for their Protestant religion. With a sympathetic understanding of the Church of Scotland, M.P.'s might heed the arguments that the Oath should not be required of Scots or should even be revised in their favor. By using such a vivid narrative style, Defoe hoped to hold his readers' interest and bring the church's struggle to life. His narrator, "an officious Stranger," called the church's history, which came as a revelation to him, a "*Terra incognita,* a vast Continent of hidden, undiscovered Novelties" (1). Had he used a Scot as narrator, Defoe's readers would not have identified with the speaker and might have seen melodramatic self-pity rather than a brave, persecuted people. As he wrote it, the reader can discover the same qualities in Scotland's church that the narrator had.

Memoirs of the Life . . . of Daniel Williams and *Memoirs of Publick Transactions in the Life . . . of . . . Shrewsbury* used the lives of the subjects to praise the men and comment critically on political events. In both, the narrator lacked personal acquaintance with the subjects but had unusual knowledge of their public concerns. Defoe had used a similar ploy in the *Memoirs of the Church of Scotland*, in which his narrator had claimed to have obtained sufficient material from "*Books, by just Authorities, by Oral-Tradition, by living Witnesses,* and by all other rational Means . . . to furnish out Memoirs, tho' not a perfect History." In *Williams,* the narrator said, "no single Person remains alive, that has had so general and so long, a knowledge of, and so particular an intimacy with the Doctor's Conduct in the Things here spoken of" (85). In *Shrewsbury* he argued that "particular intimacy with the Business which he has been employ'd in, and in which he has with a happy success illustrated his personal Character, are opportunities far beyond long Acquaintance, or indeed even Friendship" (ii) and included material from a friend "who was more intimate with" Shrewsbury than he (102–3). The idea that actions revealed intentions and even character jarred unpleasantly with the portraits of Harley, who allegedly acted a part in order to keep the government functioning. These memoirs came from somewhat less propagandistic motives than any of the others. Williams' life was done for Edmund Curll, a bookseller who published a large number of biographies of celebrities. *Shrewsbury* was written to counter one of Curll's "patch'd together" lives by an "ignorant Compiler." It draws considerable thematic unity from the character of Shrewsbury as indolent and withdrawn, yet constantly consulted and brought into the government: "Safety was the height of his Ambition, and his Ease was more than Wealth to him."[42]

One of Defoe's cleverest secret histories was the *Minutes of the Negotiations of Monsr. Mesnager* (1717). Alleged to be a translation from the French of the "private Remembrance . . . of some particular Secret Negotiations," the *Minutes* traced France's long and subtle maneuverings toward the Peace of Utrecht. Defoe made his narrator the lowly undersecretary who worked his way into the trust of King Louis XIV and became an important agent in the negotiation of "the separate peace." Mesnager had been the earliest French contact with the Harley ministry, and Defoe's fictional minutes showed him gaining intimate knowledge of the English court through his meetings and the gossip of his contacts.

Published a month before Harley came to trial, the book was a sensation. Like Defoe's earlier pamphlets, it portrayed the queen as determined to have peace at any price and showed her surrounded by Jacobite schemers and self-interested manipulators. It drew heavily upon the ideas in Defoe's 1710–1712 work to explain how faction in England helped the French. For example, "Mesnager" tells how he did not even need to go to England because the "new managers" were doing his work for him by calling the war too bloody and expensive to continue and how France rejoiced when the campaign in Spain became England's first priority. The French king's need for peace, his cleverness, and his perfidy are of a piece with Defoe's portrayal of him in countless *Reviews* and pamphlets.

What is new about the *Minutes* is the subtlety of Defoe's propaganda for Harley and the detail of the fiction—Mesnager reacts to some English customs and events as though he were as foreign as Defoe's Turkish merchant; he struggles with nuance and connotation in his attempts to understand English speeches, and he has tea and gossips with women as well as men. Some touches could be expected; Mesnager says he did not meet Harley on his first visit to England, for instance, and Harley's attempt to form a coalition government is presented sympathetically and as explanation for some of his later actions. In the *Minutes* Defoe puts Harley on trial and gives his most balanced picture of Harley's weaknesses and his personal appeal. He admits the qualities that Swift, Bolingbroke, and others found enormously frustrating, and he even includes anecdotes that seem to reveal his own difficulties in working with Harley. "I have heard of some who have waited upon him, by his own appointment, on Business of the Greatest Consequence, and have been entertained by him, from one Hour to another, on some Trifle, 'till at last the main Affair has been confin'd to a Minute or two, or perhaps deferred to another Occasion," he says (183). Although many individual passages and the conclusion that Harley was innocent because he was powerless damn Harley, Defoe's point was that Harley should be found not guilty at his trial before Parliament. Defoe's ambivalence toward Harley and his past and present collaborations could be expressed even as Defoe loyally—and honestly—concluded that Harley did not deserve execution.

These critical passages are always softened, first, by Mesnager's respect for Harley and his inability to manipulate him and, second, by descriptions of Harley's personal charm and modesty. Most clever and significant is the fact that these passages are in the early part of the book. Finally, Mesnager is relieved and happy to see Harley's influence fading and reflects that without Harley's management in the Commons and the court, France can look forward to achieving her ends. Harley would have seen through some of the French tricks and successfully opposed some of their proposals. Abel Boyer and others declared the book a forgery and saw its intentions clearly. Defoe had succeeded in raising doubts about some commonly held opinions, however, and the Harley of *Minutes* was both more human and more charismatic than the Harley of *The Secret History of the White Staff*.[43]

In the same years Defoe published epistles and letters from a variety of fictional points of view, "accounts," a "declaration," and an "appeal." Thus, even as he worked in the most overwrought of fictional forms, he began to try to develop narrative voices that would be the exact opposites of the insinuating, coded secret histories. He began to experiment with narrators who had no reason to distort material, who might be too simple and artless to do so, who might be incapable of doing so because of their lack of knowledge. Thus, several times, he used ordinary soldiers and Turks as narrators. Except for the Quakers and Turks, few of these voices are distinctive, and no personalities come to life. Defoe had not yet learned to see the world exclusively through the eyes of his character and, thus, to realize the full potential of his narrative strategy. The "officer" who narrates *An Apology for the Army* (1715) speaks with considerable energy and outrage, but the reader learns nothing at all about him; the Turkish spy in *Continuation of Letters Written by a Turkish Spy at Paris* (1718) can indulge in digressions in which he rejoices that he is not French or English, use a few phrases such as "land of infidels," and give quaint histories of things like the Order of the Garter, but his account of the French/English war from 1687 to 1693 is basically straightforward and unmarked by personality. In dialogues Defoe eliminated a narrator who might filter or color or even edit his story. *The Quarrel of the School-Boys at Athens* (1717) purports to be nothing but a story told by "a Grave Instructor" "in the Days of the ancient Philosophers, when People acted by the Light of Nature; and when Reason was the Guide of Politicians" (1–2). Although the beginning provides this frame, the story simply ends without returning to the persona who introduced it.

Defoe's 1714–1719 works go beyond providing a panorama of witnesses to making fine distinctions among kinds of witnessing and kinds of statements of authenticity. Several explain that they intended their writing for personal use alone. Mesnager says his were for "private Remembrance," and he never "put it into such Shape as to appear publickly in the World" (3). The rebel of *Proceedings at Perth* explains, "My Design was only to record in my own Memorial, which I keep of things as they come to view." Others, like the "author" of the manuscript "found" and published as *An Account of Proceedings against the Rebels* (1716) are presented as having been written in outrage. One who had fought with Monmouth, as this author appears to have, would be expected to detest all who fought with the Pretender or compared their cause to his. The powerful introduction begins, "The Faction having now lost all Hopes of Success . . . apply themselves with the utmost

Industry and Malice to cry down the Proceedings of Justice against the Rebels who are taken, as Barbarous and Cruel. . . . This Clamour is so very . . . remote from Truth" (iii). These witnesses approximate clear windows, and others require readers to perform a fairly sophisticated act of opposite judgment. For instance, the narrator of *A True Account of the Proceedings at Perth* looks back on the Jacobite rebels' defeat in Scotland and regrets nothing but losing.[44] Although he begins by explaining that they lost "not by the formidable Power of the National Forces . . . but by the ill Conduct of those on whose Councils all Things at that Time depended, as well . . . as the want of Resolution to act their part in the Field," the reader must put together the full extent of the treachery, cowardice, and incompetence of those in England, France, and Scotland. The nameless rebel suffers for his gullibility, yet is still dangerous because he would fight again if he could.[45] The propaganda purposes of this work—to stigmatize Ormonde and other still-popular Jacobites, to warn readers against Jacobitism, to encourage firm legal measures against them, and to increase support for the Hanoverian government—deliberately appear to ordinary readers to be incidental to the lively, suspenseful story that takes them behind the scenes of the rebellion. Defoe's hope, of course, was that the lessons would be remembered and acted upon because they came from example rather than precept.

This nameless rebel is an eyewitness to events and as such shares the advantages and disadvantages of all eyewitnesses. He sees and experiences events, and his account therefore has immediacy, drama, and some built-in credibility. He is also limited by being a witness; he has to discover what went before and what the causes were, and he has a bias because he was a witness—what he thinks he saw and the interpretations he gave at that moment can be replaced only with great difficulty. That the narrator of *Proceedings* is a defeated, unrepentant rebel dictates that he will probably make excuses, rationalize, and find reason to hope for better days. Defoe turns this psychological truth into powerful propaganda. Were the narrator persuaded of his error, drastically disaffected with the Pretender, and longing for reconciliation with his Hanoverian countrymen, he would not illustrate the seductiveness of the Jacobite leaders or the necessity for the policies toward the rebels of George's administration that some saw as unduly harsh. Moreover, the narrator's very extremes prevent reader empathy; he can be read only as a deluded, defeated pawn sacrificed without regret or honor.

Defoe did not stop at building reliability into his narrators through their relationship to events and their class. Many of them call upon readers themselves to witness to their truth. The events in *The History of the Wars* (1715), his preface says, were "transacted within the View, and perhaps in the Memory of most that shall now read them, and need no better Appeal for their Authority and Truth." The *Memoirs of Shrews-bury* repeats nearly the same words as *The History of the Wars*: "Things transacted in our view, and in the Days which we have constantly in Memory, Affairs of yesterday; . . . *of to day*; Things . . . if wrong repre-sented, the Town is full of Living Testimonies to confute" (5). *The Memoirs of Major Ramkins* says, "The History of that Battle [Boyne] has so many Eye Witnesses still alive" (288). *An Account of the Proceedings against the Rebels* challenges anyone who might disagree: "These Things are still remember'd by Thousands of Eye-witnesses, and therefore can admit of no Contradiction, but from such as have bid defiance to Truth" (iii). *The Danger of Court Differences* uses, "But as it is a real History, the Matters of Fact upon Record, and the Truth of them not to be disputed" (16).

While these works demanded credence on the basis of history and memory, others drew upon another kind of experience. They de-manded acceptance because the characters and incidents were so famil-iar, and, therefore, veridically accurate. In the prefatory letter to *The Family Instructor*, the Reverend Samuel Wright had said that he could "put *Names* and *Families*" to some of the dialogues, and Defoe explained that he wanted the book to function as parable and general reproof rather than as history.

By 1715, of course, it was absolutely conventional for prose fiction writers to claim that their books were true and their narrators eyewit-nesses. Epistolary fiction, continental novellas and memoirs, and par-tially autobiographical books like Francis Kirkman's *Unlucky Citizen* had made claims of authenticity completely conventional. Writer after writ-er claimed to be a witness as Aphra Behn had in *Oroonoko*: "I was myself an eye-witness to a great part of what you will find here set down; and what I could not be a witness of I received from the mouth of . . . the hero himself." Defoe even participates in the "found manuscript" tradi-tion with his *An Account of the Proceedings against the Rebels* (1716). Claims similar to that in *The Family Instructor* were somewhat conventional, too, though far less frequent. John Bunyan, for instance, had described "all" the incidents in *The Life and Death of Mr. Badman* as "acted upon the stage of this world, even many times before mine eyes."[46]

Throughout these years a new imaginative impulse grew in Defoe. At first it seemed wish-fulfilment or rationalization. When Defoe turned Atterbury into Milton's Satan, filled out conversations among conspirators, and described Queen Anne's intentions had she lived, familiar psychological defenses seem to be operating. In secret histo-ries he often moved from real events to events that might be real to incidents that he wished real; all had the same political and moral purposes. He became more and more willing to use events to make particular points. His propaganda works become longer and longer.

Details of character and setting, fleshed-out incidents, and other things irrelevant to the primary purposes of the writing emerge and become characteristic. Some pamphlets give a version of a story and say, "Others relate it otherwise; so the Matter is left doubtful in History, but this they all agree in." Some pamphlets include disclaimers: "Whether this happened or no, I . . ." or "This Discourse, whether true or not. . . ."[47]

In whatever he wrote the flow into fantasy became a possibility. Swept away into a battle, a palace intrigue, or a man's dreams, Defoe published longer and longer works of a more dramatic nature. In 1712 he would never have used a 400-page book to help a delegation to Parliament argue a case, and the readers of ordinary monthly papers must have been surprised at the detail and excitement of his accounts of battles in *Mercurius Politicus*. Sure of a market for whatever he wrote, Defoe began to indulge himself and to subordinate historical truth unapologetically to ideological and personal considerations.

CHAPTER 16

A PENETRATING EYE

*I have study'd the advancement and encrease of knowledge for
those that read, and shall be as glad to make them wise, as to make
them merry; yet I hope they will not find the story so ill told, or so
dull as to tyre them too soon, or so barren as to put them to sleep
over it.*

——DEFOE, *A Tour thro' the Whole Island
of Great Britain* (1727)

*And now we are come to the last Part of a Man's Life . . . now he
examines, weighs, and looks into Things with a most penetrating
Eye.*

——DEFOE, Mist's *Weekly Journal, Collection
of Miscellany Letters* (1727)

    Near the end of April 1719 Defoe published *Robinson Crusoe.* It was
printed in an edition of 1,000 like almost all of his works, and a second
edition of the same size came out on 9 May and a third around 6 June.
Within a year the book had been translated into French, German, and
Dutch.[1] Defoe does not appear to have been especially impressed with
his milestone in literary history. Several of his secret histories and a few
of his works on the Jacobite rebels had begun as well or nearly as well,
and the 1715 *Family Instructor* was in its seventh edition by then. Soon,
however, the newspapers began to carry advertisements for books such
as *The Adventures and Surprizing Deliverances of James Dubourdieu and His
Wife,* "very proper to be bound up with" *Robinson Crusoe,* and William
Taylor, Defoe's publisher, began a Chancery suit against Thomas Cox
to protect his copyright.[2]

    When goaded into defending *Robinson Crusoe* Defoe called it "alle-
goric history," and some readers have always found the book autobiographical. In the year of its publication, for instance, Charles Gildon
in *The Life and Strange Surprizing Adventures of Mr. D . . . De F . . .*
represented Defoe as telling Crusoe that he was "the true Allegorick
Image of thy tender Father *D . . . l*; I drew thee from the consideration
of my own Mind; I have been all my Life that Rambling, Inconsistent
Creature, which I have made thee" (x). Several statements in Defoe's

ROBINSON CRUSOE.

Robinson Crusoe, from the first French edition, 1722.

Serious Reflections during the Life and Surprising Adventures of Robinson Crusoe (1720) have often been taken to mean that Defoe intended *Robinson Crusoe* as an allegory of his own life. For instance, he says that, had he given his readers the "life of a man you knew, . . . whose misfortunes and infirmities perhaps you had sometimes unjustly triumphed over," the book might "scarce have obtained a reading, or at best no attention" (xiii). He describes the life of Crusoe as he often had his own in the *Review* and in *An Appeal to Honour and Justice*. Crusoe, he says, "suffered all manner of violences and oppressions, injurious reproaches, contempt of men, . . . corrections from Heaven, and oppositions on earth; have had innumerable ups and downs in matters of fortune, . . . been raised again and depressed again, and that oftener perhaps in one man's life than ever was known before; shipwrecked often, though more by land than by sea" (ix). More specifically, he refers to a dream of being taken by messengers and arrested by officers and to representations of imprisonment.

Serious Reflections, however, was written a year after *Robinson Crusoe*, and responds specifically to ridicule of the novel. In fact, it largely repeats the theory of "fable" that Defoe had explained in *The New Family Instructor*. In both Defoe insists upon the value and antiquity of fictions, which he speculates may provide "the only way of Teaching." *Robinson Crusoe* is not an allegory of events in Defoe's life any more than *The Family Instructor* is the history of a real family. Its autobiographical elements are states of mind, not events. Defoe's first impulse in everything he wrote was to imagine a person and project feelings. From this impulse came a dramatic situation and an individual; undergirding his work was the age's firm belief that human beings are more alike than different. Writers of the eighteenth-century often took as one of the aims of their fiction to depict how ordinary people would react to extraordinary events. Horace Walpole explained that the characters in his gothic novel, *The Castle of Otranto* "comport themselves as persons would do in their situation."

Defoe took for granted what Samuel Johnson felt it necessary to put into words:

All joy or sorrow for the happiness or calamities of others is produced by an act of the imagination, that realises the event however fictitious . . . by placing us, for a time, in the condition of him whose fortune we contemplate; so that we feel, while the deception lasts, whatever motions would be excited by the same good or evil happening to ourselves. (*Rambler*, no. 60)

In writing of Crusoe's experiences, Defoe drew upon his own emotions and created symbolic parallels. The progression of emotions in Crusoe reflects the succession of emotions, recollected and imagined, in Defoe and is transmitted to the reader who recognizes the state of mind, supplies a personal analogy, and, therefore, shares in the emotional experience.

In the powerful evocation of states of mind, in the representation of emotional experience, Defoe had made uncommon experience accessible and even personal. If he was not aware of this aspect of his work before writing *Robinson Crusoe*, he certainly became so either during or immediately after the writing of it. In the essays in *Serious Reflections* he eschewed the opportunity to point out the religious, economic, or political themes, to elaborate upon the moral lessons of the book, or to emphasize the practical ingenuity that Rousseau and other contemporaries praised. Rather, he began his essays with a meditation on solitude and forced confinement. The movement in his work was toward going beyond the commonplace illustrative anecdotes and analogies in all of his writing to making demands that his readers enter emotionally into fantastic situations and into the minds of characters whose experiences were less and less like their own. He had used human nature as a commonsense touchstone, and, in his pamphlets, quick references to such things as the behavior of people confronted with a burning house or a dishonest tradesman had been used to identify motive or recommend action. He used situations as familar as most of those in *The Family Instructor*, drew upon familiar examples from the classics, history, and especially the Bible, and provided his readers with a bridge between their experience and the idea he was trying to explain.

Robinson Crusoe, however, moved as swiftly from the commonplace as *The Consolidator* had. Although many, many Englishmen knew people captured by the Sallee pirates, those who sailed from Salé on the Moroccan coast,[3] to imagine being the captive of one and then a castaway for twenty-eight years was almost as great an act of imagination as the trip to Asia and then the moon in *The Consolidator*. In both books Defoe was careful to move from the somewhat familiar to the less familiar or even fantastic. As readers gave themselves over to the life of the imagination, they read differently. Not only did they accept more, but they tested the fiction by the credibility of the characters' responses to events rather than by the probability of the events themselves.

The clear objectives and somewhat limited length of the political pamphlets had taught Defoe to manipulate reader response through the selection of details and circumstances. He tried to assure that they would feel the conflicts, pressures, and nuances of a situation as the central actor had. The form demanded the most scant elements of setting and plot, and maneuvered to assure that the reader would say, "In his place, I, too, would. . . . " Defoe could also factor in personality and, between 1714 and 1719, the importance and individuality of character increased. This added dimension is especially obvious in the secret histories and memoirs. The hypocrisy and deceptiveness of the

Jacobite characters, for instance, seem to be the product and natural manifestation of their mistaken notions and self-deceptions. Especially in these defenses of Harley, Defoe makes the situation and Harley's personality the walls of a cage that determine the answer to the unspoken question: "In his place, would you not have done as he?"

That Crusoe is imprisoned and alone on the island is obvious, but, significantly, he feels confined and alienated at home with his parents, "castaway" and alien on his Brazilian plantation, and he has been the slave of a Moroccan. The originality of Defoe's rendering of the mentality of a prisoner resides primarily in his ability to create the mood swings and hyperactivity of the mind and imagination. In such captivity time has no signification, no meaningful referent. Crusoe's mind devours time, is itself whirled into itself. Crusoe says, "my Head run mightily," "I spent whole Hours . . . whole days, in representing to my self in the most lively Colours, how I must have acted"; "Night and Day, I could think of nothing but how I might destroy some of these Monsters"; "the innumerable Crowd of Thoughts that whirl'd through that great thorow-fare of the Brain, the Memory, in this Night's Time: I ran over the whole History of my Life." Backwards and forwards, remembering and projecting, reviewing and recasting, his mind races, and the narrative speeds up and takes on the intensity found only in the most dramatic of events. "I imagin'd," "I imagin'd," "I imagin'd," he says as he thinks about the disappearance of the shipwrecked Spaniards, and the mind is the only reality, as it becomes when Crusoe thinks about the single footprint.[4]

Surely Defoe's own mind worked as frenetically in Newgate, and later he would write rather abjectly that he lacked "passive" courage. He could carry a Protestant flail or dare a journalistic rival to carry out a threat, but the specter of time in jail turned him into a fugitive or a groveler. That actions ordinarily praised as heroic—Crusoe's fight to save the Spaniard—fade before efforts to resist despair and to build boats testify to their relative value for Defoe. To risk his life seemed easier and even "more natural" than living without companionship behind "the Eternal Bars and Bolts of the Ocean."

Reactions to imprisonment but begin the emotions Defoe took from his life, and the knowledge of some of Defoe's metaphors for his experiences give passages in the novel considerable allusive depth. At one point Crusoe remarks that being cast up on that safe and fruitful island was as great a miracle as Elijah's being fed by the ravens. In the preface to the eighth volume of the *Review* (1712), Defoe had written,

I have gone through a Life of Wonders, and am the Subject of a vast Variety of Providences; I have been fed more by Miracle than *Elijah*.

In Prison I have learnt to know that Liberty does not consist in open Doors.
The same Checquer-Work of Fortunes attends me still. . . .

In another place Crusoe reflects on the cannibals and concludes that men are "the Clay in the Hand of the Potter" and that no vessel should ask, "Why hast thou form'd me thus?" In 1681 Defoe had written a meditation on this subject; one of the vessels angrily demands to know why it is "This Rude ill-fashon'd [*sic*] Nasty Pott Destin'd to Every Slavish use." The potter punishes this pot by making it useless, and the meditation ends with a reminder to concentrate on what he is and how many "gifts" there are in life rather than on what he might be or have. Crusoe calls himself "a *Memento* to those who are touched with the general Plague of Mankind, whence, for ought I know, one half of their Miseries flow: I mean, that of not being satisfy'd with the Station wherein God and Nature has plac'd them" (1:225). *Robinson Crusoe* uses the analogy to accept, and, therefore, tolerate, the cannibals' existence. In fact, half of his conclusion about them is a restatement of his youthful meditation: "Still as we are all the Clay in the Hand of the Potter, no Vessel could say to him, Why hast thou form'd me thus?" (1:245) Yet here and in Defoe's meditation is an undertone of questioning of Providence and the suppressing of discontent and of the tendency to second-guess God.

The mind and experience of Defoe are everywhere in *Robinson Crusoe*. His political and economic ideas provide a sturdy spine for his story, the conflicts of his age give immediacy and profundity to the character of Crusoe,[5] and evidence of his most recent work and personal life abounds. In fact, *Robinson Crusoe* dramatizes Defoe's position on the very recent Salters' Hall controversy. His novel illustrates deliberately and in great detail that Scripture and revelation without dogma are sufficient. In his writings about the Salters' Hall meeting, Defoe had repeatedly complained that the controversy that grew out of it gave the impression that some ministers considered the Scriptures "inextricable, and past our Understanding." He believed that such an opinion not only might discourage people but certainly strengthened the position of the High Church and Catholic clergymen who emphasized the authority of the priest and of dogma. Since boyhood he had heard sermons that taught, "True Religion is more affection and Practice, than Doctrine, or Notion, and is seated more in the heart than in the head." It is no coincidence that at the height of the Salters' Hall debate, Crusoe finds his way to God while alone on an island and then converts Friday. Defoe has Crusoe praise God for the "infinite and inexpressible . . . Blessing . . . that the Knowledge of God . . . is so plainly laid down in the Word of God." The novel states firmly that, with the grace of revelation, anyone can understand the Bible. The concerns raised by the Salters' Hall debate appear in Defoe's work until the end of his life; his *New Family Instructor* (1727), for instance, includes extensive sections on the divinity of Christ and ends with a long blank verse poem called *Trinity: Or, the Divinity of the Son*.

The pattern of salvation as presented in the lives of several characters in *The Family Instructor*s is repeated in Crusoe, Friday, and Atkins's wife. Crusoe's repentance and ultimate salvation is assured at the moment he says, "I look'd back upon my past Life with such Horrour, and my Sins appear'd so dreadful, that my Soul sought nothing of God, but Deliverance from the Load of Guilt that bore down all my Comfort." He moves then, haltingly and with some setbacks, through the process made familiar in *The Family Instructor*. The fact that Friday asks questions that Crusoe cannot answer in no way detracts from Defoe's point. When Friday asks why God does not "kill the Devil now," Crusoe has no answer, but, by analogy to himself, Friday concludes that God may be giving even Satan a chance for repentance and pardon. Defoe takes the opportunity to comment on the natural, universal aspects of Friday's questions and on the necessity for revelation. He goes on to contrast the intuitive grasp of essential questions to esoteric theological disputes. Crusoe observes, "I cannot see the least Use that the greatest Knowledge of the disputed Parts in Religion which have made such Confusions in the World would have been to us, if we could have obtain'd it." In this implied commentary on recent church history, he sides with those who agree with Dryden's "Faith is not built on disquisitions vain; / The things we *must* believe, are *few*, and *plain*."[6]

Robinson Crusoe is, of course, Defoe's most extended exploration of God's relationship to his creatures, but how fully it communicates his experience of God's love is seldom noticed.[7] Crusoe's relationship with God goes through many stages, and Defoe uses it as a vehicle to explain the most pressing, universal questions about God even as he provides his conclusion to the Salters' Hall controversy. At the beginning of the book Crusoe is a "professor of religion," a nominal Christian, and the book quickly shows how shallow and mistaken his faith is. On the island Crusoe quickly asks why he has been "singled out" and why Providence would "thus compleatly ruine its Creatures, and render them so absolutely miserable . . . so entirely depress'd that it could hardly be rational to be thankful for such a Life." God here is adversary. When Crusoe believes the barley to be a miracle for himself alone, he thanks God, but he is quickly disabused by the discovery of the bag of chicken feed, and his piety evaporates. Even storms and an earthquake fail to move him to more than a terrified, empty "Lord ha' Mercy upon me." His fever and the dream about the angel with the flaming sword, however, lead him to ask a profound and significantly broad question: "What is this Earth and Sea of which I have seen so much, whence is it produc'd, and what am I, and all other Creatures, wild and tame, humane and brutal, whence are we?" He has stopped thinking of himself alone; soon his conscience awakens, and he begins to experience regret and guilt. Finally he has weeks and months when he feels deeply happy because he experiences God's "Presence . . . supporting, comforting, and encouraging [him] to depend upon his Providence here, and hope for his Eternal Presence hereafter" (1:129). He believes he is completely resigned to the will of God, and it is in this state that he realizes that the earth is a beautiful, abundant storehouse and that the barley was a sign of God's care for his creatures. He decides to learn "the Vertue and Goodness" of the fruits and plants; suddenly the island abounds with food, and he masters the environment in order to farm successfully. The island becomes a new Eden for it looks "in a constant Verdure, or Flourish of *Spring* . . . it looked like a planted Garden." He looks over "that delicious Vale," and his thoughts prefigure the pleasure he imagines any English king would have on surveying his country.

This condition, like the time he believed the barley to be a special miracle, is partly a delusion. The discovery of the footprint "banish'd all my religious Hope," and Crusoe moves into a state of intense fear, one which reminds him of the bitter ironies of the human state—he who had longed so desperately for human companionship is now terrified at the prospect, just as he had felt "cast away" and lonely in Brazil, only to become a real castaway, and as he had failed to appreciate the New World's abundance of rum and tobacco, only to wish for them frequently on the island. At his lowest point Crusoe vomits "with an uncommon Violence" at the thought of the depths of human "hellish" brutality and degeneracy.

His next dream promises the coming of Friday, and Friday's arrival is the turning point. Crusoe describes him as "a comely handsome Fellow" with "Sweetness and Softness" in his countenance. Shortly thereafter, Crusoe observes that God had "bestow'd upon [the natives] the same Powers, the same Reason, the same Affections, the same Sentiments of Kindness and Obligation . . . the same Sense of Gratitude, Sincerity, Fidelity, and all the Capacities of doing Good and receiving Good, that he has given to us." Coleridge greatly admired *Robinson Crusoe*, and like his Ancient Mariner, Crusoe has learned to bless and find beauty in all God's creatures. At first terrified of the animals, the sea, and the earthquake, he learns to use nature to feed and clothe himself; his "summer home" is in a beautiful natural setting, and he uses his knowledge to produce more food and even to capture the mutineers. The affirmation of what nature offers is even more clear in *Captain Singleton*. Crusoe teaches Friday to be a Christian, and this act brings him to thank God more passionately than he ever has before:

I reflected that in this solitary Life. . . . I had not only been moved my self to look up to Heaven, and to seek to the Hand that had brought me there; but was now . . . made an Instrument under Providence to save the Life, and *for ought I knew*, the Soul of a poor Savage . . . a secret Joy run through every Part of my Soul, and I frequently rejoyc'd that ever I was brought to this Place. (2.6)

When Crusoe names Friday, he is not committing an imperialist act but "christening" a man given not only his mortal life but hope for eternal life. Crusoe says he called him "Friday" "for the Memory of the Time" he saved his life and, at the same time, lets Friday know "I was very well pleas'd with him." The echo of the voice from Heaven at Jesus' baptism in the wilderness and the fact that christenings and confirmations often were the occasions for the bestowing of new names on children make the symbolism of baptism—and the English colonial mentality— unmistakable.

When Crusoe is rescued he says he looks on the captain "as a Man sent from Heaven to deliver me," as evidence of "a secret Hand of Providence governing the World" that will "send Help to the Miserable whenever he pleased." Crusoe has learned to "wait on the Lord," to trust his purposes and his benevolence, and understands that God works through natural means, but means that express his loving care as eloquently as miracles. The novel, then, explains how people may teach themselves religion and what God's nature and relationship to his creation are. Crusoe has learned that his sin was indifference to God—not disobedience to his father—and that the punishment is desperate loneliness. His "disobedience," after all, comes only after a year of obedience and continued restlessness, and, significantly, he has no calling. Moreover, the Puritan literature of the period, much of it known to Defoe, is full of real and fictional stories of such children. The message of these stories is almost uniformly against the stance taken by Crusoe's father and against the disobedience of parents theory. Thomas Shepard, for instance, says of his own life, "I saw in prayer that my great sin was continual separation, distance from God, not so much this or that particular sin."[8] The sense of calling, the opportunities for personal and national benefits, and the need to respect the feelings of those who want what is not "in it self sinful" come up repeatedly. The duke of Atholl faced a situation almost exactly like that of Robinson Crusoe's father about the time Defoe wrote his book, and Defoe may have heard about it from one of his Scottish friends. The duke's son wanted to go to sea, and the father listed the certainty of "profligate company," the danger, and the "little probability of a Scotchman's making their fortune that way," but then he writes, "Since you still persist in this design in so singular manner, I shall allow your going to Sea, since you appear so very much to set your heart upon it, since you have so much uneasiness and discontent, And that it is not sinfull or unlawfull in it self . . . I allow

Robinson Crusoe and the footprint, by Thomas Stothart, 1790.

Robinson Crusoe and his father, from the first French edition, 1722.

it." He adds that his son must return if the "uneasiness" does not end.[9]

Charles Gildon and others criticized Defoe for discouraging men from going to sea. Even Robert Knox, one of Defoe's recognized sources, records a conversation in which friends rebuke his father for opposing Knox's desire to go to sea. The men argue that the ship "will be as good as a plentifull estate to your Son & it is a pitty to crosse his good inclination, since commondly younge men doe best in that Calling they have most mind to be in." In fact, a year or so before *Robinson Crusoe*, Knox had given his publisher a manuscript that included this incident and an account of his life after captivity, an account particularly notable because Knox had turned pirate and entered the slave trade.[10] Crusoe considers what he has done to deserve to be on the island alone, he weighs and deliberates about whether and how much he should feel guilty. His conclusion is that he has been indifferent to God, not that he should have obeyed his father. He learns that in disaster there may be deliverance. Defoe's characters fully accept, as he himself did, the mysteries of God's intentions even as they occupy a providential world in which their own intentions and motives are fully known and cast in the balance.

Robinson Crusoe begins with the dilemma of a dutiful son who wants to reject the occupation that his parents have chosen for him in order to go to sea. This occupation is the law, the same profession that Defoe's own son Benjamin had recently rejected. The opening pages of the novel seem to add to the evidence that Defoe's relationship with his older son had been stormy at least since 1711 when Russell had written Defoe, "I hope you'll wiselie consider his youth leads him to many things now that his [riper] years will amend" (169). In fact, Benjamin was newly married, and Hannah Coates of Norwich was pregnant with their first child. Defoe felt strongly that marriage should wait until a young man had settled in an occupation; he and his father had, and all of his conduct books emphasize the point. *The Family Instructor* of 1715 had ended with the harrowing death of a disobedient older son. Defoe's younger son, Daniel, had moved to Cornhill, begun the life of a merchant, and was about to marry Mary Webb of Aldermanbury, London. Sons were in the public eye as well. Recent news of the break between King George and the Prince of Wales made much of the setting up of a rival court and childish rivalries and snubs over, among other things, a christening and the honorary directorship of a trading company, and Defoe knew that this breach had contributed to the defeat of the bill to repeal the Test and Corporation Acts. In Russia Czar Peter had just put his son to death.[11]

At one point, Defoe had remarked that there was a conduct book for every season of life, and in 1718 he had published a second volume of *The Family Instructor*. This sequel turned from the dialogues of parents with rebellious teenagers and of masters and servants to the behavior of fathers, especially in their responsibility for spiritual guidance in their extended households. He considered problems between husbands and wives, the discipline of children, and the education of young children and apprentices. In this book he stressed the benefits of family worship, considerate communication, and control of passions. Although conservative computations estimate the annual expenses of a contemporary upper-middle-class London household at £450–500,[12] Defoe gives his characters few concerns about money. His children, after all, seem to have married respectably, and it was one of the few economically stable periods of his life. The problems his characters in this *Family Instructor* experience come from the deficiencies in the head of the family. *Robinson Crusoe*, too, is concerned with the establishment of Crusoe's government of himself and of his "regulating" his "family" and finding comfort in their presence. Especially in the second *Family Instructor*, Defoe had worked out a portrait of the ideal master. His control of his passions, his deliberative nature, and his attention to all of the circumstances in a situation set him apart from others. Defoe even insists that such men—and they are all men—act out of affection; Crusoe, for instance, comes to understand and pity the cannibals just as the child in *The Family Instructor, II* pities Tobey and the other Barbados blacks, and he says that he came to "love" Friday. The good master teaches his extended family religion and sets a good example; those in such a family learn their duty to God and each other and live in exemplary harmony. The self-control of the master seems to be a major factor in his control over the others. They respect him and trust in his desire for their good.

Whereas the first *Family Instructor* had stressed the reform of established habits, the second deals much more heavily with the kinds of adjustments newly married people must make and with the establishment of a virtuous, happy family life. Defoe's daughter Maria, like her brothers, was newly married, and her husband, Henry Langley of Queenhithe, came from a family long friendly to the Tuffleys.[13] Eighteenth-century people felt deeply the excitement and symbolism of setting up a new household.[14] It was, of course, a rite of passage and brought great changes to the parents' as well as to the new couple's lives. The common assumption was that the couple would not marry until they could find and support a home of their own. Young men and women often saved for years, and both sets of parents helped. The housing shortage in London often delayed marriages as much as the wait for a country cottage with land or the need for a new shop of a certain kind. Marriage gave the man full membership in the community and made the woman mistress of her home; both people, therefore, attained position and responsibilities as governors. Books like Fénelon's *Traité de l' éducation des filles* (1687) based their educational plan on the concept of the woman as *maîtresse de la maison* and prepared her to manage the children, servants, and household or estate budget.[15] Moreover, Defoe's generation took added pleasure in the idea that God had ordained the family for the happiness of individuals and the welfare of the community. The family, a microcosm of the well-governed state, had Christian education and service at its core and benefited society even as it fulfilled the person. A common opinion was that marriage existed partly so "that the infinite troubles which lie upon us in this world might be eased with the comfort and help one of another."[16]

Defoe, then, watched the birth of three new spiritual and economic undertakings with a parent's customary pride and anxiety. His second *Family Instructor* with its numerous masters and mistresses of homes, their problems, their diverse personalities, and their attempts to establish happy, efficient, pious homes has far more unity than the first *Family Instructor* because of its concern with personal and family control. It conformed to the purpose of earlier books of practical divinity such as *Some Considerations concerning the Present State of Religion* (1702), which showed religion to be the means of "regulating" lives "so as it may be consistent with their own Good, and the Good of Humane Society."[17]

In *The Family Instructor, II* Defoe illustrates how sudden disputes about trifles can become "a terrible Flame" with "fatal" consequences for a whole family and how husbands and masters of family often make use of trifles as reasons for omitting their duty (173–74). In the same book he spends a significant amount of time defining "correction," illustrating ideal practice with analogies to breaking and schooling a horse. The only precepts many young people in Defoe's time heard about obedience, authority, and the social and political order came from the catechism.[18] Crusoe takes great pains with Friday and each addition to his island society, explaining and questioning in catechismal style. The Englishmen he leaves on the island make little effort with their slaves and constantly provoke their Spanish neighbors. They live in sloth and strife and provide a contrasting lesson in the need for self and family government.

Even some of the dialogue in *Robinson Crusoe* resembles sections of both *Family Instructor*s. The most obvious parallels are not in the conversations between adult sons and their fathers but in passages that resemble the catechism. Small children and Tobey in the *Family Instructor*s ask the same questions that Friday and Will Atkins's native wife do in *Robinson Crusoe* and *Farther Adventures of Robinson Crusoe*. All of these books repeat the simple truths of Christianity. Each of the four sections begins with the question, "Who made you?" From there, the inquiry takes up the same issues: what mankind is to do; what is properly meant by the fear of God; the necessity and pleasure of prayer; and the progress and joy of repentance, sanctification, and faith.[19] The stress upon people's duty to love and serve God and to obey the commandments is the same in each.[20] The first *Family Instructor* quotes more directly from the catechism, and the child interrupts his father frequently because he does not understand the words. The tot is understandably bewildered when told, for instance, that God is "one, infinite, eternal, incomprehensible, invisible BEING, the first Cause of all things; the Giver of Life and Being to all things; existing prior, and superior to all things, infinitely perfect, great, holy, just, wise, and good."[21] In the later books Defoe paraphrases more and quotes Scripture rather than the secondary church literature.

In both *Family Instructor*s and both parts of *Robinson Crusoe*, the responses of those innocents who hear about God are identical. They feel deep gratitude to God, regret their previous ignorance, fear the consequences of their failure to thank him, and express the simple desire to please him entirely. Their simple promises come in terms like those of Atkins's wife: "I no makee him angry, I no do bad wicked Thing" (2:50). The desire to know God better and to study the Bible is insatiable. This faith and hunger for religion contrasts strongly with the characters who know God and either neglect religion or even work to discourage the piety of others. The natives and children often become the instruments for the salvation of their families, and, especially in the conduct books, the narrative becomes strikingly sentimental. Once confirmed in faith, all of the characters, the newly converted and the reclaimed, feel the same happiness. All have followed the pattern summarized in *The Family Instructor* as conviction of sin, faith and repentance, sanctification, and justification (16, 25).

In 1720 Defoe would have Crusoe say, "I must have made very little use of my solitary and wandering years if, after such a scene of wonders, as my life may be justly called, I had nothing to say, and had made no observations." In another place he wrote that old age was the time to consider and meditate on everything seen and read, for "he is now arrived at an Age, when the Senses being no longer hurried away by the Passions . . . he examines, weighs, and looks into Things with a most penetrating Eye; he distinguishes . . . the Solid from the Trifling; . . . he tries every Thing by the Touchstone of Reason; and, this is the Man that's qualified to serve both his Country and his Friends."[22] Making useful observations had come to mean a great deal to Defoe. In the introduction to the third volume of his *Tour thro' the Whole Island of Great Britain*, he would divide travelers into two groups: the foolish who record "trifles" and the wise who note "critical" and "significant" sights that call to mind entire experiences and provide substance for useful "observations." In *A Journal of the Plague Year* Defoe turned observations about the 1665 plague into a comprehensive plan for lessening the spread and suffering of future plagues. His evaluation of which actions hindered and which helped, of what was done well and what needed to be done, put to use years of experience with the City and its government and months of careful reading and analysis of 1665. In *A Tour* and in *Serious Reflections* Defoe said, "I have study'd the advancement and encrease [*sic*] of knowledge for those that read, and shall be as glad to make them wise, as to make them merry, yet I hope they will not find the story . . . ill told."[23]

In no other work does he state so clearly the "wisdom" he believes his fifty-nine years have given him. What Defoe reveals is the secret of his resiliency. He had the power to make himself happy, and, if *Robinson Crusoe* shows a transforming imagination, it is because Defoe had a transforming will. Over and over he explains that in no condition is mankind without something for which to be thankful, that God will never "leave his Creatures so absolutely destitute" that they should despair. Sometimes he has Robinson Crusoe find the good in comparison to other people's conditions, sometimes in comparison to what he might have expected, and sometimes in comparison to what he deserved. Sometimes Defoe points out that an event that seems a catastrophe, "destruction," is really the beginning of a "deliverance." Over and over, he gives Robinson Crusoe a double perspective, as he does when Crusoe speaks of being "in the sixth Year of my Reign, or my Captivity."

If *Robinson Crusoe* has elements of an allegorical address to his sons, Defoe's message is a rigorous one. When he came to summarize the lessons of the novel in *Serious Reflections*, he named the necessity for "invincible patience," "indefatigable application," and "undaunted resolution" (xiii). These are, of course, the qualities that make Robinson Crusoe heroic and the book immortal. The way Defoe works these qualities out in the book defines them. Patience seems forced upon Robinson Crusoe. The alternatives—despair, rage, hasty action—are all self-destructive. Year after year after year Crusoe does not give up his hope for rescue, does not succumb to a savage state, and continues to consider consequences and possible problems. "Undaunted resolution" seems to be endurance, not single-minded movement toward a goal.

Crusoe lives "indefatigable application" more than any of the other qualities; the words "infinite Labour," "laborious and tedious," and "inexpressible Labour" occur over and over, sometimes four or five times within a page or two. He reckons the "cost" of various tasks in days, weeks, and even months, and when he sets his colonists to work, he makes sure they understand what "indefatigable Pains," "What prodigious Labour," he had expended to make a single board. In making boards, pottery, a canoe, Crusoe lives out undaunted resolution; in neither long-term plans nor extended time does he show resolution beyond enduring and living up to personal standards of conduct. That the message of *Robinson Crusoe* seems to be to trust in God and his mercy does nothing to diminish the sense of underlying frustration that Crusoe feels as he waits for understanding and deliverance. In fact, Providence seems more adversary than aid in *Robinson Crusoe*, and there is a sense that it is futile for human beings to plan.[24] Crusoe's desires and arrangements are not only thwarted but often seem at odds with "fate." In later novels Defoe will refer to "unseen Mines" blowing up plans, just as he had spoken in his pamphlets of seemingly unrelated events destroying the hopes of groups. The heroes of epics and romances seize their own destinies; Defoe's character will have destiny thrust upon him. Although Crusoe may be denied a place among great mythic heroes,[25] he may be a more inspiring example of patience, application, and resolution because he perseveres in a life that is an unpredictable "checquer work," as Defoe calls his own and most of his fictional protagonists' lives, rather than in a quest he chooses. Courage and confinement were on Defoe's mind anyway. His *An Apology for the Army* (1715) included a lengthy meditation on courage, and Harley's and the defeated rebels' imprisonments and conduct surely awakened his memories of prison.

The lesson of *Robinson Crusoe* is the lesson of Job. At the end of the book Defoe refers to the biblical story twice, and his point is not just that Robinson Crusoe has his prosperity restored and increased, but also that he and Job never entirely understand why they suffered as they did, why God had singled them out, and what their experiences meant. Patience, diligence, resolution held firm long after most would surrender but, above all, the power of the mind to transform the experience, to invert the terms of the experience from, for instance, "destruction" to "deliverance" or "Captivity" to "Reign" explains the resiliency of Defoe's characters—and of Defoe. Resolution and diligence, however, do bring success—Crusoe becomes a wealthy and respected man.

Robinson Crusoe contains other, more eccentric bits of Defoe's "wisdom." Three times, for instance, he exhorts his reader, "Let no Man despise the secret Hints and Notices"; "let no Man slight the strong Impulses of his own Thoughts." Defoe had commented that "an inclination" in his young manhood dissuaded him from accepting an advantageous offer to settle in Portugal as a merchant. As he got older such instincts seemed to take on more reliability for him. For instance, as he retells the story of Chief Justice Parker's intercession in his behalf in 1715, he increasingly emphasizes the "promptings" that motivated his letter and speaks of "certain" evidence of "an invisible World." He also seems to believe that people have a positive Genius for making the

wrong choices. Usually their blunders come from their human limitations—to leave the ship or not, to settle on one side of the island or the
other—but their restless natures and mistaken notions contribute. Defoe's heroes, real and fictional, are improvisers—punters, not quarter-
backs.

༄

Defoe's work always showed a keen understanding of the reading
public, and *Robinson Crusoe* is no exception. The best-selling books of
this time were sermons and travel literature, and Defoe probably conceived *Robinson Crusoe* along the lines of travel books. He had read them
with pleasure since childhood and owned many of them. Peace and
optimism about open seas inspired new books like Daniel Beeckman's
Voyage to and from the Island of Borneo and new editions of a number of
earlier works such as Woodes Rogers' *Cruising Voyage round the World*
(both 1718). Travel books often began with a restless son and included
religious elements. Some, like *Mr. James Janeway's Legacy to his Friends*
(1674), specifically collected "Deliverances" at sea as examples of God's
Providence. In the travel book personal salvation was usually subordinated to revelation of God's plan and the deliverance of the voyager
from danger.

Defoe's special contribution to travel literature is the power of his
protagonist's personality. As might be expected, the heroes, real and
fictional, before Crusoe are decisive leaders with laudable fortitude
and resourcefulness; most of them are also religious, and their courage, expectations, and interpretations seem to spring fairly consistently
from their faith. The similarities between some of the earlier travel
books and *Robinson Crusoe* illustrate how derivative Defoe's book is but
also how much Defoe contributed to the development of the novel. For
instance, in Robert Knox's *An Historical Relation of Ceylon*, Knox, like
Defoe, presents a mind in motion. Their protagonists debate with
themselves, weigh and balance choices, and struggle palpably to foresee the future. Time after time they are conscious of what they cannot
know or reason out—details of geography, locations of settlements,
characteristics of tribes. To a lesser extent they try to interpret actions,
words, and events—and understanding is often complicated by language differences. The fact that their lives may be at stake intensifies
these reflective passages. Knox, however, may be indecisive for a few
paragraphs; Crusoe may be obsessed for days, and he returns and
returns to some crucial questions. The amount of detail Defoe gives
subverts the form of the travel book.

In these extended presentations of a person reasoning, choosing,
struggling for, if not understanding, acceptance of his fate, the mind
of Crusoe becomes full and even somewhat individual. What he sees as

crucial questions define his personality. As he debates why he has been "singled out" and often feels that God is adversary as often as aid, his religion and his conception of himself in the world become increasingly individualized. Defoe shows Crusoe wrestling with ideas as Jacob wrestled with the angel. What and how he wrestles set him apart. For instance, he broods over killing the cannibals and about their purpose on earth, but he is untroubled about leaving the Spaniard and Friday's father. What might be a moral dilemma for one person is not for Crusoe and vice versa. As close as Crusoe is to the heroes of the spiritual autobiography and of the travel narrative, he is closer yet to the hero of the modern psychological novel. For the history of the novel, what Crusoe debates is as important as how he debates.

Knox, for instance, seems not to have felt ethical or religious conflicts. He reports discussions about the morality of marriage to native women, but his own opinion—like his judgments about the natives' customs—seems completely fixed. In fact, it is the rigidity of his judgments and his religious certainty that separate him most dramatically from Crusoe. His statements about God are completely formulaic and unshakable. These phrases of Puritan faith carry the religious theme: "By the Providence of gracious God"; "We prayed God to direct us"; "By the blessing of God." Although he reports such things as his youth upon capture, the death of his father, and the frustrated escapes as hard, he does not complain about God or question his will. He looks neither for special punishment nor special favor. Only once does Knox approach the emotional intensity Defoe gives Crusoe's religious experiences. When he has a chance to buy an English Bible, he cannot rest until it is his; he says it was as if "an Angel had spoke to me from Heaven. To see that my most gracious God had prepared such an extraordinary Blessing for me; which I did, and ever shall look upon as miraculous, to bring unto me a Bible in my own Native Language, and that in such a remote part of the World, where his Name was not so much as Known."[26] When Crusoe is similarly transported over the "miracle" of the barley, he must adjust his interpretation because of the mundane means by which the plant grew and find God's care in natural laws rather than in miracles. Crusoe actively seeks to know God and his will; Knox trusts and waits. The result is that Knox gives us an exciting adventure tale in an exotic setting, and Defoe gives us a suffering human being.

*

At the time Defoe published *Robinson Crusoe*, his life was nearly as vexed as it had been in 1715, and his reputation was hardly better. In the spring of 1717 he managed to infiltrate Mist's *Weekly Journal*. Nathaniel Mist, a rabid Tory and something of an eccentric, had been a common seaman. His first paper, the *Citizen*, had failed, but the *Weekly Journal, or Saturday's Post*, begun in mid-December 1716, attracted the readership abandoned by Charles Leslie and other extreme Tory writers silenced by George's accession. In only a few months the *Weekly Journal* had become the most successful Tory paper in England.[27] To associate himself with such a man and such a paper opened Defoe to accusations that he had fallen to yet new depths.

Mist himself was no writer, and he especially needed help translating the foreign news. Defoe had been offered positions as translator of foreign news in the past, and he seized an opportunity to apply to Mist. By April 1717 Mist was in legal trouble on two counts. Employing Defoe now appealed especially to him because of Defoe's proven ability to keep a periodical interesting and because of his experience in gauging just how much the government could be baited. Defoe undoubtedly did some hack translating for Mist, but he also wrote hundreds of items on a wide variety of subjects; he also repeated or expanded many of the anecdotes he used in *Mercurius Politicus*.[28] Some of his contributions were in the form of the question/answer periodical and others were "letters introductory" to the editor, a form Defoe invented. By filling the paper with essays and reports of topical, but not political, interest, he diluted Mist's radical Tory voice considerably. He transformed the *Weekly Journal* into a magazine filled with a variety of subjects and into a forum for opinion. Mist employed eleven people, circulation reached 11,000 copies a week, and Mist's remained the most popular journal in England for years. The paper seemed equally popular with City residents, Oxford and Cambridge men, rural folk, and the seamen of Deptford and Portsmouth.[29]

Defoe's time with Mist was difficult. Mist was an irascible, fiercely independent man and looked upon Defoe as one of several employees. Sometimes he ignored Defoe's advice, and sometimes he seemed to feel no compunction about turning Defoe in to the authorities. Surviving papers and Defoe's letters give some sense of his frustration. Although Defoe said he managed the *Weekly Journal*, he also noted that it was not his property and that he could not always prevent the publication of individual items. He seems to have left his copy at Mist's shop, and Mist—or his printers—sometimes followed the common practice of the day when their own copy was insufficient: they plagiarized from other papers.[30] On 10 May 1718 Defoe wrote to Delafaye that this very thing had happened, and an offensive paragraph from the *Post Boy* had been inserted.[31] In November 1718, under examination by the secretaries of state, Mist admitted that he had made "some few Alterations" in one of Defoe's contributions but did not think he had altered "the Substance."[32]

By December 1717 Defoe's work for Mist had been recognized, and the kind of vicious attacks he had suffered throughout 1715 resumed. Just as his association with Keimer had been met with amazement and incredulity, so was his work for Mist. Defoe was irrefutably "the hireling of a disreputable printer" and in the company of Mist's other writers, "Seddon, and the debauch'd author of the Entertainer, a poor un-benefic'd Parson."[33] Mist's singular notoriety and the opinion of his contemporaries did nothing for Defoe's hopes for respectability:

Towards the later End of Queen *Anne's* Reign, indeed, some very considerable Writers had drawn their Pens on each Side of the Politicks that then divided the Nation, but these were asleep for some Years after the Accession of King *George*. A Printer, one *Mist*, by writing for one Party, however, gain'd a consider-able Name, and many Readers . . . tho' he had not one Qualification, either as an Author or a Man, to recommend him. But in this Country it is enough for a Man, if he gets himself talk'd of, to succeed.[34]

A poem in Read's *Weekly Journal* stripped Defoe of his disguises:

> *A fawning, canting, double hearted Knave*
> Is the Inscription fittest for his Grave.
> Look there's the Bribes with which this Wretch was paid
> When he his Country and its Right betray'd.
> . . . .
> Lo that False Vizard which this K[nave] put on;
> Wrote one day *Pro* and th'other day writ *[C]on*.
> There's no such *Proteus* to be found in Story,
> One hour a *Whig* and the next hour a *Tory*.
> Sometimes Dissenter and sometimes High Church
> Strait turns his Coat leaves both sides in the Lurch.
> He wrote for all cause that did yield him most.[35]

Mist paid Defoe twenty shillings per week for his work until some time in 1718, when Defoe began to receive forty shillings a week.[36]

These years saw Defoe in and out of trouble with the government. Francis King of York sued John Morphew, one of Defoe's printers, for a report in *Mercurius Politicus* for September 1716. In March 1718 the Grand Jury found King an "Injur'd Innocente" who had suffered in his trade and reputation. Morphew had been committed until sentenced, and the sentence might be severe because the story reflected on the court as well as on King (*Mercurius Politicus* called the verdict "a piece of Justice Unmix'd with Mercy"). Defoe shows concern only for himself. "The Thing . . . was not Myne, neither can any One Pretend to Charge it o[n] me," he protested, implying that it had been printed before he became editor, but basing his case primarily on the fact that, since its publication, "all former Mistakes of Mine We[re] forgiven."[37]

In October of that same year, when Mist and the printer, Thomas Warner, swore that Defoe had written an offending Sir Andrew Politick letter in the *Weekly Journal*, his reaction was similarly defensive. When

Warner was examined by the secretary of state, he described Defoe's "daily" visits to his print shop, during which Defoe appeared "much concerned at the proceedings against Mr. Mist, Saying that he, Defoe, would not on any account be known to be the author," and he allegedly asked Warner "to exhort Mr. Mist to stand by it, & not declare the Author" as, he said, Mist had promised. Mist's *Weekly Journal* for 8 November carried a similar notice insisting upon Defoe's innocence. The *Whitehall Evening Post*, a Whig paper Defoe wrote, carried an advertisement on 15 November signed "DE FOE" in which he denied being "the Author or Writer" of the *Weekly Journal*, admitted translating foreign papers but never "meddling with" the "home Part of his Paper," and claimed that he "now had no connection with it at all."[38] The government had decided that Defoe was not doing enough to control Mist and that it needed to take harsher measures with the *Weekly Journal*, for "it is scarce credible what numbers of these papers are distributed both in Town and Country, where they do more mischief than any other Libel being wrote."[39] In August 1718 the ambassador from Moscow, Fedor Pavlovich Wesselowsky, wanted the author of no. 85 of the *Weekly Journal* prosecuted, and the attorney general considered it; Defoe, of course, was suspected. Again in 1720 Mist identified him as the author of an offending piece in the 2 January *Weekly Journal*, and in June he had to provide sureties of £400 for his appearance on the first day of Trinity term at the King's Bench.[40]

Defoe continued to participate in acrimonious personal exchanges. In some of the milder ones, he reverted to the methods of the 1704 Scandal Club. *A Letter to the Author of the Flying Post* (1718) chided George Ridpath, "How can you say Mr. *Mist daily affirms, or daily contradicts*, when his Paper comes out but *once a Week*?"(11) At one moment he pretended to be Ridpath's "old friend" and offered to do him justice by giving an example of his erudition and eloquence from "that sublime Paper of yours . . . in which you insert that celebrated Letter from the *Grecian* Coffee-house to the Bailiff of *Brecon*" (13). At the next moment, he accuses Ridpath of being like a spider that "lives upon his own Venom" by depending upon scurrility and lies (6, 11, 15–16).

Some of his most heated remarks were directed at Abel Boyer, especially when Boyer exposed Defoe's authorship of political works. When Boyer accused Defoe of writing *Minutes of Mesnager* and boasted that he was "detecting and exposing the most notorious and grossest Piece of FORGERY that was ever fobb'd upon the Publick," Defoe demanded Boyer produce some proof. He challenged Boyer "*as he values the Character of* an Honest Man, *and the Esteem of Honest Men*." Boyer went on to name fourteen other pieces by Defoe that he said he had identified by their "*longwinded, spinning way of Writing*" and the "Blunders" in Latin and French quotations.[41] That Boyer was wrong about some of his attributions hardly mattered. He had added to the perception that Defoe wrote on both sides of a question and contradicted himself frequently. Defoe's adversaries knew that this charge of a deficient education could enrage Defoe. One of his earliest and most extended tirades had been directed at such a statement printed in Swift's *Examiner* for 16 November 1710. In the *Review* Defoe gave over nearly two whole columns to invective and self-defense. Here he claimed knowledge of five languages, science, logic, and other subjects and proclaimed that he "despised" such learning as the *Examiner* had exhibited (7:455). In 1725 Defoe returned to this rankling charge; in *Applebee's Journal* he wrote,

> I remember an Author in the World, some Years ago, who was generally upbraided with Ignorance, and called an "Illiterate Fellow." . . .
> I happend to come into this Person's Study once, and I found him busy translating . . . *Bleau's* Geography, written in *Spanish*. Another Time I found him translating some Latin Paragraphs out of *Leubinitz Theatri Cometici*. . . . In short, I found he understood the *Latin*, the *Spanish*, the *Italian*, and could read the *Greek*, and I knew before that he spoke *French* fluently,—*yet this man was no Scholar*.
> In Geography and History, he had all the world at his Fingers' ends. (Lee 3:435–36)

In yet another altercation, Defoe provoked the bookseller Edmund Curll into calling him an "Old Man" and "a super-annuated *Letter-Writer*."[42] Defoe's 5 April 1719 *Weekly Journal* had placed "Curlicism" on "the Roll of Sodom" and demanded that Curll's "indecent" books be suppressed. In fact, Curll made journalistic history by becoming the first man successfully indicted for an obscene libel. In an unusually personal ad hominem attack, Defoe described Curll as "mark'd by Nature, for he has . . . a debauch'd Mien . . . and Filthiness drivels in the very Tone of his Voice."[43] Curll defended his list of books, partly by correcting Defoe's facts and partly by drawing a comparison between his "Cases of Impotency and Divorce" and what he called the "Cases of Conscience" Defoe created for Mist's *Journal*. He laughed at Defoe's "formal Gravity" and thanked Defoe for helping him publicize his list of books.

In 1718 David Dalrymple had reason to investigate Defoe, and the incident shows how Defoe worked and what many ordinary people thought of him. Dalrymple had been "much surprised" to find a "Postscript" to the *Whitehall Evening Post* that read: "We are told from good Hands . . . That his Excellency the Earl of Stairs in a Letter to his Uncle Sir David Dalrymple hath the following Paragraph. . . . " This letter, Defoe wrote, told that a French cardinal had "administer'd the Sacrament in both Kinds to great Numbers of People." He went on to comment that such an action, ordered by Henry VIII, "was one of the first Steps to the Reformation."

Dalrymple complained to the printer about the unauthorized use of his family name with the politically sensitive material, and Defoe sent an apology "by one of his people" and asked how he should retract. Dalrymple replied, and the 1 November *White-Hall Evening Post* carried a suggestive paragraph:

As we are careful to give the best Intelligence, so we shall always be careful to publish it in a right Manner. This obliges us to confirm the Truth of that important Article mentioned in our last Postscript . . . but with this Addition, in Justice to the Honourable Persons mentioned, That it was a Mistake, that the said News was written by the Earl of Stairs to Sir David Dalrymple; but came by other Hands.

Dalrymple grumbled,

I can get no more of him. The news takes, and will be dressed in four or five papers more, to be sure. . . . One thing I have learned . . . that Defoe is partner in some Whig newspaper, as well as in "Mist's Journal," but in the Whig papers he serves only to give hints of news to support the credit of his Tory journal. He is a very great rogue, that is certain.[44]

Dalrymple's investigation uncovered what public men thought of Defoe and showed how completely he was carrying off his guise of Tory commitment.

Charles Gildon's satire of *Robinson Crusoe* is of a piece with these attacks. "The Fabulous *Proteus* of the Ancient Mythologist was a very faint Type of" Defoe, he writes.

If his Works should happen to live to the next Age, there would in all probability be a greater Strife among the several Parties, whose he really was, than among the seven *Grecian* Cities, to which of them *Homer* belong'd: The Dissenters first would claim him as theirs, the *Whigs* in general as theirs, the Tories as theirs, the *Nonjurors* as theirs, and so on to what Sub-divisions there may be among us.

Thomas Cox, the man who had pirated *Robinson Crusoe*, called Defoe "one of the most prostituted pens in the whole world" in the *Flying Post* for 29 October 1719.[45] Almost every opponent accused Defoe of apostasy. John Toland, in a typical passage, approvingly quoted Abel Boyer who had written that Defoe was "a *Scribler* (Trium Litterarum) *famous for Writing* upon, *for, and against all manners of Persons, Subjects and Parties.*"[46]

Defoe was accused of publishing "notorious falshoods," "precarious suppositions," "perfect nonsense," "foul and rascally stuff," malicious and dangerous insinuations, and misrepresentations, as well as of "prostituting" his pen.[47] His adversaries described his style as "raving," "fulsome ribaldry," "incoherent," "loose," "longwinded," and ungrammatical—proof that he was "an illiterate blunderer" incapable of recognizing or speaking truth. Boyer spoke of Defoe's "Forge of *Politicks* and

Scandal" in Stoke Newington.[48] Endlessly called extreme, raving, sanctimonious, and bigoted, Defoe found himself still used as a symbol for all the dangerous qualities assigned the Dissenters by those who wanted to maintain the legal restrictions on them.

Even when his hand was not recognized in a work, his opponents kept his painful past before the public. *An Answer to the Character and Conduct of R—— W——, Esq.* (1717) quoted Defoe without appearing to identify him and observed, "We all know an Instance, where an Hymn has been made even to the Pillory it self, by a Wretch that was just come out of it" (18). *The Art of Railing at Great Men* (1723) referred to him as a negative example: "No body pities M—ST or DEF—E in the Pillory, who reads Dr. SWIFT . . . with Admiration" (12). Those who knew his work—or thought they did—had no mercy. A typical description read, "This Man has formerly put his Name to some of his *Low-Productions*, but having been stigmatized by an *ignominous Punishment*, he has since conceal'd it with all possible industry, and, at the same Time, prostituted his Pen to the *vilest Purposes*."[49] Gildon tells a fanciful story of Defoe's life and has Defoe say, "By a plaguey Irony, I got myself into the damnable *Nutcrackers*" (xii).

Just as pamphlet writers had listed lapses in argument, errors in historical information, and contradictions, so did Gildon. Abel Boyer's complaints that Mesnager never served in the military and died before his king merely added to the notoriety of Defoe's *Minutes*, and Gildon's quibbles about Crusoe's pockets and Friday's English meant even less to the readers of *Robinson Crusoe*. Defoe called criticism of the novel "Abortive" and "impotent," and even the great Samuel Johnson would say that it was one of only three books that anyone ever wished longer.

CHAPTER 17

THE WHOLE WORLD
IN MOTION

There appeared a young Man with a Book, ready to enter the Names of such as came to Subscribe, and to take five Shillings of them; giving them a PERMIT *to be received as Subscribers, to a certain Subscription, to be made sometimes or other,* they did not know when; *to some certain Scheme or other,* they did not know what; *proposed by some Person or other,* they did not know who.

—DEFOE, *The Commentator,* 1720

Defoe began to find new pleasure in his work. The fourth edition of *Robinson Crusoe* came out shortly before the August 1719 publication of *The Farther Adventures of Robinson Crusoe.* Both quickly appeared in pirated editions, imitations, and abridgements, and a 164-part serialization in the *Original London Post* gave some truth to Charles Gildon's chagrined statement, "Not an old Woman that can go the Price of it, but buys thy Life and Adventures." By the end of 1719 Taylor's fifth edition of *Robinson Crusoe* and the second of *Farther Adventures* had been published as a set with a map and six plates.[1]

In the next two years, Defoe published another travel novel, *The Life, Adventures, and Pyracies, of the Famous Captain Singleton* (also serialized in the year of its first edition), a number of monographs on trade and colonization, *Memoirs of a Cavalier,* an augmented second edition of *The History of the Wars,* and a reissue of his 1710 collected works. He wrote or contributed to ten different periodicals. During this time he began more and more Whig papers and happily noted that he was "back among friends." No longer traveling or finding bailiffs at his door, he took his place among the prosperous, established citizens of Stoke Newington.

Defoe indulged himself as never before. He wrote one book after another about men who made "the whole Earth the Theatre of their Life."[2] Just as he had been caught up in Crusoe's situation, and, in the same manner that Crusoe found ways to fill his time, Defoe filled his pages and lost himself in the older Crusoe's travels and Captain Singleton's adventures. He gave free rein to his imagination and exulted in the evidence that his analysis of "the modern Vice of the reading Palate" was correct. He believed novelty sold books, and he provided it. In a time when, as Crusoe said, "The whole World is in Motion," Defoe's travel books captured his readers' imaginations. Defoe had claimed that the success of *Robinson Crusoe* came from "the surprising variety of the subject" and "the agreeable manner of the performance."[3]

In the preface to *Farther Adventures* he promises more "novel" incidents than those in *Robinson Crusoe*, and he does indeed provide more "incidents" in *Farther Adventures*. Within the first hundred pages Crusoe's ship has rescued another ship (with a passenger who has stayed alive partly by eating gloves), Crusoe has heard the stories of battles among the survivors on his island, of wars between cannibal bands, and of an invasion of the island by cannibals. In the last hundred pages Crusoe goes by land from the coast of China, through Peking to Archangel where he takes a ship to Hamburg, travels by land to the Hague, and finally arrives in London. During this odyssey, he sees the Great Wall, battles Tartar raiders, burns an idol before the eyes of enraged priests, and rescues a royal political prisoner. The book is an amazing compendium of material. In the island survivors' conversion to Christianity, the natives play the parts of some of the little children in conduct books, and the English and Spanish sailors those of repentant parents. Drawn-out tales of elaborate ruses stand next to brief, funny descriptions of people met on the road. Defoe describes two "amazing" houses (one of wicker and one of china), defines irony as "speaking in colors," and has a boatload of natives defiantly bare their bottoms at the English seamen. Crusoe, like the reader, is often drawn along by curiosity alone. "I lik'd this very well"; "I confess . . . [it] was exceeding entertaining to me," he remarks and explains, "to divert our selves, we . . ." and "I had the Curiosity to go and see. . . ."

Captain Singleton covers the part of the known world that Crusoe missed. He sails to Newfoundland and the East Indies before he is marooned on Madagascar for his part in a mutiny. He and his fellow conspirators then walk across the wide part of Africa from Mozambique to Guinea. The last half of the book traces Singleton's career as a pirate in the West Indies, along the coast of South America, on Madagascar (in order to prey on East Indian ships), in the Red Sea, Persian Gulf, Moluccas, the Philippines, and then below Australia and concludes with his retirement in England. Singleton's adventures are as exciting, varied, and exotic as Crusoe's. The march across Africa naturally results in encounters with threatening native tribes and wild animals. Lions, tigers, leopards, crocodiles, and elephants appear, and

Defoe is artful enough to make them both beautiful and menacing; moreover, he can turn the dry, formulaic travel-book descriptions of the animals into episodes like the one where the gunner kills the crocodile that is mangling a gun as though it were a stick. The land itself is the greatest adversary. The waterfalls, jungles, and deserts amaze and horrify the men. At one point some of the men believe a huge lake is the ocean, but the travelers must walk around it. In another place, Singleton says, "Having with infinite Labour mounted these Hills [we saw] a vast howling Wilderness, not a Tree, a River, or a Green thing to be seen, for as far as the Eye could look; nothing but a scalding Sand, which as the Wind blew, drove about in Clouds, enough to overwhelm Man and Beast" (96–7). Singleton tells how walking in the burning sand was more difficult than anything before and more painful than their barefoot travel over stones and thorns. With such details does Defoe bring the experience to life.

Defoe also treats the earth and animals as nature's bounty. They feed and clothe the men; unfamiliar trees provide a pitchlike substance for their boat and the long grasses provide matting for their desert shelters. And the land offers great wealth. The men collect gold and ivory almost without effort, and the animal hides are so plentiful as to be endlessly disposable. "There's not a River here but runs Gold, not a Desart but without Plowing bears a Crop of Ivory," Singleton is told (154).

Many of Defoe's contemporaries held just this opinion of Africa and of South America as well. El Dorado might be just beyond the next bend in the river; the poor adventurer might return to England with a sugar fortune. In fact, the wealth of these continents in the eighteenth century would be quite different from the gold and silver the Spanish ships carried. England would find and create huge new markets for her goods there, and the raw materials from these places would develop new industries. Sugar, cotton, tobacco, and molasses would pour into London; refined sugar, cloth, and rum would be produced and then exported with English wool, tools, and a thousand other manufactured goods. The demand for slaves would rise, and over two million blacks would be received in the colonies before 1786.

Defoe's contemporaries calculated the income brought England and the number of manufacturers, tradesmen, artisans, and seamen employed in supplying each colonists' needs.[4] "The Prosperity of the Kingdom, is not to be attain'd by the Consumption, of our own Produce and Manufactures at home, but by the encouraging our Trade and Navigation as much as possible," one of the critics of Defoe's pamphlets supporting the weavers had said.[5] Defoe already knew this fact and had been a tireless proponent of colonization and the development of new markets and improved trade routes; moreover, he was far from alone in his vision of London as a great hub, a central collection and distribution point for all the world. That the wealth Singleton gains from his gold and ivory goes quickly symbolizes Defoe's opinion of the ephemeral nature of contemporary dreams of picking up ivory, gold, and silver from the ground.[6] Singleton makes his fortune as a pirate, and his plunder truly represents the wealth of nations. He can count on gold and coins in the Spanish and Turkish ships, spices and silk on the ships in the Pacific, pearls and meat on Arab boats; a Dutch ship off the coast of South America carries African slaves, Irish beef, Newfoundland fish, French cloth, and Portuguese wine. Crusoe secures an annual income of £1,000 from his plantation in Brazil, but remarks of one trading venture in the South Pacific: "I got so much Money . . . and such an Insight into the Method of getting more, that had I been twenty Year [sic] younger, I should have been tempted to have staid here and sought no farther, for making my Fortune" (3:110).

These rambling novels were held together by the presence of the hero and the series of adventures. Characters who would have been examples in 1712 became narrators or full-blown protagonists. Even his 1720 address to the South Sea Company took the form of a life of Raleigh.[7] Defoe's propensity to lose himself in his narrative appeared unmistakably here. He has sailed away into Raleigh's expeditions, into visions of the wealth of South America and the details of building a settlement, and suddenly what the South Sea Company was really like came back to him. His conclusion bluntly asked the company to sail for South America or give some other company the right to do so.

Some elements of *Captain Singleton* seem to develop latent narrative strains in *Robinson Crusoe*. Singleton is one of a group of mutineers set on an island; a mutiny in *Robinson Crusoe* has marooned the Englishmen on Crusoe's island. The twenty-seven men set down on Madagascar must "practise twenty Trades that we knew little or nothing of," just as Crusoe had. The final twenty pages of *Captain Singleton* try a new way to teach religion and develop some of the ideas expressed in the second *Family Instructor* about despair being no part of repentance. In that conduct book, when an apprentice quotes a multitude of frightening Scriptures, a wise woman offsets them with verses about mercy, forgiveness, and hope. Singleton learns from the quick-witted, optimistic William and becomes a penitent.

Singleton himself may have developed out of Will Atkins, the bold, trouble-making Englishman on Crusoe's island. For instance, Singleton describes how a Portuguese captain refused to give him any wages and began to mistreat him; then, in the most matter-of-fact way, he says, "I resolved to murther him."[8] He joins the mutiny before he has the opportunity, however, and soon suggests that the men seize one boat after another from the peaceful natives until they get one big enough to sail away in. When they run out of things to trade for food, he is "for falling upon them with our Fire Arms; and taking all the Cattel from them, and send[ing] them to the Devil." When others express fear of the Turks and Arabs, he says, "Are we not able to board almost any Vessel . . . and instead of their taking us, we to take them?" He is consistently predatory and bold, but it is his ingenuity that makes him a leader. His pirate career (predicted by a sailor when Singleton was but fourteen) seems entirely suited to his nature and abilities.

In many ways Singleton is the ultimate example of narrators whom Defoe created to be clear windows for his plots and themes. He has almost no education and, more important, has had no opportunity to learn any ethical code. He is kidnapped as a toddler, used by a beggar to increase alms, and sold to a gypsy for twelve shillings. After the gypsy is hanged, he is shifted from parish to parish because none will admit responsibility for him. At twelve he is taken to sea by a sympathetic captain. The Turks capture the ship and kill the captain. Almost at once the Portuguese take the ship from the Turks, and Singleton is abandoned by his countrymen; he becomes the servant of a brutal, abusive Portuguese captain. By page 6 (or age fourteen), all of this has happened to him, and he has already stolen twenty gold coins.

Repeatedly Singleton tells us that something was "all one" to him. Without home, family loyalties, or scruples, going or staying, trading with the natives or killing them seem neutral choices to him. Although he is one of Defoe's repentant, retrospective narrators, he seems intent on telling his story without excuse or self-justification. He had no reason to act differently, and he feels no need to influence our opinion of him. Crusoe never stops longing for and trying to re-create England; Singleton is quick to say that his worst treatment has been in England and that he does not know the meaning of the word *home*. He can say the same thing shortly before his retirement that he said at fourteen, "It was not one Farthing Matter to me . . . I had no home, and all the World was alike to me." He is both an intriguing and highly functional narrator. Shocking rather than average, foreign rather than common to our experience, he contrasts markedly with Crusoe and points to the next series of Defoe's characters: Colonel Jack, Moll Flanders, and Roxana, criminals all.

Editions of *Robinson Crusoe* and *Captain Singleton* often came with maps, and Defoe was fascinated by the publication of new maps, the topographical details in some of the recently issued travel books, and the intense interest in improving navigational aids. Singleton mentions "the infinite Attempts which had been made from *Europe*, as well by the *English* as the *Dutch*" to discover an Arctic passage to the Far East, and there is ample evidence that Defoe knew the best maps and descriptions of Africa available in England and took his geographical details from them.[9] Some time in 1719 Defoe contracted with William Taylor, the publisher of *Robinson Crusoe*, for an ambitious economic geography. Eventually *Atlas Maritimus* would appear in 1728 on elephant paper* with huge fold-out maps and sell for the very unusual sum of three guineas. In it Defoe would treat the history, geography, ports, commerce, natural resources, cities, and people of almost the entire known world. About Africa he would ask,

What will not the Thirst of Gold do? and what Risques will not Mankind run in search of such a Wealth as is found upon all this Coast? We therefore see great Numbers of *Europeans* . . . continually arrive there . . . most of these . . . die, and very few return to their own Countrys; yet bad Circumstances at home, and the Hopes of bettering them abroad, bring daily new Supplies of People to the Place. (251)

In that book, in *A General History of Discoveries and Improvements* (1726–27) and in *The Plan of the English Commerce* (1728), he wrote about navigation, trade, and "the world in motion" in yet other ways.

The travel and adventure novels gave Defoe rich opportunities for making observations as he catered to his generation's great interest in foreign places and people. He had called his *Continuation of Letters Written by a Turkish Spy at Paris* (1718) a "Record of History" with "fruitful Observations" on "Subjects . . . Religious and Moral" (vii), made these novels similar, but developed fiction as a far more effective way to reach his readers. He continued to subsume aspects of his conduct books into the novels and, for his time, gave his characters unusual psychological and spiritual depth. The end of the War of the Spanish Succession, competition with Spain, and the rise of the South Sea and other stock companies made the idea of London as the market of the entire world seductive. Sables, ivory, gold leaf, spices, teakwood—the exotic wealth of every continent—tantalized English readers.

❧

If fortunes could be made in a relatively short time in South America, China, or Madagascar, they could be lost as fast in English politics. From the time of Anne's death until after the Atterbury plot in 1722,† Defoe wrote fictions designed to discourage Jacobitism. His heroes were lucky if, by the ends of their stories, they were not destitute exiles; Defoe often cast these books in the form of fictional journals or memoirs told by miserable men. A number of works, including *A True Account of the Proceedings at Perth, A Journal of the Earl of Marr's Proceedings* (both 1716), *Minutes of the Negotiations of Monsr. Mesnager* (1717), and *The Memoirs of Major Ramkins* (1718), have the same intentions, use

---

*Drawing-weight paper, 28″ × 23″, used in the largest portfolio editions.
†Correspondence from the Pretender's court implicated Francis Atterbury in an elaborate but aborted invasion plan timed for the general elections of spring 1722.

many of the same rhetorical strategies, and tell variations on the same story. Defoe called Jacobitism "an uncurable Distemper" and a vice so strong "that nothing but the Grave and the Gallows can put an End to it,"[10] but most of his fictional heroes are cured. Each uses a slightly different narrative slant, and they become increasingly plain and didactic. *A True Account* is by a rebel who would fight again, *A Journal . . . of Marr's Proceedings* is an edited version of Mar's own self-justifying journal[11] and has much in common with *A True Account.* Mesnager is an admiring negotiator for Louis XIV; Ramkins is a thoroughly disaffected exile, and Colonel Jack nearly ruins his life by taking a curious look at the battle at Preston. All of these books require rudimentary acts of interpretation, and some demand inversion—Louis's clever treachery must be discovered in *A True Account* and praise of it turned into revelation and appropriate censure in the *Minutes of Mesnager.* In many ways *Minutes of Mesnager* and *Memoirs of Ramkins* are obverses, for Mesnager is an insider—he has the confidence of the king of France—and Ramkins is an outsider. Mesnager can explain the king's strategies, but Ramkins must observe and surmise.

The character and motives of Louis XIV are the same in both books. Mesnager's approval and admiration become Ramkins's bitter rhetorical questions. Of the Battle of the Boyne, for example, Ramkins asks twice: "Were not 300000 Men driven like Sheep from the Banks of the *Boyne* for want of Arms, while what would have furnish'd a Million of Men, were Rusting in the Magazines of *France*?" (287, 302) In both stories Louis acts in self-interest and gets what he wanted: Spain, peace when he needs it, and a gullible set of Englishmen to threaten England whenever Louis wants fewer troops sent to Flanders. "Let the Tory and Roman Catholick Party sum up their Losses since 1688, and it will convince 'em how foolish they acted," Ramkins concludes (333). Mesnager as well has revealed a duped and self-destructive England in his historical summary.

Between 1714 and 1719, even as his work became increasingly fictional, Defoe experimented relentlessly with methods of adding credibility and persuasiveness to his work. One direction he took was toward narrators who appeared to lack the motive or the ability to distort the material. Defoe repeatedly used the convention of a private manuscript never intended for publication or an ordinary man who discovered his ruinous mistakes only through bitter experience. Ramkins, for instance, gullibly left better prospects several times to join the Pretender; it took him years to figure out that English lives and fortunes had been sacrificed each time France had needed a Jacobite feint at the English coast.

The protagonist of *Memoirs of a Cavalier* [1720] could be any of these characters. Another of Defoe's restless young men, he, too, wants to seek "Preferment in Fire and Smoak."[12] His story is historical allegory, however. It bears the same relationship to the earlier Jacobite fictions as the conduct books and many of the pamphlets do to *Robinson Crusoe*,* *Captain Singleton*, and other novels. What had been presented in didactic terms in modified but conventional genres is subordinated to the creation of a character and a series of intrinsically interesting incidents, even as the didactic themes provide major elements of the character's personality and experience. Thus, the "calling back" of an adult to God and the catechismlike dialogue between an adult and a child (or a native) become major elements of Crusoe's personal experience on the island and of conversations with Friday, Will Atkins, Atkins's native wife, and others.

Defoe's writing at this time is as full of fighting as it is of religion and travel. Readers of his *Annals* and *Mercurius Politicus* must have been surprised at the fullness of the descriptions of even minor Jacobite skirmishes; *Continuation of the Letters of a Turkish Spy* and many of the Jacobite fictions include long passages about fighting, and all of the novels have battles. In *Robinson Crusoe* everyone seems to make war, and the result is a leveling of men. Spaniards (then at war with England and reputed to be merciless slavemasters in South America) show mercy; English sailors go berserk and massacre two villages; blacks fight each other; whites fight their own countrymen. At one point Crusoe says, "I thought it was a sad Life, which we must be always oblig'd to be killing our Fellow-Creatures to preserve [*sic*]" (3:129). Singleton and the marooned Portuguese fight the natives, and, of course, the pirates fight ship after ship. They even lay siege to a hollow tree full of Asian Indians.

Memoirs of a Cavalier, published nine months after *Farther Adventures* and a month before *Captain Singleton*, also shows Defoe indulging his own interests. The first part of the book follows the campaigns of Gustavus Adolphus, long a hero of Defoe's, and the second covers the defeat of the Royalists in the civil war of the 1640s. Defoe had just revised *The History of the Wars* and turns away from the disappointing Charles XII to his famous grandfather. In the *Review* and other places Defoe had often compared the two Swedish kings and regretted Charles's lack of devotion to the Protestant cause that Gustavus Adolphus had defended so valiantly.[13]

Defoe had always been attracted to the military life. He had fought with Monmouth and, significantly, offered to raise and lead a troop of horse to make amends for offending the queen with *The Shortest-Way*

---

*From this point on, unless noted, I shall speak of *Robinson Crusoe* and *Farther Adventures* as a single book.

with the Dissenters. In his pamphlets about the rights of Dissenters, he never failed to lament their inability to serve in the military. The Jacobite rebellion had awakened his memories and his desire to fight. For instance, in a classic "I should have done/said this" episode, a clever man tests the depth of a stream in *Memoirs of a Cavalier* as Defoe's compatriots should have done at Sedgmoor in 1685. Defoe made propaganda of the country's "need" for the loyal, willing Dissenters to join the king's troops. In fact, the rebellion was over so quickly and the Jacobites so easily defeated that additional soldiers were not needed. But that is the point—Defoe's enthusiasm for joining the fight against this hated enemy blinded him to the exaggerations in his arguments. The military life, he said in *An Apology for the Army* (1715), was chosen by "such whose *Complexion* inclines to *Activity*, rather than *Sloth*" and who "conceive *high Enterprizes*, and attempt *Difficulties*, rather than decline *Labour* or *Hazard*" (13). Defoe himself, of course, was just this kind of man. Some of his happiest times had been sampling election opinion and working for the Union with Scotland. He delighted in travel and often described his writing in military terms. His affinity and admiration for this kind of man invigorated all of his battle narratives.

Memoirs of a Cavalier, however, is far more than an adventure story of a different kind. It is a subtle and artful warning about the miseries of civil war.[14] Coming soon after yet one more Jacobite invasion attempt, it offered a historical analogy to Defoe's countrymen. In 1719 Spain had contributed twenty-nine ships carrying 5,000 soldiers and arms for another 30,000 to the forces of the duke of Ormonde. England was well informed of the plan to invade and made vigorous preparations to repel the attack. A storm nearly destroyed the Spanish fleet before it reached the port where the Pretender waited to join it, however, and the attempt was over.[15]

The first part of *Memoirs of a Cavalier* serves to make the readers connoisseurs of armies and generals. The second strips away any illusions people may have about the glory of civil wars.[16] First, the Cavalier realizes that he is not only fighting his own countrymen but his former comrades in arms. He now must try to kill men he has fought to protect and who would have died for him. The king's "rabble" of footmen, servants, and gentlemen face Parliament's motley group of Scots, London trained bands, and poorly mounted squires. Leadership on both sides is frequently inept. Englishmen reading *Memoirs* could certainly remember the mixture of pitiful, untrained men fighting beside second-rate, disaffected military men in the Jacobite rebellion of 1715. In reading of the mistakes of Prince Rupert and others, Defoe's audience might think of Mar and Forster in '15. Defoe realistically shows victory to be the result of superior equipment, training, weapons, and numbers but emphasizes his lesson about war by showing how often the sides are equal. In that case, the morale of the soldiers and mere accidents determine the outcome.

The Cavalier's frustration and helplessness build during the years of battle and become a settled "melancholy" in his retirement. He now knows that winners are often no better off than losers; Gustavus Adolphus's empire is gone; the Protectorate lasted less than a generation, and Charles XII's recent meaningless death certainly would have come to readers' minds. The Cavalier describes his world as one of "Confusions" and concludes his story with a series of lists of depressing "observations." Some, however, are unmistakably descriptive of the Jacobites. The Cavalier remarks that the Royalists "could not be content to sit still, and reserve themselves for better Fortunes . . . but must hasten their own Miseries by frequent fruitless Risings" (316). His last warning is against internal divisions that defeat any army, no matter how good. Englishmen divided by religion, divided again by party, and then again by competitions for power within parties are ripe, Defoe suggests, for the destruction of their own best interests.

Defoe had come to believe that he could gain a hearing and persuade more effectively by developing his plots and the psychology of his characters—by giving more diversion and disguising his intentions a bit more. In his novels he continued to choose middle- or even lower-class narrators. The early protagonists have no motive for deception. Defoe carefully deprives them and the Cavalier of the kind of education or noble family that would have provided historical examples. Instead, experience is their teacher and discovery their mode. After several years of experimentation Defoe decisively chose narrators who complicate their lives through impetuous or short-sighted actions and who lead the reader to interpret as they do by retracing their own convoluted paths to disillusionment and revelation. The Cavalier, for instance, comes to wish for the same uninvolved private life that Ramkins and Colonel Jack dream of. He reflects upon his experiences in two wars and the outcomes of those wars, weighs the possible changes against the costs of civil war, and concludes with a powerful case for peace. "Religion rightly practiced on both sides would have made us all better Friends," he observes once, and he speaks to the Jacobite, Bangorian, and Salters' Hall disputants by analogy.

The restless men of Defoe's novels provide novelty, diversion, and even fantasy, yet they also live out, albeit in exaggerated form, some of the changes in the reading public that Defoe understood. In an essay he had described "the Dawn of Politicks among the Common People." He could remember, he said, when newspapers were read only by a few of "the meaner sort"—the chairmen near Whitehall, for example. In 1720, however, everyone read the papers, and politics not only interested but affected everyone. People in 1720 had no place in Thomas Gray's nostalgic picture:

> Th' applause of list'ning senates to command,
> The threats of pain and ruin to despise,
> . . . .
> Their lot forbad: nor circumscrib'd alone
> Their growing virtues, but their crimes confin'd;
> . . . .
> Far from the madding crowd's ignoble strife,
> Their sober wishes never learn'd to stray;
> Along the cool sequester'd vale of life
> They kept the noiseless tenor of their way.[17]

In fact, Defoe has Crusoe quote two lines of a song called "The Country Life" near the beginning of *Farther Adventures*: "Free from Vices, Free from Care, / Age has no Pain, and Youth no Snare" (2:116). This song begins,

> Happy is a country life,
>   Blest with content, good health and ease!
> Free from factious noise and strife,
>   We only plot ourselves to please.[18]

Defoe's contemporaries could not choose a "sequester'd vale." Estates had been confiscated in the late seventeenth century and again after the 1715 uprising; ordinary people knew firsthand that they were not immune to the influence of political parties, to factions that alternately rewarded and penalized landowners, to administrations that arbitrarily imposed and lifted restrictions on religious sects, and to the vicissitudes of a war economy. Even the lowest merchant might suffer substantial losses when the enemy sank or seized ships, anyone's son might be imprest into the military, and all paid the heavy taxes.

❧

As Defoe wrote these global books, the South Sea mania gripped the nation. The South Sea Company had been created in 1711 as a means to restore public credit and fund the War of the Spanish Succession. It appealed to Tory financiers shut out of the directorships of the Bank of England and the East India Company, and to the large number of people who held the widespread belief in easy wealth on the continent of South America. The grant had been the stuff of fantasy:

the sole trade and triffick into, unto, and from all the kingdoms, lands, countries, territories, islands, cities, towns, ports, havens, creeks, and places of America, on the east side thereof from the river of Aranoca [Oronoko], to the southermost part of the Terra del Fuego; and on the west side thereof, from the said southermost part of the said Terra del Fuego, through the South Seas, to the northermost part of America, and into, unto, and from all countries, islands, and places within the same limits, which are reported to belong to the

Crown of Spain, or which shall hereafter be found or discovered within the said limits, not exceeding three hundred leagues from the continent of America.[19]

The company turned out to be surprisingly inert. The closest it came to meaningful activity as a trading company was in 1713 with the Asiento contract; in fact, however, the company made little profit on that. From its inception it contented itself with acting primarily as a financial corporation; its trading interests were small, and it undertook no expeditions even in the years when cargoes returned profits of from 350 to 450 percent. Consequently, although its stock never fell below its par value, it had never held above par* for any significant amount of time prior to 1719.[20]

At the time Defoe was writing *Robinson Crusoe*, the South Sea Company was beginning to move to increase its capital dramatically. In 1719 it had made a solid profit when the 1710 lottery holdings converted† into South Sea stock.[21] Partly on the basis of this success, partly because of the possibilities offered by such a large amount of working capital, and partly because of the political advantages of being the government's creditor, the company proposed and then bid aggressively against the Bank of England to convert the £31,000,000 of the national debt in the form of annuities into South Sea stock.

Defoe had been a very interested observer of the South Sea Company since its inception. He had been critical of the company since 1711. Skeptical about England's ability to displace or even coexist with the French *or* Spanish, whose trade and military presences were already well established, he even objected to the fundamental structure which joined funding the 1711 national debt and the company's assets. He described the original proposal of the South Sea Company to be against the wills of most of the people to whom the debts were owed and to have inspired the "universal Dislike of the whole Nation." From the beginning, too, Defoe saw the effect of public opinion; he complained that, within a year, the greatest opposers of the company had bought up all the stock, and the government, therefore, had "erected . . . a Scheme both for ascertaining a precarious Debt, and appointing an unpracticable Commerce."[22] When the plan became reality, Defoe dreamed of a vigorous company devoted to bringing the abundant treasures of South America to England; he wanted the establishment of new colonies and the harassment of the French. He recommended the expan-

---

*Par was £100.

†Winners in the royal lotteries held to finance England's wars and holders of government bonds received annuities. The lottery winners had been offered the opportunity to trade their annuities for South Sea stock; most "converted" their holdings in the hope that the stock would pay higher dividends longer. The advantage to the company, or whoever took over the government debt, was a huge increase in capital, enabling new ventures.

sion of the war against France into the South Seas, the seizure of its ships, the conquest of its colonies, and the licensing of privateers to capture the silver and gold on the way to Europe. In 1719 he wanted determined prosecution of the war against Spain and the same aggressive measures against its ships and colonies. He also imagined new settlements in Chile and Argentina whose wealth would attract Spanish trade.

But by tying the company to the national debt, Defoe saw, Parliament had created a political animal rather than an enterprising force. The company's stock rose and fell somewhat with public confidence in the government; politicians rather than commercial men controlled it, and the spirit of Sir Walter Raleigh seemed foreign to it.[23] He summarized his opinion in *The Secret History of the White Staff, Part III* (1715) when he called the company "one of the Mistakes of the Management of the Time" and argued that, had the plan to pay the debts not been joined to the company, England would have had "a Company of Men of Honour, Merchants, whose Business it would have been to propagate the Interest of Commerce, and not fallen into Factions and Tumults . . . till honest Men should withdraw from them, and leave them to ruin the Trade" (46). He signed his own South Sea stock away in 1719.[24] In August 1720, he contrasted the stock companies to plans like Sir Walter Raleigh's expeditions:

But . . . our Projects are all Bubbles, and calculated for *Exchange-Alley* Discoveries, not for enlarging our Commerce, settling Colonies, and spreading the Dominions of our Sovereign. . . .
Why has no bold Undertaker follow'd the glorious Sir *Walter Raleigh* up the River of *Amazon*, the *Rio Parano*, and the Great *Oroonoque*, where thousands of Nations remain undiscover'd, and where the Wealth . . . exceeds all that has ever been conquer'd or discover'd in the *American* World?
. . . instead of Merchants carrying on useful Commerce, we see Throngs of Setters and Cullies Sharping and Cheating one another.[25]

He spoke partly in disappointment here, for the year before he had addressed his *Historical Account of the Voyages . . . of Raleigh* to the South Sea Company. In this book he proposed that the company undertake Raleigh's plan to explore and settle the Oronoko and offered it the charts and plans he had prepared for King William. Defoe described the vast treasures and unmatched opportunities in South America. Unlike the North American Indians or the Africans, he said, the natives of South America were populous, rich, and sociable. Their mineral wealth and "the most Fertile Country in the World" promised nearly unimaginable trade of the most favorable kind: they would pay in silver and gold.[26] And Defoe wanted the Spaniards humiliated; it was, he said, a reproach to England that Spain held land that the English had discovered.

Robert Walpole, first earl of Orford.

Whatever hopes for exploration and expansion Defoe might have held faded quickly before the events of the spring and summer of 1720. Robert Walpole's resignation in 1717 had come as he was about to present Parliament with the details of his plan for reducing the national debt. Stanhope delayed for months, then steered the General, Bank, South Sea, and Sinking Fund Acts through Parliament. The major alteration in Walpole's plan was the acceptance of the proposal made by the South Sea Company to convert the national debt into their stock.[27]

Defoe had known Walpole's plan well. At the time of the death of Queen Anne, the national debt stood at £54,145,363 with an annual interest due to creditors of £3,351,358. For the nation that had launched inquiries and considered impeachments over an unfunded debt of £9 million in 1710, this figure seemed staggering. Such a debt guaranteed continued high prices and more taxes. In fact, excise taxes doubled in 1715. By 1720 taxes made up 12.9 percent of the national income as opposed to 8.9 percent in 1710, and the national income had fallen from £59.8 million to £47.5 million. In this period, taxes on raw materials such as yarn, dye, and iron for British industries averaged between 15 and 25 percent of their costs. Prices rose alarmingly. The bushel of wheat that cost 4s. 2d. in 1701 and 4s. 10d. in 1714 cost 6s. 3d. by the end of 1715.[28]

It was soon clear that it was essential that the interest and annuities paid on the debt be reduced. Defoe and others saw that additional capital had to be available for the increase of manufacture and for the expansion of domestic and global trade.[29] Robert Walpole put together a plan, and Defoe's *Fair Payment, No Spunge* and *Mercurius Politicus* supported it and implicitly answered the objections to it. William Paterson's *An Enquiry into the State of the Union of Great Britain, and the Past and Present State of the Trade and Publick Revenues Thereof. By the Wednesday's Club* (1717) had presented information about the debt and calculations prepared "by the express Order of Mr. W——, or at least by his Approbation and Encouragement."[30] Defoe's *Fair Payment, No Spunge* took up the cause by vigorously spelling out the detrimental effects of Britain's present means of raising money and by endorsing Walpole's recommendations enthusiastically. Although naive about national debt in the modern world, Defoe saw consequences clearly and produced one of his best pamphlets in Walpole's cause.

In *Mercurius Politicus* and *The Conduct of Robert Walpole* (1717), he claimed that *Fair Payment, No Spunge* was written "by Order of the first Contrivers," "in concert with" them, and had "some Things of weight in it." Walpole's plan was to fix the interest on the national debt at a uniform rate of 5 percent and to reduce the debt itself by a Sinking Fund. Defoe confirmed Paterson's figures and agreed that the nation would be "effectually clear of Debt in 22 years."[31] His pamphlet, he felt, explained the reasons for lowering interest on the government's loans as a means of equalizing the tax burdens of all of the citizens and was superior to William Paterson's.

Once again Defoe found himself an uncomfortable co-worker with Paterson. In the March 1717 *Mercurius Politicus* Defoe said that the notoriety of Paterson's work could be explained by the identity of the author, a man "fam'd for being the Author of Miscarrying Projects," and a rumor that Paterson had been set to the work "by a Great Person who sits in Publick pretty near the Head of these Matters" increased sales of his pamphlet. Defoe grumbled that Paterson had been introduced to the king, kissed his hand, and been referred to the lords of the Treasury (141–42).

Defoe's special contribution, he felt, was in his argument regarding the justice of reducing interest on loans, some made at 7 or even 8 percent.[32] He made an eloquent case for Walpole's plan being just to the public and to the people who pay taxes. The Parliament who gave such high rates on "unredeemable" loans "sold a Free People to Usury" (28–30). "Justice," he said, demanded that these notes be redeemed, for "our Trade, our Manufactures, our Navigation, in a Word our Prosperity depends" on the plan. He compared the loans not just to usury but to "Extortion . . . for 85 Years" (58). His final argument appealed to the interests of those who held the bonds; the decrease in prices, the growth of trade, and increase in cash and credit for purchases and investments would more than compensate for their lost interest payments. The pamphlet shows Defoe's awareness of the hardship of individuals as well as the forces affecting the worldwide trading network.

Defoe watched Stanhope's modifications with interest. Bribery and corruption had played a part in the creation of the company in 1711 and was used again to outbid the Bank of England in 1719. Over £575,000 worth of stock went to politicians before the debt was converted; at that time the company's capital assets amounted to only £12,000,000. At the time of the conversion, counting the sale of this stock, the £7,500,000 due the government for the privilege of converting the debt, dividends due, and other commitments, the South Sea Company had contracted obligations of £11,400,000 by the time it began to sell the new stock in April 1720. More stock would change hands before the Bubble Act, intended to eliminate unchartered rival companies, glided through Parliament. Stock stood at £128 on 1 January, rose to £200 by March; stock from the conversion came on the market on 14 April at £300, rose to £400 by the thirtieth, to £755 in June, and £1,000 in July. In May alone, the company made a gross profit of £22,750,000, or a net profit of about £13,500,000. This news, the conspicuous spending of the newly wealthy early investors, and wild rumors such as the one that predicted England would trade Minorca and Gibraltar for Spanish Peru, "the land of gold and silver," pushed the desire to buy South Sea stock into a frenzy.

Defoe repeatedly remarked that he had never seen anything like the behavior of his countrymen. At first his reproaches fell on the stock jobbers, whom he called "the most dangerous and destructive Kind" of gamblers.[33] He began to describe the "Bubble-Market," the numerous stock companies that had sprung up to take advantage of the people's desire to invest in schemes such as copper and silver mines, and to use satire and story to show exactly how the most common frauds worked. His amazement at what he saw never entirely died. Several times he described rich men "Jobbing every Day" but remembered the bargains only if they were profitable. By June he was comparing such men to highway robbers and depicting the victims of such practices. He satirized the discontented and crazed women investors and chided the "City gamblers" who risked the money of widows, children, and creditors.[34]

By September he portrayed a nation infected by avarice. The *Manufacturer* carried the story of a landowner clever enough to sell his land at an exorbitant price to a "*South Sea* Man." However, the landowner rushed to town and invested in four bubbles, thereby losing his fortune. Defoe marveled at men who "turn Cheats and Pick-Pockets in *Exchange-Alley*" and did things they would never do in their own shops and counting houses. "The Biting, the Sharping, and Circumventing one another, practis'd . . . is like a Contagion," he wrote; many transactions are "shameless Fraud" in which "the Seller is a Cheat, for he takes the Price, and delivers nothing; the Buyer is a Cheat . . . on purpose to cheat another; and as he buys Air, so he sells a Bubble." Over and over he said that "every Exorbitance tends by the Nature of the Thing to its own Reformation," and "when Crime grows audacious," justice is sure to follow.[35]

Experienced investors soon realized what was happening and began to sell. By October stock was £190, and a crisis of credit resulted. The public creditors alone, mostly finance houses, banks, insurance companies, and trustees for estates, numbered over 30,000 individuals, groups, and corporations. There was a run on the Bank of England and its cash ratio* fell to 25 percent, a very low figure for this period. Gold rose in price from £3.10.0 in January to £4.10.6 in August. New loans became extremely difficult to negotiate, and almost every note and bill in England became an object of suspicion, and, therefore, heavily discounted or even non-negotiable. People complained that it was as hard to borrow £50 in February as it was £5,000 the summer of 1720; interest rates of 3, 4, and even 10 percent *per month* could be charged on short-term loans. Among individuals, the small speculator and the owner of redeemable debts suffered most, and many of them were ruined. The number of bankruptcies in 1721 was the highest in British history and double the number for 1719.[36]

The nation faced two immediate, devastating problems: a severe shortage of coins and the disorganization of credit. Although the Mint

---

*Liquid assets. Even with the federal regulations of today, the reserve requirement for banks is 15–20 percent.

set to work at once to strike new money, nearly every person, business, and institution suffered by the refusal or severe discounting of all forms of paper currency—stocks, bonds, notes, bills, receipts—even those backed by solid assets. In many cases people could not collect money owed them and therefore could not pay their creditors. Bankers, financiers, craftsmen, and laborers all suffered even if they had never invested in the South Sea Company. The result of the company's collapse was rage and chaos, however, not long-term economic devastation. Most experienced merchants seem to have sold in time, and the trade and manufacture of the nation showed few serious, long-term effects.

Once the stock fell, Defoe might have reminded his readers that he had predicted that only one in ten thousand would win the "gamble" they had turned South Sea stock into.[37] Instead he contented himself with, "the good People have been imposed upon. . . . The *Ignes fatui* of *Exchange-Alley* have danc'd before them . . . They have been . . . catch'd in the Snare . . . running innocently after one another like a flock of Sheep, and now they are left to get out as well as they can."[38] Until a parliamentary committee uncovered the £575,000 worth of stock distributed before the act passed, Defoe put most of the blame on the stock jobbers and the "madness" of the people: "Had Men been contented, in any Bounds of Reason; had they not been push'd on with an Ambition, which, 'tis plain, could never be gratified, we had not groaned under our present Misfortunes: And are such extravagant Gamesters to be encouraged?"[39] The South Sea Company, he argued, had accepted too many schemes and projects, then made "a weak and scandalous Loan" to try to support credit; the cause was the directors' lack of experience and probity rather than criminality.

In fact, Defoe had been fairly supportive of the South Sea Company throughout 1720, and his criticism of it had actually decreased over the summer. He had used anecdotes and parables, directed his attacks at the other stock companies, and moved his objections into the mouths of fictional characters like Steele's Sir John Edgar,* who called the South Sea scheme an "infamous and unjust Design."[40] In February 1720 Defoe had equated South Sea Company investment with gambling and told the story of a man for whom "His next Game was in *Exchange-Alley*, and *South-Sea* was his last Card." In March he called this South Sea gambling craze "a Spirit raised, that cannot easily be laid." Already private lotteries, many of them fraudulent, were being held in such numbers that the attorney general had ordered mass prosecutions with mandatory fines of £500. In April he reproached the company for

---

*Steele's pseudonym in the *Theatre*; twenty-eight issues were published between January and March 1720.

buying its own stock,[41] but on 3 June he denied that the company was adversely affecting trade and on 5 September was still saying that the company could support the price of its stocks.

Later Defoe remarked that some people had considered his early 1720 cautions unpatriotic. In *The Case of Mr. Law, Truly Stated*, a pamphlet written near the end of 1721, he explained that "Power" and "popular Rage" had prevented criticism and free inquiry in England. "Nor do I say thus much without good Reasons" (28–29), he adds ominously. Evidence survives that many felt similar pressure to remain silent if they could not praise the scheme and that those who spoke or wrote critically of the company were accused of being disaffected from the government. As Archbishop William King wrote, "I send you the queries about the South Sea, but would not on any account have it known that I am concerned in it, for I think, if the debts of the nation may be paid by the folly of particulars . . . I know no obligation on me to hinder it."[42] That was the position the government expected Defoe to take.

With the disclosure of the £575,000 of stock distributed and the mutilation of all records that might have allowed full identification of the men who had accepted the stock and who had participated in other forms of fraud such as allowing favored stockholders to withdraw their allotments of stock after the price fell,[43] the motive for "Power" to suppress criticism of the sale of South Sea stock becomes clear and thoroughly reprehensible. Defoe's response to the pressure shows how he had learned to maintain some measure of his integrity. Although he would go so far as to predict stock could reach £1,500, he never did so without mentioning the safeguards the company needed to take.[44] He had continued to depict the irrational conduct of the people, to describe the frauds and tricks of stock jobbers, to insist upon inquiries into the foundations and management of projects, and to report on increasing numbers of problems including the shortage of coins, noticeable as early as June, and rumors of corruption, such as that South Sea directors were "buying" stock without credit or cash, selling, and then paying for their original puchase with their profits.[45] By using characters like Sir John Edgar and naive countrymen, by reminding people of similar corrupt practices by the old East India Company under Sir Josiah Child,[46] by attacking the unchartered companies and their investors for the practices obviously carried out by the South Sea Company and their investors, and by discussing the schemes of John Law in France,* Defoe managed to draw telling parallels to the South Sea Company and, by doing so, offered a warning to those able to hear

*John Law, a Scot, founded a national bank in France in 1716 and amalgamated the foreign trading companies into one great trust, which controlled trade to India, Africa, and French America by 1719. In August 1719 this company was authorized to convert

reason. In *The Case of Mr. Law* he summarized the specific parallels between the company's and Law's mistakes and reminded his readers of the sight of "Gentlemen crowding every Day to *Exchange-Alley*" to buy stock "at the most monstrous and extravagant Prices."[47]

Defoe's analysis of the dangers of the scheme conform remarkably to modern conclusions. He expressed concerns about artifical stock short- ages, about inadequate regulations for buying and selling, about slov- enly records of transactions, about the misuse of the surplus credit, about the company's April decision to make loans on its own stock, about buying for future delivery, about traffic in options, and about individuals' excessive optimism and increasing indebtedness. Of the dividend to be paid in stock in July that the company had declared in April, Defoe said, "It was evident these Subscriptions on which they were founded . . . could never be paid for . . . not all the Money or Credit of the Nation cou'd perform it."[48] In fact, the pretended value of all the sorts of stock in the scheme market reached £500,000,000, al- though the rental of all the lands, houses, buildings, and other proper- ties in the British isles was calculated not to exceed £14,000,000 a year.[49] As a modern economist has explained events, the company's policy all along had been to inflate the price of its scrip rather than to invest and increase its resources:

Not only were loans made on the stock, but there was a sustained effort to corner it. Necessarily those, who borrowed on their holding, had to pawn their stock, and there was a great delay in issuing new scrip against the annuities converted in May. Thus, the market was kept bare of stock. . . . The price of the stock, being artificially enhanced through the loans on it, to support the mar- ket, it was necessary to continue the policy.

Thus, further issues of stock had to be made and, in order to generate the additional stock, lists for a second conversion of debts had to be opened.[50]

What Defoe could not see, of course, was the corruption that had put the company in debt before the act passed and determined the desper- ate efforts to elevate stock prices. He also failed to predict the ramifica- tions of the Bubble Act, although he was quick to recognize its conse- quences. When the government began to enforce it in August, people who had invested in companies without charters such as York Buildings or the Welsh Copper Company had to sell their South Sea Company stock in order to meet their liabilities. The fact that writs of *scire facias* had been issued at all shook public confidence, and attempts to sell all kinds of stocks rose. Foreign investors quickly sold as the market dropped, and the drain of gold and silver reserves accelerated. With

---

the existing government debt into its stock. That debt amounted to 1,500,000,000 livres, about £34,000,000.

the issue of the writs, Defoe quickly saw that the market was flooded with stock and "which was still worse. . . . It check'd the adventurous Humour of the People, [and] made them sick of Bubbles in general."[51]

His response to the collapse of the value of the South Sea stock was to do the same things he had done during the economic crisis of 1710: he did all in his power to bolster public credit and to maintain confidence in the government. He continued to insist that the value of South Sea stock was 400, an amount well over par and, incidentally, that set by the Bank of England on 23 September 1720, the day before the Sword Blade Company, the South Sea Company's banker, failed.[52] He explained the calculations that would hold the stock at 400 and argued that reasonable dividends would certainly be paid. As he had in 1710, he tried to persuade wealthy merchants and manufacturers that it was in their own interest to do all they could to restore credit. With their resources and their knowledge of trade they could do more than Parliament to bring the nation back to health and prosperity, he insisted. Some of his claims about the company were exaggerated, some of his ideas impossible, but his faith in the City, in the basic soundness of his country's financial institutions, and in the responsiveness of Parliament was justified. Although Parliament had to intervene* and the company was unable to make a payment to the government until June 1723,[53] England—and most of her citizens—recovered within eighteen months, and Defoe bought stock in the South Sea Company for his daughter.[54]

In this crisis Defoe had succeeded fairly well in keeping his integrity and being a loyal employee of the ministry. When he could, he endorsed the company, and he wholeheartedly joined in efforts to support credit and public confidence in the government. Although he yielded to pressure, he used analogy and anecdote extremely freely and effectively. When he had to, he said nothing, and he refused to join the witch-hunt after the directors that followed the collapse of the value of the stock.[55]

❧

At the time of the publication of *Robinson Crusoe*, Defoe was in charge of the *White-Hall Evening Post*, *Mercurius Politicus*, and *Mercurius Britannicus*, writing *Dormer's Newsletter*, and contributing to Mist's *Weekly Journal*.† In many ways these papers are exemplary of the state of journal-

---

*Parliament "ingrafted" £9,000,000 of the stock to the Bank of England, an equal amount to the East India Company, extended the time for the South Sea Company to begin repaying the loan, made provisions for a possible default, and reabsorbed some of the stock into the national debt.

†Defoe should be regarded as a very active editor and contributor, not the author of every piece. In fact, attributions of individual numbers to Defoe, especially those in Lee, should be regarded cautiously.

ism in England at that time. A loophole in the Stamp Act encouraged weekly and monthly papers, for tax was on each copy of whole and halfsheet publications under six pages in length but on each *edition* of works of six or more pages. Thus, the tax on the *White-Hall Evening Post* was one penny per copy, but the entire monthly tax on *Mercurius Politicus* only three shillings.[56]

Although party divisions were less severe by the end of 1719, papers routinely maintained some party bias. To compare *Mercurius Politicus*, the monthly Tory paper, with *Mercurius Britannicus*, the monthly Whig paper, is to see how the same news item could be given more or less space or slanted to please readers even as the encouragement of moderation and support for the government remained one of Defoe's objectives. He probably handled the extreme Tory *Dormer's* much as he did *Mercurius Politicus*,[57] and his contributions to Mist's *Weekly Journal*, another Tory paper, included news reported in the manner of *Mercurius Politicus* and satires and parodies of extremists. His primary strategy in Mist's was to transform the paper into a kind of magazine of human interest stories.

The *White-Hall Evening Post*, the Whig paper Defoe began in September 1718, should be classed with the best of the true newspapers of the time. Many items were reported in a completely objective manner, and the Whig bias might not be apparent to the modern reader. Defoe managed this feat by putting opinion in letters, as he often did in Mist's *Weekly Journal*. For instance, a long letter in the 30 December 1718 *White-Hall Evening Post* reproved the author of the paper for neglecting the bill in Parliament to "take off the Bonds and Fetters" from the Dissenters. It remarked on how much the nation had needed the Dissenters to fight the Jacobites during the rebellion, congratulated the Church of England for demonstrating in the present case that "Persecution is contrary to [their] Doctrine," and stated that it was time to reward the Dissenters for their loyalty. These propagandistic points were, of course, the ones Defoe was making most frequently in his pamphlets. The news items themselves varied little if at all from those in papers like the *London Gazette*. For instance, Defoe merely announced the royal assent for the "Bills for strengthening the Protestant Interest" (the bill that repealed two of the restrictive laws against the Dissenters) and printed the Declaration of War against Spain without comment. Just as he did in Mist's paper, he included a very large number of items that had no political aspect at all. He gave the Newmarket racing schedule, reported on the results of the trials of pirates and common criminals, and described (or made up) novel accidents such as apprentices falling into vats in their workplaces.

Defoe's other Whig periodical, *Mercurius Britannicus*, underscored his gradual move away from obvious party journalism. It justified government actions and provided its Whig readers with argument to use against critics, but this paper was much tighter and more businesslike than *Mercurius Politicus*.[58] Defoe took over this paper in January 1718 and began with a light-hearted, rather bantering, preface that promised impartiality if not neutrality. He intended this Whig paper to "make Collections, give an Account of Publick Transactions, and Methodise the News of the World, that what occurs in . . . Fragments may be read in Bulk." Using many of the *Review's* strategies, Defoe presented the Whigs as moderate, patriotic, and capable. He gave considerable space to such public controversies as the suppression of the dying speeches of some of the Jacobite rebels in order to defend the king's actions so that readers could understand and explain them to others.

In October 1719 Defoe began two more papers, the *Daily Post* and the *Manufacturer*. When he began the *Daily Post* there was only one daily paper in London, the *Daily Courant*, which under Samuel Buckley had reported foreign and domestic news with unusual accuracy and judiciousness all through the Queen Anne years in spite of its Whig affiliation. In October 1719, however, the *Daily Courant* had declared itself in opposition to the government and had passed out of Buckley's capable hands into those of a man named Meers, who happened to be in the Old Bailey at the time.[59]

The *Daily Post* is only superficially like the *Daily Courant*, and it is incontrovertible evidence of Defoe's journalistic mastery. Although the claims he made in the paper's opening number are not unusual, the paper itself was. It began with the familiar statement that the town had much news "but little Intelligence," that readers were "vilely impos'd upon," and that this paper, in contrast, would give "just Accounts of Facts in plain Words . . . with clear and unbyass'd Reasonings . . . we resolve to be of no Party, and to meddle with no Quarrels, Publick or Private, Civil or Religious: Our Business is to give an Account of the News, Foreign and Domestick, in the best and clearest Manner we can."[60]

There were, however, three things about the *Daily Post* that all but guaranteed its solid success. Like Defoe's other recent papers, it reported on an unusually wide variety of subjects, and many items included specific, factual detail lacking in the standard single-sentence entries found in the other papers. For instance, in the 27 October 1719 paper he listed the groups from whom the Lord Commissioners of Trade intended to take information. By naming the Turkey and Italy merchants, mercers, weavers, East India Company representatives, drapers, dyers, and calico printers and classifying them by certainty of being summoned and by position on the controversy over the import of calicoes, he gave people much information in little space, went beyond the stark report in other papers that the woolen weavers' petition to the

Lords Justices had been referred to the Commissioners of Trade, and, by naming specific groups, appeared to be well informed and accurate.

In addition to its attractive subject matter, the style of the *Daily Post* was among the best of the London papers. The introduction had promised plain words and clear reasoning, and Defoe here acted upon a theory of prose style that he was articulating with increasing frequency and confidence. In *A Continuation of the Letters Written by a Turkish Spy* (1718) he had said, "The best Rule in all Tongues [is] to make the Language plain, artless, and honest, suitable to the Story, and in a Stile easie and free, with as few exotick Phrases and obsolete Words as possible, that the meanest Reader may meet with no Difficulty in the Reading" (v). The *Daily Post* shows a gift for lively, concise prose and especially for effective adjectives. Defoe calls the weavers "mutinous and troublesome" and captures their mood and the population's general lack of sympathy; he describes potential investors in the South Sea Company as having "the utmost Eagerness to engage with the Company upon any Terms" and catches the mindless frenzy that would inflate the stock. And he shows his Whig colors now and then; for instance, he reports the king's return from Hanover in words designed to encourage a bandwagon effect: "The Evening concluded with Illuminations and other publick Demonstrations of Loyalty and Joy."

The greatest advantage the *Daily Post* had was probably the number and quality of its advertisements. From the beginning advertisements took up about one third of the space, and they complemented the variety of news reported. Advertisements for books, medicines, plays, and household items, some with illustrations, vied for attention, and they increased in number quickly. So important were advertisements to readers that one plan to put politically offensive papers out of business proposed that the government start a general advertising office that would publish papers of such notices. "It is evidently true that the certain, Excessive profits arising from Advertisements, are the chief Support of the proprietors, Writers and printers of Newspapers and chiefly promotes the Sale of them," the proposal read. It went on to explain that public and private houses took in so many papers to get the advertising, for everyone knew that it was "undeniable that the Newswriters, mostly either copy after one another, or translate foreign Papers, or forge themselves unaccountable Stories, and thereby pick People's Pockets." With a general advertising publication, these people "would gladly decline such a Useless Expence, and find one Daily paper, one Evening post, and one Weekly Journal sufficient." Defoe could count on over ten pounds a week profit on advertising alone.[61] The success of Defoe's paper might be measured in the rise in the quality of the goods and services advertised, including large sales of books and fine furniture and large houses or even groups of buildings for rent.

Even chariots evidently found a market among Defoe's readers. New novels and plays were routinely announced, and the very best editions of Locke, Ovid, Dennis, and poetry miscellanies were advertised along with a large number of books of practical divinity, many of them obviously Anglican.

The *Manufacturer* was a different kind of paper altogether. The City Company of Weavers engaged Defoe to write it during the time Parliament was debating a bill to restrict the import of calico. So important did legislators think this debate that they gave it about twice the attention they gave the creation of the South Sea Company. Defoe had reported on the weavers' cause—and the riots and vandalism perpetrated by weavers in London, Norwich, and other cities—and had written three sympathetic pamphlets explaining the economic situation and reasons the nation should be concerned.[62] He believed the English woolen industry was threatened, and, in pamphlets like *A Brief State of the Question, between the Printed and Painted Callicoes and the Woollen and Silk Manufacture* (1719), he recommended protective legislation. He spoke frankly about the detrimental effects of the widespread smuggling that officials either dismissed or denied. In *The Trade to India Critically and Calmly Consider'd* (1720) he devoted seventeen pages to exposing the extent of the "clandestine trade." He dared to explain how the East India Company itself avoided paying duties and carried out the same frauds with tea, coffee, and pepper. In another place he created a female weaver who begged "Mrs. Woollpack" to make calico unfashionable and help save women like herself and the woolen trade from ruin.[63]

Defoe's sympathy and virtuosity appealed to the Company of Weavers, and the first number of The *Manufacturer* appeared on 30 October 1719. Defoe made it clear it was their paper:

> Their Design in this Paper, is, to have their Grievances laid open, and their Story fairly told, in a Manner less offensive than they have been able to tell it in the Street; that they may complain without Rabbling . . . and be answer'd with milder Arguments than those of a Prison and a Pillory.

In fact, at least one weaver would be hanged for his part in a mob, and it was not uncommon for weavers on the public streets to slash or tear women's calico clothing.[64]

Their cause—and, therefore, Defoe's—was not very good.[65] The English woolen industry's competition was not exclusively or even primarily calico cloth. English weavers of fashionable, light, colorful cloth, continental and Irish producers of high-quality wool, Chinese and Indian silk weavers, and Asian and colonial cotton spinners produced the cloth that people demanded because of its attractiveness, comfort, ease of cleaning, price, or all four. That the woolen material the angry weavers produced tended to be broadcloth—a fabric heavier than that used in many modern coats—did not matter to Defoe. Part of Defoe's advocacy of the woolen industry came from the fact that it was a "home industry." The wool could be grown, processed, spun, woven, and made into garments in England. It supported the agriculture, manufacture, and then transportation industries. At that time English workers could not compete with the cheap labor in the Far East and the colonies, and Parliament finally passed an Act Prohibiting the Use and Wear of Printed Calicoes in March 1721. This legislation gave England time to industrialize its cloth manufacture, and technology underlay the boom in prosperity that came after Defoe's death.

Defoe believed in the weavers' cause, however, and the first numbers of the *Manufacturer*, which outline his position, are entirely consistent with everything he wrote about the trade. Defoe argues that the entire nation should be concerned with what he labels the cause of "the labouring Poor." He describes a ripple effect that would finally impoverish tradesmen, shopkeepers, merchants, and seamen, and he appeals to patriotism and brotherly love. Week after week, he managed to explain the weavers' case, answer the East India Company's counterarguments, and appear to give new facts.

Two months after the first edition of the *Manufacturer*, Defoe began the *Commentator*. An essay periodical, it gave him a vehicle for his opinions on subjects other than the woolen trade. He intends, he says, "to pry into the Faults and Follies of Mankind," and typical essays consider self-love, advertisements, education, superstition, and freak shows. A favorite subject is journalism itself. He explains that his essays are "Commodities" that have to suit "the Humour of my Customers." The second paper, for instance, says newspapers are ruining trade and conjures up a vision of empty shops and business at a standstill, for all of the drapers, hosiers, hatters, glovers, barbers, tailors, and shoemakers are in the taverns reading the news.[66] The 8 January paper describes "bales" of news shipped out of London every day and calls printing houses the main support of the coffeehouses. Defoe calculated that an innkeeper in the West made at least £20 a year by subscribing to and supplying papers like the *Post Boy*, Mist's, and the *White-Hall Evening Post*, which he calls "a rascally Paper."[67] The *Commentator* sparkles with light-hearted satire and humorous anecdotes. Defoe gives us a barber who assures his customers that the widowed Queen Anne will take Prince Eugene of Savoy-Carignon, commander of the Empire's forces during the War of the Spanish Succession, as her second husband; a clergyman's nephew who has a trunk of his deceased uncle's literary compositions for sale; and a delightful tongue-in-cheek analysis of advertisements for medical products:

There runs throughout in them such an Air of Veracity, Candor and Disinterestedness, and such an universal Benevolence to our afflicted Fellow-Creatures, that I cannot but recommend them to the Perusal of the curious Reader. . . .

. . . [They] take in all the Diseases incident to human Nature, and supply all the Comforts, as well as the Conveniencies of Life. (15 February 1720)

The Commentator himself becomes an object of satire as a result of his attempts to be fashionable. He laments not receiving letters and poems like his fellow journalists; he goes to Jonathan's to join the bubble market where brokers and jobbers cry "their Trade as loud as the *Hawkers* do *Mist's-Journal*"; and he remarks "A Man that is out of the *Stocks* may almost as well be out of the World."

Early on Defoe had jokingly suggested a newspaper bubble, a stock company for his paper, and in some ways, the *Commentator* was part of "bubble-mania." Its comments on the South Sea Company, trade, and the people who invested, jobbed, and discussed the bubbles supported its sales. When he said on 5 September that the paper might have sold even better had it been named "The Bubble Journal," he probably spoke the truth. When Parliament was prorogued for the summer, Defoe wrote a number of lively essays on other commercial topics. *Manufacturer* no. 44, for 18 May 1720, developed an idea he had introduced in the *Commentator*. In this witty paper he extended the idea of writing as a branch of manufacture. Writers, he said, support the building of print shops, coffeehouses, and "News-houses"; they weave politics and "the Country People wear them." They employ poor authors, printers, and publishers. In another paper he had described the way Mist, who "has for some Time been most in Vogue" and is "the great Oracle of the common People," worked: "He is not the Author of the *Journal* that passes under his Name. . . . His Part of it is to hire *Runners*, and *News-gatherers*, as the Paper-Makers hire Beggars and Vagrants to pick up Rags, and accordingly . . . his Paper . . . 'tis a piece of Patchwork gather'd from all the dirty Corners of the Town" (1 April 1720). He learned from Mist, though, and became a great collector of news and surprising items himself. A few years later, he returned to the metaphor of writing as a branch of commerce and said,

Writing . . . is become a very considerable Branch of the English Commerce; Composing, Inventing, Translating, Versifying, &c., are the several Manufactures which supply this Commerce. The Booksellers are the . . . Employers. The several Writers, Authors, Copyers, Sub-Writers, and all other Operators with Pen and Ink, are the Workmen employed by the said Master Manufacturers, in the forming, dressing, and finishing the said Manufactures; as the Combers, Spinners, Weavers. . . .

If a Clothier employs a Master Workman to weave him so many Pieces of Cloth . . . the Weaver brings them home finished, and puts his own Mark on them. . . . At the same Time, this Clothier knows very well that the said Weaver could not be able to weave them all himself; perhaps also he knows that some of them are of a much meaner Workmanship than that Weaver used to Work. . . . Nay, sometimes the Weaver brings a better Workman than himself into the Loom. . . . And thus, a Medley of Goods are put off together, all under the Mark, and in the Name of the Master Weaver.

As to Writing . . . Do we expect that every Man that publishes a Book, and sets his Name to it, should *Bona fide*, be the Author *of it all* himself? . . . have not several Authors, who are particular for being voluminous, their several Journeymen that work for them?[68]

Here Defoe may be giving an allegorical description of the way he worked. His papers, like those of his fellow journalists, obviously depended upon plagiarism from the *London Gazette*, other papers, and even books. The *White-Hall Evening Post* and *Daily Post* often printed the same items and gave the same sources. Some sections of his papers were surely collected and prepared for printing by others, and the employees of his publishers surely treated his papers as they did everyone else's when they needed filler or had to cut lines. In light of the way we know he used his two sons in 1713, it is almost certain that Defoe continued to develop his practice of composing the framework of a piece and letting others fill in quotations and even sections. Surely not even Defoe would try to produce novels and write for so many periodicals simultaneously; he would, however, take great pleasure in running a "branch of commerce."

The *Manufacturer* ended in March 1720, shortly before the final approval of the Act Prohibiting Calicoes. Defoe gave up the *Commentator* with the 20 September 1720 issue and on 5 October published the first *Director*.[69] By that time, he had begun writing for Applebee's *Original Weekly Journal*, a moderate, Hanoverian Tory paper.[70] The *Director* promised to investigate the collapse of credit and reveal its causes. Defoe used his favorite quotation from Sir Walter Raleigh to describe the risky nature of his undertaking: "If in pursuing Truth too close at the Heels, the Author runs some Hazard of a Kick in the Face, he takes that to himself."[71] Defoe, however, was ignorant at that time of the risk he took. In his first paper he had said he did not expect to find the greatest people involved in "the Cheat," but, of course, they were. Among them were Secretaries of State Stanhope and Craggs, Sunderland, and the treasurer of the navy, Richard Hampden.[72] Fortunately Defoe used parables and fables from the beginning, and his first targets were companies like York Buildings and the Sword Blade Company. One of his best papers treated the stock companies like booths at a fair. In this story the South Sea Company set up the largest booth in the center of the fair, and fraud occurred primarily when other stock companies without sufficient resources imitated it. Here, as in the *Commentator*, Defoe carefully tempered his criticism of the company. Almost from the beginning the *Director* failed to please readers. The 17

October number promised fewer allegories, similes, tales, fables, and satire. Again in January the paper answered reader complaints, and the last number was 16 January. This paper had tried to persuade people to hold on to their South Sea stock and to support public credit and never revealed much about the scandal.

Some of Defoe's own eight periodicals made substantial profits, altogether perhaps as much as £1,200 a year, and by the beginning of 1721 he lived the prosperous, serene life of the prominent citizens of Stoke Newington. Now and then he vacationed at Tunbridge Wells, and he seems to have spent his weekends away from the city. When he was in Stoke Newington, servants, including his gardener, Jonathan Marshal, carried manuscripts and proofs between London and his home.[73] The papers show us a happy man going from coffeehouse to coffeehouse, mingling easily with the financiers at Jonathan's and Garraways, with the churchmen at Child's, dropping in at the Temple coffeehouses, and talking politics and economics or exchanging jokes and good-natured gibes. He laughs over the people who have told him that they think the *Commentator* is being written by "poor pastoral Philips,"[74] and his papers are full of the anecdotes and strange "sights" people have told him.

The Stoke Newington parish vestry made him one of the surveyors of the highways in 1717; in this office, he would help organize the repair and building of the streets and roads, collecting money and recruiting laborers from parish residents. Three years later he was chosen to the very responsible office of churchwarden and overseer of the poor, a position his father had held in St. Benet Fink parish many years earlier. Like many Nonconformists and elderly men, however, Defoe paid a £10 fine to be excused from the office.[75] Defoe's children, too, were doing well. His grandson Benjamin, Jr., had been baptized in Norwich in June 1719, and young Daniel was prospering in the City. When Defoe had to provide a £400 recognizance for his appearance at yet another court hearing regarding Mist's seditious libels, young Daniel had enough capital to stand for £100 for his father.[76] After this June 1720 appearance Defoe seems never again to have been accused of seditious libel.

The large profits from the periodicals, the success of his novels, and his ability to withdraw gradually from the most heated political debates gave Defoe unprecedented security and satisfactions. Although he probably made less than £100 on any of the novels, even *Robinson Crusoe*, he had a genuine affinity for the adventures and travels of their heroes.[77] He enjoyed writing the informal essays for Mist enough to begin contributing similar ones to Applebee's paper, and he clearly felt he could speak comfortably in his own voice in *Mercurius Britannicus*, the *White-Hall Evening Post*, the *Daily Post*, and the *Manufacturer*. In his *Commentator* he casually referred to his friend "Daniel" as the author of the *Manufacturer*, and the economic point of view the weavers wanted him to present was his own. In the *Manufacturer* he wrote, "The Author, is known, has had the Felicity to please formerly, and being now in the Hands of his Friends again, 'tis hoped former Prejudices shall not obstruct a good Design."[78] As he went from coffeehouse to coffeehouse and spun out his tales, he did indeed feel he was back among friends.

CHAPTER 18

PROJECTS AND DESIGNS

*My unlucky Head . . . was all this two Years fill'd with Projects
and Designs.*

—DEFOE, *Robinson Crusoe* (1719)

*Avarice did for them all that the extravagant Vices and Follies of
youth us'd to do.*

—CHARLES GILDON, *All for the Better* (1720)

On 6 August 1722 Defoe agreed to pay £1,000 to the Corporation of
the Borough of Colchester. For this impressive sum of money, he got a
99-year lease on some hundreds of acres of land and the timber rights
to them. This land, heavily mortgaged property of the Baronet of
Colchester, had been rented to as many as sixteen people and had
brought in over £180 a year in tenants' rents alone.[1] Defoe was to pay
the Colchester Corporation rent of £120 a year, and he intended to use
part of the land himself. Located in the parish of St. Michael Mile End
(now Myland), Essex, the land included Kingswood, the Severalls
Brinkley farms (sometimes called "Kingswood Heath"), Tubswick in
Lexden Hundred, and Pound Marsh. All of the messuages, tenements,
houses, buildings, fences, "feedings and premises with their and every
of the Appurtenances by whatsoever names called" went to Defoe also.
The Corporation had rented and mortgaged these lands before, but it
had always withheld the timber rights; future holders of the land would
be bound to leave every tree under six years old inviolate. Defoe, however, received the right to "fell, cut down, and sell" "all and all Manner
of Timber and Timber Trees, pollingers, logg Trees, straddles and
wavers* now standing Growing or being or that at any time during this
demise shall Stand Grow or be on any part of the . . . premises." He had
only to leave twenty-eight "up right" trees on one acre at the end of his
lease. The existing trees were beautiful, healthy oak, ash, and elm trees
and, if carefully managed, worth thousands of pounds. About the same
time, Defoe leased Broomfield in nearby Earlscolne parish. Also

---

* The archaic words describe various tree sizes, including those left to replenish a
forest.

Memorandum of receipt on the record of Defoe's agreement
to lease the Colchester land with his signature.

known as Pound Farm,* it was located on the Colne River and had rich
clay soil.[2] In these negotiations Defoe was dealing with Edmund
Raynham, a Whig alderman and former town clerk, who would become mayor of Colchester that October. Raynham often handled the
legal work for the corporation, had been charged with finding a lessee
for the land, and was the kind of leading citizen Defoe had cultivated in
Scotland.

When Defoe signed the official papers, he added his second daughter as co-signatory and reported that the lease was "on the Account and
Benefit" of her and that the money was hers. Hannah had an income
from South Sea stock; her dividend in August of that year had been
£706.13.4. Hannah apparently was in Colchester with Defoe, for she
signed the document with him.[3] The next year Defoe put a £200 mortgage on the land, probably to buy stock and make improvements, and
he began to think about setting up a new brick and tile works there.

Defoe had equally ambitious writing plans. He began *Atlas Maritimus*,
a huge economic geography with maps protected by a royal patent, and
A Tour Thro' the Whole Island of Great Britain, the only book written by
Defoe that has consistently been described as approaching belles

---

* Pound means an enclosure for cattle, and the farm was so named because of its rich
soil and long use as a pasture.

lettres. In the next few years Defoe also wrote *The Complete English Tradesman*[4] and three more conduct books, contributed to collections of Mist's periodical essays, and produced four more novels.

வ்

In 1722 Defoe began traveling again. He visited many of the places where he had carried on his hosiery trade in the late 1680s and where he had sampled political opinion for Harley in 1704 and 1705. In April he was in Essex,[5] and, as he had followed prosperous City men to Stoke Newington, he was following the same men in investing in estates in Essex. In his *Tour thro' the Whole Island of Great Britain* he wrote,

> It is observable, that in this part of the country, there are several very considerable estates purchas'd, and now enjoy'd by citizens of London, merchants and tradesmen. . . . the present encrease of wealth in the city of London, spread it self in the country, and plants families and fortunes, who in another age will equal the families of the antient gentry. (1:15)

He intended, he said, to make a list of all the "families of citizens and tradesmen thus established in the several counties." Here is Defoe's dream. His family would come to "equal" the ancient families and take its place among the settled, prosperous leaders of the country. His descendants would even have a base from which to be elected to Parliament. The upper "middle station" of life that Robinson Crusoe's father had praised would be theirs.

Twice on this page Defoe used the word "tradesman," and he intended to use his money to become a tradesman again. He and many others believed that the work of a tradesman was superior to most others, for the tradesman was such an active agent in society. A contemporary explained that the tradesman's "way of living seems preferable to the living of gentlemen and husbandmen, as requiring more industry than the former, and more ingenuity than the latter."[6] Land gave reputation and, as Captain Singleton said, a residence, a "Place that has a Magnetick Influence upon his Affections" (334). Defoe reverted to the ambitions of his young manhood. He planned to use his rich farm lands to breed cattle and raise corn; he could sell some of the corn and market cheese, butter, veal, and beef, all established Colchester products. He would be a merchant again; as he said in *Roxana*: "the best Gentleman in the Nation; that in Knowledge, Manners, in Judgment of things . . . out-did many of the Nobility . . . able to spend more Money than a Gentleman of 5000 l. a Year Estate. . . . [for] an Estate is a Pond; but . . . Trade was a Spring." His timber would find a market at the royal building yards in Chatham, if not in Ipswich or Harwich where shipbuilding was in a recession. In the *Tour* Defoe had speculated that Providence would not have made Ipswich so ideal a port were the time not coming when it would prosper and flourish, but he had calculated that, in any event, Chatham was "but one tide away." If he could not sell his timber, he believed he could produce pitch, tar, rosin, and turpentine. Over the next few years Defoe added honey and oysters to the commodities he sold from Colchester and even began to sell metal buttons, tanned leather, cloth, and imported anchovies. Some of the produce went to London, but Defoe also established markets in St. Neots, Lichfield, Coventry, and other Cambridgeshire towns. He kept at least some of his goods in a warehouse on Brewer's Key, a small street on Tower Dock off Thames Street.[7]

So intent was Defoe on a second chance that he began to plan a tile factory on the Colchester land. Late in 1723 or early in 1724 he began to try to persuade John Ward, a Nuneaton mercer and linen draper, to become his partner. Ward, the son of a Dissenting minister, had moved away from his native Coleshill, Warwickshire, partly because of religious persecution.[8] According to Ward, Defoe sent "several pressing Letters" asking him to come to Stoke Newington. Defoe insisted that he "had Something to Communicate that would be of great Advantage to him."

In Stoke Newington Defoe told Ward that he had a farm of Hannah's to rent with "Extraordinary good Tyle Clay." He went on to explain that he knew the pantile manufacture well, for he had once had "such a business at Tilbury Fort" where he made several hundred pounds a year profit. He felt "a great kindness for" Ward and was, therefore, offering him a partnership. The original plan was for the two men to stock the farm, work it for maintenance and profit, and begin to build the brick and tile works. In fact, Defoe, at sixty-four, seems actually to have planned to live on the farm, for he signed an agreement on 23 November 1724 to "jointly occupy and Carry on" the farm and brick works. Ward put up his £150 share, and furniture, rugs, dishes, and blankets for the house and stock for the farm began to arrive. Workmen began the kiln and buildings.

Robinson Crusoe had set up just such a farm in Bedford (2:116) when he returned to England and had rejoiced by comparing himself to the Old Testament Job. "I might well say, now indeed, That the latter End of *Job* was better than the Beginning" (2:81), he observed, and Defoe intended to bring his life to the same kind of closure. Some time shortly after his agreement with Ward, however, Defoe's wife became uneasy about his travel and may even have found out about the agreement. According to Ward, Defoe asked him to sign new papers in which Defoe was no longer a partner. This paper would, Defoe said, ease his wife's and children's anxieties, yet Defoe intended to keep all of his original commitments.

By 1724 Defoe's health was not good, and Mary must have thought her husband an old fool with crazy schemes. Defoe suffered from gout, bladder stones, and recurrent respiratory problems. Why he felt dissatisfied and restless probably puzzled the family, too. Hannah, Henrietta, and Sophia all lived at home, and the house and gardens showed the effects of prosperity and careful attention. A man who visited the home frequently described Defoe's home and ordinary occupations in pastoral terms. Defoe's house, he said, was "a Retirement from London," and Defoe

> amused his Time either in the Cultivation of a large and pleasant Garden, or in the Pursuit of his Studies, which he found means of making very profitable. He was now at least sixty years of Age, afflicted with the Gout and Stone, but retained all his mental Faculties intire.
>
> [He and Defoe] met usually at the Tea Table his three lovely Daughters, who were admired for their Beauty, their Education, and their prudent Conduct.[9]

Descriptions of the pleasures of Defoe's garden seats, walks, and bowers create a picture of harmony and ease. The man speaks several times of the group having refreshments outdoors, of walks through the gardens, and of Sophia gathering flowers.

The "studies" that Defoe "found means of making very profitable" ranged from books like *A Tour thro' the Whole Island of Great Britain* to some of the most common forms of popular reading matter. He continued to edit the *Daily Post* and to write for Mist and Applebee, but he published almost no political essays at all. Although his name appeared in none of the advertisements for *Atlas Maritimus*, it was surely one of his profitable undertakings. The 21 November 1721 *Post-Boy* carried the announcement of the book:

> *This Day is publish'd,* PROPOSALS for printing a complete SEA-ATLAS, from a true Globular Projection; approved by several of the Ablest Judges of Navigation and Astronomy, and warranted his Majesty's Letters Patent under the Great Seal of Great Britain, granted to John Harris, John Senex, and Henry Wilson. Containing a Description of all the Ports and Harbours in the World . . . , of the Seaports, as to their Situation, what Navigable Rivers flow up to them; of their Trade, Shipping, Product, Manufactures, Customs, &c. To which will be prefix'd, A General Treatise of Navigation . . . Revised by Dr. Edmond Halley.

The proposal promised to print the names and engrave the arms of subscribers, who were to pay a guinea of the three guineas price in advance at any of six booksellers' shops. The publisher of *Robinson Crusoe* and *Farther Adventures*, William Taylor, may have advertised a draft plan of the atlas in the first edition of *Farther Adventures*,[10] but this 1721 proposal is the first certain announcement of the ambitious book. Taylor and his conger of [Thomas] Taylor, William Innys, H. Wilson, and E. Symson had added the engraver Andrew Johnston to prepare the book and share the high production costs.

The proposal would have caught the eye of the scientific, literary, and mercantile communities. In fact, a passion for learning geography swept the nation. Defoe's *White-Hall Evening Post* carried advertisements for educational playing cards that promised benefits such as "the principal Nations of the World, and the Habits of each Country, Prospects of the capital Cities . . . ; Observations of the Fruitfulness, Religion and Trade" and "Map-Cards of the 52 Counties of England and Wales; shewing . . . the Latitude." In his *New Family Instructor* Defoe portrayed the children, including the daughters, happily using maps and globes "to observe which Way the several Armies march'd, where the Towns and Cities stood" (13). The maps of Harris, Senex, and Wilson had indeed been granted a royal patent on 20 June 1721. Such patents were infrequently requested and rarely granted. Theirs asserts in part that "after much labour, time, & expence they have invented a new Method of projecting Sea Charts for the use and Improvement of Navigation, which being agreable [*sic*] to the Globe, as truly representing the Globular Surface of the Sea, they humbly apprehend may be properly called a Globular Chart." Their application was endorsed by Admirals George Byng, Charles Wager, and John Jennings and by Edmund Halley, by then Savilian Professor of Geometry at Oxford and Astronomer Royal, who "had vouchsafed, for the promoting so publick a Benefit . . . to recommend it to all Navigators for it's [*sic*] use at Sea." It is to them that the endorsement of the proposal for *Atlas Maritimus* alludes; they are "the Ablest Judges of Navigation and Astronomy." The maps promised navigators "more Facility, certainty & Security." John Harris had engraved Halley's charts of the constellations in 1690 and his world charts and isogonic maps in 1702.[11] By 1721 Halley was one of the two greatest living English scientists; only Isaac Newton could surpass him. His expeditions to map the stars and later to study longitude and magnetic fields had made him famous, and he was Britain's brightest hope for a breakthrough in navigational technology.

The subscription list for *Atlas Maritimus* includes the Mathematical Society of London, Harley, Walpole, the three admirals who had endorsed the patent application, and Sir John Norris. Most of the subscribers, however, were merchants and professional men, and they included John Arbuthnot, Pope's friend and a physician to Queen Anne. The most remarkable thing about the list is the number of Scots, and particularly, the number of families who had subscribed to Defoe's 1706 poem *Caledonia*. Anstruther, Baillie, Campbell, Dalrymple, Douglas, Erskine, Elliott, Findlater, Forbes, Hamilton, Haddington, Montrose, Queensberry, Roxburgh, Stair, Tweedale, Wemyss—they were all there. In all, 435 subscribers paid their one guinea* deposit and pledged two more; nonsubscribers would pay a higher price when the

---

* After Newton's Assay Report, the guinea was officially worth £1.3s.

book came out. Defoe was to write a preface to the book and be responsible for the descriptive text.

Other things pushed *Atlas Maritimus* aside, however, and the economic geography would not be published until 1728. Before 1715 Defoe had been deeply engaged with the politics of Parliament and court. His movement from pamphlet to periodical literature and from propaganda to subversive journalism had marked a shift in subject matter as well. He continued to be a keen observer of domestic politics, but Great Britain was enjoying a relatively tranquil time, and he had no desire to be embroiled in party sniping again. He reverted to his happy life as a coffeehouse habitué and became a practicing reporter rather than a political essayist.

The connection between Defoe's journalistic subjects and his 1720s publications is very close.[12] Many of the reports in his papers became grist for his novels. For instance, on 8 October 1719 the *Daily Post* reported the death of Paul Lorrain, Ordinary of Newgate* and one model for the greedy Ordinary who cannot save Moll Flanders's soul. Moll describes Jemy as having the reputation of "Hind, Whitney, or the Golden Farmer," all contemporary criminals whose exploits had reached near-mythical proportions thanks to the popular press.[13] Defoe's *Commentator* for 1 August 1720 published a short poem that prefigures passages in *Moll Flanders* and *Roxana*:

> What makes a homely Woman fair?
> About Five Hundred Pounds a Year.
> What makes a Virgin of a Whore?
> Much about Five Hundred more.
> 'Tis Money guides the World and Fate,
> Makes Virtue Vice, makes Crooked Strait.

The 13 October 1719 *Daily Post* also printed a report from the Amsterdam *Courant* that sounds like the robbery that led to the death of Roxana's first benefactor. This "most notorious Robbery committed upon a Merchant" involved bonds, diamond earrings, and many other items of jewelry, and Roxana's lover was killed for the case of jewels he habitually carried to show his clients.

Some of Defoe's writing was still on political issues, but not as obviously so. The plague in Marseilles and the ways it had been used in the debates over restricting the import of calicoes as well as the Quarantine Act of 1721 helped shape *Due Preparations for the Plague* and *A Journal of the Plague Year*;[14] the South Sea and stock company schemes and his reports of crimes and trials contributed to *Moll Flanders* and

---

*The Church of England clergyman whose assigned "parish" was Newgate Prison. He was to counsel all of the prisoners and prepare the condemned for death. Many published collections of short biographies of those who were hanged; these "*Accounts*" always included descriptions of how offenders met death.

Colonel Jack; the end of the Great Northern War, the death of Peter the Great's son, and England's growing rivalry with Russia suggested *An Impartial History of the Life and Actions of Peter Alexowitz, . . . Czar of Muscovy*. All of these books, however, could be read without recognition of the political issues behind them.

Defoe's periodicals indicate his renewed interest in the City, his growing fascination with new kinds of people and situations, and his deep engagement with different kinds of social problems. Always topical and alert to people and stories that might serve as exempla, he carried these qualities into his fiction. A number of characters besides Crusoe himself have been speculatively identified with actual people in both *Robinson Crusoe* and *Farther Adventures*.[15] As early as *Major Ramkins* Defoe used an actual person for thematic emphasis. The Irish prebendary Francis Martin had recently published a book, *Scutum Fidei contra Haereses Hodiernas* (1714), in which he recommended that English Catholics accept George I, and in 1715 he had proposed a plan for the union of Protestants and Catholics. What was highly pertinent was that Martin, like Ramkins, had changed his mind about Jacobitism. Defoe's contemporaries would have recognized his name and remembered how different and how extreme his position had been at the time of William.[16]

Characters like Martin are part of the trappings that contributed to the illusion of an authentic memoir or journal, and they also provide an external referent. That men like Martin have changed their minds makes Ramkins's change that much more credible and makes the anti-Jacobite propaganda more persuasive. Robert Clayton, the long-term London alderman and former lord mayor who had recently joined the trend (noted in Defoe's *Tour*) of prominent City men buying estates in neighboring counties, appears in both *A Journal of the Plague Year* and *Roxana*. In the *Journal* Defoe mentions the house Clayton built on Hand Alley and the burial ground unearthed by digging for the foundation. Clayton plays a bigger part in *Roxana* where he provides a reminder of the everyday London business world, of the opinions ordinary people held, and, in Roxana's life of corruption and predatory conduct, of honesty and straightforwardness. Without Clayton, whom John Evelyn called "that prince of citizens," the dark, paranoid world into which Roxana sinks might seem less her own private one and readers might come to believe her radical egoism justified. Shortly after she refuses to marry the Dutchman, Roxana expounds her philosophy to Clayton. He hears her out, then laughs and observes that she talks "a kind of *Amazonian* Language." Like the Dutchman, he finds her views quite singular and provides a barometer for readers.

Defoe uses actual people in his novels in all of the ways he uses historical events and fictional characters. One of the most absorbing "adventures" in *Captain Singleton* is the men's meeting with an English-man in central Africa. In the novel the man has lost his employment and gradually moved deeper and deeper into Africa until he has no hope of escape. Defoe exploits the contradictions in him. His hair and beard have grown until they cover his back and chest; without clothing for over two years, his skin is blotched, dry, and peeling. So indifferent is he to life that he owns no weapon and if so minimal an action as building a fire to scare off wild animals is done the natives must do it for him. Yet he remembers his English, Latin, French, and Italian and quickly reveals himself to be a shrewd merchant, a mathematician, and a gentleman.

Many of Defoe's readers would have recognized him as John Free-man, an agent of the Royal African Company stationed in Sherbro. Freeman had served under Defoe's old friend Dalby Thomas, the Gold Coast agent-general for the company, who, along with most of the other company agents, had been accused of "arbitrary conduct." He had been dismissed after he abandoned the company's stock to the French during an attack in 1705. After his unsuccessful defense in London, he returned to Africa and tried to succeed as an independent—and therefore illegal—trader. He failed, and notes in the Royal African Company archives trace his retreat to Sierra Leone, follow his increasing poverty, and, finally, record his death in 1713. In *Atlas Maritimus* Defoe cites Freeman as a source for some of his information.[17] Defoe has the Englishman admit his independent trade, some-thing Freeman had been accused of before being dismissed, but sup-presses accusations of embezzlement and theft. In *Captain Singleton* Freeman is one more example of the kind of man who goes to that harsh land; his experience and his descent into a primitive state show how necessary Singleton's companions are to one another in their own struggle against the continent. Freeman, reduced to a man without a country, reinforces the thematic concern with community and belong-ing. He offers a poignant comment on Singleton's own end; retired to England, Singleton disguises himself as a Greek and refuses to speak English. More alienated and solitary even than Freeman, Singleton, too, remains a man without a country.

These examples testify to Defoe's keen, even lifelong observation of some of the notable men of his generation. Whatever dreams he might have had of becoming an alderman or lord mayor like Robert Clayton or Josiah Child had died with his bankruptcies and the pillory. His knowledge of the careers of these men, however, goes beyond casual information to sustained fascination. The brief portrayal of Robert Clayton, for instance, manages to include a surprising number of facts about Clayton's business practices: that he was a pioneer in deposit banking, specialized in mortgage and loan contracts, recommended investments in land, and even served as a matchmaker for some of his clients.[18] That they are largely City men whom Defoe would have seen, perhaps even spoken to, rather than ministers of state and under secretaries whom we know he knew cannot be dismissed as either discretion or fear of prosecution; he had, after all, included greater men in secret histories, political allegories, and fictional memoirs.

✌︎

Between 1718 and 1721 Defoe became increasingly concerned and analytical about crime. He and his contemporaries believed that crime had never been so common. In fact, the so-called Black Act (1723), the most extensive increase in the number of offenses classified as capital instituted in that century, passed because Walpole and its supporters introduced it with a description of the rising incidence of crime in "clearly lurid and alarmist terms."[19] Americans who read that, in any year, three of every one hundred of them will be the victims of a violent crime,[20] who dare not walk alone in any city in the nation, and who turn comparisons of dead-bolt locks and burglar alarms into dinner party conversation would have felt at home in Defoe's London. Defoe's own house had numerous, expensive locks;[21] his September 1716 *Mercurius Politicus* had remarked on the unusual number of robberies and housebreakings, saying: "No House seem'd sufficiently Fortified" (242). In one of the most feared maneuvers, a member of the gang disguised himself as a servant and opened the door for his pillaging comrades. In *The Great Law of Subordination* Defoe said that Jonathan Wild, the famous "thief-taker," had a "List of 7000 *Newgate*-Birds, now in Services in this City, and Parts adjacent, all with Intent to rob the Houses they are in" (210). Defoe's periodicals carried innumerable reports of crimes and trials. The 22 January 1719 *White-Hall Evening Post*, for instance, included a letter in which a Reading gentleman complained that it was impossible to go to or from the town, morning or evening, without being robbed by footpads. He described the county gaol as "pretty well throng'd." The next month, the same paper described the sight of "Above 100 Convicts" being taken from Newgate to Blackfriars for transportation. Defoe's *Daily Post* was equally full of the news of crime; its 24 October 1719 issue reported another large number of Newgate convicts taken to a ship for transportation, and nearly every paper listed housebreakings, muggings, and highway robberies. The activities of pirates and privateers claimed almost as much space. The *Daily Post* often mentioned as many as seven taken in a single river, and the *White-Hall Evening Post* covered the trials of the most noted pirates, including Stede Bonnet. On the day it reported that Bonnet had received a temporary reprieve, the paper announced that thirty-six other pirates were to be executed in South Carolina. *Applebee's Journal* specialized in the lives and trials of pirates and felons.[22]

Crime had increased and increased in frightening ways. "So many . . . robberies happen daily that 'tis almost incredible," one contemporary journalist remarked. A modern historian has concluded that "some areas were virtually 'lawless zones.'"[23] The troubled economy drove some to theft, but urbanization and the return of military men gave a new character to crime in England. Many of Defoe's contemporaries blamed the increase in crime on the return of these men, many of whom were on half pay or less and unable to find jobs. An eighteenth-century ballad has seamen sing: "I have no trade. . . . I will take to the road . . . And every one that comes by, I'll cry, 'Damn you, deliver your purse.'"[24] These men were accustomed to violence, comfortable with swords and guns, and unafraid of civilians. Some of them joined together in gangs or became pirates, but people believed that, even when they acted alone, they added to the number of personal injuries inflicted during robberies.

The movement of the population into the cities as the rural economy faltered meant that waves of unskilled, naive men and women became the victims and then the perpetrators of yet more crime. In Defoe's youth almost every person in a parish or even a ward had been known by everyone else. Now the criminal could fade into the amorphous crowd. A man or woman could be assaulted and robbed in daylight on a London street and the thief never identified. Strangers moving through the crowded streets attracted no attention.

With the growing concern about crime came greater interest in criminals. The weekly journals increased the number of items and joined the sessions papers, broadsides, pamphlet lives, *The Ordinary of Newgate, His Account,* the *Old Bailey Sessions Papers,* and collections such as Alexander Smith's *A Compleat History of the Lives and Robberies of the Most Notorious Highway-Men, Footpads, Shop-Lifts, and Cheats of Both Sexes.* Always alert to what his contemporaries were interested in and eager to analyze, explain, and point out the implications of social change, Defoe began to publish extensively on crime and criminals. Still convinced that novelty drew the most readers, Defoe found it in three intriguing groups of criminals: pirates, gangs, and women.

At first most of his serious attention went to pirates, for they discouraged trade and colonization. Pirates were on everyone's mind. In 1718 Captain Woodes Rogers had defeated a huge pirate colony in the Bahamas, and in the aftermath some 2,000 surrendered and received royal pardons. The center of pirate operations became Madagascar, and by 1721 the English had dispatched navy squadrons to protect East India Company ships. Reports of the capture and subsequent trials of pirates appeared almost daily in the papers. Defoe's *Colonel Jack* records the booty taken by a French privateer and comments in the words of many of his creator's contemporaries, "This was a Terrible Loss among the *English* Merchants." The State Papers include numerous petitons from merchants, shipmasters, traders, and planters for protection.[25] In September 1717 Secretary of State Addison responded to a report on West Indies trade made by the Lord Commissioners of Trade and Plantations, "His Majesty [was] sensible that the British Trade in those parts is thereby in great danger." In December 1718 a royal proclamation set rewards for the discovery and capture of the pirates.[26]

Defoe's first book about a pirate, *The King of Pirates*, was in the form of two fictional letters allegedly written by Captain John Avery, the most glamorous pirate of his time. Stories about Avery's marriage to a beautiful, wealthy Muslim lady whom he had captured and about his "castle" on St. Mary's made him one of the few romantic pirate heroes. He was even the subject of ballads and a play,[27] and Defoe's book shows familiarity with these works and some of the best stories, many of them true, about him. For instance, according to an East India Company petition of 1696, Avery left a "declaration" for the company that began, "To all English Commanders, let this satisfie. . . . I have never as yet wronged any English or Dutch, nor ever intend whilst I am Commander." He continued with directions for a signal English ships could use to identify themselves to him. In Defoe's book Avery does not attack English ships except during the time he serves under "Captain Redhand," a time he calls "in the service of the devil" and "at war with all mankind." Again the accounts of Avery's capture of the Great Mogul's ships and women conform to the testimony of contemporaries.[28]

The King of Pirates sold well enough for a second 1720 edition, and the title page of *Captain Singleton* aims at the same readership as well as at the average buyer of travel books:

The Life, Adventures, and Pyracies of the Famous Captain Singleton: Containing an Account of his being set on Shore in the Island of *Madagascar*, his Settlement there, with a Description of the Place and Inhabitants: Of his Passage from thence . . . to the main Land of *Africa*, with an Account of the Customs and Manners of the People . . . As also Captain *Singleton*'s Return to Sea, with an Account of his many Adventures and Pyracies with the famous Captain *Avery* and others.

Singleton, who demonstrates the temper and "inclination" of a pirate from his youth, describes his reaction to the beginning of his career as finding himself "in [his] Element." "[I] never undertook any Thing in my Life with more particular Satisfaction," he says (170–71). Singleton, like the Avery of one of the ballads, has found England a "false-hearted nation" and disowns the land of his birth and the cheats he met there. In spite of his enthusiasm for the career of a pirate, his life and those of Defoe's other pirates seem empty and fit Defoe's description of the state of nature. Desperate, fearful, insecure, unhappy, and existing in a perpetual state of anxiety, pirates had no reason to expect anything but a short, brutish life. Their lack of long-term relationships and their crimes drove them to keep quiet about their pasts and made a lonely, even solitary, existence the only one open to them.[29] The eighteenth-century novel is full of characters telling each other their "whole life stories"; even Crusoe does it before he leaves the island. In contrast, fictional pirates evade, lie, and say, as Singleton does, "'tis Time to . . . say no more . . . lest some should be willing to inquire too nicely after . . . Captain Bob" (335).

In the *Commentator* and *A Plan for the English Commerce* Defoe had argued that the destruction of the pirates on the coasts of Africa would be a worthy work for a great, far-sighted king like George I; he envisioned the European nations joining together to make the sea safe and open to merchants of every nation. The War of the Quadruple Alliance, in which France and England fought Spain, meant that privateers were again licensed in large numbers and joined the hoard of pirates in the sea lanes.[30] Moreover, some of the Madagascan pirates were negotiating with Sweden to become its privateers. Not only would they be joining an enemy of George I's Hanover, but they had Jacobite sympathies.[31] At a time when England knew of Sweden's and Russia's contacts with the Pretender and was at war with Spain, this specter of an additional group of experienced enemies on the sea alarmed the ministry and informed citizens like Defoe.

In contrast to the opinions he expressed in his nonfiction, Defoe gives a more complex and sympathetic portrayal of pirates in the novels. Crusoe is in danger of being mistaken for a pirate simply because of the ship he has bought (3:121). John Avery cannot figure out a way to give up his life as a pirate without risking arrest. Singleton has nowhere to go. The pirates threaten to take Moll's husband on her first voyage to Virginia but leave him when she pleads. Descriptions of sailing "up and down," chasing ships, and deciding more on whim than anything else to try another part of the world alternate with brief and often bloody fights and lists of prizes that give the men wealth they seem unable to enjoy. Singleton says his Wealth is "all like Dirt under my Feet . . . no great Concern about me for the leaving of it" even before he comes to think of it as "the Devil's Goods," the reason he could expect "to be hanged . . . here, and damned for hereafter." It is significant that this fictional extension of a pirates' life is a good story partly because of the interpolated tales (the hollow tree siege, the section from Knox's *Ceylon*) but primarily because of William, the witty, resourceful Quaker who becomes Singleton's friend. For better or worse, William lightens the tone and distracts the reader from the pirates' cruelty and destructiveness so much that even the multiple, violent deaths of men who sail with

Singleton and Singleton's suicidal despair and paranoid retirement in England make little impression.

~~~

"Land pirates," highwaymen and gangs, became Defoe's next subject. Particularly frightening because they outnumbered their prey and often encouraged each other in reckless and violent acts, the gangs seemed alarmingly numerous around 1720. One Englishman spoke for many when he said that they threatened "life and safety, as well as property: and . . . render the condition of society wretched, by a sense of personal insecurity."[32] Among the most famous gangs operating around the time that Defoe was completing *Captain Singleton* were the Hawkins, Lemon, Spiggott, Field, Shaw, and Carrick gangs. Carrick was said to have fifteen members in his group and to have loose alliances with four other gangs.[33] By 1720 the gangs threatened inland trade as the pirates did foreign.

Defoe had already described William Spiggot's refusal to plead in an *Applebee's* essay and had occasionally reported on gang activities and arrests. He surely knew some of the victims, including the Scot Sir David Dalrymple, who was robbed by the Hawkins gang in 1720. The trials of some of the gang leaders and members in the early 1720s and the publication of books like *A Compleat and True Account of All the Robberies Committed by James Carrick, John Malhonie, and Their Accomplices* and Ralph Wilson's *A Full and Impartial Account of All the Robberies Committed by John Hawkins, George Sympson . . . and Their Companions* (both 1722) made the inside operation of gangs common knowledge. Moll Flanders had felt uncomfortable with gangs and could not even operate with an accomplice, but Colonel Jack commits a robbery with a gang. In the latter novel the gang is presented as a loose association of men who split an evening's take with those who participate. Brought into the gang by Will, the person who taught him to pick pockets, Jack follows them on a typical evening: first they will be footpads, then housebreakers. One of the gang has become a servant in the household in order to let his cronies in. Jack's evening, however, persuades him that he does not want to be part of the gang, for he robs a poor old woman and a maidservant whom he cannot get off his conscience and learns what a murderous crew of men the gang would be had the disguised member not become drunk and been unable to let them into the house.

This part of the novel shows how homeless boys become "a Gang of naked, ragged Rogues" and progress to adult gangs. In 1718 Henry Newman was making a second effort to set up a charity school for the "blackguard boys," the common term for them and one Defoe uses in the novel. Newman had noted that many of them were the children of military men, as Jack probably is, and "are strictly of no parish" and, therefore, not eligible for parish charity. The nation, he believed, should take care of the children left because their "parents have been knocked in the head in the service" of their sovereign.[34] Other prominent people deplored the way "the distressed children called the Blackguard" "are vagrants and exposed to a multitude of temptations."[35] They learned as children to beg and steal and, as *Colonel Jack* shows, encouraged each other. As a former member of the Society for the Reformation of Manners and an interested observer of the S.P.C.K., Defoe was undoubtedly aware of Newman's efforts.

This section of *Colonel Jack* exploits the preconceptions and fears people of Defoe's time had of the gangs. Their random crimes and their willingness to commit violence, their youth and lack of principles, and the number of men in the population like them made them especially frightening. Will's gang includes three members who take positions in the houses of wealthy people in order to let their cohorts in to rob the family. Defoe shows them overpowering and threatening their victims in groups numbering between four and thirteen. When caught, they "peach on"—inform against—each other in order to save their own lives. Defoe captures their empty lives, too. Will seems a little better than most of the gang members, for he does not implicate Jack and warns him that his brother is about to be arrested as a member of the gang. Yet another of Defoe's brave, resolute, evil characters named Will, he is last seen in Newgate loaded with chains and headed for the gallows. Without prospects, hope, or morals, the blackguard boys have nothing to discourage them from leading such lives.

Women criminals always fascinated people, and in 1720 they were appearing in court more frequently than ever before. Without good employment opportunities and displaced from jobs by the returning military men and by the depressed state of the woolen trade, women turned to prostitution and robbery to support themselves. Social change hit women hard. Bad times had sent men to sea and to the colonies; the natural dangers of ocean travel and the wars had contributed to the imbalance of numbers of men and of women, and spinsters, widows, and deserted wives found their fathers and brothers unable to maintain them. With the end of the self-supporting family and the cottage industry, they could contribute little or nothing to the family.

In the seventeenth century communities tended to handle female offenders privately, but the urban courts had begun to see sizeable numbers of them. In rural Surrey, for instance, only 19 percent of the women arrested for property crimes were actually prosecuted, whereas 81 percent were in London. In the city, women were more likely to be on their own, subject to economic hardship, and with the opportunity to commit crimes.³⁶ The village woman would have been deterred from risking apprehension as a shoplifter by the fact that the shop-keeper would know her, that she would probably be handed over to her disgraced family, and that she would be shamed in front of her neighbors and family.

Although scarcely new, even petty female thieves were more intriguing than ordinary male footpads, and some of them received as much attention from the press as notorious male murderers. More unusual criminals like Moll King, Sally Salisbury, and Betsy Careless captured London's imagination, and convicted females on the scaffold and the carts headed for ships to the colonies were familiar sights. Moll Flanders, of course, resembles the common thieves, but Roxana comes closer to Moll King and Sally, both famous whores whose houses entertained men like the duke of Richmond and the earl of Mansfield. How close Defoe's novels could be to popular ephemera can be seen by comparing the plot of *Moll Flanders* to the title of an eight-page criminal life:

An Account of the Birth and Education, Life and Conversation of Mary Raby; Who was Executed at *Tyburn* on *Wednesday* the 3d of November 1703 . . . Particularly the manner of her several pretended Marriages . . . her many *Cheats, Robberies, Shop-liftings, Clipping, Coyning, Receiving Stolen goods*, and other strange and astonishing Actions of her Life.

In fact, Mary Raby had some of Moll's airs—she was twice "burnt in the hand for acting Quality in Disguise." One of her best-known escapades was stealing a set of pearls, and, like Moll, she confessed in Newgate and admitted to loving an Irish husband.

By the time Defoe wrote *Roxana*, Sally Salisbury's story was as familiar and romanticized as Captain Avery's. The daughter of a bricklayer, Sally was one of the first English courtesans from the ranks of the poor. Her story and Roxana's have several striking similarities. Sally rejected "a rich Dutch Merchant," just as Roxana does, and, as a member of Mother Whyburn's brothel, Sally had affairs with Lord Bentinck, by then "ageing and wither'd," Viscount Bolingbroke, and a number of other noblemen. Roxana alludes to the courtiers who came to her entertainments and to a "retreat" from which she returned "blown . . . like *a cast-off Mistress*" (1:213). Defoe puts Roxana's house on Pall Mall, where "the 'Misses' of the courtiers, often lodged near Whitehall." Sally claimed to have slept with the Prince of Wales, subsequently George II, and Roxana is intoxicated with the idea that she may have danced with the king. The fact that this mysterious person seems too young to be the king associates him with the Prince of Wales and his rival court. Sally was known for wit, daring, exhibitionism, and a magnetic personality—qualities Roxana also has, especially in her Turkish costume.³⁷ In 1721

PORTRAIT *of the Celebrated* MOLL FLANDERS
Taken from Life in Newgate

The famous Moll Flanders, of beauty the boast,
Belov'd and distinguish'd, long flourish'd the toast,
But beauty is frail and soon comes to decay,
When shift and contrivance must enter in play;
Her arts of intrigue, as this book shall unfold,
Will keep you awake while her story is told.
Pub.d by C. Johnson.

Moll Flanders.

the Act against Prophaneness and Immorality included masquerades and pleasure houses, and *Roxana* illustrates the vices the law was intended to curb.

These criminal novels show the influence of Defoe's observations during the South Sea saga. Avarice in particular fascinated him, and he came to see personality as more addictive than he had earlier in his life. In *The Case of Mr. Law* (1721) he called avarice "an unwearied and impatient Vice" (21–22). At the height of the investment frenzy, he remarked,

AVARICE has a Kind of natural Assurance with it, that steels the Countenance against Blushes, and repels all the Objections rais'd from Modesty, from Reason, from Justice, and even from the Laws of the Land. So true it is, that the Love of Money increases with the Money.

There's a strange Charm in this Sort of Trade of getting Money; they never surfeit of the Quantity, never weary with the Labour.[38]

It is avarice, of course, that takes over Moll and from which she must wean herself. From the time Moll is "more confounded with the money than . . . with the love" of the elder brother to the day she is caught robbing a silk factor, she never tires of money. She insists that poverty makes her what she is and several times resolves "to leave it quite off, if I could but come to lay up money enough to maintain me." She sets amounts of money as targets for retirement but always raises the sum when she reaches her goal. On the day she commits her last robbery, she has over £1,000. She has become so addicted to crime that she takes whatever opportunity puts before her—including a horse that she must abandon at an inn. "Avarice kept me in, till there was no going back; as to arguments which my reason dictated for perswading me to lay down, avarice stept in and said, Go on . . . go on," she says.

Even more extreme is Roxana's case. In one of his *Applebee's* essays Defoe had asked,

What can be said in Favour of that Luxury, which is not content with the Equipage of a Lord; a Coach and Six, a Revenue, with Servants and Establishments in proportion; but that, to have two Coaches and Six, and two Sets of Servants, and two Revenues, &c. would Mortgage Faith and Honour, Character and Principles, and even run the Risk of losing the Estate they had, and starving their Posterity?

He goes on to ask the question that is often central to disputes over the interpretation of *Moll Flanders* and *Roxana*: "Are these Men to be pity'd, or to be punish'd?"[39] Roxana not only builds her fortune by investing shrewdly, she collects plate, jewels, dresses, lovers, and even titles. She and Moll become hardened and lose awareness of the meaning of their actions. In *The Fears of the Pretender Turn'd into the Fears of Debauchery* (1715), one of Defoe's earliest reflections on the effects of social immorality, he wrote, "How easily, and by what insensible Degree they are drawn to a general Defection of Vertue, and to follow a Practice, which in time will be the Ruin . . . of Religion it self." (25–26). Moll Flanders laments that she became "harden'd to a pitch above all the reflections of conscience or modesty." Roxana notes that she has £2,800 coming in yearly from her investments and lives "without the least Signals of Remorse; without any Signs of Repentance; or without so much as a Wish to put an End to it."

~~~

So powerful is this addiction that only some powerful, external force can wean the characters from their ways of life. In *Roxana* that force is Susan's determination to be recognized as Roxana's daughter.[40] In *Moll Flanders* and *Colonel Jack*, Defoe recommends a solution open to the state and to individuals: transportation.

The Transportation Act of 1718 allowed courts to sentence even clergied felons* to transportation to America. On a very limited scale, transportation had been used before the Restoration as an alternative to capital punishment, and by 1700 it had become a fairly common form of conditional pardon. The judge could pronounce it, or the criminal could petition as Moll Flanders did for transportation. A typical text written by a justice of the peace read:

I reprieved them because it did not appear to me that either of them had committed any such offense before, or were ingaged in any society of offenders . . . But they are lewd idle fellows, and it is fitting the country should be clear'd of them. they are strong able body'd men and may do good service either in her Majestys Plantations or army.[41]

The secretary of state would then endorse the pardon upon condition of the prisoner joining the army or accepting transportation. Until 1718 merchants or the prisoners themselves paid their passages to the New World. Because the infirm and female had no market value there, they and the indigent were hanged or simply released.[42] Defoe himself had transported people to Maryland in 1688. He paid £1.7.6 for the transporation of each, and another £1.7.0 for shoes and a coat for them.[43] His expenses were typical. Transportation and board never cost more than £5 or £6 pounds, and Defoe, then a partner for the ship's voyage, was probably paying the actual cost rather than cost plus the profit expected by the captain or shipowner. The trade was profita-

---

* Some lesser felonies (such as damaging trees or poaching) allowed the offender to claim the ancient "benefit of clergy" for the first conviction only. Before the Restoration, *male* criminals read "the neck verse," Psalm 51, and were turned over to a representative of the Church for punishment. By the early eighteenth century, such offenders were simply released, as were women who committed these "clergyable" crimes. Public dissatisfaction grew, and demands for fewer releases led to a decrease in the number of clergyable offenses and then to the provision for the transportation of clergied felons.

Print for a forty-four page book, *The Fortunate Transport*, [1741].

ble; for instance, Defoe made an £8.5s. profit on one of the men he sold. Not all people shipped were convicts; companies and colonies recruited servants, and unemployed people chose to immigrate. Some courts paid up to £8 per person to merchants willing to take women, but so sure were profits from the sale of the prisoners that most required the merchant pay jail fees and even the clerk's charge for drawing up a pardon. Between 1580 and 1650 some 80,000 people went, voluntarily or otherwise, to be servants in the North American colonies; between 1651 and 1700 the figure rose to 90,000. Colonial planters sometimes purchased them by the shipload.[44]

The 1718 act gave merchants contracts granting them £3 for each convict transported. In addition, the merchants could sell the prisoners' services at auction in the colonies where men brought an average of £10, women £8 to £9, and craftsmen as much as £25. By 1722, the year *Moll Flanders* was published, about 60 percent of the convicted male, clergyable felons and 46 percent of the women were transported. In fact, about 70 percent of all the felons convicted at the Old Bailey were deported and only about 7.5 percent executed. Between 1718 and 1775 the courts sent 30,000 convicts to the North American colonies, primarily Maryland and Virginia, Moll's and Jack's destinations. Although the contract holder might protest, prisoners could still arrange their own passage to the colonies.[45] The experience of Moll Flanders is authentically rendered.

Defoe's depiction of her life and Jack's included powerful propaganda for the recent act. Because convicted felons had often been released with a punishment as mild as being branded on the thumb, large numbers of criminals were quickly and repeatedly released. Because there were no satisfactory penalties between branding and whipping at one extreme and hanging at the other and judges and juries often felt the inappropriateness of either, the lighter sentences were imposed.[46] Moll's and Jack's cases were designed to show the appropriateness of transportation. Jack's crimes were just the kind committed by most of the felons sent over, but he had not been caught, tried, and sentenced. In any event, his kidnapping and sale were realistic. The Mansion House Justice Room Charge Book records several instances of men "spirited" "beyond the Sea without Consent," and Virginia seems to have been the most frequent destination (2 December 1701, fol. 130). So frequently were people tricked, made drunk, or forced that a series of laws against kidnapping were passed in England and the colonies. Even the most prominent merchants were occasionally prosecuted; a 1682 diary entry reads, "Two great Merchants are this Term Cast for Kidnapping, you know how many merchants use to buy young people that say they are willing to goe into forraine Plantations."[47] Moll, although an old offender, is tried only once, for theft of goods valued at

£46. To have hanged a person who was technically a first offender for that crime would have seemed cruel indeed.

Defoe presents transportation as both opportunity and the means to break an addictive pattern. Transportation gives Moll and Jack, and other characters in both books, a new chance. Had Moll's husband not been her brother, she might have lived as peaceful and productive a life as her mother had.[48] Jack's experience perhaps reflects Defoe's opinion that the colonies offered men greater opportunities and benefits. Sold like any other transported person, Jack can count on "the custom of the country." The captain tells him that this phrase means he will be given land, and his master does provide 300 acres and £40 or £50. In fact, Defoe is exaggerating the benefits of transportation. The custom of the country was an increasingly formal body of legislature governing the lives of "white servants." These laws specified the terms of those arriving without indentures or convictions, assured their masters' legal right, for instance, to sell them and forbid marriage, and gave them some rights, such as the capacity to sue. At the time Jack was a servant, the grant at the end of service was only fifty shillings and ten bushels of corn, no land at all. Indentured servants could, however, learn trades, and some, like Jack, extended their terms with their masters in order to learn more.[49]

In order to illustrate how ordinary Jack is, when a group of felons arrives at the plantation where he works, at least one has had a career almost exactly like his own. The master's speech about the mercy of the change in their sentences, the opportunity they now have, and the custom of helping them start their own farms after serving their terms touches Jack deeply and rehearses the purpose and benefits of England's policy. Defoe repeatedly refers to the men as having the chance to "begin the World again" and promises that "no Diligent Man" can fail to prosper. As Jack says, "A Transported Felon, is . . . a much happier Man, than the most prosperous untaken Thief in the Nation."

Defoe is careful to show the colonies in a favorable light, and he is informed enough to set his novels in the colonies where land was most easily obtained. Although without amenities, the characters live almost as they might in England. Defoe includes no threatening Indians and gives no sense of the wilderness or, compared to England, the extremes of climate. In *A Plan of the English Commerce* (1728) Defoe describes the North American colonies as "wild," "barren," and "inhospitable" and the Indians as fierce, treacherous, "bloody and merciless" (228–29). *Atlas Maritimus* adds that the Indians are "gigantick," carry seven- to eight-foot-long bows, and resist all overtures (294). Although Maryland and Virginia planters routinely allowed a three-hour midday break in summer and thousands died of the heat anyway,[50] Jack never mentions the heat and humidity of the Virginia summer or the damp cold of winter. With his background he might not be expected to complain of the diet or the limited selection of consumer goods, but Moll has learned to appreciate fine clothes. It is notable that half of Defoe's first six novels show their characters' prosperity based upon New World plantations.

The integration of discussions of transportation illustrate one of the ways Defoe's political writing had changed. He had used *A Journal of the Plague Year* and *Due Preparations* to support and comment upon Walpole's Quarantine Act in a similar way. Woven into the narrative, the clauses of the Quarantine Act are worked out in H.F.'s observations. Defoe obviously approves of quarantining ships, of the attempts to stop smuggling, and of the setting up of adequate numbers of lazarets to which infected people were required to go. The act also allowed watchmen to use "any kind of Violence that the Case shall require" against infected or exposed people who left the places of their quarantine. Entire parishes and towns could be quarantined, and the same force used to compel citizens to remain inside the lines. Anyone who eluded the watchmen would be "adjudged guilty of Felony, and suffer Death." Moreover, the crime was not clergyable. Defoe had reported on the slaughter at Toulon, where 315 people attempting to leave the infected city had been shot. He described them as "made desperate by their Diseases, and quite raging by their Hunger."[51] Defoe's two books reflect the impression this event had made on him, and he proposed evacuating as many people from an infected place as possible, even if public funds had to be used. Both explicitly and by narrative examples, he offers modifications of the act's clauses. For instance, he offers plans for the supply of food and other necessities and emphasizes the impracticality and undesirability of shutting healthy people up for excessive amounts of time. Although City merchants had begun a determined resistance to some of the clauses affecting trade, Defoe treats these issues as independently as he does the ministry's proposals.[52] Above all, he lays out plans for a steady supply of food. Citizens who followed his advice could live safely and legally, and magistrates could learn from the details of his carefully worked out examples. In praising the lord mayor and aldermen for going among the people and using public money for charity in 1665, he offers a plan for the 1722 City officials to follow.

After *Colonel Jack*, *Moll Flanders*, and *Roxana* came the lives of some of the most famous criminals of the 1720s, including those of John Sheppard and Jonathan Wild, and a series of pamphlets proposing ways to control street crime. Sheppard achieved his greatest fame by escaping repeatedly from prisons, and Defoe's *History of the Remarkable Life of Sheppard* and *A Narrative of all the Robberies, Escapes, &c. of John Sheppard* (both 1724) portray Sheppard as a clever jester who exchanges jokes with those who come to gawk at him and tells his own story. "[I] made the door my humble servant," he says, describing how he broke a lock.[53] Sheppard was rather easily captured, however, and, like most of the subjects of eighteenth-century criminal lives, went to the gallows penitent.

Jonathan Wild was another kind of subject. He had come to the public's attention first as the proprietor of his "Office for the Recovery of Lost and Stolen Property" and then as the thief-taker chiefly responsible for the destruction of London's four largest gangs. Two years later, Wild was exposed as the monstrous lord of criminals who directed them, received their plunder, and sold it back to their victims. He decided whether his followers would live or die by turning some over to the authorities and providing witnesses against them. Moreover, he recruited thieves, hired specialists for big robberies, divided the city into districts and deployed gangs to each, and made enormous profits.[54] Convicted in May of 1725, Wild went to the gallows disheveled and stupefied from the effects of laudanum taken in an unsuccessful suicide attempt.

Defoe called him a "wretched subject," but he saw Wild's deceptive art for what it was more clearly than any of his other biographers. Defoe judged Wild's "game" more difficult than those of Machiavelli or "the greatest Statesmen, who have been at the heads of Governments," for "he was to blind the Eyes of the World, to find out Tricks to evade the Penalties of the Law; and on the other Side, to govern a Body of People who were Enemies to all Government; and to bring those under Obedience to him, who, at the Hazard of their Lives, acted in Disobedience to the Laws of the Land."[55] Defoe saw that Wild's roles had been more contradictory than his own during the elections of 1704 and 1705, in Scotland, or even with Mist. Here was a criminal who had been "all things to all people," one "without Learning or Education," whose life was a wonder. Defoe repeatedly used the metaphor of steering between dangers to describe Wild's double role: "he steered among rocks and dangerous shoals, so he was a bold pilot . . . no man ever did the like before him, and I dare say no man will attempt to do the like after him."[56]

In fact, Wild's criminal activities were strikingly similar to those of Mother Midnight in *Moll Flanders*. Both of them recruited and trained thieves, encouraged them to continue, received stolen goods, and brokered them back to their original owners. Mother Midnight allows some of her associates to hang and makes serious efforts to save others, as she does Moll. The way Will and Jack scheme to return stolen goods they cannot use for profit also resembles Wild's technique. Rather than suggesting that Defoe was on to Wild two years before anyone else, the similarity to incidents in his novels shows that Wild had improved existing criminal practices. In fact, one of the satiric targets of Defoe's *Reformation of Manners* (1702), Sir Salathiel Lovell, had practiced Wild's game of hanging one thief in order to protect another who happened to be in his employment.[57]

In Wild, Defoe saw the validation of many of his considered opinions about crime. Wild had learned his trade as an imprisoned debtor and could say with Moll's mother that prison made thieves. Defoe concluded bluntly, "Jonathan's avarice hanged him" (16:263). Defoe always relished a good trick, and some of Wild's crimes, particularly his early ones when he used his double hip joint, delighted him. Perhaps he also saw an aspect of his own personality in Wild. The thief-taker's mistake, Defoe said, was "in his gay Hours, when his Heart was open, he took Pleasure in recounting his past Rogueries." Had Wild been able to keep his own counsel, he might never have been caught. The clause, "when his Heart was open," recalled the moment of healing in *Moll Flanders* when the minister "broke into [her] very soul." The desire to confide and be known that warred so often with the need to disguise, deceive, and hide appeared as a key to interpret Wild's life story and underscored the rather poignant longing, combined with deep suspicion and fear, found in Defoe and in his major characters. Crusoe hid himself and spoke as governor, armed himself and stared ferociously, and felt himself both king and captive; Moll Flanders had more disguises than could be counted and told her story even more sparingly than she shared her money. Defoe wanted to be recognized but felt the consequences to be unpredictable and condemnation as likely as appreciation.

Defoe wrote to be useful, and exposition was his most natural voice. Whenever he dealt with things he cared about, he attempted to reach readers with a variety of genres and personae, but he always included straightforward essays. He genuinely believed that all "Members of the Community" were struggling with street violence, and he wrote several pamphlets proposing ways to control crime. Using one of his most characteristic metaphors, he summarized his habitual method as well as it can be done: "The first reasonable Step towards the Cure of a distemper'd Body, is to find out the Nature and Original of the Disorder; whence it proceeds, and what Progress it has made in its Attacks upon the Health of the Patient." In *Some Considerations upon Street-Walkers* [1726],[58] *Second Thoughts Are Best: Or, a Further Improvement of a Late Scheme to Prevent Street Robberies, Street Robberies Consider'd, Augusta Triumphans* [all 1728], and *An Effectual Scheme for the Immediate Preventing of Street Robberies* (1731), Defoe made the inquiries into causes and described kinds of crimes just as his method outlined and then proposed cures.

As much as he deplored the fact that "the streets swarmed with rogues" and that "the Armies of Hell" possessed the streets after 10 P.M.,[59] he never loses sight of the part poverty and lack of a trade played in making criminals. His suggestions are as characteristic of him as these pamphlets: they begin with bedrock practicality and become elaborate baroque creations. For example, he begins by suggesting better lighting for the streets; younger watchmen, for now they have "one Foot in the Grave, and t'other ready to follow"; and robbers prosecuted at the public's, not the witnesses', charge. Soon, however, he wants the city divided into tiny squares with an impossible number of watchmen and a national reformation of manners. Ridiculous as a few of his individual suggestions are, his pamphlets are full of shrewd observations, common sense, and unmistakable public spirit. His "chequer-work" life had left intact the spirit of the young man who wrote *An Essay upon Projects* for the benefit of his country, and, in his sixty-eighth year, Defoe subtitled *Augusta Triumphans* "The Way to Make London the Most Flourishing City in the Universe."

Colonel Jack required three editions by 1724; *Moll Flanders* also had three and was serialized in the *London Post* between 14 May 1722 and 20 March 1723. In 1724 *A Narrative of All the Robberies . . . of Sheppard* went through eight editions and *The History of the . . . Life of Sheppard* three, and *The Life of Wild* had two in 1725. Before he died Defoe had come to compete with the Newgate Ordinary as the most productive and popular crime writer and to write the "effectual schemes" for the reduction of street robberies that helped establish the reputation his obituaries would celebrate.

CHAPTER 19

CHANGES AND DISASTERS

Human Affairs are all Subject to Changes and Disasters.
　　　—DEFOE, *Robinson Crusoe* (1719)

All the Sorrows and Anxieties of Men's Lives . . . rise from their
Restless pushing at getting of Money, and the restless Cares of
keeping it when they have got it.
　　　—DEFOE, *Colonel Jack* (1722)

In 1725 Defoe had surgery for the bladder stones that had troubled him for years; he describes the operation as follows:

Here's a Man . . . torn and mangled by the merciless Surgeons, cut open alive, and bound Hand and Foot to force him to bear it; the very Apparatus is enough to chill the Blood, and sink a Man's Soul within him. What does he suffer less than he that is broken alive upon the Wheel?[1]

At that time surgeons performed the operation fairly frequently but advised,

If the Severity of the Disease therefore brings the Patient to a Resolution to undergo the Operation it should be a matter of the last Importance with a prudent Surgeon, to be previously satisfied with regard to the Probability of his success. . . . For notwithstanding we at present possess many Advantages over our Ancestors in this Operation . . . the operation of Lithotomy is still very dangerous.[2]

Anyone in the eighteenth century faced surgery of any kind with horror. Anesthetics, of course, did not exist, and the excruciating pain of the operation often led to months of infection and putrefaction and an agonizing death. Lithotomies, like any surgery on the excretory system, added embarrassment to the other pains of an operation. Since lithotomies were common, hospitals had special tables on which the reclining patient was bound and held. Defoe would be strapped to the board at his back and his wrists tied to his ankles; the "three or four strong and courageous Attendants" "generally necessary" "to secure the Patient firmly in the proper posture" would hold him down and keep his bent legs apart. The surgeon would insert a long, silver catheter through the opening in the penis so that he could locate the uretha

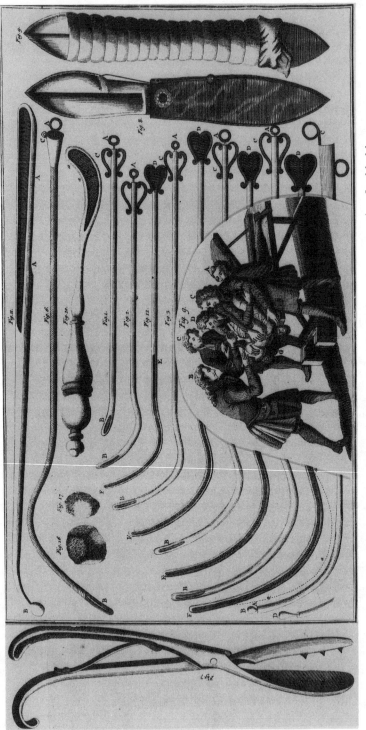

Surgical instruments and drawing of procedure for eighteenth-century operation for bladder stones.

and bladder easily. He then would make a small incision from behind the scrotum toward the anus, cut open the uretha there, and insert a probe, a catheter, and then forceps to remove the stone. In some cases a scoop or even special forceps with teeth to crush large stones had to be used. Throughout the operation, the surgeon pressed the stones forward with fingers inserted in the rectum.

Healing time, if healing took place without infection, was three to five weeks. Such surgery left the patient humiliated and sore, and, at age sixty-five, Defoe was feeling vulnerable and angry. The *Applebee's* essay in which he described the operation went on to reflect that hanging was an easier way to die than "the Tortures of the Stone, the Strangury, the Cholick," and other "terrible Distempers" (3:431). For the first time, some of Defoe's criminal lives included scenes of explicit torture.[3] His pamphlets on reducing street crimes showed a new awareness of age. *An Effectual Scheme for the Immediate Preventing of Street Robberies,* for instance, noted that some people, "especially if they are in Years," "seldom fully recover" from the blow street robbers often used to knock their victims down (29). Other works, like *The Protestant Monastery* (1726), particularly addressed the problems of older people. Defoe described how they were a "standing jest" and mistreated by their children. Calling himself "an over officious *Old Man,*" he proposed a group home in which the elderly would share expenses and find dignity and independence. *Chickens Feed Capons* (1730) reprinted the part of *The Protestant Monastery* about the elderly man who was starved, shut away, neglected, and consistently insulted by his daughter, and *Conjugal Lewdness* (1727) mentioned the need for wifely tact and indulgence should the husband experience occasional "Weakness and Impotence."

Until *Roxana,* there had been an optimism in all Defoe wrote. He explains a problem and proposes a way to prosper; Crusoe, Singleton, Jack, and Moll find God; the City of London endures the plague and the fire, and *A Journal of the Plague Year* ends with a vision of the City grown greater. The novels have comic touches and happy endings, the characters energy, ingenuity, and resilience. Jack yearns for human warmth and a normal life. Moll Flanders rises from each catastrophe with a new name and a few coins in her pocket. She can be nearly as witty as Quaker William,[4] and the conclusion is the happiest in all of Defoe's novels. A prosperous Moll has Jemy, the husband whom she enjoyed and loved most, and even recovers one of her children to complete a family portrait. Her repentance has been a thing of joy.[5] Like the rock that poured clear, refreshing water when struck, Moll has told her story to the minister who "broke into my very soul" by his honest, friendly manner. She and Jemy find salvation in the blessings that seem to pour on them. When she receives the unexpected reprieve, Moll describes herself as feeling the deepest "Impressions upon my Mind . . . of the Mercy of God . . . and a greater Detestation of my Sins, from a Sense of that goodness" than at any other time (2:117). Later Jemy exclaims, "What is God a doing! . . . for such an ungrateful dog as I am!" Their escape from the gallows, their comfortable trip to the colonies together, and their growing prosperity seem almost miraculous, and they bask in the life they can finally lead. The wife that Moll wanted to be with the older brother, was briefly with her own brother, and tried to be with the banker is realized with the man of her heart's choice. Moll insists from preface to conclusion that she is a sincere penitent, and Jemy comments, "So is Heaven's Goodness sure to Work the same Effects in all sensible Minds, where Mercies touch the Heart" (2:171). Crusoe compares himself to Job, and Moll Flanders, now a picture of family harmony and social forgiveness, can also end her story by observing that "the latter End . . . was better than the Beginning."

The same could not be said of Defoe's life. "Ruin and wild destruction sport around him, and exercise all their fury on all he has to do with," one of his sons-in-law remarked.[6] Certainly that was true in his business affairs and perhaps in his family life. No better analysis of Defoe's troubles exists than the words he gave Robinson Crusoe to describe the cause of his misfortunes: they were owing to his "not being satisfy'd with the Station wherein God and Nature ha[d] plac'd [him]." Several times, Crusoe describes how his "Head began to be full of Projects and Undertakings . . . such as are indeed the Ruine of the best Heads in Business." Crusoe laments his "unlucky Head, that was always to let me know it was born to make my Body miserable; was . . . fill'd with Projects and Designs." These words accurately describe the cause of Defoe's 1691 bankruptcy and even his too-clever maneuver with the *Flying Post* that led to his 1713 arrest. The "wisdom," then, of fifty-nine years appeared in these direct, didactic statements, but by 1724 Defoe was destined to repeat some of the mistakes of his youth.

With his plans for the Colchester land and in his trading ventures, Defoe tried to expand and diversify too quickly. He could have made a profit on the rents alone, but he began to remove tenants and start too many projects. The land around Earl's Colne was suitable for brick and tile making, but setting up a factory was expensive. The nearby heath would allow Defoe to make the more profitable place bricks he preferred,* but it would be several years before he could hope to see a profit. To begin stocking a farm and developing a trade in a number of commodities stretched his resources beyond common sense, and,

* Because place bricks were dried in rows on the ground instead of in straw-covered hacks, workmen received 1 shilling less per 1,000 for making them, and materials were cheaper.

above all, Defoe was an elderly man living in Stoke Newington. No matter how good John Ward's intentions were, he lacked the experience and the manpower to bring Defoe's dreams to reality. Confused, out of capital, and unable to make the farm pay for itself, Ward gave up and returned to Warwickshire in October 1725. When Defoe's rent collector, Henry Bevan, died, Defoe was so out of touch with the property that he was surprised to learn that a lawyer whom he had never met had been collecting the rent for at least three years. Eventually, he would have to file suit against this lawyer to get his records.[7]

Many of the things Defoe traded were likely to get him in exactly the same trouble he had been in thirty-five years before. He was again subject to the frailties, problems, and dishonesties of suppliers, transporters, collectors, and debtors. Lacking mobility and declining in energy, he was less able than before to oversee and control any kind of wholesale trade. In no Chancery case had he ever been able to produce good records, and he was to suffer severely again for this negligence.

Major changes at home complicated Defoe's life. In 1725 Mary's brother Samuel Tuffley died and left her financially independent. She inherited property in London, Essex, and perhaps Surrey, and the estate left her was valued at £5,000 to £6,000. Her will mentions three houses in White Cross Alley and a farm in Dagenham, Essex, and lists other "lands, goods, chattels."[8] Since Samuel Tuffley was a resident of Croyden, Surrey, at the time of his death and owned property in Nutfield and Bletchingly, it is possible that Mary had inherited and kept property there too.[9] The penal bond required of trustees shows that she received about £1,500 in addition. Optimistically, Defoe wrote John Ward to tell him that the death of a relative gave him "a considerable estate," and they signed another agreement. Defoe's share of the rent, stock, and building of the brick works would be subtracted from Ward's rent; in other words, Ward would pay no rent until the arrears from Defoe had been covered. Defoe never paid anything, however, and Ward left for good at the end of 1726 or the beginning of 1727.

Tuffley had been careful to leave the money to Mary alone. His will stipulated that his estate would be managed in trust by John Pettit, the elder, John Pettit, junior, and Henry Langley, Maria's husband, and was to be "free and independent" of Daniel and of any claim or demand that might be made by him or anyone else. Mary had the power to sell, dispose of, or transfer the property and would receive faithful accounts and all the profits and rents from the trustees. Tuffley went on to specify that, should Defoe die, she would enter the whole estate in her own right as if the trust had never been appointed. Suddenly Mary was not only independent but well off; she could provide for some of the children's futures as well or better than Daniel. Mary seems to have kept her inheritance separate. Defoe appears to have had no money to send Ward, did not redeem the £200 mortgage, and, in fact, began to have additional financial problems.

John Ward took out a commission of bankruptcy to protect himself from his creditors and threatened an action in the Court of Common Pleas against Defoe to recover money he said Defoe owed him. Defoe began a suit in Chancery. Ward claimed that Defoe had not only failed to pay his share of the costs of stocking the farm and building the brickworks but had actually cultivated another part of the Colchester land with the stock that had been purchased jointly for Ward's farm. He concluded that Defoe owed him £253.1.11, run up over a year and a half in £3 to £4 amounts. For instance, Defoe had not paid him for bacon and cheese, for oyster barrels, and for two mares.

Defoe insisted that he had rented the land to Ward at Ward's initiative and, again at Ward's request, provided "cattle, horses, sheep, waggons, a cart and the servants necessary for cultivating" the land. Even though Defoe reduced the rent from £100 to £60, Ward had never paid any rent at all and owed Defoe £256 for the stock and £196 for materials and workmen. He noted small sums of money Ward had allegedly borrowed from his son and other family members and asked for a total of £747.7.11.[10]

Ward replied in outrage that Defoe had encouraged him to rent the land, repeated the tale of the projected partnership, and complained of promises broken. His story has credibility because of the pattern of Defoe's business conduct and because of Defoe's age and infirmity. Additionally persuasive is the fact that Ward's account rings with the words and phrases of the novels. For instance, Ward quotes Defoe as saying that he "had Something to Communicate that would be of great Advantage to him." The older brother asks Moll how she can refuse a marriage "apparently so much to your Advantage." Moll sees that she could marry "very much to my Advantage" in Virginia, and later she stays in Bath hoping something "for my Advantage will come up." Ward says that Defoe told him that he felt "a great kindness for" him. Both Moll and Jack describe times when people have expressed or shown unusual "kindness" toward them. For instance, Moll finds it in her husband-brother, the banker, Jemy, and Mother Midnight. The younger brother tells her "that the Kindness he had" for her has been noticed by the family. Jack remarks of the planter, "I had too much Knowledge of the Honesty of his Principles, as well as of the Kindness he had for me; to doubt his being as good as his Word."

Defoe had always been especially hard on people who risked their children's or their wards' security. He had consistently deplored this irresponsibility during the South Sea frenzy and had agonized over his own bankruptcy in these terms. The Colchester land was Hannah's.

Now he had lost a tenant, the manager of one of his farms and of the brick works under construction. He was already in arrears to the Corporation of Colchester for his rent.[11] He was in the position of losing an investment that had seemed utterly secure in 1722.

In addition to whatever abashment he felt because of the optimistic, unfulfilled promises he had made Ward based on the inheritance was embarrassment caused by two of his children. Benjamin had left the Temple and embarked on a career as a journalist and hack writer. In August 1721 one of his essays in the *London Journal* was declared seditious, and he was sent to Newgate on 14 August 1721. He was released on bail the next day,[12] but the fact remained that a child of Defoe's had been in Newgate, the place he would describe in *Moll Flanders* only a year later as "that horrid place! my very blood chills at the mention of its name. . . . the hellish noise, the roaring, swearing and clamour, the stench and nastiness . . . an emblem of hell itself."

Benjamin's publication not only worried but angered Defoe. Benjamin had written the introduction to excerpts from the testimony of some of the South Sea Company directors before the Committee of Secrecy, and he confessed to the offending words. Among them were "Here we find the Source of all our Misery and Woe; here we see who have been Traytors, Harpies, and Parricides . . . to whom we owe the National Calamities we labour under" (12 August 1721). What followed revealed that pages from the South Sea account books were missing; that there were erasures, alterations, blanks and fictitious entries, and that the directors had sold stock that did not exist. Under interrogation Benjamin claimed sole credit for composing the essay and named "Mr. Gordon" as the man who had set him to work. Gordon's desire, he said, was to discredit "some great Men" and to incite the people to petition for a new Parliament. Thomas Gordon was an experienced journalist who had joined with John Trenchard and Lord Molesworth in a sustained campaign against Robert Walpole in the pages of the *London Journal*; this campaign would be taken over by Bolingbroke in the *Craftsman*.[13] At that time, the *London Journal* was beginning to outsell Mist's *Weekly Journal* and was the most influential and troublesome of all the opposition papers.

The earl of Sunderland, whose interest Gordon served, wanted to force early elections in the hope of gaining control of Parliament. Walpole wanted to put off the elections required by the Septennial Act as long as possible, perhaps even beyond the legislated time. He hoped to have his plan for refinancing the South Sea Company through Parliament and, thereby, to keep the Bubble, discontent, and corruption from being election issues.[14] Not only was Benjamin writing against his father's employer and taking a line utterly opposed to Walpole's and Defoe's, but he was brazen to the point of arrogance and broke the code

Defoe had lived by throughout his own career as a political propagandist: he named names at once.[15] Walpole, the minister accused of believing every man had his price, brought Benjamin into line with money and, the next September, bought the *London Journal*.[16]

Although Benjamin now had a deal with the government somewhat like his father's and, therefore, a fairly reliable income, he still gave Defoe cause to worry. In the nineteen years of his marriage, his wife gave birth to seventeen children. Although only three survived infancy, Benjamin's family was always on the edge of destitution.[17] *Conjugal Lewdness*, the conduct book Defoe released in 1727, may have been published with Benjamin in mind.[18] The third from the last chapter condemns resuming intercourse too soon after childbirth, and the conclusion is an eloquent essay in favor of "Temperance and Moderation."

Benjamin's character is plain in this incident. He thinks nothing of implicating his employer and is obviously on the make. He accepts a deal with Townshend readily and does for money what Defoe did largely to serve the causes of moderation and national unity. Seven months later, Benjamin wrote Delafaye: "You are Sensible Sir I must submit every thing to your Direction; but I must beg leave to Intreat that if my Lord Townshend will not be so kind to me as he has given me reason to Expect I may have the Liberty to pursue any other measures I may think for my advantage to Enter into." Benjamin met Delafaye every Monday evening and was so little trusted that he always had to submit everything he wrote to the undersecretary.[19] In all of his life, Defoe never threatened to sell his pen to another; Benjamin did it within the year.

As Townshend and Walpole tried to gain control of the *London Journal*, they negotiated with the paper's proprietor. Elizée Dobrée did not trust Benjamin either. He asked that his negotiations with the ministry be kept secret from Benjamin and, when they made a deal about the paper, he made it a condition that he would know when and how much Benjamin was paid.[20] Benjamin's mercenary lack of principle continued. Sniveling letters to Walpole and then to the duke of Newcastle survive in which he describes small services he has performed, pleads desperate poverty, demands money, makes excuses, and promises not to ask again. In 1737, for instance, he tells Walpole that he will perish in prison "for a Debt Contracted Endeavouring to Serve the Government" and later insists that he wrote for the *Craftsman* only because his children were starving after Walpole reneged on his promises to "Support and provide" for him.[21]

Even Sophia, his youngest child, the one he sometimes called his favorite, had begun to cause Defoe trouble. She had fallen in love with Henry Baker, a former bookseller's apprentice who had devised a

Henry Baker.

method of teaching the deaf to read, write, lip-read, and speak. In 1724, when he was twenty-six, Baker began staying in Stoke Newington four days a week in order to teach a fourteen-year-old boy named White. By that time Baker had spent four years with the John Forsters in Enfield teaching their deaf child and had published some poetry.[22] Baker had his afternoons free and often took tea with the Defoes. Sophia, then twenty-three, was one of the cultivated, pretty daughters Baker praised in his "Autobiographical Memoranda":

Elegance of Form . . . fine turn'd Neck and Bosom white as Snow, her beau-teous fair blew Eyes beaming all Goodness, her auburn glossy Tressies, her Face where every Feature spoke Perfection, and over all that Bloom of Health that tinctur'd every Charm! . . . from Time to Time Occasion showed her manly Sense, her Sentiments refined, her sprightly Wit, her delicate Expression, the extensive Knowledge by her Reading gained . . . the Sweetness of her Manners. (1–2)

Allowing for a lover's hyperbole, the description nevertheless shows the success Daniel and Mary had had with their daughter and demonstrates that Defoe practiced what he asserted about women's education. In *An Essay upon Projects* he had called a well-bred, well-taught woman "the Finest . . . Part of God's Creation; the Glory of her Master." It is, he continued, "the sordid'st Piece of Folly and Ingratitude in the world, to withhold from the Sex the due Lustre which . . . Education gives."[23] He recommended that girls be taught French, Italian, music, dancing, and "the Graces of Speech," and he encouraged wide reading, especially of history, so that they would understand the world, be able to judge what they hear, and make conversation "as Profitable . . . as Pleasant." The man who had given his fiancée the *Historical Collections* would certainly have encouraged his daughter's studies and taken pride in her "manly Sense" and "extensive Knowledge."

Baker was a cautious, thrifty—perhaps even avaricious—man in spite of his diary's romantic flights about Sophia. Before he accepted a student, he required a seven-year contract, an entrance fee of ten guineas, and a salary of one and a half guineas per lesson; his contract included a promise to keep his methods secret and specified a penalty of £100 should the full seven-year term he deemed necessary for success not be concluded. The earl of Buchan, for instance, owed Baker £728.7s. for his 1727–1734 work. Baker usually accepted five or six students at a time, and his income averaged £308 a year.[24] By 1727, when Baker finally declared his love to Sophia, he had saved £1,000.

At first Sophia delayed the engagement with words that could have come from her father's *Religious Courtship* (1722): "We may both be wretched should we come together before we know each other well."[25] When she agreed to marry Baker in 1727, Sophia opened a distressing subject with her father. Because of the way Defoe lived, Baker expected "a decent Portion" for Sophia's dowry. Defoe, however, told Baker that "he did not know the true State of his own Affairs," could not give the couple any cash at that time, and had already disposed of his property for the security of other members of the family; he offered £500 upon his death. A man like Baker who recorded every penny could not accept Defoe's word. Baker said that he "expostulated," "complained," and "besought" Defoe and that Sophia took up the case. Two years of negotiations began; Baker described Defoe as "pretending" that things could not be otherwise.[26] They became so angry at each other that they seldom met, and their letters are careful exercises in barely suppressed dislike and resentment. In a typical exchange Defoe writes, "The first Proposal you have rejected, and also a second," and Baker, in a note he revised several times, defends his request for a renegotiation of Defoe's lease on the Stoke Newington house and says, "I wonder'd you should call that a Hardship & I persum'd [*sic*] . . . it was not unreasonable to desire you would attempt gaining" what Baker wanted. In spite of their uncomfortable negotiations Defoe wrote the first article for Baker's *Universal Spectator*, a periodical he began on 12 October 1728.[27]

It was the worst possible time for anyone to inquire closely into Defoe's affairs. When Baker's friend and relative John Forster told Baker that the Essex property was already mortgaged, Defoe felt that his privacy had been invaded and sent a resentful letter to Baker: "I am Very Sorry to Hear that Mr. Forster should Say I have not acted with Honour in this affair. I must ask your leav to think quite otherwise, and that I am not Well used atall" (H 465). By this time he knew that Ward and Ward's creditors had begun a suit against him, and an even more serious court case for debt threatened. Elizabeth Stancliffe, the widow of his friend Samuel, had suddenly brought up the matter of a very old debt.[28] Her husband was the man to whom Defoe had surrendered his assets and the power to settle with his creditors, including Samuel himself, in 1695. Elizabeth became Samuel's executrix but turned Defoe's affairs over to her brother-in-law, James Stancliffe. James died intestate, and a man named Samuel Brooke was appointed administrator of the estate. Brooke died, and suddenly Elizabeth Stancliffe and Brooke's widow Mary demanded money that they claimed Defoe had never paid the Stancliffe brothers. They produced a note for £800 signed in September 1691. In 1728 Elizabeth filed suit, and after her death Mary Brooke continued the case.

Defoe was in danger of losing the Essex property and everything else he had. To admit all of his fanciful plans and the full extent of his mismanagement in Colchester would have been humiliating indeed. Without the most rudimentary records of his transactions with Ward or of the 1706 settlements, he would look the fool indeed. As Baker questioned him and demanded he try renegotiating contracts, Defoe's discomfort grew. The Corporation of Colchester became uneasy about Defoe's unpaid rent and sent the town chamberlain to Stoke Newington. Defoe had paid off the £200 mortgage and obtained Mary Newton's release in November 1727, but he had not kept up with the rent. The chamberlain's accounts show that he made two trips in 1726 to Stoke Newington to talk to Defoe, and another record states that Defoe was habitually delinquent. In May 1728 Defoe mortgaged the property for £1,000 to a man named Rodwell.[29]

In an attempt to salvage what he could and put the Colchester property on a sound basis beyond the reach of Ward or Stancliffe, he had to appeal to his younger son. Daniel, by then an established Cornhill merchant, took over the Essex farms in a series of rather complicated maneuvers. In October the Corporation had transferred the problem to one of its own mortgage holders. Defoe was to pay the arrears of his rent to the executors of Mr. Cooke's estate.[30] On 25 November Defoe assigned the Essex property to his son for £1,400 and the money due on the mortgage. At once young Defoe mortgaged it for £600 to Richard Micklefield.

A year later young Daniel mortgaged the property to Edward Stanley for £1,200 and the right to live on the property free and collect the rents. With the money and £400 of his own, Defoe paid the principal and interest on the mortgages held by Rodwell and Micklefield. By August of 1729, however, young Daniel had mortgaged the property again.

~≈≈~

The one thing in Defoe's life that never failed him was his writing. Whenever he had been on the verge of bankruptcy, "the God that gave him brains" had given him bread, and the means had been his pen. Whevever he had felt disgraced with fortune and men's eyes, he had published a popular and useful work. He looked proudly on *An Essay upon Projects*, *The True-Born Englishman*, *The Family Instructor*, and surely upon *Robinson Crusoe*. As his personal life became more troubled, Defoe turned to the arena he could control, and an almost unimaginable two and a half million words flowed from his pen.*

Perhaps because of his own situation and the time in which he lived, his work shows a preoccupation with order and disorder. He tended to begin with turbulent scenes and inchoate situations and to impose on them explanations of causes and characteristics. In his solutions and "improvements," he offered a vision of regularity and prosperity. Defoe's yearning for order and regulation had been exhibited as early as his *Essay upon Projects* and is seldom absent from his work. In the 1720s, however, it becomes a dominant theme and primary motive for his work. In many ways *A Journal of the Plague Year* is the introduction to its artistic implications and one of the earliest signs of how pervasive this need had become in his thought. Unlike the earlier travel and adventure novels, the *Journal* is full of beautiful rhythms. The opening pages establish the pattern of severe anxiety followed by complacency that continues in the early weeks of the plague, is repeated at the end, and mirrors H.F.'s vacillations about whether to go or stay, to shut himself up or walk the streets. The phrase "all the 97 parishes" becomes a refrain, and the regular appearances of the bills of mortality that Defoe

---

* This estimate is conservative; it begins with the first volume of the *Tour* (May 1724) and concludes with *An Effectual Scheme* (December 1730, but dated 1731) (Moore nos. 459–516). It includes no periodical essays, editions with new titles, collections (*Miscellany Letters*), or items about which I feel attribution to Defoe is uncertain.

uses to integrate individual anecdotes into mass casualties become visual markers. As the months pass and the plague moves from west to east, the patterns in the book come together. The confused deaths of hundreds are punctuated first by anecdotes of people who are not so much individuals as representatives, and, second, by yet sharper moments conveyed in single violent images, such as the scream "O Death! Death! Death!" and the pregnant woman kissed. Underlying all of the action of the book is the fierce struggle between the city officials and a city on the verge of breakdown. The lord mayor and aldermen impose order, maintain order, and repeatedly take additional measures to shore up the structure that keeps the death carts rolling, the grave diggers at work, the quarantine enforced, and food distributed.

H.F. fulfills one of the duties of a witness. Witnesses are to testify to truth, to remember and pass on what they have seen. Above all, they often bear the responsibility for an alternate history, as survivors of American slavery, of the holocaust, of the Soviet Gulag, or of South African torture do. Because H.F. records the efforts of the City officials, the courage of the Dissenting divines who stayed and openly assumed empty Anglican pulpits, and the plight and behavior of the poor, he offers a history quite at variance with that found in the *London Gazette*, Pepys's *Diary*, Dryden's *Annus Mirabilis*, and other contemporary sources.[31] Dryden, for instance, represents the assumption of vacant pulpits by Nonconformist clergymen during the plague as a sign of disorder, whereas Defoe considers such assumptions heroic actions and forces for calm. His scornful remarks about the king and court and his criticism of some of the quarantine regulations stand in contrast to the "history" of the time as it was offered immediately after the plague. Once told, alternate histories become challenges both to existing versions of history and to current belief and even conduct. The *Journal*, then, becomes preparation for the kinds of recommendations offered in *Due Preparations for the Plague* and *A Plan of the English Commerce* that occupied the last eight years of his life.

In the early eighteenth century the family was the foundation and the microcosm of society, and, as he wrote his novels, Defoe returned to writing conduct books. *Religious Courtship* and even *Due Preparations for the Plague* have much in common with *Moll Flanders* and *Colonel Jack*, two of the novels published in that same year (1722). *Religious Courtship* begins with a situation much like Defoe's own. A father, a man formerly "hurried in the world," has retired to a house "a Mile or two out of Town" with his three unmarried daughters. His business—and theirs—is to marry them to good husbands. The title places it with other tracts, sermons, and books that expressed concern about marriages between members of different Christian churches.[32] The full title read,

*Religious Courtship: Being Historical Discourses, on the Necessity of Marrying Re-
ligious Husbands and Wives Only. As Also of Husbands and Wives Being of the Same
Opinions in Religion with One Another.*

In form, it is like the *Family Instructor*, a series of dialogues most commonly between two speakers at a time, and with all of the repetitions
and tedium of actual conversations.

Published a month after *Moll Flanders* and eleven months before
Colonel Jack, Religious Courtship develops ideas present in the two novels.
The conduct book preaches the need for women to question their
suitors closely, and Moll helps a neighbor woman inquire into the character, morals, and "substance" of the captain who is courting her. Moll,
however, learns a perverted lesson colored by her observations that
"men made no scruple . . . to go a fortune-hunting" and "money only
made a woman agreeable." She neglects character, morals, and background and checks substance alone. The neighbor marries happily;
Moll's own quest continues, but the lesson from *Religious Courtship* that
the woman must be wary, inquisitive, and even tricky in order to determine the true nature of a lover is repeated here. Moll's experiences
surely second one of the daughter's observations: "the Times terrify
me; the Education, the Manner, the Conduct of Gentlemen is now so
universally loose, that . . . for a young Woman to marry, is like a Horse
rushing into the Battel [*sic*] . . . in the Gross ten Rakes [are] to one Sober
Man" (13).

The suspicion and warfare between the sexes that has been an un-
dercurrent in these books break out in Colonel Jack's disastrous marriages. Although there may be "ten Rakes to one Sober Man," Jack finds
that four out of four wives are adulterous. Three of them cuckold him,
and the book contains terrible scenes of resentment, frustration, malice, and rage. His first wife says she will not be restrained and threatens
him with other men; he spends "whole Nights" planning the murder of
his second wife, and his third becomes an alcoholic who commits adultery in their marriage bed. That Jack, the young man incapable of
violence as a thief, could descend to the "fierce Thoughts, and foment-
ing Blood" that drove him to leave off "debating whether I should Murther her or no" and turn to considering only how to do it and get away
with it emphasizes the central importance of the family. The most
violent acts Jack commits are against a wife and an agent of a wife: he
shoves the Italian wife with such force that he knocks her down, and he
leaps upon the agent and even tries to trample him. In *Conjugal Lewdness* (1727) Defoe characterizes marriages like these as "a *Bedlam*," "an
Emblem of real Hell" (214, 217), and it is hard not to wonder if he and
Mary were having problems adjusting to Defoe's most extended time at
home since 1701. At least by 1728 Defoe kept lodgings in London (H
463).

In contrast to this strife and disorder Defoe offers a vision of domestic happiness in a "sober, regular, well-govern'd Family, a most pleasant, comfortable, agreeable Conversation with one another, suitable in Temper, Desires, Delights . . . exemplar [*sic*] in Piety and Virtue."[33] His longing for harmony and order surfaces repeatedly. Chores, meals, family prayers, and retirement to bed mark the hours of the day, and respect, patience, and understanding characterize the ideal relationship among family members. He explains the necessity for shared religious principles in *Religious Courtship* primarily in terms of the "Comfort of Family-Society" and the government and guidance of children and servants (215). Those characters who complain of its lack tell tales resonant with longing for greater intimacy and respect. Without it, they cannot talk on the same level about what they see as the most pressing family problems, and they find evidence of insensitivity to their feelings in their mutilated prayer books.[34]

Defoe worried about servants even more than he did about husbands and wives. Always alert to social change, he was among the first to write about this large population group[35] at the time when it was being transformed into strangers whose work was a commodity for which they received wages. As Defoe said, "the common People of this Country have suffer'd a kind of general Revolution, or change in their Disposition, Temper and Manners, within a certain Term of Years."[36] Defoe held the somewhat old-fashioned but far from unusual opinion that servants should be "adopted children" in the household who owed their masters and mistresses gratitude and faithful service.[37] Years later Samuel Johnson was still referring to the family and their servants as "the household." Moll Flanders occupies such a position in the Colchester family, and the ambiguity and confusion she feels about her situation contribute in part to her seduction. She has no way of knowing that the older brother is simply living out a common master-servant sexual practice,[38] one Defoe saw as a violation of the master's responsibility for his servant. Before the eighteenth century servants often received bed, board, and even clothing from the family in lieu of wages;[39] when Singleton asks for wages, his master refuses on just these grounds. Singleton, in the spirit of modern servants, is infuriated and "resolves" to kill him.

In his conduct books Defoe uses the seventeenth-century concept of "relative duties," which included mutual obligations between servants and masters as well as those between husbands and wives and between parents and children. *Religious Courtship* breaks away from the discussions of, for instance, the duties of masters to provide family worship for apprentices and drastically reduces the amount of space given to examples of the salvation of a master by a servant and the conversion of a black servant to Christianity.[40] In this later conduct book Defoe recognizes that many servants have come to resent efforts to regulate their behavior as parents do that of children. The appendix dramatizes conflicts over the way to spend Sunday, over attendance at family prayers, and over respect for the family's piety. A servant girl says that she works hard and "Sunday's my own" (298). In a more pointed speech, she says, "I go to Service to work, not to learn my Catechism" (304). In *The Great Law of Subordination* Defoe describes servants who "take it very ill to be examin'd," even when they return from long absences drunk or when household goods are missing. Defoe describes ugly arguments and even fights between masters and servants. "Thus you are obliged to hold your Tongue, and sit down quietly by your loss," he concludes.[41] Work left undone, contracts broken, and the steady drain of pilfering and outright theft by those brought trustingly into the shop or home destroyed the bonds that had made servants part of the family and created a state of war between frustrated, frightened masters and, in Defoe's scenario, surly, rebellious servants.

James Guthrie, one of the Newgate Ordinaries, described theft as "directly contrary and destructive to all Society in general, turning everything into Disorder and Confusion." This opinion, common to Defoe and his contemporaries, reflected not only the challenge to property but also the disruption of bonds among human beings. To live in fear of people hired as servants or met on the street is to live in a state of nature, and to be unsafe outdoors after ten P.M. is to be in a hostile country. Defoe was especially conscious of the disruptions in trade. People could not cash bonds, carry goods, or make payments or deliver a manuscript safely late at night. Unsafe streets and roads worked against the possibility of the kind of constant movement of goods in and out of London and among the town and cities that Defoe believed best for trade. When he described a merchant robbed by his apprentice or by a highwayman on the road, he provided synecdoches for a serious hindrance to the realization of his dream for English commerce.

Here Defoe shows how servants like Mary ruin the "peace of families" by causing strife and encouraging others to be rude and resistant to authority, and some of his other books clarify the importance of the subject for him. Insolent servants set a bad example for children, apprentices, and other dependents, and soon family government is at an end. In a series of books including *The Great Law of Subordination Consider'd* (1724), *Every-body's Business, is No-body's Business* (1725), and *Augusta Triumphans* (1728), he delineates servants' part in England's economic stagnation. Bad servants, he believes, are responsible for "the Husbandmen . . . ruin'd, the Farmers disabled, Manufacturers and Artificers plung'd, to the Destruction of Trade, and Stagnation of Business." Like most people of his generation, he counted apprentices, clerks, tutors, and all household servants including stewards as servants.[42] These people and the common workmen, watermen, carters, drivers, threshers, day laborers, husbandmen, weavers, spinners, and miners were the backbone of English prosperity and the heart of the ability to compete in world markets. "By their Industry our Manufactures, Trade, and Commerce are carried on," he wrote in *Second Thoughts Are Best* (4).

He could praise them above all other nations' workforces for their skill, but he began to concentrate on the "black History of the Degeneracy of *English* Servants." Besides their insolence, he complained of their habitual drunkenness, dishonesty, and undependability. Most serious for the nation's economy was their complete disregard for contracts. Defoe gave case after case of servants who quit just when their work was most needed, as at the peak of a harvest; who failed to complete work so that the master lost contracts and had to pay penalties; and who neglected customers in shops and coffeehouses.[43] He gives a picture of people jostled and threatened in streets that ring with curses, shouts, and arguments between master and apprentice, nobleman and footman, and shopkeeper and clerk; of hordes of pilfering, malingering, arrogant servants, and of a social reversal in which employers feared their employees. It is the world of Moll Flanders, where she presumes—correctly—that a woman she meets at a house fire is also a thief.

In some ways *Roxana*, the novel advertised as "Just Publish'd" on the last page of *The Great Law of Subordination*, partakes of this threatening disorder. Roxana's husband has wasted their fortune and destroyed their business, and she comes to refuse marriage to a good man, to be a courtesan, to be called "Amazonian," and to wish her own daughter dead. Above all, Amy, her loyal maid, manifests this world of evil and disorder that Defoe feared. Again the confusion and violation of the roles of employer and servant evident in Moll Flanders' Colchester experience surface. Amy dresses herself up "like a Gentlewoman" and entertains Roxana and the landlord; Roxana confides everything to her and finally perverts the mistress's role as guardian of the morals of her servants by putting Amy in bed with her lover. Several times, the narrator observes how Amy imitated Roxana, who admits, "I had been her wicked Example; and I had led her into all." Defoe's observation was a commonplace of the time, and he dramatizes Steele's *Spectator* no. 96 in which a fictional servant traces his moral decline and concludes, "We are what we are, according to the Example of our Superiours." Amy and the prince's man mimic Roxana and the prince. "*Like* Mistress, *like* Maid," Roxana says. "Why might not they do the same thing below, that we did above?"

In *The Great Law of Subordination Consider'd*, Defoe hinted ominously at "three or four several Ladies of Fortune, sold, or rather deliver'd into

the Hands of Scoundrels, by their *Maid-Servants*," and Amy introduces
the idea of sex with the landlord.[44] Roxana denies that that is the
landlord's intention, but Amy argues vigorously that it is, that Roxana's
desperate situation makes it essential, and that "necessity" will excuse
her. In none of these things does Roxana agree with her. In fact, the
landlord insists, before Amy as witness, that he has no "ill Design" and
acted in "meer Kindness." Later he tells Roxana that he will not withdraw his support if she declines his advances, and *she* "press'd him" to
spend the night. The name Roxana most consistently gives Amy is
"jade," a term of reprobation in the eighteenth century meaning "wan-
ton," "insolent," and "lascivious." Defoe listed "Jade" as one of the "hard
names" judges called Dissenters in the 1680s. So intense is the role
confusion, that Roxana describes Amy as "the Skin to my Back" and
"my Right Hand," and modern critics have called them alter egos.[45] By
the end of the novel Amy has become "a Woman of Business" who eats
every meal with the family. She calls herself "half a Servant, half a
Companion" (2:14), and both women describe her as Roxana's
"agent"—the person who acts *for* another, the one who does the actual
work. Conversations between the two women become frenetic, reflective chatter. They often say the same things and begin to rave; they
swear, express great passion, and release frustration, terror, desperation, and rage. When Amy disappears, Roxana feels deprived of her
conversation at least as much as she fears Amy's actions. "I was, for want
of *Amy*, destitute," she says (2:145). The jumble of names Defoe has
Roxana call Amy in the space of a few pages illustrates what Amy has
become: Agent, Friend, faithful Friend, Steward, Trusty Agent, Jade,
Devil, Monster, Tyger—Murderer. Roxana says that *Susan* "haunted"
her imagination, but so does Amy. Amy becomes the personification of
Roxana's self-loathing; Roxana wants Amy, her confidante, friend, and
confessor, but the very thought of her raises the death's head. Amy has
committed murder, she believes, and, therefore, acted out Roxana's
most monstrous wish, and, furthermore, has done it because of Roxana's wicked past. Amy, Roxana says, "knew all the Secret History of my
Life"; Amy is the visible representation, the emblem, of this life and its
consequences. The most desired, then, becomes the most hideous. In
this final study of desperation and guilt, Defoe creates two hellhounds
to punish Roxana: Susan, the abandoned child of her body, and Amy,
the rejected product of her secret thoughts.

꧂

   In opposition to these phantasms of disorder, Defoe began to invent
an astonishingly detailed, carefully ordered construct toward which
Great Britain might aspire. This construct is worked out primarily in *A
Tour, The Royal Progress* (both 1724), *The Complete English Tradesman, A*

General History of Discoveries and Improvements (both 1726), *Plan of the English Commerce, Atlas Maritimus and Commercialis* (both 1728), and several shorter works such as *An Humble Proposal to the People of England, for the Encrease of Their Trade, and Encouragement of Their Manufactures* (1729). In these books Defoe characterizes the English people, identifies their strengths and advantages, and charts their course to greatness. Typically, he begins with surveys—of the present state of England (*A Tour*) and of their place in worldwide commercial history (*A General History of Discoveries and Improvements*)—and with guides for the most basic cogs in the machine (*The Great Law of Subordination Consider'd* and *The Complete English Tradesman*).

Defoe's plan for his country was nothing less than world domination. Trade, not military might, would make this conquest. In *Plan of the English Commerce*, he wrote, "Trade is the Foundation of Wealth, and Wealth of Power" (39), and, in *The Advantages of Peace and Commerce* (1729), he said, "If any one Nation could govern Trade, that Nation would govern the World" (6). At the heart of Defoe's conception was the City of London, because he believed that it was the only city in the world on which every sea captain could depend to buy his cargo and then reload his ship. As Defoe put it in *The Complete English Tradesman*, "Here is always a Market, and here they can be consum'd . . . many [cities] can send Ships Loaden out, but few can bring them Loaden home" (3:128). In his opinion England was ideally poised to realize this goal. The "Growth and Product of our Lands and Seas" and "the Labour and Manufacture of our People," combined with a large, prosperous, materialistic population and her very great number of ships, gave England an unchallengeable advantage.[46] In book after book Defoe catalogued what England had to sell and enumerated the luxuries she bought. In contrast to her substantial exports of wool, corn, minerals, and manufactured goods, he listed imports of wine, brandy, raisins, currants, oranges, coffee, tea, chocolate, olives, nutmeg, cinnamon, and pepper. He always added the sugar, tobacco, cotton, rice, cocoa, furs, and other imports from the colonies to the account of English wealth and was quick to point out how many imports became more expensive exports, as raw silk and flax became cloth, cochineal and indigo dyed material, and plantation molasses went into rum.

Defoe challenged his countrymen to duplicate the pattern of English commerce in their foreign trade. In *A Tour, Complete English Tradesman,* and other books, he presented London as the hub of a great wheel. Every part of Great Britain had something to contribute and, equally significant, seldom duplicated the produce and industries of any other part. All of these things flowed to London and were redistributed. Cheshire cheese, for instance, came to London and then fed the city but was also sent on to Norfolk, Exeter, and Halifax which produce different things. In a series of lists in *Complete English Tradesman*, Defoe showed how ordinary household furnishings and daily attire proved his point; he counted, for instance, eleven regions that contributed to a man's everyday outfit.

Modern historians confirm Defoe's portrayal of London as a prodigious market. "This whole Kingdom . . . are employ'd to furnish something . . . , the best of everything, to supply the city of London with provisions . . . corn, flesh, fish, butter, cheese, salt, fewel, timber, &c. and cloths also; with everything necessary for building . . . or for trades," Defoe says. In 1725 London consumed "60,000 calves, 70,000 sheep and lambs, 187,000 swine, 52,000 suckling pigs, 115,000 bushels of oysters, 14,750,000 mackerel, 1,398 boatloads of cod, haddock, and whiting, 16,366,000 pounds of butter, 21,066,000 pounds of cheese, and 5 million gallons of milk." That farmers, manufacturers, and consumers were scattered all over England meant that the transportation industry employed thousands of people: "So all the manufactures are brought [to London], and from hence circulated again to all the country" "so that all the manufactures of *England* . . . are to be found in the meanest village, and in the remotest corner of . . . *Britain*."[47]

If England could replicate this orderly spoke-and-hub model in international trade, she would be the richest, most powerful nation on earth. Defoe imagined the produce of the world flowing into London to be redistributed and, of course, augmented with English goods and produce. Books like *A Plan of the English Commerce* and *Atlas Maritimus* target countries and products and challenge Englishmen to develop trade with them. His plan included establishing England's independence; very high on his list of priorities, therefore, is getting timber, hemp, turpentine, resin, and masts from the American colonies rather than from the Baltic and Scandinavian countries. That shipbuilding and repair had to depend on these fractious countries alarmed him. Another part of the plan was to identify the imports that worked against a favorable balance of trade or were, in his opinion, exorbitantly expensive. He argued that by studying climate as Crusoe had done, Englishmen could plant more effectively and, for example, bring the price of coffee and spices down. He saw Africa as the most promising place for this endeavor. England's west coast territory,* the part he called "Guinea," was but two weeks away from London; in contrast, Jamaica, with its similar climate, was six to ten weeks over the treacherous open Atlantic. Defoe compared such things as latitude and chided the British for letting "fruitful Soil [lie] waste." He reminded them that even the slothful Portuguese now grew coffee in Brazil, as did Britain's arch-rivals the Dutch in Java.

---

* Albreda, Fort James, Cape Coast, and Accra.

In books like *Atlas Maritimus* Defoe surveyed the globe, determined what each part of the world had to offer, drew the lines of the spokes of the wheel, and set priorities for his countrymen. He urged the establishment of new settlements and colonies in addition to improving territory England already held. North America, in spite of its relative barrenness, had a high priority because England was nearly without competitors there for land, and "a Fundamental" of improving trade was the establishment of additional colonies where "People may plant and settle." They would become consumers and producers. He also recommended East Africa, because it was the "one considerable Country in the World . . . to which the Inhabitants of *Europe* have no Commerce." Because of what he knew about its culture and degree of civilization, he saw East Africa as a promising market for England's cloth and hardware. He returned to his arguments for settlements in what is now Argentina. He saw great promise in this "uninhabited and uncultivated" land. Not only was it fertile and level but in a temperate climate, perfect for the English constitution and "for the Production of . . . all the most useful Product [*sic*] of the Earth . . . much beyond any part of the yet inhabited Quarter of the World call'd *America*."[48]

Defoe developed a picture of England becoming the richest, most powerful nation on earth through trade. By taking advantage of opportunities, by developing land already held, by establishing additional trading posts even within other nations' territory, and by moving into relatively unoccupied places, England could expand almost without opposition. "The rising greatness of the *British* nation" he reminded his countrymen, was "not owing to war and conquests, to enlarging its dominion by the sword, or subjecting the people of other countries to our power; but it is owing to trade." In the aftermath of the disappointing Treaty of Utrecht, Defoe's countrymen could hardly disagree. Returning to the arguments of his 1712 pamphlets, he reminded people how necessary peace was for a flourishing trade and that the longest purse, not the longest sword, wins wars. Conquest, he reminded them, is "a Thing attended with Difficulty, Hazard, Expence, and a Possibility of Miscarriage." In *A General History of Discoveries* he argued that war, tyranny, and ambition beggar the world.[49]

Defoe's recommendations, however, are aggressive. Many imply the pushing aside (or back) of natives or even European settlers. He explains how the English can "introduce" a fashion and create a new market for luxury goods. The example of calico in his own country, much as he had deplored the passion for luxury cloth, had taught him a method of exploitation. He continues to challenge the East India Company. When he recommends a settlement within its charter, he says, "No exclusive Privilege of Commerce is granted to any Men, or Company of Men . . . but to improve and carry it on; and if they . . . will not trade, their Right is so far void." In one case, he even suggests conquest: the maritime nations of Europe should band together, coordinate an attack, take the North African seaports, and divide them "in Proportion to the Forces employed in the Conquests."[50]

Part of the attraction of this uncharacteristic, violent idea was the admiration Defoe had for Carthage, the great trading city destroyed by Rome. In defining the character and strengths of the English nation, he had concluded that Englishmen were not great inventors, explorers, or conquerors, but that they had a genius for "improvement." "Most of our great Advances in Arts, in Trade, in Government, and in almost all the great Things, we are now Masters of . . . are really founded upon the Inventions of others," he says, going on to give examples, such as the dependence of the modern wool industry upon Flemish methods and of glass manufacturing on Venetian techniques.[51] He portrays the Phoenicians as "naturally Industrious, and addicted to Commerce"; "they carry'd on Trade to all the Parts of the World, planted Colonies, built Cities Abroad, and Ships at Home; and wherever they came . . . they planted the Country . . . carry'd People to it . . . made them rich." Here is the vision he had for his countrymen and the rejection of the parallels drawn between England and Rome at least since Dryden's *Astraea Redux.*

Defoe insisted that the Phoenicians were the Englishmen "of that Age"[52] and used his propaganda skills to try to persuade his people to see themselves as such and act accordingly. Now and then, he would slip and admit that England neglected some of her colonies as the Romans had, but exhortation and praise are his major tones. Carthage's rival, the Romans, were "not at all addicted to the true glories of Peace, the improvement of the industrious, the employment of the Poor, the encrease of Navigation and Commerce, or the making new Discoveries, in order to the better cultivating abandon'd Countries." He contrasts the Phoenicians to the English in a way that seemed flattering but carried an underlying message, "they planted for Conquest, we planted for Commerce."[53] Sometimes he complained, "we are not that industrious, applying, improving People that we pretend to be, and that we ought to be, and might be," but he genuinely believed that Englishmen were "addicted" to commerce and more capable than other nations of "indefatigable Application." He often used the New World colonies to support his opinion. They were, he said, compared to the Spanish ones, "the Fag-end of the Discovery . . . cold and barren Parts, without Silver and Gold, without Mine or Mineral, without any apparent Product," and yet, by English hard work and commercial instincts, these very colonies had become "the richest, the most improved, and the most flourishing Colonies in all that Part of the World."[54]

The seductiveness of Defoe's vision is its comprehensiveness. It includes a nation of shopkeepers so numerous that they cannot be calculated and moves to a world of trading posts; describes the island's and then the world's produce flowing into London and moves to the wealth of all the world flowing to the "most remote village" in Great Britain and also to the most distant parts of the globe; it offers a path for advancement to the humblest individual and a means of world domination for his country. "Trade is the readiest way for men to raise their fortunes and families," he says. Trade leads to new discoveries in "lands unknown," creates new settlements, colonies and markets, promotes navigation, invention, and manufacture, provides the capital needed for stock, laborers, machinery, and cultivation, and makes a nation so wealthy, with a vast fleet that can instantly be converted from merchant vessels into warships, that the world is in awe and, therefore, kept in peace. Moreover, this endeavor, Defoe promises, is "the undoubted design of that Providence which made the World, it may . . . be fully Improv'd, its Treasures fully Discover'd, and all that . . . Wealth which Heaven furnish'd the Globe with, be . . . made use of, as he certainly at first intended it shou'd be"; "I cannot believe that God ever design'd the Riches of the World to be useless." Moreover, it is as if England had been "singled out [by Heaven] to be great, opulent, powerful, above all your Neighbours, and to be made so by your own Industry and [God's] Bounty."[55]

Defoe's love for his native country is everywhere in these books. He begins his *Tour* with the statement that his subject is "the most flourishing and opulent country in the world" (1:1). "Like *Eden* Fruitful, like *Arabia* Gay, / So blest, they scarcely know for what to pray: / ENGLAND in native Glory ever springs," he exults. "With what inexpressible Satisfaction must a Prince naturally look on a Country so populous, so rich, so powerful; and see them all under his Government." Alive to landscape as he had seldom shown himself to be before *Captain Singleton*, he describes scene after scene for his readers and invests these descriptions with the expansiveness and harmony of his vision for his country. He remarks upon "the glorious interspersing of capital Cities," the "safe and capacious Havens," "magnificent Buildings," "innumerable Beauties [that] render the . . . View desirable and pleasant, and that in the most solid and significant manner."[56] The adjectives—"glorious," "capacious," "magnificent," "innumerable"—pile up, and the cumulative effect joins with and explains the "flourishing," "easy," and "pleasant" life he describes the citizens leading and then opens into the "solid and significant" implications: England's place in world commerce and, therefore, among the nations of the world.

❧

About this time Defoe came to accept what seems obvious to us: he was meant to be a writer. In fact, as he took stock of his life, he began to define his "calling." In 1728 he wrote, "I have but a short time to live, nor would I waste my remaining Thread of Life in Vain."[57] Here and in many other places, the biblical admonition to work for "the night cometh when no man can work" (John 9:4) springs to mind. In *The Complete English Tradesman*, Defoe writes,

> The life of man . . . is a measure of allotted time; as his time is measured out to him, so the measure is limited, must end, and the end is appointed.
> The purposes for which life is given, and life bestow'd, are very momentous . . . time is no more to be unemploy'd, than it is to be ill employ'd. Three things are chiefly before us in the appointment of our time, 1. Necessaries of nature. 2. Duties of religion, or things relating to a future life. 3. Duties of the present life, viz. business and calling. (1:63)

In *The Protestant Monastery* he says, "Alas I have but small Health and little Leisure to turn Author, being now in my 67th Year, almost worn out with Age and Sickness" (vi). The choice of the phrase, "to turn Author," suggests his new conviction. In *Augusta Triumphans* he explains that "many Schemes having occur'd to my Fancy, which to me carried an Air of Benefit; I was resolv'd to commit them to Paper before my Departure, and leave, at least, a Testimony of my good Will to my Fellow Creatures" (4).

His sense of duty and his pleasure in that duty are expressed repeatedly in his late work. There is a tranquillity in these statements and a sense of a larger personal context than has been present before. He says that the *General History of Discoveries* has been written to "prompt the Indolent to retrieve those Inventions that are neglected, and animate the diligent to advance and perfect what may be thought wanting" (iii) and that he tries to advance what is practical and beneficial without self-interest. In *The Protestant Monastery* he explains, "A Commonwealth is a Machine actuated by many Wheels, one dependant on the other, yet the Obstruction of a small Wheel may stop the Motion of the whole. Every Man ought therefore as much as in him lies, to contribute in his Station, to the publick Welfare, and not be afraid or ashamed of doing, or at least, meaning well" [iii]. Here Defoe's statement echoes a common idea in Puritan writing, that politics is a moral activity. In fact, it is a moral duty: "he who withholds his service from the public is, in my opinion, little less criminal than he that by downright treachery and corruption betrays it," intones a 1682 *Observator*. In the forthcoming books of practical divinity, the pamphlets on relations with Spain and on crime, the "projects" in the books on the supernatural, he would attempt to set his countrymen straight, to guide them, and to help them make distinctions between, for example, the case for peace versus the case for war against Spain and between a weak or "distemper'd" idea of spirits and pious respect for inexplicable phenomena.

Under the name of "Andrew Moreton," Defoe published *Every-body's Business, Is No-body's Business* (1725), *The Protestant Monastery* (1726), *Parochial Tyranny* (1727), *Augusta Triumphans* (1728),[58] and *Second Thoughts Are Best* (1729). He developed this modest persona to propose projects for the improvement of the quality of London life. "Moreton's" books, with *The Great Law of Nature Subordination*, return to some of Defoe's 1697 concerns—gambling, education, the treatment of seamen—and all show a keen awareness of human cruelties. The Moreton he created was a somewhat crotchety old man who huffed about the indignities of old age and took a firm stand on the duties of citizens:

Every Man ought . . . to contribute in his Station, to the publick Welfare, and not be afraid or ashamed of doing, or at least, meaning well.

I hope therefore the Reader will excuse the Vanity of an over officious *Old Man*, if like *Cato*, I enquire whether or no before I go hence and be no more, I can yet do anything for the Service of my Country.[59]

This voice, tempered by a hint of self-deprecating humor, casts in gentler form the Defoe of the *Essay upon Projects* and even of the Queen Anne propaganda, but here individual and domestic concerns take precedence. In *Augusta Triumphans*, for instance, he rails against the treatment of foundling children and the use of private madhouses to confine unwanted wives. Not until Mary Wollstonecraft's *The Wrongs of Woman* (1798) would such stark protests be made against the confinement of healthy women. "How many poor Women in Labour have been lost, while two Parishes are contending to throw her on each other[?]"* he asks in *Parochial Tyranny* as part of a complaint that money collected for the poor goes instead to "Parish Feasts" (8–9).

This old man's voice suited Defoe well. Like many older people, he criticized others for their crimes, their love of luxury, their sexual immoralities, and their public short-sightedness. We are, Defoe said, inundated with vice; Englishmen have lost their "good Humour" and "seem to be quite another Kind of People than their Ancestors . . . even than as I myself remember them to be." "The Parson's Rate, the Church Rate, the Poor's Rate, the Over-Rate . . . besides the Scavenger, the Sewers, the Watch, the Highways, the Orphans, . . . the Trophies, and other Rates without Number . . . our Doors are eternally haunted at a most unreasonable Rate," "Moreton" raves.[60] Defoe enjoyed the verbal play, the histrionics, the stance of the put-upon, down-to-earth elder

---

* The parish in which a child was born was responsible for its expenses; it was therefore to the benefit of a parish to get rid of indigent pregnant women. Hints of this anxiety appear in *Moll Flanders*.

statesman, and the character developed a bit as the years passed. "Moreton" came to talk about his "friends," to reminisce about the days when he was "no despicable Performer on the Viol and Lute, then much in Vogue," and even to recommend plays.[61] He became something of a controversialist; when part of *The Protestant Monastery* was reissued in abridged form as *Chickens Feed Capons*, a pamphlet attack, *No Fool Like the Old Fool*, and perhaps some objections from a family who believed themselves described followed.[62] So popular did Moreton become that later editions of *A System of Magick* were attributed to him in order to boost sales.

In every pamphlet attributed to Moreton, Defoe attacked John Gay's *Beggar's Opera* and, finally, in *Second Thoughts Are Best*, he recommended the John Vanbrugh/Colley Cibber play *The Provok'd Husband* as a model for the theatre. The play appealed to Defoe partly because, as Cibber said in his dedication to the queen, its design was "to expose and reform the licentious irregularities" that disrupt marriages.[63] The wife who reforms bears many similarities to Colonel Jack's frivolous, headstrong first wife. Both gamble, keep bad company and late hours, spend extravagantly, and speak insolently to their husbands. The quarrels between spouses are highly similar as is the ideal marriage, described by Lord Townly in the play: "I proposed the partner of an easy home. . . . hoped to find a cheerful companion, an agreeable intimate, a faithful friend, a useful helpmate, and a tender mother" (5.251–54). Struck by her husband's kindness and firm principles, Lady Townly reforms, as many Defoe characters do, because she is touched by kindness and feels gratitude and her own unworthiness. "How odious does this goodness make me!" she says, in lines Defoe would have heartily applauded.

Defoe's objections to Gay's *Beggar's Opera* were that thieves were presented in "so amiable a Light . . . that it has taught them to value themselves on their Profession, rather than be asham'd of it" and that the criminals were not punished at the end. He blamed the play, as other contemporaries did, for a new increase in street crime after a few years' decrease. "Every idle Fellow, weary of honest Labour, need but fancy himself a *Macheath* or a *Shepherd*, and there's a Rogue made at once," he complained.[64] In truth, Defoe's own *Moll Flanders* was liable to the same charges. Moll is rescued from the gallows and allowed a happy ending after an almost equally improbable set of events. Both works broke with the most common conclusion to criminal lives, a hanging,[65] and, as Defoe did with Quaker William in *Singleton*, he distracts the reader from the fact that Moll commits despicable crimes against small children and people in crisis. If *Street Robberies Consider'd* is his, he produced another happy ending to a life of crime. All three works are essentially comic. The narrator of *Street Robberies*, for instance, is the son of eight pirates, was left tied to a coffeehouse door knocker, and makes his victims' consternation funny. Defoe's language, no less than Gay's, makes his works amusing rather than didactic. Moll, for example, describes one theft as "made my purchase."

Certainly Defoe's attitude toward the theatre had softened since he had castigated the *Spectator* for doing more evil by "recommending the Play-Houses . . . running up the Humour of following Plays to such an Extream . . . than all the Agents of Hell ever employed before." Here and in the 1715 *Family Instructor* Defoe had railed against the bad effects that play reading had on the young.[66] The *New Family Instructor*, however, seems to imply that plays can be judged as fiction should be. Defoe approves those "where the Moral of the Tale is duly annex'd . . . enforcing sound Truths; making just and solid Impressions on the Mind; recommending great and good Actions, raising Sentiments of Virtue in the Soul, and filling the Mind with just Resentments against wicked Actions" (52). In *A System of Magick* Defoe praised the actor and pantomimist John Rich for exposing modern magicians: "Never was the popular Frenzy better exposed. . . . Mr. *Rich* shows you what foolish things you are just now doing" (A5v).

Defoe's appreciation of *The Provok'd Husband* put him in good company. The play's first run was twenty-eight nights; it opened the next two Drury Lane seasons and was popular into the nineteenth century. Contemporary criticism of *The Beggar's Opera* agreed with Defoe's objections and added harsh specifics. A letter in the 30 March 1728 *London Journal*, for instance, found shocking the presentation of criminals "as a proper Subject of Laughter . . . braving the ignominous Death they so justly deserve, with . . . undaunted Resolution." It is the author's duty, the letter continued, to "heighten the Terror of the Penalties annexed . . . to flagrant Crimes." Boswell noted, as Defoe had, that Gay made honest work seem tedious and even less certain of profit than theft.[67]

Certainly Defoe had become more interested in the theatre. Whether he read or saw the plays is not known, but the increasing number of comments and epigraphs from plays that appear in his works show far more than casual familiarity with a wide range of plays. On his *Conduct of Robert Walpole* (1717), he uses a quotation from the *manuscript* of George Sewell's *Tragedy of Sir Walter Raleigh* a year and a half before its first performance,[68] and in *Some Considerations upon Street-Walkers* he quotes from Otway's *Orphan* five months after it had been revived at Drury Lane. He is obviously familiar with pantomimes and plays about Wild and Sheppard other than *The Beggar's Opera*, including the obscure *Quaker's Opera*.[69]

One of the most remarkable signs of Defoe's knowledge of the theatre is one of the names Moll Flanders assumes. She tells us only two of her countless aliases. The first, "Mrs. Flanders," she adopts with tongue-in-cheek wit—it occurs to her because her second husband has deserted her but left her his most valuable, though illegal,* property: twenty pieces of fine holland cloth, the most expensive made into lace and commonly called "flanders." The second, when Moll disguises herself as a man, is "Gabriel Spencer," the name of the actor Ben Jonson killed in a duel. What exactly Defoe knew about Spencer is hard to say. Spencer had been an extremely promising actor and had gone to prison with Ben Jonson the year before the duel for acting in an allegedly seditious play, *The Isle of Dogs*. Defoe may have known about the duel from his time in Scotland. One of his Scottish printers, James Watson, had published an account of the fight in *The Works of William Drummond* in 1711, and Robert Sibbald, a prominent Edinburgh antiquary, had made a transcript of Drummond's manuscript sometime before 1710. Drummond did not give Spencer's name, but Defoe may have heard a fuller account in Scotland, and the actor was buried in St. Leonard's Shoreditch,[70] a place Defoe knew well. An account of Jonson's trial may have been published in one of the many collections of "notable" Old Bailey trials coming out around the time of the composition of *Moll Flanders*. Moll, of course, is acting a part, and the name of the doomed Gabriel Spencer may be one of the many indicators that Moll's criminal career is near its end.

✌

Not all Defoe wrote was so realistic and topical. In addition to the conduct books, the travel books, the treatises on crime, the "projects" for the City of London, and the works on foreign and domestic economy, Defoe wrote *The Political History of the Devil* (414 pages), *A System of Magick* (411 pages) (both 1726), and *An Essay on the History and Reality of Apparitions* (404 pages) (1727). These books, usually regarded with bewilderment by modern readers, come out of another of Defoe's lifelong interests[71] and have nothing strange about them. Charles Morton had taught him material preserved in his *Compendium Physicae* that approved "natural astrology" (the planets' influence on the weather and human body with applications to farming and medicine), discussed alchemy, and ridiculed fortunetellers. Raleigh and Boyle, whose work Defoe admired, defended astrology, and men like Bacon, Newton, and Dryden took the study of the occult seriously. Even legal indictments still occasionally spoke of someone "Being moved by the instigation of the devil." Human beings have always been interested in the occult, and Defoe captures the subject's standing in the 1720s when superstition, folklore, and magic were rampant.[72] Magicians like Isaac Fawkes made

---

* Because of wars and legislation to protect English manufacturing, import of this lace was prohibited as early as 1673, but smuggling abounded.

fortunes and even entertained King George. Books such as William Andrews' *Great News from the Stars* (1724), Job Gadbury's *Ephemeris: Or, a Diary Astronomical, Astrological, Meterological* (1725), and Salem Pearse's annual *Coelestial Diary* sold well. Even Addison's unpopular *The Drummer*, a comedy about the supernatural, went in to a second edition (1722). As late as 1764 the second largest group of chapbooks dealt with the supernatural, the mystical, and the religious (the most popular were traditional fictions such as *Robinson Crusoe* and *Robin Hood's Tale*); the largest number of these works were prophecy.[73]

Defoe's material is both sacred and secular, and his tone is both serious and comic.[74] Rather than these variations in tone proving confusion, they allow Defoe to give his subject comprehensive treatment. He mixes the Bible, *Paradise Lost*, and folktales, as the people and books of his time jumbled religion and magic. The intellectual might say that magic and religion "are nothing but theories of thought" that "[postulate] the controlling power of the supernatural in everyday life." Even clergymen who published books to combat superstition and magical rituals never absolutely denied the possibility of the devil, apparitions, spirits, and omens appearing in the world. To deny the supernatural seemed to them atheistical.[75] By necessity, then, these books include material we would view with skepticism if not amusement.

In fact, the parish church and the Anglican faith were remote from many people in the eighteenth century.[76] Far too few churches existed, some charged high pew rental fees or were proprietary, entire rural counties might have but a single church, and snobbery, pluralism,* and absenteeism contributed to the ignorance of the common people. Bishop White Kennett, for instance, discovered that no one had held a confirmation in Rutland between 1682 and 1722; the Reverend Oliver Heywood describes a meeting with a ten-year-old who could not tell him "how many gods there be," and a 1733 traveler described meeting some colliers who thought the Commandments were "a family living in their parts, but they did not know them personally."[77]

In the *Tour* Defoe had noted that few "take Notice of the common People; how they live, what their general Employment is" (1:49), and his novels reveal a deepening interest in their folklore, aphorisms, and belief in apparitions. Moreover, he believed that the threat of the plague and a decline in religion had encouraged this "popular Frenzy" for a new army of fortunetellers and astrologers. Both *A Journal of the Plague Year* and *Moll Flanders* are full of peasant lore. Out of these interests and the sensibility that had Robinson Crusoe admonish his

---

* Many clergymen had two parishes, one in London and one in the country; in 1700 there were forty-three. Most put an underpaid curate (sometimes an unlicensed one) in the country and neglected the church.

readers always to heed "those secret Hints, or pressings of [the] Mind" and led Defoe to defend these statements in *Serious Reflections* grew these three intriguing books.

Folk medicine and superstition are very much a part of the ambience of plague-ridden London. As the poor people begin to fear the disease, Defoe depicts them turning to astrologers, fortunetellers, and interpreters of dreams. The city "swarmed" with them, and the signs of Roger Bacon, Merlin, and Mother Shipton appeared on doors to advertise their predictive "arts." As the plague spread, quacks and mountebanks who sold strange cordials, pills, potions, charms, and amulets multiplied, and people appeared on the street wearing the signs of the zodiac, intricately knotted ribbons, and odoriferous necklaces. Defoe's three books on the supernatural go into great detail about these and other charms. Both *History of the Devil* and *A System of Magick* describe spells, charms, and incantations from several nations as well as some of the magic tricks performed by the Egyptians and trace the way magic fell from the pursuit of useful knowledge into corrupt and dishonest practices. Because they wanted to perform surprising things, magicians experimented with drugs, and out of their interest in the "Arcana of things *Divine*" came strange rites.[78] Moreover, these books, like many of Defoe's other late writings, are full of folk sayings such as one that appears in *Conjugal Lewdness* as well, "He that lives *a Gallop*, goes to the Devil *a Trot*."

Folk customs and popular beliefs abound in *Moll Flanders*. Moll and her lovers "bundle," a semi-acceptable courting practice in which the couple went to bed together fully clothed, and they write alternate lines of poetry as lovers had since at least the sixteenth century. She says that Jemy is meant for her, and a number of signs, like their extrasensory communication, are inserted to suggest that they are.

Like many of the class she represents, Moll believes that a promise to marry is a contract that the elder brother will keep. In *Conjugal Lewdness* Defoe condemns this practice and refers to it as a custom on the Isle of Man. In fact, betrothal *in verbis de praesenti* viewed as a valid marriage as well as the popular practice of self-marriage and self-divorce continued even after the Marriage Act of 1753. Just as the lack of a legal divorce never prevented Moll from remarrying, neither did it hinder the lower classes.[79] Mother Midnight represents yet another subculture, one removed from the mores of society and redolent with superstition, evil, and anarchy. Her name was a cant term for a midwife or a bawd or both together, and such a figure usually functioned in literature as "an agent of fate." Traditionally associated with the power of touch and with "Art and Dexterity," she teaches Moll to be a consummate pickpocket. "It was to this wicked Creature that I ow'd all the Art and Dexterity I arriv'd to," Moll says.[80] In *Augusta Triumphans*, Defoe calls such women part of "a set of Old Bedlams," a phrase implying they were like the "lunatics" released from madhouses with license to beg and therefore to prey on people.

The people in *A Journal of the Plague Year* see apparitions, messages in clouds, and angels. Most of Defoe's characters have extrasensory experiences and feel the presence of the devil.[81] Crusoe's and Singleton's religious dreams, Crusoe's prophetic dream about Friday, Moll's "call" to Jemy, and Roxana's visions of the death's head and murdered bodies are powerful, influential experiences, and Satan is equally real to them. Crusoe is ready to do battle with him when he finds the footprint, Singleton batters the wall of his cabin in an imagined confrontation, and Moll insists she hears Satan's "prompting." Crusoe has been in an almost constant dialogue with God, and Moll and Jack are sometimes as intimately engaged with the devil. *Roxana*, that powerful exploration of the nature and sources of evil, objectifies Satan and explores personality partly in terms of satanic characteristics.

The Political History of the Devil went into a second edition in 1727 and before Defoe died was translated into French (1729) and German (1730). Six months after its first appearance, Defoe's *A System of Magick* came out, and four months later he published *An Essay on the History and Reality of Apparitions*. *A System of Magick* traces the history of magic, defines three kinds that developed, discusses spirits, dreams, and the devil again, and exposes modern magicians and fortunetellers as frauds and cheats. *An Essay on Apparitions* collects stories about angels, dreams, omens, phantoms, and spirits, describes the workings of conscience and imagination, and offers some help in "one of the greatest Difficulties of Life": "to distinguish between . . . real Apparitions, and such as are only the Product of an incumbr'd Brain, a distemper'd Head, or . . . worse, a distemper'd Mind" (211). As late as 1764 John Wesley noted in his journal that he had been reading Richard Baxter's *The Certainty of the Worlds of Spirits* (1691) and exclaimed, "How hard is it to keep the middle way; not to believe too little or too much!" (5:103) All of these books, as might be expected, repeat each other in a number of passages; they are full of amazing and funny stories, but also have strongly didactic elements. He is not merely writing "a History of all the Chimney-Corners in three Kingdoms," Defoe says. From *An Essay on Apparitions* some idea of his serious thinking about his method can be gained: "But hold! . . . This looks like Religion, and we must not talk a Word of that, if we expect to be agreeable. Unhappy Times! where to be serious, is to be dull . . . . so we may quote prophane History . . . a Story out of . . . *Plutarch* . . . but not a Word out of *Moses*" (42).

Defoe's big books on the preternatural attempt to separate the legitimate from the superstitious. What falls into the first category ranges from serious, pious beliefs to things deserving respectful consideration all the way to matters arousing considerable skepticism. The existence of the two categories helps explain the sometimes distracting varieties of tones in the works. Moreover, that the group in the first category that arouses skepticism has grown substantially since Defoe's time complicates the reading of Defoe's books. The modern reader feels that Defoe's comic tone is appropriate for things that Defoe has treated fairly seriously. The problem may be the greatest in *The Political History of the Devil* in which Defoe explores the reality, actions, and influence of Satan in the world. It attempts to define the ways people use the devil as an excuse or as an ignorant explanation and to separate these "abuses" from Satan's active force in the world. As in the novels, Satan is real and threatening in human inclinations and passions. He can "stupefy" the soul, first, as the person "sins on" and "hardens" until conscience sleeps, and, second, as the person despairs and becomes paralyzed in the first stage of repentance: awareness of sin. Such a state results in desperation and self-loathing, both apparent in Roxana's agonized description of her married life: "This good-humour'd Gentleman embrac'd the most cursed Piece of Hypocrisie that ever came into the Arms of an Honest Man . . . a She-Devil, whose whole Conversation for twenty five Years had been black as Hell" (300–301). The novel works because we understand the psychological experience of self-loathing. *The Political History of the Devil* glosses *Roxana* as *Serious Reflections* was intended to elaborate on ideas in *Robinson Crusoe*. Today, however, *Roxana* helps illuminate the *History of the Devil*.

A concern with how evil takes possession is woven into these books and often glosses the novels. To some extent all of Defoe's novels are about guilt, and *Robinson Crusoe* and *Roxana* are extended studies of it. Crusoe is trying to discover the nature and degree of his, and Roxana is the obverse: she is certain about hers. Defoe repeats an idea found in the *Review* and some of his early pamphlets in *An Essay on Apparitions*: "Guilt only is the reason of Fear . . . Fear is a Horror of the Soul, in apprehension of some farther Evil yet out of view; unseen, and therefore terrible; merited and therefore dreadful" (191). Roxana's last days are spent immobilized by phantoms of future Evil, and "the Blast of Heaven," which she tells us is her fate, is its synonym. "Conscience, indeed, is a frightful Apparition," Defoe says and explains the theory that produced this passage in *Roxana*: "[Susan] was ever before my Eyes; I saw her by-Night, and by-Day; she haunted my Imagination . . . I saw her with her Throat cut . . . her Brains knock'd out . . . hang'd upon a Beam . . . drown'd . . . all these Appearances were terrifying to the last Degree" (325). "The Soul of the Murther'd Person," Defoe explains in *An Essay*, "seeks no Revenge . . . but the Soul of the Murtherer is like the Ocean in a Tempest . . . in continual Motion, restless and raging: and the Guilt of the Fact . . . lies on his Mind . . . 'till it becomes a meer Mass of Horrour and Confusion" (104).

When Defoe describes the state of mind he calls hell or the devil in *The Political History*, he says it is "Absence from . . . all Beatitude . . . Despair is the reigning Passion in his Mind, and all the little Constituting Parts of his Torment, such as Rage, Envy, Malice, and Jealousy . . . make his Misery compleat . . . he is without Hope, without Redemption, without Recovery." This "devilish spirit," he says, "forms a hell within us, and . . . imperceptibly . . . transforms us into devils." Here, in truth, is Roxana's portrait. When she and Amy curse Susan, their individual voices blend and become a cacophony of evil reminiscent of the hideous hissing of Milton's demons. Defoe's novel is one of several literary treatments of diabolism, incarnations of evil.

The best known of these works may be William Congreve's *Double Dealer*, and it has puzzled modern readers in some of the same ways that Defoe's books have. Critics routinely object to the "mixed tone" and fail to understand the kind of comedy Congreve wrote. In fact, the character and actions of Maskwell, the villain, shed light on *Roxana* as well as on Defoe's books on the supernatural. Amy and Maskwell share a number of qualities that eighteenth-century readers would immediately associate with Satan. In fact, other characters speak of Amy and Maskwell in similar ways. Both are called devils, identified as agents of hell, and described as having supernatural powers. "O *Maskwell*, in Vain do I disguise me from thee, thou knows't me, knows't the very innermost Windings and Recesses of my Soul," one character exclaims.[82] Roxana, of course, speaks of "Amy, who knew my disease," by which she means that Amy understands exactly how vain and ambitious she is.

Defoe's three books on the supernatural are, however, far more for his reader's enjoyment than for their instruction. His tone is jocular, his "history" largely familiar—a bringing together of, for instance, all the Bible says of Satan—as opposed to a speculative or polemical work, and his anecdotes largely what can only be called jokes. Satan could tell us, he says, of Noah's voyage around the world, how he "wheedled" Eve, and whether the story of Helen of Troy is fable or history. He could even confirm or put to rest Thomas Burnet's theory* and, among the points to be cleared up, he could "tell us whether, as there was a natural necessity of the deluge, there is not the like necessity and natural tendency to a conflagration at last" (21). We read of a man who constantly dreamed of beautiful ladies in his bed ("he seldom slept without some such entertainment," Defoe remarks); of a man who tries to get the devil to reveal the name of his wife's lover; of housebreakers who find a fat old man, rocking in every room; and of a girl on her way to meet her lover who meets the apparition of her parson.[83] These books sold well.

* The reference is to *The Theory of the Earth*, 2 vols. (London, 1684–1690).

Before Defoe died *A System of Magick* went into four editions and *An Essay on Apparitions* into three. *The Complete English Tradesman* and *A Plan for the English Commerce* both required two editions.[84]

⁊⳥

Ironically, *The Complete English Tradesman* has a long, detailed passage on how tradesmen should keep their books and how necessary scrupulous attention to them is, for just this lapse destroyed the happiness and prosperity of Defoe's final years. The Stancliffe/Brooke suit inexorably worked its way through the courts. The women continued to insist that Defoe had never paid the bond due the Stancliffes in January 1692. In January 1729 Defoe appeared in Chancery and swore that he had paid the debt but had had to give all of his records, "this Instrument of Composition, Mortgages, Bonds, Bills, Notes, and Securities for Money," all other deeds, writings, books, papers, evidences, vouchers, receipts, acquittances, and releases to James Stancliffe "in 1704 or thereabouts." He said he never asked for his records, explained that he and the Stancliffe men "trusted each other," and insisted that Brooke herself had the records, which she must have "Obliterated Burnt or destroyed." Over the next year the two sides exchanged "demurrers" and answers and appeared in court; Mrs. Stancliffe died. Upon the court's order, Defoe handed in an affidavit swearing that he had none of the records and did not know where they were if Mrs. Brooke herself did not have them. The exception, he said, was "an Instrument of Composition," in this case a crucial piece of evidence because it would have certified that Defoe had settled his debts. He said that Aaron Lamb, an Islington scrivener and a surety for Mary for the administration of Samuel Tuffley's estate, held it and would not return it because he claimed, incorrectly in Defoe's opinion, that Defoe owed his father money.[85] In October 1729 Brooke took her case to the Court of Exchequer, then superior to Chancery because a court of record; after a hearing, the sheriffs of London were ordered to investigate Mrs. Brooke's claims, and, in the next Easter term, a jury found against Defoe. He owed Mary Brooke £800 plus £16.10.5 damages and £14.9.11 for costs.[86]

Defoe owned almost nothing. On 5 April 1729 he had signed a bond to provide Sophia with a dowry of £500 at 5 percent, payable upon his death. On 25 April he had given Baker a 34½ year mortgage on his Stoke Newington house as pledge for the bond. He and Mary continued to live there for a while, but the house was Baker's. In fact, on 6 May 1730 Baker took possession.[87] After the judgment Defoe could have been prosecuted and jailed for the debt. During the final year of his life, he moved between various London lodgings and a village in Kent. Still listed as a citizen of Stoke Newington, he defaulted on his church and poor rates in both 1730 and 1731.[88] His last letter is that of a tired old man "sinking under the Weight of an Affliction too heavy for my Strength," "under the Load of Insupportable Sorrows." His need to remain undiscovered makes him a lonely exile. "It would be a greater Comfort to me than any I now Enjoy that I could have your Agreeable Visits with Safety," he writes to Baker, lamenting that he will never see Sophia's first baby (H 474).

Even in this last year, he continued to write; his handwriting remained remarkably small, firm, and clear. *An Effectual Scheme for the Immediate Preventing of Street Robberies* came out in December 1730, and he was writing *Of Royall Education* when he died on 24 April 1731. A finished manuscript, *The Compleat English Gentleman*, for which he had begun correcting proofs in 1729, had been left in his Stoke Newington house.[89] His last days were embittered by the conduct of his son Daniel, whom he believed to be "living in a profusion of Plenty" (H 475). He knew that Mary and his unmarried daughters needed her property and its income. Benjamin and his wife were poverty-stricken; on 25 March 1730 Benjamin had written to Walpole, "I have now three Children Sir, one being Born on Monday last, and in most Destitute Circumstances, not having a guinea Left in the world."[90] But Defoe thought his son Daniel should help him. Not only was he a successful merchant, but it was to him Defoe had turned over the Colchester lease.

Appropriately, Defoe died in his lodgings on Rope Makers' Alley, a winding street in the heart of the City then inhabited chiefly by shop owners and workers at the Exchange, and his death was recorded in the St. Giles, Cripplegate, General Registry, the registry holding his sisters' baptismal records. He would have been pleased to know that he was styled "Gentleman," and that his obituaries called him "the famous Mr. Daniel De Foe" and "a Person well known for his numerous and various Writings." "Mr." and "Gentleman" would have told his contemporaries that he was a person with some power, an "active agent in the record we call historical," and that he did not work with his hands. Although most were but a few lines long, Defoe's death received unusual notice; after all, the *London Gazette*'s obituary for Queen Anne had been but twelve lines long. The papers reported that Defoe died of a lethargy, a variety of apoplexy, what we call "a stroke," probably of the hemorrhagic variety. He spent his last hours, then, in a heavy sleep. A contemporary medical book described such patients as capable of being roused for brief periods but with "an utter loss of rational powers, and inaptitude of motion." Usually beginning with "Loss of Speech, Depravation [*sic*] of Senses, inability of Motion in all Members of the Body, [and] Distortion of Countenance," such attacks, medical authorities believed, primarily afflicted older people; grief, worry, and cold were thought to increase their likelihood.[91] Two days after his death, on 26 April 1731,

Defoe was buried in Bunhill Fields, the great Dissenting cemetery that holds at least 100,000 Dissenters including John Bunyan, George Fox, members of the Cromwell family, Daniel Williams, Isaac Watts, and Susannah Wesley, the daughter of Defoe's first pastor, Samuel Annesley. His coffin bore a metal plate that read "Foe." In July, Mary made her will and, on 15 November 1731, many of Defoe's books were sold by the bookseller Olive Payne, in the Strand. Mary died in December 1732 and was buried in a single grave beside her husband on the nineteenth. Each burial cost 13s. 6d., and no record of headstones was made in the Bunhill Fields registry.[92]

Mary Brooke pursued Defoe beyond the grave. After several court appearances, the court of Canterbury granted her letters of administration in September 1733, and she finally believed she possessed all that Defoe had. Among the papers are proof that she was his principal creditor, that she erroneously believed he died in 1732, that she swore that Benjamin was believed dead or "to be beyond the seas,"* and that all of Defoe's children had been subpoenaed, but that none appeared to challenge her right: "the Relict of the said deceased dying before she took Administration and Daniel ffoe otherwise Deffoe, Benjamin ffoe, otherwise Deffoe, Hannah ffoe . . . , Henrietta ffoe . . . , Sisters, Sophia Baker . . . and Maria Langley . . . , the natural and lawful children of and only Issue the said deceased being first cited with Intimations etc., but in no wise appearing."[93] There was no reason why they should; as that of a freeman of the City of London who died without a will, Defoe's estate was automatically divided according to the "Custom of London": four-ninths went to his wife and the rest to his children.[94] His house was safely in Baker's hands, and, before Mrs. Brooke discovered his death, his books had been sold and his furniture and possessions divided.

---

* This statement is all but meaningless; litigants used it whenever someone could not be found or evidence was missing.

EPILOGUE

BRED IN THE BONE

What is bred in the Bone will not go out of the Flesh.

—DEFOE, *The Farther Adventures of Robinson Crusoe* (1719),
and *Chickens Feed Capons* (1730) (cf. Horace, Epistle
1.2.69)

An Error fatal to all manner of Charity and good Meaning in the
World: . . . our judging and censuring the greatest and best
Actions of Men by the Success only, and not at all by the real
Prospect, true Reason, or plain Design of the Actors.

—DEFOE, 27 August 1706

Defoe was prepared for death. His letters to Baker show that he had
thought about a will and decided that the City Customs assured the
provisions he wanted. Several times he mentioned his estate, and he
told Baker that he expected Sophia's settlement to "bar" any claim upon
City Custom (H 464). Nowhere does he show any concern about death.
Death is, he said, "a mere passing out of life," and he seems to have
maintained his unwavering faith that God took "the real Prospect, true
Reason, or plain Design" of people's actions into account. In the 1727
preface to *Conjugal Lewdness* he wrote that he was "soon to come before"
the great judge of his life and intentions (v–vi). If there is fear of death,
he says, its only source is guilt, not regret for "what we pass out of" or
"what we part with."[1] This preface and everything Defoe wrote show a
hope for understanding and vindication; he explains himself endlessly
to his readers, but he seems absolutely confident that his God sees him
aright. His last surviving letter displays a state of mind found in every
period of his life:

I Would Say (I hope) with Comfort That tis yet Well. I am So Near my
Journeys End, and am Hastning to the place where the Weary are at Rest, and
where the Wicked Cease to Trouble; be it that the Passage is Rough, and the
Day Stormy, by what way So ever he please to Bring me to the End of it, I desire
to Finish life with this Temper of Soul in all Cases, Te Deum laudamus—(H
476)

Twenty-six years earlier he had written, "I Never Despaird and In the
Worst Condition allways believ'd I should be Carryed Thro' it, but

which way, has been and yet Remaines a Mystery of Providence Unexpounded" (H 17). Eight years after that he explained, "I submit with an
entire Resignation to what ever happens to me, as being by the immediate Direction of that Goodness, and for such wise and glorious Ends, *as
however I may not yet see through*, will, at last, issue in good, even *to me*, fully
depending, that I shall *yet* be deliver'd from the Power of Slander and
Reproach . . . and if not, *Te Deum Laudamus*" (*Review* 8: preface).

Defoe's assurance comes from a dynamic, personal, even intimate
relationship with God. He may not have been a regular part of any
congregation—in fact, he may have been excommunicated, as many
Presbyterians were for bankruptcy[2]—and he certainly did and wrote
reprehensible things, but he was never out of communion with God. He
probably did attend church regularly; descriptions in his letters and *A
Tour* suggest so, and in *Serious Reflections* he calls it "unlawful" not to go
to public worship. In this book he describes "the voice of his soul to
speak to God and to himself" as comfort and sustenance (5). Read's
Weekly Journal described him taking his place "demurely on Sundays in
the Meeting" (20 Sept. 1718). The words of contemporaries noted for
their piety seem clichés beside his. William Bradford and Isaac Barrow
may praise God and begin hundreds of sentences with the words, "It
pleased God that . . ," and Samuel Pepys and men like him may write,
"Blessed be God! Praised be God!" in their diaries, but Defoe's phrases
are individual, entirely his own. Unlike most of his respected contemporaries, he constantly explores and comments on God's relationship
to men and to events in the world. He may sometimes question and
express skepticism or even annoyance with God as H.F. and Crusoe do,
but it is a living, not a perfunctory, faith. Quite simply, he is in conversation with God. He habitually, even characteristically, thinks about God
in the world and, therefore, thinks typologically.

He had called his work "a Testimony of my good Will to my Fellow
Creatures," and his obituaries recognized him in these terms:

A few days ago dy'd Mr. Daniel Defoe, sen. a person well known for his numerous and various writings. He had a great natural genius; and understood very
well the trade and interest of this Kingdom. . . . he was in the interest of civil
and religious liberty, in behalf of which he appeared on several remarkable
occasions.[3]

Defoe's greatest contributions to his contemporaries were his conception of what Great Britain could become and a style of writing effective
for its propagation. He took an interest in every thing that might better
individuals, society, and his country, and his wide-ranging sympathy
and tireless sense of justice invigorated all he did. His late economic
writings offered the most detailed description of what became Eng-

land's vision of herself for 150 years and what drove her imperial ambitions. At the time he wrote, Walpole and Bolingbroke debated domestic economic policies, but Defoe made the globe his study. A protectionist like Walpole, Defoe differed from the prime minister in casting a critical eye on the great companies' monopolies and by defending high wages. Like Bolingbroke an enemy of stock jobbing and the political liaison with the great companies, he had no patience with Bolingbroke's idealized picture of laissez faire or his complaints that the power of the Commons meant that men "who, born to serve and obey, have been bred to command even government itself."[4] Even as Defoe applauded the measures Walpole took to lessen manufacturers' costs, encourage exports of manufactured goods, and raise the prices of imported goods not used as raw materials, he chafed over the lack of colonial investment and encouragement. None of these men was an original economist and each in his own way was conservative, but Defoe grasped the global reverberations of historical and contemporary actions and saw better than either of them how symbiotic world trade was.

Walpole's policies, however, began the creation of the environment that allowed Defoe's vision of England's future to materialize. In his late pamphlets, Defoe had called on his countrymen to do what he had despaired of his government and the companies doing, and his "nation of shopkeepers" and enterprising tradesmen and manufacturers gradually wrote England's Epic of Trade, the saga that made Great Britain the wealthiest and most powerful nation on earth. The dominant mode of political thought in the last decade of Defoe's life was certainly political economy, and Defoe saw more clearly than either Walpole or Bolingbroke how a new partnership of the interests of land, trade, and credit could be served by international opportunities to give England the power to change the balance of world power and, in fact, provide a means for "a new conquest of the planet" nearly without risk.[5] Defoe had studied English history and English character deeply for forty-five years—even the historical anecdotes in A Tour define and analyze the psychology of his countrymen—and he could, therefore, describe a part they could play on every continent. In The Four Years Voyages (1726) Captain Roberts reminds his readers, "No Man was born a Carpenter . . . it was Necessity which put Mankind on many Inventions at first" (273). In fiction after fiction, book after book, Defoe describes in concrete terms ordinary individuals' triumphs in new lands. Like Roberts, they say, "I resolv'd to do what I could, and depend upon Providence for the rest" (118). "Trade is a spring," Defoe repeats, and within thirty years Great Britain had added eight colonies to her empire, including Canada, Florida, and North America as far west as the Mississippi, and the signs of unrivaled permanence had become unmistakable.[6] Fifty

years later, the colonies, England's and those of other European nations, had helped raise the percentage of exported manufactured
goods from 8 percent to 20 percent, and London was established as the
great center for world banking, insurance, and finance. By the end of
the century the value of English imports had gone from £5.9 million to
£28.4 million, while exports—the all-important determinant of a
favorable balance of trade—had gone from £6.9 million to £40.8
million.[7]

Defoe wanted to write so that he could not be misunderstood:

> A man speaking to five hundred people, of all common and various capacities,
> Ideots and Lunaticks excepted, should be understood by them all, in the same
> manner with one another, and in the same sense which the speaker intended to
> be understood.

> the best Rule in all Tongues, (viz) to make the Language plain, artless, and
> honest, suitable to the Story, and in a Stile easie and free . . . that the meanest
> Reader may meet with no Difficulty in the Reading, and may have no Obstruc-
> tion to his searching the History of things by their being obscurely repre-
> sented.[8]

The phrase, "understood by them all in the same manner," shows that
he hoped to make even elementary interpretation unnecessary. He had
outlined the most effective means of education in *A New Family Instructor*, and perhaps no better description of his theory of writing exists:

1. Bring all things under "short and concise Heads of Dispute" so that they
can be more easily remembered.
2. Endeavor to bring "solid and sufficient Vouchers to prove every Thing"—
he recommended ancient and "authentick Authors," especially the Scriptures,
as authorities.
3. Digest all "in a familiar Way," one easy "to be understood by the meanest
Capacity."
4. Put as much as possible into Story "that it might be pleasant and diverting."
(248)

Although Defoe's style is not praised as often as Addison's, Swift's, or
Johnson's, it has far more versatility and has always attracted admirers.
William Robertson, for instance, recommended it as the ideal model
for history writing; Adam Smith once quoted some of Defoe's poetry
and commented that it "breathed . . . the true spirit of English verse."
James Joyce described the style of *A Journal of the Plague Year* as "master-
ly" and even "orchestral"; countless other novelists have cited Defoe's
influence, as Thomas Hardy did. Willa Cather, no great admirer of
some of Defoe's work, said, "There is a strong weave in the sentences as
they follow each other that gives pleasure . . . as the feel of good hand-
woven linen does to the fingertips." The idea that the phrase "imme-
thodical homespun garrulity" characterizes his writing has long been
out of fashion.[9] The manuscript of *The Compleat English Gentleman*

shows many corrections, additions, deletions, and revisions as well as a substantial number of the tricks of an experienced, confident, voluminous, and somewhat repetitious writer (abbreviations, sketched or shorthand sections).

His desire to be useful and his style made Defoe the pioneer journalist and propagandist he was. During his lifetime, both professions were transformed, and his contributions dwarf all others. Before Defoe, what news was printed was without elaboration, interpretation, or even context. The *Review* worked diachronically and synchronically, demonstrated the possibilities of using history and news for propaganda purposes, and pointed out the advantages of a sense of discrete audiences. By the time Defoe died his innovations had become matter-of-course, signs of the changes to which he was primary contributor. Around 1745 *An Essay on the Manner of Writing History* asserted that the beginning of "intermingling" party politics and historiography could be dated to that century. The 1732 *Memoirs of the Society of Grub Street* computed the number of London writers at six thousand, "four thousand that are concerned in Political Discourses; one in Dramatick Performance, and the other odd thousand in petit Pieces." William Oldys supported an ambitious plan to reprint the best pamphlets of the seventeenth and eighteenth centuries, describing them as "the liveliest Pictures of their Times."[10] Defoe had more than a little to do with the changes these statements record.

For us, however, Defoe will always be the novelist. The novel is a great form when it captures the temper of its time even as it incorporates the timeless concerns of the human race. Defoe's novels give us the eternal struggle of the individual versus the "wilderness of this world," but he also demonstrates new ways for literature to participate in immediate debates, to become an instrument of persuasion, and to be "useful." Every novel by Defoe not only records but contributes to the concerns of his contemporaries. The issues, large and small—*Robinson Crusoe* and Salters' Hall, *A Journal of the Plague Year* and the Quarantine Act, *Roxana* and the increase in fashionable gambling houses,[11] *Moll Flanders* and transportation, and *Colonel Jack* and the need for schools for the blackguard boys—are too numerous to identify. And yet we also find the most enduring themes of life and literature: survival; the search for happiness; man against nature; the desire to escape urban complexity.

Defoe's fictions gave literary history the defining characteristics of the form we call "novel," those characteristics that set it apart from, for instance, poetry and drama: what Henry James called its "loose and baggy form" and its "obsession" with the mind, with identity. In fact, the form serves this kind of exploration of character and becomes a source of radical power because it is the structure of the mind and experiences of the character. Those impulses and techniques are biographical expressions.

For instance, self-dramatization came naturally to Defoe. His earliest surviving writings showed this characteristic. In the 1681 Meditations he imagined himself as fugitive, rebel, and clay pot. He saw himself as a player in the world and was intensely aware of the parts open to him. In the *Review* he slid from a familiar, friendly voice to high-pitched prophecy to righteous self-pity to exhortation and back again, and he became his own subject by writing about his "Early Disasters, and frequent turns of Affairs" and describing himself as "fed more by Miracles than Elija." *An Appeal to Honour and Justice* broke down because he could not sustain the role of martyr that he had created for himself. Later he observed that "man may be properly said to be alone in the midst of the crowds and hurry of men of business. All the reflections which he makes are to himself."[12] In *A System of Magick* he wrote, "We live in a general Disguise, and like the Masquerades, every Man dresses himself up in a particular Habit" (336). Assuming, then, willingly or unwillingly, the guise of the rising City merchant, the public poet, the bankrupt, the defender of liberty, the pilloried martyr, the spy, the government apologist, the retired controversialist, the elderly sage, and the betrayed father, he remained intensely aware of the self within, the personality that "precedes and resists alteration," seems "to have existed before events and continues to exist," and that could never be contained in any one role.[13] His part was played on the stage of Great Britain and in a providential world that he knew he could never fully understand or predict. Over and over he refers to "changes and disasters," to "new scenes of life," to "unseen Mines" blowing up tranquil lives, and to "mysteries of Providence." As the future and his part are unpredictable, so are the roles that Defoe will be called on to play. His work reveals a continued struggle to direct his actions within this framework. The very acts of self-dramatization are attempts to place himself in familiar stories in order to understand his experiences and moral courses of action.[14]

His intense desire to touch and change people moved him to attempt to translate every idea into an experience about which his readers would *feel*—not just understand—as he wanted them to. In order to do so, he drew deeply upon his own reactions and feelings and relentlessly projected how others would respond. An understanding of Defoe's life reveals how eloquently he could charge apparently impersonal art with personal meaning—and how well he could hide it.[15] His greatest talent as a fiction writer is probably this ability to generalize about human emotional experiences, create symbolic parallels, and then embody them in a character who appears both individual and even removed from the experiences of his readers. That he did so in order to explain and persuade his readers, and in the service of his considered economic, social, and religious theories, explains much of the power and resonance of his fiction.

The most traumatic, influential experience of Defoe's life was not the pillory but his bankruptcy, and the ways he transformed this experience illustrate his means of creating empathetic experience. The autobiographical elements in "Letter VII. Of the Tradesman in distress, and becoming Bankrupt" of the *Complete English Tradesman* have long been recognized. The chapter begins with a little-quoted description of the violent break-up of the family: the father hiding, the mother returning to her parents, the children divided among relatives. The conclusion rises to the highest emotional pitch:

> I might instance here the miserable, anxious, perplexed life, which the poor Tradesman lives under before he Breaks; the distresses and extremities of his declining state; how harass'd and tormented for money . . . how many little, mean, and even wicked things will even the most religious tradesman stoop to in his distress, to deliver himself? even such things, as his very soul would abhor at another time; and for which he goes, perhaps with a wounded conscience all his life after?
>
> By giving up early, all this, which is the most dreadful part of all the rest, would be prevented. I have heard many an honest unfortunate man confess this; and repent, even with tears . . . by which they had avoided falling into many foul and foolish actions, which they afterwards had been driven to by the extremity of their affairs. (1:79–80)

The primacy of conscience and the fact that it is the greatest source of suffering recalls *Roxana*, the novel in which Defoe explored the depths of self-condemnation and that marked his turn to the "useful" works of his last years. Its tone of desperation makes an experience now thirty-five years in the past immediate and points to dozens of reworkings in Defoe's prose. Any close reader of *Moll Flanders* or *Roxana*, for instance, will surely recognize the state of mind of the "declining state," "harass'd and tormented for money."

In a 1722 *Applebee's* essay Defoe described "the natural Progresson of Crime in the nature of Man" and worked through a rather moving comparison of the destitute thief with the bankrupt. "There are Extremities," he says, "which the Nature of Man cannot support, and which no Virtue, no Principle, will be a Protection against." He then describes the excesses to which desperation can drive people and says that "great Spirits" are particularly susceptible.[16] *Roxana* develops these ideas and records the powerful effect of memory. Defoe's spare descriptions of emotion, which rely as heavily upon the symbolic power of gesture as the drama of his time did, merely hint at the depth of Roxana's desperation after her first husband deserts her. She says she

was "reduc'd to such inexpressible Distress, that is not to be describ'd";
the scene where she sits among the rags begins with an account of her
"stripp'd, and naked" house and ends with the children divided between the parish and their relatives. Just how deeply this experience is
supposed to have affected her, however, cannot be measured until she
tells a disguised version of her story to the Dutchman:

In the middle of what she thinks is her Happiness and Prosperity, she is in-
gulph'd in Misery and Beggary . . . her Visiters [sic] and good Company, all
about her to-Day; to-Morrow surpriz'd with a Disaster; turn'd out of all by a
Commission of Bankrupt; stripp'd to the Cloaths on her Back . . . left to live on
the Charity of her Friends . . . or follow . . . her Husband, into the *Mint* . . . till
he is forc'd to run away from her, even there; and then she sees her Children
starve.

The Dutchman can only comment, "what . . . terrible Apprehensions."
Roxana's speech summarizes the *Complete English Tradesman* passage
and captures the desperation and hardening stated explicitly in it and
in the *Applebee's* essay. In fact, Roxana says her misery "hardened my
Heart." The opening paragraph of the *Complete English Tradesman* letter uses "desperate" twice and "harden'd" once, and the *Applebee's* essays
include the macabre story of a man who kills his wife, two children, and
himself "purely because he could not see them starve." Defoe insists
here that people could be "driven out of themselves" and would then
commit nearly unimaginable atrocities.

   "Poverty presses, the soul is made desperate by distress, and what can
be done?" Moll Flanders remarks. She, like Roxana and the hypotheti-
cal case in *The Complete English Tradesman*, is described as "distracted"
and, a few minutes later, she steals the bundle and feels a "horror of
soul." Defoe's experience as a bankrupt underlies Moll's psychology
from the beginning. What is she if not bankrupt when her nurse's
daughter turns her out in the street? In fact, Moll uses one of the
phrases found frequently in Defoe's descriptions of bankruptcy; of her
former home, Moll says, the daughter came and "swept it all away." She
explains that she was "left . . . to rob the creditors for something to
subsist on" when her second husband deserts her. She hides in the Mint
and sees men who are "almost mad" and find "darkness on every side."
Once married to the banker, she describes herself in a "safe harbour"
but reflects that "there are temptations which it is not in the power of
human nature to resist, and few know what would be their case, if
driven to the same exigencies." In *The Complete English Tradesman* Defoe
writes, "Absolute Necessity forces many a poor distressed Tradesman
to do Things . . . which his very Soul abhorr'd" (2:186). Defoe is never
far from the reality of bankruptcy. It is not lost on him that Jonathan
Wild learned his criminal trade while an imprisoned debtor, and Roxana says that a debtor, should he rise again in the world, "is a certain

Benefactor to Prisoners there, and perhaps to every Prison he passes by, as long as he lives; for he remembers the dark Days of his own Sorrow."

Some of Defoe's Nonconformist contemporaries managed to make most people forget most of the time that they were Dissenters. Robert Harley and Matthew Prior, for instance, illustrate the possibility that Defoe vigorously rejected, and his identification with a group he knew to be persecuted provided another of the enduring qualities of his fiction. Defoe understood social alienation and the violence of threats to his sense of himself. Much of the social aggression in his characters and their sense of extreme alienation spring from his Nonconformity.[17] Four of his major characters deny that they are Englishmen or pose as foreigners in their own country. Even those who don't— Crusoe, H.F., and the Cavalier—sometimes feel that their native land is as strange to them as the surface of the moon, and all feel confined by it. Even *The Great Law of Subordination Consider'd* purports to have a French author. Dissenters after the Restoration went beyond the idea that "this earth is not our home" to assimilate the legal and social restrictions placed on them into a kind of alien mentality. One modern scholar has pointed out that Puritans no longer perceived themselves "fixed in society," and another shows that the Dissenters "conceived themselves to be . . . 'a tribe' . . . in tension with their neighbours just as ancient Israel was." Isaac Watts, who had been educated in Stoke Newington, wrote,

> We are a Garden wall'd around,
> Chosen and made peculiar Ground;
> A little Spot inclos'd by Grace
> Out of the World's wide Wilderness.[18]

The Dissenters were sharply aware of the contradictions in a society that required a series of contradictory oaths, and Defoe often wrote about the deceptions, hypocrisies, and downright lunacies in, for instance, the bill to prevent occasional conformity; did it supersede the Toleration Act? was occasional conformity really a crime? As he pointed out in *The Shortest-Way*, "To talk of 5s. a Month for not coming to the Sacrament, and 1s. per Week for not coming to church . . . is such a way of converting People as never was known, this is selling them a Liberty to transgress for so much money" (128). Just as Dissenters lived in a kind of moral Never-Never Land, so did Defoe's characters. Singleton, of course, is innocent of any ethical code, but his men are soon forced by circumstances to inhabit a similar land. Without loyalties, without roots, Singleton is truly a man without a country and may, therefore, prey on the world, but Crusoe, Moll, Jack, and Roxana are reduced to comparable situations. The underworlds of the glass house boys and of

Mother Midnight, the high life of Roxana's Pall Mall house, H.F.'s plague-stricken city, and the novels' numerous vexed moral situations cut Defoe's characters loose from the ethical and legal mores of his time.[19] They render moral codes insufficient or even irrelevant.

Moreover, the need for individuals to define themselves and resist the community's perceptions was part of every Dissenter's experience. To continue to be guilty of "schism" demanded introspection and conscientious definition of principles, and to dissent automatically carried membership in the group labeled potential rebels and regicides at heart. Moll Flanders refused to accept the identity of a criminal. She was a lady; she was comfortable only when dressed as one and carried the "habit of good breeding" with her everywhere. Roxana came to detest the name "Roxana" so intensely because it was forced upon her and contradicted what she wanted to believe she was at the core. Crusoe liked to hear the parrot say his name because it reminded him that he was once a civilized, successful man. Nothing threatened Moll as severely as Newgate,[20] because it alone had the power to impose a label that would define and, therefore, confine her, and, once Roxana is branded "Roxana," her destruction is inevitable. Throughout his life, Defoe resisted the abuse heaped on him. Pope portrayed him in the pillory "un-abash'd" (*Dunciad Variorum* 2.139), and his sense of himself, his insistence on his right to name himself finds imaginative expression in his character's central struggles. His childhood as a Dissenter had prepared him for the pillory and the abuse; his bankruptcy shook his conception of himself and his place in the world.

As a writer Defoe had great success; as a human being he did deplorable things. In his life as in his characters we can see the struggle between expediency and idealism. Some of the weakest and most reprehensible human motives are inextricably woven into a life of striving after service and courage. Repeatedly faced with disapprobation, hatred, and prison, responsible for a large family and longing for the comforts, even some of the ostentatious signs, of a middle-class life, Defoe did what he thought he had to do and took what opportunities he was offered. He often persuaded himself that he could turn a situation into a chance to do good, or rationalized an outcome when he couldn't. He failed as a tradesman in the 1720s for the same reasons that he failed in the 1690s. He made rash, immoderate statements and alienated people throughout his life. He could never be entirely candid. Although he revealed a great deal about himself and often exposed personal vulnerability in a way unusual in any time and nearly unknown in his own, he also habitually exaggerated and strove to be obscure. Just as characters like Moll Flanders seem to hide things that do not need hiding, so did Defoe. His letters are full of coy, deliberately mysterious remarks: who invited him to a certain place, how he acquired a paper, and when he received information remain stubbornly unspecified. He could be a compassionate friend; a fragment of a 1724 letter reads,

And poor distressed I left alone, and no one to go and speak to, save only Mr. Deffoe, who hath acted a noble and generous part toward me and my poor children. The Lord reward him and his with the blessing of upper and nether spring, with the blessings of basket and store &c.[21]

Yet he could exasperate his favorite children to the point of a near-permanent break. A contemporary could conclude, "Mr. De Foe, who possessed a resolute temper, and a most confirmed fortitude of mind, was never awed by the threats of power, nor deterred from speaking truth by the insolence of the great."[22] Yet he would tell demeaning lies about his finances to those most concerned.

His contemporaries expressed wonder at his energy, his output, his intelligence, and his resilience, and any reader of more than a few of Defoe's works will react as the writer of a modern book on Defoe did. First, Peter Earle noted, "To my horror I discovered that Defoe was probably the most prolific writer in the English language, a writer moreover who wrote on every conceivable topic from angels to annuities and from adultery to agriculture." But he came to ask respectfully, "How could the old man have remembered so much?"[23]

One of the noblest purposes of biography is to show how people have overcome the difficulties and griefs inherent in human life. If Defoe did not always triumph, he always coped with energy, resolution, and ingenuity. He left the record of a man of great intelligence, comprehensive knowledge, imagination, devotion to his country's interests, and admirable resilience. Regardless of what happened and how distraught or despairing Defoe might be, his underlying faith in his ability to "earn his bread" and his trust in a purpose for his life never disappeared entirely. He would always say, "I Never Despaird and In the Worst Condition allways believ'd I should be Carryed Thro' it," and his confidence that "he that gave him Brains would give him Bread" never wavered.

If Defoe could have attained his youthful ambitions, he would have been a successful merchant like Sir Robert Clayton and a popular coffeehouse companion. He would have reveled in participating in England's growing international trade and perhaps risen to be an alderman, lord mayor, or M.P. for London. It was not to be. Many things worked against Defoe. The times were too unsettled, and he sometimes had to tack and trim to stay afloat. One of the letters in Mist's *Weekly Journal* that he probably wrote reads, "A dozen, a score, perhaps a hundred Men, may by an uncommon Greatness of Soul, by an extraordinary Force of Genius, break thro' the thick Clouds of Difficulties which surround them."[24] Few have broken through so much, and few have written books like *Robinson Crusoe*. His story, like those of his characters, is one of infinite variety, a chain of wonders. Barred by his religion from the major educational institutions and from the most prestigious and promising civil and crown positions, he could not follow the familiar paths to greatness or even serve his country as he wanted. Even his faith, the faith that carried him through hard times and gave him his belief in a purpose for his life, was an obstacle, for he thought that it demanded that he be an obedient servant. "Te deum laudamus," he often wrote, and he learned by bitter experience that he could not will or even work enough to attain his goals. With his characters, he could indeed have said more than once:

And now I began to think my Fortunes were settled for this World, and I had nothing before me, but to finish a Life of infinite Variety. . . . But an unseen Mine blew up all this apparent Tranquility at once.

and

But in the Middle of all this Felicity, one Blow from unforeseen Providence unhing'd me at once.

The repressive reign of King James, Monmouth's rebellion, the effect of international hostilities on shipping, the introduction of the bill to prevent occasional conformity, the Sacheverell trial, the Treaty of Utrecht, the malice and avarice of an elderly woman who claimed an old debt—all changed the course of Defoe's life suddenly.

Yet the same faith that he felt determined his destiny and therefore could deny his youthful ambition, that acted to take away the possibility of a quest, any single-minded, noble, personal pursuit, provided the convictions that finally made him great. He believed that every person was born with inalienable rights. These rights included freedom of conscience, religion, speech, and property. He believed that every person had the right to the chance to reach his or her greatest potential—to attain economic security, to live in safety, to learn, and to think. He vibrated to the injustices all around him, published them so that others would be ashamed, and demanded this birthright for the insignificant, the poor, the criminal, the old, the unfortunate, and even the great when he felt them unjustly maligned. Time and again, he championed this birthright. He stated it fearlessly. He went to prison for it repeatedly. He created great characters who lived it and suffered for it. Crusoe, Moll, Jack, and even Roxana, simply want to reach their farthest star, to live the life that is in them unhindered by unjust legal, economic, and social restrictions. It is no accident, I believe, that generation after generation Defoe's reputation has been revived and given additional magnitude by the likes of a Scot (Sir Walter Scott, 1810), women (Virginia Woolf, 1919, and Dorothy Van Ghent, 1953), and a distinguished modern scholar without a Ph.D. (Ian Watt, 1957).

We have forgotten *The Original Power of the Collective Body of the People of England*, and few of us would single out Defoe as the person who published in "able, plain and courageous" prose "the doctrine on which . . . all free political constitutions rest."[25] Yet his ideas ring in our constitution, and the lasting power of his novels—novels always read by the ordinary person as well as the intelligentsia—comes from his passionate belief in human rights. He once wrote what he called "The Vindication of the Original Right of all Men to the Government of themselves." In it he told Parliament, "You may Die, but the People remain; you may be Dissolved . . . Power may have its Intervals, and Crowns their *Interregnum;* but Original Power endures to the same Eternity the World endures to. . . . Nor have I advanced any new Doctrine, nothing but what is as ancient as Nature, and born into the World with our Reason." Bred in a religion in which men fought under the banner "Fear nothing but God," and in a City rich in the history of resistance to tyranny and encroachment, he told a deep truth about himself when he wrote, "While such publick, scandalous Practices are found among us . . . it shall never be said, that my Father's Son liv'd to see it, and fear'd to speak it."

NOTES

These notes are in the "shortened reference" form of the *Chicago Manual of Style*, 13th ed., except that only author's name and page number are given when the note immediately preceding cites the same source. Thus, in note 4, "Pepys 6:274" follows note 3, "Pepys, *Diary* 7:272." Publications of the Historical Manuscripts Commission (HMC) are given by volume number, and Portland and Bath volumes are cited as such. Full references for works cited here are in the bibliographies with two exceptions. Defoe's letters as printed in George H. Healey's *The Letters of Daniel Defoe* are often cited in the text with the page prefixed by an "H," as "H 16" for "Healey, *Letters*, p. 16." Manuscript references are found in the notes alone; the following abbreviations are used in them:

BL: British Library
CLRO: City of London Record Office
MHS: Massachusetts Historical Society
Morrice: Roger Morrice's "Entring Book," Dr. Williams Library, London, manuscript. 3 vols.
NCBEL: *New Cambridge Bibliography of English Literature*. Vol. 2.
POAS: *Poems on Affairs of State*
PRO: Public Record Office, Chancery Lane and Kew
SRO: Scottish Record Office
V&A: Victoria and Albert Museum, London

CHAPTER 1: FIRE AND PLAGUE

1. Information on the Foe family is from Mundy, "Ancestry of Daniel Defoe," 112–13; Bastian, *Defoe's Early Life*, 8–11, 15; Sutherland, *Defoe*, 1–3; Moore, *Citizen*, 1–3, 8–12. I have searched the London records as well as all of those that survive in Essex and Surrey. The quoted entry is from the register of Chadwell, near Grays, Essex; I am grateful to the Essex Record Office, Chelmsford, for permission to quote.

2. On the fire damage in the Broad Street Ward, see the records in the CLRO, Alchin Box F, no. 65, and for some of James Foe's pledges, see CLRO Ass. Box 46.10 for 23 Feb. 1673/74; CLRO Misc. MS. 64.13; Guildhall MSS. 7332 and 6443. See also Walter G. Bell, *Great Fire*, 210–29, 264–68.

3. Pepys, *Diary* 7:272; Baxter, *Reliquiae Baxterianae* 3:17.

4. Respectively, Evelyn, *Diary* 3:453; Pepys 7:274; Vincent, *God's Terrible Voice*, 76; Evelyn 3:451, 453–54; Pepys 7:272, 274. Robert A. Aubin, *London in Flames* is a collection of contemporary writings on the Great Fire; descriptions of the chaos in the streets and comparisons to Sodom and to Troy are common; see, for example, "The Dreadful Burning of London," 35, "London Undone," 53; "Seasonable Thoughts in Sad Times," 64, 69–70, and Henry, *Diaries of Philip Henry*, 192–93.

5. The list of burned-out citizens does not include the Foes. See CLRO, Alchin Box F, no. 65.

6. Evelyn, *Diary* 3:459–62; Leasor, *Plague and Fire*, 254–55, for the survey.

7. Reddaway, *Rebuilding of London*, 247.

8. St. Benet Fink, Guildhall MS. 4097.

9. Evelyn, *Diary* 3:417–18; Reresby, *Memoirs and Travels*, 167–68; St. Botolph, Aldgate, Register, Guildhall MS. 9224; St. Giles, Cripplegate, Vestry Minute Book, entries for 4 and 28 Sept. 1665 and 16 Jan. 1665/66, Guildhall MS. 6048/1.

10. *Letter from Some Aged Nonconforming Ministers*; J. R. Jones, *Country and Court*, 143–52; Keeble, *Literary Culture of Nonconformity*, 28–37, 45–55, see especially 35; Drysdale, *History of the Presbyterians*, 383–86; Cragg, *Puritanism in the Period of the Great Persecution 1660–1688*, 241–42.

11. Information about Annesley is from Walter Wilson, *History and Antiquities* 1:363, 369; Whitehead, *Life of John Wesley*, 20–22; Daniel Williams, *Excellency of A Publick Spirit*; "Cripplegate Ward," Lyon Turner MS. (89.3), Dr. Williams Library; Calamy, *Continuation of the Account* 1:65–73, and *Account of the Ministers* 2:47–49; Denton, *Records of St. Giles, Cripplegate*, 54; Morrice; Drysdale, *History of the Presbyterians*, 456–57.

12. "Cripplegate Ward," 30, 31, 39, 56, 77, 78a, 79, in the Lyon Turner MS, Dr. Williams Library MS. 89.3; it is Turner who estimates Annesley's fines. Baxter, *Reliquae Baxterianae* 3:19; Walter Wilson *History and Antiquities* 1:363; John A. Newton, "Samuel Annesley," 29–45; George I. Turner, "Papers concerning a Ward by Ward Survey," Dr. Williams Library MS. M89.3, p. 22; Dunton, *Impeachment*, b2r.

13. Tong, *Some Memoirs of John Shower*, 49–51; *Review* 2:498; Defoe, preface to *Delaune's Plea for the Non-Conformists*, ii. In *Wise as Serpents* Defoe describes the persecution of Dissenters as "such Fines levied upon them, so many ruined, so many imprison'd, and so many murthered" (9–10); see also 40–41; *Delaune's Plea*, ii, v–vi; and *Review* 3:317 and 4:126. Morrice's Entring Book describes numerous instances of injustice (1:344, 346, 423, 437–38, 578, 634 and 2:9). Cf. Bogue and Bennett, *History of Dissenters*, 87, 353, and Whiting, *Studies in English Puritanism*, 9–17. Scholars agree that the most severe persecution of Dissenters followed the renewal of the Conventicle Act in 1670; cf. Bebb, *Nonconformity and Social and Economic Life*, 70, 76; Henry W. Clark, *History of English Nonconformity* 2:66–106; Watts, *Dissenters*, 228, 239; M'Crie, *Annals of English Presbytery*, 233, 244, 256, 264–65; Keeble, *Literary Culture of Nonconformity*, 25–67, 74–78; Cragg, *Puritanism in the Persecution*, 11, 18, 26, 38.

14. Beecham, "Samuel Wesley, Senior," 85.

15. Defoe, *Serious Reflections*, xii.

16. M'Crie, *Annals of English Presbytery*, 247; Baxter, *Reliquae Baxterianae* 3:17; Davys, *Familiar Letters*, 273. Englishmen persisted in thinking of the Dissenters as dangerous and rebellious throughout Defoe's lifetime. See Christopher Hill, *Society and Puritanism*, 21–23, 27; Michael Watts describes the lingering distrust of Dissenters: "What motivated the majority party in the Commons, apart from naked revenge, was loyalty to the Laudian conception of the church and fear that 1642 would come again, a belief that every Presbyterian was a potential rebel and every Independent a regicide at heart" (*Dissenters*, 222). See also Collinson, "Towards a Broader Understanding of the Early Dissenting Tradition," 23–25; Henry W. Clark, *History of English Nonconformity* 2:102; J. R. Jones, *Country and Court*, 146–47; Defoe, *Jure Divino*, xxv; Whiting, *Studies in English Puritanism*, 4.

17. Sprat, *History of the Royal Society*, 121; Reresby, *Memoirs and Travels*, 169; Dryden, *Annus Mirabilis* 1:48–49.

18. Reddaway, *Rebuilding of London*, especially 254; Bell, *Great Fire*, especially 175–212, 270, 276, 337–38; Vincent, *God's Terrible Voice*, 78, 79, 83; Defoe describes the slow growth of some of the trades after the fire in *Complete English*

Tradesman 2, pt. 2:162–67; see also his *Journal of the Plague Year*, 272, 281–84.

19. George Clark, *Later Stuarts*, 10–16, 55–115; Christopher Hill, *Century of Revolution*, 191–200; J. R. Jones, *Country and Court*, 164–96.

20. I accept Bastian's and Moore's conjectures on the death of Defoe's mother. They cite evidence from the Marsh family wills. Bastian, *Defoe's Early Life*, 32–33; Moore, *Citizen*, 10.

21. Calamy, *Nonconformist's Memorial* 1:124, 126.

22. Whitehead, *Life of John Wesley*, 21; John A. Newton, *Susanna Wesley and the Puritan Tradition*. Newton cites Defoe as a source.

23. Annesley, ed., *Morning-Exercise at Cripple-gate*, 1–28. The fourth edition identifies the writers of the sermons. Annesley's sermon, "How Is the Adherent Vanity of Every Condition Most Effectually Abated by Serious Godliness?" is in Annesley, *Continuation of Morning-Exercise* and was selected by his grandson John Wesley for inclusion in his *Christian Library* 46:333–34. This sermon is a particularly good example of Annesley's casuistical method. The 1690 edition was titled *Casuistical Morning-Exercises*. See also, Walter Wilson, *History and Antiquities* 1:369. Annesley's prayer is in *Compleat Collection of Farewell Sermons*, 626.

24. Information about Morton's life comes from Calamy, *Continuation of the Account* 1:177–211; Tong, *Some Memoirs of John Shower*, 9–10; [Samuel Wesley], *Letter from a Country Divine to His Friend in London*, 4–5; Morison, *Harvard College in the Seventeenth Century* 1:223, 238–51; 2:476–79; introduction to Morton, *Compendium Physicae*, xii–xxiv; Whiting, *Studies in English Puritanism*, 465–67. Morton's Royal Society Paper was "The Improvement of Cornwall by Sea-sand," no. 113 for April 1675, 10:293–96. The warrants for their arrests are described in Morrice's *Entring Book* 1:444.

It seems irrefutable that Morton was invited to America to assume the presidency of Harvard College, but the threat to Harvard's charter should a Nonconformist be selected prevented his appointment. In 1681 the presidency had been offered to Increase Mather and to the Rev. Samuel Torrey, both of whom declined. In 1683 the Rev. John Rogers was selected and inaugurated but died in the same year. In 1684 the Rev. Joshua Moody declined the position, and Michael Wigglesworth refused to be considered. In June 1685 Increase Mather was asked to be acting president, and he accepted subject to dispensation of the rule that the president had to live in Cambridge.

A 1686 letter from Edward Randolph, an English agent in Boston, to the archbishop of Canterbury reads: "This day is a commencement at our collidge. . . : They are all at present more taken up in puting in one Morton of Neventongreen, a rank independent, to be theire president, than to shew any respect which is due to youre graceouse present." ([Hutchinson], *Collection of Original Papers Relative to the History of Massachusetts Bay*, 551). Randolph's official position is confirmed in his "Report on New England," 1676, American Antiquarian Society Misc. MS. R, Box 1, Folder 8. Increase Mather continued as acting president for sixteen years and finally accepted the presidency for eight more; Morton wrote and signed many crucial documents as vice president of Harvard College. See *Collections of the Massachusetts Historical Society* 1:161–62, 2:115–16; Quincy, *History of Harvard University* 1:38, 69–71, 85, 89–91, 495–97; Morison, *Harvard College in the Seventeenth Century*, xix; David Levin, *Cotton Mather*, 48.

25. Toulmin, *Historical View of the State of the Protestant Dissenters*, 218–24; Morton published a defense of himself and other Dissenting academy teachers, which is reprinted in its entirety in Calamy, *Continuation of the Account* 1:177–97.

26. Information about Dissenting education is from Defoe, *More Short-Ways*

with the Dissenters, 5–6; *Present State of the Parties*, 316–19; *Compleat English Gentleman*, 218–22; Palmer, *Vindication of the Learning of the Dissenters*; Samuel Wesley, *Reply to Mr. Palmer's Vindication*, 26–40; [Samuel Wesley], *Letter from a Country Divine*; [Palmer], *Defence of the Dissenters Education in the Private Academies*; [James Owen], *Defence of the Private Academies and Schools of the Protestant Dissenters*; Girdler, "Defoe's Education," 573–91; J. W. Ashley Smith, *Birth of Modern Education*, 59–61 et passim; McLachlan, *English Education under the Test Acts*, 18–26; Whiting, *Studies in English Puritanism*, 465–67; Watts, *Dissenters*, 366–68. This is not to say that university students did not read the likes of Gassendi. See, for example, Margaret Jacob's review of Richard Westfall's *Never at Rest: A Biography of Isaac Newton*, 318.

On the importance of the changes made in scientific instruction, see Christopher Hill, *Change and Continuity*, 148; Hans, *New Trends in Education in the Eighteenth Century*, 11, 59; J. W. Ashley Smith, 246; [Palmer], *Defence of Dissenters' Education in the Private Academies*, 4–7; and [Samuel Wesley], *Letter from a Country Divine*.

27. *Review* 6:341, for 22 October 1709.

28. Morton, *Spirit of Man*, 21–22.

29. [Samuel Wesley], *Letter from a Country Divine*, 7.

30. The 1723 Harvard College overseers' report lists the book among texts in use; see *Publications of the Colonial Society of Massachusetts* 28:421. Education at Harvard was still very much like that at Morton's academy; cf. 365–66.

31. Printed in Calamy's *Continuation of the Account* 1:199, 206.

32. Morton, "Advice to Candidates," in Calamy 1:208; the deathbed statements are quoted in Sewall, *Diary of Samuel Sewall* 5:476. Daniel Williams, *Excellency of a Publick Spirit*, 29, 46, 133.

33. Defoe, *Augusta Triumphans*, 4; Daniel Williams, 29; Defoe, *Protestant Monastery*, [iii], respectively.

34. Preface to Timothy Lindall's copy of Morton's "System of Logic," MHS MS. C.81.11 (19.4); I am grateful to the Massachusetts Historical Society for permission to quote.

35. Morton, *Of Ethicks and Its End*, Harvard MS. Am. 911*. I am grateful for permission to quote.

36. Defoe, *Serious Reflections*, xiii, ix; *Moll Flanders*, 1:ix.

37. Morton illustrates nearly every section of the *Compendium Physicae* with two to six lines of verse, and *Pneumaticks or the Doctrine of Spirits* depends upon the question-and-answer format for a significant part of the argument. The *Compendium* is most easily accessible in the *Publications of the Colonial Society of Massachusetts* edition; *Pneumaticks* is Harvard MS. Am. 911*. Cf. John A. Newton, "Samuel Annesley," 43–44.

38. Samuel Wesley, *Defence of a Letter Concerning the Education of Dissenters*, 2.

39. The "Postscript" survives in the Lindall copy of Morton's "System of Logic."

40. MHS, 2d ser., 2:116.

41. See Starr, *Defoe and Casuistry*, v–xiii and 1–50, and my *Being More Intense*, 126–30, 141–44.

42. Annesley, "Serious Godliness," 46:360; Annesley, *Continuation of Morning-Exercise Questions and Cases of Conscience*, 12; Defoe, *Complete English Tradesman* (1727) 2:183.

CHAPTER 2: MERCHANT-REBEL

1. Information about the the City of London is from Cumberlege, *Corporation of London*; Gomme, *Governance of London*; Morrison, *How London Is Gov-*

erned; Webb, *English Local Government*, vol. 3, pt. 2; Sharpe, *London and the Kingdom*, vols. 1 and 2; Henderson, *London and the National Government*, 3–24.

2. *Review* 8:207; the entire essay is pertinent, 8:205–8; CLRO Jor 55: 251v, 252r, and Rep. 115, fol. 319r.

3. Guildhall MS. 6440/2 for May 1644, "Presentiments of Apprentices." I am grateful to the Butchers' Company for permission to quote from its records.

4. Guildhall MS. 6440/2. The records of the company are incomplete, but, since Wardens were elected from Assistants, Levitt must have held office before his election to Warden in 1631.

5. Webb, *English Local Government* 2:571–72.

6. Information about the companies is from Philip E. Jones, *Butchers of London*, 13–30; Pearce, *History of the Butchers' Company*, 4–85; Salters' Company, *No. 1. Minute Book, 5th May 1685 to 15 June 1726*; I am grateful to the company for access to its archives.

7. Aitken, "Defoe's Wife," 232, and "Defoe's Birth and Marriage," 257; Stancliffe will, PCC 155 (135); PRO CO5/1081, 68 and 681; Mundy, "Wife of Defoe," 296–98; Bastian, *Defoe's Early Life*, 165–66 and Sutherland, "Early Troubles," 280–90; Sutherland, *Defoe*, 40–41, respectively.

8. Philip Jones, *Butchers of London*, 185; Clarendon, *History of the Rebellion* 1:278.

9. Clode, *London during the Great Rebellion*, 23; [Sewell], *Trained Bands*; Emberton, *Skippon's Brave Boys*, 63–70, 81.

10. Quoted in Gomme, *Governance of London*, 240.

11. Guildhall MSS. 9234/8; Vellum and Quarterage Books, Honourable Artillery Company. The vestry minutes are severely damaged and incomplete; the earliest surviving record of Levitt's attendance seems to be 10 June 1641 and the last in 1663.

12. Monier-Williams, *Tallow Chandlers of London*, 18, 35–36, 39.

13. For Henry Foe, CLRO Ass. Boxes 23.17, 24.17, 25.9, 66.22, and 111.13; for James Foe, CLRO Ass. Boxes 4.15, 7.12, 11.9, 18.19, 19.7, 21.3, 22.18, 25.1, 25.13, 34.20, 56.18, 57.7, 61.21; CLRO Misc. MS. 87.4; Guildhall Churchwarden's Accounts, MS. 1303/1, and Vestry Book, Guildhall MS. 4458, vol. 1; Butchers' Company Minutes, Guildhall MS. 6443/1; Bastian, *Defoe's Early Life*, 10.

14. Guildhall MSS. 6441, 6443.1, and 6443A.

15. Jennifer Levin, *Charter Controversy in the City of London, 1660–1688*, 1–59.

16. Guildhall MS. 6443A for 3 July 1684; PRO S.P. 44/336, fols. 98–99; the full text is fols. 19–20.

17. See J. R. Jones, *First Whigs*, 198–99.

18. Defoe, *Present State of the Parties*, 316.

19. Sponsored by prominent London merchants, the Pinners' Hall "lectures" were sermons given on Tuesday mornings by carefully chosen, leading Presbyterian and Congregational divines. In 1694 the Presbyterians withdrew over a theological controversy and started the rival Salters' Hall sermons. See Matthews, *Calamy Revised*, 127–28; Calamy, *Nonconformist's Memorial* 3:511. Collins's St. Bartholomew's Day sermon is included in the *London Collection of Farewell Sermons*.

20. Thirsk, "Fantastical Folly of Fashion," 51, 55, 56–58.

21. Guildhall MS. 5602/3 for 8 Jan. 1651/52; 5602/4 for 4 Oct. 1659; 5602/5 for 7 Dec. 1669, *Minute Books of the Cooper's Company*, and PRO PROB 11/385/156, John Tuffley's will, dated 25 Aug. 1686 and proved 22 Nov. 1686. Kilby, *Cooper and His Trade*, 15, 48, 134; Elkington, *Coopers*, 158, 262–65.

22. Sutherland, "Note on the Last Years of Defoe," 137–41.

23. Aitken, "Defoe's Birth and Marriage," 257; Moore, *Citizen*, 83–87; Bastian, *Defoe's Early Life*, 99–102; Quarrell and Mare, *London in 1710*, 15.

24. CLRO Ass. 22.18, 26.13, 34.2, 61.21; Guildhall 1303/1; Butchers' Company, Guildhall 6441; Bastian, 10, 32–33.

25. Luttrell, *Historical Relation* 1:341; see also Sharpe, *London and the Kingdom* 2:506–11.

26. Watts, *Dissenters*, 254.

27. Defoe, Preface to Delaune's *Plea for the Non-Conformists*.

28. Defoe, *Account of the Late Horrid Conspiracy*, 28.

29. Nuttall, *Richard Baxter*, 110; the classic account is still Macaulay, *History of England* 1:455–59.

30. 22 May 1685; Evelyn, *Diary* 4:445.

31. Defoe, *Account of the Proceedings against the Rebels*, iv; *Wise as Serpents*, 11.

32. Earle, *Monmouth's Rebels*, ix, 4–5, 10, 19–25, 142; the proclamation of war is Harl. 6845, fols. 256–59. Among the occupations listed on warrants after the rebellion were, typically, woolen draper, pewterer, glassmonger, merchant, and cheesemonger; see PRO S.P. 44/337 (124).

33. Burnet, *History* 3:60–61.

34. Clifton, *Last Popular Rebellion*, 154; Wigfield, *Monmouth Rebellion*, 46. Warrants for the arrests of Matthews and more than a dozen others, including at least one woman, were issued on 19 May (PRO SP 44/336, fols. 88–91); see also Morrice 1:469–71.

35. Macaulay, *History of England* 1:551; Earle, *Monmouth's Rebels*, 59–62; PRO SP 44/336, cf. fols. 100 and 103; *Lieutenancy Minute Books, 1684–1687*, 13, 21, 23, and 30 June 1685. These minutes identify the two Quaker meeting houses (CLRO 441A).

36. Clifton, *Last Popular Rebellion*, 245.

37. Cf. Defoe, *Tour* 1:269. In his account of the battle Morrice says it was a sentinel (1:472–74). For other comments by Defoe, see *Memoirs of Shrewsbury*, 10, and *Expostulatory Letter, to the B—— of B——*, 9–10.

38. Quoted in Earle, *Monmouth's Rebels*, 141.

39. Little, *Monmouth Episode*, 198–205; Earle, 141–58.

40. For representative passes, see the Lord Mayor's Waiting Books in the CLRO; cf. bk. 14, fols. 294 and 296, and PRO SP 1685. I have found no evidence that Defoe had such a pass, but significant gaps exist in both records. In March 1689 passes became valid for only eight days because of "abuses."

41. Cf. Defoe, *Tour* 1:266 and 279–80; Earle, *Monmouth's Rebels* 156–58.

42. CLRO *Journal of Common Council* 50, fol. 138, for 9 July 1685; CLRO Misc. MS. 64.13; Defoe is not on the list.

43. Witnesses at Defoe's hearing on his debts thought he lived in Kingsland; other trial evidence and the manuscript of the Meditations in the Huntington Library establish that Defoe's travels were commonplace.

44. Burnet, *History* 3:56; for typical warrants, see PRO SP 44/337, fols. 124 and 129; Macaulay, *History of England* 1:602–3; Clifton, *Last Popular Rebellion*, 231–42; Earle, *Monmouth's Rebels*, 162–82. According to eyewitnesses, Monmouth was struck three times by the hangman, then given three more blows with a borrowed ax, and was finally beheaded with a knife. Burnet called Jeffreys's conduct at the trials of the rebels "behavior . . . beyond any thing that was ever heard of in a civilized nation" (3:55–56). CLRO *Court of Lieutenancy Minute Book*, 441a, fols. 61–62; Defoe, *Account of the Proceedings against the Rebels*, xxvi.

45. Defoe's pardon is dated 31 May 1687, PRO SP 44/337/281. See also

Earle, 180. Defoe's classmate Shower was pardoned on 5 Nov. 1686, PRO SP 44/337, fol. 125; Kitt Battersby, William Jenkyns, and the Hewling brothers were executed. "Early Nonconformist Academies," 281; [Tutchin], *Western Martyrology*. The king's General Pardon was issued 10 March 1686.

CHAPTER 3: BANKRUPT

1. Description of Defoe in Cornhill tax records, CLRO Ass. Box 35.12.

2. On prosperity required, see Philip Jones, *Butchers of London*, 23; for Defoe's admission to the Butchers' Company, see Guildhall MS. 6443.1.26v. Defoe was elected to the petty jury in 1684–86 and again in 1688, Guildhall MS. 4069, vol. 2, Cornhill Wardmote Book. It was not unusual for a break to occur in jury service: Guildhall MS. 6641 and 6451/1–3; Bastian, *Early Life*, 124.

3. So solid was this tradition that a house in Tooting had a plaque reading, "Daniel Defoe lived here." See Dr. Williams Library MS., Thompson Records of Nonconformity 10, pp. 295–96; Cleal concludes that the house was not built until fifty years after Defoe's death (*Story of Congregationalism in Surrey*, 208–9). The earliest mention of Defoe's connection to the congregation that I can find is [Josiah Thompson], "A Collection of Papers Containing an Account of the Original Formation of Some Hundred Protestant Dissenting Congregations" [1731], Dr. Williams MS. 38.10, no. 11 for Tooting. See also, *DNB*; Harris, *Sermon Occasioned by the Death of Oldfield*; Defoe surely knew Oldfield by 1710, when both were in Scotland (H 301–2, 310).

4. CLRO, Lord Mayor's Waiting Book, 14, 503; CLRO Sessions of the Peace, SF 399, Recognizances 1, 7, 9, 15, and SM 57, Recognizances 7 and 9. For other prosecutions, see Morrice 1:543, 578, and 2:9; Mansion House Justice Room Charge Book, 1686–1689, CLRO MS. 487, vol. 1 for 22 Aug. 1686 and 5 Sept. 1686. Information about the women and Tenter Alley: CLRO Ass. Box 6.3, 11.9, 19.7, 25.13, 46.24, 61.21.

5. From King Charles's answer to a 1681 Whig petition; quoted in J. R. Jones, *First Whigs*, 199.

6. Guildhall MS. 6443.27v–r; 46v and MS. 6443A.

7. Hume, *History of England* 8:251.

8. Downie, *Harley and the Press*, 24.

9. All of the major libraries contain collections of pamphlets made by private men. One of the best known is George Thomason's in the British Library; some are bound and annotated. Very rare works are in the Guildhall Library's A.5.4. no. 34.

10. Defoe, *Appeal to Honour and Justice*, 223. The pamphlet in question has never been identified.

11. Ibid., 233.

12. G. N. Clark, *Later Stuarts*, 107–9.

13. J. R. Jones, *Country and Court*, 236–46.

14. *Letter to a Dissenter*, 4; J. R. Jones, 238.

15. Goldie, "Revolution of 1689," 476.

16. Tutchin, *Civitas Militaris*, 2; on the regiment, see Luttrell, *Historical Relation* 1:556; Morrice, 2:570 and 633. Peterborough was in the Tower (PRO SP 44/81).

17. Ll. 7–10, *POAS* 5:95–99.

18. Guildhall MS. 4069, vol. 2, *Cornhill Wardmote Book*.

19. Commonwealth of Massachusetts Archives, 37:7, 8. The petition can be dated between Feb. and Apr. 1689 by a number of events. William and Mary were proclaimed in Feb. 1689. In Apr. 1689 they restored the colonies' charter

rights, and on 15 Apr. they gave the colonies notice of their intention to go to war with France. Petitions from the colonies for protection from the French increased in Dec. after the Sept. loss of £332,800 to French privateers. This petition was one of several bearing Henry Ashurst's name and serving his desire to be appointed "Representative to their Majesties in all matters concerning the Colony of Massachusetts." I can find no copy of the petition Defoe signed among the Colonial, Treasury, Admiralty, or State Papers in England. Such petitions ordinarily went to the Commissions of Trade and Plantations (after 1696 the Board of Trade), but the request for a frigate (which was ordered by the king himself after months of delay on 14 Jan. 1691/92) might have gone to the Admiralty. Ashurst's maneuver, however, was so transparent as to render the petition redundant. See PRO CO 5/858, CO 324/5, CO 5/1, CO 5/905, CO 5/855. A very similar petition from merchants trading in New York, also signed by Meriwether, is dated 19 Dec. 1689 (CO 5/108). H 108.

20. Lillywhite, *London Coffee Houses*, 155–56; John Ashton calls this coffeehouse "Sew's" (*Social Life in the Reign of Queen Anne* 2:266). The club met at least from 1700 to 1729. Dudley Ryder mentions Sue's as a comfortable Dissenters' meeting place and club (*Diary*, 233, 374).

21. Goldie, "Revolution of 1689," 476–77.

22. Walter Wilson, *History and Antiquities* 1:59.

23. Many scholars have felt that Defoe used natural law primarily; see Goldie, 508 et passim for a typical characterization of Defoe's stance.

24. Defoe, *Reflections upon the Late Great Revolution*, 28, 40, 36, and 48 respectively. J.A. Downie has questioned this attribution.

25. Goldie, "Revolution of 1689," 490.

26. Defoe, *Advantages of the Present Settlement*, 12.

27. Defoe, *Account of the Late Horrid Conspiracy*, 19.

28. Guildhall MS. 4063/1, St. Michael's burial register for 7 September 1688. This lower vault was a common burial place that year; one intriguing entry notes the burial of "John Foe," "son of John and ———his Wife," 12 Feb. 1686/87. Tuffley's will is PRO PROB 11/385/156; see also PRO C7/580/114.

29. Essex Record Office, Chelmsford, D/DU 68/2; I am grateful to the archivist, Victor Gray, for pointing out this material.

30. Sutherland, *Defoe*, 34–42, and "Early Troubles," 280–81; PRO C5/84/9.

31. PRO C7/179/188; C24/1129, pt. 1, item 44; Sutherland, "Early Troubles," 276–77. Lodwick is identified as "brother to Secretary Clarkson" in PRO CO 391/7; see also PRO T 1/88 and CO 51/113 for 19 May 1690; CO 5/1037, 17 Mar. 1691; New York Historical Society MSS, Bayard Papers (Letters from Lodwick to Nicholas Bayard and Jay Family, Misc. Papers); he was assessor and tax collector for Portsoken Ward in 1689, CLRO Ass. Box 44.17.

32. CLRO, Lord Mayor's Waiting Book, 14, 32, for 15 Oct. 1685; Entick, *New History of London* 3:307; Mansion House Justice Room Charge Book, 1686–1689, Ms. 487, vol. 1.

33. Sutherland, "Early Troubles," 277–80; PRO C33/275/674; C33/277/116, 176, 177, and 290; C33/273/702; C31/58 pt. 1, item 130; C7/122/9; C7/179/188. The number of servants can be surmised from the Gravesend record. Some of these documents have not been discovered before.

34. Calendar of Treasury Books 9, pt. 2, p. 545, and Reference Book 6:145; cf. Bastian, *Defoe's Early Life*, 148–51.

35. CLRO Ass. Box 4.15.

36. Sutherland, "Early Troubles," 286–88; Bastian, *Defoe's Early Life*, 144–45, 190; PRO C5/214/5.

37. Webb, *English Local Government* 2:576–80, and Trevelyan, *England under Queen Anne* 1:79.

38. Campbell, *Defoe's First Poem*, 16.

39. Sharpe, *London and the Kingdom* 2:556–57.

40. See, for example, the Yale edition of *Poems of Affairs of State*.

41. The most famous example is Swift's essay, *Conduct of the Allies*; see Ehrenpreis, *Swift* 2:500.

42. In fact, Defoe believes the English to be worse than Dryden's Hebrews; cf. ll.92–131.

43. Nevo, *Dial of Virtue*, 37–42, and Cherniak, "Heroic Occasional Poem," 523–35.

44. Trickett, *Honest Muse*, 85; my *Defoe*, 13–41.

45. Campbell, *Defoe's First Poem*, 15–20.

46. Bastian, "James Foe Merchant," 82–86; Guildhall MS. 6641; CLRO Ass. Box 6.10 respectively.

47. Defoe, *Complete English Tradesman* 1:73.

48. Piesse, *Art of Perfumery*, 242, 245–46; *Encyclopaedia Britannica*, 15th ed., s.v. "civet" and "mammals."

49. T. Newton, "Civet-Cats," 10–19; Sutherland, *Defoe*, 40–42.

50. Sutherland, "Early Troubles," 284; Bastian, *Defoe's Early Life*, 167; PRO C6/499/41; C33/280, fol. 316; C7/373/22 (Sutherland's reference is incorrect), C33/280/587 and 590.

51. Sutherland, "Early Troubles," 281–83; C33/278/497; C8/548/96; C6/330; C8/353/220 (Sutherland also has this reference wrong); KB 27/2093, mem. 336, previously unpublished. [Cokayne], *Various Families of the Name of Marsh*, 22; Surrey Record Office, QS 7/5/1 for 1659–61, 1661–63, 1663–66 ("Returns of Men Eligible for Jury Duty"; Roger Cooper is listed until 1710).

52. Moore, *Citizen*, 89; Bastian, *Defoe's Early Life* 173; Sutherland, *Defoe*, 42.

53. PRO PRIS 1/1A, p. 533; this document was discovered by Pat Rogers, "Defoe in Fleet Prison," 451–52. See Bastian, 173–74. I am grateful to James P. Derriman for this and other translations of legal documents, as well as for his careful searches of the De Banco and Coram Rege Rolls in my behalf. Rogers and Bastian had only the commitment entries.

54. This previously unnoticed case is PRO CP 40/3112, mem. 101v. Defoe may have known the Selbys well. John Tuffley had been the executor for Robert Selby, who died at sea. Robert's mother-in-law sued Joan Tuffley, as her husband's executor in 1686. Joan Tuffley won the case (PRO C7/580/114 and C31/57 item 655). I could not find the Lambert case, but a John Lambert had had brandy and other goods on the ship seized in Ireland for taxes (Bastian, 149).

55. PRO PRIS 1/1A, p. 533; CP 40/3112, mem. 108 (also an unnoticed case); Fairfax has not been found.

56. Also newly discovered: KB 27/2093 mem. 196.

57. Also new: KB 27/2094 mem. 191.

58. Also new: KB 27/2093 mem. 336.

59. Also new: KB 27/2095, pt. 2, mem. 916.

60. PRO C 33/280/316, 334, 587, and 590; C 6/499/41; some of these documents have never been recognized. *Clerk's Associate*, 21–23 and 41–42; Sutherland, "Early Troubles," 284–86.

61. PRO C 33/282/530; C 33/282/379; C 33/284/26.

62. PRO KB 27/2093 mem. 336.

63. Defoe describes such an event in *Complete English Tradesman* 1:65–73.

64. CLRO Small MS. Box 19.3.
65. Whiting, *Studies in English Puritanism*, 127–28.
66. CLRO MS. 40/112, entry 118; CLRO Ass. Box 35.12. CLRO Ass. Box 4.15, 6.10, and Guildhall MS. 1303.1 show one child in 1690 and two in 1691. Defoe was also missing from his precinct in Jan. 1693, CLRO Ass. Box 13.26 and 32.13.

CHAPTER 4: RECOVERY

1. Thomas Chapman so testified on 24 Feb. 1692/93 in the diving-bell case (Sutherland, "Early Troubles," 286).
2. Robbins, "Daniel Defoe," 285. Commons Journal 2:8 et passim; Lords Journal 15:381–82 and 390, House of Lords Record Office; House of Lords MS., n.s., I.
3. Bastian first proved that Defoe worked for the private 1695 lottery, not the government's Million Pound Lottery, *Defoe's Early Life*, 188–89. The 1693 lottery is described in PRO SP 9/247/72. See *London Gazette*, 4 Sept., 2 and 23 Oct. 1693, and *Post Boy* for 1695, especially 9 July and 12 and 16 Nov. The licensing requirement was printed in the *Gazette*, 24 July 1693.
4. Pat Rogers, "Defoe's First Official Post," 303; Bastian, *Early Life*, 186–89; PRO T 29/11 for 7 Sept. 1699 and T 54/18 for 1703.
5. Moore, *Citizen*, 287–89. Neale's office is registered in the Privy Seal Docket Books for February 1696/97; cf. PRO IND 1/6757, and his work with the mint mentioned throughout.
6. The date is not entirely certain. It appears that the clerk transposed the last two digits on the document, which unmistakably reads "1678." Defoe would have been about eighteen years old, and it is unlikely that he would have contracted for the land several years before that; the Essex mortgage payment also argues for the later date.
7. Essex Record Office, Chelmsford, D/DU 68/2. Sainthill was the eldest son of the Rev. Peter Sainthill of Southwark, rector of Ovington, Essex. Upon his death he left land in East, West, and South Hanningfield, Chelmsford TG/6, genealogical notes collected by "Mr. Sainthill" (1939).
8. PRO C 5/214/5; Sutherland, "Some Early Troubles," 286–90.
9. Bastian, *Early Life*, 144–46, 190–95.
10. "An Act to Prevent Abuses in the Making of Bricks and Tiles" [London, 1726]; *Builders Dictionary*, s.v. "Bricks" and "Tyles"; Quarrell and Mare, *London in 1710*, 20–21; Drysdale, *History of the Presbyterians*, 443; Charles T. Davis, *A Practical Treatise on the Manufacture of Bricks*, 142–53 and 403.
11. Sutherland, *Defoe*, 51; H 17; PRO C. 7/377/91 clearly shows Defoe to be the proprietor, a fact in some doubt until now.
12. PRO ADM 67/2/5, 11, 16, 25, 29, 32, 36, 44–45, 60, 85, 92, and 184; ADM 68/670 and 671; ADM 69/1 and 2; ADM 67/1. These records show Dalby Thomas to be a faithful and influential committee member. For criticism of Goodwin's works, see ADM 67/2/98, 104, 105, 115, 141. Cf. Peterson, "Defoe and Westminster," 319; Sutherland, *Defoe*, 51.
13. PRO C 33/284/26 (previously unnoticed).
14. PRO C 5/171/5, the previously unrecorded C 33/286/16, and C 33/286 fol. 107; Sutherland, "Early Troubles," 289–90.
15. Sutherland, "Early Troubles," 287–89; PRO C. 5.214/5.
16. All information on this plan comes from Peterson, "Defoe and Westminster," 306–38.

17. Henry Fielding satirizes this practice in *The Author's Farce* (1730), act 2, scenes 3 and 4. For an account of one such writer, see McBurney, "Edmund Curll, Mrs. Jane Barker, and the English Novel," 385–99.

18. Quoted in Schwoerer, "Literature of the Standing Army Controversy, 1697–1699," 193.

19. On the economic situation, see Doubleday, *Financial, Monetary, and Statistical History of England*, 62–65 and 72–77; J. R. Jones, *Country and Court*, 64–66; G. N. Clark, *Later Stuarts*, 174–79.

20. Some of Neale's patents are recorded in PRO SP 44/81; see 2, 4, 12, 21, and 24 Aug. and 17 and 21 Sept. 1691.

21. Defoe, *Complete English Tradesman* 2, pt. 1:110–11 (and see 2, pt. 1:26–27); *Plan of the English Commerce*, 280.

22. Cf. Defoe, *Essay upon Projects*, 81 and 90–92 with the St. Mary's parish register, Stoke Newington, now in the Hackney Archives, for 16 Dec. 1717, P/M 1; at that meeting Defoe was chosen one of the Surveyors of High Wayes (fol. 206).

23. Kennedy, "Defoe's *An Essay upon Projects*," 170–75.

24. The best studies of John Dunton are Parks, *John Dunton and the Book Trade* from which I have also used information about Defoe's publishers, and Hunter, "The Insistent I," 19–37. The location of Dunton's home on Seven Stars Alley is in Dr. Williams Library MS. M 89.3, p. 22, and Hearth Tax records, PRO E 179/252/32.

25. Myers, *British Book Trade*, 57 and 329; Keeble, *Literary Culture of Nonconformity*, 120–26.

26. Dunton, *Life and Errors* 1:180.

27. Kennedy, "Defoe's *Essay upon Projects*," 174; Dunton 1:214.

28. For a full discussion, see Schwoerer, *No Standing Armies!* especially 137–90.

29. Downie, *Harley and the Press*, 31; and Downie, "Growth of Tolerance," 50.

30. Schwoerer, "Literature of the Standing Army Controversy," 195–96, and "Chronology and Authorship," 382–90.

31. For a discussion of the poem as part of this controversy, see Rosenberg, "Defoe's *Pacificator* Reconsidered," 433–39.

32. Rosenberg, 437–38.

33. Schwoerer, *No Standing Armies!* 163–64; Downie, *Harley and the Press*, 24, 28–29, 33.

34. Schwoerer, 164.

35. Schwoerer, "Chronology and Authorship," 383.

36. J. R. Jones, *Country and Court*, 302-10; on the divisions within the Church of England, see E. L. Ellis, "William III and the Politicians," 130, and Bennett, "Conflict in the Church," 165–67; Horwitz, *Parliament, Policy and Politics*, 277, 284–85.

37. Downie, *Harley and the Press*, 35.

38. Luttrell, *Historical Register* 5:40 and 43.

39. Evelyn, *Diary*, 18 May 1701, 5:461; Burnet, *History* 4:497.

40. J. R. Jones regards these petitions as instigated by Junto Whigs (*Country and Court*, 314).

41. G. N. Clark, *Later Stuarts*, 195–96; Evelyn, *Diary* 5:457–58.

42. Evelyn 5:457–58.

43. Evelyn 5:457–58 n. 2; Oldmixon, *History*, 235.

44. J. A. Downie believes so (*Harley and the Press*, 46); J. R. Jones, *Country and Court*, 314.

45. Quoted in Downie, 46.

46. Luttrell assiduously collected news each day, but he occasionally took it from contemporary periodicals. See 15 May 1701, *Historical Register* 5:50.

47. Chalmers' uncatalogued correspondence, Edinburgh University Library; Chalmers, 14. In *History of the Kentish Petition* Defoe acknowledges the rumor but calls it "a mistake" (91).

48. *History of the Kentish Petition*, 14.

49. CLRO, minutes of Common Council. A typical advertisement for the effigies is in *Post Boy*, 12 July 1701. Newspaper reports of the banquet: *Post Boy*, *Post Man*, and *Flying Post* for 3 July 1701. Five hundred horsemen, the gentry in coaches, and "great numbers of the Gentlemen and Freeholders" met the five as they returned to Kent (*English Post*, 14 July 1701).

50. *Account of . . . Designs to Create Misunderstanding*, 17.

51. Defoe, *Original Power of the Collective Body of the People of England*, dedication and 12 respectively.

52. *Account of. . . Designs to Create Misunderstanding*, 17, 7; *LEGION's Humble Address to the LORDS, Answer'd Paragraph by Paragraph*, 8.

53. *The Ballad, Or; Some Scurrilous Reflections in Verse . . . With the Memorial, Alias Legion Reply'd to Paragraph by Paragraph*, 38.

54. Peterson, "Defoe and Westminster," 322-25, 329.

CHAPTER 5: FUGITIVE

1. *View of the Present Controversy about Occasional Conformity*, 2; *Dialogue between a Dissenter and the Observator*, 5-6, 8; see also Calamy's marginal note: "The beginning of the Grand Debate about *Occasional Conformity*," in *Abridgement of Mr. Baxter's History of His Life and Times* 1:576. Even modern church historians are coming to this opinion; cf. Roger Thomas, "Presbyterians in Transition": "Perhaps the earliest shot in the agitation was Daniel Defoe's *An Enquiry into the Occasional Conformity of Dissenters*" (124).

2. [Owen], *Moderation a Virtue*, 13-14; Calamy 1:622; Whiting, *Studies in English Puritanism*, 19. Baxter called occasional conformity a "healing custom" (Henry Clark, *History of Nonconformity*, 214).

3. Roger Thomas, "Presbyterians in Transition," 124; Thomas gives the date of the thanksgiving service as 2 December, which is substantiated in the *Journal of the Court of Common Council*, CLRO *JNL* 52, fol. 158. Thomas's source is *Postman*, 30 Nov.-2 Dec. 1697. If it were Defoe's pamphlet, then the publication date is much earlier than that given in Moore's *Checklist* but seems to correspond with events better. See Morrice 1:634. Cf. Hickes, *Passive Obedience in Actual Resistance*.

4. Quoted in Dale, *History of English Congregationalism*, 486.

5. *Shortest-Way with the Dissenters . . . with its Author's . . . Name Expos'd*, 2-3, 25. J. G. W., "History of the Old Meeting Houses," 129-31. Watson, *History of the Salters' Company*, 94; [Gillespy], *Some Account of the Worshipful Company of Salters*, 58-60; Tong, *Some Memoirs of the Life and Death of John Shower*, 72.

6. Defoe, *Enquiry into the Occasional Conformity of Dissenters* (1702 edition), 303-4.

7. Roger Thomas, "Presbyterians, Congregationals and the Test and Corporation Acts," 119; Thomas quotes Calamy. Beaven, *Aldermen of the City of London* 2:193; Morrice 2:190, 193, 196, 200, 235. Shorter's Company, the Grocers, elected the king Sovereign Master of the company on 24 Oct. 1689 and gave him the freedom of the City in a gold box (*London Gazette*, 31 Oct. 1689). Hornby, *Caveat against the Whigs*, called occasional conformity "a sacrilegious

Design," a "scandalous Practice," and "occasional Hypocrisy" in describing the events of 1702.

8. Defoe, *Enquiry into the Occasional Conformity of Dissenters, In Cases of Preferments*, 12.

9. CLRO, Repertory for the Court of Aldermen, 102, fol. 11, for 9 Nov. 1697.

10. Carstares stopped the messenger sent to Scotland with orders for oaths required of clergymen ("An Abstract of the History of the Statesmen," MS in the library of the earl of Hyndford marked "written for use of Princess Sophia").

11. Guildhall MS. 2145/1, see especially fol. 5.

12. *Some Considerations of a Preface to An Enquiry Concerning the Occasional Conformity of Dissenters.*

13. Horwitz, *Parliament, Policy, and Politics*, 223–24; Watts, *Dissenters*, 264; Higgons, "The Mourners" (1702) in *POAS* 6:362–63.

14. Queen Anne's speech is in *Collection of All Her Majesty's Speeches*, 7 (25 May 1702). Sacheverell, *Political Union*, 9; Common Council had voted against publishing the sermon.

15. Cunningham, *History of Great Britain* 1:319–20; Calamy, *Abridgement of Mr. Baxter's History* 1:622.

16. See the explanation of amendments by the House of Lords as printed in *Select Documents for Queen Anne's Reign*, ed. Trevelyan, 33–34, 37; Journals of the House of Lords 17: 178ff. (minutes of the Free Conference between the Managers for Lords and Managers for Commons, 2 Dec. 1702); Journals of the House of Commons (minutes of the same meeting) 14:180–82; *Clamours of the Dissenters, against the Bill to Prevent Occasional Conformity Examined*, 8; *Case of Dissenters as Affected by the Late Bill Proposed in Parliament, for Preventing Occasional Conformity*, 18–22; Watts, *Dissenters*, 484. Already elections were battlegrounds between High Church and moderates; cf. Sacheverell, *Character of a Low-Churchman*, 3.

17. *Case of the Experience of Dissenting Acts against the Protestant Dissenters Consider'd in a Dialogue*, 15; Journals of the House of Commons 14:182; *Observator*, 19 Dec. 1702.

18. Compare Defoe's 1717 pamphlets when he believed King George I might repeal the Occasional Conformity, Schism, Corporation, and Test Acts.

19. The opinion that Dissenters caused strife began before Defoe's birth. See Christopher Hill, *Society and Puritanism in Pre-Revolutionary England*, which documents the fact that they were called "turbulent and factious spirits," "ever discontented with the present government" (21–23, 27). Watts describes the lingering distrust of Dissenters: "what motivated the majority party in the Commons, apart from naked revenge, was loyalty to the Laudian conception of the church and fear that 1642 would come again, a belief that every Presbyterian was a potential rebel and every Independent a regicide at heart" (*Dissenters*, 222). See also Collinson, "Towards a Broader Understanding of the Early Dissenting Tradition," 23–25, and Henry Clark, *History of Nonconformity* 2:102. M. Dorothy George describes prints that show, for example, "Presbytery" and "Rebellion" trampling on "Loyalty" (*English Political Caricature to 1792*, 69–70).

20. Defoe, *Present State of the Parties in Great Britain*, 15-18.

21. Astell, *Fair Way with the Dissenters and Their Patrons*, 7.

22. Leranbaum, "'An *Irony Not Unusual*,'" 227–45; Alkon, "Defoe's Argument in *The Shortest Way with the Dissenters*," 512–23; Novak, "Defoe's *Shortest Way with the Dissenters*," 402–17; Downie, "Defoe's *Shortest Way with the Dissenters*: Irony, Intention, and Reader-Response," 120–39; Oliphant, "Author of *Robin-*

son Crusoe," 743–44. The proverb is no. 552 in *Witts Recreations. Selected from the Finest Fancies of Moderne Muses with a Thousand Outlandish Proverbs*; the Outlandish Proverbs were allegedly collected by George Herbert.

23. *Letter to a Peer, Concerning the Bill against Occasional Conformity*, 15. *Establishment of the Church*, 3.

24. All quotations from *Shortest-Way* are from the Shakespeare Head edition, 127.

25. See Alkon, "Defoe's Argument in *The Shortest Way*," 14-15, and Leranbaum, "'An *Irony Not Unusual*,'" 229, on Defoe's narrative stance, which they identify as that of a party, not an individual.

26. Defoe, *New Test of the Church of England's Honesty*, 10.

27. *Reflections upon some Scandalous and Malicious Pamphlets*, 10. See also *Reflections upon a Late Scandalous and Malicious Pamphlet*.

28. Quoted in Calamy, *Abridgement of Baxter's History* 1:623.

29. Cf. *Political Union*, 52, and *Shortest-Way*, 116, 133, and 125, for typical usage of the phrases. See Edmund Bohun's translation of *Apology for the Church of England*.

30. Leranbaum draws a perceptive parallel to a hoax perpetrated by Charles Blount in 1693 ("'An *Irony Not Unusual*,'" 246–50).

31. Sutherland, *Defoe*, 86.

32. Leslie, *New Association*, 6; *Review and Observator Review'd*, 5–6; Oldmixon, *History of England*; "Remarks on the Author of the Hymn to the Pillory," 1; *Observator*, 26 Dec. 1702; quoted in Moore, *Citizen*, 112–13 respectively. [Leslie], *Cassandra. Number II*, 13. King, *Vindication of the Rev. Dr. Sacheverell* (1711), 9. Blenheim MS., HMC 8th report, 43. The author of *Reflections upon a Late Scandalous and Malicious Pamphlet* assumed the author of *Shortest Way* to be High Church; cf. 20–24.

33. *Observator*, 2 Jan. 1702/3; [Dunton], *Shortest Way with Whores and Rogues . . . Dedicated to Mr. Daniel de Foe*, dedication; cf. *Reflections upon a Late Scandalous and Malicious Pamphlet*, 14, 22; *Shortest Way with the Dissenters. . . . With Its Author's . . . Name Expos'd* (the final quotations are from p. 9).

34. *Shortest Way. . . . With Its Author's . . . Name Expos'd*, 22; see Moore, *Citizen*, 114; warrants for Defoe's arrest are *Calendar of State Papers Domestic*, 1703–4 2:473, PRO SP 44/352 (fols. 103–4) for 3 Jan.; the warrant for Bellamy is fol. 105, and Entry Books, 350:103, 104. In his review of Healey's edition of the correspondence, Secord notes that there is no reason to think that Harley knew Defoe wrote *Shortest Way* (50–51). Cf. accounts of Defoe's arrest and imprisonment in Moore, *Citizen*, 104–49; Sutherland, *Defoe*, 77–125; Bastian, *Defoe's Early Life*, 270–301. I have noted only the most important corrections and additions to their work; see my "No Defense: Defoe in 1703."

35. H 1–3.

36. Luttrell, *Historical Register* 5:187, 189, 191 (see especially 23 June and 4 July). Defoe, *Essay on the Regulation of the Press*, 20. Preface to *De Laune's Plea for the Non-Conformists* (1706), viii; Morrice 2:27–28; Dunton, *Whores and Rogues*, dedication. "The Scribler's Doom" is a dialogue between Defoe and Fuller that ends with their drinking like brothers.

37. Luttrell 5:300–301; information about rewards is from Radzinowicz, *History of English Criminal Law* 2:86.

38. The notices appeared in the *London Gazette*, 11 and 14 Jan. Moore prints and discusses them in *Citizen*, 117–18; cf. "Defoe in the Pillory," plates opposite pp. 80 and 94 in Sutherland, *Defoe*, and plate in chapter 4; Horner, *Brief Account of the Interesting Ceremony of Unveiling the Monument . . . to the Memory of Daniel Defoe*, 6. Horner describes how an earth mover uncovered Defoe's body.

39. Bastian, *Defoe's Early Life*, 188; Rogers, "Defoe's First Official Post," 303; Peterson, "Defoe and Westminster," 320. All of Defoe's 1703 letters are signed "D.F." or "DeFoe." Defoe signs the following published works "D.F.": *Some Reflections on a Pamphlet . . .*; *An Essay upon Projects*; *The Poor Man's Plea*; 2d ed. of *An Enquiry into the Occasional Conformity of Dissenters*; *A Letter to Mr. How*; *The Present State of Jacobitism Consider'd*; *The Original Power of the Collective Body*; all before *Shortest-Way*. Most of the debt cases against Defoe, however, refer to him as "Daniel Foe."

40. PRO SP 44/352. fol. 106.

41. CLRO, Sessions of the Peace, SF 472. I am grateful to Linda Merians of La Salle University for this reference. A legend survives that Croome refused to plead and was subjected to pressing, *peine forte et dure*, but the warrant and release dates show that this did not happen.

42. I am grateful to J. A. Downie, Goldsmith's College, University of London, for the Bellamy reference, Oyer and Terminer Sessions Files, 7 July 1703, fol. 14; SP 44/352 fol. 105; Entry Book 350: 103, 104; Croome is CLRO SF 472, Recognizance 2. CLRO SM 72 for 24 Feb. shows that Croome did appear and give evidence.

43. The resolution and debate are in Journals of the House of Commons 14:207, for 25 Feb. 1702/3. Concern over their privileges had begun with the Kentish petition, and the Houses' perhaps unconstitutional imprisonment of the petitioners. A House committee had been appointed to study their prerogatives.

44. Journals of the House of Commons, House of Lords Record Office 14:207; *English Post*, 1 Mar. 1702/3. This was a rare action for the House; only a few other books even came up for discussion, and they tended to be blasphemous rather than seditious. Defoe's was the first book ordered burned since 1697. A few cases in 1699-1700 concluded with an order that the author be discovered.

45. CLRO SF 472. No other Defoe scholar seems to have found the trial records before or beyond the Sessions Minute Book 73 for July 1703-Mar./Apr. 1703-4, which records only Defoe's sentence (see Moore, *Citizen*, 372, n. 34). I am grateful to Mrs. Pauline Sidell for the translation of the Latin.

46. Jacob, *New Law Dictionary*; Crompton, *Practice Common-placed*, vii.

47. H 4-7; Paterson's proposal is BL MS. 4654; he wanted to set up a library to study "the effects of [how] wars, Conquests, Fires, Innundations, Plenty, Want, good or bad Direction, Management or Influence of Governments and Such Like, have more immediately Affected the rise or Declension of the Industry of a people whither Home or Foreign."

48. PRO T 1/85, 25 May 1703; T 38/737, 27 May 1703; SP 44/352 (fol. 162). See also the *Daily Courant*, which said Defoe was taken "on Thursday last in a private House in Spittle-Fields" (24 May 1703).

CHAPTER 6: PRISON

1. BL MS. Harl 7034 (fols. 440-41); Norfolk goes on to say that Nottingham "heap'd up vast Riches" and withdrew them "out of all danger"; Trevelyan, *England under Queen Anne* 1:335-36; Morgan, *English Political Parties and Leaders*, 50-51; CLRO SF 472; Downie, "Defoe's Shortest Way," 130.

2. In a letter to Harley, Defoe says he burned some of his papers (H 345). PRO 44.352.162; PRO T 54/8 (fol. 362-66), "A State of Mr. Borrett's Account . . . for one whole year ended 15th Oct. 1703."

3. Holdsworth, *History of English Law* 10:670-71. Baxter's books and papers

were seized when he was fined for preaching in 1675 (Powicke, *Reverend Richard Baxter under the Cross*, 88–89.

4. *The Reformer Reform'd*; the passage is quoted in full in Moore, *Citizen*, 126. See also "to the Keeper of Negate [*sic*] or his Deputy," PRO 44.352.f.162, and Nottingham's Letter Book. The contemporary description of Newgate is in *An Accurate Description of Newgate*, by B.L. of Twickenham, 1–3, 5–12, 35, 43. See also *Glimpse of Hell*, especially 4–5, 8, 15–18. PRO C 110/72 for 22 May. For this reference, I am grateful to Joanna Innes of Somerset College, Oxford.

5. [Leslie], *New Association, Part II*, 6; Oldmixon, *History*, 235.

6. This important note seems to corroborate Defoe's acquaintance with his king. BL Add. MS. 29595 (fol. 241) for 22 July 1703. In a conclusion added to Defoe's pamphlet *The Original Power of the Collective Body of the People of England*, he had congratulated King William for heeding the people's wishes, especially as expressed in petitions, and calling the new elections. Defoe described the people having "recourse" to the king in order to "depose" a Parliament "misapplying power" (24).

7. Davis was married to Defoe's sister Elizabeth. Earlier biographers of Defoe are probably correct to speculate that Defoe spent some of the time he was in hiding with Davis. He is referred to as a Tilbury shipbuilder in the recognizance for Defoe's bail; Moore, *Citizen*, 128, with reference to Sessions Roll for 7 July 1703.

8. By his account, Defoe was paying most of them the full amount owed rather than the percentage agreed upon in the bankruptcy settlement. See his *Dialogue between a Dissenter and the Observator* (1703), 7, and his letter to Harley (H 17). The nature of the debts outstanding in 1705 and, especially, the 1702 Annesley versus Foe case (PRO CP.40/3210 mem. 393) cast serious doubts on his claims, however.

9. This previously unnoticed circumstance is clear from the facts in Defoe's writing. In *More Reformation*, published 16 July 1703, Defoe says he has six children; his spring 1704 letter says seven (H 17). Mary Defoe would have gotten pregnant before 21 May or between 5 June and 7 July. Since Defoe does not mention the coming child in his personal summer writings, it is more probable that he was certain of her pregnancy in Sept. 1703. This child, Martha, was buried in 1707. As those who have studied Dissenting baptismal records note, there are many obstacles to finding those of any child. Few registers for the years before 1750 seem to have survived. Furthermore, Dissenters were more likely to travel great distances to their churches than Anglicans. Cf. Capewell, "Exploring Nonconformist Registers," 5–13.

10. Quarrell and Mare, *London in 1710*, 124–25.

11. Information from Defoe's poems; *DNB*; *Reformation of Manners*, 7; Sharpe, *London and the Kingdom* 2:509, 553–54; Orridge, *Some Account of the Citizens of London and Their Rulers*; Beaven, *Aldermen of the City of London* 2:113, 115. The City militia were surprisingly anti-Nonconformist. As late as 1690 five Nonconformist colonels were ejected from the trained bands (Beaven 2:113).

12. Journals of the House of Commons, House of Lords Record Office 13:732–35, 767; *Review* 1:97–105, and discussed more fully in ch. 8.

13. Beattie, *Crime and the Courts*, 459; *Observator*, 10 July 1703; this quotation was part of Tutchin's indictment for seditious libel, see Howell, *State Trials* 14:1098–99. The judgment in Defoe's case follows the indictment in CLRO SF 472; see also SM 73 for 5 July, the first day of session, which records Bellamy's and Croome's appearances as well as Defoe's. Defoe's reads, "Daniel de foe of the City of London, Gent. To answer. Appeared and Indicted." SM 73 for 7 July 1703 records Defoe's appearance for trial.

14. My interpretation of seditious libel is based on Pollock and Maitland, *History of English Law* 2:503; Holdsworth, *History of English Law* 8:333–45; Thomas A. Green, *Verdict According to Conscience*, 318–24, and "Jury, Seditious Libel, and the Criminal Law," 40–43; Hamburger, "Development of the Law of Seditious Libel and the Control of the Press," 661–765.

15. Hamburger, 734–35 and 701 respectively. See also Hawkins, *Treatise of the Pleas of the Crown* 1:193–94.

16. PRO KB 33/24/2; Woodfall, *Summary of the Law of Libel*, 2, 23–24; *Complete Collection of State-Trials, and Proceedings for High-Treason, and Other Crimes and Misdemeanors* 5:534 and 2:1035 respectively. "Trial of Benjamin Harris in 1679," *State-Trials* 2:1035. The privilege of the judge to determine seditious words was reaffirmed as late as 1731 in R. versus Francklin. In a 1792 protest against a "Bill to Remove Doubts respecting the Functions of Juries in Cases of Libels," "leaving to the Jury the Trial of fact, reserv[ing] to the Court the decision of the Law" was called "a fundamental and important principle of English jurisprudence" (PRO KB 33/24/2).

17. See Defoe's *Brief Explanation of a Late Pamphlet, Entituled The Shortest Way with the Dissenters*, 1–4; *Dialogue between a Dissenter and the Observator*, 26.

18. CLRO SF 472; Hamburger traces the government's attempts to use these laws in "Development of the Law of Seditious Libel," 673–74, 714, et passim.

19. Burn, *Justice of the Peace* 2:122–24; H 8; *Applebee's Journal*, 8 July 1721, in Lee, *Defoe* 2:403. Here Defoe says no sedition, treason, or malice is usually intended and indictments should read "greedily, avariciously." See also *Review* 1:165.

20. William Bohun, *English Lawyer*, 317; *Narrative of the Tryal and Sufferings of Thomas Delaune*, no pag.

21. *Applebee's*, in Lee, *Defoe* 2:401–4; quotation from *Essay on the Regulation of the Press* (1704), 18–20; Woodfall, *Summary of the Law of Libel*, 157.

22. Hull, *Female Felons*, 121; *Tryal and Examination of Mr. John Tutchin*; Holdsworth, *History of English Law* 8:341.

23. Moore, *Citizen*, 130; *Applebee's*, in Lee, *Defoe* 2:402–3.

24. PRO T 54/18 (fols. 362–66) and T 61/16 for 23 Oct. 1702 and 5 May 1703.

25. Entick, *New and Accurate History . . . of London* 2:329–30; J.G.W., "History of the Old Meeting Houses," 213–14; [Tutchin], *Western Martyrology*, 78.

26. Drysdale, *History of Presbyterians*, 456–57.

27. Dobrée, *William Penn*, 228–34, 259, 377. Penn's son had come to represent his father frequently; for example, in May 1701 he had appeared before the Lords with his father's petition (*Journals of the House of Lords*, House of Lords Record Office 16:676 et passim).

28. Penn, *Papers* 4:58, 66, 74 n. 7; Penn, *Considerations*, 2–3.

29. H 7 n. 2, 8 n. 3; BL Add. MS. 29589, fols. 28–29.

30. Burton, *History of the Reign of Queen Anne* 1:97; BL Add. MSS. 29589. 628; Beattie, *Crime and the Courts*, 464–66; Jewitt, "Pillory," 209–24; *Remarks on the Letter to the Dissenters*; *Post Man*, 31 July 1703; Old Bailey Sessions Papers, *Proceedings for . . . 8, 9, 10 July 1719*; Burn, *Justice of the Peace*, s.v. "Pillory."

31. H 7 n. 2; PRO SP 34.33; BL Add. MS. 29589 (fols. 28–29). Moore is mistaken in his assertion that Penn's letter was to Godolphin; in fact, the content contradicts him and his uncatalogued notes in the University of Illinois Library show that he did not read the entry correctly; see *Citizen*, 136.

32. PRO SP 44.104 f.316; Nottingham's Entry Book 104, p. 316. See Moore, 137.

33. H 7; BL Add. MSS. 29,589 fol. 46, and 29595 fol. 241.

34. PRO SP 44/104 for 27 July 1703; Luttrell, *Historical Register* 5:300-301, 323.

35. *Whole Life of Mr. William Fuller*, 107; Jewitt, "Pillory," 222–24; see also Luttrell 5:189.

36. Luttrell 5:300-301, 323.

37. Pittis, *Hugonot*, 4, 11; *Heraclitus Ridens* no. 2, 3 Aug.–Sept. 1703; *Wolf Stript of His Shepherd's Clothing*, 59–60 respectively.

38. Oliphant, "Author of *Robinson Crusoe*," 744.

39. From the 1700 judgment; see ch. 3; Aitken, "Defoe's Brick Kilns," 472–73. PRO PRIS 10/157, cited in Pat Rogers, "Defoe in Fleet Prison," 452, and Bastian, *Defoe's Early Life*, 272. Defoe's case is PRO PRIS 1/1A/533, CP 40/3210, mem. 393, judgment 20 Nov. 1702; *Biographical Dictionary of the Judges of England*, s.v. "Blencowe, John." See Whitehust versus Defoe, PRO C. 7/377/91.

40. Weiss, *Early Brickmaking in New Jersey*, 58–59; Nicolson, *British Encyclopedia or Dictionary of Arts and Sciences*, s.v. "Bricks"; Berendsen, *Tiles, 167 and 244; Builders Dictionary*, s.v. "Bricks"; Dobson, *Rudiments of the Art of Making Bricks and Tiles*, 21–24; Defoe, *Storm*, 72.

41. HMC Portland 4:64 (30 June 1703). Defoe, *Appeal to Honour and Justice*, 199–200.

42. *Fees of the Sheriffs' Court, Chamberlain's Office, Woodstreet and Poultry Compters, and Ludgate*; cf. Guildhall MSS. 17046 and 13672.

43. Quoted in Snyder, "Daniel Defoe, the Duchess of Marlborough, and *The Advice*" 5.

44. HMC Portland 4:75 for 4 Nov. 1703. Information on Harley's influence at this time is from David Green, *Queen Anne*, 85-129, and Hamilton, *Backstairs Dragon*, 49–81.

45. Defoe, *Minutes of Mesnager*, 49–50.

46. Quoted in *Queen Anne* from BL Add. MSS. 28055 (9 Aug. 1702).

47. In these months alone, see HMC Portland 4:69 on parties; 4:64 and 66 on Scotland; and 4:69 on Bills of Supply.

48. BL Loan 29/208 fol. 298.

49. BL Loan 29/191; Moore, *Citizen*, 145; Hamilton, *Backstairs Dragon*, 60.

50. CLRO SF 478, Recognizance 35. The terms of the surety are explained in Burn, *Justice of the Peace* 2:437–53. Offenses against the crown such as Defoe's nearly invariably required four sureties in addition to the offender's; other felonies required two (Hawkins, *Treatise of the Pleas of the Crown* 2:88).

51. These important notes are preserved in Lowndes' receipt book, PRO T 38/737 (97); see also T 48/17 for 8 Nov. 1703.

52. Cf. BL Loan 29/263 (fol. 154) for 4 Oct. 1705 for an example of Harley's. Others are scattered through the secretaries of state's Letter Books.

53. *Heraclitus Ridens*, 6 Nov. 1703. The record of Defoe's summons is in CLRO Sessions Minute Book 73, July 1703–Mar./Apr. 1703/4.

54. *Enquiry into the Occasional Conformity of Dissenters*, 20; cf. *Peace without Union*, 6–12; *Serious Inquiry into This Grand Question*, 5–21.

55. *Sincerity of the Dissenters Vindicated*, 2.

56. Trevelyan, *Select Documents*, 40.

57. I am grateful to the Bristol City Archivist, Mary E. Williams, for the description of Defoe's dress in that city; her source is Hutton, *Bristol and Its Famous Associations*, 185. Wagner, *Heralds of England*, 167, 120. There is a possibility that Defoe's arms came from the Painter-Stainer's Company rather than the College of Arms. Merchants often went to the City company, which insisted it did legitimate searches and was the most common source for arms for City funerals (Wagner, 237, 365). "City" coats of arms, often plainer than those for

the gentry and nobility, were done by the College of Heralds; cf. BL Stowe MS. 670.

58. For a discussion of Defoe's poetry, see my *Defoe*, 12–41.

59. *Elegy*, preface; see also 2:69 of the poem; *Storm* 2:90; and *Dissenters Misrepresented* 2:363.

60. *Dissenter[s] Misrepresented* 2:363 and 360 respectively.

61. Quoted in Bolam et al., *English Presbyterians*, 85, 89; Whiting, *Studies in English Puritanism*, 10; H 11. The conception endured; in 1721 Cotton Mather preached of the power of "the *silent Saint*" whose "very *silence* will have in it a *Voice* to be greatly hearken'd to" (*Silentarius*, 1). Defoe thinks of himself as a persecuted righteous man; ironically, these sermons counsel the good man's duty to "hold his peace" and be patient; cf. Mather, 2, 5, 11.

62. Defoe, *New Test of the Church of England's Honesty* 2:315; *More Short-Ways* 2:295.

63. *New Test* 2:315.

64. Defoe, *More Short-Ways* 2:277; *Dissenter[s] Misrepresented* 2:358.

65. Defoe, *Dissenters Answer to the High-Church Challenge* 2:189.

66. [Owen], *Moderation a Virtue*, 5; Defoe, *Letter from a Dissenter in the City*, 2–3; Calamy, *Abridgement* 1:622; *Principles of the Dissenters concerning Toleration and Occasional Conformity*, 48.

67. [Owen], 7, 11, 13; Trevelyan, *Documents*, 39.

CHAPTER 7: FOUR HUNDRED THOUSAND WORDS

1. Defoe was probably rewarded for *The True-Born Englishman*, perhaps in combination with the standing army tracts. See H 17; *Appeal to Honour and Justice*, 195. On Harley's agents in France and Scotland, see Snyder, "Daniel Defoe, the Duchess of Marlborough, and *The Advice*," 55–56.

2. Luttrell, *Historical Register* 5:363–67. *Chambers' Book of Days* calls it "one of the most terrific storms recorded in our national history" (2:622–23). Cf. Evelyn, *Diary* 5:550–52.

3. Defoe is listed as a contributor after "The Contents." Turner's *History* had been started by Matthew Poole "some 30 years ago," the advertisement for contributors said in the *Athenian Gazette; or, Casuistical Mercury*, 22 May 1695. Poole was a Presbyterian ejected from St. Michael le Querne, London, in 1662. He devoted himself to abridging a Bible commentary until he was forced to emigrate to Holland in the year he died, 1679. I am indebted to my research assistant, Maryellen Potts, for bringing this work to my attention.

4. Cf. Defoe, *Storm*, 89, 91, 127, 128, 131. For the circulation of papers in 1704, see Sutherland, "Circulation of Newspapers and Literary Periodicals, 1700–30," 111; and Snyder, "Circulation of Newspapers in the Reign of Queen Anne," 216. These sources give 7,000 for the *Gazette*, but that figure seems low considering that in Nov. 1705, 950 copies of each issue were given away and around 9,000 sold. The paper brought Harley over £150 per quarter (BL MS. Loan 29/162).

5. Cf., e.g., "A Letter from the Reverend Mr. William Derham, F.R.S. Containing his Observations concerning the Late Storm," *Philosophical Transactions of the Royal Society* 24:1530–34, with Defoe, *Storm*, 26–33; and Bohun's *Discourse on Wind* (1671) with *Storm*, 128.

6. Cf. Pat Rogers, "Defoe as Plagiarist," 771–74, and my *Defoe*, 98–100, 250 nn. 51, 52.

7. Defoe's thinking conformed to that of the majority of his contemporaries. For instance, when John Evelyn heard a series of sermons arguing that no

affliction comes by chance, he found them "true" and moving (*Diary* 5:554 and 548–49).

8. Michael Seidel gives a good synopsis of the Gill case in his notes to the *Consolidator*, MS, 107–10; I am grateful to him for use of this forthcoming edition. Cf. Luttrell, *Historical Register* 5:429.

9. Ellis, *POAS* 7:75; Defoe's *To the Honourable the C——s of England Assembled in P——t* (1704) was also circulated in a cheap printed version in April; see Downie, "An Unknown Defoe Broadsheet on the Regulation of the Press?" 54. Information on press production is from Ewald, *Rogues, Royalty and Reporters*, 6. *Life and Character of John Barber*, 8–9.

10. See Ellis 7:639, who points out that Darby can be identified as the printer through the *Observator*, 23–26 May 1705, and *Review*, 6 Oct. 1705; the *Whipping Post*, 17, 20. Cf. Ellis 7:75; Plomer, *Dictionary of Printers and Booksellers . . . from 1688 to 1725*; Barber allegedly gave Bolingbroke, then Harley's secretary-at-war, credit for introducing him to the Scriblerians (*Life of Barber*, 10–11).

11. *Hymn to Victory*, 5; see, for example, HMC Portland 4:69, 26 Sept. 1703, a letter in which Godolphin admits he is not paying as much attention to domestic affairs as he is to funding the war.

12. Marshal Maurice de Saxe spoke for the age when he said, "I am not, however, at all in favour of battles, particularly at the start of a war, and I believe an able general can, throughout his life, manage affairs without being forced to engage in one" (quoted in H. C. B. Rogers, *British Army of the Eighteenth Century*, 107).

13. Smithers, *Life of Joseph Addison*, 93–101; PRO T 52/22 for 1 Nov. 1704; the fact that *Diverting Post* no. 1 is carefully preserved in SP 9/251/207 emphasizes its official connection.

14. Defoe, *Dissenters Answer to the High-Church Challenge* 2:189.

15. BL Loan 29/209, De Fonvive to [Harley], 18 July 1705; *Gazette*: Stevens, *Party Politics and English Journalism, 1702–1742*, 6. Jones's Coffeehouse on Finch Lane was on the Southside of Mumford's Court on Milk Street (Guildhall MSS. 19501 and 8674/3, p. 255, which notes that it was one of four buildings owned by Joseph Collins, mercer, insured for £200).

16. Cf. *Review* 1:1 and Harley's 9 Aug. 1702 letter to Godolphin quoted in Downie, *Harley and the Press*, 58–59. Downie interprets the early *Review* differently (64–67).

17. Dunton, "Secret History of the Weekly Writers," in *Life and Errors* 2:423; McEwen, *Oracle of the Coffee House*, 49.

18. Downie quotes William Ettrick to Lord Weymouth (Aug. 1705) on coffeehouse reading; Ettrick uses the word *still* to describe continued high interest in reading the *Review* ("Mr. Review and His Scribbling Friends," in *Harley and the Press*, 346); Leslie, "Preface" to the *Rehearsal*, iv.

19. HMC Bath 1:58–59, quoted in part by Downie, *Harley and the Press*, 65–66.

20. [Tutchin], *The Prophet No Conjuror*, 8.

21. This pamphlet reprinted the entire "Proclamation for Restraining the Spreading of False News, and Printing and Publishing of Irreligious and Seditious Papers and Libels" (*Moderation, Justice, and Manners of the Review* [2], 22).

22. *New Cambridge Modern History* 6:658–60.

23. Hamilton, *Backstairs Dragon*, 63–65; Evelyn says Harley accepted the secretaryship "after a month's delay" (*Diary* 5:140); see Luttrell, *Historical Register* 5:416 and 418. Harley's memorandum is BL Loan 29/9/1; PRO T 52/22 records many payments to Harley made in 1704 and up to 12 May 1705.

24. McCormick, *State-Papers and Letters Addressed to William Carstares*, 66; BL Loan 29/209 n.d., fol. 234; the letter can be approximately dated by its reference to Pittis's recently published praise of Marlborough.

25. This letter may be dated approximately by Admiral Rooke's activity in the Mediterranean and the fact that Defoe was out of London on 30 May (*Review* 1:119) and on 14 June (HMC Portland 4:93).

26. See, for example, HMC Portland 4:64–65.

CHAPTER 8: THE LITERARY EFFORT OF A LIFETIME

1. Ashcraft, *Revolutionary Politics*, 172.

2. *Review* 1:268; H 72; *Queries upon the Bill against Occasional Conformity*, 25.

3. The conclusion states, "The Dissolution of the last Parliament has been subsequent to the Writing these Sheets," and Defoe congratulates the king for listening to the people (23–24).

4. Locke's *Two Treatises* had been published anonymously in 1690 and appeared with a preface by Locke in 1694. Cf. the previous quotation from *The Original Power of the Collective Body of the People of England* to Locke's *Second Treatise*, sections 222 and 243, and Defoe on *Salus Populi, suprema Lex*, 2, to *Second Treatise*, sections 124 and 222 (Locke uses the same quotation to make the same point in 158). On the purposes of government and their "dissolution," cf. Defoe, 5–6, 9, and 10 with Locke, sections 123, 124, and 131. Quotations from Locke's *Two Treatises* are from Laslett's edition.

5. For a detailed discussion of this form and its popularity, see my "Verse Essay, John Locke, and Defoe's *Jure Divino*."

6. My discussion of this poetry has benefited from Trickett, "The Idiom of Augustan Poetry," 111–26, and Cohen, "Augustan Mode in English Poetry," 3–32.

7. Colie, *Resources of Kind*, viii, 3, 30, 79–80.

8. The phrase is Krueger's; see his edition of *The Poems of Sir John Davies*, liv.

9. *Boswell's Life of Johnson* 4:286–87 n. 3.

10. On the reality of the threat to the Protestant succession, see Kenyon, *Revolution Principles*, 104–5, 126–27.

11. Leslie, *Cassandra*, 1.

12. Leslie, *New Association, Part II*, 28, 43, 50.

13. This opinion now seems generally accepted. See, for instance, Pocock, "John Locke," 5; Martyn Thompson, "The Reception of Locke's *Two Treatises*," 187–90; Ashcraft, *Revolutionary Politics*, 184, 572–89.

14. See especially Locke, *Two Treatises*, 243. On the contemporary radical associations of Locke's *Civil Government*, see Martyn Thompson, 186, 188–90. Kenyon points out that parliamentary debates in 1688–89 first rejected words like *forfeit* and even *abdicate* and that the Declaration of Rights makes no mention of the "Original Contract" ("Revolution of 1688," 48–49, 51, 68–69; see also 53, 56–58, where Kenyon links Locke's arguments to Hobbes and the Jesuits). See also Ashcraft, *Revolutionary Politics*, 184, 327, 558–69, 572–89; Goldie, "Revolution of 1689," 479–80.

15. Defoe repeats this paragraph in *Review*, 18 Dec. 1708, 5:454. I am grateful to my graduate assistant Maryellen Potts for the reference from *The Storm*.

16. Morton's lectures, called *Eutaxia*, have been lost. My account of them is from Toulmin, *Historical View*, 233. Toulmin appears to have seen *Eutaxia* but quotes Samuel Palmer's description from *Vindication of the Dissenters* (1704). On Defoe's reading, see Girdler, "Defoe's Education," 575.

17. Defoe, *More Short-Ways with the Dissenters*, 6.

18. For a more detailed discussion, see my "Verse Essay, John Locke, and *Jure Divino*."

19. Cf. Locke, *Two Treatises* 2:200 and Defoe, *Jure Divino* 7:27. *Forfeit* and *compact* are among the words used in the same special sense; Barclay is another unusual source both men quote; see Ashcraft, *Revolutionary Politics*, 296–97 n. 44.

20. See Downie, "Unknown Defoe Broadsheet," 51–58 from BL Add MSS. 28094, ff. 165–66, and BL Loan 29.162.5.

21. HMC Portland 4:93.

22. HMC Portland 4:138.

23. Warrant and Newgate delivery, PRO SP 44/349; examination of Sammen, SP 34/5/69 (for 1704); Hedges to attorney general, SP 44/105/135, 5 Oct. 1704.

24. Luttrell, *Historical Register* 5:469; Ellis and Snyder, "Introduction" to *Master Mercury*, v and ix n. 28, from Luttrell 5:469 and Folger Library Newdigate Collection, LC 2799.

25. Information about the Mediterranean campaign is from J. H. Owen, *War at Sea under Queen Anne*, 71–100.

26. Owen calls it "luck," 81; Clark, *Later Stuarts*, 204.

27. Defoe, *Spanish Descent*, 3.

28. *Review* for April and May 1704, see especially 1:97–105; Defoe, *True State of the Difference between Sir George Rook, Knt. and William Colepeper, Esq.*, gives the history of the quarrel, minutes of the trial, and its outcome. Most Defoe scholars believe Defoe wrote part of this pamphlet; except for parts of the appendix, the evidence seems slim to me.

29. *Master Mercury*, 21 Aug. 1704, 17. Rooke had reported on 25 July 1704 that he could not "attempt" Barcelona because the Dutch were short of provisions and the "Forces" could not get to the fleet in time to help. He estimated he could besiege Cadiz only until 15 Sept. This report and his accounts of battles and his councils of war are in the House of Lords Main Paper, MS. 2058.

30. Trevelyan, *England under Queen Anne* 1:420; Owen, *War at Sea*, 97.

31. Quoted in Wilson, *Memoirs of the Life* 3:335.

32. *Life of Barber*, 9.

33. Dunton, *Whipping-Post*, 9; Dunton, *Life and Errors* 1:180; H 84; see the other ten letters between Defoe and Fransham in my "Russell to Defoe," 164.

34. This was David Erskine, earl of Buchan, who became godfather to Sophia's first child in Jan. 1730. Her husband, Henry Baker, taught one of the earl's deaf children.

35. I am grateful to my colleagues Marjorie Curry Woods and Ella Schwartz for the translation.

36. Dunton, *Whipping-Post*, 91.

37. On Defoe's family, see H 15, 17 et passim; on inherited offices, see Aylmer, *King's Servants*, who points out that Europeans were firmly committed to providing for the eldest son and that the Restoration gave the "'old administrative system' a longer lease of life than it might otherwise have had" (433; see also 9, 107–8, 123). See also Thirsk, "European Debate on the Customs of Inheritance, 1500-1700," 177–91. Evidence in the manuscripts of Defoe's contemporaries is abundant. The warden of Fleet Prison was appointed for life in 1713 with "reversion to his son" (who sold the position for £5,000) ([Brown], *The Fleet*, 9–11, 14); the *Post Boy* for 8 May 1701 announced the appointment of "Mr. Wright, Eldest Son to the . . . Lord Keeper" to "the Place of Clerk of the Crown, vacant by . . . death." One of the Clerks of the Signet asked to resign his

place to his nephew, and the queen approved (1 Apr. 1706; BL Portland Loan 29/263). For arrangements for Charles Davenant's son, see BL Add. 4291; Lansdowne requested the position of Master Swan-Herd, held by his deceased father and brother, for a friend and said: "Your Lordship could not well refuse it, if I asked it for my self" (20 Feb. 1713/14; BL 29/203).

38. Defoe asked Harley to send money to his family in Kingsland on 30 July 1705 (H 96); Fransham quotes *Dyers* as saying Defoe was a tenant (H 65); Defoe received mail at a tavern in Essex Court where Robert Davis's home was in the Middle Temple (H 124); Oliphant, "Author of *Robinson Crusoe*," 740–53.

39. H 18, 84; Defoe, *Jure Divino*, xxxv.

40. Ashcraft, *Revolutionary Politics*, 172–73.

41. *Review* 1:226; H 59.

42. I am grateful to Alan P. Voce, curator of the Tiverton Museum, for this item and for friendly assistance. His sources were the Burnet Morris Index and Martin Dunsford's *History of Tiverton* (1790).

43. I am grateful to Anthony Carr, local studies librarian, Shropshire, who sent this material, which is in "Mayors of Shrewsbury," 24.

44. Ogden, "Antiquarians at Ovenden" (1905), 214; (1925), 93–94; (1929), 219, provided by M. E. Corbett, Calderdale central librarian, Northgate, Halifax.

45. Provided by A. Heap, Leeds Local History Library, from R. G. Wilson, "Gentleman Merchants: The Merchant Community in Leeds, 1700–1830," 244.

46. Information about Kinderley is from Gill Rayment, library assistant, Wisbeck and Fenland Museum; about Jardine from J. M. Farrar, Cambridgeshire county archivist, who cites the *Cambridge Chronicle*, 13 June 1767, and BL Add. MS. 5825, fol. 25. I am grateful to them for bringing these references to my attention.

47. Jane E. Isaac, Suffolk County Archives, provided J. Duncan's "Daniel Defoe and His Connection with Bury St. Edmunds," 2, 4, and 5. I appreciate her help.

48. Cf. H 98, 96, 101–2 especially n. 3, and 108–13; the name of the tavern is from Hamilton, *Backstairs Dragon*, 83.

49. I am grateful to the archivist at the Liverpool Record Office, Janet Smith, for sending me copies of the Norris letters (920 NOR 1/283, 920 NOR 2/393, and 595). The ordinance is quoted in a report on the Coventry riot written by the mayor and aldermen, BL Loan 29/192.

50. I am grateful to D. Wilkinson of the Weymouth Library for bringing the court records to my attention and for providing Groves, "Daniel De Foe in Dorsetshire," 67–75, and Moule, *Descriptive Catalogue of the Charters, Minute Books . . . of Weymouth and Melcombe Regis*, 86–87. See *Minute Book* (1699–1724) 3:142, fols. 74–78, and H 97–98.

51. H 97–102 (includes Stafford's warrant and letter to Hedges); PRO SP 44/105/287; SP 34/6/128, and Weymouth Library, *Minute Book* 3.142 (1699–1724), fols. 74–78.

52. *Review* 2:214; 2:231–32; H 106.

53. *Reviewer Review'd*, 1 and 8; *Moderation, Justice, and Manners of the Review*, 3, 4–20; *Republican Bullies*, 4; Harley may have silenced this paper, see Downie, "Mr. Review and His Scribbling Friends," 351; *London Gazette*, 21 June 1705.

54. Sutherland, "Circulation of Newspapers and Literary Periodicals, 1700–30," 111.

55. Defoe, *Review* 3:11–12 and *Jure Divino*, xxvii; *Proceedings*, 3.

56. HMC Portland 4:188.

CHAPTER 9: NEW LIFE

1. Published alone in July 1706, Defoe's *True Relation* appeared with the fifth edition of Drelincourt in 1707. By 1768 the combination had seen twenty legitimate editions and dozens of pirated ones; Baine, "Defoe and Mrs. Bargrave's Story," 390; Powell, "Defoe and Drelincourt," 98. There is extensive literature on Defoe's sources and the publication history of *True Relation*; cf. Secord, "September Day in Canterbury," 639–50; Parsons, "Ghost Stories before Defoe," 293–98.

2. H 85. Defoe tells Fransham to read it, and asks for permission to publish one of Fransham's anecdotes in it. See also *Review* 1:355, 26 Dec. 1704.

3. Defoe, preface to *Jure Divino*, xxvi.

4. Quoted in Hamilton, *Backstairs Dragon*, 82.

5. Although Downie does not cite the familiar figure of 1,400 copies, his "Mr. Review and His Scribbling Friends" is the best study of Defoe's readership in 1705 (345–66).

6. H 86; Snyder, "Daniel Defoe, the Duchess of Marlborough, and *The Advice*," 56–57; BL Add. MS. 61458, Halifax to the duchess, 12, 15, and 22 May 1705. Later she resented Halifax and wrote, "If he did give . . . the whole Sum, I dare swear that he gave it in his own Name: For I never heard any thing . . . to thank me for it" (24 Sept. 1744 in Portland Loan 29/200). In 1705 Halifax had told her he would "follow your Directions, till you give Me leave to let him know his Benefactress, which I hope shall not be long concealed" (15 May 1705, BL Add. 61458).

7. Cf. *An Essay upon Projects* (1697), 312–34, the *Review* for 13 and 16 Jan. 1705, and the proposal printed in Healey for Defoe's evolving plan. The act passed is in *Manuscripts of the House of Lords, 1706-1708* 7:518–37. On the Bolton Committee, see H 73–78; House of Lords Committee Book, no. 7, entries for 14 and 20 Jan., 3, 7, 10, 12 Feb., and 3 and 9 Mar. 1704/5. I am grateful to the House of Lords for permission to use and quote this material. Defoe's proposal considers at least two problems raised by Marlborough, Byng, and Shovel, the higher wages paid by merchant ships and the competition from the collieries. *Manuscripts of the House of Lords* (HMC vol. 17, pt. 10), 6:116, 223–26. Defoe's handwritten proposal is in the House of Lords Record Office, Main Papers, MS. 2058, pt. 2; it is printed in H 73–74.

8. *Some Considerations on the Reasonableness and Necessity of Encreasing and Encouraging the Seamen* (1728), 35–38.

9. Ll. 110–13. A more literal translation reads: "Dare some deed to merit scanty Yíatos and the gaol, if you wish to be somebody. Honesty is praised and starves." Defoe made mistakes in his Latin, but many "errors" cited by earlier scholars reflect his use of medieval Latin, commonly used in England until at least 1740, rather than classical. I have reproduced his Latin exactly. For this observation I am grateful to Marjorie Curry Woods. Defoe's Latin usage seems most like that in historical and diplomatic documents but is marked by usage indicative of a person who learned Latin in school but did not use it daily and cannot be idiomatic. Medieval Latin was the means of international contact and slowly gave way to the revival of classical Latin, now called Neo-Latin.

10. Defoe, *Reply to H——'s Vindication*, 7.

11. Bastian, "James Foe, Merchant, Father of Daniel Defoe," 86; CLRO Ass. Box 32.6, 33.6 (records wife and one child), 21.6.

12. I am grateful to my research assistant Laurie Sterling for this information. Her major sources were Cunnington and Lucas, *Costume for Births, Marriages and Deaths*; Gittings, *Death, Burial and the Individual in Early Modern Eng-*

land; Pepys, *Diary*, vol. 1; Puncle, *Funeral Customs*. The *Universal Spectator and Weekly Journal*, 30 Aug. 1729, reported that 200 attended a funeral and were "treated with *Newberry* Beer and Plumb cakes."

13. James's will is PRO PROB 11/492/31/246, written 20 Mar. 1705/6 and proved 25 Feb. 1706/7.

14. Defoe's other biographers, Sutherland and Moore, are probably reading this period aright; cf. Moore, *Citizen*, 124–26.

15. Sutherland, "Some Early Troubles," 288–89; see Sessions Roll for 7 July 1703; Bastian, *Defoe's Early Life*, 222–23; Moore, *Citizen*, 284; Peterson, "Defoe and Westminster," 329–31. Davis's good fortune is recorded in BL Loan 29/201 for 20 Oct. 1713 and PRO T 53/17 (fol. 210).

16. See *London Gazette* advertisements for 18–22 July and 5–8 Aug. 1706.

17. The motion for a second reading of the Bankrupts Relief Bill was negatived, House of Lords Record Office, Main Papers, 14 Apr. 1707, MS. 2385. For amendments, see *Statutes of the Realm* 8:461–65, and 600–602. See also Defoe's *Remarks on the Bill* (1706), and the anonymous *Observations on the Bankrupts Bill* (1706). The latter gives some questionable descriptions of Defoe's commission hearings; cf. 35–36; H 123, 401; Moore, *Citizen*, 98; *Review* 3:575–76.

18. Sutherland, "Note on the Last Years," 138–39; PRO C.11.679.2 and c11.1473.18. Healey, Moore, and Bastian repeat the Stancliffe story. *Review* 3:397–400 (note that both 22 Aug. and 20 Aug. bear the date of 20 Aug.).

19. McCormick, *State-Papers to Carstares*, 719; Secretary Johnstone, quoting Harley, in a letter to George Baillie of Jerviswood, 21 Dec. 1704 (*Correspondence of George Baillie of Jerviswood*, 27).

20. 6 July 1706, SRO GD.124.15.413, and BL Add. MS. 6420 for 31 July 1706.

21. 16 Sept. 1706, SRO GD.124.15.462. On Stewart's opposition, see Omond, *Lord Advocates of Scotland* 1:270–71.

22. H 125, and 24 Aug. 1706 in HMC Portland 4:324 respectively.

23. HMC Portland 4:296. On Harley's spies and correspondence, see Moore, *Citizen*, 183–84; Snyder, "Daniel Defoe, the Duchess of Marlborough, and *The Advice*," 55–56; and John H. Davis, *Robert Harley as Secretary of State, 1704–1708*, 14, 18, 20–25.

24. HMC Portland 4:303.

25. HMC Portland 4:78, 331.

26. Hamilton, *Backstairs Dragon*, 105. For a typically high-quality report from Greg, see HMC Portland 4:240–42 for 4 Sept. 1705, the day that Hamilton made his suprising move to allow Queen Anne to select the Scots commissioners. Evidence of Harley's correspondence is in BL Loan 92/221 and BL Portland Loan 29/208 (Carstares), 29/191 (Leven); 29/371 (Lockhart).

27. *Consolidator*, 341 and 344 respectively; see also 103–5, 116–19, and 339–46, especially 118 and 345.

28. Phillipson to [George Tilson], a friend in Secretary Boyle's office, later secretary to Bolingbroke, 15 July 1708, PRO SP 54/3 (31); and BL Add. MS. 34, 180 for 14 June, no year. Henry Hunter, *Brief History of the Society in Scotland for Propagating Christian Knowledge*; Burnet, *History* 5:171.

29. Defoe, *Jure Divino* 12:19 and 21; *Reply*, 13–16. Haversham's speeches are collected in *Memoirs of the Late Right Honourable John Lord Haversham, from the Year 1640 to 1710*.

30. J. R. Jones, *Country and Court*, 331; Riley, *Union of England and Scotland*, 2–11, 171–206; Ferguson, *Scotland's Relations with England*, 245. On the historic connection between Scotland and France, see Fenwick, *Auld Alliance*; Smout calls France "Scotland's best trading partner" ("Union of the Parliaments," 149).

Manuscripts recording the Scots part in appointing the commissioners include Nairn to Gleneagles, who relates how Stair, Hew Dalrymple, James Murray, and Nairn took the list to Gleneagles, 4 Dec. 1705, SRO GD 124/15/263/5; for Queensberry and Argylle's part, see Clerk's Journal, SRO GD 18/3132; Queensberry and Mar, HMC Bath at Longleat 1:67.

31. For a fuller discussion of these men, see my "Defoe and the Clerks of Penicuik"; see also Graham, *Annals and Correspondence of the Viscount and First and Second Earls of Stair*, especially 1:201–20. Many historians consider Stair and Mar to be the architects of the passage of the treaty in Scotland. Defoe would soon know another "Lord President," James Graham, Montrose, who became Lord President of the Privy Council in March 1706, but he was not a commissioner and not in London in May.

32. LA II.63. I would like to thank Roger Emerson of the University of Western Ontario for bringing this item to my attention and to the University of Edinburgh for permission to publish the pertinent parts in full here. Rosebery, too, was a firm supporter of Union. In March 1706 he had written Mar that in spite of the expense, he was glad to be a commissioner to the negotiations, "for I do believe nothing will ever make this country easy but an intire compleat union" (SRO GD 124/15/341/9, 11 Mar. 1706).

33. I am grateful to Iain Brown of the National Library of Scotland, for useful suggestions and for making his Ph.D. dissertation, "Sir John Clerk of Penicuik," available to me. Dr. Brown is preparing a full study of Clerk and his circle, the family's cultural patronage and its contributions to archæology, antiquarian thought, architecture, painting, and poetry. For a fuller discussion of this episode in Defoe's life, see my "Defoe and the Clerks." Nairn to Gleneagles and Glasgow, 4 Dec. 1705, SRO. GD. 124.15.263.5.

34. Defoe, *History of the Union*, "Of the Carrying on of the Treaty in Scotland," 5. There were at least two Edinburgh editions. Both print the second *Essay at Removing National Prejudices* immediately after the first, beginning on p. 27. One edition is fifty pages (see National Library of Scotland copy 1.52) and the other 51 (NLS 1.519). Defoe explained that he had written these essays to allay *English* fears.

35. For contemporary descriptions of routes and inns, see SRO GD RH 9.17.266, and SRO GD 18.3131; Defoe, *Tour* 2:283. The Coldstream route was more popular; Defoe probably chose his route in order to stop at Hew Dalrymple's North Berwick home. Hamilton, Tweedale, and three more men shared expenses and paid about £8.10.9 each; Hamilton private papers, F2.605.

36. *Tour* 2:299 and 301; see also [Morer], *Short Account of Scotland*, 70–73.

37. [Morer], 70; Taylor, *Journey to Edenborough in Scotland*, 100.

38. *Tour* 2:298–301; [Morer], 73; Graham, *Social Life of Scotland in the Eighteenth Century*, 83–85.

39. For the sentiments of the common people, see the Rev. Mr. Robert Wylie to Hamilton, 1 July 1706, GD. 406.1.C.9747; earl of Selkirk to Hamilton, 2 Sept. 1706, Hamilton private papers, 7251; Riley, *Union of England*, 282–84; Mar to Godolphin, 16 Sept. and 26 Oct. 1706, GD. 124.15.462; Smout, "Union of the Parliaments," 158. The quotation is from [William Black], *Reply to the Authors of The Advantages . . . of an Incorporate Union, and The Fifth Essay*, 14; H 147. On the influx of people, see H 182, 184, 187; Lockhart, *Memoirs*, 218–19; W. C. MacKenzie, *Andrew Fletcher of Saltoun*, 146–47. The description of the Highlander is Taylor's (*Journey to Edenborough*, 138).

40. Information on the Riding and Parliament House is from MacKenzie, *Fletcher of Saltoun*, 145–48, and Terry, *Scottish Parliament*, 94–102 and 78–85.

41. Marchmont to Wharton, 9 Nov. 1706, in *Selection from the Papers of the Earls of Marchmont* 3:311; see also 313.

42. Ferguson says "the evidence which supports the view that many Scottish politicians regarded the union as a political job from which profit could be made is wide, varied and irrefutable" (*Scotland's Relations with England*, 250). This discussion is based on Ferguson, 232–53; Riley, *Union of Scotland*, 254–59, 273.

43. Clerk, *Letter to a Friend*, 9–10.

44. PRO T 48/17; private papers of the duke of Buccleuch, TD 86/62, vol. 127, no. 131. BL Loan 29/210, fol. 166 is especially revealing. £4,500 for the earl of Glasgow went through "John Campbell Goldsmith" and an account by Glasgow shows Atholl, Tweedale, and Marchmont receiving about £1,000 each and many payments of several hundred pounds. On awarding of positions or money, see especially Ferguson, *Scotland's Relations with England*, 246–50; Riley, *Union of England and Scotland*, 254–59; Burton, *History of Scotland* 8:178–86. On 20 July 1707 Seafield and Glasgow wrote a letter "to be read [to] Godolphin and then burnt" explaining that they could account for only some of the £20,000 "advanced" by Godolphin and would pay that part back. The rest, given to Atholl, Tweedale, Roxburgh, Marchmont, "and sixty or seventy others" could not be "asigned" "unless it were to bring discredit upon the management off [*sic*]that parliament" (BL Add. MS. 34, 180).

45. Information about the duke of Hamilton comes primarily from the papers on deposit at the SRO and the private Lennoxlove and Hamilton papers made available to me by the present duke. I am grateful for his generosity. See HMC Portland 4:339; Lennoxlove 406.1.6037 and 406.1.5294; private papers 7854 and 7263 for 8 Oct. 1706; Defoe, *Strict Enquiry into the Circumstances of a Late Duel*, 37–38; Taylor, *Journey to Edenborough*, 117–18; private papers of the duke of Buccleuch, TD 86/62, vol. 127, no. 150; on the magnates, see Riley, *Union of England and Scotland*, 11–19. Halifax confirms that the Union now "cannot fail of succeeding" in a letter to Robethon, 26 Oct. 1706; he also describes the opposition's tactics in this letter (BL Stowe 241, 72–73).

46. See Defoe, *History of the Union*, "Minutes of the Parliament in Scotland," 4–50; Riley, *Union of England and Scotland*, 287–90; GD 406.1.c.8104 and in the private papers, GD 406.1.M.9.273; see my "Cross-Purposes," 173–75. No two sources agree on the exact vote, partly because Queensberry insisted upon being counted although he had no official vote; see Ferguson, 261; Riley, 289, 328. The quotation is from "Of the Carrying on of the Treaty in Scotland," *History of the Union*, 45.

47. Backscheider, "Cross-Purposes," 171–73; GD 124.15.449.65 and 67 for 14 and 19 Nov. 1706; Mar to Nairn, 23 Oct. 1706, GD.124.15.449.41; MacKenzie, *Fletcher of Saltoun*, 270; H 133–36 and 151; Bennet of Grubbet, "Diurnalls of the Parliaments of Scotland," SRO GD 90.2.172; Anderson, SRO PA 3.7. On Leven's order, GD 26.7.124; according to Bennet, Provost McClellan shed tears as he watched the troops enter his city; Mar had predicted a riot in a letter written that morning (GD 124.15.449.41).

48. H 134, 146, 147, and 163; Ker, *Memoirs* 1:27–30; private papers of the duke of Buccleuch, TD 86/62/1202 for 24 Oct. 1706.

49. HMC Portland 4:335 for 1 Oct. 1706, Bell to Harley.

50. As Macaree says, the two churches were really not identical, especially in forms of government. See his "Daniel Defoe, the Church of Scotland, and the Union of 1707," 62–65. For Defoe's explanations, see H 141, 143, 158.

51. Cf. HMC Portland 4:335 for 1 Oct. 1706 and 4:336 for 4 Oct. The difference in tone is striking; at the first meeting Bell doubts Defoe's word

about authorship of a work under discussion. Bell had worked for Harley at least since 1704; in one letter Harley writes to Bell, "[I] greatly approve your Diligence & discreet management of this affair, I desire you will continue" (9 Sept. 1704, Portland Loan 29/263).

52. Taylor, *Journey to Edenborough*, 112; Defoe mentions the batons in his *History of the Union*; a [1707] attack on Defoe accuses him of pretentious behavior at Sue's (Novak, "A Whiff of Scandal," 37); see ch. 3, n. 20, above.

53. H 133, 148, 151–52, and 161: "This Terrible people the Churchmen have not yet done." Others saw the church as a major source of unrest; see Mar to Erskine, 16 Nov. 1706, GD 124.15.474. The commission was very large and included, in addition to Hew Dalrymple, William Carstares, Archibald Campbell, and Colonel Erskine, the man who would be next moderator, John Stirling, and the present moderator, William Wishheart. So important did they feel their work to be that members were "enjoyned" to stay in Edinburgh. Stirling was principal (president) of the University of Glasgow, the position Carstares held at the University of Edinburgh. Representation is recorded on 8 Nov. in SRO PA 7/20. Pertinent minutes are SRO CH 1/3/8 for 29 Oct. and 8 Nov. 1706; CH 1/4/2 for 9, 11, 14, 23, 28, 29 Oct., 1 and 25 Nov., 4 and 19 Dec. 1706; CH 1/2/25/3 for 11, 14, and 16 Oct., 22 Nov., 12 Dec. 1706; CH 1/3/9 for 6, 11, and 24 Dec. 1706, and 14 and 16 Jan. 1707.

54. *Papers of Marchmont* 3:304–5 (Marchmont to Somers); private papers of the duke of Buccleuch, TD 86/62/1202 for 21 Sept. 1706; Mar to Nairn, 23, 26 Nov. and 2 Dec., SRO GD. 124.15.449.

55. Mar to Nairn, SRO GD. 124.15.449, and James du Pré to William Paterson in "Two Treatises Relating to the Union of the Two Kingdoms," BL. MS. Add. 10,403.

56. Belhaven's speech is reprinted entirely in Defoe's *History of the Union*. See also Macaree, "The Flyting of Daniel Defoe and Lord Belhaven," 72–80, and Burton's *History of the Reign of Queen Anne* 1:343–45. Mar relates the story of how Belhaven believed that Haddington had written the verse satire of his speech in a letter on 26 Nov.; Mar says, "I send you inclosed ane answer to [the speech] in rime, wch is the true way of answering such a Speech, I believe it was done by Defoe" (SRO GD 124.15.449).

57. This letter is in BL Loan 29/370; I am grateful to the British Library for permission to publish it here and in *Modern Language Review*. H 160; this letter can now be dated the thirteenth with certainty.

58. H 86; Snyder, "Daniel Defoe, the Duchess of Marlborough, and *The Advice*," 56–67; BL Add. MS. 61458, Halifax to the duchess, 12, 15, and 22 May 1705. Cf. correspondence in BL Loans 29/151, 29/197, 29/198, 29/200, and 29/203; the years covered are 1711 until shortly before Halifax died in 1715. The quotation is from 29/200, Halifax to Harley, 9 Mar. 1712/13.

59. Defoe, *History of the Union*, "Minutes with Observations," 33–34.

60. Backscheider, "Defoe and the Clerks," 375–76.

61. Backscheider, 375.

62. Privy Council Minutes, rough and fair copies; a manuscript note lists Defoe's petition as a "Note of Business" for 3 Dec., Minute Book of Privy Council, SRO PC 4.3; "Sederunt and Minutes of Councill the 3d. Decemb" has a rough copy of the petition, but the fair copy says specifically that the petition was "read and granted" on the earlier date. Rough copy, SRO PC 12, Box 11, as is the membership/attendance list. Membership included Queensberry, Mar, Loudon, Leven, Argyll, Buchan, Cessnock, Erskine, Hew Dalrymple, and the lord provost of Edinburgh. In a letter to Mar, Baron Clerk called Forbes "my friend" and asked Mar and his friends to support Forbes in the 1709 election

(25 Dec. 1708, SRO GD 124/15/920). Hew Dalrymple made the same request (SRO GD 124/15/928).

63. SRO GD 124.15.474; GD 220/5/101, and 124.15.449; cf. 26 Nov. 1706, Nairn to Mar summarizing efforts to persuade various members of the English commission and Mar to Nairn on the same day in which he says that "all is lost" if the English will not accept a few alterations.

64. Mar to Godolphin, 26 Oct. 1706; James Ogilvy to Godolphin, 7 Nov. 1706, *Correspondence between George Ridpath and the Rev. Robert Wodrow* 1:176–77; GD 124.15.462.

65. Beatrice Curtis Brown, ed., *Letters and Diplomatic Instructions of Queen Anne*, 190–91, for 31 July 1706.

66. Carstares' correspondence is in McCormick, *State Papers to Carstares*, HMC Portland, and other papers. He wrote Mar that he was afraid considera-tion of an incorporate union would delay the settling of the succession to the throne, a matter he considered essential and pressing (2 Mar. 1706, GD 124.15.315). Defoe wrote that "Carstares in perticular [*sic*] Merits Great Con-sideration" for his work for the Union (H 193).

67. BL Stowe MSS. 241.f.72, also quoted in Green, *Queen Anne*, 152–53, Halifax to Robethon; Ferguson, *Scotland's Relations with England*, 253.

68. SRO CH 1/3/9, fols. 114–19. The queen's letter to Queensberry is dated 21 Nov., BL Add. MS. 6420.

69. Hamilton private papers, 8122, Charles, earl of Selkirk, to his mother, the duchess of Hamilton; Atholl to her, SRO GD 401.1.7092.

CHAPTER 10: A TERRIBLE PEOPLE

1. PRO T 27/18; SRO GD 124/15/413, 534, 581, 747, and 763. Correspon-dence of the powerful Scots contains numerous requests for help in securing positions. In a typical letter, Thomas Burnet reminds the earl of Mar that he "did to the utmost of my power" to serve the queen and asks for help in getting a post in the Commission of Customs (SRO GD. 124.15 for 29 July 1708). George Lockhart complained that far too many positions in Scotland went to English-men (*Memoirs*, 342). The *Edinburgh Courant* makes it a point to record informa-tion such as that four of the twenty-five commissioners for settling the Equiv-alent were Englishmen (6–9 June 1707). P. W. J. Riley details the problems with setting up the Customs and Excise system in *The English Ministers and Scotland, 1707–1727*, 38–46.

2. "A brave man is not rendered contemptible by being brought to the scaffold; he is, by being set in the pillory. His behaviour in the one situation may gain him universal esteem and admiration. No behaviour in the other can render him agreeable" (Adam Smith, *Theory of Moral Sentiments*, 1:138). Laetitia Barbauld also describes the punishment as "severe and degrading" in her preface to *Robinson Crusoe* (British Novelists series, 16:iii); ten years after the incident Defoe described himself as "suffering the Indignity of the Pillory" (*Review* 9:183).

3. H 221; SRO GD 18.3135, correspondence to his father, Sir John; PRO T 27/18, Godolphin to Queensberry, 6 May 1707. See Moore, *Citizen*, 188–89.

4. HMC Bath 1:152, reprinted in H 224; BL Loan 29/194 for 14 May 1707.

5. Defoe, *Review* 4:201, 223–24; *Modest Vindication of the Present Ministry*, 6–7.

6. Payments to William Paterson and John Ker of Kersland were larger than those to Defoe. For instance, Paterson received £200 in the summer of 1706 and Ker £700 on 4 Nov. 1707 (PRO T 48/17). Bell supplied Ker and Fearne as

well as Defoe on occasion, cf. BL Loan 29/194, 4 Jan. 1707 and 10 Apr. 1707. For Montrose's letters, cf., GD 220/5/107, and on other noblemen's letters, SRO TD 86/62, vol. 127. Harley heard periodically from Atholl, Seafield, Leven, Annandale, Mar, Roxburgh and others; Carstares wrote frequently, and Hamilton addressed Harley as "Gawen Mason," cf. BL Add. MS. 28055 and BL Loan 29/210; HMC Portland 4:382.

7. HMC Portland 4:421; BL Loan 29/194.

8. Defoe says almost the same thing in *Review* 3:577; these quotations are H 187, and *Review* 3:470, 473.

9. Luttrell, *Historical Register* 6:195–96; *Review* 4:314–16.

10. SRO CH 1/4/2 for 7 Aug. 1707; SRO GD 124/15/419 and 491 for 15 May and 9 Aug. 1707; SRO GD 220/5/159 for 24 Jan. 1708; BL MS. 34,180 for 5 Aug. 1707.

11. Peterson, who also believes some knew Defoe's mission ("Defoe in Edinburgh, 1707," 28–29); *Review Review'd*, 38; *Welsh-Monster* [1708].

12. Clerk, *Memoirs of the Life of Sir John Clerk*, 63–64.

13. "Memorial for Major James Coult," SRO GD 26.9.79; petition to Mar, SRO GD 26.9.468; H 397; Russell to Defoe, printed in my "Russell to Defoe," 167–68; Wodrow, *Analecta* 2:88–89.

14. The canon of Defoe's writings in 1706–7 is vexed. Cf. Moore, *Checklist*, Moore numbers 109–54 with Novak's contribution to *NCBEL*, 887–89; see also Downie, "Defoe and *The Advantages of Scotland by an Incorporate Union with England*," 489–93.

15. We know the location of Mrs. Anderson's print shop because of efforts to remove her. On 8 Dec. 1703, the chamberlain of the Burgh of Edinburgh was instructed to "persew a Removeing" of Anderson from the space "below the Bibliotheck." On 31 July 1713 she finally had found a place to move her presses but asked for "some encouragement" for renovation (Armet, *Extracts from the Records of the Burgh of Edinburgh, 1689 to 1701*, 65, 251).

16. H 211, and *Review* 4:513. Unfortunately the Privy Council minutes end abruptly on 25 Jan. 1707 (SRO PC 4.3), and Defoe's letter is dated 27 Jan.

17. SRO GD 124.15.1027 dated 19 Feb. 1711; see my "Cross-Purposes," 167–68; Johnson, *Journey to the Western Islands*, 50.

18. *Review* 4:82; H 197, where Defoe writes, "I talk of Manufactures and Employing the poor."

19. Edinburgh Town Council Minutes, 20 Sept. 1704, 16 Mar. 1705, and 5 Sept. 1707 Edinburgh City Chambers archives; SRO RD 4:110 and RD 14.52.266; the deed was registered 9 Apr. 1712. The council complained that the linen trade was not being supported by England as it it had promised on 3 Feb. 1710 (Minutes, vol. 39). Sutherland cites one copy of the deed (*Defoe*, 164–65, 289 n. 119). Reports on the poor at New Greyfriars appear at several points in the Minutes; the numbers are given for 5 Dec. 1711 (40:304; see also 40:258–59 and 41:25).

20. Edinburgh University MS Laing III.339 for 25 Mar. 1707; see Burch, "Defoe and the Edinburgh Society for the Reformation of Manners," 306–12.

21. Information about the Edinburgh Society is from Laing III.339; Burch, "Defoe and the Edinburgh Society"; McElroy, "A Century of Scottish Clubs, 1700–1800," 1:6–1 through 12–1; Portus, *Caritas Anglicana*, 141–55.

22. Woodward, *Account of the Rise and Progress of the Religious Societies*, 85. See also *Brief Account of the Nature, Rise, and Progress, of the Societies for Reformation of Manners*, which classifies some sixty societies in England and Ireland; *Representation of the State of the Societies*, 14–15. Calamy notes in 1699 that the Dissenters

had been as active as Church of England members "from the first erection" of the London societies (*Historical Account of My Own Life* 1:410-11). See Dunton's *Athenian Mercury* (cf., 4 Aug. 1691) and, for example, *Proposals for a National Reformation of Manners*, licensed Feb. 1694.

23. Dunton describes how the societies operated in the *Athenian Oracle* 3:30–31; Shower's sermon was 15 Nov. 1697, printed 1698; Oldmixon, *History*, 175.

24. [Owen], *Moderation a Virtue*, 25. Curtis and Speck also note the trend in the societies to dwindle to "low Church" Whigs and Dissenters ("The Societies for the Reformation of Manners," 59).

25. Information about the societies and their work comes from Rawlinson, D.1312 and D.129, manuscripts at the Bodleian Library; Woodward, *Account of the Rise and Progress*; Portus, *Caritas Anglicana*, 38–57, 60–61, 73–75. For the extent of book distribution, see Bahlman, *Moral Revolution of 1688*, 54–58. The quotation is from *15th Account of the Progress Made towards Suppressing Profaneness and Debauchery, by the Societies for Reformation of Manners*.

26. On Cotton Mather and his involvement with the religious and reform societies, see Middlekauff, *The Mathers*, 268–77; Wendell, *Cotton Mather*, and Silverman, *Life and Times of Cotton Mather*. Mather refers to his correspondence with Defoe in his *Diary* 2:74, and his daughter said that her father received letters from Defoe and read them to the family.

27. McElroy, "Century of Scottish Clubs," 6–1 [*sic*]; SRO GD 95.10; SRO CH 1/4/2 for 7 Nov. 1707, 22 Jan. and 3 Mar. 1708; Minutes of the Greyfriar's Kirk Session, 2 Oct. 1710; Allen and McClure, *Two Hundred Years*, 122–25.

28. SRO GD 95.10, minutes beginning 27 May 1708; see the General Assembly minutes for 20 Apr. 1708. The SPCK in London had been working to establish lending libraries in the Highlands since 1705 (Allen and McClure, 125). Bahlman, *Moral Revolution*, 72–74.

29. University of Edinburgh MS. Laing III.339.

30. SRO GD 95/10/3; *Review* 6:441. Defoe here expressed an opinion held by many Scots. As late as 1748 Robert Walker wrote that the Highlanders "are not quite civilized . . . further, That they are, many of them, wild and barbarous" (*Short Account of the Rise, Progress, and Present State*, 50).

31. Gilbert Elliot, too, was a substantial man, for he pledged £20 (SRO GD 95.10; these records are very badly damaged). I am grateful to the SPCK for permission to use the information from its Abstract Letter Books (1708-9, 1709–11) and Minutes of the SPCK (1706-9, 1709–12); see especially to 28 July 1709 and 2 Feb. 1709. Other rebuffs are dated 17 and 24 Nov. 1709 and 7 Dec. 1710. The English SPCK did not seek a royal charter until 1969. Hunter, *Brief History of the Society in Scotland*, 2–8, 14–16, 19.

32. H 246; SRO CH.2.154.6; see also Kirkcaldie Kirk session records at Kirkcaldie Old Church, Scotland. I am grateful to the Rev. John Sim and his wife for giving me access to these records.

33. Quoted in Story, *William Carstares*, 309; Calamy, *Historical Account* 2:152.

34. Information about the Clerks' acquaintances is from the National Library of Scotland Advocates' MS. 29.1.2, SRO GD 18/5278; Peterson, "Defoe in Edinburgh," 25–28; and Moore, "Defoe and the Rev. James Hart," 404–9. In a 25 Oct. 1719 letter Hart mentions that he has been staying at Penicuik for some time (National Library of Scotland Advocates' MS. 29/1/2). The description of Penicuik is in a letter to Boerhaave by John (Clerk, *Memoirs*, 237–40); the description of Sir John is by his son ("A Short Account of My Father," SRO GD.18.2092). On Sir John's coal mines and his "Calvinistic" management style, see Marshall, *Presbyteries and Profits*, 235–47.

35. Sir John Clerk was a subscriber; *Caledonia* was published in Edinburgh in early December. Clerk occasionally had editions he purchased bound. See Clerk's Account Book, SRO GD.18.2096.

36. Queensberry's order and the receipts signed by Defoe are in the Taylor Collection, Princeton University.

37. Defoe alludes to "Ecclesiastic Frenzy" (18 Mar. 1707, H 208) and calls the Scottish clergy "the worst Enemies of the Union" (10 June, H 226). Others substantiate Defoe's opinion; see, for example, HMC Portland 4:460–61; Luttrell, *Historical Register* 6:182, 195–96; SRO GD 220/5/159. Unrest in Scotland is discussed in Mar's 29 July letter to Leven ordering him to stay in Edinburgh to give stability and "preserve the Peace" (SRO GD 26.13.139); Mar to James Erskine, 28 June, SRO GD 124.15.496 (20); Riley, *English Ministers and Scotland*, 30.

38. Defoe called the clergy's suggestions regarding the Oaths "rational" (H 192); he told Harley he had spies on the commission and in General Assembly (18 Mar. 1707, H 211). Whenever Defoe gives the dates of attendance at church meetings, his truthfulness is supported by Church of Scotland records. For example, the Presbytery of Dumfermline did meet on 14 May 1707; Archibald Campbell was moderator and "Col. Areskin" one of the ruling elders, both acquaintances of Defoe's (SRO CH 105/4; H 153, 176).

39. Cf. *Passion and Prejudice*, especially 4, 7, and 15. It appears that copies of this pamphlet survive only in the National Library of Scotland, the Glasgow University Library, and the Canterbury Cathedral Library; H 210.

40. H 211; also 195, 201, and 209–10 on the Webster controversy. The exchange began with Webster's *Lawful Prejudices against an Incorporating Union with England*, which was published before the middle of January 1707; Defoe answered with his sixth essay, *Two Great Questions Considered*, and *The Dissenters . . . Vindicated*. Webster then published *The Author of the Lawful Prejudices . . . Defended*, to which Defoe replied with *Passion and Prejudice* and *A Short View of the Protestant Religion*. At this point, William Adams entered the fray and Webster published *A Second Defence of the Lawful Prejudices*.

41. H 241–42 and 244–45; BL Loan 29/194 for 20 Sept. 1707.

42. Sums are from Defoe's correspondence and Bell's letters to Harley preserved in the Portland papers; see especially BL Loan 29/193 and 194 (quotations are from 1 Oct. and 19 Nov. 1706); see especially 4 Jan. 1705; H 159; Snyder, "Reports of a Press Spy," 330 n. 1. The average cost of lodging in Edinburgh in 1707 was half that sum; the earl of Mar, for example, paid £10 Scots per month, about £9.2 sterling for the year (SRO GD 124/15/413). In *Passion* Defoe says he rents from a friend (5), perhaps John Clerk, whose family owned one of the largest houses on the High Street; see the Register of Assessments for the September 1711 window tax, Edinburgh Town Council Archives. Alexander Campbell, Leven, and Robert Sandilands also owned very large houses. Some of Harley's other agents experienced the same problems with irregular payments and contact; see, for example, Ogilvie's letter in HMC Portland 4:303.

43. H 180; Guildhall MS. 4093/1, St. Peter the Poor registry, 21 Dec. 1706; will proved 25 Feb. 1706/7, PRO PROB 11/492/31/246. Lee dates Martha's death (*Defoe*, 1:59). See also Moore, *Citizen*, 326.

44. H 247, for 28 Nov. 1707; HMC Portland 4:464. Bell's letter telling Harley that he had given orders to pay Defoe is dated 2 Dec., BL 29/194.

45. H 227, for 12 June 1707. Descriptions of Godolphin are quoted in Snyder, "Godolphin and Harley," 243–44.

46. John H. Davis examines Harley's mode of correspondence (*Robert Harley as Secretary of State*, 6–8); see also Hamilton, *Backstairs Dragon*, 3–6, 12–13, and my "Personality and Biblical Allusion," 1–20.

47. Letters in BL Loan 29/370, 7 Oct. 1706 to Carstares and 21 Nov. 1706 to Leven. One note Harley wrote for a meeting on 13 Jan. 1708 read, "joyne in nothing which is ill & wrong" BL 29/9, vol. 2, bundle 51; see also 29/10. Pope, "Epistle to Robert, Earl of Oxford," ll. 23–26.

48. HMC Portland 4:179. See also HMC Bath, 180, 182, 189–90, and especially 183 (Godolphin, 18 Sept. 1707).

49. See especially, on the one hand, *Legion's Memorial*; *Original Power of the Collective Body of the People of England*; *Review* 3:559, 561–64; and on the other, Defoe's sixth *Essay at Removing National Prejudices*, entitled *Two Great Questions Considered*.

50. "Edinburgh, January 1707" is printed at the end of the text of "A Short Satyre on . . . the Albanian Animal," see 3, 14, 17–18. *A Scots Poem, POAS* 7:239–82.

51. See Luttrell, *Historical Register* 6:216 and 224. Part of Defoe's interest in Charles may have come from descriptions being printed in the *Edinburgh Courant*; see especially 12–14 March 1707.

52. See Luttrell; Hearne, *Collections*, cf. 6:107, and the London periodicals for that time period. Defoe refers to Tutchin's "MURTHERER" in *October Club* 2:56.

53. Hamilton, *Backstairs Dragon*, 90-114; Holmes and Speck, "Fall of Harley in 1708 Reconsidered," 673–98, and Snyder, "Godolphin and Harley," 241–71.

CHAPTER 11: POLITICAL MAELSTROM

1. We can date Defoe's departure as soon after 22 Mar. 1708 because of a letter he carried to the earl of Leven (H 254–55). How low Harley had fallen shows in the letter he received on 3 Feb.: the queen had granted his petition to "give such accounts and produce such Papers to Commons" as he should "think necessary for your justification, in case any thing should be objected to you" (PRO SP 44/107/166).

2. HMC Bath 1:171; Edinburgh Town Council Minutes (20 Feb. 1708) 39:30–31 City Chambers archives; Mar wrote David Nairn on 14 June 1708 that he, Seafield, and Loudoun were trapped at a dinner until 1 A.M. by such a mob (SRO GD 124/15/831).

3. Downie argues that this phrase demonstrates Defoe's "utter ignorance of the state of relations between Godolphin and the Junto" ("Daniel Defoe and the General Election of 1708," 321–22).

4. Green, *Queen Anne*, 190 and 198; Riley, *English Ministers and Scotland*, 140.

5. H 251–52; Snyder, *Correspondence* 2:967. Ample evidence is also in the HMC Portland papers; see, for example, 4:535–38.

6. H 256. Strong evidence points to Sunderland; see H 452–53, 26 Apr. 1718, in which Defoe describes his association with Sunderland. The edition of *HMC Eighth Report* names Sunderland. Moreover, his activities in 1708 strongly argue his identity. Godolphin and Sunderland distrusted each other; see, for example, Trevelyan, *England under Queen Anne* 2:348. Correspondence between Sunderland and Godolphin (about Shute, for example) suggests at least some serious collaboration; cf. BL Add. MS. 6420, fols. 82–83.

7. Riley, *English Ministers and Scotland*, 114, 143–44.

8. On Queensberry and Defoe's *History*, see *Review* 3:114, 611, 657–58, 682.

Riley and other modern historians say that Queensberry was not as powerful as Defoe thought (*English Ministers and Scotland*, 150–51; Ferguson, *Scotland's Relations with England*, 211–19).

9. SRO GD 220/5/159, 7 May 1708, Sunderland to Montrose; GD 124/15/831, Mar to Nairn, 14 June 1708.

10. The release of other noblemen was also negotiated. See MacKinnon, *Union* 399–400; Riley, *English Ministers and Scotland*, 104–8; and Downie, "Defoe and the General Election," 322–23, 326.

11. Godolphin to Marlborough, 18 June 1708, in Snyder, *Correspondence* 2:1016.

12. Loudoun to Hew Dalrymple, 8 May 1708, and 21 June 1708, in the private papers of the marquis of Bute, Bundle A235; Rothes to Montrose, SRO GD 220/15/135; GD 124/15/831/20; the Leven papers, SRO GD 26/15/23.

13. *Review* 5:142; on the election abuses, see Riley, *English Ministers and Scotland*, 108-10; SRO GD 220/5/135, 172, 763; BL Add MS. 41340, fols. 104–6. The earl of Rothes' report to Montrose explained that Cessnock and his father, Marchmont, were to contact Lord Somers and attempt to overthrow the Fife election of "trash" (SRO GD 220/5/159); Phillipson concurred with Defoe's opinion that the Squadrone had little influence with the "Generality," PRO SP 54/3 (31).

14. *Review* 5:146; cf. Riley, *English Ministers and Scotland*, 108–10, and Downie, "Defoe and the General Election," 324–25.

15. Novak lists this tract as "probably" by Defoe in *NCBEL*, and I believe it to be by Defoe, perhaps with some help from his Scottish friends. Edinburgh Town Council Minutes 39:31, City Chambers archives.

16. HMC Bath 1:178; Godolphin to Marlborough, 2 July 1708, in Snyder, *Correspondence* 2:1025; H 264, respectively.

17. See *Equivalent for De Foe*; *Second Defence of the Scotish* [sic] *Vision*; *Paper concerning Daniel De Foe*; *Review Review'd*, 38–39; Couper, "Writings and Controversies of Clark," 88–92. *Second Defence* calls Defoe's intention to move to Scotland "cant." The record of John Frewen's efforts to have the pamphlet answered are in the Minutes of the SPCK, 1706–9 for 29 July and 12 Aug. 1708, and in the Abstract Letter Book for 1708–9 for 24 July, 30 Sept., and 30 Oct. 1708, SPCK archives. Because of the dates of comments on events in the *Review*, we can tell that Defoe was still in Edinburgh on 28 Oct. when Prince George died but was back in London by 12 Dec.

18. See Jones, *Compleat History of Europe*, 494; it is quoted on p. 7 of *Paper concerning Daniel De Foe*.

19. "Second Defence of The Scotch Vision"; *Review Review'd*, 39–40; "A Short Satyre on the Albanian Animal," and [Abercromby], *The Advantages of the Act of Security Compar'd with Those of the Intended Union*, 18–19.

20. *Answer to a Paper concerning Mr. De Foe* is usually assigned to Defoe, but the attribution is not certain.

21. Defoe had been advertising for subscribers for months and even printed a special proposal (Pafford, "Defoe's *Proposals* for Printing the *History of the Union*," 202–6).

22. Couper, "Writings and Controversies of Clark," 91–92.

23. Few copies of *History of the Union* are identical. This collation is of two copies in the National Library of Scotland, DF.4.56 and E.D.F. 9 (4106)DEF. Defoe explains Anderson's culpability in *Reproof to Mr. Clark, and a Brief Vindication of Mr. De Foe*, 5. Couper's manuscript evidence suggests that the lord provost of Glasgow urged the compromise between Defoe and Clark (92). Couper erroneously states that Defoe made no changes in *History of the Union*.

His defense, *Advertisement from Daniel De Foe to Mr. Clark*, is signed "D.F."

24. Secord, "Defoe in Stoke Newington," 212–15; St. Mary's Parish Record, Stoke Newington, in the Hackney archives, PM 1.fol.129 for 15 Aug. 1709.

25. *Review*, for 25 Aug. 1709 (6:245–46); *Brief History of the Poor Palatine Refugees*; PRO SP 44/108; Moore, *Citizen*, 303–4; Fernsemer, "Daniel Defoe and the Palatine Emigration of 1709," 103–10. Defoe's ideas about the Palatines are consistent with his economic theories; see Earle, *World of Defoe*, on "population." The private papers of the marquis of Bute include an "Answer of the Commissioners of Trade and Plantation to an Order of the . . . Parliament 21 March 1710/11" by the earl of Stamford discussing the settling of 3,000 Palatines on the Hudson River in New York to make turpentine, "rozen," tar, and pitch from pine trees (Bundle A245). Nearly 5,000 arrived in London in May 1709 alone; for a description of their ages, sexes, occupations, and living conditions, see PRO SP 34/10 (236–37).

26. Ellis, "Defoe's 'Resignaçon,'" 338–54.

27. Ellis notes these four lines in the 22 Oct. 1709 *Review* (6:342), the entire version in the 28 Jan. 1710 Edinburgh *Review*, and the expanded version in the preface to vol. 8 of the *Review*, written July 1712 (Ellis, 341–42); *Robinson Crusoe* 1:156.

28. *Edinburgh University Matriculation Roll: Arts, Law, Divinity*, vol. 1, *1623–1774*, 24 Mar. 1710, and Matriculation Accounts for the same day. Benjamin Defoe paid £3; only five of the twenty-seven students paid that amount, with £1.10s. appearing to be usual, Edinburgh University Library. See Burch, "Benjamin Defoe at Edinburgh University, 1710–1711," 343–48. Grant to Defoe: Town Council minutes, 19 Oct. 1709, in the archives of the Edinburgh City Chambers. A number of Defoe's friends including Adam Brown were on the council. On the *Scots Postman:* the Minutes show that Fearne received exclusive right to print on Tuesday, Thursday, and Saturday, 39:413–14. SRO RD.4.107, contract between David Fearne and Daniel De ffoe, Esq., dated 13 Dec. 1710.

29. See, for example, *Review* 6:422, 445, 475, and especially the monster Jacobite he creates in 6:465 (5 Jan. 1709/10). My discussion of Sacheverell and his trial is based upon Holmes, *Trial of Dr. Sacheverell*; Scudi, *Sacheverell Affair*; Kenyon, *Revolution Principles*, and Madan and Speck, eds., *Critical Bibliography of Dr. Henry Sacheverell*.

30. Cf. *Reviews*, 7 and 10 Jan. 1709/10 (6:469–71 and 473–76).

31. "Articles of Impeachment," Holmes, *Sacheverell*, 180–81; H 265–66; Defoe prints a "Certificate" from the three men who made these charges against Sacheverell in the 13 Apr. 1710 *Review* (7:31). A printed copy of Sacheverell's speech "at the Bar of the House of Lords" is in PRO SP 34/12.

32. Holmes, *Sacheverell*, 226. The sermons to be burned were the 15 Aug. Derby Assizes sermon, "The Communication of Sin," and the 5 Nov. St. Paul's sermon, "The Perils of False Brethren."

33. Holmes, *Sacheverell*, 231; Scudi, *Sacheverell Affair*, 126–31.

34. *A Speech without Doors* (London, 1710) is an attack on Non-Resistance. I have omitted "The Age of Wonders," an anti-Sacheverell doggerel ballad attributed to Defoe by J. R. Moore, from this discussion, because, in my opinion, it may not be his work.

35. Argyll and his brother, the earl of Islay; Somerset; Rivers; Shrewsbury; and Harley had banded together during the Sacheverell trial. Halifax and Newcastle soon moved more firmly into Harley's circle. See Holmes, *Sacheverell*, 226–27; Trevelyan, *England under Queen Anne* 3:57–58.

36. Cf. *Remedy Worse than the Disease*, 12; *Brief Survey of the Legal Liberties of the Dissenters*, 6–9.

37. Stock quotations are from the *Post Man* and the *London Gazette* for those dates. See also B. W. Hill, "Change of Government," 395–413.

38. PRO T 48/16 and 17; this was the source of Ker's and Paterson's money. Defoe is always called "Claude Guilot" and signed his receipts in an inverted script. He endorsed the 27 Sept. 1710 receipt for £100, but "James Turner" received £50 "for the use of Claude Guillott" on 27 Dec. (PRO T 48/16).

39. For a more detailed discussion of some of these essays, see my "Defoe's Lady Credit," 89–100.

40. BL Loan 29/371 for 23 Aug. 1710. The Scots habitually used "Queen's Servants" to mean men who supported the ministry, regardless of party; Harley's use quoted in Trevelyan, *England under Queen Anne* 3:74.

41. On election numbers, see Trevelyan 3:72–74; Clark, *Later Stuarts*, 217–18; Holmes, *Sacheverell*, 250–55; Dickinson, "October Club," 155–58.

42. A 1708 report to Godolphin from a press spy identifies Matthews as Defoe's printer and Morphew as his publisher; if this report is accurate and Defoe is using "publisher" in the same way, then it was Morphew who was kidnapped. The report is quoted in Stevens, *Party Politics and English Journalism*, 51. Secord, however, says that it was Matthews who was kidnapped (*Review* 1:xxi). George identifies Defoe as the chief target of the pro-Sacheverell propagandists and discusses the satiric prints in *English Political Caricature to 1792* 1:67–71.

43. *Medley*, no. 1, 5 Oct. 1710. On the creation of this paper and its opposition to Defoe, see Oldmixon, *Life and Posthumous Works of Arthur Maynwaring*, especially 168–69. These two pamphlets were provoked primarily by the re-issue of Defoe's 1706 preface to *De Laune's Plea for the Non-Conformists* in a book entitled *Dr. Sacheverell's Recantation.* [King], *Vindication of the Rev. Dr. Sacheverell*, 2, 12. In the new edition of *Jure Divino*, each book has its own title page. The woodcut labels the pillory "For Jure Divino" and an onlooker's "bubble" recalls *Shortest Way with the Dissenters*. See Madan and Speck, *Critical Bibliography*, for titles of other works aimed at Defoe.

44. Holmes, *Sacheverell*, 225–29, 284, 287; Ferguson, *Scotland's Relations*, 156–57; Riley, *English Ministers and Scotland*, 153–54, 157.

45. On the elections, see Riley, *English Ministers*, 147–57; private papers of the marquis of Bute, Hew Dalrymple to Loudoun, 23 Aug. 1710, and Queensberry to Loudoun, 26 Oct. 1710 (Bundle A245); BL Loan 29/220, Mar to Harley, 10 Nov. 1710; H 293; the earl of Islay's letters in the Portland papers reveal the character of his efforts and his conviction that he acted at "the Queen's commands," see especially 4:622–23, 625–26. On abuses, see Royal Burgh Convention records, Bundle 227, in the Edinburgh City Chambers Archives; for example, James Scott, 4 Nov. 1710.

46. H 313–15. For patronage reasons, Harley appointed Annandale, whom Defoe had described (correctly) as having no reputation because he could never be counted on except to oppose Queensberry.

47. Contemporary descriptions of Leith are from [Morer], *Short Account of Scotland*, 89; Irons, *Leith and Its Antiquities* 2:120–21, 246–47. The Royal Burgh Convention in April 1710 compiled a list of "Ships, Barks, Boats, and other small craft" for Scotland's seaports; Leith had 33 ships and 92 seafaring men. The nearest competitor, Aberdeen, had 13 ships and 31 skippers and seamen. This report also includes the information about the men who sailed the Leith ships and boats. See Bundle 226, Edinburgh City Chambers archives. The contract with Hislop is SRO RD 4.111 and RD.14.52.269, dated 1 Sept. 1712, but contracted on 7 Mar. 1707. The record of Davis's guild brothership is in

Edinburgh Town Council Minutes, 39:331, 6 Apr. 1709, and in the Edinburgh Roll of Burgesses, City Chambers archives.

48. Minutes of the Town Council of Edinburgh 39:831–43; Loudoun to Harley, June 1710, in the private papers of the marquis of Bute, Bundle A.245; PRO SP 44/109, 29 Aug. 1710, Boyle to Commission of the Treasury.

49. H 283 and 284. Strangely enough, the only report the lord high admiral received was in favor of Queensferry, Edinburgh Council minutes, 5 Mar. 1712. "Ancient Letters" 8:90, Edinburgh City Chambers archives.

50. Edinburgh Town Council Records, 13 Dec. 1710, 39:1026–28. The council inserted a clause specifying its right to void Davis's contract without reimbursement to him should Parliament fund a wet or dry dock and Davis's lease prove "prejudiciall thereto."

51. SRO RH 14/52/269/5 gives the details of the contract. Heislop's investment was to be £150 sterling, but he was to pay Davis £30 "for his Contryvence and attendence upon the . . . erecting of the said milne" (Edinburgh Town Council records, 22 Oct. 1712); the contract was between Davis and the treasurer, Robert Tod, and was entered in the Burrough Court records on 23 Oct. 1712. (Edinburgh Town Council Minutes 40:542–43). The Edinburgh marriage register dates the license 24 June 1716 and the marriage 2 July 1716. Helen's estate can be estimated as sizeable because of a variety of legal documents about it; see, for example, RD.4.105, 29 Oct. 1709.

52. Edinburgh marriage register, license 2 Nov. 1718; the marriage 17 Nov. 1718.

53. The contract with Ochiltree for the tablecloths is dated 9 Apr. 1712, but begins with a reference to 30 Sept. 1710 (SRO RD 4.110 and RD 14.52.266). There was no requirement to register such contracts; the dates before registration refer to private agreements usually drawn up by the men's solicitors. On Defoe's import/export involvement, see the Russell letters in my "Russell to Defoe."

54. Russell tried to help Defoe secure "ane exclusive privilledge" for printing, but the council would agree only to order that no other papers be printed on the three days Defoe selected for the *Courant*; Edinburgh Town Council records, 1 Feb. 1710; Russell to Defoe, 14 Mar. 1710, reprinted in my "Russell to Defoe," 163.

55. BL Loan 29/45A, Sir Rowland Gwynne to Robethon, 31 Oct. 1710, and quoted in Dickinson, "October Club," 159.

56. This discussion is based upon J. R. Jones, *Country and Court*, 339–46, and Dickinson, "October Club," 161–62.

57. Swift, *Journal to Stella*, 7 Jan. 1711.

58. J. R. Jones says that the appointments were often lucrative but not influential; he gives as an example the appointment of Sir William Wyndham to Master of Buckhounds (*Country and Court*, 346); see also Dickinson, "October Club," 163–64, 167.

59. *Letter from some Protestant Dissenting Laymen*, 14; *Letter to the Dissenters*, 26.

CHAPTER 12: THE GOLIATH OF THE PARTY

1. Quoted in MacLachlan, "Road to Peace," 198.

2. McKay says Hanover became England's "enemy" after Utrecht ("Bolingbroke, Oxford and the Defence of the Utrecht Settlement in Southern Europe," 265). See also Holmes, "The Commons' Division on 'No Peace without Spain,' 7 December 1711," 224, 230; Hatton, *George I*, 105; J. R. Jones, *Country*

and Court, 297–98, 351–52; *New Cambridge Modern History* 6:477; Thomson, "Parliament and Foreign Policy," 138–39; Green, *Queen Anne,* 257–58. Hill reminds us that one of the first actions of George I's rule was to impeach those responsible for the Peace of Utrecht ("Oxford, Bolingbroke, and the Peace of Utrecht," 241–42). Defoe's deprecating attitude toward Hanover can also be seen in *Succession of Spain Considered,* 1, 36–37.

3. In *Ballance of Europe,* for instance, Defoe had listed the "principals" in the war and added, "it needs not for any Light that it will give to our Discourse, that we should enumerate the Kings of *Portugal* and *Prussia,* the Duke of *Savoy,* or Electors of the Empire" (26); see also 38–41. Sill, "Report to Hanover on the 'Insolent De Foe,'" 224–25, speculates that the report concerns such pamphlets as *Reasons against the Succession of the House of Hanover* and that it does not recognize Defoe's irony.

4. Secret Service accounts cited in Hanson, *Government and the Press,* 95–96; Stevens, *Party Politics,* 57; Downie, "Secret Service Payments to Daniel Defoe," 437–41. Treasury Records, PRO T48/16, Lowndes' accounts for 27 Sept. 1710; 24 Feb. and 6 Mar. 1712/13; 16 Jan., 1 and 10 Feb., and 2 and 26 July 1714, each for £100 to "Claude Guilot." I have confirmed these figures and found an additional £50 on 27 Dec. 1710, in PRO T48/15 and in T48/17, and an additional £100 for 10 July 1711 in BL Loan 29/45A. Some of the payments are easy to miss: on one occasion, Lowndes paid James Turner, Defoe's 1705 Weymouth contact, for him (see T 48/16, 27 Dec. 1710, entry marked "in Satisfaction of Money expended for Her Maty. Service"). Defoe mentions his allowance on 13 Feb. 1710/11 (HMC Portland 4:658–59) and again on 26 July 1714 (H 442).

5. PRO SP 44/77, fols. 157, 161, 162, 167, 179, 182, and 196. Walpole and Townshend signed warrants. Even a woman who had made her mark because she could not sign her name was arrested "for causing to be printed or published" Philo Basilius's *Letter to Richard Steele* (Maria Atkins, 19 July 1715, fols. 179 and 182). See Stevens, *Party Politics,* 104–5; Nicholas Rogers, "Popular Protest in Early Hanoverian London," 70–100; Downie, "Secret Service Payments," 439–41.

6. *Secret History of the October Club,* 65.

7. John, "War and the English Economy," 334–37.

8. *Ballance of Europe,* 28–29; see also *Review* 4:187, 4:247, 6:29, 6:114, and preface, 7:3. On 31 May 1709 Defoe had written: "At last the wish'd for Hour is come. . . . And the Peace IS MADE" (6:97).

9. J. R. Jones, *Country and Court,* 290–98; *New Cambridge Modern History* 6:428–40; Coombs, *Conduct of the Dutch,* 195; quoted in B. W. Hill, "Oxford, Bolingbroke and Utrecht," 251; Grange to Bruce, 8 Dec. 1710 (SRO GD 124/15/986). The correspondence of the time is full of such sentiments. Mungo Graham wrote Montrose in December 1708 that the news from the Continent was "most seasonable" and expressed hopes that "a vigorous prosecution of the advantages already gott may bring this war to a very speedy and happy Conclusion" (SRO GD 220/5/803). See also Francis Philipson to George Tilson, 9 Dec. 1709 (SRO RH 2/4/299).

10. Trevelyan, "'Jersey' period," 100–101.

11. Trevelyan, 105; B. W. Hill, "Oxford, Bolingbroke and Utrecht," 245–46.

12. Sachse, *Lord Somers,* 307. On the propaganda campaign against the allies, see Coombs, *Conduct of the Dutch.* Coombs traces "a determined policy on the part of the Tory ministry of publicly reproaching and abusing the Allies" (277).

13. Defoe's part in the formation of the South Sea Company has been largely misunderstood. His own plan, offered in the time of King William, differed

significantly from the one Harley adapted from that presented by the City financiers. See Sperling, *South Sea Company*, 4–5; B. W. Hill, "Oxford, Bolingbroke, and Utrecht," 249–51; BL Loan 29/200, 14 Oct. 1712. I am grateful to my research assistants, David Ames and Laurie Sterling, and my colleague Cliff Smith, for their contributions to my discussion of the South Sea Company.

14. H 339–40, 343, 346–49; *Review* 8:177–79. Defoe's plan as outlined in *The Succession of Spain Consider'd* was to make the duke of Savoy, the king of Lombardy, and Prince Eugene governors of the Spanish Low Countries. The succession question had been hopelessly complicated in April 1711 when Emperor Joseph I died of smallpox at age 32. His brother, the archduke Charles, subsequently Emperor Charles VI, thus inherited the claims of the house of Hapsburg. Were Charles to rule Spain as well as the Empire, the balance of power would have been distorted at least as much as by a union between France and Spain. Philip V, the French candidate, was therefore permitted to be king of Spain.

My discussion of Swift is based on Ehrenpreis, *Swift*, especially 2:406–542. For a judicious appraisal of Swift's influence, see Downie, *Jonathan Swift: Political Writer*, 146–50, 184. See also Ellis, ed., *Swift vs. Mainwaring*, xxxi; Speck, "*Examiner* Examined," 153–54.

15. In August 1710 the Bank of England had offered Harley £50,000 for two months instead of the £100,000 he requested (B. W. Hill, "Change of Government," 402). In April 1711 nineteen Whigs and four Tories had been elected to the board of directors of the East India Company and twenty-four Whigs and no Tories to that of the bank in spite of vigorous Tory campaigns and the preparation of lists of candidates (Sperling, *The South Sea Company*, 7). For a discussion of Defoe, the company, and his tracts, see Sperling, 14–19; on Harley and the company rivalry see J. R. Jones, *Country and Court*, 343, and Hamilton, *Backstairs Dragon*, 189–91.

16. In content *Reasons Why This Nation* is much the same as his shorter *Reasons for a Peace* (1711); both offer the same alternatives (stop the funds, impose a general excise, or stop the war), propose new partition schemes, and refer to the "caprice" of the allies. No London publication date has been assigned this pamphlet; the Edinburgh edition reads, "*London* Printed, and *Edinburgh* Re-printed by *John Reid Junior*, 1711."

17. Defoe, *Reasons Why This Nation*, 6.

18. J. R. Jones says, "These moves destroyed the last obstacles to the conclusion of peace" (*Country and Court*, 346–47).

19. Owens and Furbank believe that *Defence of the Allies* may not be Defoe's, but I agree with Novak and Downie that it is. I find Defoe's defense deliberately half-hearted, and his argument that England was the "Principal," his justification of a land war, and his points about trade the same as found in his *Reasons Why This Nation* (cf. 43); the preparation of the loss of Spain (26) is consistent with Defoe's other 1712 pamphlets. Moreover, nothing in the style gives reason to question the authorship. See Downie, "Daniel Defoe's *Review*," 248–49; Owens and Furbank, "Defoe and the Dutch Alliance," 176–77.

20. During the war Defoe definitely believed in "no peace without Spain." He explains that it was necessary for the balance of trade and the balance of power (cf. *Review* 4:187–88). As the years passed Defoe hoped treaty concessions after the repudiation of the Barrier Treaty and the death of Emperor Joseph I would protect English interests. PRO SP 34/8/86 for 5 Oct. 1706; Edinburgh Town Council Minutes, 6 June 1712, 40:447–48, City Chambers archives.

21. Defoe, *Validity of the Renunciations*, 2; in *Ballance of Europe* Defoe noted that "if any Man enquired what we Fought for in this War, the Answer was

short, we Fought for *Spain*," but now, "tho' the King of *France* should come and say to us, that his Grandson was ready to Evacuate *Spain* . . . we are now uncertain whether we had best take it or no" (4). Defoe introduced the aphorism "Tempora Mutantur, nos & Mutamur" in *Review* 8:43 [469], 22 Dec. 1711, and followed with a series of essays on the idea. See also *Review* 8:339, 6 Oct. 1711; H 428. Other critics who see consistency in Defoe are Poston, "Defoe and the Peace Campaign," 1–20; John Forster, *Daniel De Foe*, 132–34; Illingworth, "Economic Ideas," 2:1097–1100; Owens and Furbank, "Defoe and the Dutch Alliance," 170–72, and Furbank and Owens, *Canonisation*, 151–60.

22. Defoe, *Justification of the Dutch*, 34; *Further Search*, 60. Owens and Furbank question Defoe's authorship of *Justification* (177–78). Their case, that it is a "bland and unconvincing pamphlet," is negligible and not my impression of the work. It begins dramatically, as do many of Defoe's 1712 pamphlets: "Oh Unfortunate *Britain*! Unhappy and Infatuated Nation!" This prophetic tone is one often found in Defoe's middle period and an object of ridicule and a means of identification for his contemporaries. The pamphlet warns the English not to trust the French again, an entirely characteristic position for Defoe, who had great respect for France and its diplomats. The characteristic elements of Defoe's style are present. Owens and Furbank do not consider the impact the publication of the eleven resolutions made on the country, and *Justification*'s publication before that could explain the contradictions they cite. On the court's reaction to the publication of the peace preliminaries, see Green, *Queen Anne*, 257–60.

23. *Review* 8:432. Such statements occur repeatedly in his work during these years in these and other words; cf. *Review* 4:248 and 7:190. *Defence of the Allies*, 23–24; the conclusion of *Justification of the Dutch* and *Modest Vindication of the Present Ministry*. *Conduct of Parties*, 34. See also Novak's discussions of heroes and the duke of Marlborough in *Defoe and the Nature of Man*, 129–61, especially 137 and 152–54.

24. Coombs, *Conduct of the Dutch*, 291–92, 339–41. Defoe quotes some of these resolutions regarding the deficiencies of the allies' efforts in *Further Search*; cf. *Resolves and Address to the Queen Ordered to be Printed by Parliament*, House of Lords Record Office, and the Admirality Resolves with *Further Search*, 12–13, 59–61, 62, and *Resolves*, 1–3 with *Further Search*, 59–61. See the eleven resolves in the Journal of the House of Commons for 5 Feb. 1711/12 (17:69–70); the resolves, *Report of the Commission of the Admiralty*, and *Address to the Queen* were printed. Defoe gives the figures from the Admiralty report, which differed from *Explanation of the Eleven Resolves* for the years 1705, 1708, and 1709. He seems to have had the Admirality charts and tables as well as the resolves before they were printed, for he assures his readers they will be printed "for the Conviction" of "the Queen's Subjects."

25. H 360–61. For a detailed discussion of Swift's polarizing rhetoric in *Conduct of the Allies*, see Ehrenpreis, *Swift* 2:497–99.

26. *Defence of the Allies*, 21. Downie, *Swift*, 159–60; Ehrenpreis 2:483–84; Ellis suggests that writing *Conduct of the Allies* may have been suggested as early as April (*Swift vs. Mainwaring*, xxxiii).

27. *A Defence of the Allies*, 26. Other representative examples are "entailing long and large Debts . . . it is evident is the Thing" (43) and "a Notion of being run on Ground in their Strengths" (44).

28. Ehrenpreis, *Swift* 2:484–85 and 500; Downie notes that Harley bought 200 copies of *Conduct of the Allies* (*Swift*, 363 n. 88).

29. *Review* exchanges with the *Examiner* include *Review*s nos. 88, 105, 113, 114, 149, 153, and 155. *Armaggedon* (1711), 29; *Secret History of the October Club*,

Part II (London, 1711), 27 and 42. See also *Representation Examined* (1711), 11–12; *Present Negotiations . . . Vindicated*(1712), 12 and 19. *Hannibal at the Gates* (London, 1712), a pamphlet that might fit in this category, I do not believe to be by Defoe. It lacks Defoe's characteristic sentence paragraphs and other distinguishing stylistic traits. The use of "Republican," "Presbyterian," and "liberty," as well as the description of Queen Anne as "too affectionate to the *True Church*" (emphasis added), is simply not like Defoe. Nothing in the response to this pamphlet (*Hannibal Not at Our Gates*) or the 1714 reply with the same title, *Hannibal at the Gates*, indicates Defoe's authorship. In fact, *Hannibal Not at Our Gates* attacks Steele, Dunton, Ridpath, Toland, Asgill, and Burnet—but not Defoe.

30. Defoe, *The Re-Representation*, 10; *Defence of the Allies*, 21.

31. Cf. *Review* 7:477. The *Examiner* in question is no. 15, 16 Nov. 1710. The delay in Defoe's response occurred because he was in Scotland.

32. Barber had printed Defoe's *Dyet of Poland* and would print the *Mercator*; on Barber's friendship with Swift, see Downie, *Swift*, 175, and *Harley and the Press*, 169–70; Ehrenpreis, *Swift* 2:446, 610, 633–35. Downie compares Defoe and Swift and suggests that Swift's "most important" propaganda function may have been as "organizer," not writer (*Harley and the Press*, 168–70, and *Swift*, 174–75).

33. See my "Personality and Biblical Allusion," 6–7; H 379. Defoe frequently identified with St. Paul; cf. *Review* 9:167 and 177. Years ago Ian Watt noted Defoe's tendency toward "vicarious identification with the supposed speaker" (*Rise of the Novel*, 126). See also Horsley, "Rogues or Honest Gentlemen," who says that pamphleteers felt it necessary to create "an idea of themselves that would draw attention and produce conviction" and, therefore, the "thread of their lives was naturally woven into the fabric of [their papers]" as a "compound of conventional and personal self-justification" (198, 200).

34. See my "Russell to Defoe," 164–71. Defoe had wanted to buy Harley claret in the spring of 1707; see H 206, 207.

35. Cf. *Mercator*, no. 56, 1 Oct. 1713, on reduction of duties on linen since the Union and minutes of the Convention of Royal Burghs, 12 April 1710, with reference to the 6th Act of the General Convention of 1708, Edinburgh City Chambers Archives, Royal Burgh Convention, Bundle 226. The treaty guaranteed £2,000 a year for seven years to encourage Scots woolen manufacture (Riley, *English Ministers*, 212). Determined efforts to improve Scots linen in Defoe's time had little effect; shortly after the Union, the linen industry was in deep trouble from the Irish and the Dutch (Durie, *Scottish Linen Industry in the Eighteenth Century*, 9–10, 12–15).

36. SRO RD 4/109/462–63; see also RD 14/51/262, "General Register of Deeds." The heading reads "Anna Goodale," but the text throughout is clearly "Hanna." On the coinage project, see my "Russell to Defoe," 164, and H 391–92 and 392 n. 1. I am grateful to Frank Ellis, Smith College, for this clarification.

37. SRO RD 4/107, no. 1817, and Edinburgh Town Council minutes, 9 Jan. 1710.

38. 4 Jan. 1709 (Advocates' recommendation), quoted in Pinkerton, ed. *Minute Book of the Faculty of Advocates* 1:278. Edinburgh Council minutes, 17 Aug. 1709, 39/3/413–14 in City Chambers' archives.

39. SRO SP 44/77, 14 June 1706 (committal of Gildon); *Edinburgh Courant*, 19 Dec. 1705, 13 and 15 Mar. 1706.

40. Edinburgh Town Council Minutes, 11 June 1708, 39:100; Moses Bundle, no. 222, vol. 7; miscellaneous papers of the Royal Burghs in Edinburgh Town Council Archives.

41. Burch says that Defoe wrote for the *Courant* between October 1708 and December 1709 ("Defoe's Connections with the *Edinburgh Courant*," 437–40). Although discussions of ideas such as population as wealth seem new to the *Courant*, nothing in the style or content seems to be certainly Defoe's. Moses Bundle, no. 222, vol. 7. A contemporary wrote that Boig died "this day" on his 27 Jan. 1710 paper, now preserved in the NLS Advocates' Library; see J.S., "Scotch Newspapers of the Age of Queen Anne," 386. The transfer to Defoe is in the Edinburgh Town Council minutes, 109/628. The quoted letter is in Backscheider, "Russell to Defoe," 163–64.

42. SRO GD 222/5/802 for 10 July 1708.

43. See Stevenson, *List of the Deans of Guild of the City of Edinburgh, 1403–1890*, 9. Information about the Merchant Company comes from the Minutes of the Merchant Company of the City of Edinburgh, 1681–1696 and Minute Book Belonging to the Merchant Company of the City of Edinburgh, 1704–1714. I am grateful to the company and its archivist, Mr. Berryl, for permission to quote from this material. See also Heron, *Rise and Progress of the Company of Merchants of the City of Edinburgh*; and *"Stock of Broom."*

44. Russell and Leven continued to be friends for years, cf. Russell to Leven, 2 Sept. 1717 (SRO GD 26/13/525) and 15 Nov. 1719 (GD 26/13/544); GD 26/9/79 for family relationships. An example of business executed by Russell for Leven are deeds making Coult Leven's factorie, 20 and 27 Nov. 1707; see especially RD 4/104 and a discharge of the earl of Melville to Leven, 1 Jan. 1708. See RD 4/106 for evidence of sizeable sums of money negotiated by Russell for Edinburgh Castle (28 Jan. 1710). On Helen Russell and her estate, see SRO RS 3/110 (fols. 453–58), SRO General Register of Sasines, 17 May 1717.

45. Backscheider, "Russell to Defoe," 167–68; Letterbook SRO GD 26/13/482 and 26/9/52; see, for instance, 16 June 1711 for £21 10s. Among the documents linking Defoe and these men are H 397; SRO GD 26/9/79; BL Loan 29/219 for 25 Oct. [1712]. Russell tells Defoe that Carstares intends to see him in August 1711 (Backscheider, 167–68).

46. Backscheider, 163.

47. Grant, *Story of the University of Edinburgh* 1:262–65. I am grateful to Roger Emerson of the University of Western Ontario for additional information about John Goodale.

48. Edinburgh Town Council Minutes, 39/2/219 and 270 City Chambers' archives.

49. Backscheider, "Russell to Defoe," 171; H 389–90; Moore, "Defoe and the Rev. James Hart," 404–9.

50. HMC Portland 8:196–97; BL Loan 29/209, 13 July 1705; for Fearne's account of his own life, see BL Loan 29/193, 19 Nov. 1705. Bell seems to be acting at Harley's orders when he keeps the men's activities secret from each other (HMC Portland 4:353); by the time Defoe had received £103 8s. Fearne had had only £15 (4:377–78). Harley's description of Fearne is 4:421, 19 June 1707. Cf. HMC Portland 8:275–76 and 4:357 and 402.

51. H 163–64, 180–81. It has been suggested that Defoe's Pierce is Ker; although it is true that both worked with the Cameronians, the dates in Healey and the HMC Portland papers do not coincide very well, especially that for Pierce's departure for London in March 1707. Cf. H 206–7; HMC Portland 8: 312–13. Payments to Ker in 1710 and 1711 were made in £100 grants; see PRO T 48/16. On 15 Nov. 1707 Ker signed a receipt for £700, "expended by her Maty Command and for her Majty Speciall Service" (PRO T 38/737). On 19 Feb. 1708/9 he received £300; also £400 on 21 July 1709 and £300 on 1 Oct.

1709 (T 38/737). Paterson received £100 on 29 Sept. 1710 (T 48/16); he asked for more money and often claimed he deserved more from funds such as the Equivalent; cf. BL Loan 29/151, 3 Apr. 1710. He continued to get "Royal Bounty" throughout the Oxford years; cf. 3 March 1713/14, T 53/23.

52. H 184–85, 256, 259; Calamy, *Historical Account* 2:44–49.

53. Anderson claimed to have built the paper mill at her own expense (Bute private papers, Bundle A30, Section 2, Loudon Rowallen). She paid £5 a year rental for the mill; see SRO GD 18/2096 (vol. 2) for 23 July 1709 for one receipt. On her litigious nature, see Couper, *Watson's Preface*, 49–54.

54. Watson, "Publisher's Preface to the Printers in *Scotland*," 16–17; [Lee], *Memorial for the Bible Societies in Scotland*, 116–23, 128, 135; 159–62 lists many individual errors. Her contemporary, Watson, called two of her proudest works, "Two voluminous Botches" (Couper, *Watson's Preface*, 49); SRO CH 1/4/2, 25 Nov. 1706.

55. Edinburgh Town Council Minutes, 17 Jan. 1696, City Chambers' archives; Couper, *Watson's Preface*, 12–17. Watson says Anderson "persecuted all the Printers in *Scotland*" ("Publisher's Preface to the Printers in *Scotland*," 15). [Lee], *Memorial for the Bible Societies*, 167–68; Edinburgh Town Council Minutes, 4 Feb. 1687. Anderson expanded her space on 20 Dec. 1699; the college made efforts to remove her, 8 Dec. 1703 and 31 July 1713, and to get her to repair her roof, 10 Sept. 1712.

56. Couper, *Watson's Preface*, 6.

57. H 330, 341–42, and 357–58. Some of Anderson's memorials addressed to Harley are in BL Loan 29/222 and 10/1864 and 1866; see also Anderson's letter to Mar SRO GD 124/15/536.

58. The reference is to Defoe's *Seasonable Warning and Caution against the Insinuations of Papists and Jacobites*. The quotation is from "Memorial for Mr. Watson" [1713], in George Chalmers' notes, University of Edinburgh Library, MS. LA II.448. Other typical statements that express shock at Anderson's work for Defoe are *Letter from a Gentleman in Edinburgh, to a Member of Parliament*, which quotes several of Defoe's *Review*s including nos. 9, 58, and 135 from vol. 6, and *Letter from a Gentleman at Edinburgh to his Freind* [sic] *at London*, 3. "The Case of James Watson one of Her Majesties Printers," fair copy preserved in University of Edinburgh, MS. LA. II.448. An answer to Freebairn's letter preserved in the State Papers rules that "The Gift is now become Mr. ffreebairns property and cannot be taken from him without a Fair Tryal att Law," and no one but the queen could prosecute an action to take it away (PRO SP 34/38 [no date]). Watson's patent was never disallowed, but on 8 Dec. 1714, Anderson received a grant from the Scottish Court of Session upon its ruling that Freebairn's patent had been granted in an irregular manner. In 1715 Freebairn joined the Pretender's rebellion, and a new grant was issued to Anderson and Basket in 1716. She and Watson both held patents and royal warrants until her death in 1716 (Couper, *Watson's Preface*, 23–25; [Lee], *Memorial for the Bible Societies*, xv).

59. SRO GD 135/140, Bundle 11, no. 80, 5 Jan. 1715.

60. On Edinburgh degrees, see Defoe, *Memoirs of the Life of Williams*, 36–43; Calamy, *Historical Account* 2:187–88, 201–2, 212; for Glasgow, *Munimenta alme universitatis Glasguensis* 3:304; Calamy as burgess, Edinburgh Town Council records, 6 Apr. 1709, 39:332; City exchanges, McCrie, ed., *Correspondence of the Rev. Robert Wodrow* 1:17–20 (letters from 2 and 17 June 1709); Coutts, *History of the University of Glasgow*, 209; John Stirling's correspondence, 4 Sept. and 21 Nov. 1709, Dr. Williams Library, BE III 82 and 85.

61. The correspondence between Calamy and Carstares outlines the prob-

lems; see University of Edinburgh MS. LA 2/407/6; MS. DK 1/1, June 1709; LA 2/407, 8 July 1709; [Morer], 78–79, 110.

62. This proposal is printed in Burch, "Benjamin Defoe at Edinburgh University in 1710–1711," 344–45. Other evidence of Defoe's authorship can be drawn from his habitual usages compared with this proposal: the use of subordinating elements noting the relationship between paragraphs to begin paragraphs, with "as," "but," and sequence numbers as most frequent; the use of rhetorical signifiers to answer objections and to weigh and balance points; use of phrases such as "of more consequence" and "nothing of more consequence" to underscore his ideas; phrases frequently used when writing about youth, such as "visible hazard," "committing him wholly to his own management," "without any opportunity of improvement."

63. Calamy reports: "It is a very frequent subject of inquiry in conversation, what North Britain has gained by the Union, and what it has lost" (*Historical Account* 2:219).

64. Journal of the House of Lords, petition from William Carstares, Thomas Blackwell, and Robert Baillie for time for the Commission of the General Assembly to lay their concerns before the House, 11 Feb. 1711/12 and 11 Apr. 1712 House of Lords Record Office; Royal Assent, 22 May. The official objections of the Convention of the Royal Burghs with the queen's response are in Edinburgh Town Council Ancient Letters 1:135. For modern discussions of these issues, see Burton, *History of Scotland* 8:198–249; Riley, *English Ministers and Scotland*, 188–229, 233–34, 242–43, who calls the imposition of the malt tax "a technical breach of the Union"; MacKinnon, *Union of England and Scotland*, 374–431; Lenman, *Jacobite Risings in Britain*, 97–99, 103–6; Ferguson, *Scotland 1689 to the Present*, 59–63.

65. Cf. Anstruther to Montrose, 23 Feb. 1709, SRO GD 220/5/119; Mar to Harley, 10 June 1711, GD 124/15/1024. Mar joined the Pretender in 1715. MacKinnon, *The Union*, 426–31; *Review* 9:207–8, 4 June 1713.

66. Cf. H 216–18, 220–25, 234–35 et passim, with *Review*s 5:7, 14, 318; 6:86, 95–96, 176, 235, 310, 378; 8:65, 73–74, 548, 595–96; 9:61, 203 and 206, and *Trade of Britain Stated, Present State of the Parties*, and *Union and No Union*.

67. H 251, 258, and 223; *Review* (Edinburgh ed.) 6:347; *Scot's Narrative Examin'd*; *Judas Discover'd* [sic], 3.

68. Cf. H 222–23; *Scots Nation and Union Vindicated*, 23.

69. H 321–25; see also 369, 382, 396–98, and Backscheider, "Russell to Defoe," 166–71.

70. Quoted in Pat Rogers, "Dunce Answers Back," 37.

71. Backscheider, "Russell to Defoe," 167–69, and Moore, *Citizen*, 331.

CHAPTER 13: A TEAM OF WRITERS

1. The term *double game* is common; it is used by Coombs as the heading for *Conduct of the Dutch*, ch. 9. See also MacLachlan, "Road to Peace," 204–7; *Collection of All Her Majesty's Speeches*, 39. Swift's first three *Examiner*s strongly reflect this policy.

2. Downie, *Harley and the Press*, 141.

3. Harley once described himself when allied with the Tories as "a captain of bandits" and described the Tories as "naturally selfish, peevish, narrow-spirited, ill-natured" (quoted by MacLachlan, "Road to Peace," 201–2). Downie calls Harley a "Shaftesburian Whig of the Old School" (*Swift*, 136). Dickinson describes Harley's continued clandestine meetings with Whigs as late as 1713

(*Bolingbroke*, 106), and evidence abounds in the uncatalogued Portland papers, British Library.

4. *Essay at a Plain Exposition of . . . a Good Peace* (1711), *Felonious Treaty* (1711), and *Some Thoughts upon the Subject of Commerce with France* (1713) are examples.

5. Cf. Defoe, *Essay at . . . Peace*, 20, 23–24, 28–29, and *Felonious Treaty*, 34–44.

6. Cf. *Felonious Treaty*, 14, 22, 45–48.

7. In addition Baker did Defoe's first group of peace pamphlets and those on Dissenting issues, including *Essay on the History of Parties* (1711) and *Wise as Serpents* (1712).

8. The phrase is Ehrenpreis's; Downie quotes it in *Harley*, 131.

9. Cf. *Ballance of Europe*, 42–45, 48.

10. *Ballance*, 32.

11. *Enquiry into the Real Interest of Princes* (1712).

12. *Conduct*, 40; Defoe attacks the Junto in *Present Negotiations*, 4.

13. Respectively, *Peace, or Poverty*, 15; *Further Search into the Conduct of the Allies*, 66–67.

14. *Further Search*, 21.

15. See *Medley*, July 1712; *Moderator*, June and July 1710; *Examiner*, 16 Nov. 1710; *Two Letters concerning the Author of the Examiner*; preface to *Infernal Congress*. Abel Boyer wrote that Swift's *Conduct of the Allies* was "written with the same Spirit, if not by the same Pen, that writ [Defoe's] *Reasons Why This Nation . . .*" (*Quadriennium Annae Postremum* 1–2:652). Oldmixon, too, linked Swift and Defoe. He accused Defoe of "taking over Harley's craft and dissimilation, whilst Swift inherits his apostacy" (Pat Rogers, "The Dunce Answers Back," 34). Note that it is Swift, not Defoe, who is accused of apostasy. Defoe wrote, "Behold, both sides fall upon me, and . . . one Bullies me for Injuring the Episcopal Party in *Scotland, and the other*, will have me in a Plot *with the Examiner*" (*Review* 9:115). In this case, he referred to *Post Boy* and *Flying Post*. Horsley, "Rogues or Honest Gentlemen," 212–13, also notes the attacks from both parties.

16. *Review*, preface to vol. 6; 7:49, 25 Apr. 1710; the advertisement explaining where to get the *Review* ran until this first number printed by Baker; Edinburgh *Review* no. 147.

17. *Review* 8:283, 315–20; *Flying Post*, 20 September 1711; *Supplement* 14 and 26 Sept. 1711; Trent, "New Light on Defoe's Life," 260–61.

18. H 123, 401–2, 402 n. 1.

19. Defoe, *Reasons against the Succession*, 13.

20. Lord chief justice to [Bolingbroke], 15 Apr. 1713, the letter and informations are in PRO SP 34/21, pt. 1; duplicate informations except for William Jackson's in PRO KB 33/5/5; *Review* 9:169–70; H 405. The information in this section is based on these sources, with special reliance on Healey's useful notes. I am grateful to Vincent Liesenfeld, University of Oklahoma, for bringing KB 33/5/5 to my attention. See also Oldmixon, *History of England*, 509; Sutherland, *Defoe*, 196–99.

21. PRO SP 44/114/126; Dartmouth's cabinet minutes are in the Stafford Record Office, D742/U/3/27; I am grateful to Linda Merians of La Salle University for this reference.

22. Ryder, *Diary of Dudley Ryder*, 4; H 405.

23. *Review* 9:170; H 407, 410–12; *Flying Post*, 16 Apr. 1713.

24. *Flying Post*, 23 Apr. 1713; *Review* 9:177–78, 181–82; Oldmixon, *History of England*, 477, 509. Trent records the fine from a *Weekly Packet*, 9 May 1713 ("New Light on Defoe's Life," 261).

25. Defoe's appearances are in PRO KB 372, Easter 1713, mem. vij recto, rot. 33, and KB 372, Trinity 1713, mem. xxiij verso; the indictment is KB 10/15 pt. 2 (Indictment file, Trinity 12 Anne). The indictment is badly creased and is torn at the top edge; some words are therefore illegible or missing; except for brackets around innuendoes, the document has almost no punctuation. I am grateful to James P. Derriman for the translation of these previously unpublished documents.

26. Quotations from Defoe's pamphlets are all taken from the indictment, PRO KB 10/15 pt. 2, but have been collated with Defoe's pamphlets; this one is from *And What If the Pretender*, 24.

27. Cf. *Reasons against the Succession*, 11, 13–14, and *What If the Pretender*, 4–5 and 23–24.

28. PRO SP 34/37/11, petition in Defoe's own hand; H 415, 418, 422.

29. Bolingbroke's copy is SP 44/356/435–38; Northey's is SP 34/37/12–15 with a dated annotation on the back. Earlier Defoe scholars have confused the drafts for the pardon and therefore dated it incorrectly. See IND 8911 for December 1713; Noli prosequi, PRO KB 372, mem. xxiij, Michaelmas 12 Anne.

30. Snyder, "Circulation of Newspapers in the Reign of Queen Anne," 206–35; Downie, *Harley*, 10; Stevens, *Party Politics*, 6, 61–63.

31. One of the earliest recognitions of Defoe's influence was Laetitia Barbauld in her *British Novelists* series: [Defoe's] "fiction of a club . . . in all probability gave the hint to Steele and Addison for the frame they used afterwards with so much success" (iii). Bond also noted this in *The Tatler: The Making of a Literary Journal*, 129; *Tatler* 1:12.

32. Both Defoe and Steele mention the *Mercure Galant*; cf. Steele, *Tatler*, no. 67, 3:336, and *Guardian*, nos. 99 and 156 (both by Addison). *Review* 1:15 alludes to the French source; Defoe was still reading it in 1708; see H 263. The *Mercure* was widely read in England; the *Daily Courant*, for instance, had translated and printed an earthquake description from it on 12 Nov. 1708. Winton identifies the similarity in tone and gives the *Mercure* some credit for the *Tatler*'s success in *Captain Steele*, 105–6. In Defoe's time the *Mercure* included all the items that might have been found in a variety of periodicals—political and literary news, reviews, gazette items (promotions, appointments, marriages, deaths), sermons, official declamations, poetry, madrigals, essays on scientific and philosophical topics, and anecdotes (*Bibliographia histoire et crit. de la presse périodique française* and Grente et al., eds., *Dictionnaire des lettres française*, vol. 2, s.v. *Mercure Galant*).

33. *Review* 7:70, 9 May 1710; the pagination is incorrect for no. 19.

34. BL MS. 7121, fol. 67, for 6 Oct. 1709. Steele may have been recently released from a spunging house for debt. See Blanchard, ed., *Correspondence of Richard Steele*, 265 n. 1.

35. *Tatler* 4:56–57 and 96–97; *Tatlers* nos. 214 and 220; 4:130 for 5 Sept. and 4:102–3 for 22 Aug. Page 11 of *Condoling Letter* refers the reader to the *Consolidator*, 18.

36. Some of Steele's highly partisan numbers are 183, 187, 190, 191, 193, and 195; quotation is from 191. Quotations from Biddle, *Bolingbroke and Harley*, 34 and 36. Bolingbroke's *Letter* is in *Prose Works of Swift* 3:221.

37. *Review* 8:97, 246, and 525 respectively; see also 8:255 for the use of the *Spectator* in an amusing, mock-instructive essay on dullness.

38. *Mercator* no. 55, 26–29 Sept. 1713; cf. *Review* 8:97–98, 122–24, 525.

39. Peter I had visited Western European nations in order to learn how to develop Russia. *Spectator* 2:47–50 and *Review* 8:261.

40. *Review* 9:4; *Guardian*, 427. Cf. Defoe on Dunkirk, *Review* 8:843–44. The quotation is from a copy of Walpole's speech sent to Harley via Lynn and Cambridge (BL Loan 29/201, 29 Sept. 1713). See also Moore, "Defoe, Steele, and the Demolition of Dunkirk," 279–87 and 297–302.

41. See especially *Importance of Dunkirk* in *Tracts and Pamphlets*, 114, 115, 121.

42. *Mercator* no. 55, responding to *Guardian* no. 170 for 25 Sept. 1713. Note the implied contrast of the rhetoric of Steele to that of Swift.

43. *The Crisis* in *Tracts and Pamphlets*, 173–74, 180. See Downie, *Swift*, 186–87.

44. Blanchard, *Correspondence*, 86–87 n. 1; H 430. On his association with the Junto, see Winton, *Captain Steele*, 108–9 and 184–87.

45. *Mercator* no. 55 for 26–29 Sept. 1713; *Fears of the Pretender Turn'd*, 22; see also 19–21 and *Mercator* no. 57.

46. H 335. On 17 July Defoe refers to Harley's "Orders" and repeats nearly verbatim the double directions of 13 July (338 and 340).

47. *Present State of the Parties* says it was in manuscript (102).

48. Quoted in Basil Williams, *Stanhope*, 136–37.

49. H 364; *Review* 8:465–82 (quotation is from 466, misnumbered 465); [*Speech of a Stone Chimney-Piece*], *Present State*, 102. *Essay on the History* was advertised in the *Review* as "This Day is Publish'd" on 22 Dec. and [*Speech*] was quoted there on 25 Dec. Moore discusses the publication of [*Speech*] in the *Review* and in *Present State* in "Defoe's Lampoon," 139–42.

50. Historians are unanimous in describing Harley as more furtive and drunken than usual; cf. J. R. Jones, *Country and Court*, 350; Hamilton, *Backstairs Dragon*, 256; Dickinson, *Bolingbroke*, 129–30.

51. Defoe's awareness of the way the vote was being used can be surmised from H 416, 419–21, and his essays. See also Illingworth, "Economic Ideas of Daniel Defoe" 2:685–88.

52. Cf. H 408–9, 422, 426, and 442, for references to Defoe's illnesses; they are also mentioned in the informations (PRO KB 33/5/5).

53. Cf. *Review* for 9, 14, 16, and 19 May 1713 in vol. 9.

54. I share Alan Downie's skepticism about any close connection between Defoe and Bolingbroke's employee, one of the commissioners of trade, Arthur Moore; see his *Harley*, 171–72. Defoe's letters do show he knew and saw Moore (H 415 and 446); most Defoe scholars have assumed a working relationship. Detailed analysis by a number of scholars, however, finds Defoe's, not Bolingbroke's opinions; Defoe had printed many of these ideas as early as 1704; cf. Illingworth, "Economic Ideas of Defoe" 2:635–50; Sill notes that there were some points Defoe was reluctant to argue (*Defoe and the Idea of Fiction*, 33–41). Snyder gives the sales figures for the *Mercator* ("Circulation of Newspapers," 209).

55. Addison's essay is in *Miscellaneous Works of Joseph Addison* 2:267–72; other discussions of Defoe's *Count Tariff* are in Goldgar, *Curse of Party*, 119–21, and Sill, 17–18, 47–53.

56. H 423–24, 426–27; note especially plans to send pamphlets into the West of England.

57. Biddle, *Bolingbroke and Harley*, 277–81; Dickinson, *Bolingbroke*, 126–28; H 441.

58. Backscheider, *Defoe*, 65–68; *Manufacturer*, 2 Dec. 1719; Illingworth, "Economic Ideas of Defoe" 2:623–26, 1099–1102; Novak discusses Defoe's discomfort with the Tory treaty in *Economics and the Fiction of Daniel Defoe*, 25–28; Sill disagrees with Novak's interpretation of Defoe's use of trade statistics (*Defoe and the Idea of Fiction*, 33–35, 37–38), and his figures should be accepted.

59. SRO GD 124/15/1129, 7 Aug. 1714.

60. Prior to Swift, 25 April 1721, in *Correspondence of Jonathan Swift* 2:382.

61. *Flying Post*, 25 Dec. 1714, 2 and 16 April 1715; PRO T 38/180, accounts from August to August, 1714–1715. Beattie's *English Court in the Reign of George I* describes the nature and value of appointments in the king's household; see especially appendix, 279–82; see also Stevens, *Party Politics*, 82–103 who notes that by 18 Oct. 1715 Steele had received a grant guaranteeing him £1,000 a year (83).

CHAPTER 14: SIX HUNDRED THOUSAND WORDS

1. Paul Dottin says that the horse incident "was a big factor in making [Defoe] lose caste with his British public" (*Daniel Defoe*, 145). For sources and discussion, see Moore, "Defoe's Use of Personal Experience in *Colonel Jack*," 362–63; Novak, "Whiff of Scandal in the Life of Daniel Defoe," 35–36 (Novak lists a number of contemporary items on Sammon; see especially 35–36 and 40); *Hue and Cry after Daniel De Foe and His Coventry Beast*; *Welsh-Monster*.

2. Calamy, *Historical Account* 2:274–77; *Letter to the People of England. Occasion'd* [sic] *by the Letter to the Dissenters*, 1; *Remarks on the Letter to the Dissenters. By a Churchman*, 4 and 28. Defoe's *Letter to the Dissenters* was first published 3 Dec. 1713; a second edition with a new preface appeared 29 May 1714 (Moore, *Checklist*, 108).

3. *Advice to the People of Great Britain*, 3, 13, 15–16. Before George landed Defoe had published a reassuring description of George I in a fictional letter from the point of view of a man who had lived at George's court for twelve years (*Flying Post*, 14 Aug. 1714, reprinted in Lee, *Daniel Defoe* 1:231–32).

4. *Reasons for Im[peaching] the L[or]d H[igh] T[reasure]r*, 4; the reference is to Jonah. *Letter to Mr. Steele*, 21; the reference is to Joshua 9:21–27. *Brief Survey of the Legal Liberties of the Dissenters*, 11; the reference is to a fleet-footed man killed in battle, 2 Samuel 2:18; *Pernicious Consequences of the Clergy's Intermeddling*, 35–38.

5. Sill in *Defoe and the Idea of Fiction* reads Defoe's defenses of Harley, most specifically the *Secret History* pamphlets as a "fiction," an "interpretation of faithful service and the tragedy of good designs thwarted" (87–93). Cf. Downie, *Harley*, 186–88, who points out some of the quite accurate parts of the series. Independent evidence that the meeting after the queen's death took place is in Williams, *Whig Supremacy*, 150–52; and for the queen's last conference with Harley in BL Loan 29/294, 27 July 1714. See also Lenman, *Jacobite Risings in Britain*, 113, and Bennett, *Tory Crisis in Church and State*, who sorts out some of the accurate and inaccurate statements (189–92).

6. Burnet, *History* 6:45n.

7. Defoe, *Secret History*, pt. 1; pt. 3:73–76; *Account of the Conduct of Robert Earl of Oxford*, 57, 60–70.

8. *Secret History*, pt. 3:3, 7.

9. *Secret History*, pt. 3:20; *Memoirs of Publick Transactions in the Life and Ministry of . . . Shrewsbury*, 104. In the latter book Defoe does not repeat the stories of Harley's resignation and shows Shrewsbury as independent of both factions.

10. Cf. *Account of the Conduct of . . . Oxford*, 53ff.; *Secret History*, pt. 3:28–30.

11. *Secret History*, pt. 3:52–53.

12. [Atterbury], *Considerations upon The Secret History of the White Staff. Humbly Address'd to the E——— of O———*, 28 and 25–26; Oldmixon, *Detection of the Sophistry and Falsities of the Pamphlet, Entitul'd, the Secret History of the White Staff*, 5.

13. Oldmixon, *Detection of the Sophistry* . . . *Part II*, 32; [Pittis], *Queen Anne Vindicated*, 16.

14. *Detection of the Sophistry* . . . *Part II*, 32; [Pittis], 11–12, 16; Boyer, *Quadriennium Annae Postremum* 5:343.

15. *Secret History*, pt. 3:18, 46. These were the Scots accused of conspiring to aid the Pretender's 1708 invasion; see ch. 10 above.

16. A typical example of Defoe's reference to having "ruined" his family is in *Some Thoughts upon the Subject of Commerce with France*, 47.

17. Ryder, *Diary*, 39, 129.

18. This, the longest list I found, is in PRO SP 9/217.

19. E. Anthony James argues that the entire essay is an artful, unified piece. "Defoe's Autobiographical Apologia," 69–86. *Appeal to Honour and Justice* has traditionally been treated as honestly autobiographical; even the skeptical Furbank and Owens call it "his best-known apologia" (*Canonisation*, 11).

20. PRO KB 33/5/5 and SP 34/21, pt. 1.

21. Perkins, *Treatise of the Vocations or Callings of Men*, quoted in Ryken, *Worldly Saints*, 30; [Simon Brown], preface to *Caveat against Evil Company*; see also Walker, *Of Education*, 202–4.

22. Defoe's preface to the second edition; Ewing, "First Printing of Defoe's *Family Instructor*," 269–72.

23. Among Defoe's publications on the reformation of manners are *Poor Man's Plea* (1698), *Free-holders Plea* (1701), *Reformation of Manners, A Satyr* (1702), *Fears of the Pretender Turn'd into the Fears of Debauchery*, and *Friendly Epistle by Way of Reproof* (both 1715). A royal proclamation on 5 Jan. 1714/15 for the encouragement of piety and virtue and the preventing and punishing of vice, profaneness, and immorality made the subject even more fashionable.

24. See my "Defoe's Prodigal Sons," 3–18, for a comparison of Defoe's and Steele's conduct books. Cruso's book, as most conduct books do, also has a substantive section on obedience to parents (cf. 20). The preface to *The Gentleman's Library* (1715) describes the great success of *The Ladies' Library*; it did not, however, approach that of *The Family Instructor*. In 1720 Defoe's conduct book was in its eighth edition; Steele's only in its third in 1723.

25. *Union and No Union*, 11–13; *Scots Nation, and Union Vindicated*, 13–18.

26. Some writers have linked *The Family Instructor* very closely to the Schism Act; see Rothman, "Defoe's *The Family Instructor*," 201–20, and Iványi, "Defoe's Prelude to The Family Instructor," 312. Defoe's comments on George's court are in *Fears of the Pretender*, 24–26, 29–37; gaming, 32–34 and excessive celebrations, 29. The ideas these men associate with the Schism Act, however, were very old. See, for example, [Brokesby], *Of Education With respect to Grammar Schools, and the Universities*, 1; and [Mortimer], *Advice to Parents; or, Rules for the Education of Children*: "[Education] 'tis the best Inheritance can be left to Children, and what will be out of Reach, either of Fortune or Time" (3).

27. I deduce this from Samuel Tuffley's will, in which he names Langley as a trustee of his estate (PRO PROB 11/604/383). Queensberry's father had written a guide ("Instructions to Mr. Fall anent my sones way of liveing," private Buccleuch paper, TD 86/62/1131), and John Clerk would write one ("Advice about the Education of My Male Posterity," SRO GD 18/2329).

28. Ryder, *Diary*, 128–29, 140, and my "Russell to Defoe," 168–69, for Aug. and Sept. 1711.

29. PRO PROB 11/604/383.

30. SRO GD 18/5249 and 18/5250, see especially 28 Jan. 1702.

31. Baxter's "To the Reader" explains that Arthur Dent's *Plain Man's Pathway*

to Heaven "was so well accepted, because it was a plain, familiar dialogue" and that he has imitated it. His dialogues are divided into nine days' conversations (*Practical Works* 19:296). John E. Mason calls Darrell's book "important and influential" (*Gentlefolk*, 183–84). On Defoe's originality, see my "Defoe's Prodigal Sons," 5, 13–14, and Hunter, *Reluctant Pilgrim*, 44–45.

32. Mason, 144; Powell, *English Domestic Relations*, 139–41.

33. For a discussion of *The Family Instructor* and some of Defoe's novels, see my "Defoe's Prodigal Sons," 3–18.

34. Barbauld, ed., *British Novelists* 16:iv.

35. Defoe uses the crown, scepter, and sword as the symbols of power; see especially *Secret History of the Scepter; Memoirs of the Conduct of Her Late Majesty*, 10–30, 50–51, 75, 80; *Secret History of the White Staff*, pt. 1:35, 57; 2:51–52; *Secret History of State Intrigues*, 34–35, 52–53; *Account of the Conduct of Robert, E—— of O——*, 73–74; *Strike While the Iron's Hot*, 12–13.

36. Defoe, *The Secret History of State Intrigues*, 4–7, 35.

37. Michael, *England under George I* 1:91. George, however, was unable to follow this advice; see Michael, 106–7.

38. This important, unpublished evidence is in an advertisement in the *Weekly Packet*, 9–16 July 1715:

> The King of Sweden's Minister has represented in the strongest Terms to the Emperor, the Pressures which that Heroick Prince is encompass'd with, and has receiv'd Assurances of all possible Dispositions in his Favour, his Imperial Majesty being very ready to interpose his good Offices, for a Monarch so highly deserving of all Brotherly Love and Assistance, having given Orders for an English Book, call'd *The History of the Wars of his Present Majesty Charles XII* . . . which gives a lively Discription of that Prince's political and martial Virtues to be translated into the German and Sclavonian Tongues.

Samuel Keimer, one of Defoe's printers, published *History of the Wars of His Late Majesty* and *Serious Reflections during the Life and Surprizing Adventures of Robinson Crusoe* in Philadelphia in 1725; this fact offers an additional bit of circumstantial evidence pointing to Defoe's authorship.

Furbank and Owens have questioned the attribution of this book to Defoe. They offer no concrete evidence and suggest no other author; their objections are that it does not conform to the "balanced but predominantly critical attitude" of the *Review*, is "innocent of ideas," and is of uncharacteristically poor quality without narrative "gift" ("What If Defoe Did Not Write the *History of the Wars of Charles XII*?" 333–47; *Canonisation*, 17–28).

Although the text of this chapter implicitly refutes these points, it may be useful to cite two of the many places where Defoe is specifically critical of Charles in *History of the Wars*, 148–52 and 275–76. Rather than being different from the *Review*, it was in the *Review*, the periodical he called "history writing by inches," that Defoe laid the ground work for this book. He had paused several times in the nine years of the *Review*'s life to give the entire history of the war from its beginning to the present (6:261–63, 266–67, 269–71). The most significant political fact for Defoe was that Charles's "Hereditary Dominions, especially in *Germany* [were] the great Prop and Support of the Protestant Interest" (8:259). Charles, he concludes, never thought of the glorious responsibility to the Protestants of Europe which he had inherited from the great Gustavus Adolphus. "But while the Fate of all *Europe* . . . the Subversion of the Protestant Religion, of which his Ancestors were the Glorious Protectors, while the Sovereignty of *French* Power over all the Kingdoms of *Europe*, is in the Scale against . . . his Personal Pique at the *Pole*; what shall we say to the Matter?"

(1:167) Gustavus Adolphus, of course, was the model leader in Defoe's *Memoirs of a Cavalier*. Almost every opinion expressed in *History of the Wars* appeared first in the *Review*, and Defoe used the conclusions he reached about Charles's personality in 1704 and 1709 as a sturdy frame in 1715. Several of the subsequent notes point out significant parallels.

39. *Review* 6:235, 279. Cf. *History of the Wars*, 59–60, 86–91, 139, 322, 329.

40. Michael, *England under George I*, 72; M. S. Anderson, *Britain's Discovery of Russia*, 51–53; Chance, *George I and the Northern War*.

41. Michael, 285.

42. See *History of the Wars*, 85, 100, 281, 282, 287.

43. Information on news comes from Sutherland, *Restoration Newspaper*, 123–45; Black, "Russia and the British Press in the Early Eighteenth Century," 16–31, and "British Press and Europe in the Early Eighteenth Century," 64–79. On the uncertainties facing journalists, see, for example, *Review* 6:247.

44. Quoted in Sutherland, 124.

45. Sutherland makes clear how ambiguous references to these correspondents were, especially since contemporaries talked of such small numbers of them in the employ of a person as five or six for all of Europe (138–40).

46. Sutherland cites, among others, a May issue of *Post-Boy* almost completely devoted to it (140). See also Black, "Russia and the British Press," 17.

47. Clerk thought it important enough to give it one of his longest entries—seven pages of closely written script (SRO GD 18/5078/36).

48. *Review* 9:91; Cf. Defoe, *Royal Religion*, 6, on the beginning of the war ("without so much as declaring War, without Quarrel, without Pretence, without the least Shadow of Honesty . . . depending upon the Minority of the King of *Swedeland*") to *History of the Wars* 85, 100, 147–48, 295–96, 354.

49. Matthews quotes Ned Ward on the Temple's law students: "His *Books* were of no other use but to Adorn his Study; and he never thought of Pleading at any other *Bar* but a *Vintners*" (*Diary of Ryder*, 7–8). Benjamin is not among the students Ryder describes studying or discussing court sessions. PRO KB 33/5/5, 10 Apr. 1713.

50. Information on Defoe's composition methods is in PRO KB 33/5/5 and SP 34/21, pt. 1; see also my *Defoe*, 91–99.

51. Pittis's payment is recorded in PRO KB 33/5/5, testimony of John Baker, 10 Apr. 1713. On edition sizes, see Rostenburg, *Literary, Political, Scientific, Religious, and Legal Publishing, Printing and Bookselling in England, 1551–1700* 2:425.

52. *Reasons against the Succession*, 38–39. These six pages (13–16 and 19–20) of the same pamphlet could be Benjamin's but the metaphors and sentence structure seem to me to be Defoe's. Benjamin's handwriting appears to be a scrawl to me. Defoe may have disguised his writing—one contemporary complained that he was hard to prosecute because he had six styles (PRO KB 33/5/5, testimony of the compositors and pressmen, 10 Apr. 1713). Lee, *Defoe* 3:410–12.

53. "A Health to be Sung and Drank by all Honest Britons"; Dunton, *Golden Age*, 57; see also *Hudibrastick Brewer* and *White Staff's Speech to the Lords*.

54. Defoe, *Protestant Jubilee*, 25.

55. Many Englishmen did not know that George was divorced, and there was some confusion over whether Sophia Dorothea's name should be added to the prayers in the Anglican liturgy (Michael, *England under George I*, 78–80).

56. A good account of George's arrival at Greenwich and London is in Michael, *England under George I*, 74–76. See also Lenman, *Jacobite Risings*, 115–

17; Oldmixon, *History*, 579; Hatton, *George I*, 170–71. Hatton argues rather unconvincingly that George's English was not as limited as is generally thought (130–31).

57. Records from Bristol, Taunton, Canterbury, Norwich, Hertford, Reading, Tewkesbury, Birmingham, Salisbury, and others on Coronation Day, along with encouragements of mayors, aldermen, sheriffs, and justices of the peace to suppress unrest and "execute" the laws are in PRO SP 44/116. See Nicholas Rogers, "Popular Protest," 83; Speck, *Stability and Strife*, 180–81; Lenman, *Jacobite Risings*, 115.

58. H 444. On some of the forces behind the hostility to George and the Whigs, see Rogers, 83–94 and Foord, *His Majesty's Opposition, 1714–1830*, 15–38; Speck, 172–74, and Michael, *England under George I*, 80–88.

59. Defoe, *Strike while the Iron's Hot*, 17.

60. Defoe, *Letter from One Clergy-Man to Another*, 11; *Flying Post*, 14 Aug. 1714, in Lee, *Defoe* 1:231.

61. *Strike while the Iron's Hot*, 12–13.

62. Myers, *British Book Trade*, 57, 329. Janeway and Baker describe their agreements for Defoe's pamphlets between themselves and between Defoe and themselves in PRO KB 33/5/5. Mumby, *Publishing and Bookselling*, 129–30; Mumby, Hodgson, and Blagden, *Notebook of Thomas Bennet and Henry Clements*, 67–68, 81–86. Defoe notes how printers will no longer print in the mere hope of sales (H 424).

63. *Two Letters concerning the Author of the Examiner*, 8–9.

64. Howard gives the example of the Queen Mother in "Truth Preserves Her Shape," 199; on Defoe's tendency to use his own material, see Moore, "Canon of Defoe's Writings," 155–69, and "Defoe Acquisitions at the Huntington Library," 47–53. *Immorality of the Priesthood* is the same as *Justice and Necessity of Restraining the Clergy* except that the latter has no preface; *Secret History of State Intrigues* is the same as *Secret History of the Scepter* (all 1715).

65. Information on Keimer is from PRO SP 35/2, 30 May 1715; Pittis, *Queen Anne*, 16; Bloore, "Samuel Keimer," 255–87; Benjamin Franklin, *Autobiography*, 23–26 and 50–54; Schwartz, *French Prophets*, 124, 128, 193; H 448–49, 448 n. 2.

66. Both Keimer and Defoe personified the Quakers successfully enough that the Quakers published statements to the effect that the authors were not Quakers (Lee, *Defoe* 1:245; Bloore, 271–72). Maxfield gives evidence from another source that Keimer was disowned by the Quakers ("Daniel Defoe and the Quakers," 180 n. 6, and on Defoe, 183–86). Lee discusses Defoe's early Quaker personae (1:244–54). Sutherland also dates Defoe's Quaker voice to this period but does not discuss Keimer (*Defoe*, 211). Moore attributes *The Quaker's Sermon: or, A Holding-forth concerning Barabbas* (1711) to Defoe, but I am unpersuaded by his case. Without evidence, Ireland says that Defoe's entire family was Quaker and attended the Bull and Mouth, the most famous meeting location in London ("The Defoe Family in America," 61–62).

Sill recognizes the importance of these years in shaping the novelist (*Defoe and the Idea of Fiction*, 24–26), as does Novak ("Fiction and Society in the Early Eighteenth Century," 66–69). See, also, my *Defoe*, 42–69.

67. Information about printers from Plomer's *Dictionary* and Moore's *Checklist*; on Anne Dodd, PRO SP 35/1.

68. An intriguing link may exist between *The Candidate* and Susannah Centlivre's unacted play, *The Gotham Election* (1715). After the play was refused a license by the Master of Revels, Samuel Keimer printed it. The printed version begins very prominently with act 1, but only that act seems to survive.

69. H 446; *Flying Post and Medley*, 27 Aug. 1714; Sutherland, *Defoe*, 204–6, 213–17.

. 70. Lee, *Defoe* 1:233–34; J. R. Jones, *Country and Court*, 350–51.

71. Examinations of Baker and Hurt are dated 23 Aug. 1714; BL Loan 29/8 newsletter for 24 Aug. 1714 says "yesterday": the examinations were enclosed in Bromley's letter to Attorney General Northey and recorded as dated 23 Aug., PRO SP 44/115 for 27 Aug. 1714. Warrant for the seizure of papers, PRO SP 44/79A for 24 Aug.

72. PRO SP 44/115 and SP 35/1 pt. 1, fol. 29.

73. PRO SP 44/115 and H 446–47.

74. Speck, *Stability*, 171.

75. Oldmixon, *History*, 554; Defoe, *Letter from a Member of the House of Commons*, 43–44.

76. Beardwell is identified as the printer in PRO SP 44/79A, fols. 12–13, SP 44/115, for 3 and 7 Sept. 1714. Dunton calls him "generous and obliging" (*Life and Errors* 1:251).

77. Controllment Roll for 1 George I, PRO KB 29/374, mem. xvj verso, rot. 82 (Mich. 1714); KB 28/52, Crown Roll, Hilary term 1 George I. I am grateful to James P. Derriman for transcribing these documents.

78. The date of Defoe's move is not entirely certain, but I read the evidence as Secord does ("Defoe in Stoke Newington," 216). Details about the house are from this article (211–15); Shirren, "Daniel Defoe in Stoke Newington," 18–19 and 22–23; and Henry Baker's description in "Autobiographical Memoranda," V&A, Forster MS. 48. D. 4, 1–2, 6. Unfortunately Defoe's library was sold with another person's. Defoe scholars agree that most of the books on the list were his; I believe he was a collector and that his son-in-law kept the most valuable editions, because multiple copies of many books were sold but special editions of them and other books do not appear on the list. See *Librorum ex Bibliothecis Philippi Farewell. D.D., et Danielis De Foe, Gen., Catalogus* (BL C. 57. C); Heidenreich, *Libraries of Daniel Defoe and Philip Farewell*, and Kropf, "Sale of Defoe's Library," 123–33.

79. *Universal Spectator*, 12 Oct. 1728; Lee, *Defoe* 3:467.

80. *Weekly Journal*, 16 July 1715, allows us to date the trial as 12 July (Lee 1:252). Even hawkers were the objects of mass arrests throughout 1715. For summer 1715 warrants, see PRO SP 44/77 and SP 44/117.

81. PRO KB 29/374 (Hil. 1714/15), mem. xlvj recto, rot. 41.

82. Michael, *England under George I*, 130; Moore, *Citizen*, 206–7.

83. Defoe, *View of the Scots Rebellion*, 28–29. Sources for the account of the rebellion are Speck, *Stability*, 179–83; Lenman, *Jacobite Risings*, 126–62; Bennett, *Tory Crisis in Church and State*, 196–98. See Moore's "Defoe's Hand in *A Journal of the Earl of Marr's Proceedings*," 209–28, for one of the ways Defoe discredits Mar. Macaree summarizes Defoe's contribution in *Daniel Defoe and the Jacobite Movement*, 72–91.

84. Defoe, *Pernicious Consequences*, 15; he also cites Matthew 13.

85. *His Majesty's Obligations to the Whigs Plainly Proved*, another refutation of *English Advice*, is often included in the Defoe canon, but I am not convinced it is his.

86. PRO T 29/22, fols. 166–70, and T 54/23 (Mr. Borret's accounts, 7 Apr. 1715); Lee, *Defoe* 1:254–55 quotes the *Weekly Packet*.

87. For Defoe's accounts, see H 450–54, and *Serious Reflections of Robinson Crusoe* 3:290–92. On Parker, see *Biographical Dictionary of the Judges of England*; see also Moore, *Citizen*, 208–9, and Sutherland, *Defoe*, 214–17.

CHAPTER 15: A DISCONTENTED PEOPLE

1. Defoe, *Considerations on the Present State of Affairs in Great Britain*, 3; Michael, *England under George I*, 130–32.

2. On party struggle, see Speck, *Stability*, 172–81; Hatton, *George I*, 123–28.

3. Hanson, *Government and the Press*, 102; on the devious method of payment, see Alsop, "Defoe and His Whig Paymasters," 225–26. The receipt is printed in HMC, 8th report, appendix, 27.

4. "Preface" to *The True-Born Englishman: A Satyr. Corrected and enlarg'd by the AUTHOR*; I am grateful to Spiro Peterson and the Miami University, Oxford, Ohio, library for a copy of this rare poem. Defoe inserted 49 lines between lines 540 and 541, cut lines 624–53, changed a phrase in the conclusion, and added a couplet. He removed the lines satirizing John Tutchin, author of *The Foreigners*, the poem that had originally inspired *The True-Born Englishman*. Cf. pp. 17–21 and 35–36 to the 1700 poem in *POAS* 6:283–87 and 308–9. He changes "Fools do the Wise, and Wise Men Fools succeed" (6:308) to "Fools for wise Men, and wise Men Fools succeed."

5. On the paper's appeal, see Moore, "Daniel Defoe, Ambidextrous Mercury," 1–2, and my *Defoe*, 159–73 et passim. On the reporting of parliamentary news, see Sutherland, *Restoration Newspaper*, 7–8, 157–59, and Peter Thomas, "The Beginning of Parliamentary Reporting in Newspapers," 623.

6. PRO SP 44/79A for 9 Jan. 1716 and 8 Oct. 1718; SP 35/3 for 25 and 26 July 1715, complaint from Bristol against Dormer's newsletter and Dormer's apology. Snyder, "Newsletters in England, 1689–1715," 3–19.

7. It is clear from the HMC Stuart Papers that the Pretender and his circle did not trust Harley before the death of Queen Anne; see 1:291, 294, 318, 321, 333. In fact, the duke of Berwick expresses relief at the news that Harley will be dismissed, just as Defoe says in *Minutes of Mesnager* (1:318, 27 Apr. 1714). Harley's oldest daughter was married to Mar's brother-in-law, and Harley had made Mar secretary of state for Scotland upon Queensberry's death in 1711 (Gregg, "Jacobite Career of John, Earl of Mar," 180). By 21 Sept. 1716 a "settled way of correspondence" had been set up between Harley and the exile court (Stuart Papers 2:458–60; 464–66; 3:151, 5:538). The way Ogilvie worked is explained in 4:124. For some of Harley's advice, see 4:60–62, 146, 273–74; 544–45, 5:121–22. See also Green, *Queen Anne*, 249. Defoe favored establishing a "barrier" to protect the North American colonies (*Review* 8:519, 538–39). I am grateful to Beth Neman for bringing some of this material to my attention and for sharing the manuscript of her forthcoming edition of *Major Ramkins*. She quotes a letter from Dubois to Craggs, BM Stowe MSS 247, fols. 35–39, in her manuscript; cf. Stuart Papers 5:539–40. As Neman says, biographies of Harley have ignored this late Jacobite collaboration.

8. Speck, *Stability*, 183–84; Michael, *England under George I*, 215–19; Hatton, *George I*, 211–12. Michael quotes Steele (217). Defoe also wrote extensively in support of the administration's prosecutions of the rebels and, later, of the Act of Grace. He answered such opposition pamphlets as Matthias Earbery's *History of the Clemency of Our English Monarchs* (1717); see Defoe, *History of the Clemency of Our English Monarchs* (1717) and *Mercurius Politicus*, Sept. 1717, 56off.

9. Lord Trevor, quoted in Michael, *England under George I*, 216.

10. *Review* 2:374 and 5:143 respectively.

11. *Some Considerations on a Law for Triennial Parliaments* (1716), 17–19. The authorship of the Triennial pamphlets has attracted some controversy. After examining them carefully and considering Defoe's own and his contempo-

raries' statements about them, I feel confident that Defoe wrote the two named in the text.

12. Defoe, *Annals of King George, Year the Second . . . for the Year MDCCXVI* (1717), 281–82.

13. Sainty, "Huguenot Civil Servant," 398–413. See *Review* 1:163–64, 167–68, 188.

14. Oldmixon, *History*, 671–72; Basil Williams, *Stanhope*, 384–86; cf. Defoe, *Vindication of Dr. Snape*, 5–6. Some examples of these pamphlets are Lowman, *Defence of the Protestant Dissenters; Dissenters Claim of Right to a Capacity for Civil Offices; What the Dissenters Would Have;* and Boyer, *Impartial History.*

15. Defoe, *Layman's Vindication of the Church of England*, 3; *Faction in Power*, 47–48; *Question Fairly Stated*, 4–7, 26–29; *Danger and Consequences of Disobliging the Clergy*, 19–30.

16. Barlow, *Citizenship and Conscience*, 67–70. *Mercurius Politicus*, May 1717, blames reports of such meetings for stiffening resistance (300-301).

17. "A Presbyterian Getting on Horse-back" (2d ed., 1717), 14, 34; the first edition, also 1717, is about a page shorter. As is typical of attacks on Defoe, the author attributes pamphlets to him that he did not write—but also identifies one he did write. Barlow, 70–76.

18. Hatton, *George I*, 243; Oldmixon, *History*, 671; Defoe, *Impartial Enquiry*, 75–76. Defoe speaks specifically of Walpole's change of position in *Mercurius Britannicus*, January 1718, 10–12.

19. Defoe, *Some Thoughts upon the Subject of Commerce with France*, 7; *Danger and Consequences of Disobliging the Clergy*, 5 and 33 respectively.

20. On this policy, see Speck, *Stability*, 93. On the defeat, see Basil Williams, *Stanhope*, 384–92.

21. Locke, *Letter on Toleration*, 59 and 155 respectively.

22. Information on the Bangorian controversy is from Overton and Relton, *English Church*, 14–19; Carpenter, *Eighteenth-Century Church and People*, 130–39; and *Mercurius Politicus*, May 1717, 301–32.

23. *Mercurius Politicus*, May 1717, 302 and table of contents; *Annals, Year the Third*, 264 respectively. Defoe makes the same point in *A Reply to the Remarks upon the Lord Bishop of Bangor's Treatment of the Clergy and Convocation*, in which he says thirty or forty individuals have written or preached on the subject (4–5).

24. Defoe, *Annals, Year the Third*, 262–63.

25. Novak says that the issue of sincerity is central to an understanding of Defoe's interest in the controversy in "Sincerity, Delusion, and Character," 109–10.

26. Carpenter, *Eighteenth-Century Church and People*, 130–31 and n. 3.

27. *The Monthly Catalogue* dates it in January 1717. For this and other *Monthly Catalogue* dates, I have relied upon Pat Rogers, "Addenda and Corrigenda," 60–64.

28. Defoe, *Vindication of Dr. Snape*, 5–6. This pamphlet is attributed to Defoe in Moore's *Checklist* and listed as "Probably by Defoe" in Novak's *NCBEL* entry, but the style and details of the argument do not allow me to believe it is certainly his. The argument that Hoadley is more extreme than the Presbyterians and that he made a fine "Independent sermon" seems counterproductive for Defoe. The authorship is not important for my point. For another example of the Nonconformists' involvement in the Bangorian controversy, see Lowman, *Defence of the Protestant Dissenters.*

29. Novak notes this groundbreaking quality of the dispute in "Sincerity, Delusion, and Character," 112.

30. Defoe, *Reply to the Remarks*, 6, 9, 13, 19, 35 (quotations from 34–35); *Conduct of Christians*, 29–31 (quotation from 30); *Expostulatory Letter*, 2.

31. Calamy, *Historical Account* 2:418.

32. Stogdon denied the equality of Christ to God, but that issue was settled outside of Salters' Hall; the issue there was sufficient tests for orthodoxy. On the beginning of the controversy, see Thomas, "Presbyterians in Transition," in *English Presbyterians*, 151–61; Watts, *Dissenters*, 371–82; Walter Wilson, *History and Antiquities* 3:515–22.

33. Quoted from Gough's 1730 *Enquiry into the Causes of the Decay of the Dissenting Interest* by Speck, *Stability*, 102. Wilson concurs; he notes it provided the opportunity for "their enemies to speak all manner of evil against them" (*History and Antiquities* 2:7–8); Wodrow, *Analecta* 2:377, says it was still a factor in the "weakened interest" as late as 1723. Defoe called the Dissenters' behavior "scandalous" in *Mercurius Politicus*, March 1719.

34. Defoe, *Letter to the Dissenters*, 17.

35. *Mercurius Politicus*, Feb. 1719, 80.

36. Black, "British Press," 68–69.

37. On parties, see Bolingbroke's *Dissertation upon Parties* 3:4–172, and Pocock, *Machiavellian Moment*, 483–84, 488–89.

38. Richetti, *Popular Fiction*, 125. My discussion has been influenced by his 119–67. On Manley's political effectiveness, see Needham, "Mary de la Rivière Manley, Tory Defender," 253–88.

39. Cf. Defoe, *Secret History of the October Club*, pts. 1 and 2 in 1711, *Memoirs of Count Tariff* in 1713, and *Memoirs of John, Duke of Melfort*, published in February 1714.

40. Cf. Defoe, *Secret Memoirs of the New Treaty*, 2–3.

41. *Mercurius Politicus*, April 1717, 247–48. Defoe says that he began *Memoirs of the Church of Scotland* nine years earlier. On the basis of evidence from the *Review*, Moore dates it to 1708, a highly probable surmise (Moore's uncatalogued notes in the University of Illinois Library). Wodrow complains of numerous errors in the book, but Wodrow was a competing author at the time. His own *History of the Sufferings of the Church of Scotland* came out in 1721–22. Some of Wodrow's citings are misreadings; see, for example, his objections to the purpose of the commission's trip to London, xlii–xliii.

42. Defoe, *Memoirs of Publick Transactions in the Life . . . of Shrewsbury*, 3–4, 50–54, 104, 120–21; quotation from 120.

43. See, for instance, *Mesnager*, 183–85; Sill finds autobiographical passages in this work and discusses it as fiction and the treatment of the character of Shrewsbury (*Defoe and the Idea of Fiction*, 23–25 and 141–44).

44. Defoe, for instance, depicts the king laughing that he means he will not help the Pretender only as long as Anne lives (*Proceedings at Perth*, 2–32). Cf. Boyer, *Political State of Great Britain*, June 1717, 13:627–39, and Defoe's comments in *Mercurius Politicus*, July 1717, 471–73.

45. See Sill's discussion of this work and *Journal of the Earl of Marr's Proceedings* (*Defoe and the Idea of Fiction*, 115–18).

46. Behn, *Works* 5:129; Lennard Davis gives Behn credit for "inaugurating" the claim that her work was true (*Factual Fictions*, 106–10); in fact, the claim was already convention. I have used examples from Davis's book and from J. Paul Hunter. On evidence and the shifting weight of oral versus written testimony, see Staves, *Players' Scepters*, 224–34.

47. Defoe, *Quarrel of the School-Boys*, 30; *Secret Memoirs of the New Treaty*, 30.

CHAPTER 16: A PENETRATING EYE

1. *Robinson Crusoe* was entered in the Stationers' Register on 23 Apr. 1719 and went on sale a few days later (Pat Rogers, *Robinson Crusoe*, 4–7). Maslen usefully documents how edition numbers compared to those of other eighteenth-century books ("Edition Quantities for *Robinson Crusoe*," 145–50).

2. Rogers, 7–8; Walter Wilson, *Memoirs of . . . Defoe* 3:433–34; Gove, *Imaginary Voyage in Prose Fiction*, 124ff. *Daily Post* advertisement for 9 Oct. 1719: "This Day is publish'd (very proper to be bound up with *Robinson Crusoe*) . . . Written by himself." Defoe's recent works that had done as well included *Secret Memoirs of a Treasonable Conference*, the first two parts of *Secret History of the White Staff*, *Remarks on the Speeches of Clerk and Hall*, *Proceedings at Perth*, and *Account of Proceedings against the Rebels*.

3. A petition to Secretary of State Craggs set the number of English seamen "now miserable Slaves . . . in Sally" (Salé, on the Atlantic coast of Morocco) at three hundred (PRO SP 44/119, fols. 305–6). News of the captures, ransoms, and thanksgiving services were commonly reported in the papers; see my "Barbary Ransom," 239. Defoe called on the allies to destroy the pirates and reminded his readers of the suffering of their captives, saying, "the chief of these People are the *Moors* of SALLEE" (20 June 1720).

4. See Alkon, "The Odds against Friday," 29–61; Knox-Shaw, *Explorer in English Fiction*, on "projection," 4–9, 24–49.

5. This chapter is strictly limited to biographical matters. Among the many fine studies of Defoe's art and ideas are Novak's *Defoe and the Nature of Man*, *Economics and the Fiction of Daniel Defoe*, ch. 2 of *Realism, Myth, and History in Defoe's Fiction*, and "Crusoe the King and the Political Evolution of His Island"; Starr, *Defoe and Spiritual Autobiography*; Hunter, *Reluctant Pilgrim*; ch. 2 of Zimmerman's *Defoe and the Novel*, ch. 1 of Seidel's *Exile and the Narrative Imagination*, ch. 2 of Richetti's *Defoe's Narratives*, Braudy's "Defoe and the Anxieties of Autobiography," 76–97. See also ch. 8 of my own *Defoe*.

6. *Robinson Crusoe* 2:7; the quotation is from Dryden's *Religio Laici, or a Laymans* [sic] *Faith* (1682), ll. 431–32. The quotation from the sermon is from a sermon Defoe may have heard by John Collins, "How Are the Religious of a Nation the Strength of it?" Defoe satirized the Arian heresy in *Mist's Weekly-Journal*, 30 May 1719 (Lee, *Defoe* 2:129–31). See Adams, *Travel Literature and the Evolution of the Novel*, 39, 59–60, 113, 123, 126, 182.

7. Richetti has; see his *Defoe's Narratives*, 46–47; see also my "Defoe's Prodigal Sons," 3–18.

8. Quoted in Damrosch, *God's Plot and Man's Stories*, 48. Damrosch notes, "Defoe's story curiously fails to sustain the motif of the prodigal" (188).

9. Private papers of the duke of Hamilton, Atholl to his son William, no date, MS. M2/66. I am grateful to the duke for access and permission to quote.

10. Knox, *Autobiography*, as quoted in Goonetileke's edition, xi; see viii, x–xi, xvii, xxii–xxiii.

11. Information about the marriages of Defoe's sons, Moore, *Citizen*, 331–32, 334. Defoe had reported on the royal rivalry and on Czar Peter in *Mercurius Politicus*, *Mist's Weekly-Journal*, and other places; see, for example, Lee, *Defoe* 2:58–59 and 61–66. A number of critics have related the conduct books and *Robinson Crusoe*; see, for example, Starr, *Defoe and Spiritual Autobiography*, 75–76 et passim; Hunter, *Reluctant Pilgrim*, 26–46; Marks notes in *Sir Charles Grandison* that Defoe's conduct books "seem poised" between the traditional conduct book and the modern novel (39).

12. *Annual Matrimonial Expenses in London*.

13. Moore, *Citizen*, 326. Langley was an executor of Samuel Tuffley's will (PRO PROB 11/604/383). In the 5 Dec. 1719 *Weekly-Journal* there is an amusing story of a Queenhithe man who has been married for three whole years and has not yet come to regret it (Lee, *Defoe* 2:177–78).

14. Information in this paragraph is from Ryken, *Worldly Saints*, 73–87, Trumbach, *Rise of the Egalitarian Family*, and Laslett, *World We Have Lost*, 81–105.

15. Laslett, 99–103.

16. Quoted in Ryken, *Worldly Saints*, 74.

17. [Mortimer], *Some Considerations concerning the Present State of Religion*, 4. Mason lists two of the four types of courtesy books as the book of parental advice and the book of polity (*Gentlefolk*, 5, 58, 86, 294–99).

18. *Family Instructor* (1718), 181–88, 193–96; the section on horses is mis-numbered 686 [186]–187. See Laslett on the catechism (*World We Have Lost*, 218–19).

19. Cf. *Family Instructor* (1715), 10–16 and 25–26; *Family Instructor* (1718), 297, 320–24; *Robinson Crusoe* 2:1–5, and *Farther Adventures* 3:47–53. See Hunter on the verisimilitude of the dialogue ("Friday as Convert," 243–48).

20. *Family Instructor* (1715), 6–7, 371; *Family Instructor* (1718), 320; *Robinson Crusoe* 1:243; *Farther Adventures* 2:47.

21. *Family Instructor* (1715), 18; cf. *Westminster Confession*, "Of God, and Of the Holy Trinity."

22. *Serious Reflections*, 3; *Collection of Miscellany Letters* (no. 18) 4:99, and 103.

23. Introduction to vol. 3 of the *Tour*, 136; cf. introduction to *Serious Reflections*, 3.

24. Bell makes this observation in *Defoe's Fiction*, 88–89.

25. Two good discussions are Watt, "Robinson Crusoe as a Myth," 311–32; Price, *To the Palace of Wisdom*, 266–69.

26. Knox, *Historical Relation of Ceylon*, 205. Some of the best sources studies are Secord, *Studies in the Narrative Method of Defoe*; *Biographia Britannica* (1793) 1:68–70; Brink, "*Robinson Crusoe* and *The Life of the Reverend Mr. George Trosse*," 433–51; Percy Adams, *Travel Literature*, 126–34. Secord notes the significance of Knox, 32–49, 109. Downie usefully reminds us of the importance of travel literature to *Robinson Crusoe* ("Defoe, Imperialism, and the Travel Books Reconsidered," 66–83).

27. On the influence of *Mist's Weekly-Journal*, see Sutherland, *Defoe*, 221; Sutherland, *Restoration Newspaper*, 38–40, and Hanson, *Government and the Press*, 103–5.

28. Most biographies of Defoe date his work with Mist to August 1717; Alsop guesses that one of Mist's arrests facilitated Defoe's acceptance by Mist ("New Light on Nathaniel Mist and Daniel Defoe," 57–60). The August evidence seems slim to me. Novak suggests February in his *NCBEL* entry, and that date, although perhaps a bit early, is not out of the question. See Stevens, *Party Politics*, 109; Hanson, *Government and the Press*, 102–3. Both Sutherland, *Restoration Newspaper*, 212–13, and Rogers, *Grub Street*, 277, conclude that Mist did little writing.

29. Mayo, *English Novel in the Magazines*, 49–50, and Sutherland, *Restoration Newspaper*, 40, 229–30.

30. Sutherland, *Defoe*, 215, 230; H 453–55, 460–61.

31. H 454–55.

32. Quoted in Sutherland, *Restoration Newspaper*, 212.

33. Rogers, *Grub Street*, 326.

34. *Historical View of the Principles, Characters, Persons, &c. of the Political Writers in Great Britain.*

35. Quoted in Stevens, *Party Politics*, 109–10.

36. Testimony of Thomas Warner, 1 Nov. 1718 (PRO SP 35/13); Aitken, "Defoe and Mist's *Weekly Journal*," 287–88.

37. PRO SP 44/79A for 3 Mar. 1717/18 and KB 1/1, pt. 2, items 48 and 72; H 456 for 23 May 1718.

38. PRO SP 35/13 for 1 Nov. 1718. *Mist's Weekly-Journal*, 8 Nov. 1718, and *White-Hall Evening Post*, 15 Nov. 1718.

39. A long memorial, including this quotation, on the "mischief" of Mist's paper is in PRO SP 35/3, 1 Nov. 1718; on the paper's wide distribution, see Sutherland, *Restoration Newspaper*, 38–39.

40. The prosecution of Mist and the frustration Craggs and his staff felt can be traced in PRO SP 44/79A, 1 Aug. 1718; SP 44/79, 334–39; SP 35/12, 6 Sept. 1718; SP 44/119, Craggs to attorney general, 6 Sept. 1718, fol. 212; SP 35/13, 18 and 31 Oct. and 1 and 6 Nov. 1718. Delafaye told Mist that Buckley had "the Care of the Affair relating to you" (1 Oct. 1718), and Mist identified Defoe as the author of the offending paper in a memorial dated 1 Nov. 1718 (SP 35/13).

41. Boyer, *Political State of Great Britain* 13:627–33 (June 1717); Defoe, *Mercurius Politicus* (July 1717), 471–73. Furbank and Owens "question" the attribution of *Letter to the Author of the Flying-Post* to Defoe; their argument is that the writing is too poor to be Defoe's, but surely any reader of *Jure Divino* can testify that Defoe's style—in prose or poetry—could have all of the characteristics that they object to. See *Canonisation*, 161–64.

42. [Curll], *Curlicism Display'd* 2 and 26.

43. Lee, *Defoe* 2:30–36. In the *Commentator*, 14 Mar. 1720, Defoe had pitied newsmen without a war to write about and suggested they follow the lead of "honest *Curl*, [and] transcribe last Wills and Testaments from *Doctor's-Commons*." On the prosecution of Curll, see Thomas, "Press Prosecutions," 320.

44. Dalrymple's letter is misdated 3 Oct. 1718, probably for 3 Nov., SRO GD 135/141, vol. 18/24. The postscript was in the 30 Oct. *White-Hall Evening Post* (no. 19), and the retraction in no. 20 for 1 Nov. 1718. Dalrymple's letter is printed in *Annals and Correspondence of the Viscount and the First and Second Earls of Stair* 2:58–60. A clear contemporary account of the affair of the French cardinal is in Boyer's *Political State of Great Britain* 16:264 (September 1718).

45. Gildon, *Life*, preface, iv. Cox is quoted in Rogers, *Robinson Crusoe*, 8.

46. [Toland], *Second Part of the State Anatomy*, 27; Boyer, *Political State* 13:632.

47. Respectively Toland, *Second Part of the State Anatomy*, 27, 32, 28, 29; Hart, *Bulwark Stormed*, 22–23; Boyer, *Political State* 13:627, 632.

48. Respectively Toland, 32, 29; Boyer 13:631; Gildon, *Life*, 1, 23–24, 31; Toland, 27; Boyer, 13:632–33.

49. Boyer 13:632.

CHAPTER 17: THE WHOLE WORLD IN MOTION

1. Rogers, *Robinson Crusoe*, 6–9 and "Classics and Chapbooks," 27–39; Gildon, *Life*, ix–x. Maslen points out that the third and fourth editions of *Robinson Crusoe* each exist in two distinct settings of type and that the number of 1719 editions should, therefore, be six ("Edition Quantities," 145–47). The two parts of *Robinson Crusoe* were serialized from 7 Oct. 1719 to 19 Oct. 1720 (Wiles, *Serial Publication in England before 1750*, 27).

2. Defoe's most frequent grammar error is agreement, and he is most care-

less with pronoun/noun agreement. The quotation is from his *Memoirs of Majr. Alexander Ramkins*, 269.

3. Preface to *Farther Adventures*; cf. the preface to the second *Family Instructor*; *Robinson Crusoe* 3:108.

4. Eric Williams, *Capitalism and Slavery*, 51–53; Spate, *Pacific since Magellan*, 204–7; Gipson, *Southern Plantations* 2:228–85, 312–42. Williams quotes Josiah Child and Dalby Thomas among others. William Wood, secretary to the commissioners of Customs and Britain's "leading mercantilist writer" agreed that foreign trade was England's "staff of life" (*Survey of Trade* quoted in Mathias, *Transformation of England*, 46–47).

5. *Further Examination of the Weavers Pretences*, 40.

6. Hulme comments on Defoe's cautious attitude toward easy wealth and examines his ideology of trade in *Colonial Encounters*; see especially 180–86. See also Downie's important article "Defoe, Imperialism, and the Travel Books Reconsidered," 74–83. Defoe calls London "Magazine of the whole World" in *What If the Swedes Should Come?* 16–17; see also 17–21.

7. *Historical Account of the Voyages and Adventures of Sir Walter Raleigh* (1719). Furbank and Owens question the attribution of this item to Defoe; I believe it to be by Defoe and find it consistent with Defoe's references to Raleigh throughout his life and indicative of the way Defoe's work took changing historical situations into consideration. See *Canonisation*, 164–66.

8. Knox-Shaw calls Singleton "by a long way the most appalling" of all of Defoe's creations (*Explorer in English Fiction*, 54–55).

9. Secord, *Studies in the Narrative Method*, 130–39; Scrimgeour, "Problem of Realism in Defoe's *Captain Singleton*," 21–37.

10. *Ramkins*, 324; *Commentator*, 18 Mar. 1720.

11. Moore, "Defoe's Hand in *A Journal of the Earl of Marr's Proceedings*," 209–28. Moore details Defoe's editorial changes and introduction and their effect.

12. *Ramkins*, 269.

13. Cf. *Review* 1:165ff., 178; 4:307–8; 6:103, 266; *Scots Nation and Union Vindicated*, 24–28.

14. Novak sees Defoe's intention to be to "champion" the Protestant cause in Europe and the Dissenting cause in England, but I think the book was written too late for Defoe to be intensely interested in doing either ("History, Ideology and the Method of Defoe's Historical Fiction," 109).

15. Lenman, *Jacobite Risings*, 188–94.

16. See my *Defoe* for a fuller discussion of the literary strategy of this novel, 123–35.

17. Gray, "Elegy Written in a Country-Churchyard," ll. 61–62, 65–66, 73–76.

18. Defoe was probably quoting from memory, for a few words differ from those of the song ("and" for "nor," for instance). The song "The Country Life" is from *The British Musical Miscellany* (n.d.), cited in Eirionnach [pseud.], "Quotations in 'Robinson Crusoe,'" 426–27.

19. Quoted in Glyndwr Williams, "'Inexhaustible Fountain of Gold,'" 37.

20. Dickson, *Financial Revolution*, 93–94; Spate, *Pacific since Magellan* 2:189, 200; Schachter, Gerin, Hood, and Andreassen, "Was the South Sea Bubble a Random Walk?" 325; Scott, *Constitution and Finance* 1:399, 3:296–97. Williams describes the company's single, strange proposal for an extravagant expedition ("'Inexhaustible Fountain,'" 44–55).

21. Information in this paragraph is from Speck, *Stability*, 196–98; Scott 1:400–401, 408–19 and 3:295–324, working capital could have reached £40,000,000, 3:307; Dickson, 99–104; Carswell, *South Sea Bubble*, 127; Brisco,

Economic Policy of Walpole, 43–52. Defoe reported the conversion in *Mercurius Politicus*, June 1719, to be advantageous to the company, to subscribers who chose to convert to stock, and to the government (326–28). See Dickson on the advantages to the government (97). It is worth noting that the House of Commons spent almost twice as much time on another bill then pending (on calico) than on the South Sea Company (Dickson, 103 n.7).

22. *Minutes of the Negotiations of Monsr. Mesnager*, 50–51. Although Mesnager is an unreliable narrator, there is no reason to doubt that this statement is not close to Defoe's own opinion. Williams discusses Defoe's early skepticism ("'Inexhaustible Fountain,'" 39–42).

23. Carswell contends that financial manipulation and the creation of credit was always the company's end (*South Sea Bubble*, 55–56).

24. Wilson, *Memoirs of the Life of Daniel De Foe* 3:425. Defoe owned stock worth £127 10s., one share.

25. *Manufacturer*, 10 Aug. 1720.

26. *Historical Account of the Voyages . . . of Raleigh*, 40–41, 44. Many people shared Defoe's opinion of the wealth of South America; cf. Williams, "'Inexhaustible Fountain,'" 27–28.

27. Information on Townshend and the divisions is from Hatton, *George I*, 187–210; Speck, *Stability*, 186–96; Plumb, *First Four Georges*, 46–47; and Defoe's *Impartial Enquiry into the Conduct of . . . T[ownshend]*. On the aftermath of Walpole's resignation, see Brisco, *Economic Policy of Walpole*, 37–38; Scott, *Constitution and Finance* 3:298–99; Dickson, *Financial Revolution*, 102–21; Basil Williams, *Stanhope*, 260–65; Foord, *His Majesty's Opposition*, 60–61. Walpole had objected primarily because he was in opposition to Stanhope, but he predicted some of the ways in which the plan would be detrimental to the public.

28. Information on England's national debt and economic conditions is from Speck, *Stability*, 120–42; Mathias, *Transformation of England*, 118, table 6.1; William Wood, *Survey of Trade*; Ashton, *Economic Fluctuations in England*, 142, 181; Thompson, "Moral Economy of the Crowd in the Eighteenth Century," 76–136.

29. Cf. *Fair Payment No Spunge*, 48–50, and *Mercurius Politicus*, Mar. 1717, 173–76.

30. *Mercurius Politicus*, Mar. 1717, 141–44, 153. Walpole's comments on one of the pamphlets is in Cambridge MS. CH (H) 49/1a/14. On Paterson's Wednesday Club publications, see Bannister's preface in *Writings of William Paterson*; Paterson gives the figures Defoe quotes on 2:135, 137, 177–78.

31. Defoe, *Conduct of Robert Walpole*, 57–63. On Walpole's plan, cf. *Fair Payment*, 51–56, with Brisco, *Economic Policy of Robert Walpole*, 35–41, and Scott, *Constitution and Finance* 3:298–99.

32. He quotes this part approvingly in *Mercurius Politicus* and *Conduct of Walpole*, 59–63. The quotations are from *Fair Payment*.

33. *Commentator*, 26 Feb. 1720; *Anatomy of Exchange-Alley*, 1–5; *Mercurius Politicus*, June 1719, 329–30. Rogers discusses the language of disease and gambling in "'Calamitous Year,'" 151–67.

34. *Commentator*, 27 May and 10 June 1720; *Manufacturer*, 9 June 1720; *Commentator*, 26 and 29 Feb., 20 May, and 10 June 1720 respectively; see also *Anatomy of Exchange-Alley*, 8, 26, 44.

35. *Commentator*, 27 June, 9 May, 10 June, and 1 July 1720.

36. Defoe, *Manufacturer*, 13 Oct. 1720; all quotations are from this unpaginated edition; Hoppit, "Financial Crises in Eighteenth-Century England," 39–58, especially 47–48; Scott, *Constitution and Finance* 1:427–29, 432–35, and 3:348–53; Carswell, *South Sea Bubble*, 191–200, especially 194–99; Ashton,

Economic Fluctuations, 120–21 and *Economic History of England: The Eighteenth Century*, 170–74, 177–88; Rosen, "Dictatorship of the Bourgeoisie," 49–50.

37. *Commentator*, 29 Feb. 1720.

38. *Director*, 5 Oct. 1720.

39. *Director*, 5 and 28 Oct. 1720; *Commentator*, 16 Sept. 1720; *True State of the Contracts Relating to the Third Money-Subscription Taken by the South-Sea Company*, 21–22; in *Tour thro' the Whole Island of Britain*, Defoe called the South Sea performance "a general possession" (1:90).

40. *Commentator*, 25 Mar. 1720.

41. *Commentator*, 26 Feb., 25 Mar., and 8 Apr. 1720; *Daily Post* for 9 Dec. 1719, respectively.

42. Scott, *Constitution and Finance* 1:352, 424.

43. Scott 3:314–52, see especially 329; Defoe, *Vindication of the Honour and Justice of Parliament*, 16–18.

44. For typical cautionary essays and calls for regulation, see *Commentator*, 10 and 27 June and 25 July 1720.

45. *Commentator*, 3 June 1720 on the coin shortage; representative essays on abuses and rumors of corruption, *Manufacturer*, 9 June and 8 Sept. 1720; *Commentator*, 8 Apr. and 27 May 1720. Scott shows that the directors reported high prices after the stock dropped long enough to sell their own (*Constitution and Finance* 3:337–41).

46. Defoe is especially astute here. Cf. the section on Sir Josiah Child in *Anatomy of Exchange-Alley*, 13–14, to the practice used by the old East India Company as described in Scott 3:315.

47. Defoe specifically outlines the parallels in *Case of Mr. Law*, 8–24. As early as 20 Feb. 1720 he had called the South Sea Company "the English Mississippi" (*Mist's Weekly-Journal*, in Lee, *Defoe* 2:203).

48. *Case of Mr. Law*, 15. Cf. Scott, *Constitution and Finance* 3:296, 313–14, 351; Dickson, *Financial Revolution*, 101–2, 110–12, 123–36, 140ff.

49. Doubleday, *Financial, Monetary History*, 92.

50. Scott, *Constitution and Finance* 1:423–24.

51. Dickson, *Financial Revolution*, 150–51; Sperling, *South Sea Company*, 32–33; Scott lists other companies (3:445ff.). Defoe, *Case of Mr. Law*, 23.

52. Illingworth, "Economic Ideas of Defoe," 1:541–42; Scott, *Constitution and Finance* 3:327–28.

53. Brisco, *Economic Policy of Walpole*, 53–59. Henderson, *London and the National Government*, 26–31.

54. On 22 Aug. 1722, she owned £706.13.4 worth of the stock (Wilson, *Memoirs of the Life of De Foe* 3:644 n. x).

55. One reason he may have spared the directors is that many were Dissenters, and that fact was given much publicity (Wodrow, *Analecta* 2:377).

56. Aspinall, "Statistical Accounts of the London Newspapers in the Eighteenth Century," 201–3.

57. Unfortunately I have been able to locate only a few copies of *Dormer's Newsletter*.

58. See, for example, *Mercurius Britannicus*, Mar. 1718, and, on negotiations with Spain, Sept. 1718. Moore compares *Mercurius Politicus* with *Mercurius Britannicus* in "Defoe, Ambidextrous Mercury," 1–2.

59. Hanson, *Government and the Press*, 91, 110; Stevens, *Party Politics*, 113. Stevens notes that in 1716 the *Daily Courant* was said to "speak the sentiments of much greater" Whigs than those Defoe knew (113).

60. *Daily Post*, for 3 Oct. 1719. Cf. *Review* 8:253 to see the change in Defoe's

own style and description of it. See Starr, "Defoe's Prose Style," 277–94; Richetti, *Defoe's Narratives*, 18–22 et passim.

61. Cambridge MSS. CH (H) 75/21 and CH (H) 75/1a/1 for 17 Mar. 1726 (by Thomas Robe); I am grateful to Cambridge University for permission to quote from the Cholmondelay manuscripts, and to Vincent Liesenfeld, University of Oklahoma, for bringing them to my attention. A *Daily Advertiser* began on 3 Feb. 1731 and continued with some name changes until 1809.

62. Dickson, *Financial Revolution*, 103 and n. 7. *Just Complaint of the Poor Weavers, Brief State of the Question, between the Printed and Painted Callicoes and the Woollen and Silk Manufacture,* and *Trade to India Critically and Calmly Consider'd.*

63. "Petition of Dorothy Distaff," *Mercurius Politicus* Dec. 1719, 793–803.

64. Dickson, *Financial Revolution*, 137.

65. Historical material from Earle, *World of Defoe*, 121–27; *English Historical Documents* 10:454–68; Douglas, "Cotton Textiles in England," 28–43; Coleman, "Innovation and its Diffusion," 417–29.

66. 12 Feb. 1720 and 4 Jan. 1720 respectively.

67. *Commentator*, 28 Mar. 1720.

68. Lee, *Defoe* 3:410–11.

69. Gosselink, introduction to *Manufacturer*, v–vi, xxix–xxx. This paper is probably not entirely by Defoe; he may have been paid in part by some of the Dissenting South Sea directors to manage it.

70. 25 June 1720 according to Novak's *NCBEL* entry; Lee describes its political orientation well but does not trace the legal prosecutions that may have influenced Applebee's moderation (1:337–38; PRO SP 44/79a, 20 Mar. 1717/18).

71. No. 1 for 5 Oct. 1720.

72. Dickson, *Financial Revolution*, 107–12. *Index Rerum & Vocabulorum* (1722) identifies large investors who were also on the Secret Inquiry committee and complains of conflict of interest (preface, 18, 19).

73. A conservative estimate from profits of de Fonvive, Buckley, Mist, Read, and others; a memorial by J. Peele gives some data for Defoe's papers, Cambridge MS. CH (H) 75/15. An unassigned, undated note in PRO SP 35/14 describes Marshal's role; the item regards an investigation of Mist. The *White-Hall Evening Post* continued until 10 Apr. 1739 (*British Union Catalogue of Periodicals*).

74. For Defoe's summer trips, see the July and Aug. 1720 *Commentator*s; *Commentator* for 11 Jan. et passim.

75. Parish Register of St. Mary's, Stoke Newington, MS. P/M1, fols. 206, 222. I am grateful to the Hackney Archives for permission to quote and to its archivist for her assistance.

76. Tallack, "Defoe and his Descendants," 450; recognizance, PRO SP 44/79a, 13 June 1720. I have searched to the end of Defoe's life; Hipwell, "Daniel De Foe," 105; Moore, *Citizen*, 331–32, 334–35.

77. Defoe probably received around £50 for the manuscript of *Robinson Crusoe*. It was common for publishers to purchase a book outright. Records of the sale of Taylor's copyrights in 1724 suggest that Defoe received £10 more for each subsequent edition of *Robinson Crusoe* and 10 guineas for each additional edition of *Farther Adventures*, with a bonus of £5 upon the sale of each 500 copies. If this money did go to Defoe, he had negotiated a better deal for *Farther Adventures* than for *Robinson Crusoe*. Rogers, *Robinson Crusoe*, 4, 10.

78. *Manufacturer*, 18 May 1720; *Commentator*, 5 Aug. 1720; see Gosselink, introduction to *Manufacturer*, v–xxx, and Earle, *World of Defoe*, 121–27, 143–44.

CHAPTER 18: PROJECTS AND DESIGNS

1. Assembly Book of the Corporation of Colchester, 1712–1741, entries for 9 July and 6 Aug. 1722, fols. 126–27, 129–34. Representative entries on the mortgage are 17 Dec. 1706, 24 Aug. 1714, 20 Aug. 1717, 18 Aug. 1720, and 6 Aug. 1722; on leases: 19 May, 30 June 1702, and list of leases in "Schedule of leases of the Estates belonging to the Borough of Colchester in the Iron Chest at the Moot Hall in the year 1737." Assembly Book, 1693–1712, fols. 254, 259; Morant MS. D/Y 2/1 (180): "One Bundle of Leases of Several Estates in the said parish all which are let to Mr. Deffoe" (some of these leases are for more than 100 acres). Leases recorded as late as 1702 reserve the timber rights (Assembly Book, 1693–1712, fol. 259; see also Colchester Muniments, legal brief, 1756, concerning ejectments on the Severalls Estate 1750–56, for Aug. 1756; (the latter document is not numbered). I am grateful to P. R. J. Coverley, branch archivist, and John Bensusan Butt for their careful assistance and to the Essex County Record Office for permission to publish; these documents are in the Colchester branch. Information about Defoe's Colchester land comes from these documents and PRO C.11.2578/31.

2. Essex County Record Office, Chelmsford, D/DU 256/21. A 1736 indenture sets the rent of "Broomfield" at £90 and mentions "Tyle Kiln and Pound Farm." The youthful Moll Flanders meets her lover in Mile End (26).

3. Lee, *Defoe* 1:362–64; Lee says an indenture dated 29 Sept. 1723 "now in my possession" bears Hannah's signature and Defoe's; the signatures are reproduced facing 1:364.

4. Pat Rogers points out that these works were the basis of Defoe's reputation; the identification of him as a novelist is modern (introduction to *A Tour thro' the Whole Island of Great Britain*, 17).

5. Evidence of Defoe's travel comes primarily from his *Tour*; his assertions are supported by internal evidence, see, for example, 1:15, 32, and 48, and Rogers, introduction to *Tour*, 15–16; "Defoe at Work," 431–50, and "Making of Defoe's *A Tour*," 133–34. Defoe says he was "in the West," at Rochester, visiting a "manufacturing town" in the north, and at Tunbridge Wells in 1720 (see *Commentator* for spring and summer months). The Assembly Book minutes state that Defoe was present in Colchester on 6 Aug. 1722, and his signature is in the Assembly Book. See also *Colonel Jack*, 1:105–7, 111–12.

6. Schlatter, *Social Ideas of Religious Leaders*, 161. Cf. *Complete English Tradesman* 1:305–6, 310–15.

7. *Tour* 1:44; Defoe suggests that the South Sea Company plan for the Greenland fishery might have this effect. *Tour* 3:416; Duckworth, "'Whig' Landscapes in Defoe's *Tour*," 457–58, 463 n. 26. Starr, "'Sauces to whet our gorg'd Appetites,'" 531–33; PRO C.11.2578/31 (Ward's Schedule); Sutherland, *Defoe*, 253; *Tour* 1:40–42, 44, 106–8. The location of the warehouse is given in CLRO SF 689, Indictment 8 (file 289) and Recognizance no. 9. The printed copy used by Starr incorrectly transcribed "Brown's" for "Brewer's" Key; the error is not Professor Starr's.

8. Information in these paragraphs is from PRO C.11.2578/31; Essex, D/DU 256/21; Sutherland was aware of some, but not all, of the Chancery documents and used them. Walter Wilson identifies Ward (*History and Antiquities*, 4:172).

9. Baker, "Autobiographical Memoranda," V & A Forster MS. 48.D.4. The description of Defoe's life is for 1724.

10. See the entry in Moore's *Checklist* where he reprints the proposal (216–18).

11. PRO SP 44/361, fols. 44–46. "Grants" signed by Townshend. Halley received the position of Royal Astronomer in Feb. 1720 and took it up in 1721 (MacPike, *Helvelius, Flamstead, and Halley*, 67–68). See also Thrower, "Edmund Halley and Thematic Geo-Cartography," 23–25; *Oxford Historical Register, 1220–1900*, 53, 706.

12. This point has been made by Novak and others; see, for example, Novak, "Defoe's Theory of Fiction," 650–68, 664–66.

13. Lorrain was the Ordinary from 1698 to 1719. See Singleton, "Defoe, Moll Flanders, and the Ordinary of Newgate," 407–13, and Faller, "In Contrast to Defoe," 59–78. On Hind, Whitney, and the Golden Farmer and their place in the literature of crime, see Faller, *Turned to Account*, 6–20, 136–44, et passim.

14. That Defoe frequently wrote about the plague in his periodicals is well known. See Novak's "Defoe and the Disordered City," 245–48; Landa's introduction to the Oxford edition of *Journal*, xi–xiv, and Henderson, *London and the National Government*, 44–45, 54.

15. The "Robinsons" and "Crusoes" in Defoe's life seem legion. Some, like Defoe's schoolmate Timothy Cruso are well known (see Hunter, *Reluctant Pilgrim*, 47 and n. 46). Among the interesting ones I have encountered are Mary Robinson, Mary Defoe's aunt (PRO PROB 11/385/156, John Tuffley's will); a minister whose last name was "Cruyo" kept a Presbyterian meeting house on the street on which Defoe lived, Freeman's Yard, in 1683 (BL 491-K4, no. 12), and Benjamin Crusoe, pastor of Little St. Helen's (formerly Annesley's church), one of the mainstays of the Merchants' Lecture at Salters' Hall, and a participant in the Salters' Hall controversy.

16. I am grateful to Beth Neman for the information about Martin from the manuscript of her forthcoming edition of *Majr. Ramkins*.

17. Davies, *Royal African Company*, 139–40, 255–56; Knox-Shaw, *Explorer in English Fiction*, 60–65; *Atlas Maritimus*, 238, 251–53.

18. I am grateful to one of my students, Rafe Schoenfeld, who allowed me to include the results of his research. Among his chief sources was Melton, *Sir Robert Clayton and the Origins of English Deposit Banking*.

19. Radzinowicz characterizes the Black Act as an "emergency law" (*History of English Criminal Law* 3:15–16). Thompson, who has done the most thorough study of the legislation, points out the confusion exhibited by modern scholars, however, and concludes that a general feeling of fear played a substantial part in the passage of the act "under colour of emergency" by a "compliant and partially corrupted House of Commons" (*Whigs and Hunters*, 23–24, 190–97).

20. *Statistical Abstracts of the United States, 1986* (Washington, D.C.: Bureau of the Census, 1987).

21. Shirren, *Daniel Defoe in Stoke Newington*, 19.

22. *White-Hall Evening Post*, 5 Feb. 1719; Harris says John Applebee was the leading publisher of criminal lives for twenty-five years; he did both the *Original Weekly Journal* and the Ordinary's *Accounts* ("Trials and Criminal Biographies," 5).

23. Quoted in Beattie, *Crime and the Courts in England*, 217; Brewer and Styles, *Ungovernable People*, 13.

24. To some extent, Beattie's statistics support this opinion; see especially figure 5.4, 215 and 213–28. Firth, *Naval Songs and Ballads*, 229, 230. On highwaymen, see Parkes, *Travel in England*, 152, 160–84.

25. Cf. PRO SP 44/119, May and July 1717.

26. PRO SP 44/119, 3 Sept. 1717; PRO T 27/24, 21 Dec. 1718.

27. Charles Johnson's *Successful Pirate* (1712) has some similarities to Avery's life; Jameson, *Privateering and Piracy in the Colonial Period*, 153–87; "Copy of

Verses, Composed by Captain Henry Every, Lately Gone to Sea to Seek His Fortune," in Firth, *Naval Songs*, 131–33 and 346–47; Schonhorn, *General History of the Pirates*, xix–xx, 667, 668 n. 3.

28. Cf. *King of Pirates* 8:6–7 with Grey, *Pirates of the Eastern Seas*, 154; and *King of Pirates* 8:53–59 with Grey, 158–61, and Jameson, 159–62.

29. The definition and sources for Defoe's man in a state of nature come from Novak, "Robinson Crusoe's Fear and the Search for Natural Man," 238–40, 244–45. See also *King of Pirates* 8:4.

30. *Commentator*, 17 and 20 June 1720; Little, *Crusoe's Captain*, 158–59.

31. Baer, "Complicated Plot of Piracy," 14; Lenman, *Jacobite Risings*, 188–89; Karraker, *Piracy Was a Business*, 48–58.

32. Quoted in Beattie, *Crime and the Courts*, 148.

33. Howson, *Thief-Taker General*, 106–7, 171–86, 190 (see especially "Appendix III: Principal Gangs," 312–14); Beattie, 252–63. Beattie describes the same loose associations without fixed members found in *Colonel Jack*, 256–58.

34. Newman's first effort had been in 1713. Cowie, *Henry Newman*, 75–76.

35. Quoted in Cowie, 101; the quoted speech by Robert Nelson was published in 1715. See deGategno, "Daniel Defoe's Newgate Biographies," 157–60.

36. Beattie, *Crime and the Courts*, 237–43, 436–39.

37. Burford, *Wits, Wenchers, and Wantons*, 46–50; *Daily Post*, 18 Jan. and 29 Apr. 1723; Thompson, *Unfit for Modest Ears*, 62.

38. *Commentator*, 10 June 1720.

39. Lee, *Defoe* 2:349 and see the entire essay, 348–50.

40. See Richetti, "Family, Sex, and Marriage in Defoe's *Moll Flanders* and *Roxana*," 34–35, and my *Defoe*, 194–200.

41. BL Loan 29/369, letters from justices of the peace, for 27 and 28 Feb. 1704/5.

42. Beattie, *Crime and the Courts*, 470–73, 479–83; Abbott Smith, *Colonists in Bondage*, 62–63; BL Loan 29/369, letters from justices of the peace, 27 and 28 Feb. 1704/5; *Proceedings on the King's Commission of the Peace* collected in Guildhall show that after 1718 transportation became the "order of the day." The State Papers include numerous references to problems before the act; in 1706 merchants had to bring women prisoners back to England at their own expense because none of the women could pay their fare and the plantations would not receive them (PRO SP 44/105, for 6 Feb. 1706); here and elsewhere the secretary of state tried to get the City to accept them in the workhouses, see also PRO SP 44/117, Dec. 1714. Information on transportation comes from these sources.

43. PRO C 5/84/9 and C 7/122/36.

44. Beattie, *Crime and the Courts*, 479, 483; Smith, *Colonists in Bondage*, 35–36, 99–100, 103, 105–6; Galenson, *White Servitude*, 100; Dunn, "Servants and Slaves," 159–61, 171.

45. Beattie, 504–5; PRO C 5/84/9 and C 7/122/36; Smith, 110–19, 125; Dunn, 170.

46. Beattie, 454–55, 469–70 et passim; Smith, 91–92, 128–29.

47. Smith, 60–62, 68–86; Morrice 1:346 (28 Nov. 1682).

48. See her mother's story, *Moll Flanders*.

49. Abbott Emerson Smith, *Colonists in Bondage*, 226–52, 291–92; see especially 233–39. In fact, Pennsylvania, Maryland, Virginia, and the Carolinas tried to make it easy for men to get land (296, 298–99).

50. Smith, 254–57, 303–5; Jack's experience there otherwise is fairly accurate.

51. *Applebee's*, 20 May 1721, printed in Lee 2:378–79; see also *Applebee's*, 10

Sept., 1 Oct., and 5 Nov. 1720, 1 July, 16 Sept., and 4 Nov. 1721.

52. Examples of alternate plans are in *Journal*, 46–59, 219–26, and *Due Preparations*, 11–12, 15–24. Henderson, *London and the National Government*, 33–45.

53. Defoe, *Narrative of All the Robberies, Escapes, &c. of John Sheppard*, 226.

54. Howson notes that not one conviction of a highwayman is recorded between 1723 and Wild's death in 1725 (*Thief-Taker General*, 5). Information about Wild is from this book.

55. Defoe, *Life of Jonathan Wild*, v–vii.

56. Defoe, *True and Genuine Account of the Life and Actions of the Late Jonathan Wild*, 256.

57. Howson, *Thief-Taker General*, 38–43.

58. Defoe, *Effectual Scheme for the Immediate Preventing of Street Robberies*, 15.

59. Quotations are from Defoe, *Brief Historical Account of the Lives of the Six Notorious Street-Robbers, Executed at Kingston*, 371–72, and *Effectual Scheme*, 64.

CHAPTER 19: CHANGES AND DISASTERS

1. *Applebee's*, 25 Sept. 1725, in Lee, *Defoe* 3:430; in *General History of Discoveries and Improvements*, Defoe laments that the ancient secret of operating for the stone has been lost (94).

2. Heister, *General System of Surgery in Three Parts* 2:104. Details of the operation are from this book, 2:104–26.

3. See, for example, *Unparallel'd Cruelty: Or, the Tryal of Captain Jeane of Bristol*.

4. Cf. *Moll Flanders* 2:81,76. Moll's use of the language of commerce is particularly amusing, as when she says of her booty: "I brought off my purchase" (2:79).

5. I realize not all critics agree with this reading. Among those who find Moll's repentance dubious at best are Bender, *Imagining the Penitentiary*, 46–47, who finds Moll rehabilitated but unrepentant. Homer O. Brown, among others, however, believes her "converted"; see "Displaced Self," 578–79.

6. Henry Baker to Sophia Defoe, quoted in Wright, *Life*, 202.

7. PRO C.11.2578/31; Sutherland, "Note on the Last Years of Defoe," 138 and 141; Guimaraens, "Daniel Defoe and the Family of Foe," 241–43. For the suit against Turner, see PRO C 11/366/72 for 11 Dec. 1729.

8. PRO PROB 11/604/383, proved 25 Aug. 1725; Mary's will gives additional details of the estate (PROB 11/655/282).

9. PRO PROB 11/385/156; PROB 11/655/282; Essex Record Office, Chelmsford, D/DH5 TJ6, D/P 69, and E44 (1726–69).

10. PRO C. 11/2578/31; C. 3/353/83; C. 33/351/63; C. 33/353/15; see especially John Ward's schedule attached to C. 11/2578/31.

11. Chamberlain's Account Roll, Essex Record Office, Colchester, D/B 5; Aa1/33; a note on the Chamberlain's balance sheet reads: "A great deal of the Rents was not rece'd by Mr. Grey a Great while after he has charged himself with it, particularly Mr. Deffoes"; Aa 135.

12. PRO SP 44/79a, fols. 313, 420, 422, 426; SP 35/28 for 12 and 14 Aug. 1721.

13. PRO SP 35/28; Realey, "*London Journal* and Its Authors, 1720–1723," 2–3 and 17–18; Kramnick, *Bolingbroke and His Circle*, 243–56; Dickinson, *Walpole and the Whig Supremacy*, 150; Stevens, *Party Politics*, 113–14, 117.

14. PRO SP 35/28 for 14 Aug. 1721; Realey, 54–55, 57, and 105–16; Dickinson, 150.

15. On 14 Aug., Benjamin talks about the "person who put him up to it" and about Gordon (PRO SP 35/28).

16. Realey, "*London Journal*," 19–20, 23–26, 34; Sutherland, "Circulation of Newspapers and Literary Periodicals, 1700–30," 116–18; Kramnick, *Bolingbroke and His Circle*, 18, 116; PRO SP 36/48, in which Benjamin refers to Walpole's "most solemn" promise (19 Oct. 1739).

17. Pleading letters to Walpole and his ministers provide information about Benjamin Defoe. See BL Add. MS. 32692, fols. 454–55, 480–81; BL Add. MS. 32691, fols. 390–91; Cambridge MS. CH (C) 2712 for 11 Oct. 1737 and 80/181 (I am grateful to the Cambridge Library for permission to quote). In BL Add. 32692, fol. 480–81, for instance, Benjamin says he has buried fourteen children and their mother.

18. Defoe says in the preface that it is "almost thirty Years" since he "began" the book, *Conjugal Lewdness*, iv.

19. Realey, "*London Journal* and Its Authors," 19–20.

20. Realey, 23–24; Sutherland, "Circulation," 116–17.

21. CH (C) 2712 for 11 Oct. 1737, Benjamin to Walpole, and BL Add. MS. 32692, fol. 454–55, 11 Nov. 1739; BL Add. MS. 32691, fols. 390–91 (Benjamin to Newcastle, 2 Oct. 1738). Benjamin would be tried and convicted for his *Craftsman* essays before his old friend Dudley Ryder.

22. Information about Henry Baker is from V & A Forster MS. 48.D.4. "Autobiographical Memoranda" by Henry Baker (Potter prints this document in "Henry Baker, F.R.S.," 310–17; I have used the manuscript copy); Yale University, Beinecke Library manuscript, Osborne fc 109/1; G. L'E. Turner, "Henry Baker, F.R.S.," 53–79; Secord, "Defoe in Stoke Newington," 216 n. 17.

23. *Essay upon Projects*, 294, and see the entire "project," 282–304.

24. Turner, "Henry Baker," 58; Yale Osborne fc 109/1, items 28, 89, and 92; Baker, "Autobiographical Memoranda," 4; for novelistic scenes, see 6–9.

25. Baker, 12; see also 6 and 10.

26. Baker, 13–15; H 461–71.

27. H n. 4, 461–62 and 462; Bodleian MS. Dep. c. 128. Healey's version of Baker's note, taken from Wright's *Life*, is very incomplete, especially the part Baker revised. The note reads,

I never supposed you could force Sutton but {I wonder'd you should call that a Hardship & I persum'd I might expect reasonably desire it was not unreasonable to desire you would attempt gaining what so evidently was for your/the/own Advantage/of us both advantage of us both/It seems you have, but without Success} presumed I might without offence desire your Endeavours towards another Lease.

You have try'd it seems in vain: if then it can't be done, we must make the best of things without it. I never shall exact Impossibilities. but indeed wonder'd at your unwillingness to attempt it But I never intended it as the sine qua non.

To have the House is not my wish {otherwise than} & if you please {any day to} as yourself propos'd to secure the yearly payments I shall not only rest well contented, but be in the sincerest manner. Your most obliged humble Servt.

I am grateful to Mrs. Violet De Foe Vasey for permission to publish the full text. The list of authors of the *Universal Spectator* issues is preserved in the Bodleian Library; see Potter, "Henry Baker, F.R.S.," 305; Lee, *Defoe* 3:466–69.

28. Information about this case is from PRO C 11/1473/18; C33/351/154; C11/579/2; C33/353/191; E13/880/ rot. 3. Compare Sutherland, "Last Years," 138–40.

29. Colchester Chamberlain's Accounts, Essex Record Office, Colchester, "Discharges" in Aa/35 shows "2 Journeys from London to Newington to Mr.

Deffoes £5," fol. 133 for 1725–26; Aa1/33 and D/B 5; Colchester Muniments, misc. deeds 1–17 (the document pertinent to Defoe, "Cooke against Todd and others" has no number).

30. The summary of young Daniel's transactions is in "Cooke against Todd": Defoe was ordered to pay Cooke's estate his past due rent on 14 Oct. 1728, *Assembly Book of the Corporation of Colchester*, fol. 243, Essex Record Office, Colchester.

31. Novak and others note the contrast; cf. *Realism, Myth, and History in Defoe's Fiction*, 65–66.

32. Watts, *Dissenters*, 329–32. Watts sees a significant concern about the decline of "practical religion" among Dissenters in the 1720s and 30s (331–32, 384–85).

33. Defoe, *Religious Courtship*, 181.

34. For instance, one husband in *Religious Courtship* puts ballads in the book of Psalms and pastes words over the text of devotional books, thereby changing the sense and producing nonsense; see 87–88.

35. Speck, *Stability and Strife*, estimates 20 percent of the London population and 13 percent of the country were *domestic* servants in 1694. To this should be added at least another 7 percent of the population who were laborers and outservants (56, 57, 297–98); cf. Hecht, *Domestic Servant Class*, 33–34. Cissie Fairchilds' estimates for Paris are about the same and suggest that London's should probably be higher (*Domestic Enemies*, 1–2). In fact, Trumbach presents evidence that English houses kept more servants (*Rise of the Egalitarian Family*, 132).

36. Defoe, *Great Law of Subordination Consider'd*, 50; Trumbach, 123, 134; Stone calls the servant revolution "the only fundamental changes in the household in the last five hundred years" (*Family, Sex, and Marriage in England*, 29, and see 27–29, 254–55); Hecht says that "the evolution of service from a system based upon fixed status to one that is almost entirely contracted" "was far from complete" (71); Fairchilds, 3, 138–40.

37. This section is influenced by Fairchilds' fine book; see particularly 17–20, 52–53, 71–77; Trumbach, *Rise of the Egalitarian Family*, 141; Hecht, 74–77. Johnson, *Life of Savage*. Schochet says that servants and apprentices "owed their masters and employers the same filial obedience that parents could expect from their children" ("Patriarchalism, Politics, and Mass Attitudes in Stuart England," 415). For other contemporaries who shared Defoe's opinion, see Darrell, *Gentleman Instructed* (1727), and Fleetwood, *Relative Duties of . . . Masters and Servants* (1705).

38. Stone, *Family, Sex, and Marriage*, 642–43, 646–47; Trumbach, 130, 147–50; Fairchilds, 171ff.; Seaton, *Conduct of Servants in Great Families*, 143–46.

39. Hecht, *Domestic Servant Class*, 102–24. In 1720 boarded footmen and ladies' maids received about £6 a year in wages (144–45).

40. Cf. William's teaching the husband-to-be of the first daughter and the conversion of Negum in *Religious Courtship* with the *Family Instructors*.

41. *Every-body's Business is No-body's Business*, 9; *Complete English Tradesman* 1:152; cf. Hecht, *Domestic Servant Class*, 78–80.

42. *Great Law of Subordination Consider'd*, ii, 8–9.

43. Ibid., 15–16, 91ff.; *Every-body's Business is No-body's Business*, 21–22. Trumbach also notes difficulties enforcing contracts (*Rise of the Egalitarian Family*, 139); Hecht, *Domestic Servant Class*, 81–82, 88–92; Malcolmson notes that few servants stayed in a position for more than a year and discusses insubordination (*Life and Labour in England*, 71 and 108–10 respectively).

44. Like *Roxana*, *Great Law of Subordination Consider'd* also illustrates abuses

of "liberty" (285). Aikins and Blewitt also link these two books; see Aikins, "Roxana: The Unfortunate Mistress of Conversation," 533–35, and Blewitt, *Defoe's Art of Fiction*, 7–8.

45. See, for example, Castle, "'Amy, Who Knew my Disease,'" 81–96, and Marshall, *Figure of the Theatre*, 133.

46. Defoe, *Plan of the English Commerce*, 55, 58, 115–16, 124–25, 144–45.

47. Defoe, *Tour* 1:12; Speck, *Stability*, 127; George Rudé, *Hanoverian London*, 21; Defoe, *Complete English Tradesman* 1:328.

48. Defoe, *Atlas*, 317; cf. *General History of Discoveries and Improvements*, 287–98.

49. Defoe, *General History of Discoveries*, 123; *Advantages of Peace and Commerce*, 20, 23–24; the quotations are from *Plan of the English Commerce*, 246.

50. *Plan of the English Commerce*, 259 and 242 respectively. As early as 1706 proposals for "reclaiming" Madagascar from the pirates had been sent to the secretaries of state; see PRO SP 34/8.

51. See, for example, *Plan of the English Commerce*, 224–29.

52. Defoe, *General History of Discoveries*, 68; *Plan for the English Commerce*, 235; *General History of Discoveries*, 78–79 respectively. See also *Plan of the English Commerce*, 234–38 and *General History of Discoveries*, 44, 100–125.

53. *General History of Discoveries*, 124, 169.

54. Defoe, *Humble Proposal to the People of England*, 4; *Plan of the English Commerce*, 229 and 227 respectively.

55. Defoe, *Plan of the English Commerce*, 79; *Complete English Tradesman* 1:306; *Atlas*, iii, 100; *Advantages of Peace and Commerce*, 6; *General History of Discoveries*, 6, 18; *Humble Proposal*, 9.

56. Defoe, *Royal Progress*, epigraph and 70–71; *Plan of the English Commerce*, 60. See Pat Rogers, "Guidebook as Epic," 115–50.

57. Defoe, *Augusta Triumphans*, 4.

58. *Augusta Triumphans* is listed in *Second Thoughts Are Best* as by Moreton. Where Defoe got the name is a mystery. "Moreton" is close to the "Morton" of Defoe's Newington Green Academy teacher. An Arabella Moreton's house in Long Walk was a licensed meeting house in 1710 (Guildhall MS. 9579). Sill shows that Defoe was known to be Moreton by 1728 ("Rogues, Strumpets, and Vagabonds," 75 and 78 n. 10).

59. Defoe, *Protestant Monastery*, [iii]–iv; cf. *Augusta Triumphans*, 4.

60. Defoe, *Great Law of Subordination*, 4, 43; *Parochial Tyranny*, 3. In April 1721 Defoe had paid a £10 fine to avoid being Stoke Newington churchwarden (St. Mary's Parish Registry, Hackney archives, P/M 1, fol. 222).

61. Defoe, *Protestant Monastery*, 6–15; *Augusta Triumphans*, 16; *Second Thoughts Are Best*, 4.

62. Moore, *Checklist*, 225–26.

63. Cibber, "To the Queen," in *Provoked Husband*, 3.

64. *Augusta Triumphans*, 48; *Second Thoughts Are Best*, 2–4; Mackay says that magistrates' records, including Henry Fielding's, substantiate increases in crimes after the *Beggar's Opera* (*Extraordinary Popular Delusions and the Madness of Crowds*, 643–44).

65. Faller, *Turned to Account*, 4; Price, *To the Palace of Wisdom*, says, "Ultimately, one might call Defoe a comic artist" (266–69).

66. Defoe, *Fears of the Pretender Turn'd into the Fears of Debauchery*, 20, 31–32; Defoe also attacks *Cato*, 22. In the *Family Instructor*, the children's playbooks are burned.

67. Schultz, *Gay's Beggar's Opera*, 230–52; see also 226–69.

68. Sewell's *Tragedy of Sir Walter Raleigh* saw three editions in 1719, and there

was a fifth edition by 1722; the first recorded performance was on 16 Jan. 1719, a year and a half after Defoe's publication. Marshall notes how often Defoe uses theatrical effects and metaphors in *Moll Flanders* and *Roxana* (*Figure of the Theater*, pt. 1); Richetti, *Defoe's Narratives*, 216.

69. Thomas Walker's obscure three-act play *The Quaker's Opera* was first performed at Bartholomew Fair (24 Aug.) and Southwark Fair (6 Sept.) before a four-night run at the Haymarket (31 Oct., 1, 5, 6 Nov. 1728) (Schneider, *London Stage*); Schultz says it is an adaptation of *The Prison Breaker* (*Gay's Beggar's Opera*, 286). Otway's *The Orphan* was performed at Drury Lane on 13 Feb., 20 May, and 16 Oct. 1725 and 19 Mar. and 9 May 1726, and at the Haymarket on 24 Feb. 1726; Defoe's pamphlet appeared in Oct. 1726. S. M. Ellis, "Epilogue: Jack Sheppard in Literature and Drama," 71–76, and see the long list of plays and other literature, 64–136.

70. On Moll's first alias, see Novak, *Realism, Myth and History*, 77. I am grateful to Cyrus Hoy for identifying Gabriel Spenser and for these references: Chute, *Ben Jonson of Westminster*, 75, 81, 51; *Ben Jonson*, ed. Herford and Simpson 1:18–19, 128–30, 139.

71. Only Baine has given the subject serious attention; see his *Daniel Defoe and the Supernatural*. More typical is Sutherland's confusion (*Defoe*, 263–65). For a more psychoanalytical reading, see Curtis, *Elusive Daniel Defoe*, 184–97. Defoe's lifelong interest in the occult may have begun at Morton's school; Morton's *Compendium Physicae* discussed most of these subjects. Defoe had contributed to Turner's *Compleat History of the Most Remarkable Providences* (1697), which had as its stated purpose to combat atheism, and published *True Relation of the Apparition of One Mrs. Veal*, probably in 1705; see also *Commentator* on the Devil, 24 June 1720. See his "Vision of the Angelic World" in *Serious Reflections*, 242–325. Baine cites a number of Defoe's scattered writings on the supernatural, "Daniel Defoe and *The History and Reality of Apparitions*," 335–47.

72. Thomas, *Religion and the Decline of Magic*, 645–46 and 665; Malcolmson, *Life and Labour*, 86–87; Valenze, "Prophecy and Popular Literature in Eighteenth-Century England," 85 and 91–92; Faller, *Turned to Account*, n. 7, 228–29.

73. Price, *Magic: A Pictorial History of Conjurers in the Theater*, 29–30; Valenze, "Prophecy and Popular Literature," 76–91; Baker, "Witchcraft, Addison, and *The Drummer*," 174 n. 1. Wodrow was collecting and publishing material for *Analecta: or, Materials for a History of Remarkable Providences* while Defoe was in Scotland (1701–1731).

74. Sutherland calls *Political History of the Devil* "irritating" and complains that Defoe "has not decided whether to treat the subject seriously or comically. He does both in turn. He is willing to awe, and yet ashamed to strike too hard" (*Defoe*, 264).

75. All note the frequency of mixing religion and magic. Frazer, *The Golden Bough*, 826; Malcolmson, *Life and Labour*, 93; Thomas, *Religion and the Decline of Magic*, 79, 91, 225–26; 267, 591, 599–600, 668; Donald Baker, "Witchcraft, Addison," 177–78; Valenze, "Prophecy and Popular Literature," 79–88. On clergy hostility, see Thomas, 253–79. A controversy over the existence of witches attracted considerable attention in the early 1720s; the chief disputants were Richard Boulton and Francis Hutchinson (Baker, 177–88).

76. Malcolmson, *Life and Labour*, 81–93; Rudé, *Hanoverian London*, x, 103–4, 106; Thomas, *Religion and the Decline of Magic*, 151, 159–66; Hultin, "Medicine and Magic," 349–53, 365–66.

77. Thomas, 151 and 166; Malcolmson, 85.

78. Defoe, *System of Magick*, 27–60; *Political History of the Devil*, ch. 9.

79. "Bundling" is described by Laslett, *Family Life and Illicit Love*, 110–16. See, for example, "A Play with Proverbs" by Michael Drayton (1563–1631), which begins: "As Love and I, late harbour'd in one Inne, / With proverbs thus each other intertaine, / *In Love there is no lack, thus I begin* . . . " (2:340); [Herbert], *Witts Recreations*, nos. 223–25; *Conjugal Lewdness*, 275–76; Gillis, "Married but Not Churched," 33–36.

80. Erickson, *Mother Midnight*, 4–11, 18, 46–47.

81. Novak, *Myth, Realism and History*, 105–6; *History of Apparitions*, 201–2. See my *Defoe*, 116–19.

82. Aubrey Williams, *Approach to Congreve*, 129, 130–33, 156. Williams agrees that "the best minds of the period" took "such goings-on seriously" (131), and "the demonical attributes and behavior . . . would have prompted, in a contemporary audience, a sense of old acquaintance with a maleficent intelligence somehow still at large in the world" (132). See also Snow, "Diabolic Intervention in Defoe's *Roxana*," 52–60.

83. Defoe, *Political History of the Devil*, 383; *System of Magick*, 253–75; *History of Apparitions*, 90, 132–51.

84. *Complete English Tradesman* had 1726 and 1727 Dublin editions too.

85. PRO C 11/679/2; other information on this case is in C 11/1473; C 33/351/154, and C 11/1473/18.

86. PRO E. 13/880. rot. 3, *Exchequer of Pleas*, plea roll for Hilary 2 George II and IND 4533. Opening 52. This document has never been published before.

87. Secord, "Defoe in Stoke Newington," 217; Peterson, "Daniel Defoe and 'City Customes,'" 400 and 400 n. 4; Turner, "Henry Baker," 55 and 71 n. 12. The house was valued at £700 according to the Sun Fire Insurance records (Moore, *Citizen*, 383 n. 25).

88. H 460–76; Stoke Newington vestry minutes in the Hackney archives for 1730 and 1731, pp. 332, 346, 348, 358. In 1730 he owed 13s. 4d. church rate and 15s. poor rate; in 1731, 6s. poor rate. See Secord, "Defoe in Stoke Newington," 218.

89. "Forewords" [*sic*], *Compleat English Gentleman*, ix–xi, and Moore, *Checklist*, 230. See the 28 Aug. 1728 letter (V & A MS. Forster 48.E.23) and manuscript of *Compleat English Gentleman* in the British Library.

90. A few records suggest that the younger Daniel was an active merchant dealing in fairly large sums of money. Three bills in the books kept by the Wiltshire clothiers Ussher and Jeffries show that they owed Daniel £30 in 1721, that he paid them £54 16s. in 1723, and that this note was given to a John Ellis (Wiltshire Record Office, 927/2); I am grateful to K. H. Rogers for bringing these items to my attention. The estate of Gilbert Page shows that Daniel owed Page £200, (inventory, 12 Apr. 1737, CLRO, Orphans' Inventories Box 51, Common Serjeant's Book 6, fol. 160). In the past, these bills have been thought to be the elder Defoe's. The addresses of Defoe, of young Daniel, and the notation "Cornhill," however, prove otherwise. Cambridge University MS. CH (H) 2712, Defoe to Walpole.

91. *Grub Street Journal*, 29 Apr. 1731, and *London Journal*, 1 May 1731, identify them as Defoe's lodgings; other obituaries are in the *Universal Spectator*, 1 May 1731; *Read's Weekly Journal*, 1 May 1731; and the *Courant* and *Daily Journal* are quoted in the *Grub Street Journal*. Laslett, *World We Have Lost Further Explored*, 27–29. Motherby, *New Medical Dictionary*. That what we call a stroke was meant is clear from contemporary descriptions; see *Diary of Samuel Sewall* 1:178–79. Richard James calls lethargy "related to . . . paralytic Disorders, and often accompanying them" (*Medicinal Dictionary*, s.v.).

92. Horner, *Brief Account of an Interesting Ceremony*, 5–6, 22. Unfortunately

Defoe's books were sold with the Rev. Philip Farewell's; see n. 78, ch. 14 above.

93. PRO PROB 6/109, Sept. 1734; PROB 31/117/376, 26 June 1733; PROB 29/125, fol. 181, 7 Sept. 1733.

94. *Clerk's Instructor in the Ecclesiastical Courts*, 221–27; Peterson points out that the City Custom remained in force until 1856 ("Daniel Defoe and 'City Customes,'" 400–401). His account of the division of the estate, based on Holdsworth, differs from that given in early eighteenth-century legal handbooks.

EPILOGUE: BRED IN THE BONE

1. Defoe, *History of Apparitions*, 191.

2. Watts says that bankrupts were "*usually* excommunicated from the gathered churches" (*Dissenters*, 335–36; emphasis added).

3. *Grub Street Journal*, 29 Apr. 1731.

4. This discussion of Walpole and Bolingbroke depends upon Kramnick, *Bolingbroke and His Circle*, 46–51, 70–78, 245–51; Dickson, *Financial Revolution in England*, 200–210; Basil Williams, *Whig Supremacy*, 187–91; Dickinson, *Walpole and the Whig Supremacy*, 93–96 and 102–8.

5. The phrase "Epics of Trade" is Howard Weinbrot's. See Pocock, *Machiavellian Moment*, 423–26, 454.

6. Briggs lists Canada, the thirteen colonies, Florida, the Falkland Islands in the New World; Minorca; St. Louis and Ningo in Africa, and Bassein and Madras in Asia (*Social History of England*, 168). During this time, England resumed the charters of territory granted individuals and companies (Basil Williams, *Whig Supremacy*, 290–98).

7. Speck, *Stability and Strife*, 126; Rudé, *Hanoverian London*, 20–24 and 32–35; Ashton, *Economic History of England*, 151; Dickinson, *Walpole*, 107.

8. Defoe, *Complete English Tradesman* 1:26, *Continuation of the Letters Written by a Turkish Spy at Paris*, v.

9. Starr, "Defoe's Prose Style," 277–94; other studies of Defoe's style are Furbank and Owens, "Defoe and the 'Improvisatory' Sentence," 157–66; Novak, "Fiction and Society in the Early Eighteenth Century"; Braudy, "Daniel Defoe and the Anxieties of Autobiography," 76–97; Brougham's biography of Robertson in *Lives of Men of Letters* 1:304 (I am grateful to Jeffrey Smitten for locating this reference); James Joyce, "Daniel Defoe," 17; the Adam Smith anecdote is from *Lectures on Rhetoric and Belles Lettres*, 230; Cather, *On Writing*, 79.

10. [Whalley], *Essay on the Manner of Writing History*, 13; *Memoirs of the Society of Grub Street*, no. 108, 27 Jan. 1732, 224; Oldys, *Dissertation upon Pamphlets*; Hanson calls Defoe "the ablest political journalist of his generation" (*Government and the Press*, 94); Mayo calls him "the presiding genius during [the] formative period" (*English Novel in the Magazines*, 49, and see also 61, 64); Stevens, *Party Politics and English Journalism*, 59–60, 64; Sutherland, *Defoe*, 228.

11. For the similarity to contemporary gambling houses, see Burford, *Wits, Wenchers, and Wantons*, 135–43; at one point, Roxana calls her house a "gambling Ordinary." Dijkstra argues that *Roxana* is a "systematised" version of Defoe's economic opinions (*Economics and the Fiction of Defoe*, see especially x, 53, 67–69).

12. Defoe, *Serious Reflections*, 4.

13. This Lockean idea has been applied to Defoe's characters; see Damrosch, *God's Plots*, 196; Richetti, *Defoe's Narratives*, 93, 101, 140 in order to emphasize the similarity. Richetti points out how many of the changes of fortune experienced by characters are without transition (51); because Defoe felt

they were unpredictable, "unseen Mines," transitions would have been unrealistic.

14. For some of the biblical parts Defoe assigned himself, see my "Personality and Biblical Allusion in Defoe's Letters," 1–20.

15. See Edel, *Literary Biography*, 49.

16. There are two essays reprinted in Lee, *Defoe* 3:15–19.

17. Damrosch, *God's Plot*, 188–89; Richetti, *Defoe's Narratives*, 130, 194; Schonhorn, too, recognizes the "displacement of aggression" ("Defoe's *Captain Singleton*: A Reassessment with Observations," 51).

18. Quoted in Davie, *Gathered Church*, 28; Damrosch, 17; Watt, *Rise of the Novel*, 90; Keeble, *Literary Culture of Nonconformity*, 268–82.

19. Starr's *Defoe and Casuistry* discusses many of the vexed moral problems.

20. Cf. Richetti, *Defoe's Narratives*, 134–35; Homer O. Brown, "Displaced Self in the Novels of Daniel Defoe," 562–90.

21. Secord, "Correspondence of Daniel Defoe," 51.

22. Theophilus Cibber, "Defoe," in *Lives of the Poets* 4:315.

23. Earle, *World of Defoe*, vi, 45.

24. Defoe, *Collection of Miscellany Letters* 3:2.

25. I am grateful to Ian Watt for the biographical information above. Forster, *Defoe*, 56.

BIBLIOGRAPHY

WORKS BY OR ATTRIBUTED TO DEFOE

Unless otherwise noted, place of publication is London. Dates are as printed on the title pages and may be Old Style. For discussions of attribution, please consult the index.

An Account of the Conduct of Robert Earl of Oxford, 1715.
An Account of the Great and Generous Actions of James Butler. [1715].
An Account of the Late Horrid Conspiracy to Depose Their Present Majesties K. William and Q. Mary, to Bring in the French and the Late King James, and Ruine the City of London. 1691.
An Account of the Proceedings against the Rebels. 1716.
The Advantages of the Present Settlement, and the Great Danger of a Relapse. 1689.
The Advantages of Peace and Commerce; with Some Remarks on the East-India Trade. 1729.
Advertisement from Daniel De Foe, to Mr. Clark. [Edinburgh, 1710].
Advice to the People of Great Britain, with Respect to Two Important Points of Their Future Conduct: I, What They Ought to Expect from the King; II, How They Ought to Behave by Him. 1714.
"The Age of Wonders." 1710.
The Anatomy of Exchange-Alley. 1719.
And What if the Pretender Should Come? Or Some Considerations of the Advantages and Real Consequences of the Pretender's Possessing the Crown of Great-Britain. 1713.
The Annals of King George, Year the Second. 1717.
The Annals of King George, Year the Third. 1718.
An Answer to a Paper concerning Mr. De Foe, against his History of the Union. Edinburgh, 1708.
An Answer to a Question that No Body Thinks of, Viz. But What if the Queen Should Die? 1713.
An Answer to the Late K. James's Last Declaration. 1693.
An Apology for the Army. 1715.
The Apparent Danger of an Invasion. 1701.
An Appeal to Honour and Justice. 1715. In *The Shortest-Way with the Dissenters and Other Pamphlets*. Shakespeare Head edition. Oxford: Blackwell, 1974.
Applebee's Original Weekly Journal. See *The Original Weekly Journal*.
An Argument Shewing that a Standing Army, with Consent of Parliament, Is Not Inconsistent with a Free Government. 1698.
Arguments about the Alteration of Triennial Elections of Parliament. 1716.
Armageddon: Or, the Necessity of Carrying on the War. [1711].
Atalantis Major. 1711.
Atlas Maritimus & Commercialis. 1728.
Augusta Triumphans. 1728.
The Ballad: Or, Some Scurrilous Reflections in Verse . . . with the Memorial, Alias Legion Reply'd to Paragraph by Paragraph. [1701].
The Ballance of Europe: Or, an Enquiry into the Respective Dangers of Giving the

Spanish Monarchy to the Emperour as Well as to King Phillip. 1711.

The Ban[bur]y Apes: Or, the Monkeys Chattering to the Magpye. [1710].

A Brief Explanation of a Late Pamphlet, Entituled The Shortest Way with the Dissenters. [1703].

A Brief Historical Account of the Lives of the Six Notorious Street-Robbers, Executed at Kingston. 1726. In vol. 16 of *Romances and Narratives by Daniel Defoe,* edited by George A. Aitken. London: Dent, 1905.

A Brief History of the Poor Palatine Refugees, Lately Arrived in England. 1709.

A Brief Reply to the History of Standing Armies in England. 1698.

A Brief State of the Question, between the Printed and Painted Callicoes and the Woollen and Silk Manufacture. 1719.

A Brief Survey of the Legal Liberties of the Dissenters. 1714.

Caledonia. Edinburgh, 1706.

The Candidate: Being a Detection of Bribery and Corruption as It Is Just Now in Practice All Over Great Britain. 1715.

Captain Singleton. 1720. Shakespeare Head edition. Oxford: Blackwell, 1974.

The Case of Dissenters as Affected by the Late Bill Proposed in Parliament for Preventing Occasional Conformity. 1703.

The Case of Mr. Law, Truly Stated, in Answer to a Pamphlet, Entitul'd A Letter to Mr. Law. 1721.

The Character of the Late Dr. Samuel Annesley. 1697.

Chickens Feed Capons. 1731.

Colonel Jack. 1723. Shakespeare Head edition. Oxford: Blackwell, 1974.

A Collection of Miscellany Letters. 4 vols. 1722, 1727.

A Collection of the Writings of the Author of the True-Born English-Man. 1703.

Commentator. 1 Jan.–16 Sept. 1720.

The Compleat English Gentleman. Edited by Karl D. Bülbring. London: David Nutt, 1890.

The Complete English Tradesman. 1726.

A Condoling Letter to the Tattler: On Account of the Misfortunes of Isaac Bickerstaff, Esq. [1710].

The Conduct of Christians Made the Sport of Infidels. 1717.

The Conduct of Parties in England, More Especially of those Whigs Who Now Appear against the New Ministry and a Treaty for Peace. 1712.

The Conduct of Robert Walpole, Esq. 1717.

Conjugal Lewdness. 1727. Edited by Maximillian E. Novak. Gainesville, Fla.: Scholars' Facsimiles & Reprints, 1967.

Considerations in Relation to Trade Considered. [Edinburgh], 1706.

Considerations on the Present State of Affairs in Great-Britain. 1718.

Considerations upon the Eighth and Ninth Articles of the Treaty of Commerce and Navigation. 1713.

The Consolidator. 1705. Edited by Malcolm J. Bosse. New York: Garland, 1972.

A Continuation of Letters Written by a Turkish Spy at Paris. 1718.

Daily Post. 3 Oct. 1719–c. 27 Apr. 1725.

The Danger and Consequences of Disobliging the Clergy. 1717.

The Danger of Court Differences. 1717.

The Danger of the Protestant Religion Consider'd. 1701.

Daniel Defoe's Hymn for the Thanksgiving. 1706.

The Defection Farther Considered. 1718.

A Defence of the Allies. 1712.

A Dialogue between a Dissenter and the Observator. 1703.

Director. 5 Oct. 1720–16 Jan. 1721.

The Dissenter[s] Misrepresented and Represented. [1704].

The Dissenters Answer to the High-Church Challenge. 1704. In *A Second Volume of the Writings Of The Author Of The True-Born Englishman.* 1705.

The Dissenters in England Vindicated. [Edinburgh, 1707].

[*Dormer's News Letter.* June 1716–Aug. 1718?]

The Double Welcome: A Poem to the Duke of Marlbro. 1705.

Due Preparations for the Plague as Well for Soul as Body. 1722.

The Dyet of Poland: A Satyr. 1705.

The Dyet of Poland, A Satyr. Consider'd Paragraph by Paragraph. 1705.

An Effectual Scheme for the Immediate Preventing of Street Robberies. 1731.

An Elegy on the Author of the True-Born-Englishman. 1704.

An Encomium upon the Parliament. 1699.

The Englishman's Choice, and True Interest. 1694.

An Enquiry into Occasional Conformity, Shewing That the Dissenters Are in No Way Concerned in It. 1702.

An Enquiry into the Danger and Consequences of a War with the Dutch. 1712.

An Enquiry into the Disposal of the Equivalent. Edinburgh, 1706.

An Enquiry into the Occasional Conformity of Dissenters, in Cases of Preferment. 1697.

An Enquiry into the Occasional Conformity of Dissenters Shewing that the Dissenters Are No Way Concern'd in It. 1702. In *A True Collection of the Writings Of The Author of The True Born English-man.* 1703.

An Enquiry into the Real Interest of Princes. 1712.

An Essay at a Plain Exposition of That Difficult Phrase A Good Peace. 1711.

An Essay at Removing National Prejudices against a Union with Scotland, to Be Continued during the Treaty Here. Part I. 1706.

An Essay at Removing National Prejudices against a Union with Scotland, to Be Continued during the Treaty Here. Part II. 1706.

An Essay, at Removing National Prejudices against a Union with Scotland. Part III. [Edinburgh], 1706.

An Essay on the History and Reality of Apparitions. 1727.

An Essay on the History of Parties, and Persecution in Britain: Beginning with a Brief Account of the Test-Act and an Historical Enquiry into the Reasons, the Original and the Consequences of the Occasional Conformity of Dissenters. 1711.

An Essay on the Late Storm. 1704.

An Essay on the Regulation of the Press. 1704. Edited by J. R. Moore. Luttrell Society Reprints, no. 7. Oxford: Blackwell, 1948.

An Essay on the South-Sea Trade. 1711.

An Essay on the Treaty of Commerce with France. 1713.

An Essay upon Projects. 1697. Menston, England: Scolar, 1969.

An Essay upon Publick Credit. 1710.

Every-body's Business, Is No-body's Business. 1725.

The Experiment: Or, the Shortest Way with the Dissenters Exemplified. 1705.

An Expostulatory Letter, to the B[ishop] of B[angor]. [1717].

Faction in Power: Or, the Mischiefs and Dangers of a High-Church Magistracy. 1717.

Fair Payment No Spunge. 1717.

The Family Instructor, in Three Parts, with a Recommendatory Letter by the Reverend Mr. S. Wright. Newcastle, 1715.

The Family Instructor, in Three Parts . . . The Second Edition. Corrected by the Author. 1715.

The Family Instructor, in Two Parts. I. Relating to Family Breaches, and their obstructing Religious Duties. II. To the Great Mistake of Mixing the Passions in the Managing and Correcting of Children. . . . Vol. II. 1718.

The Farther Adventures of Robinson Crusoe. 1719. Shakespeare Head edition. Oxford: Blackwell, 1974.

The Fears of the Pretender Turn'd into the Fears of Debauchery. 1715.

The Felonious Treaty. 1711.

A Fifth Essay, at Removing National Prejudices. [Edinburgh], 1607 (for 1707).

The Fortunate Mistress: Or, A History of the Life and Vast Variety of Fortunes of Mademoiselle de Beleau, Afterwards Call'd the Countess de Wintelsheim, in Germany. Being the Person known by the Name of the Lady Roxana. [1724]. Shakespeare Head edition. Oxford: Blackwell, 1974.

The Fortunes and Misfortunes of the Famous Moll Flanders, &c. 1721. Shakespeare Head edition. Oxford: Blackwell, 1974.

The Four Years Voyages of Capt. George Roberts. 1726.

A Fourth Essay, at Removing National Prejudices. [Edinburgh], 1706.

The Free-holders Plea against Stock-Jobbing Elections of Parliament Men. 1701.

A Friendly Epistle by Way of Reproof from One of the People Called Quakers. 1715.

A Further Search into the Conduct of the Allies. 1712.

A General History of Discoveries and Improvements. Oct. 1725–Jan. 1726; 1727.

A General History of the Pyrates. 1724. Edited by Manuel Schonhorn. Columbia: University of South Carolina Press, 1972.

The Great Law of Subordination Consider'd. 1724.

Hannibal at the Gates. 1712.

Hanover or Rome. 1715.

His Majesty's Obligations to the Whigs Plainly Proved. 1715.

An Historical Account of the Bitter Sufferings, and Melancholly Circumstances of the Episcopal Church in Scotland, under the Barbarous Usage and Bloody Persecution of the Presbyterian Church Government. Edinburgh, 1707.

An Historical Account of the Voyages and Adventures of Sir Walter Raleigh. 1719.

Historical Collections: Or, Memoirs of Passages Collected from Several Authors. William Andrews Clark Library, UCLA. Manuscript. 1682.

A History of the Clemency of Our English Monarchs. 1717.

The History of the Kentish Petition. 1701.

The History of the Remarkable Life of John Sheppard. [1724].

The History of the Union Of Great Britain. Edinburgh, 1709.

The History of the Wars, of His Late Majesty Charles XII. King of Sweden. 1720.

The History of the Wars, of His Present Majesty Charles XII. King of Sweden. 1715.

The Honour and Prerogative of the Queen's Majesty Vindicated and Defended against the Unexampled Insolence of the Author of the Guardian, in a Letter from a Country Whig to Mr. Steele. 1713.

An Humble Proposal to the People of England, for the Encrease of Their Trade, and Encouragement of Their Manufactures. 1729.

A Hymn to Peace. 1706.

A Hymn to the Pillory. 1703. In *The Shortest Way with the Dissenters and Other Pamphlets.* Shakespeare Head edition. Oxford: Blackwell, 1974.

A Hymn to Victory. 1704.

The Immorality of the Priesthood. 1715.

An Impartial Enquiry into the Conduct of the Right Honourable Charles Lord Viscount T[ownshend]. 1717.

An Impartial History of the Life and Actions of Peter Alexowitz, the Present Czar of Muscovy. 1723.

Instructions from Rome, in Favour of the Pretender. [1710].

A Journal of the Earl of Marr's Proceedings. [1716].

A Journal of the Plague Year. 1722. Shakespeare Head edition. Oxford: Blackwell, 1974.

A Journey to the World in the Moon. [1705].

Jure Divino: A Satyr in Twelve Books. 1706.

The Just Complaint of the Poor Weavers. 1719.
The Justice and Necessity of Restraining the Clergy. 1715.
A Justification of the Dutch. 1712.
The King of Pirates. 1720. Vol. 8 of *The Works of Daniel Defoe,* edited by G. H. Maynadier. Boston: Brainard, 1904.
The Lay-Man's Sermon upon the Late Storm. 1704.
The Layman's Vindication of the Church of England. 1716.
Legion's Humble Address to the Lords. [1704].
Legion's Memorial. [1701].
Legion's New Paper. 1702.
A Letter from a Dissenter in the City to a Dissenter in the Country, Advising Him to a Quiet and Peaceable Behaviour in this Present Conjuncture. 1710.
A Letter from a Member of the House of Commons. 1713.
A Letter from Mr. Reason. [Edinburgh, 1706].
A Letter from One Clergy-Man to Another. 1716.
A Letter from Some Protestant Dissenting Laymen. 1718.
A Letter from the Man in the Moon. [1705].
A Letter to a Dissenter from His Friend at the Hague, concerning the Penal Laws and the Test. [1688].
A Letter to a Merry Young Gentleman. 1715.
A Letter to Mr. How. 1701.
A Letter to Mr. Steele. 1714.
A Letter to the Author of the Flying-Post. 1718.
A Letter to the Dissenters. 1713, 1714.
A Letter to the Dissenters. 1719.
The Letters of Daniel Defoe. Edited by George H. Healey. 1955. Oxford: Clarendon Press, 1969.
The Life and Strange Surprizing Adventures of Robinson Crusoe. 1719.
The Life of Jonathan Wild. 1725.
The Livery Man's Reasons, Why He Did Not Give His Vote for a Certain Gentleman either to be Lord Mayor: or Parliament Man for the City of London. 1701.
Manufacturer. 13 Oct. 1719 –17 Feb. 1720. Introduced by Robert N. Gosselink. Delmar, N.Y.: Scholars' Facsimiles & Reprints, 1978.
The Master Mercury. Introduced by Frank Ellis and Henry Snyder. ARS no. 184. Los Angeles: Clark Library, 1977.
Meditaçons. Huntington Library Manuscript. 1681.
The Meditations of Daniel Defoe Now First Published. Edited by George Harris Healey. Cummington, Mass.: Cummington, 1946.
Memoirs of a Cavalier. [1720]. Shakespeare Head edition. Oxford: Blackwell, 1974.
The Memoirs of an English Officer. 1728. In *Memoirs of an English Officer and Two Other Short Novels,* introduced by J. T. Boulton. London: Gollancz, 1970.
Memoirs of Count Tariff, &c. 1713.
Memoirs of John, Duke of Melfort. 1714.
The Memoirs of Majr. Alexander Ramkins. 1719. In *Memoirs of an English Officer and Two Other Short Novels,* introduced by J. T. Boulton. London: Gollancz, 1970.
Memoirs of Publick Transactions in the Life and Ministry of His Grace the D. of Shrewsbury. 1718.
Memoirs of Some Transactions during the Late Ministry of Robert, E. of Oxford. 1717.
Memoirs of the Church of Scotland. 1717.
Memoirs of the Conduct of Her Late Majesty and Her Last Ministry. 1715.
Memoirs of the Life and Eminent Conduct of That Learned and Reverend Divine, Daniel Williams, D. D. 1718.

A Memorial to the Nobility of Scotland, Who Are to Assemble in Order to Choose the Sitting Peers for the Parliament of Great Britain. Edinburgh, 1708.
Mercator: or Commerce Retrieved. 26 May 1713–20 July 1714.
Mercurius Brittanicus. Jan. 1718–March 1719.
Mercurius Politicus. May 1716–Oct. 1720.
Minutes of the Negotiations of Monsr. Mesnager. 1717.
The Mock-Mourners: A Satyr. 1702
A Modest Vindication of the Present Ministry. 1707.
More Reformation: A Satyr upon Himself, by the Author of the True-Born Englishman. 1703.
More Short-Ways with the Dissenters. 1704.
A Narrative of All the Robberies, Escapes, &c. of John Sheppard. 1724. In vol. 16 of *Romances and Narratives by Daniel Defoe,* edited by George A. Aitken. London: Dent, 1905.
A New Discovery of an Old Intreague. 1691.
A New Family Instructor. 1727.
A New Map of the Laborious and Painful Travels of Our Blessed High Church Apostle. 1710.
A New Test of the Church of England's Honesty. 1704.
A New Test of the Church of England's Loyalty. 1702.
A New Test of the Sence of the Nation. 1710.
No Queen, or No General. 1712.
Novels and Selected Writings. 2d ed. Shakespeare Head edition. Oxford: Blackwell, 1974.
Observations on the Fifth Article of The Treaty of Union. [Edinburgh, 1706].
Of Royall Educacion: A Fragmentary Treatise. Edited by Karl D. Bülbring. London: Nutt, 1895.
On the Fight at Ramellies. Review 3 (1706): 242–44.
The Original Power of the Collective Body of the People of England. 1702.
Original Weekly Journal (later called *Applebee's Original Weekly Journal*). 25 June 1720–14 May 1726 (and occasionally thereafter).
The Pacifactor: A Poem. 1700.
Parochial Tyranny. [1727].
Passion and Prejudice. Edinburgh, 1707.
Peace, or Poverty. 1712.
Peace without Union. 1703.
The Pernicious Consequences of the Clergy's Intermedling with Affairs of State. [1714?].
"The Petition of Dorothy Distaff." *Mercurius Politicus,* Dec. 1719.
A Plan of the English Commerce. 1728, 1730. Shakespeare Head edition. Oxford: Blackwell, 1974.
The Political History of the Devil. 1726.
The Poor Man's Plea. 1698.
Preface to *De Laune's Plea for the Non-Conformists.* 1706.
Preface to *De Laune's Plea for the Non-Conformists.* In *Dr. Sacheverell's Recantation.* 1709.
The Present Negotiations of Peace Vindicated. 1712.
The Present State of Jacobitism Considered. 1701.
The Present State of the Parties in Great Britain. 1712.
The Protestant Jubilee. 1714.
The Protestant Monastery. 1727.
The Quarrel of the School-Boys at Athens. 1717.
Queries upon the Bill against Occasional Conformity. [1704].

The Question Fairly Stated, Whether Now Is Not the Time to Do Justice to the Friends of the Government as Well as to Its Enemies? 1717.

Reasons against a War with France. 1701.

Reasons against Fighting: Being an Enquiry into This Great Debate, Whether It Is Safe for Her Majesty, or Her Ministry, to Venture an Engagement with the French. 1712.

Reasons against the Succession of the House of Hanover. 1713.

Reasons for a Peace: Or, the War at an End. 1711.

Reasons for Im[peaching] the L[or]d H[igh] T[reasure]r. [1714].

Reasons Why a Party among Us, and Also among the Confederates, Are Obstinately Bent against a Treaty of Peace with the French at This Time. 1711.

Reasons Why This Nation Ought to Put a Speedy End to This Expensive War. 1711.

Reflections upon the Late Great Revolution. 1689.

Reformation of Manners. 1702.

Religious Courtship. 1722.

Remarks on the Bill to Prevent Frauds Committed by Bankrupts. 1706.

Remarks on the Speeches of William Paul Clerk, and John Hall. 1716.

The Remedy Worse Than the Disease. 1714.

A Reply to a Pamphlet Entituled, the L[or]d H[aversham]'s Vindication. 1706.

A Reply to a Traiterous Libel Entituled English Advice to the Freeholders of Great Britain. 1715.

A Reply to the Remarks upon the Lord Bishop of Bangor's Treatment of the Clergy and Convocation. 1717.

The Representation Examined: Being Remarks on the State of Religion in England. 1711.

A Reproof to Mr. Clark, and a Brief Vindication of Mr. De Foe. [Edinburgh, 1710].

The Re-Representation: Or, a Modest Search after the Great PLUNDERERS of the NATION. 1711.

Resignacion. 1708. In Frank Ellis, "Defoe's 'Resignacion' and the Limitations of Mathematical Plainness." 1985.

Review. 9 vols. 19 Feb. 1704–11 June 1713. Edited by A. W. Secord. 22 vols. New York: Columbia University Press, 1938.

The Royal Progress: Or, a Historical View of the Journeys or Progresses, Which Several Great Princes Have Made to Visit Their Dominions. 1724.

Royal Religion: Being Some Enquiry after the Piety of Princes. 1704.

The Scot's Narrative Examin'd. 1709.

The Scots Nation and Union Vindicated; from the Reflections Cast on Them, in an Infamous Libel, Entitl'd the Publick Spirit of the Whigs. 1714.

A Scots Poem: Or, a New-Years Gift, from a Native of the Universe, to his Fellow-Animals in Albania. Edinburgh, 1707.

A Seasonable Warning and Caution against the Insinuations Of Papists and Jacobites. 1712.

A Second, and More Strange Voyage to the World in the Moon. [1705].

Second Thoughts Are Best: Or, a Further Improvement of a Late Scheme to Prevent Street Robberies. 1729.

A Second Volume of the Writings of the Author of the True-Born Englishman. 1705.

The Secret History of the October Club. 1711.

The Secret History of the October Club. . . . Part II. 1711.

The Secret History of State Intrigues. 1715.

The Secret History of the Scepter. 1715.

The Secret History of the Secret History of the White Staff. 1715.

The Secret History of the White Staff. [Pt. I] 1714.

The Secret History of the White Staff. . . . Pt. II. 1714.

The Secret History of the White Staff. . . . Pt. III. 1715.

Secret Memoirs of a Treasonable Conference at S[omerset] House. 1717.

Secret Memoirs of the New Treaty of Alliance with France. 1716.

A Serious Inquiry into This Grand Question, Whether a Law to Prevent the Occasional Conformity of Dissenters, Would Not Be Inconsistent with the Act of Toleration. 1704.

Serious Reflections during the Life and Surprising Adventures of Robinson Crusoe, with His Vision of the Angelick World. 1720. Vol. 3 of *The Works of Daniel Defoe*, edited by G. H. Maynadier. New York: Crowell, 1903.

A Short Letter to the Glasgow-men. [Edinburgh, 1706].

A Short Narrative of the Life and Actions of His Grace John, D. of Marlborough. 1711.

A Short View of the Present State of the Protestant Religion. Edinburgh, 1707.

The Shortest Way to Peace and Union. 1703.

The Shortest-Way with the Dissenters: Or, Proposals for the Establishment of the Church. 1702. In *The Shortest Way with the Dissenters*. Shakespeare Head edition. Oxford: Blackwell, 1974.

The Sincerity of the Dissenters Vindicated. 1703.

The Six Distinguishing Characters of a Parliament-Man. 1700.

Some Considerations on a Law for Triennial Parliaments. 1716.

Some Considerations on the Reasonableness and Necessity of Encreasing and Encouraging the Seamen. 1728.

Some Considerations upon Street-Walkers. [1726].

Some Methods to Supply the Defects of the Late Peace. [1715].

Some Persons Vindicated against the Author of the Defection. 1718.

Some Reasons Offered by the Late Ministry in Defence of their Administration. 1715.

Some Reflections on a Pamphlet Lately Publish'd Entitul'd An Argument Shewing That a Standing Army Is Inconsistent with a Free Government. 1697.

Some Remarks on the First Chapter in Dr. Davenant's Essays. 1703.

Some Thoughts of an Honest Tory in the Country. 1716.

Some Thoughts upon the Subject of Commerce with France. 1713.

The Spanish Descent. 1702.

[A Speech of a Stone Chimney-Piece]. [1711].

A Speech without Doors. 1710.

The Storm: Or, A Collection of the Most Remarkable Casualties and Disasters Which Happen'd in the Late Dreadful Tempest, Both by Sea and Land. 1704.

Street-Robberies Consider'd. [1728].

A Strict Enquiry into the Circumstances of a Late Duel. 1713.

Strike while the Iron's Hot: Or, Now Is the Time to Be Happy. 1715.

The Succession of Spain Considered. 1711.

The Succession to the Crown of England, Considered. 1701.

A Supplement to the Faults on Both Sides. 1710.

A System of Magick. 1727.

"To the Athenian Society." In *The History of the Athenian Society*, by Charles Gildon. [1692].

To the Honourable, the C——s of England Assembled in P——t. 1704.

A Tour thro' the Whole Island of Great Britain. 1724–27. Introduction by G. D. H. Cole. 2 vols. New York: Kelley, 1968.

The Trade of Britain Stated. [Edinburgh, 1707].

The Trade of Scotland with France, Consider'd. 1713.

The Trade to India Critically and Calmly Consider'd. 1720.

Treason Detected, in an Answer to That Traiterous and Malicious Libel, Entitled English Advice to the Freeholders of England. 1715.

A True Account of the Proceedings at Perth. 1716.

The True and Genuine Account of the Life and Actions of the Late Jonathan Wild. 1725.

In vol. 16 of *Romances and Narratives by Daniel Defoe*, edited by George A. Aitken. London: Dent, 1905.

The True-Born Englishman. 1700.

The True-Born Englishman. Rev. ed. 1716.

A True Collection of the Writings of the Author of the True Born English-man. 1703.

A True Relation of the Apparition of One Mrs. Veal. 1706.

A True State of the Contracts Relating to the Third Money-Subscription Taken by the South-Sea Company. 1721.

A True State of the Difference between Sir George Rook, Knt. and William Colepeper, Esq. 1704.

"Truth and Honesty." *London Post.* 1705.

Two Great Questions Considered. [Edinburgh], 1707.

Union and No Union. 1713.

Universal Spectator and Weekly Journal. 12 Oct. 1728.

Unparallel'd Cruelty. 1726.

The Validity of the Renunciations of Former Powers. 1712.

A View of the Scots Rebellion. 1715.

The Villainy of Stock-Jobbers Detected. 1701.

A Vindication of Dr. Snape. [1717].

A Vindication of the Honour and Justice of Parliament. [1721].

A Vindication of the Press. 1718.

The Vision: A Poem. [Edinburgh, 1706].

The Weakest Go to the Wall. 1714.

Weekly-Journal: or Saturday's Evening Post. (Mist's Weekly-Journal). c. Feb. 1717–24 Oct. 1724.

What If the Swedes Should Come? 1717.

White-Hall Evening Post. 18 Sept. 1718–c. 14 Oct. 1720.

Wise as Serpents. 1712.

PRIMARY WORKS

Unless otherwise noted, place of publication is London for early editions.

[Abercromby, Patrick]. *The Advantages of the Act of Security Compar'd with Those of the Intended Union.* [Edinburgh], 1706.

An Account of Some Late Designs to Create Misunderstanding betwixt the King and His People. 1702.

An Account of the Society for Promoting Christian Knowledge. 1739.

Adams, William. *A Letter from the Country Containing Some Remarks concerning the National Covenant and Solemn League.* Edinburgh, 1707.

Addison, Joseph. *Cato.* 1713.

———. *The Miscellaneous Works of Joseph Addison.* Edited by A. C. Guthkelch. 2 vols. London: Bell, 1914.

Allestree, Richard. *The Gentleman's Calling.* 1660.

———. *The Ladies' Calling.* 1668.

Ames, William. *De conscientia et eius iure, vel casibus.* Amsterdam, 1631.

Annesley, Samuel. "How Is the Adherent Vanity of Every Condition Most Effectually Abated by Serious Godliness?" In *A Continuation of Morning-Exercise Questions and Cases of Conscience.* 1683. Reprinted in vol. 46 of *A Christian Library*, edited by John Wesley. 50 vols. Bristol, 1749–55.

———, ed. *Casuistical Morning-Exercises.* 1690.

———, ed. *A Continuation of Morning-Exercise Questions and Cases of Conscience.* 1683.

————, ed. *The Morning-Exercise at Cripple-gate: Or, Several Cases of Conscience Practically Resolved, by Sundry Ministers*. 1661.

Annual Matrimonial Expenses in London: At a Very Moderate Computation. [1740].

Astell, Mary. *A Fair Way with the Dissenters and Their Patrons*. 1704.

[Atterbury, Francis]. *Considerations upon the Secret History of the White Staff. Humbly Address'd to the E—— of O——*. [1714].

Atterbury, Francis. *English Advice to the Freeholders of England*. 1714.

Baillie, George. *Correspondence of George Baillie of Jerviswood*. Edinburgh: Bannatyne Club, 1842.

Barbauld, Anna Laetitia, ed. *The British Novelists*. 50 vols. 1820.

Basilius, Philo. *A Letter to Richard Steele*. 1715.

Baxter, Richard. *Poetical Fragments*. 1681.

————. *The Practical Works of the Rev. Richard Baxter*. Edited by William Orme. 23 vols. 1830.

————. *Reliquiae Baxterianae*. 3 vols. 1696.

Behn, Aphra. *The Works of Aphra Behn*. Edited by Montague Summers. 6 vols. London: Heinemann, 1915.

Biographia Brittannica. 5 vols. 1778–93.

Bissett, William. *The Modern Fanatic*. 1710.

Black, William. *A Reply to the Authors of the Advantages of Scotland by an Incorporate Union, and of the Fifth Essay at Removing National Prejudices*. Edinburgh, 1707.

Bohun, Edmund, trans. *Apology for the Church of England*. 1685.

Bohun, Ralph. *Discourse on Wind*. 1671.

Bohun, William. *The English Lawyer*. 1732.

Bolingbroke, Henry St. John, 1st viscount. *A Dissertation upon Parties*. In *Works*. 4 vols. Philadelphia: Carey & Hart, 1841.

Boswell's Life of Johnson. Edited by George Birkbeck Hill. Oxford: Clarendon Press, 1934.

Boyer, Abel. *History of the Reign of Queen Anne, Digested into Annals*. 11 vols. 1703–13.

————. *An Impartial History of the Occasional Conformity and Schism Bills*. 1717.

————. *The Political State of Great Britain*. 60 vols. 1711–40.

————. *Quadriennium Annae Postremum; Or, the Political State of Great Britain*. 8 vols. 1711. 2d ed. 1718–19.

A Brief Account of the Nature, Rise, and Progress of the Societies for Reformation of Manners. Edinburgh, 1700.

[Brokesby, Francis]. *Of Education with Respect to Grammar Schools, and the Universities*. 1701.

[Brown, Simon]. Preface to *A Caveat against Evil Company*. 1706.

Builders Dictionary. 1703.

Bunyan, John. *Grace Abounding & The Life and Death of Mr. Badman*. Introduced by G. B. Harrison. New York: Dutton, 1956.

Burn, Richard. *The Justice of the Peace, and Parish Officer*. 2 vols. 1755.

Burnet, Gilbert. *A History of My Own Time*. 6 vols. Oxford: Clarendon Press, 1823.

Calamy, Edmund. *An Abridgement of Mr. Baxter's History of His Life and Times*. 2 vols. 2d ed. 1713.

————. *An Account of the Ministers, etc., Who Were Ejected*. Vol. 2 of *An Abridgement of Mr. Baxter's History of His Life and Times*. 1713.

————. *A Continuation of the Account of the Ministers . . . Who Were Ejected and Silenced after the Restoration in 1660*. 1727.

————. *An Historical Account of My Own Life*. Edited by John T. Rutt. 2 vols. London: Colburn & Bentley, 1829.

————. *The Nonconformist's Memorial . . . Originally Written by Edmund Calamy, Abridged, Corrected and Methodized by Samuel Palmer.* 3 vols. London, 1802–3.

Calendar of State Papers, Domestic Series, of the Reign of Anne. Edited by Robert P. Mahaffy. 2 vols. London: HMSO. 1916–24.

Calendar of State Papers, Domestic Series, William III. Edited by William J. Hardy. 6 vols. London: HMSO. 1908–37.

Calendar of Treasury Books. Prepared by William A. Shaw. 32 vols. London: HMSO. 1904–57.

The Cambridge Chronicle and University Journal. [Stamford], 1762–1898.

The Case of the Experience of Dissenting Acts against the Protestant Dissenters Consider'd in a Dialogue. 1717.

Centlivre, Susannah. *The Gotham Election.* 1715.

Cibber, Colley, and Sir John Vanbrugh. *The Provoked Husband.* Edited by Peter Dixon. Lincoln: University of Nebraska Press, 1973.

Cibber, Theophilus. *The Lives of the Poets of Great Britain and Ireland.* 5 vols. 1753.

The Clamours of the Dissenters, against the Bill to Prevent Occasional Conformity Examined . . . by a True Church-of-England-Man. 1703.

Clark, James. *A Just Reprimand to Daniel De Foe.* Edinburgh, 1708.

————. *A Paper concerning Daniel De Foe.* Edinburgh, 1708.

Clerk, John. *A Letter to a Friend, Giving an Account How the Treaty of Union Has Been Received Here.* Edinburgh, 1706.

————. *Memoirs of the Life of Sir John Clerk.* Edited by John M. Gray. Publications of the Scottish History Society, vol. 13. Edinburgh, 1892.

The Clerk's Associate: Containing an Account of the High Court of Chancery. 1737.

The Clerk's Instructor in the Ecclesiastical Courts. 1740.

A Collection of All Her Majesty's Speeches, Messages, &c. from Her Happy Accession to the Throne to the Twenty First of June 1712. 1712.

Collins, John. "How Are the Religious of a Nation the Strength of It?" In *A Continuation of Morning-Exercise Questions and Cases of Conscience,* edited by Samuel Annesley. 1683.

————. "Contend Earnestly for the Faith, &c." In *A Compleat Collection of Farewell Sermons.* 1663.

A Complete Collection of State-Trials, and Proceedings for High-Treason, and Other Crimes and Misdemeanours. 6 vols. 2d ed. 1730.

Cowley, Abraham. *Davideis: A Sacred Poem of the Troubles of David.* 1656. In *Poems.* Edited by A. R. Waller. Cambridge: Cambridge University Press, 1905.

Crompton, George. *Practice Common-placed: or, the Rules and Cases of Practice in the Courts of King's Bench and Common Pleas.* 1780.

Cruso, Timothy. *God the Guide of Youth.* 1695.

Cunningham, Alexander. *The History of Great Britain: From the Revolution in 1688, to the Accession of George the First.* Translated from the Latin by William Thomson. 2 vols. 1787.

[Curll, Edmund]. *Curlicism Display'd.* 1718.

Daily Advertiser. 1731–1809.

Daily Courant. 1702–35.

Daily Post. 1719–46.

Darrell, William. *The Gentleman Instructed.* 1727.

Davenant, Charles. *Essays upon Peace at Home and War Abroad.* 2 parts. 1704.

Davies, Sir John. *The Poems of Sir John Davies.* Edited by Robert Krueger. Oxford: Clarendon Press, 1975.

[Davys, Mary]. *Familiar Letters betwixt a Gentleman and a Lady.* [1720].

De Laune, Thomas. *Dr. Sacheverell's Recantation.* 1709.

Dennis, John. "The Causes of the Decay and Defects of Dramatick Poesie." [1725]. In *The Critical Works of John Dennis*, edited by Edward Niles Hooker. 2 vols. Baltimore: Johns Hopkins University Press, 1943.

Dent, Arthur. *The Plain Man's Path-way to Heaven.* Glasgow, 1731.

Derham, William. "A Letter From the Reverend Mr. William Derham, F.R.S. Containing his Observations concerning the Late Storm." *Philosophical Transactions of the Royal Society of London* 24 (1704): 1530–34.

The Dissenters Claim of Right to a Capacity for Civil Officers. 1717.

Diverting Post. 1704–5.

Drayton, Michael. *The Works of Michael Drayton.* Edited by J. William Hebel. 5 vols. Oxford: Blackwell, 1931.

Dryden, John. *Works.* Edited by Edward Niles Hooker and H. T. Swedenberg, Jr. 13 vols. Berkeley and Los Angeles: University of California Press, 1956–84.

Dunsford, Martin. *History of Tiverton.* 1790.

Dunton, John. *The Athenian Gazette: Or, Casuistical Mercury.* 1691–97.

——. *The Athenian Mercury.* See *Athenian Gazette.*

——. *The Athenian Oracle.* 1703–4.

——. *Dunton's Whipping-Post.* 1706.

——. *The Golden Age.* 1714.

——. *The Impeachment.* [1714].

——. *The Life and Errors of John Dunton.* 2 vols. 1818. New York: Burt Franklin, 1969.

——. *The Post-Angel.* 1701–2.

——. *Queen Robin: Or, the Second Part of Neck or Nothing, Detecting the Secret Reign of the Four Last Years.* [1714].

——. *The Shortest Way with Whores and Rogues . . . Dedicated to Mr. Daniel de Foe.* 1703.

Dyer's News Letter. 1706–7.

Earbery, Matthias. *The History of the Clemency of Our English Monarchs.* 1717.

Edinburgh Courant. 1707.

English Post. 1700–1709.

Entick, John. *A New and Accurate History and Survey of London, Westminster, Southwark, and Places Adjacent.* 1766.

An Equivalent for De Foe. 1706.

The Establishment of the Church, the Preservation of the State: Shewing the Reasonableness of a Bill against Occasional Conformity. 1702.

Evelyn, John. *The Diary of John Evelyn.* Edited by E. S. de Beer. Oxford: Clarendon Press, 1955.

An Explanation of the Eleven Resolves. 1712.

The Fees of the Sheriffs' Court, Chamberlain's Office, Woodstreet and Poultry Compters, and Ludgate. 1709.

Fielding, Henry. *The Author's Farce.* Edited by Charles B. Woods. Lincoln: University of Nebraska Press, 1966.

The 15th Account of the Progress Made towards Suppressing Profaneness and Debauchery, by the Societies for Reformation of Manners. 1710.

Fleetwood, William. *The Relative Duties of . . . Masters and Servants.* 1705.

Flying Post. 1696–1731.

Forster, John. *Daniel De Foe and Charles Churchill.* 1855.

Franklin, Benjamin. *Autobiography.* Boston: Houghton Mifflin, 1958.

A Further Examination of the Weavers Pretences. 1719.

Gentleman's Library. 1715.

Gildon, Charles. *The Life and Strange Surprizing Adventures of Mr. D . . . De F . . . of London, Hosier.* 1719.

A Glimpse of Hell: Or, a Short Description of the Common Side of Newgate. 1705.

Gough, Strickland. *An Enquiry into the Causes of the Decay of the Dissenters' Interest.* 1730.

Gray, Thomas. "Elegy Written in a Country-Churchyard." 1751.

Greville, Fulke. *Of Humane Learning.* In *The Works in Verse and Prose . . . of Fulke Greville, Lord Brooke,* edited by Alexander Grosart. 4 vols. Printed privately, 1870.

Grub Street Journal. 29 April 1731.

Hannibal Not at Our Gates. 1712.

Harris, William. *Sermon Occasioned by the Death of the Late Reverend Joshua Oldfield.* 1730.

Hart, Edward. *The Bulwark Stormed.* 1717.

Haversham. *Memoirs of the Late Right Honourable John, Lord Haversham, from the Year 1640 to 1710.* 1795.

Hawkins, William. *A Treatise of the Pleas of the Crown.* 2 vols. 1716–21.

Healey, George H. *The Letters of Daniel Defoe.* 1955. Oxford: Clarendon Press, 1969.

"A Health to be Sung and Drank by All Honest Britons." In *Political Merriment: Or, Truths Told to Some Tune.* 1714.

Hearne, Thomas. *Remarks and Collections of Thomas Hearne.* Edited by C. E. Doble. Oxford: Clarendon Press, 1885.

Heister, Lorenz. *A General System of Surgery in Three Parts.* 1743.

Henry, Philip. *Diaries and Letters of Philip Henry, M.A.* Edited by Matthew Lee. London: Kegan Paul, Trench & Co., 1882.

[Herbert, George]. *Witts Recreations. Selected from the Finest Fancies of Moderne Muses with a Thousand Outlandish Proverbs.* 1640.

Hickes, George. *Passive Obedience in Actual Resistance or, Remarks upon a Paper Fix'd up in the Cathedral Church of Worcester.* 1691.

Higgons, Bevil. "The Mourners." 1702. In vol. 6 of *Poems on Affairs of State,* edited by Frank Ellis. 7 vols. New Haven: Yale University Press, 1963–75.

Historical Manuscripts Commission. *Calendar of the Manuscripts of the Marquis of Bath.* 5 vols. London: HMSO, 1904–80.

———. *The Manuscripts of His Grace the Duke of Portland.* 9 vols. London: HMSO, 1891–1923.

An Historical View of the Principles, Characters, Persons, &c. of the Political Writers in Great Britain. 1740.

Hornby, Charles. *A Caveat against the Whiggs.* 3d ed. 1712.

Howell, T. B. *A Complete Collection of State Trials.* 33 vols. London, 1812.

The Hudibrastick Brewer. 1714.

A Hue and Cry after Daniel De Foe and His Coventry Beast. 1711.

Hume, David. *History of England.* 6 vols. 1763.

Hunter, Henry. *A Brief History of the Society in Scotland for Propagating Christian Knowledge.* 1795.

[Hutchinson, Thomas]. *A Collection of Original Papers Relative to the History of the Colony of Massachusetts Bay.* Boston, 1769.

Index Rerum & Vocabulorum. 1722.

The Infernal Congress: Or, News from Below. 1713.

Jacob, Giles. *A New Law Dictionary.* 10th ed. 1782.

James, Richard. *A Medical Dictionary.* 1743.

Johnson, Charles. *The Successful Pirate.* 1712.

Johnson, Samuel. *A Journey to the Western Islands*. Edited by Mary Lascelles. New Haven: Yale University Press, 1971.

——. *An Account of the Life of Mr. Richard Savage*. 1744.

——. *Life of Cowley*. In *Lives of the Poets*. 1779–81.

Jones, David. *Compleat History of Europe*. 8 vols. 1701–20.

Judas Discuver'd. 1713.

Ker, John. *The Memoirs of John Ker, of Kersland, in North Britain, Esq. Published by Himself*. In 3 parts. 3d ed. 1727.

King, William. *A Vindication of the Rev. Dr. Sacheverell*. 2d ed. 1711. In *The Original Works of William King, LL.D.* 1776.

Knox, Robert. *An Historical Relation of Ceylon*. Edited by James Ryan. Glasgow: MacLehose, 1911.

——. *An Historical Relation of Ceylon*. Introduced by H. A. I. Goonetileke. New Delhi: Navrang, 1983.

B. L. of Twickenham. *An Accurate Description of Newgate*. 2d ed. 1729.

Lawson, George. *Politica sacra et civilis*. 1660.

LEGION's Humble Address to the LORDS, Answer'd Paragraph by Paragraph. 1704.

Leslie, Charles. *Cassandra*. [1702]. In *A Collection of Tracts Written by the Author of the Snake in the Grass*. N.d.

——. *Cassandra. Number II*. In *A Collection of Tracts Written by the Author of the Snake in the Grass*. N.d.

——. *Heraclitus Ridens*. 1703–4.

[——]. *The New Association*. In *A Collection of Tracts Written by the Author of the Snake in the Grass*. N.d.

——. *The New Association, Part II*. 1703.

——. *Reflections upon a Late Scandalous and Malicious Pamphlet*. 1703.

——. *The Rehearsal*. 1704–8. 6 vols. 1750.

——. *The Wolf Stript of His Shepherd's Clothing*. 1704.

A Letter from a Dissenter in the City, to his Country-Friend. 1705.

A Letter from a Gentleman at Edinburgh to his Freind [sic] *at London*. Edinburgh, 1711.

A Letter from a Gentleman in Edinburgh, to a Member of Parliament. Edinburgh, 1712.

A Letter from One Clergyman to Another. 1716.

A Letter from Some Aged Nonconforming Ministers. 1702.

A Letter to a Country-Gentleman: Setting Forth the Cause of the Decay and Ruin of Trade. 1698.

A Letter to a Peer, concerning the Bill against Occasional Conformity. 1702.

A Letter to the People of England. [1714].

The Life and Character of John Barber, Esq; Late Lord-Mayor of London, Deceased. 1741.

Locke, John. *Letter on Toleration*. Translated by J. W. Gough. Oxford: Clarendon Press, 1968.

——. *Locke's Two Treatises of Government*. Edited by Peter Laslett. 1960; Cambridge: Cambridge University Press, 1980.

Lockhart, George. *Memoirs concerning the Affairs of Scotland from Queen Anne's Accession to the Throne to the Commencement of the Union of the Two Kingdoms of Scotland and England in May, 1707*. 1714.

London Gazette. 1665–1800.

London Journal. 1720–34.

Lowman, Moses. *A Defence of the Protestant Dissenters; in Answer to the Misrepresentations of Dr. Sherlock*. 1718.

Luttrell, Narcissus. *A Brief Historical Relation of State Affairs*. 6 vols. Oxford: Oxford University Press, 1857.

————. *The Parliamentary Diary of Narcissus Luttrell*. Edited by Henry Horwitz. Oxford: Clarendon Press, 1972.

McCormick, Joseph, ed. *State Papers and Letters Addressed to William Carstares*. London: Strahan & Cadell; Edinburgh: Balfour, 1774.

Marchmont, Patrick Hume, 1st earl of. *A Selection from the Papers of the Earls of Marchmont*. London: Murray, 1831.

Mather, Cotton. *The Diary of Cotton Mather, 1681–1724*. 2 vols. Boston: Massachusetts Historical Society, 1911–12.

————. *Silentarius*. Boston, 1721.

Medley. 1710–12.

Memoirs of the Society of Grub Street: Selections from the Grub-Street Journal. 1730–37. 2 vols. 1737.

Mercure Galant. Paris, 1672–1716.

Milton, John. *Animadversions upon the Remonstrants Defence, against Smectymnuus*. In vol. 3 of *The Works of John Milton*. New York: Columbia University Press, 1931.

The Moderation, Justice, and Manners of the Review. 1706.

Moderator. 1710.

Monthly Catalogue. 3 vols. 1725–29.

[Morer, Thomas]. *A Short Account of Scotland*. 1702.

[Mortimer, John]. *Advice to Parents: Or, Rules for the Education of Children*. 1704.

[Mortimer, John]. *Some Considerations concerning the Present State of Religion*. 1702.

Morton, Charles. "Advice to Candidates for the Ministry, under the Present Discouraging Circumstances." In vol. 1 of *A Continuation of the Account of the Ministers . . . Who Were Ejected and Silenced after the Restoration in 1660*, by Edmund Calamy. 1727.

————. *Compendium Physicae*. In vol. 33 of *Publications of the Colonial Society of Massachusetts*. Boston, 1940.

————. "The Improvement of Cornwall by Sea-sand." In *Transactions of the Royal Society* 10 (1675): 293–96.

————. *The Spirit of Man*. Boston, 1693.

Motherby, G. *A New Medical Dictionary*. 1785.

A Narrative of the Tryal and Sufferings of Thomas Delaune. 1683.

Observations on the Bankrupts Bill. 1706.

Observator. 1702–12.

The Observator's Letter to his Learned Counsel. 1711.

Oldham, John. *The Works of Mr. John Oldham*. 1685. Delmar, N.Y.: Scholars' Facsimiles & Reprints, 1979.

Oldmixon, John. *History of England*. 1735.

————. *The Life and Posthumous Works of Arthur Maynwaring*. 1715.

————. *A Detection of the Sophistry and Falsities Of the Pamphlet, Entitul'd, the Secret History of the White Staff*. 2d ed. 1714.

————. *A Detection of the Sophistry and Falsities Of the Pamphlet . . . Part II*. 1714.

Oldys, William. *A Dissertation upon Pamphlets*. 1731.

Osborn, Francis. *Advice to a Son*. 1658.

Otway, Thomas. *The Ophan*. 1725.

————. *The Works of Thomas Otway*. Edited by J. C. Ghosh. 2 vols. Oxford: Clarendon Press, 1932.

[Owen, James]. *Moderation a Virtue*. 1703.

Palmer, Samuel. *A Defence of the Dissenters' Education.* 1703.

———. *A Vindication of the Learning, Loyalty, Morals, and Most Christian Behaviour of the Dissenters . . . in Answer to Mr. Wesley's Defence.* 1705.

A Paper concerning Daniel De Foe. 1708.

Paterson, William. *The Writings of William Paterson.* Edited by Saxe Bannister. 3 vols. 1858. New York: Augustus M. Kelley, 1968.

Payne, Olive. *Librorum ex Bibliothecis Philippi Farewell, D.D., et Danielis De Foe, Gen., Catalogus.* 1731. Berlin: Heidenreich, 1970.

Penn, William. *Considerations on the Bill Depending, for Preventing Occasional Conformity.* [1703].

———. *The Papers of William Penn.* Edited by Richard S. Dunn and Mary Maples Dunn. 5 vols. Philadelphia: University of Pennsylvania Press, 1981–87.

Pepys, Samuel. *The Diary of Samuel Pepys.* Edited by Robert Latham and William Matthews. 11 vols. Berkeley and Los Angeles: University of California Press, 1972.

Perkins, William. *A Treatise of the Vocations or Callings of Men.* 1603.

Pinkerton, John M., ed. *The Minute Book of the Faculty of Advocates.* Vol. 1, *1661–1712.* Edinburgh: Stair Society, 1976.

[Pittis, William]. *Queen Anne Vindicated from the Base Aspersions of Some Late Pamphlets Publish'd to Screen the Mismanagers of the Four Last Years from Publick Justice.* 17$\frac{14}{15}$.

Pittis, William. *The True-Born-Hugonot.* 1703.

———. "Two Campaigns in One Panegyrical Essay upon . . . Marlborough's Successes." 1706.

———. *The Whipping Post, At a New Session of Oyer and Terminer. For the Scriblers.* 1705.

Political Merriment: Or, Truths Told to Some Tune. In 3 parts. 1714–15.

Pope, Alexander. "Epistle to Robert, Earl of Oxford." 1722.

———. *An Essay on Man.* 1735.

Post Boy. 1695–1728.

Post Man. 1695–1725.

"A Presbyterian Getting on Horseback." 2d ed. 1717.

A Present for Servants. 1726.

The Principles of the Dissenters, concerning Toleration and Occasional Conformity. 1705.

Proposals for a National Reformation of Manners. 1694.

Read's Weekly Journal. 1730–39.

Reflections upon Some Scandalous and Malicious Pamphlets. 1703.

The Reformer Reform'd. 1703.

"Remarks on the Author of the Hymn to the Pillory." 1703.

Remarks on the Letter to the Dissenters. By a Churchman. 1714.

A Representation of the State of the Societies for the Reformation of Manners. 1715.

Republican Bullies. 1705.

Reresby, John. *The Memoirs and Travels.* London: Jeffery, 1813.

Resolves and Address to the Queen ordered to be Printed by Parliament. 1712.

Review and Observator Review'd. 1706.

Review Review'd. 1705. In "A Whiff of Scandal in the Life of Daniel Defoe," by Maximillian E. Novak. *Huntington Library Quarterly* 34 (1970–71): 35–42.

Ridpath, George. *Correspondence between George Ridpath and the Rev. Robert Wodrow.* In *Miscellany of the Abbotsford Club.* Vol 1. Edinburgh, 1837.

Ryder, Dudley. *The Diary of Dudley Ryder, 1715–1716.* Edited by William Matthews. London: Methuen, [1939].

Rymer, Thomas. Preface to Rapin's "Reflections on Aristotle's Treatise of Poesie." In *Critical Works of Thomas Rymer*, edited by Curt A. Zimansky. New Haven: Yale University Press, 1956.

Sacheverell, Henry. *The Character of a Low-Churchman.* 1702.

―――. *The Political Union: A Discourse Shewing the Dependance of Government on Religion in General: and of the English Monarchy on the Church of England in Particular.* Oxford, 1702.

"The Scribler's Doom: or, The Pillory in Fashion." 1703.

Seaton, Thomas. *The Conduct of Servants in Great Families.* 1720.

"A Second Defence of the Scotch Vision."

A Second Defence of the Scotish [sic] Vision. Edinburgh, 1706.

Sewall, Samuel. *Diary of Samuel Sewall, 1674–1729.* Collections of the Massachusetts Historical Society, 5th ser., vol. 5. Boston: Boston University Press, 1878.

Sewell, George. *Tragedy of Sir Walter Raleigh.* 1719.

"A Short Satyre on That Native of the Universe, the Albanian Animal." Edinburgh, 1707.

The Shortest Way with the Dissenters: Or, Proposals for the Establishment of the Church. With Its Author's Brief Explication Consider'd; His Name Expos'd, His Practices Detected, and His Hellish Designs Set in a True Light. 1703.

Shower, John. *A Sermon Preach'd to the Societies for Reformation of Manners.* 1698.

Smith, Adam. *Lectures on Rhetoric and Belles Lettres.* London: Oxford University Press, 1983.

―――. *The Theory of Moral Sentiments.* 1759. 1790.

Some Considerations of a Preface to an Enquiry concerning the Occasional Conformity of Dissenters. 1701.

A Speech, Design'd to Have Been Spoken in the House of Commons, on the Resolution concerning the Terms of Peace. 1715.

Speke, George. *The Secret History of the Happy Revolution in 1688.* 1715.

Sprat, Thomas. *History of the Royal Society.* Edited by Jackson I. Cope and Harold W. Jones. St. Louis: Washington University Studies, 1958.

Stair, James Dalrymple, 1st viscount. *Annals and Correspondence of the Viscount and The First and Second Earls of Stair.* Edited by John M. Graham. 2 vols. Edinburgh: Blackwood, 1875.

The Statutes of the Realm. 11 vols. London, 1810–28.

Steele, Richard. *The Correspondence of Richard Steele.* Edited by Rae Blanchard. 1941. Oxford: Clarendon Press, 1968.

―――. *The Crisis.* 1714. In *Tracts and Pamphlets*, edited by Rae Blanchard. Baltimore: Johns Hopkins Press, 1944.

―――. *The Importance of Dunkirk.* 1713. In *Tracts and Pamphlets*, edited by Rae Blanchard. Baltimore: Johns Hopkins Press, 1944.

[―――]. *The Ladies Library.* 3 vols. 1714.

―――. *The Guardian.* Edited by John C. Stephens. Lexington: University Press of Kentucky, 1982.

―――. *Tracts and Pamphlets.* Edited by Rae Blanchard. Baltimore: Johns Hopkins Press, 1944.

Steele, Richard, and Joseph Addison. *The Spectator.* Edited by Donald F. Bond. 5 vols. Oxford: Clarendon Press, 1965.

―――. *The Tatler.* Edited by George A. Aitken. New York: Hadley & Matthews, 1899.

Stubbs, Philip. *For God or for Baal: Or, No Neutrality in Religion.* 1702.

Swift, Jonathan. *The Conduct of the Allies.* In vol. 6 of *The Prose Works of Jonathan*

Swift, edited by Herbert Davis. 14 vols. Oxford: Blackwell, 1939–68.

————. *The Correspondence of Jonathan Swift*. Edited by Harold Williams. 5 vols. Oxford: Clarendon Press, 1963–65.

————. *The Examiner, and Other Pieces Written in 1710–11*. Edited by Herbert Davis. Oxford: Blackwell, 1957.

————. *Journal to Stella*. Edited by Harold Williams. Oxford: Blackwell, 1974.

————. *The Prose Works of Jonathan Swift*. Edited by Herbert Davis. 14 vols. Oxford: Blackwell, 1939–68.

Taylor, Joseph. *A Journey to Edenborough*. Edinburgh: Brown, 1903.

[Toland, John]. *The Second Part of the State Anatomy*. 2d ed. 1717.

Toulmin, Joshua. *An Historical View of the State of the Protestant Dissenters in England*. London: Cruttwell, 1814.

Tong, William. *Some Memoirs of the Life and Death of John Shower*. 1716.

The Tryal and Examination of Mr. John Tutchin. 1705.

Turner, William. *A Compleat History of the Most Remarkable Providences, Both of Judgment and Mercy . . . Extracted from the Best Writers, the Author's Own Observations, and the Numerous Relations Sent Him from Divers Parts of the Three Kingdoms*. 1697.

Tutchin, John. *Civitas Militaris*. 1689.

————. *The Foreigners*. In vol. 6 of *Poems on Affairs of State*, edited by Frank H. Ellis. 7 vols. New Haven: Yale University Press, 1970.

[————]. *The Prophet No Conjuror: Or, His Scandal Club's Scandalous BALLAD*. 1705.

[————]. *The Western Martyrology: Or, Bloody Assizes*. 5th ed. 1705.

Two Letters concerning the Author of the Examiner. 1713.

Universal Spectator and Weekly Journal. 1728–46.

A View of the Present Controversy about Occasional Conformity. 1703.

Vincent, Thomas. *God's Terrible Voice in the City*. 1667. 1722.

Walker, Obadiah. *Of Education*. 1673. 6th ed. 1699.

Walker, Robert. *Short Account of the Rise, Progress, and Present State of the Society in Scotland for Propagating Christian Knowledge*. Edinburgh, 1748.

Walker, Thomas. *Quaker's Opera*. 1728.

Watson, James. "The Publisher's Preface to the Printers in Scotland." In *The History of the Art of Printing Containing an Account of Its Invention and Progress in Europe*. Edinburgh: Watson, 1713.

Webster, James. *The Author of the Lawful Prejudices . . . Defended*. 1707.

————. *Lawful Prejudices against an Incorporating Union with England*. 1707.

————. *A Second Defence of the Lawful Prejudices*. [Edinburgh, 1707].

Weekly Packet. 1714–21.

The Welsh-Monster; Or, the Rise and Downfall of That Late Upstart . . . Innuendo Scribble. [1708?].

Wesley, John. *The Christian Library*. 50 vols. Bristol, 1749–55.

————. *The Journal of the Rev. John Wesley*. 8 vols. London: Epworth Press, 1938.

Wesley, Samuel. *A Defence of a Letter concerning the Education of Dissenters*. 1704.

[————]. *A Letter from a Country Divine*. 1703.

————. *A Reply to Mr. Palmer's Vindication of the Learning, Morals, and Most Christian Behaviour of the Dissenters*. 1707.

The Westminster Confession of Faith. 1648.

[Whalley, Peter]. *An Essay on the Manner of Writing History*. 1746.

What the Dissenters Would Have: Or, the Case of the Dissenters Briefly yet Plainly Stated. In Three Parts. 1717.

The White Staff's Speech to the Lords. 1714.

Whitehead, John. *The Life of the Rev. John Wesley*. 1793.

The Whole Life of Mr. William Fuller. 1703.

Williams, Daniel. *The Excellency of a Publick Spirit.* 1697.

Wilson, Walter. *History and Antiquities of Dissenting Churches and Meeting Houses.* 4 vols. London: Button, Williams, Conder, 1808.

Wodrow, Robert. *Analecta: Or, Materials for a History of Remarkable Providences.* 4 vols. Edinburgh: Maitland Club, 1842.

———. *The Correspondence of the Rev. Robert Wodrow.* Edited by Thomas M'Crie. 3 vols. Edinburgh, 1842.

———. *History of the Sufferings of the Church of Scotland.* 4 vols. Glasgow: Blackie & Son, n.d. [1721–22].

Wood, William. *Survey of Trade.* 1718.

Woodfall, H. S. *A Summary of the Law of Libel.* 1771.

Woodward, Josiah. *An Account of the Rise and Progress of the Religious Societies in the City of London.* 2d ed. 1698.

———. *An Account of the Societies for Reformation of Manners.* 1699.

———. *The Necessary Duty of Family Prayer.* 1768.

SECONDARY WORKS

Adams, Percy. *Travel Literature and the Evolution of the Novel.* Lexington: University of Kentucky Press, 1983.

Aikins, Janet. "Roxana: The Unfortunate Mistress of Conversation." *SEL* 25 (1985): 529–56.

Aitken, G. A. "Defoe and Mist's *Weekly Journal.*" *Athenaeum* (26 Aug. 1893): 287–88.

———. "Defoe's Birth and Marriage." *Athenaeum* (23 Aug. 1890): 257.

———. "Defoe's Brick-Kilns." *Athenaeum* (13 Apr. 1889): 472–73.

———. "Defoe's Wife." *Contemporary Review* (Feb. 1890): 232–39.

Alkon, Paul K. "Defoe's Argument in *The Shortest Way with the Dissenters.*" *MP* 73 (1976): 13–22.

———. "The Odds against Friday: Defoe, Bayes, and Inverse Probability." In *Probability, Time, and Space in Eighteenth-Century Literature*, edited by Paula R. Backscheider. New York: AMS, 1979.

Allen, W. O. B., and Edmund McClure. *Two Hundred Years: The History of the Society for the Propagation of Christian Knowledge.* London: SPCK, 1898.

Alsop, J. D. "Defoe and his Whig Paymasters." *N&Q* 226 (1981): 225–26.

———. "New Light on Nathaniel Mist and Daniel Defoe." *PBSA* 75 (1981): 57–60.

Anderson, M. S. *Britain's Discovery of Russia, 1553–1815.* London: Macmillan, 1958.

Armet, Helen, ed. *Extracts from the Records of the Burgh of Edinburgh, 1689 to 1701.* Edinburgh: Oliver & Boyd, 1962.

Ashcraft, Richard. *Revolutionary Politics and Locke's Two Treatises of Government.* Princeton: Princeton University Press, 1986.

Ashton, John. *Social Life in the Reign of Queen Anne.* 2 vols. London: Chatto & Windus, 1882.

Ashton, T. S. *Economic Fluctuations in England, 1700–1800.* Oxford: Clarendon Press, 1959.

———. *An Economic History of England: The Eighteenth Century.* London: Methuen, 1955.

Aspinall, Arthur. "Statistical Accounts of the London Newspapers in the Eighteenth Century." *EHR* 63 (1948): 201–32.

Aubin, Robert A. *London in Flames, London in Glory*. New Brunswick: Rutgers University Press, 1943.

Aylmer, G. E. *The King's Servants: The Civil Service of Charles I, 1625–1642*. Rev. ed. Boston: Routledge & Kegan Paul, 1974.

Backscheider, Paula R. "Barbary Ransom: News—Novel." *Scriblerian* 18 (1986): 239.

———. *A Being More Intense: The Prose Works of Bunyan, Swift, and Defoe*. New York: AMS, 1984.

———. "Cross-Purposes: Defoe's *History of the Union*." *CLIO* 11 (1982): 165–86.

———. *Daniel Defoe: Ambition and Innovation*. Lexington: University Press of Kentucky, 1986.

———. "Defoe and the Clerks of Penicuik." *MP* 84 (1987): 372–81.

———. "Defoe's Lady Credit." *HLQ* 44 (1981): 89–100.

———. "Defoe's Prodigal Sons." *SLI* 15, no. 2 (1982): 3–18.

———. "John Russell to Daniel Defoe: Fifteen Unpublished Letters from Scotland." *PQ* 61 (1982): 161–77.

———. "No Defense: Defoe in 1703." *PMLA* 103 (1988): 274–84.

———. "Personality and Biblical Allusion in Defoe's Letters." *SAR* 47 (1982): 1–20.

———. "The Verse Essay, John Locke, and Defoe's *Jure Divino*." *ELH* 55 (1988): 99–124.

Baer, Joel H. "'The Complicated Plot of Piracy': Aspects of English Criminal Law and the Image of the Pirate in Defoe." *The Eighteenth Century: Theory and Interpretation* 23 (1982): 3–26.

Bahlman, Dudley W. R. *The Moral Revolution of 1688*. New Haven: Yale University Press, 1957.

Baine, Rodney. "Daniel Defoe and *The History and Reality of Apparitions*." *Proceedings of the American Philosophical Society* 106 (1962): 335–47.

———. *Daniel Defoe and the Supernatural*. Athens, Ga.: University of Georgia Press, 1968.

———. "Defoe and Mrs. Bargrave's Story." *PQ* 33 (1954): 388–95.

Baker, Donald C. "Witchcraft, Addison, and *The Drummer*." *Studia Neophilologica* 31 (1959): 174–81.

Barlow, Richard B. *Citizenship and Conscience*. Philadelphia: University of Philadelphia Press, 1962.

Bastian, Frank. *Defoe's Early Life*. Totowa, N.J.: Barnes & Noble, 1981.

———. "James Foe, Merchant, Father of Daniel Defoe." *N&Q* 209 (1964): 82–86.

Beattie, J. M. *Crime and the Courts of England, 1660–1800*. Princeton: Princeton University Press, 1986.

———. *The English Court in the Reign of George I*. London: Cambridge University Press, 1967.

Beaven, Alfred. *The Aldermen of the City of London*. 2 vols. London: Fisher, 1908–13.

Bebb, E. D. *Nonconformity and Social and Economic Life, 1660–1800*. London: Epworth, 1935.

Beecham, H. A. "Samuel Wesley Senior: New Biographical Evidence." *Renaissance and Modern Studies* 7 (1963): 78–109.

Bell, Ian. *Defoe's Fiction*. Totowa, N.J.: Barnes & Noble, 1985.

Bell, Walter George. *The Great Fire of London in 1666*. 1920. London: Bodley Head, 1951.

Bender, John. *Imagining the Penitentiary*. Chicago: University of Chicago Press, 1987.

Bennett, G. V. "Conflict in the Church." In *Britain after the Glorious Revolution, 1689–1714*, edited by Geoffrey Holmes. London: Macmillan, 1969.

———. *The Tory Crisis in Church and State, 1688–1730: The Career of Francis Atterbury, Bishop of Rochester*. Oxford: Clarendon Press, 1975.

Berendsen, Anne. *Tiles: A General History*. Translated by Janet Seligman. New York: Viking, 1967.

Biddle, Sheila. *Bolingbroke and Harley*. New York: Knopf, 1974.

A Biographical Dictionary of the Judges of England. London: Wildy, 1971.

Black, Jeremy. "The British Press and Europe in the Early Eighteenth Century." In *The Press in English Society from the Seventeenth to the Nineteenth Centuries*, edited by Michael Harris and Alan Lee. Rutherford, N.J.: Fairleigh Dickinson, 1986.

———. "Russia and the British Press in the Early Eighteenth Century." *Study Group on Eighteenth-Century Russia Newsletter* 11 (1983): 16–31.

Blewitt, David. *Defoe's Art of Fiction*. Toronto: University of Toronto Press, 1979.

Bloore, Stephen. "Samuel Keimer." *Pennsylvania Magazine of History and Biography* 54 (1930): 255–87.

Bogue, David, and James Bennett. *A History of Dissenters: From the Revolution to the Year 1808*. 4 vols. London, 1808–12.

Bolam, C. G., Jeremy Goring, H. L. Short, and Roger Thomas. *The English Presbyterians, from Elizabethan Puritanism to Modern Unitarianism*. London: Allen & Unwin, 1968.

Bond, Richmond. *The Tatler: The Making of a Literary Journal*. Cambridge, Mass.: Harvard University Press, 1971.

Boulton, James T. "Introduction. Daniel Defoe: His Language and Rhetoric." In *Daniel Defoe*. New York: Schocken, 1965.

Braudy, Leo. "Daniel Defoe and the Anxieties of Autobiography." *Genre* 6 (1973): 76–97.

Brewer, John, and John Styles, eds. *An Ungovernable People*. New Brunswick, N.J.: Rutgers University Press, 1980.

Briggs, Asa. *A Social History of England*. London: Weidenfeld & Nicolson, 1983.

Brink, Andrew W. "*Robinson Crusoe* and *The Life of the Reverend Mr. George Trosse*." *PQ* 48 (1969): 433–51.

Brisco, Norris A. *The Economic Policy of Robert Walpole*. New York: Columbia University Press, 1907.

British Union-Catalogue of Periodicals. 17 vols. 1964–80.

Brougham, Henry P. *Lives of Men of Letters and Science Who Flourished in the Time of George III*. 2 vols. London, 1845.

Brown, Beatrice Curtis, ed. *The Letters and Diplomatic Instructions of Queen Anne*. London: Cassell, 1935.

Brown, Homer O. "The Displaced Self in the Novels of Daniel Defoe." *ELH* 38 (1971): 562–90.

Brown, Iain G. "Sir John Clerk of Penicuik, 1676–1755: Aspects of a Virtuous Life." Ph.D. diss., Cambridge, 1980.

[Brown, William]. *The Fleet*. London, 1843.

Burch, C. E. "Benjamin Defoe at Edinburgh University, 1710–1711." *PQ* 19 (1940): 343–48.

———. "Defoe and the Edinburgh Society for the Reformation of Manners." *RES* 16 (1940): 306–12.

———. "Defoe's Connections with the *Edinburgh Courant*." *RES* 5 (1929): 437–40.

Burford, E. J. *Wits, Wenchers and Wantons: London's Low Life*. London: Robert Hale, 1986.

Burton, John Hill. *The History of Scotland.* 8 vols. Edinburgh: Blackwood, 1873–74.

———. *A History of the Reign of Queen Anne.* 3 vols. Edinburgh: Blackwood, 1880.

Campbell, Mary Elizabeth. *Defoe's First Poem.* Bloomington, Ind.: Principia Press, 1938.

Capewell, Janice. "Exploring Nonconformist Registers." *Cockney Ancestor* 5 (1979–80): 5–13.

Carpenter, S. C. *Eighteenth-Century Church and People.* London: Murray, 1959.

Carswell, John. *The South Sea Bubble.* London: Cresset Press, 1960.

Castle, Terry. "'Amy, Who Knew my Disease': A Psychosexual Pattern in Defoe's *Roxana.*" *ELH* 46 (1979): 81–96.

Cather, Willa. *On Writing.* New York: Knopf, 1949.

Chambers, Robert, ed. *The Book of Days.* 2 vols. Edinburgh: Chambers, 1863–64.

Chance, James F. *George I and the Northern War.* London: Smith, Elder, 1909.

Cherniak, Warren L. "The Heroic Occasional Poem." *MLQ* 26 (1965): 523–35.

Chute, Marchette. *Ben Jonson of Westminster.* New York: Dutton, 1953.

Clarendon, Edward Hyde, earl of. *The History of the Rebellion and Civil Wars in England.* 2 vols. Oxford: University Press, 1840.

Clark, G. N. *The Later Stuarts, 1660–1714.* 1934. Oxford: Clarendon Press, 1955.

Clark, Henry W. *History of English Nonconformity.* London: Chapman & Hall, 1913.

Cleal, Edward E. *The Story of Congregationalism in Surrey.* London: Clarke, 1908.

Clifton, Robin. *The Last Popular Rebellion.* London: Maurice Temple Smith, 1984.

Clode, Charles M. *London during the Great Rebellion.* London: Harrison & Sons, 1892.

Cohen, Ralph. "The Augustan Mode in English Poetry." *ECS* 1 (1967): 3–32.

Coleman, D. C. "An Innovation and Its Diffusion: The 'New Draperies.'" *EcHR* 22 (1969): 417–29.

Colie, Rosalie. *Resources of Kind.* Berkeley and Los Angeles: University of California Press, 1973.

Collinson, Patrick. "Towards a Broader Understanding of the Early Dissenting Tradition." In *The Dissenting Tradition,* edited by C. R. Cole and M. E. Moody. Athens, Ohio: Ohio University Press, 1975.

[Cokayne, G. E.] *Some Notice of Various Families of the Name of Marsh.* N.p., 1900.

Cook, R. I. "'Mr. *Examiner*' and 'Mr. *Review*': The Tory Apologetics of Swift and Defoe." *HLQ* 29 (1965): 127–46.

Coombs, Douglas. *The Conduct of the Dutch: British Opinion and the Dutch Alliance during the War of Spanish Succession.* The Hague: Martinus Nijhoff, 1958.

Couper, W. J. *Watson's Preface to the "History of Printing," 1713.* Edinburgh: Darien Press, 1913.

———. "The Writings and Controversies of James Clark, Minister at Glasgow, 1702–1724." *Records of the Glasgow Bibliographical Society* 11 (1933): 73–95.

Coutts, J. *A History of the University of Glasgow.* Glasgow, 1909.

Cowie, Leonard W. *Henry Newman, An American in London.* London: SPCK, 1956.

Cragg, Gerald R. *Puritanism in the Period of the Great Persecution, 1660–1688.* Cambridge: Cambridge University Press, 1957.

Cuddon, J. A. *A Dictionary of Literary Terms*. Garden City, N.Y.: Doubleday, 1971.

Cumberlege, Geoffrey. *The Corporation of London*. London: Oxford University Press, 1950.

Cunnington, Phyllis, and Catherine Lucas. *Costume for Birth, Marriages and Deaths*. New York: Barnes & Noble, 1972.

Curtis, Laura A. *The Elusive Daniel Defoe*. Totowa, N.J.: Barnes & Noble, 1984.

Curtis, T. C., and W. A. Speck. "The Societies for the Reformation of Manners. A Case Study in the Theory and Practice of Moral Reform." *Literature and History*, no. 3 (March 1976): 45–64.

Dale, R. W. *History of English Congregationalism*. London: Hodder & Stoughton, 1907.

Damrosch, Leopold. *God's Plot and Man's Stories: Studies in the Fictional Imagination from Milton to Fielding*. Chicago: University of Chicago Press, 1985.

Davie, Donald. *A Gathered Church: The Literature of the English Dissenting Interest*. London: Routledge & Kegan Paul, 1978.

Davies, K. G. *The Royal African Company*. London: Longmans, Green, 1957.

Davis, Charles T. *A Practical Treatise on the Manufacture of Bricks, Tiles, Terra-Cotta, Etc*. 2d ed. Philadelphia: Henry Carey Baird & Co., 1889.

Davis, John H. *Robert Harley as Secretary of State, 1704–1708*. Chicago: University of Chicago Libraries, 1934.

Davis, Lennard. *Factual Fictions: The Origins of the English Novel*. New York: Columbia University Press, 1983.

deGategno, Paul J. "Daniel Defoe's Newgate Biographies: An Economic Crisis." *CLIO* 13 (1984): 157–70.

Dickinson, H. T. *Bolingbroke*. London: Constable, 1970.

———. "The October Club." *HLQ* 33 (1969–70): 155–58.

———. *Walpole and the Whig Supremacy*. [London]: English Universities Press, [1973].

Dickson, P. G. M. *The Financial Revolution in England*. London: Macmillan, 1967.

Dijkstra, Bram. *Defoe and Economics: The Fortunes of Roxana in the History of Interpretation*. London: Macmillan, 1987.

Dobrée, Bonamy. *William Penn: Quaker and Pioneer*. London: Constable, 1932.

Dobson, Edward. *Rudiments of the Art of Making Bricks and Tiles*. London, 1850.

Dottin, Paul. *The Life and Strange and Surprising Adventures of Daniel De Foe*. Translated by Louise Ragan. New York: Macaulay, 1929.

Doubleday, Thomas. *A Financial, Monetary, and Statistical History of England*. London: Wilson, 1847.

Douglas, Audrey W. "Cotton Textiles in England: The East India Company's Attempt to Exploit Developments in Fashion, 1660–1721." *Journal of British Studies* 8 (1969): 28–43.

Downie, J. Alan. "Daniel Defoe and the General Election of 1708 in Scotland." *ECS* 8 (1974–75): 315–28.

———. "Daniel Defoe's *Review* and Other Political Writings in the Reign of Queen Anne." Master's thesis. University of Newcastle upon Tyne, 1973.

———. "Defoe and *The Advantages of Scotland by an Incorporate Union with England*: An Attribution Reviewed." *PBSA* 71 (1977): 489–93.

———. "Defoe, Imperialism, and the Travel Books Reconsidered." *YES* 13 (1983): 74–83.

———. "Defoe's *Shortest Way with the Dissenters*: Irony, Intention, and Reader-Response." *Prose Studies* 9 (1986): 120–39.

————. "Growth of Government Tolerance of the Press to 1790." In *Development of the English Book Trade, 1700–1899*, edited by Robin Myers and Michael Harris. 1981. Oxford: Oxford Polytechnic Press, 1982.

————. *Jonathan Swift: Political Writer*. London: Routledge & Kegan Paul, 1984.

————. "Mr. Review and His Scribbling Friends: Defoe and the Critics, 1705–1706." *HLQ* 41 (1977–78): 345–66.

————. *Robert Harley and the Press*. Cambridge: Cambridge University Press, 1979.

————. "Secret Service Payments to Daniel Defoe." *RES*, n.s., 30 (1979): 437–41.

————. "An Unknown Defoe Broadsheet on the Regulation of the Press?" *The Library* 33 (1978): 51–58.

Drysdale, Alexander Hutton. *History of the Presbyterians in England*. London: Publication Committee of the Presbyterian Church of England, 1889.

Duckworth, Alistair. "'Whig' Landscapes in Defoe's *Tour*." *PQ* 61 (1982): 453–65.

Duncan, J. "Daniel Defoe and His Connection with Bury St. Edmunds."

Dunn, Richard S. "Servants and Slaves: The Recruitment and Employment of Labor." In *Colonial British America: Essays in the New History of the Early Modern Era*, edited by Jack P. Greene and J. R. Pole. Baltimore: Johns Hopkins University Press, 1984.

Dunne, John. *The Political Thought of John Locke*. Cambridge: Cambridge University Press, 1969.

Durie, Alastair J. *The Scottish Linen Industry in the Eighteenth Century*. Edinburgh: John Donald, 1979.

Earle, Peter. *Monmouth's Rebels*. London: Weidenfeld & Nicolson, 1977.

————. *The World of Defoe*. London: Weidenfeld & Nicolson, 1976.

"Early Nonconformist Academies." *Transactions of the Congregational Historical Society* 3 (1907–8): 157–94.

Edel, Leon. *Literary Biography: The Alexander Lectures, 1955–56*. Toronto: University of Toronto Press, 1957.

Ehrenpreis, Irvin. *Swift: The Man, His Works, and the Age*. 3 vols. Cambridge, Mass.: Harvard University Press, 1962–83.

Eirionnach [pseud.]. "Quotations in 'Robinson Crusoe.'" *N&Q*, 4th ser., 7 (1871): 426–27.

Elkington, George. *The Coopers: Company and Craft*. London: Sampson, Low, Marston, 1933.

Ellis, E. L. "William III and the Politicians." In *Britain after the Glorious Revolution, 1689–1714*, edited by Geoffrey Holmes. London: Macmillan, 1969.

Ellis, Frank. "Defoe's 'Resignacion' and the Limitations of Mathematical Plainness." *RES*, n.s., 36 (1985): 338–54.

————, ed. *Swift versus Mainwaring*. Oxford: Clarendon Press, 1985.

Ellis, S. M. "Epilogue: Jack Sheppard in Literature and Drama." In *Jack Sheppard*, by Horace Bleackley. Edinburgh: Hodge, 1933.

Emberton, Wilfrid. *Skippon's Brave Boys: The Origins, Development and Civil War Service of London's Trained Bands*. Buckingham: Barracuda, 1984.

English Historical Documents, 1714–1783. 12 vols. London: Eyre & Spottiswoode, 1957.

Erickson, Robert A. *Mother Midnight*. New York: AMS, 1986.

Ewald, William B. *Rogues, Royalty and Reporters*. Boston: Houghton Mifflin, 1957.

Ewing, Dessagene C. "The First Printing of Defoe's *Family Instructor*." *PBSA* 65 (1971): 269–72.

Fairchilds, Cissie. *Domestic Enemies*. Baltimore: Johns Hopkins University Press, 1984.

Faller, Lincoln B. "In Contrast to Defoe: The Rev. Paul Lorrain, Historian of Crime." *HLQ* (1976): 59–78.

———. *Turned to Account: The Forms and Functions of Criminal Biography*. Cambridge: Cambridge University Press, 1987.

Fenwick, Hubert. *The Auld Alliance*. Kineton, Warwick: Roundwood Press, 1971.

Ferguson, William. *Scotland, 1689 to the Present*. 1968. Edinburgh: Oliver & Boyd, 1977.

———. *Scotland's Relations with England: A Survey to 1707*. Edinburgh: John Donald, 1977.

Fernsemer, O. F. W. "Daniel Defoe and the Palatine Emigration of 1709." *JEGP* 19 (1920): 103–10.

Firth, C. H. *Naval Songs and Ballads*. Publications of the Navy Records Society 33 (1908).

Foord, Archibald S. *His Majesty's Opposition, 1714–1830*. Oxford: Clarendon Press, 1964.

Forster, John. *Daniel De Foe and Charles Churchill*. London, 1855.

Foss, Edward. *A Biographical Dictionary of the Judges of England from the Conquest to the Present Time*. London: Murray, 1870.

Frazer, James G. *The Golden Bough*. New York: Macmillan, 1960.

Furbank, P. N., and W. R. Owens. *The Canonisation of Defoe*. New Haven: Yale University Press, 1988.

———. "Defoe and the 'Improvisatory' Sentence." *ES* 67 (1986): 157–66.

———. "What If Defoe Did Not Write the *History of the Wars of Charles XII?*" *PBSA* 80 (1986): 333–47.

Galenson, David W. *White Servitude in Colonial America: An Economic Analysis*. Cambridge: Cambridge University Press, 1981.

George, M. Dorothy. *English Political Caricature to 1792*. Oxford: Clarendon Press, 1959.

[Gillespy, Thomas]. *Some Account of the Worshipful Company of Salters*. London: Metcalfe, 1827.

Gillis, John R. "Married but Not Churched: Plebian Sexual Relations and Marital Nonconformity in Eighteenth-Century Britain." *Eighteenth-Century Life*, n.s., 9, no. 3 (1985): 31–60.

Gipson, Lawrence H. *The Southern Plantations*. Vol. 2 of *The British Empire before the American Revolution*. 10 vols. Caldwell, Idaho: Caxton Printers, 1936.

Girdler, Lew. "Defoe's Education at Newington Green Academy." *SP* 50 (1953): 573–91.

Gittings, Clare. *Death, Burial and the Individual in Early Modern England*. London: Croom Helm, 1984.

Goldgar, Bertrand. *The Curse of Party*. Lincoln: University of Nebraska Press, 1961.

Goldie, Mark. "The Revolution of 1689 and the Structure of Political Argument: An Essay and an Annotated Bibliography of Pamphlets on the Allegiance Controversy." *Bulletin of Research in the Humanities* 83 (1980): 473–564.

Gomme, George L. *The Governance of London*. London: Unwin, 1907.

Gove, Philip. *The Imaginary Voyage in Prose Fiction*. New York: Columbia University Press, 1941.

Graham, Henry G. *The Social Life of Scotland in the Eighteenth Century*. London: Adam & Charles Black, 1906.

Grant, Alexander. *The Story of the University of Edinburgh*. 2 vols. London: Longmans, Green, 1884.

Gray, John M., ed. *Memoirs of the Life of Sir John Clerk*. Edinburgh: Constable, 1892.

Green, David. *Queen Anne*. New York: Scribner's, 1970.

Green, Thomas A. "The Jury, Seditious Libel, and the Criminal Law." In *Juries, Libel and Justice*. Los Angeles: Clark Library, 1984.

———. *Verdict According to Conscience: Perspectives on the English Criminal Trial Jury, 1200–1800*. Chicago: University of Chicago Press, 1985.

Gregg, Edward. "The Jacobite Career of John, Earl of Mar." In *Ideology and Conspiracy: Aspects of Jacobitism, 1689–1759*, edited by Eveline Cruikshanks. Edinburgh: John Donald, 1982.

Grente, Georges, Albert Pauphilet, Louis Pichard, Robert Barroux, and Maxime Gorce, eds. *Dictionnaire des lettres françaises*. 5 vols. Paris: A. Fayard, 1951–.

Grey, Charles. *Pirates of the Eastern Seas*. London: Kennikat, 1933.

Groves, Thomas B. "Daniel De Foe in Dorsetshire." *Proceedings of the Dorset Natural History and Antiquarian Field Club* 2 (1878): 67–75.

Guimaraens, A. J. C. "Daniel Defoe and the Family of Foe." *N&Q*, 11th ser., 5 (1912): 241–43.

Hamburger, Philip. "The Development of the Law of Seditious Libel and the Control of the Press." *Stanford Law Review* 37 (1985): 661–765.

Hamilton, Elizabeth. *The Backstairs Dragon*. New York: Taplinger, 1969.

Hans, Nicholas. *New Trends in the Eighteenth Century*. London: Routledge & Kegan Paul, 1951.

Hanson, Laurence. *The Government and the Press, 1695–1763*. London: Humphrey Milford, 1936.

Harris, Michael. "Periodicals and the Book Trade." In *Development of the English Book Trade, 1700–1899*, edited by Robin Myers and Michael Harris. 1981. Oxford: Oxford Polytechnic Press, 1982.

———. "Trials and Criminal Biographies." In *Sale and Distribution of Books*, edited by Robin Myers and Michael Harris. Oxford: Oxford Polytechnic Press, 1982.

Hatin, Eugene. *Bibliographie historique et critique de la presse périodique française*. Paris: Editions Anthropos, 1965.

Hatton, Ragnhild. *George I: Elector and King*. Cambridge, Mass.: Harvard University Press, 1978.

Healey, George. *The Letters of Daniel Defoe*. 1955. Oxford: Clarendon Press, 1969.

Hecht, J. Jean. *The Domestic Servant Class in Eighteenth-Century England*. London: Routledge & Kegan Paul, 1956.

Heidenreich, Helmut. *The Libraries of Daniel Defoe and Phillips Farewell*. Berlin: Hildebrand, 1970.

Henderson, Alfred James. *London and the National Government, 1721–1742*. Durham: Duke University Press, 1945.

Herford, C. H., and Percy Simpson, eds. *Ben Jonson*. 11 vols. Oxford: Clarendon Press, 1925–52.

Heron, Alexander. *The Rise and Progress of the Company of Merchants of the City of Edinburgh, 1681–1902*. Edinburgh: Clark, 1903.

Hill, B. W. "The Change of Government and the 'Loss of the City,' 1710–1711." *Economic History Review*, 2d ser., 24 (1971): 395–413.

———. "Oxford, Bolingbroke, and the Peace of Utrecht." *Historical Journal* 16 (1973): 241–63.

Hill, Christopher. *The Century of Revolution, 1603–1714.* 1961. New York: Norton, 1980.

———. *Change and Continuity in Seventeenth-Century England.* Cambridge, Mass.: Harvard University Press, 1975.

———. *Society and Puritanism in Pre-Revolutionary England.* 2d ed. New York: Schocken, 1967.

Hipwell, Daniel. "Daniel De Foe." *N&Q,* 7th ser., 6 (1888): 105.

Historical Manuscripts Commission. *Eighth Report of the Royal Commission on Historical Manuscripts.* London: HMSO, 1881.

Holdsworth, William. *A History of English Law.* 12 vols. London: Methuen, 1938.

Holmes, Geoffrey S. "The Commons' Division on 'No Peace without Spain,' 7 December 1711." *Bulletin of the Institute of Historical Research* 33 (1960): 223–34.

———. *The Trial of Dr. Sacheverell.* London: Methuen, 1973.

Holmes, Geoffrey, and W. A. Speck. "The Fall of Harley in 1708 Reconsidered." *EHR* 80 (1965): 673–98.

Hoppit, Julian. "Financial Crises in Eighteenth-Century England." *Economic History Review*, 2d. ser., 39 (1986): 39–58.

Hornberger, T. Introduction to the *Compendium Physicae* in Publications of the Colonial Society of Massachusetts, vol. 33. Boston: Merrymount, 1940.

Horner, Samuel. *A Brief Account of the Interesting Ceremony of Unveiling the Monument . . . to the memory of Daniel Defoe.* Southampton: Alfred Dyer, 1871.

Horsley, L. S. "Rogues or Honest Gentlemen: The Public Character of Queen Anne Journalists." *TSLL* 18 (1976–77): 198–228.

Horwitz, Henry. *Parliament, Policy, and Politics in the Reign of William.* Newark, Del.: University of Delaware Press, 1977.

Howard, William J. "Truth Preserves Her Shape: An Unexplored Influence on Defoe's Prose Style." *PQ* 47 (1968): 193–205.

Howson, Gerald. *Thief-Taker General: Jonathan Wild and the Emergence of Crime and Corruption as a Way of Life in Eighteenth-Century England.* New Brunswick, N.J.: Transaction Books, 1970.

Hull, N. E. H. *Female Felons.* Urbana: University of Illinois, 1987.

Hulme, Peter. *Colonial Encounters.* London: Methuen, 1986.

Hultin, Neil C. "Medicine and Magic in the Eighteenth Century: The Diaries of James Woodforde." *Journal of the History of Medicine and Allied Sciences* 25 (1975): 349–66.

Hunter, J. Paul. "Friday as a Convert: Defoe and the Accounts of Indian Missionaries." *RES* 14 (1963): 243–48.

———. "The Insistent I." *Novel* 13 (1979): 19–37.

———. *The Reluctant Pilgrim: Defoe's Emblematic Method and Quest for Form in "Robinson Crusoe."* Baltimore: Johns Hopkins Press, 1966.

Hutton, Stanley. *Bristol and Its Famous Associations.* Bristol: Arrowsmith, 1907.

Illingworth, Edgar. "The Economic Ideas of Daniel Defoe." 2 vols. Ph.D. diss., University of Leeds, 1974.

Ireland, Mary E. "The Defoe Family in America." *Scribner's Monthly* 12 (1876): 61–64.

Irons, James C. *Leith and its Antiquities*. 2 vols. Edinburgh: Morrison & Gibbs, [1898].

Iványi, B. G. "Defoe's Prelude to the Family Instructor." *TLS* 7 April 1966, 312.

Jacob, Margaret. Review of Richard Westfall's *Never at Rest: A Biography of Isaac Newton*. *ECS* 16 (1983): 317–21.

James, E. Anthony. "Defoe's Autobiographical Apologia: Rhetorical Slanting in *An Appeal to Honour and Justice*." *Costerus: Essays in English and American Language and Literature* 4 (1972): 69–86.

Jameson, John Franklin. *Privateering and Piracy in the Colonial Period*. New York: Macmillan, 1923.

Jewitt, Llewellyn. "The Pillory, and Who They Put in It." *The Reliquary* 1 (1860–61): 209–24.

John, A. H. "War and the English Economy, 1700–1763." *Economic History Review*, 2d ser., 7 (1955): 329–44.

Jones, J. R. *Country and Court*. 1978. Cambridge, Mass.: Harvard University Press, 1979.

———. *The First Whigs: The Politics of the Exclusion Crisis, 1678–1683*. London: Oxford University Press, 1961.

Jones, Philip E. *The Butchers of London*. London: Secker & Warburg, 1976.

Joyce, James. "Daniel Defoe." Edited and translated by Joseph Prescott. *Buffalo Studies* 1 (1964): 5–27.

Karraker, Cyrus H. *Piracy Was a Business*. Rindge, N.H.: Richard R. Smith, 1953.

Keeble, N. H. *The Literary Culture of Nonconformity in Later Seventeenth-Century England*. [Leicester]: Leicester University Press, 1987.

Kennedy, Joyce Deveau. "Defoe's *An Essay upon Projects*: The Order of Issues." *SB* 23 (1970): 170–75.

Kenyon, J. P. "The Revolution of 1688. Resistance and Contact." In *Historical Perspectives: Studies in English Thought and Society*, edited by Neil McKendrick. London: Europa Publications, 1974.

———. *Revolution Principles: The Politics of Party, 1689–1720*. Cambridge: Cambridge University Press, 1977.

Kilby, Kenneth. *The Cooper and His Trade*. London: John Baker, 1971.

Knox-Shaw, Peter. *The Explorer in English Fiction*. New York: St. Martin's Press, 1986.

Kramnick, Isaac. *Bolingbroke and His Circle*. Cambridge, Mass.: Harvard University Press, 1968.

Kropf, C. R. "The Sale of Defoe's Library." *PBSA* 65 (1971): 123–33.

Landa, Louis A. Introduction to *A Journal of the Plague Year*, by Daniel Defoe. London: Oxford University Press, 1969.

Laslett, Peter. *Family Life and Illicit Love in Earlier Generations*. New York: Cambridge University Press, 1977.

———. *The World We Have Lost Further Explored*. 1965. New York: Scribner's, 1984.

Leasor, James. *The Plague and the Fire*. New York: McGraw-Hill, [c. 1961].

[Lee, John]. *Memorial for the Bible Societies in Scotland*. Edinburgh: Edinburgh Bible Society, 1824.

Lee, William. *Daniel Defoe: His Life and Hitherto Unknown Writings*. 3 vols. London: Hotten, 1869.

Lenman, Bruce. *The Jacobite Risings in Britain, 1689–1746*. London: Methuen, 1980.

Leranbaum, Miriam. "'An *Irony Not Unusual*': Defoe's *Shortest Way with the Dissenters*," *HLQ* 37 (1974): 234–45.

Levin, David. *Cotton Mather*. Cambridge, Mass.: Harvard University Press, 1978.

Levin, Jennifer. *The Charter Controversy in the City of London, 1660–1688, and Its Consequences*. London: Athlone, 1969.

Lillywhite, Bryant. *London Coffee Houses: A Reference Book of Coffee Houses of the Seventeenth, Eighteenth, and Nineteenth Centuries*. London: Allen & Unwin, 1963.

Little, Bryan. *Crusoe's Captain: Being the Life of Woodes Rogers*. London: Odhams Press, 1960.

———. *The Monmouth Episode*. London: Werner Laurie, 1956.

Loiseau, Jean. *Abraham Cowley's Reputation in England*. Paris: Henri Didier, 1931.

Macaree, David. *Daniel Defoe and the Jacobite Movement*. Salzburg: Institut für Anglistik und Amerikanistik, 1980.

———. "Daniel Defoe, the Church of Scotland, and the Union of 1707." *Eighteenth Century Studies* 7 (1973–74): 62–65.

———. "The Flyting of Daniel Defoe and Lord Belhaven." *Studies in Scottish Literature* 13 (1978): 72–80.

Macaulay, Thomas B. *The History of England*. New York: Harper & Brothers, 1849.

McBurney, William. "Edmund Curll, Mrs. Jane Barker, and the English Novel." *PQ* 37 (1958): 385–99.

M'Crie, Thomas. *Annals of English Presbytery: From the Earliest Period to the Present Time*. London, 1872.

McElroy, Davis D. "A Century of Scottish Clubs, 1700–1800." 2 vols. Diss., University of Edinburgh, 1969.

McEwen, Gilbert. *The Oracle of the Coffee House*. San Marino, Calif.: Huntington Library, 1972.

Mackay, Charles. *Extraordinary Popular Delusions and the Madness of Crowds*. New York: Harmony Books, 1980.

McKay, Derek. "Bolingbroke, Oxford and the Defence of the Utrecht Settlement in Southern Europe." *English Historical Review* 86 (1971): 264–84.

MacKenzie, W. C. *Andrew Fletcher of Saltoun*. Edinburgh: Porpoise Press, 1935.

McKeon, Michael. *The Origins of the English Novel, 1600–1740*. Baltimore: Johns Hopkins University Press, 1987.

MacKinnon, James. *The Union of England and Scotland*. London: Longmans, Green, 1896.

MacLachlan, A. D. "The Road to Peace, 1710–1714." In *Britain after the Glorious Revolution, 1689–1714*, edited by Geoffrey Holmes. London: Macmillan, 1969.

McLachlan, H. *English Education under the Test Acts*. Manchester: Manchester University Press, 1931.

Maclean, Hugh N. "Fulke Greville: Kingship and Sovereignty." *HLQ* 16 (1952–53): 237–71.

MacPike, Eugene. *Helvelius, Flamstead, and Halley: Three Contemporary Astronomers*. London: Taylor & Francis, 1937.

Madan, F. F., and W. A. Speck. *A Critical Bibliography of Dr. Henry Sacheverell*. Lawrence: University of Kansas Libraries, 1978.

Malcolmson, Robert. *Life and Labour in England, 1700–1780*. New York: St. Martin's Press, 1981.

Marks, Sylvia K. *Sir Charles Grandison*. Lewisburg, Pa.: Bucknell University Press, 1986.

Marshall, David. *The Figure of the Theatre*. New York: Columbia University Press, 1986.

Marshall, Gordon. *Presbyteries and Profits*. Oxford: Clarendon Press, 1980.

Maslen, K. I. D. "Edition Quantities for *Robinson Crusoe*." *The Library*, 5th ser., 24 (1969): 145–50.

Mason, John E. *Gentlefolk in the Making*. Philadelphia: University of Pennsylvania Press, 1935.

Mathias, Peter. *The Transformation of England*. New York: Columbia University Press, 1979.

Matthews, A. G. *Calamy Revised*. Oxford: Clarendon Press, 1934.

Maxfield, Ezra Kempton. "Daniel Defoe and the Quakers." *PMLA* 47 (1932): 179–90.

Mayo, Robert D. *The English Novel in the Magazines, 1740–1815*. Evanston, Ill.: Northwestern University Press, 1962.

"The Mayors of Shrewsbury." *Transactions of the Shropshire Archaelogical Society*, 4th ser., 3 (1913).

Melton, Frank. *Sir Robert Clayton and the Origins of English Deposit Banking, 1658–1685*. Cambridge: Cambridge University Press, 1986.

Michael, Wolfgang. *England under George I: The Beginnings of the Hanoverian Dynasty*. London: Macmillan, 1936.

Middlekauff, Robert. *The Mathers*. New York: Oxford University Press, 1971.

Monier-Williams, Randall. *The Tallow Chandlers of London*. London: Kaye & Ward, 1970.

Moore, J. R. "The Canon of Defoe's Writings." *The Library*, 5th ser., 11 (1956): 155–69.

———. *A Checklist of the Writings of Daniel Defoe*. 1960. Hamden, Conn.: Archon, 1971.

———. "Daniel Defoe, Ambidextrous Mercury." *Periodical Post Boy* 11 (1952): 1–2.

———. *Daniel Defoe: Citizen of the Modern World*. 1958. Chicago: University of Chicago Press, 1966.

———. "Defoe Acquisitions at the Huntington Library." *HLQ* 28 (1964): 47–53.

———. "Defoe and the Rev. James Hart: A Chapter in High Finance." *PQ* 19 (1940): 404–12.

———. "Defoe, Steele, and the Demolition of Dunkirk." *HLQ* 13 (1949–50): 279–302.

———. "Defoe's Hand in *A Journal of the Earl of Marr's Proceedings* (1716)." *HLQ* 17 (1954): 209–28.

———. "Defoe's Lampoon: *A Speech of a Stone Chimney Piece*." *Boston Public Library Quarterly* 9 (1957): 139–42.

———. "Defoe's Use of Personal Experience in *Colonel Jack*." *MLN* 54 (1939): 362–63.

Morgan, William T. *English Political Parties and Leaders in the Reign of Queen Anne, 1702–1710*. New Haven: Yale University Press, 1920.

Morison, Samuel Eliot. *Harvard College in the Seventeenth Century*. Cambridge, Mass.: Harvard University Press, 1936.

Morrison, Herbert. *How London Is Governed*. London: People's Universities Press, 1949.

Moule, H. J. *Descriptive Catalogue of the Charters, Minute Books . . . of Weymouth and Melcombe Regis*. Weymouth: Shirren & Son, 1883.

Mumby, Frank A. *Publishing and Bookselling. Part One: From the Earliest Times to 1870*. London: Jonathan Cape, 1974.

Mumby, Frank A., Norma Hodgson, and Cyprian Blagden. *The Notebook of Thomas Bennet and Henry Clements (1689–1719)*. Oxford: Oxford University Press, 1956.

Mundy, P. D. "The Ancestry of Daniel Defoe." *N&Q* 174 (1938): 112–14.

———. "The Wife of Daniel Defoe." *N&Q* 203 (1958): 296–98.

Munimenta alme universitatis Glasguensis. 4 vols. Edited by C. Innes. Glasgow, 1854.

Myers, Robin. *The British Book Trade from Caxton to the Present Day*. London: André Deutsch, 1973.

Myers, Robin, and Michael Harris. *Development of the English Book Trade, 1700–1899*. 1981. Oxford: Oxford Polytechnic Press, 1982.

Needham, G. B. "Mary de la Rivière Manley, Tory Defender." *HLQ* 12 (1949): 253–88.

Nethercot, Arthur H. "The Reputation of Abraham Cowley (1660–1800)." *PMLA* 38 (1923): 588–641.

Nevo, Ruth. *The Dial of Virtue*. Princeton: Princeton University Press, 1963.

The New Cambridge Modern History. 14 vols. Cambridge: Cambridge University Press, 1957–70.

Newton, John A. "Samuel Annesley (1620–1696)." *Proceedings of the Wesley Historical Society* 95 (1985): 29–45.

———. *Susanna Wesley and the Puritan Tradition in Methodism*. London: Epworth, 1968.

Newton, Theodore. "The Civet-Cats of Newington Green: New Light on Defoe." *RES* 13 (1937): 10–19.

Nicolson, William. *The British Encyclopedia or Dictionary of Arts and Sciences*. London: Whittingham, 1809.

Novak, Maximillian E. "Crusoe the King and the Political Evolution of His Island." *SEL* 2 (1962): 337–50.

———. "Daniel Defoe." In *The New Cambridge Bibliography of English Literature*, vol. 2, edited by George Watson. Cambridge: Cambridge University Press, 1971.

———. "Defoe and the Disordered City." *PMLA* 92 (1977): 241–52.

———. *Defoe and the Nature of Man*. London: Oxford University Press, 1963.

———. "Defoe's Shortest Way with the Dissenters." *MLQ* 27 (1966): 402–17.

———. "Defoe's Theory of Fiction." *SP* 61 (1964): 650–68.

———. *Economics and the Fiction of Daniel Defoe*. Berkeley and Los Angeles: University of California Press, 1962.

———. "Fiction and Society in the Early Eighteenth Century." In *England in the Restoration and Early Eighteenth Century: Essays on Culture and Society*, edited by H. T. Swedenberg. Berkeley and Los Angeles: University of California Press, 1972.

———. "History, Ideology and the Methods of Defoe's Historical Fiction." In *Studies in the Eighteenth Century*, vol. 4, edited by R. F. Brissenden and J. C. Eade. Canberra: Australian National University Press, 1979.

———. *Realism, Myth, and History in Defoe's Fiction*. Lincoln: University of Nebraska Press, 1983.

———. "Robinson Crusoe's Fear and the Search for Natural Man." *MP* 58 (1961): 238–45.

———. "Sincerity, Delusion, and Character in the Fiction of Defoe and the 'Sincerity Crisis' of His Time." In *Augustan Studies*, edited by Douglas Patey and Timothy Keegan. Newark, Del.: University of Delaware Press, 1985.

———. "A Whiff of Scandal in the Life of Daniel Defoe." *HLQ* 34 (1970–71): 35–42.

Nuttall, Geoffrey F. *Richard Baxter*. London: Nelson, 1965.

Ogden, J. H. "Antiquarians at Ovenden." *Transactions of the Halifax Antiquarian Society* (1905): 213–15; (1925): 92–5; (1929): 219–21.

Oliphant, M. O. W. "The Author of *Robinson Crusoe*." *Century* 24 (1893): 740–53.

Omond, George W. T. *The Lord Advocates of Scotland*. 2 vols. Edinburgh: David Douglas, 1883.

Orridge, B. B. *Some Account of the Citizens of London and Their Rulers*. London: Tegg, 1867.

Overton, John, and Frederic Relton. *The English Church, from the Accession of George I to the End of the Eighteenth Century*. London: Macmillan, 1906.

Owen, J. H. *War at Sea Under Queen Anne, 1702–1708*. Cambridge: Cambridge University Press, 1938.

Owens, W. R., and N. P. Furbank. "Defoe and the Dutch Alliance." *British Journal for Eighteenth-Century Studies* 9 (1986): 169–82.

Oxford Historical Register, 1220–1900. Oxford: Clarendon Press, 1900.

Pafford, J. H. P. "Defoe's Proposals for Printing the *History of the Union*." *The Library*, 5th ser., 11 (1956): 202–6.

Parkes, Joan. *Travel in England in the Seventeenth Century*. London: Oxford University Press, 1925.

Parks, Stephen. *John Dunton and the English Book Trade*. New York: Garland, 1976.

Parsons, Coleman O. "Ghost Stories before Defoe." *N&Q* 201 (1956): 293–98.

Payne, William L. *Mr. Review*. Morningside Heights, N.Y.: King's Crown Press, 1947.

Pearce, Arthur. *The History of the Butchers' Company*. London: Meat Trades' Journal, 1929.

Peterson, Spiro. "Daniel Defoe and 'City Customes.'" *N&Q* 203 (1958): 400.

———. "Defoe and Westminster, 1696–1706." *ECS* 12 (1978–79): 306–38.

———. "Defoe in Edinburgh, 1707." *HLQ* 38 (1974–75): 21–33.

Piesse, G. W. Septimus. *Art of Perfumery*. London, 1855.

Plomer, Henry. *A Dictionary of Printers and Booksellers . . . from 1688 to 1725*. Oxford: Oxford University Press, 1922.

Plumb, J. H. *The First Four Georges*. New York: Macmillan, 1957.

Pocock, J. G. A. *The Machiavellian Moment*. Princeton: Princeton University Press, 1975.

———. "The Myth of John Locke and the Obsession with Liberalism." Los Angeles: Clark Library, 1980.

Poems on Affairs of State: Augustan Satirical Verse, 1660–1714. 7 vols. Edited by George deF. Lord. New Haven: Yale University Press, 1963–75.

Pollock, Frederick, and F. Maitland. *The History of English Law*. 2 vols. Cambridge: Cambridge University Press, 1898.

Portus, Garnet V. *Caritas Anglicana*. London: Mowbray, 1912.

Poston, Lawrence. "Defoe and the Peace Campaign, 1710–1713: A Reconsideration." *HLQ* 27 (1963): 1–20.

Potter, George R. "Henry Baker, F.R.S. (1698–1774)." *MP* 29 (1932): 301–21.

Powell, Chilton L. *English Domestic Relation, 1487–1653*. New York: Columbia University Press, 1917.

Powell, L. "Defoe and Drelincourt." *TLS*, 7 February 1929, 98.

Powicke, Frederick J. *The Reverend Richard Baxter under the Cross (1662–1691)*. London: Jonathan Cape, 1927.

Price, David. *Magic: A Pictorial History of Conjurers in the Theater*. Cranbury, N.J.: Cornwall Books, 1985.

Price, Martin. *To the Palace of Wisdom*. Garden City, N.Y.: Doubleday, 1964.

Puncle, Bertram S. *Funeral Customs: Their Origin and Development*. New York: Stokes, 1962.

Quarrell, W. H., and Margaret Mare, eds. *London in 1710, from the Travels of Zacharias Conrad von Uffenbach*. London: Faber & Faber, [1934].

Quincy, Josiah. *The History of Harvard University*. Cambridge, Mass.: John Owen, 1840.

Radzinowicz, Leon. *A History of English Criminal Law and Its Administration*. 5 vols. London: Stevens, 1948–56.

Realey, Charles B. "*The London Journal* and Its Authors, 1720–1723." *Bulletin of the University of Kansas Studies* 36 (1935): 1–38.

Reddaway, T. F. *The Rebuilding of London after the Great Fire*. London: Jonathan Cape, 1940.

Rees, Joan. *Fulke Greville, Lord Brooke, 1554–1628*. London: Routledge & Kegan Paul, 1971.

Richetti, John. *Defoe's Narratives: Situations and Structures*. Oxford: Clarendon Press, 1975.

———. "The Family, Sex, and Marriage in Defoe's *Moll Flanders* and *Roxana*." *SLI* 15, no. 2 (1982): 19–35.

———. *Popular Fiction before Richardson*. Oxford: Clarendon Press, 1969.

Riley, P. W. J. *The English Ministers and Scotland, 1707–1727*. London: Athlone Press, 1964.

———. *The Union of England and Scotland: A Study in Anglo-Scottish Politics of the Eighteenth Century*. Manchester: Manchester University Press, 1978.

Robbins, Alfred F. "Daniel Defoe." *N&Q*, 9th ser., 5 (1900): 285.

Rogers, H. C. B. *The British Army of the Eighteenth Century*. London: Allen & Unwin, 1977.

Rogers, Nicholas. "Popular Protest in Early Hanoverian London." *Past and Present* 79 (1978): 70–100.

Rogers, Pat. "Addenda and Corrigenda: Moore's *Checklist* of Defoe." *PBSA* 75 (1981): 60–64.

———. "Classics and Chapbooks." In *Books and Their Readers in Eighteenth-Century England*, edited by Isabel Rivers. New York: St. Martin's Press, 1982.

———. "Defoe as Plagiarist: Camden's *Brittania* and *A Tour thro' the Whole Island of Great Britain*." *PQ* 52 (1973): 771–74.

———. "Defoe at Work: The Making of *A Tour thro' Great Britain*, Vol 1." *New York Public Library Bulletin* 78 (1974–75): 431–50.

———. "Defoe in Fleet Street Prison." *RES*, n.s., 22 (1971): 451–55.

———. "Defoe's First Official Post." *N&Q* 216 (1971): 303.

———. "The Dunce Answers Back: John Oldmixon on Swift and Defoe." *TSLL* 14 (1972–73): 33–43.

———. *Eighteenth-Century Encounters*. Brighton, Sussex: Harvester, 1985.

———. *Grub Street: Studies in a Subculture*. London: Methuen, 1972.

———. "The Guidebook as Epic." In *Eighteenth-Century Encounters*. Brighton, Sussex: Harvester, 1985.

———. Introduction to *A Tour thro' the Whole Island of Great Britain*, by Daniel Defoe. Harmondsworth: Penguin Books, 1971.

———. "The Making of Defoe's *A Tour thro' Great Britain*, Volumes II and III." *Prose Studies* 3 (1980): 109–37.

———. *Robinson Crusoe*. London: Allen & Unwin, 1979.

———. "'This Calamitous Year.'" In *Eighteenth-Century Encounters*. Brighton, Sussex: Harvester, 1985.

Rogers, Robert W. "The Early Vogue of the *Essay on Man*." Ph.D. diss., Harvard University, 1942.

Rosen, Marvin. "The Dictatorship of the Bourgeoisie: England, 1688–1721." *Science and Society* 45 (1981): 24–51.

Rosenberg, Albert. "Defoe's *Pacificator* Reconsidered." *PQ* 37 (1958): 433–39.

Rostenburg, Leona. *Literary, Political, Scientific, Religious, and Legal Publishing, Printing and Bookselling in England, 1551–1700*. New York: Burt Franklin, 1965.

Rothman, Irving N. "Defoe's *The Family Instructor*: A Response to the Schism Act." *PBSA* 74 (1980): 201–20.

Rudé, George. *Hanoverian London, 1714–1808*. Berkeley and Los Angeles: University of California Press, 1971.

Ryken, Leland. *Worldly Saints*. Grand Rapids, Mich.: Zondervan, 1986.

J. S. "Scotch Newspapers of the Age of Queen Anne." *N&Q*, 6th ser., 6 (1883): 386.

Sachse, William. *Lord Somers*. Manchester: Manchester University Press, 1975.

Sainty, J. C. "A Huguenot Civil Servant: The Career of Charles Delafaye, 1677–1762." *Proceedings of the Huguenot Society of London* 22, no. 5 (1975): 398–413.

Schacter, Stanley, William Gerin, Donald C. Hood, and Paul Andreassen. "Was the South Sea Bubble A Random Walk?" *Journal of Economic Behavior and Organization* 6 (1985): 323–29.

Schlatter, Richard B. *The Social Ideas of Religious Leaders, 1660–1688*. London: Oxford University Press, 1940.

Schneider, Ben Ross, Jr. *Index to the London Stage, 1660–1800*. Carbondale: Southern Illinois University Press, 1979.

Schochet, Gordon J. "Patriarchalism, Politics, and Mass Attitudes in Stuart England." *Historical Journal* 12 (1969): 413–41.

Schonhorn, Manuel. "Defoe's *Captain Singleton*: A Reassessment with Observations." *PLL* 7 (1971): 38–51.

Schultz, William E. *Gay's Beggar's Opera: Its Content, History and Influence*. 1923. New York: Russell & Russell, 1967.

Schwartz, Hillel. *The French Prophets: The History of a Millenarian Group in Eighteenth-Century England*. Berkeley and Los Angeles: University of California Press, 1980.

Schwoerer, Lois. "Chronology and Authorship of the Standing Army Tracts, 1697–1699." *N&Q* 211 (1966): 382–90.

———. "The Literature of the Standing Army Controversy, 1697–1699." *HLQ* 28 (1965): 187–212.

———. *No Standing Armies!* Baltimore: Johns Hopkins University Press, 1974.

Scott, William Robert. *The Constitution and Finance of English, Scottish and Irish Joint-Stock Companies to 1720*. 3 vols. New York: Peter Smith, 1951.

Scrimgeour, Gary J. "The Problem of Realism in Defoe's *Captain Singleton*." *HLQ* 17 (1954): 21–37.

Scudi, Abbie Turner. *The Sacheverell Affair*. New York: Columbia University Press, 1939.

Secord, A. W. "Defoe in Stoke Newington." *PMLA* 66 (1951): 211–25.

———. Review of *The Correspondence of Daniel Defoe*. *MP* 54 (1956–57): 45–52.

———. "A September Day in Canterbury: The Veal-Bargrave Story." *JEGP* 54 (1955): 639–50.

———. *Studies in the Narrative Method of Defoe*. New York: Russell & Russell, 1963.

Seidel, Michael. *Exile and the Narrative Imagination*. New Haven: Yale University Press, 1986.

[Sewell, T. D.]. *The Trained Bands of the City of London*. [London, 1907].

Sharpe, Reginald R. *London and the Kingdom*. 3 vols. London: Longmans, Green, 1894–95.

Shirren, A. J. *Daniel Defoe in Stoke Newington*. Stoke Newington: Public Libraries Committee, 1960.

Sill, Geoffrey. *Defoe and the Idea of Fiction*. East Brunswick, N.J.: Associated University Presses, 1983.

———. "A Report to Hanover on the 'Insolent De Foe.'" *N&Q* 28 (1981): 224–25.

———. "Rogues, Strumpets, and Vagabonds: Defoe on Crime in the City." *Eighteenth-Century Life* 2 (1976): 74–78.

Silverman, Kenneth. *The Life and Times of Cotton Mather*. New York: Harper & Row, 1984.

Singleton, Robert R. "Defoe, Moll Flanders, and the Ordinary of Newgate." *Harvard Library Bulletin* 24 (1976): 401–13.

Smith, Abbott Emerson. *Colonists in Bondage*. Chapel Hill: University of North Carolina Press, 1947.

Smith, J. W. Ashley. *The Birth of Modern Education*. London: Independent Press, 1954.

Smithers, Peter. *The Life of Joseph Addison*. 1954. Oxford: Clarendon Press, 1968.

Smout, T. C. "Union of the Parliaments." In *The Scottish Nation*, edited by Gordon Menzies. London: BBC, 1972.

Snow, Malinda. "Diabolic Intervention in Defoe's *Roxana*." *Essays in Literature* 3 (1976): 52–60.

Snyder, Henry L. "The Circulation of Newspapers in the Reign of Queen Anne." *The Library*, 5th ser., 23 (1968): 206–25.

———. "Daniel Defoe, the Duchess of Marlborough, and *The Advice to the Electors of Great Britain*." *HLQ* 29 (1965): 53–62.

———. "Godolphin and Harley: A Study of Their Partnership in Politics." *HLQ* 30 (1966–67): 241–71.

———. "Newsletters in England, 1689–1715." In *Newsletters to Newspapers: Eighteenth-Century Journalism*, edited by Donovan Bond and W. R. McLeod. Morgantown: West Virginia University Press, 1977.

———. "The Reports of a Press Spy for Robert Harley." *The Library*, 5th ser., 22 (1967): 326–45.

———, ed. *The Marlborough-Godolphin Correspondence*. 2 vols. Oxford: Clarendon Press, 1975.

Spate, O. H. K. *The Pacific since Magellan: Monopolists and Freebooters*. Minneapolis: University of Minnesota Press, 1983.

Speck, W. A. "*The Examiner* Examined: Swift's Tory Pamphleteering." In *Focus: Swift*, edited by C. J. Rawson. London: Sphere Books, 1971.

———. *Stability and Strife: England, 1714–1760*. Cambridge, Mass.: Harvard University Press, 1979.

Sperling, John G. *The South Sea Company*. Kress Library of Business and Economics, pub. no. 17. Cambridge, Mass.: Harvard University Press, 1962.

Starr, G. A. *Defoe and Casuistry*. Princeton: Princeton University Press, 1971.

———. *Defoe and Spiritual Autobiography*. Princeton: Princeton University Press, 1965.

———. "Defoe's Prose Style: 1. The Language of Interpretation." *MP* 71 (1974): 277–94.

———. "'Sauces to whet our gorg'd Appetites': Defoe at Seventy in the Anchovy Trade." *PQ* 54 (1975): 531–33.

Staves, Susan. *Players' Scepters*. Lincoln: University of Nebraska Press, 1979.

Stevens, David H. *Party Politics and English Journalism, 1702–1742*. Chicago: University of Chicago Libraries, 1916.

Stevenson, Thomas G. *List of the Deans of Guild of the City of Edinburgh, 1403–1890*. Edinburgh: Printed for Private Circulation, 1890.

"The Stock of Broom." Edinburgh: Swain, for the Company of Merchants and the Edinburgh Museums and Art Galleries, 1978.

Stone, Lawrence. *The Family, Sex and Marriage in England, 1500–1800*. London: Weidenfeld & Nicolson, 1977.

Story, Robert. *William Carstares*. London: Macmillan, 1874.

Sutherland, James. "The Circulation of Newspapers and Literary Periodicals, 1700–1730." *The Library*, 4th ser., 15 (1934–35): 110–24.

———. *Defoe*. 1937. Philadelphia: Lippincott, 1938.

———. "A Note on the Last Years of Defoe." *MLR* 29 (1934): 137–41.

———. *The Restoration Newspaper and Its Development*. Cambridge: Cambridge University Press, 1986.

———. "Some Early Troubles of Daniel Defoe." *RES* 9 (1933): 275–90.

Tallack, T. R. "Defoe and His Descendants." *N&Q*, 7th ser., 15 (1887): 450.

Taylor, Joseph. *A Journey to Edenborough in Scotland*. 1705–6. Edinburgh: Brown, 1903.

Terry, Sanford. *The Scottish Parliament: Its Constitution and Procedure, 1603–1707*. Glasgow: MacLehose, 1905.

Thirsk, Joan. "The European Debate on the Customs of Inheritance, 1500–1700." In *Family and Inheritance: Rural Society in Western Europe, 1500–1700*, edited by Jack Goody, Joan Thirsk, and E. P. Thompson. Cambridge: Cambridge University Press, 1976.

———. "The Fantastical Folly of Fashion: The English Stocking Knitting Industry, 1500–1700." In *Textile History and Economic History*, edited by E. B. Harte and K. G. Ponting. Manchester: Manchester University Press, 1973.

Thomas, Donald. "Press Prosecutions of the Eighteenth and Nineteenth Centuries: The Evidence of the King's Bench Indictments." *The Library*, 5th ser., 32 (1977): 315–32.

Thomas, Keith. *Religion and the Decline of Magic*. New York: Scribner's, 1971.

Thomas, Peter. "The Beginning of Parliamentary Reporting in Newspapers." *EHR* 74 (1959): 623–36.

Thomas, Roger. "Presbyterians, Congregationals and the Test and Corporation Acts." *Transactions of the Unitarian Historical Society* 11 (1955–58): 119.

———. "Presbyterians in Transition." In *The English Presbyterians: From Elizabethan Puritanism to Modern Unitarianism*, by C. G. Bolam, Jeremy Goring, H. L. Short, and Roger Thomas. London: Allen & Unwin, 1968.

Thompson, E. P. "The Moral Economy of the Crowd in the Eighteenth Century." *Past and Present* 50 (1971): 76–136.

———. *Whigs and Hunters*. London: Allen Lane, 1975.

Thompson, Martyn P. "The Reception of Locke's *Two Treatises of Government*, 1690–1705." *Political Studies* 24 (1976): 184–91.

Thompson, Roger. *Unfit for Modest Ears*. Totowa, N.J.: Rowman & Littlefield, 1979.

Thomson, Mark. "Parliament and Foreign Policy, 1689–1714." In *William III and Louis XIV: Essays 1680–1720, by and for Mark A. Thomson*, edited by Ragnhild Hatton and J. S. Bromley. Liverpool: Liverpool University Press, 1968.

Thrower, Norman. "Edmund Halley and Thematic Geo-Cartography." In *The Terraqueous Globe*. Los Angeles: Clark Library Papers, 1969.

Trent, W. P. "New Light on Defoe's Life." *Nation* 87 (17 September 1908): 259–61.

Trevelyan, G. M. *England under Queen Anne*. 3 vols. London: Longmans, 1930.

———. "The 'Jersey' Period of the Negotiations Leading to the Peace of Utrecht." *EHR* 49 (1934): 100–105.

———, ed. *Select Documents for Queen Anne's Reign*. Cambridge: Cambridge University Press, 1929.

Trickett, Rachel. *The Honest Muse*. Oxford: Clarendon Press, 1967.

———. "The Idiom of Augustan Poetry." In *Discussion of Poetry: Form and Structure*, edited by Francis Murphy. Boston: Heath, 1964.

Trotter, David. *The Poetry of Abraham Cowley*. London: Macmillan, 1979.

Trumbach, Randolph. *The Rise of the Egalitarian Family*. New York: Academic Press, 1978.

Turner, G. L'E. "Henry Baker, F.R.S.: Founder of the Bakerian Lecture." *Notes and Records of the Royal Society of London* 29 (1974): 53–79.

Valenze, Deborah M. "Prophecy and Popular Literature in Eighteenth-Century England." *Journal of Ecclesiastical History* 29 (1978): 75–92.

W., J. G. "A History of the Old Meeting Houses." *Under the Dome*, n.s., 9 (1900): 129–31.

Wagner, Anthony. *Heralds of England: A History of the Office and College of Arms*. London: HMSO, 1967.

Wallerstein, Ruth. *Studies in Seventeenth-Century Poetic*. Madison: University of Wisconsin Press, 1950.

Waswo, Richard. *The Fatal Mirror: Themes and Techniques in the Poetry of Fulke Greville*. Charlottesville: University Press of Virginia, 1972.

Watson, J. Steven. *A History of the Salters' Company*. London: Oxford University Press, 1963.

Watt, Ian. *The Rise of the Novel*. 1957. Berkeley and Los Angeles: University of California Press, 1967.

———. "Robinson Crusoe as a Myth." Revised from *Essays in Criticism*, 1951. In the Norton critical edition of *Robinson Crusoe*, edited by Michael Shinagel. New York: Norton, 1975.

Watts, Michael R. *The Dissenters*. Oxford: Clarendon Press, 1978.

Webb, Sidney, and Beatrice Webb. *English Local Government from the Revolution to the Municipal Corporations Act: The Manor and the Borough. Part II*. New York: Longmans, Green, 1908.

Weiss, Henry B., and Grace M. Weiss. *Early Brickmaking in New Jersey*. Trenton, N.J.: New Jersey Agricultural Society, 1966.

Wendell, Barrett. *Cotton Mather: The Puritan Priest*. New York: Harcourt, Brace & World, 1963.

Whiting, C. E. *Studies in English Puritanism from the Restoration to the Revolution*. New York: Macmillan, 1931.

Wigfield, W. MacDonald. *The Monmouth Rebellion*. Totowa, N.J.: Barnes & Noble, 1980.

Wiles, Roy M. *Serial Publication in England before 1750*. Cambridge: Cambridge University Press, 1957.

Williams, Aubrey. *An Approach to Congreve*. New Haven: Yale University Press, 1979.

Williams, Basil. *Stanhope*. Oxford: Clarendon Press, 1932.

———. *The Whig Supremacy, 1714–1760*. 1939. Oxford: Clarendon Press, 1962.

Williams, Eric. *Capitalism and Slavery*. 1944. London: André Deutsch, 1964.

Williams, Glyndwr. "'The Inexhaustible Fountain of Gold': English Projects and Ventures in the South Seas, 1670–1750." In *Perspectives of Empire: Essays*

Presented to Gerald S. Graham, edited by John E. Flint and Glyndwr Williams. New York: Barnes & Noble, 1973.

Wilson, R. G. *Gentleman Merchants: The Merchant Community in Leeds, 1700–1830*. Manchester: Manchester University Press, 1971.

Wilson, Walter. *Memoirs of the Life and Times of Daniel De Foe*. 3 vols. London: Hurst, Chance, 1830.

Winton, Calhoun. *Captain Steele*. Baltimore: Johns Hopkins Press, 1964.

Wright, Thomas. *The Life of Daniel Defoe*. 1894. London: C. J. Farncombe, 1931.

Zimmerman, Everett. *Defoe and the Novel*. Berkeley and Los Angeles: University of California Press, 1975.

INDEX

NOTE: Definitions and explanations of key terms are given on pages marked by **boldface** type.

ABOUT THE AUTHOR

Paula Backscheider's previous books include *Daniel Defoe: Ambition and Innovation* and *A Being More Intense: The Prose Works of Bunyan, Swift, and Defoe.* She is professor of English at the University of Rochester.

DANIEL DEFOE: HIS LIFE

Designed by Kachergis Book Design.

Composed by The Composing Room of Michigan in Mergenthaler 202 Baskerville.

Printed by the Maple Press Company on 50-lb. Glatfelter Eggshell Cream paper, and bound in Joanna Arrestox cloth with Rainbow Parchment endsheets.